# British Empire: dates of acquisition

This map shows the beginning of British rule, either directly by Government or by trading companies or settlers with royal authority. Cession sometimes preceded settlement; capture during war sometimes preceded transfer by treaty; in all cases the da[...] Territories which ceased to be ruled [...] or were ruled for fewer than 25 years, are excluded.

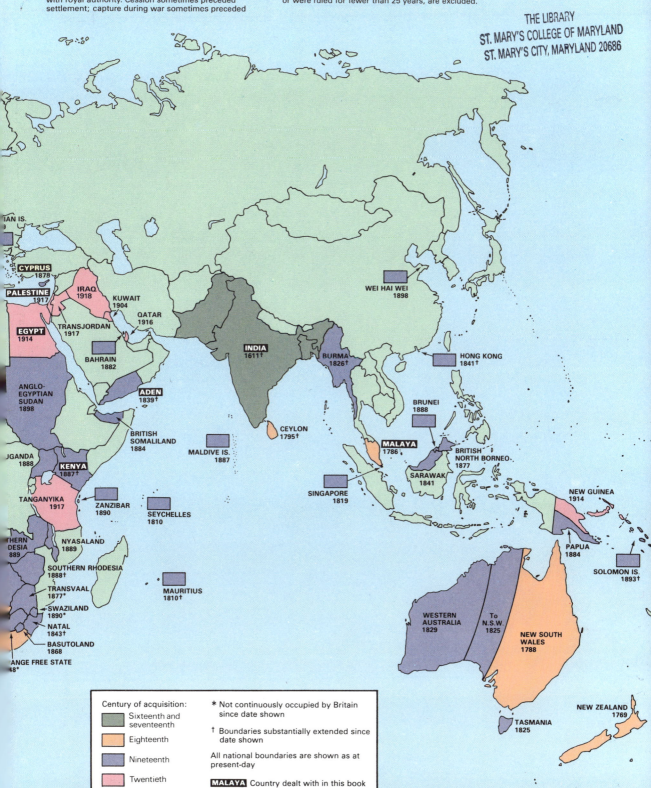

IAN IS.

CYPRUS
1878

PALESTINE
1917

IRAQ
1918

KUWAIT
1904

QATAR
1916

WEI HAI WEI
1898

EGYPT
1914

TRANSJORDAN
1917

BAHRAIN
1882

INDIA
1611†

BURMA
1826†

HONG KONG
1841†

ANGLO-
EGYPTIAN
SUDAN
1898

ADEN
1839†

BRUNEI
1888

BRITISH
SOMALILAND
1884

MALDIVE IS.
1887

CEYLON
1795†

MALAYA
1786

BRITISH
NORTH BORNEO
1877

UGANDA
1888

KENYA
1887†

SARAWAK
1841

NEW GUINEA
1914

TANGANYIKA
1917

ZANZIBAR
1890

SEYCHELLES
1810

SINGAPORE
1819

PAPUA
1884

THERN
DESIA
889

NYASALAND
1889

SOLOMON IS.
1893†

SOUTHERN RHODESIA
1888†

MAURITIUS
1810†

TRANSVAAL
1877*

SWAZILAND
1890*

WESTERN
AUSTRALIA
1829

To
N.S.W.
1825

NATAL
1843†

BASUTOLAND
1868

NEW SOUTH
WALES
1788

ANGE FREE STATE
48*

TASMANIA
1825

NEW ZEALAND
1769

Century of acquisition:

Sixteenth and seventeenth

Eighteenth

Nineteenth

Twentieth

* Not continuously occupied by Britain since date shown

† Boundaries substantially extended since date shown

All national boundaries are shown as at present-day

**MALAYA** Country dealt with in this book

# End of
# Empire

BRIAN LAPPING

# End of Empire

ST. MARTIN'S PRESS
New York

For Anne,
Harriet, Claudia and Melissa

Library of Congress Catalog Card Number 85-1759

ISBN 0-312-25071-1
ISBN 0-312-25072-X (pbk.)

# Contents

# Maps

*Maps by Richard Natkiel*

# Illustrations

# Acknowledgements

My principal thanks go to Granada Television for allowing me to make the television series, 'End of Empire', and to use in this book material gathered by the production teams.

Secondly I wish to thank the hundreds of former ministers, military men, nationalist leaders, governors and officials who have answered my questions and those of my colleagues. Many of them I have quoted. Others provided recollections and arguments in preliminary interviews which I have drawn on but, since they were not filmed, I have generally not attributed.

The producers, directors and researchers who worked on the series have helped in the writing of this book by reading and sometimes sharply criticising early drafts of chapters. I should like to thank them all:

India: Allan Segal, Liz McLeod
Palestine and Iran: Mark Anderson, Alison Rooper
Malaya: Mark Anderson, Desmond Smith
Egypt: Mark Anderson, Cate Haste
Aden: Mike Ryan, Patrick Buckley
Cyprus: Norma Percy, Bruce MacDonald, Liz Andrew
Gold Coast: Maxine Baker, Simon Albury
Kenya: Allan Segal, Polly Bide
Central African Federation: Maxine Baker, John Sheppard, Pete Connors
Rhodesia: Norma Percy, Mick Gold, Max Graesser.

In addition I have submitted draft chapters to many friends and expert advisers who have patiently read them and commented, saving me from hundreds of errors. Those who have helped in this way are: Dennis Austin, Leslie Barr, François Crouzet, Elsie Donald, Dan Gillon, John Gurney, Albert Hourani, Joe Hunt, Derek Ingram, Tim Jackson, Patrick Keatley, Tony King, Colin Legum, Peter Loizos, John Lonsdale, David McKie, Nicholas Mansergh, Peter Mansfield, Sir Penderel Moon, Richard Perle, Gowher Rizvi, Andrew Robinson, Anthony Short, Eric Silver, Tony Stockwell, Richard Trench, David Throup.

The Earl of Stockton (Harold Macmillan) kindly gave me permission to quote at length from his memoirs. Donald Simpson, librarian of the Royal Commonwealth Society, did the research for the maps inside the front and back covers.

Finally I wish to thank two people without whom the book would never have been written: Valerie Hayward, my secretary, who has typed and retyped drafts until she was sick of the sight of them, and Anne Lapping, my wife, who has lost her spouse to the Empire for three consecutive summer holidays and most of the weekends and evenings in between, but has remained willing to knock out illiteracies.

A sentence normally follows here, like one of those ritualised exemption clauses in solicitors' letters: 'But I am responsible for all errors.' It goes, of course, without saying.

B.L.

# Preface

The title of this book, *End of Empire*, may seem pretentious. After all, the book is about the end of the British Empire only. Perhaps it is too much to ask for a title to be modest, but why should it not be accurate?

The answer is that with the end of the British Empire came the end of all empires. To conquer distant lands and rule them from a home base was widely regarded as legitimate before the twentieth century. The British were the last of the great subjugators with the self-confidence to call their conquests an Empire. This species of relationship between peoples ended mainly because of an idea. The right to self-determination had since 1776 inspired nationalist leaders throughout the world and muzzled the direct assertion of imperial power. But the British, Turkish and French empires continued to suppress nationalism by the then approved method: massacre.

The British did not often use this word for the actions of their own colonial governments. The common euphemism was 'punitive expedition'. A gunboat or an army would visit the home town or village of a dissident leader and destroy him, his followers and their homes. This was considered as morally neutral an act as a tiger killing a lamb. Empires kept the peace by proving, when challenged, that they were still tigers. However William Ewart Gladstone, repeatedly British Prime Minister between 1868 and 1892, refused to accept this rule of nature. So vehemently did he thunder against the massacres perpetrated by Britain's long-standing ally, Turkey, that his political opponent, Benjamin Disraeli, was impelled to describe Gladstone's speeches as, of all the Turkish outrages, the worst. Disraeli's remark was witty, but Gladstone had caught the mood of the time. A large and growing part of the British public did not like being told that its allies were responsible for massacres – even less that its own public servants were.

Many missionaries in the colonies believed the doctrines they taught about the sanctity of human life and all men being equal, and wrote reports to their brethren in London when British governments acted in flagrant defiance of their own laws. Gladstone's followers in the House of Commons took up such reports. The arrival of the electric telegraph, allowing information to reach newspapers in London from the colonies within hours, helped this shackling of the imperial tradition. When General Dyer massacred 379 Indians and wounded a further 1,500 in Amritsar in 1919 (see page 37), his action was, by the standard of the recent punitive expeditions of the Turkish empire, modest. But the debate provoked by the Amritsar massacre – in the United States and India as well as Britain – led in a few years to the abandonment of the only method by which empires could survive. The moral sensitivity – or, as Dyer's supporters thought, the squeamishness – of the most powerful nations, expressed by the reluctance of their leaders to be publicly revealed as mass murderers, brought the End of Empire.

The Russian and American Governments can still, in the final decades of the twentieth century, exercise great sway over distant people and governments. But no longer can a 'Governor' be sent, wearing the fancy uniform of the dominant power, to administer laws enacted by its legislature and openly to enforce its policies. In 1939 the Viceroy of India declared war against Germany on behalf of all the 400 million people of India and its 650 princes. He did not consult a single Indian. That was imperial power. Neither the United States nor the Soviet Union can do that. Their critics call them both empires, but they do not use the term of themselves and they scrupulously avoid any claim to sovereign rights over distant territories. Their relationship with lesser states retains some imperial characteristics, but without massacre or direct rule, they are not empires in the sense of the Roman, Portuguese, Dutch, Ottoman and British. They cannot conceive of addressing a head of state as the Viceroy of India in 1926 addressed the Nizam of Hyderabad – ruler of a country bigger in area than Great Britain:

> The sovereignty of the British Crown is supreme in India and therefore no ruler of an Indian State can justifiably claim to negotiate with the British Government on an equal footing. Its supremacy is not based only upon treaties and engagements, but exists independently of them.

The colonial Governor, with absolute authority in his colony and subject to the absolute authority of the Government back home, has, like the dinosaur, become extinct. And the last specimens, a diminishing band of them still alive, are British.

Until 1947 – within the lifetime of half the world's population – the Government in London ruled more land and people than any other government in history. In the thirty-three years between India's independence in 1947 and Southern Rhodesia's in 1980 the British Empire ended. Until 1934 the Empire was still expanding. Territories that gained independence from Britain before then – for example the American colonies and Ireland – were part of the imperial ebb and flow. After 1980 the dozen territories that remained British – Hong King, Gibraltar and a scatter of tiny islands – were no longer an empire, merely the left-overs. Relative to its size, no great ship ever sank so quickly.

The motive behind both this book and the television series with which it is associated was the desire to seize an opportunity. Many of the people who had crucial responsibilities aboard the Empire as it sank live quietly in retirement. To film them and record their contrasting versions of the events that concluded with the lowering of the British flag seemed a worthwhile task of historical evidence-gathering.

Of the forty-nine territories that acquired independence from Britain in the years 1947–80, this book relates in some detail the history of the ten I consider the most important and exciting. Cyprus is included because the battles leading to its independence drew British and international attention, because Archbishop Makarios and the British Government reached a tragic misunderstanding, because the story is gripping. Ceylon (now Sri Lanka) is left out because, although it is a larger and more populous island, its progress to independence was smooth by comparison and overshadowed by events in neighbouring India. The Gold Coast (now Ghana) is included because it was the first African colony to become independent, with Kwame Nkrumah the inspiration of nationalists throughout the continent. Nigeria is left out because, although larger and more populous, it merely followed behind the Gold Coast. The territories I most regret leaving out are the West Indies. When the Empire was at its height, Europeans brought slaves to these mostly uninhabited islands. In the post-imperial phase, the immigration of West Indians terrified suburban Britain and its spokesman, J. Enoch Powell. The End of Empire story in the West Indies, however, the history of an attempted federation broken up by local-minded jealousies, is one of great complexity that made little impact outside the area. It had to be omitted.

The inclusion of Iran requires explanation. Many states that were never formally part of the Empire became in effect British underlings. It would have been misleading to tell the End of Empire story without including one of them. Iran is the best case for several reasons. Twice Britain played a decisive role in putting rulers on its throne. The Anglo-Iranian oil company was the largest single British overseas investment and by far the largest source of income for the Government of Iran. And the crisis of 1951–53, when Iran nationalised the oil company and Britain responded by organising a coup, is almost as important in understanding the end of the British Empire as is the attack on Egypt in 1956 – also by then an independent state.

The ten cases chosen all involved misunderstanding, double-dealing and murder. This could be misleading. If the remaining thirty-nine territories had all made a peaceful, tolerant progress to independence, this book and the accompanying television series would convey the impression that the End of Empire story as a whole was exciting when really it was rather dull. But I do not think this is so. In the several conferences leading to independence that I reported for the *Guardian*, it was the normal objective of British officials involved to persuade journalists that all was smooth, peaceful and routine. But some of the nationalist leaders always talked about abused and discontented minorities, Britain's dilatoriness in giving up power, and cases of wrongful imprisonment. At the independence conference for Zanzibar (now part of Tanzania), I saw the British Government in London formally agree to hand power to the Sultan and his party, who were promptly ousted by their own people when the independence celebrations were over. Before the independence of British Guiana (now Guyana) I heard the bitter protests of former Premier Cheddi Jagan that the British had rigged the elections. In the case of Basutoland (now Lesotho) angry opposition leaders explained to me that Chief Leabua Jonathan, to whom Britain was handing power, was merely the lackey of the British and the South Africans. My conclusion from these and from several other countries I covered, as a reporter, is that the cases included here reveal the tensions that, though often contained, were present in every colony.

Of the forty-nine cases available, I have chosen three, Palestine, Iran and Egypt, that bring out the role of the United States in bringing the British Empire to its end; one, Malaya, that enables me to describe the impact of communism; and three, Palestine, Cyprus and Aden, that show the role of the United Nations. A major reason for including the Gold Coast was to describe a country in which progress to independence was notably smooth and successful.

The chapters that follow have a consistent pattern. First comes a brief section of historical background, designed to explain why the British came to the country and why they stayed. The main section then describes the End of Empire period, drawing, among other sources, on the interviews recorded in preparing the television series. A final, brief section attempts to summarise major events since independence. The chapter on Egypt has no 'After independence' section because post-1956 actions by Egypt that affected the British Empire are partly covered in the chapter on Aden.

Throughout the book, I have used the names of territories that were in use at the time: Nyasaland for what is now Malawi, Northern Rhodesia for Zambia, the Gold Coast for Ghana. Where names have changed since independence, I have used the new name only when describing post-independence events.

The amount of use made of interviews recorded for the television series varies between chapters. This is because the best way to tell a story for television is usually not best for a book. The programmes needed anecdotes and lively talkers, which for the book sometimes seemed irrelevant. The book needed an ordered presentation of the main facts, which for the programmes sometimes seemed pedestrian. The book and the television series are thus twins, but not identical. I hope each stands independently of the other.

# The Route to Independence

The end was generally the same. At teatime or thereabouts, in any case conveniently before sundowner time or the need to change for dinner, the flag on the flagpost at Government House was lowered for the last time. For fifty, or a hundred, or even in the case of The Gambia more than three hundred years – since the place had become a British colony – the flag had been lowered at this hour every day. A sergeant-major in the local regiment shouted the order. A soldier paid out the rope hand over hand, brought the flag down, folded it neatly and gave it to the sergeant-major, who gave it to the officer in charge, who gave it to the Governor, who gave it to the British Sovereign's representative. At the independence ceremony which effectively marked the end of the British Empire – in 1980 in Southern Rhodesia (about to become Zimbabwe) – the Queen's representative was her son, Charles, the Prince of Wales. He handed the neatly folded flag to his aide-de-camp, and immediately turned away, to lead the guests to the garden party.

The garden party was generally the same. It was marked by absences. In the battle for the succession, someone always had to lose and the loser often chose not to come to the party.

The flag ceremony on the lawn at Government House and the party that followed were a semi-private event, like a funeral. Most of the British who were present – the Governor, the senior officials, the deputy governors, the top people from the big British companies – felt a lump in their throats as the flag came down. They wondered if the weed-free, closely-mowed grass would remain impeccable, and if the Prime Minister or President who was about to take over this home counties-style house would preserve its traditions. On balance they thought he would as they talked of permanent secretaries and civil service commissions, of schemes for inter-governmental co-operation and technical improvement. The garden party hinted that, though British rule was going, British ways were, to a substantial extent, staying.

Later that night, in the largest stadium in town, usually the football ground (cricket, though alleged to be the imperial sport, rarely caused big stadiums to be built), a second ceremony was to be held for the people. This promised to be a long, noisy event, with too much marching, speech-making and traditional dancing. Senior British officials shortly to leave for home

*Teatime in Salisbury: the last flag-down at a British Governor's residence in Africa. Far left, Prince Charles; beside him, the Governor, Lord Soames.*

affected boredom and said they would give midnight at the stadium a miss. But, as important persons, they had received tickets and felt their absence might cause offence. One Englishman in the stadium at Lagos on 1 October 1960, independence day in Nigeria, was asked how all this affected him. 'Tomorrow morning', he said, 'I suppose I'll have to brush my own teeth.'

As midnight approached in Salisbury, Rhodesia, on 17 April 1980, shortly before it became Harare, Zimbabwe, the vast crowd in the stadium watched the soldiery arrive with bands playing. The ZANLA and ZIPRA forces, until recently guerillas, marched in first. They were followed by more soldiers marching in step to the same tune. These were the Rhodesian forces against whom the guerillas had until a few weeks earlier been fighting. As the crowd slowly realised which force was which, a great 'Oooh' went round the banked seats of the stadium, followed by clapping and cheering as 100,000 people stood, amazed and impressed at the evidence below them that the war was really over and the integration of the rival armies was already so far advanced.

At 11.59 p.m., with the 'Ooohs' silenced and the soldiers at attention, the British flag that had been flying on a post in the middle of the pitch was quietly lowered. Then at midnight, to roars and screams of applause, the Zimbabwe flag went up, and – a flashy gesture but an impressive one nonetheless – at the exact instant the new flag reached the top of the pole a flight of jets screeched terrifyingly low across the stadium. Thoughts of the impeccable planning required to achieve such synchronisation from an airfield a dozen miles away gave Englishmen present a satisfied glow: the pride of successful showmanship. Then came the reading of the Royal message, formally transferring power, and the speeches. Thirty-three years earlier, in Delhi on 14 August 1947, Jawaharlal Nehru, first Prime Minister of independent India, summed them all up:

> Long years ago we made a tryst with destiny, and now the time comes when we shall redeem our pledge . . . At the stroke of the midnight hour, while the world sleeps, India will awake to life and freedom. A moment comes, which comes but rarely in history, when we step out from the old to the new, when an age ends and when the soul of a nation, long suppressed, finds utterance . . .

After the speeches in 1980, in what was by now Zimbabwe, the programme promised tribal dancing and singing: surely the time to go? Something then happened that appeared to be in bad taste. A choir of white girls from a Salisbury school paraded into the middle of the arena and began singing a song with slight but clear racist undertones: their school song. The packed stadium fell still. The few hundred whites in the stands felt momentarily vulnerable among so many thousands of blacks. The white girls finished their song. The vast audience stayed quiet. After a second or two, the girls resumed, this time singing in Shona, the local language; now they were singing the national anthem of the new state. The worry was defused, with smiles all round: a momentary reminder of the tensions of race and war.

                              *        *        *

No generalisation covers all the transfers of power. In Palestine in 1948 and Aden in 1967, the British lost control and scuttled to the docks and the airport. Those humiliations for the departing rulers are described in the chapters that follow. The usual pattern of the Government House flag-down, the garden party and the midnight ceremony in the sports arena – organised fifty times by a small and increasingly accomplished section of the Colonial Office will not be described again.

The series of usual steps that preceded the end will likewise be less than fully described in the chapters that follow. Some years before independence the Governor of each colony, with the approval of Westminster, brought a few of 'the better sort of natives' into Legco. Legco (short for legislative council) was to evolve in most colonies into the local parliament – not elected at first, for that would have brought in 'agitators'; no, Legco began as the Governor's sounding board to which he appointed a few selected local whites, the chairmen of the harbour board, the railway company, the chamber of commerce, then a few browns or blacks who were known to be 'responsible'. Where the British established colonies, others flocked in, finding that the enforcement of law made for good business. These others, Chinese in Singapore and Penang, Hindus in Madras and Calcutta, Arabs in Aden and Zanzibar, were soon sending their children to English schools and universities. From this English-educated group the Governor chose a lawyer or two or a wealthy trader to join the legislative council. They helped keep him informed about the concerns of the merchant classes. In Calcutta the first Indians joined the Governor-General's Legco in 1858. In Accra the first Gold Coast African joined in 1861. These were called the 'unofficials' to distinguish them from the dominant group, the 'officials' – the Chief Secretary, the Attorney-General, the Financial Secretary – who mostly found attending Legco a bore because they hated making speeches, which they regarded as a politician's job. In Legco the officials announced what would happen and the unofficials were supposed to express their views and acquiesce.

Above Legco was Exco (short for executive council), the Governor's board of management. Here none but officials could sit. In the ports that were Britain's original and most important colonies, laws concerning trade had to be enforced and Exco was long thought to have responsibilities which neither natives nor British traders could share. The arrival of the first native on Exco – in India in 1909 – marks the beginning of the End of Empire.

The British, in the twilight years of their Empire, were arrogant about many things. Above all they believed that the British system of government was the best in the world. At the apex was the constitutional monarch, nominally in charge, actually impotent: what could be cleverer than that? One step down came the party system, by means of which governments willingly alternated at elections; below that was the civil service, an intellectual and administrative élite, prepared to obey the orders of mostly less clever politicians. Learning to run such a system, like learning to play cricket, took time. Even the Americans, when, in writing their constitution, they tried to copy it, were misled by a Frenchman into getting it wrong. So the British believed they had a duty to teach the colonised peoples not only the complicated rules but also the tricks by which the rules could be bent.

From the date a colony began its slow progress towards 'internal self-government' or 'Dominion status within the Commonwealth' (euphemisms by means of which the British deceived themselves that full independence would not be demanded), the Governor and his colleagues behaved as though the last years of British rule were a university course in the British constitution for clever natives. A senior British official might say, 'That chap Eric Williams' (in Trinidad), or 'That chap Julius Nyerere' (in Tanganyika), 'he really understands the principles of British constitutional government better than I do'. Such a sentence would be intended as the sincere praise of a proud teacher, neither patronising nor impertinent.

This education in the Westminster method was willingly administered to willing pupils. It would have been impossible to run the Empire without local co-operation. Consent, a far more efficient way to keep order than coercion, required the active help of the right sort of natives at all levels. Anyway, not enough Britons could be found to do all the administrative jobs, especially the lowlier ones.

The wrong sort of natives were 'political agitators', 'self-seeking trouble-makers' and 'Communists', i.e. people who demanded that their countries be rid of British rule. Nirad C. Chaudhuri, in *The Autobiography of an Unknown Indian*, describes how, sitting in the gallery at the Calcutta opera and looking down at the well-dressed British audience in the stalls, he was seized by such a ferocity of hate that he longed to drop a bomb and kill them all. He adds that there could be no redemption for India until it could escape from 'the snake's fangs' of such hatred.

The Viceroy of India, Lord Irwin, when faced with snakes' fangs throughout the subcontinent in 1931, invited Gandhi, the leading national-ist, to meet him as an equal and join constitutional talks under the chairmanship of the Prime Minister in London. The Governor of the Gold Coast, Sir Charles Arden-Clarke, faced with apparently comparable agi-tation in his colony in 1950, did not use the disorders as an excuse to defer or even abandon the first general election in black Africa, as many of his more conservative colleagues recommended, but determinedly pressed ahead with it. Both men advanced the territories they governed towards independence at a time when many still assumed that the sun would never set on the British Empire. Their actions reveal the fundamental ambiguity in the British imperial will. Both were serving under Labour Prime Ministers, Irwin under Ramsay MacDonald, Arden-Clarke under Clement Attlee. Had Labour not come to power in Britain, such steps towards the voluntary transfer of power would probably not have occurred. An equally distinctive Labour policy was the unconditional offer of Foreign Secretary Ernest Bevin in 1946 to withdraw all British troops from Egypt. Had the Egyptian Parliament accepted that offer, instead of demanding that Britain also quit the Sudan, the disastrous errors of the Conservative Government in dealing with Egypt in 1956 would have been avoided. Some have argued that it made no difference to imperial policy whether Labour or the Conservatives were in power in Britain. They are wrong. Labour always responded more sympathetically and rapidly than the Conservatives to the growing national-ism of colonial peoples – and the Conservatives responded faster than the French, Belgians and Portuguese.

Even the arch-imperialist of the Conservative party, Winston Churchill, eventually gave up his attempts to resist the inevitable. In the 1930s and during the 1939–45 war he opposed advances towards independence for India with all his considerable strength. When, in August 1941, he was desperately seeking America's entry into the war, President Roosevelt told him that a joint statement of the aims for which they would be fighting together would help to win over American public opinion and Congress. Unfortunately, however, on one central point the two potential allies did not agree: the Americans opposed imperialism. So, in their joint declaration, which became known as the Atlantic Charter, the third paragraph was conceded by Churchill only with extreme reluctance. Its opening words declared that the two heads of government 'respect the right of all peoples to choose the form of government under which they will live' – Churchill's own formulation – but the subsequent phrase was inserted by Roosevelt over Churchill's resistance: 'and they wish to see sovereign rights and self-government restored to those who have been forcibly deprived of them'. Churchill signed only because he had to. He afterwards explained that 'those forcibly deprived of sovereignty' were Hitler's victims in Europe. Roosevelt interpreted the phrase as meaning all the subject peoples of the European empires. Attlee, the Labour Party leader and Churchill's deputy Prime Minister, agreed with the American interpretation.

After the war, although he said he had not become Prime Minister to preside over the dismemberment of the British Empire, Churchill continued to find, both in office and in opposition, that he had no choice. In 1947 when Attlee gave India independence, the principal role of Anthony Eden, Churchill's deputy as leader of the opposition, was to keep Britain's greatest parliamentarian away from the House of Commons in case he made a scene. Churchill's post-war moderation concerning the Empire becomes evident when his conduct is compared with that of Georges Bidault, President of the Resistance in the 1939–45 war and later Prime Minister of France. When,

*London actors in End of Empire dramas, on their way to a thanksgiving service at the end of the 1939–45 war: back row left, Oliver Lyttelton (Malaya, Rhodesia, Kenya); front row left to right, Anthony Eden (Egypt, Cyprus), Winston Churchill (Iran, Egypt), Clement Attlee (India), Herbert Morrison (Iran).*

after 1958, it became clear that France was about to concede Algerian independence, Bidault fought to the end, first in Parliament, later in active support of the Secret Army Organisation (OAS). He finally fled the country and was charged with plotting against the state. The contrast with Churchill's attitude towards India in 1947 is total. So is the contrast between the behaviour of the two men when they were in power. Bidault would not allow political concessions in either Vietnam or Algeria and consequently bore a large share of the responsibility for France's fighting two disastrous colonial wars. Churchill, when he became peacetime Prime Minister between 1951 and 1955, reluctantly let the Gold Coast, Nigeria, the Sudan and Malaya proceed through the constitutional stages that led inevitably to independence. He even allowed himself to be persuaded that the Suez Canal base, where 80,000 British troops were stationed in order to protect what he had long considered the vital artery of Empire, would have to be evacuated, because Egyptian and Arab nationalists demanded it. As Colonial Secretary he had sat with T. E. Lawrence and the Emir Feisal in Cairo in 1922, drawing nation states on the map of what had previously been the Ottoman Empire. What is surprising is not that he resisted the end of the British Empire, but that he did not resist it more forcibly.

The reason was that the game was over and Churchill knew it. Why, when the Ottoman and Habsburg Empires had survived for centuries after their power had declined from its peak, did the British Empire collapse so quickly? What had gone wrong with the force of inertia? Part of the answer lies in the experience of the British themselves. When the thirteen colonies that later became the United States of America broke away from the British Empire in 1776 the British learned the lesson that iron rule from the imperial capital leads to revolt, war and the risk of humiliation. This, the painful loss of their first empire, was their main education in how to run their second, the schoolmaster being Edmund Burke who lectured the House of Commons and the Government on both. So the British readily granted self-government and democracy to the colonies in Canada in the 1840s, to some in Australia in the 1850s and to New Zealand in 1856. If by the start of the twentieth century the British were forgetting the lessons of 1776, they were given two sharp reminders. In South Africa in 1899–1902 and in Ireland in the years leading up to 1922, the price of resisting nationalist movements was too high – both in money and in embarrassment to ministers of being caught out by parliamentary questions about British brutality. Rather than face another Boer War or than order another Black and Tans operation, governments in London decided they would bend before the wind of nationalism. In the colonies in Africa the people were politically and educationally centuries behind, providing grounds for lengthy delay. But by the 1930s Indian recruits to the élite bureaucracy, the Indian Civil Service, were more able than the British. Before 1914 the brightest graduates of Oxford and Cambridge had tried to get into the ICS, but after 1918 and Britain's public commitment to self-government for India, they looked elsewhere. A gradual transition to self-government was thus taken for granted in the British imperial system.

It speeded up principally because of the two world wars. Europe tore itself apart in 1914–18 and 1939–45, and all the European powers were broken as a result. So devastated was Britain by the 1914–18 war that soon afterwards the Government invented 'the ten-year rule', a remarkable principle that laid down a guideline for all departments of state: for ten years there would be no war. Each year the rule was reviewed and until 1932 reimposed. The complementary policy was to back the newly created League of Nations: since Britain could not face the prospect of another war, it eloquently supported the League's efforts to make sure war was prevented. In 1922 Britain agreed with the other great naval powers that they would all restrict the size of their navies. A traditional role of the Royal Navy was to defend the eastern seas between China and Africa, and from Malaya to Australia. But the Government decided it could no longer afford to maintain a fleet in the east. Instead it built a huge dry dock at Singapore, a kind of naval garage. The warning was issued to any potential adversary: if you attack Britain's interests in this area a fleet will sail to Singapore, taking sixty days or so, and, using the repair facilities and the stock of armaments there, will wreak terrible retribution. It was defence by bluff. When in 1935 Japan seized parts of China, threatening vast British commercial and treaty relationships there, the British Government took no action, except to appeal ineffectively to the League of Nations. When in 1936 Italy seized Abyssinia, threatening areas Britain ruled in Kenya, the Sudan and Somalia, Britain again used no weapon but the League. When in 1938 Germany seized Czechoslovakia, Britain remained determined to avoid war. The Prime Minister, Neville Chamberlain, tried to appease the German Chancellor, Adolf Hitler, partly because Britain, if compelled to fight in Europe, was likely to lose much of its Empire.

When the attempt at appeasement failed and Hitler contemptuously moved on, accepting what Chamberlain had conceded and then seizing territories in Europe that he had promised to leave free, Britain was obliged to declare the war which was to end the Empire. In 1939, 1940 and 1941, while Hitler conquered the rest of Europe, Britain mortgaged a large part of its worldwide imperial assets in order to fight single-handed. The bankruptcy brought on by the 1939–45 war – a war the British Government knew was beyond its means – was the principal reason why the British Empire ended so much more quickly than anyone expected.

Yet bankruptcy was not the whole story. In 1947 France, as economically damaged as Britain, faced a revolt in its colony of Madagascar. The French socialist Government took extreme measures, sending troops and killing more than 30,000 black people. Six Communist members of the French Cabinet resigned, but France reasserted imperial control. A few months later, in February 1948, Britain faced riots in the Gold Coast. The Governor asked for troops, but Britain's Labour Government sent instead a committee of enquiry to hurry the black people of the country on towards self-government. The motives of the British Government were, as always, mixed. Suppression by force, ministers considered, would probably lead to more trouble and would certainly cause embarrassing questions to be asked in Parliament. Encouraging African political advance was arguably the safest way to keep the colony amenable and profitable. The fact remains that Britain in the Gold Coast did the opposite of France in Madagascar. Likewise Britain, in giving independence to India in 1947 and to Burma and Ceylon in 1948, did the opposite of France and Holland in their desperate efforts in those years to hold on to power in Indo-China and Indonesia. The bankruptcy caused by the 1939–45 war doomed all the European empires. But the British bowed out comparatively gracefully – largely because a Labour Government was in power, but also because the need to grant self-determination to subject peoples was deeply etched in the Colonial Office mind. In addition the British could afford to show the magnanimity of victory whereas the French and Dutch, after five years of German occupation, had to try to reassert their national authority.

\*     \*     \*

Many colonial administrators had honourable and convincing reasons for opposing Britain's transfer of power to the nationalist leaders of its colonies. They had become closely attached to the people they governed, the rural peasants and up-country headmen and chiefs. These sturdy people generally grew their countries' food and often felt threatened by the lawyers and journalists, the 'pushy natives', who clustered around the centres of British power and demanded its removal. The rural district commissioner was often convinced that agitators, fuelled with alien ideas from the United States or Ireland or Soviet Russia, did not represent *his* tribe or region; they were on the make; their claims to speak for a united national will, determined to be rid of the British, were spurious. The district commissioner knew that the sensible majority of the population would not vote for them – his own tribes, when he asked them, always told him so. And of course his tribes would, wouldn't they? They knew what he wanted to hear. Such British officials were repeatedly surprised when radical, nationalist leaders proved able to win elections.

The man on whom the British had set their hopes often lost the election. Onn bin Ja'afar in Malaya, Dr J. B. Danquah in the Gold Coast, Joshua Nkomo in Rhodesia were each displaced by independence leaders – Tunku Abdul Rahman, Kwame Nkrumah, Robert Mugabe – whom the British had before their election victories considered thoroughly unsuitable. But having laid down the rules of the game the British accepted the results, patiently transferring their educational and administrative help to the winner. If he was prepared to learn – to make the sudden transition from nationalist agitator and speechmaker to head of a complex bureaucratic machine – they gave him all the support they could.

Sometimes this help went further than the British or the nationalist leaders would like to admit. When in 1959 Lee Kuan Yew was about to fight an election in Singapore as leader of the People's Action Party, he had a private meeting with Alan Lennox-Boyd, the Colonial Secretary, at Chequers, the British Prime Minister's country home. Lee and Lennox-Boyd reached an understanding. The British Government would arrest several leading Communists in Singapore, who were Lee's allies in the election campaign; Lee would make speeches bitterly attacking this illiberal, imperialist action; but once he had won the election and released his former allies, he would find grounds to imprison them again. And so he did. In 1962, when Dr Hastings Kamuzu Banda was on the way to assuming power in Nyasaland, his leading radical supporter, Henry Chipembere, was arrested for sedition – on the grounds that he had made bloodthirstily threatening remarks about an English member of the legislative council. It was a case where the Governor, Sir Glyn Jones, could have persuaded his Attorney-General that a prosecution was against the interests of the state. But Dr Banda assured the Governor that he approved of Chipembere's imprisonment. Thus Banda, like Lee, was helped to purge an extremist from his party. Sir Charles Arden-Clarke's partisanship for Kwame Nkrumah in the Gold Coast shows equally strikingly how, once the winner had demonstrated that he had majority support, the Governor would bend the rules to back him. It was all part of the process of graceful handover.

The exceptions to this pattern were all in the Middle East: Palestine, Iran, Egypt, Aden and Cyprus. The British in the Middle East, it was said, never saw the writing on the wall until they hit their heads against it. This was the last area of British imperial expansion. In the nineteenth century power gradually slipped from the Ottoman Empire until, in a remarkable coup at the expense of France and Russia at the end of the 1914–18 war, Britain scooped its choicest possessions. This book contains more chapters about the Middle East than about any other area because it was here that the normally bumpy but nevertheless successful processes of education in government and acceptance of the popularly elected leader went most consistently wrong. The problems were different in each country, as the chapters show, but the consistent way in which the British handled the transfer of imperial authority in the Middle East worse than anywhere else is easily explained. The Middle East was the area of the grand strategic delusion.

Britain took on the task of controlling the Middle East in order to protect the route to India. Ironically, Britain's last major acquisitions in the area, Palestine, Jordan and Iraq, were made at exactly the moment – in 1917 – when Indian nationalists exacted the promise of self-government. Thirty years later, after India had become independent, Britain continued to behave as though the defence of the subcontinent and of the sea-routes east and west of it was a British responsibility. In 1965, shortly after becoming Prime Minister, Harold Wilson summed up this view: 'Britain's frontiers', he said, 'are on the Himalayas.' If this was true, Britain did indeed have to continue to dominate the Middle East in order to be able to send men, ships and aircraft to the frontiers in time of need. But it was not true, and twenty years after Indian independence – in 1967 – the British Government realised it and decided to stop maintaining forces 'East of Suez'. During those twenty years a succession of reasons was given for Britain's staying in the Middle and Far East as a major military power: that treaties with allies had to be seen to be observed, including the promise to deliver military aid if needed; that Australia and New Zealand relied on Britain's military presence (which after the fall of Singapore to Japan in 1942 they no longer did, both countries having then turned to the United States as their principal ally); that the Communist powers had to be contained; that friendly regimes must be saved from overthrow by their own extremists; that the United States wanted a junior partner to share the role of world policeman; that without British troops on hand the flow of Middle Eastern oil to Europe would cease. All these reasons helped account for Britain's spending a higher proportion of its national income on defence in the years of imperial decline than did any of its allies.

In the Far East and Africa the British used their forces with skill, putting down a major Communist insurrection in Malaya by 1957, overcoming the Mau Mau tribal uprising in Kenya by 1956, coming out best at the end of a difficult guerilla war against Indonesia by 1966. But in the Middle East neither force nor political skill seemed to serve the British. The Colonial Office practice of putting the welfare of the local people first, which won friends and willing collaborators in so many colonies, was here overridden by a sense of strategic obligation: whether it was liked or not by the Palestinian Arabs, the Egyptians, the Cypriots and the Adenis, the British Government's perception of its need for military bases in this region overrode its normal policy of bending before the winds of nationalism. Consequently Britain's reputation as the most progressive and reasonable of the developed countries was, in the Middle East, sullied.

This reputation, however, did survive, and the credit earned in India, Ceylon, Burma, the Sudan, the Gold Coast and Nigeria brought Britain a remarkable new instrument of world influence, the reshaped Commonwealth. This organisation was much derided and misunderstood, but was the proof that Britain's manner of disengagement from Empire was approved by the bulk of the new nation-states that resulted. Although Jawaharlal Nehru had once said that India's remaining in the Commonwealth after independence was unthinkable, he himself led India and a succession of other new states in making this a uniquely effective multi-racial group of states. Still in capitals throughout the world, Commonwealth ambassadors meet regularly to share information and plan joint efforts – a function that can be as useful to the Ugandans in dealing with Western Germany as to the British in dealing with the Marxist Government of Ethiopia. The Commonwealth has developed into a partnership of nations in every continent, whose heads of government assemble every two years, rather like an old school reunion. During the 1960s the Commonwealth

*A letter like this one was taken by the monarch's representative to every independence celebration – but not to Palestine or Aden.*

I have entrusted to my Uncle the duty of acting as my representative at the celebrations of the Independence of your country. This is a great and memorable day for you; my thoughts and my good wishes are with you as you take up the great and stimulating responsibilities of independence; and it is with deep and real pleasure that I welcome you to the brotherhood of our Commonwealth family of nations. I am confident that Malaya will respond worthily to the challenging tasks of independence, and that she will continue to show to the world that example of co-operation and goodwill between all races that has been so marked a feature of her history. May God bless you and guide your country in the years that lie ahead.

Elizabeth R

31st August, 1957.

changed from being a white nations' club and primarily Britain's tool into an independent body with its own multi-racial secretariat reporting to all its member-governments: an imperial survival, but with no imperialist characteristics.

The Commonwealth was almost destroyed by the problem of the white settlers in Africa. In Kenya and Southern Rhodesia the settler communities tried desperately to override the normal practices of the Colonial Office and came near to succeeding. They demanded the right to rule over the Africans for as far ahead as they could foresee. What many of the settlers wanted, though they did not say so publicly, was for Britain to secure for them the system evolved in South Africa: *apartheid*. British public opinion and British governments were ambivalent on the issue. They professed detestation for *apartheid* and for the white supremacist designs of the settler communities, yet they found both South Africa and their own white kith and kin reliable business partners. The British in Kenya and Southern Rhodesia, like the French in Algeria, found it difficult to side with the African majority against the white settlers. Eventually, however, after long teetering on the brink, Britain backed the blacks, thus keeping the Commonwealth together and ending the Empire with some credit.

It was Harold Macmillan, the Conservative Prime Minister, who turned Britain's face away from the white settlers when in 1959 he appointed a new Colonial Secretary, Iain Macleod, to deal with them. Macmillan himself was a genius at disguising from the right wing of his party the direction in which he was leading them. In 1959 and 1960, when he and Macleod were taking decisions that Conservative backbenches thought a threat to civilised rule in Africa, Macmillan was to be seen in the smoking room of the House of Commons, flitting from group to group. He chatted in his unflappable, aristocratic way about domestic affairs, about the splendid achievements of the son of one member and of the cousin of another, about a young man commissioned into the Guards and an old man appointed Lord Lieutenant of his county, about the plentiful grouse that year. He thus preserved among them the confidence that, whatever might be happening in Africa, Macmillan was really one of them and in their world nothing had changed.

In February 1960 Macmillan decided that the time had come to announce the change. He chose to do it in the capital of white supremacy. To the amazement and horror of his host, Dr Henrik Verwoerd, South Africa's Prime Minister, and of most of the two hundred and fifty members of both houses of the South African Parliament assembled to hear him in the historic chamber of the old Cape Colony Parliament in Cape Town, he announced which side Britain was finally going to take in ending its Empire:

> Ever since the break-up of the Roman Empire one of the constant facts of political life in Europe has been the emergence of independent nations. They have come into existence over the centuries in different forms, with different kinds of Government, but all have been inspired by a deep, keen

*Harold Macmillan, on his way to South Africa in 1960, visited Ghana and its President, Kwame Nkrumah (second from right).*

feeling of nationalism, which has grown as the nations have grown. In the twentieth century, and especially since the end of the war, the processes which gave birth to the nation states of Europe have been repeated all over the world. We have seen the awakening of national consciousness in peoples who have for centuries lived in dependence upon some other power. Fifteen years ago this movement spread through Asia. Many countries there of different races and civilisations pressed their claim to an independent national life. Today the same thing is happening in Africa, and the most striking of all the impressions I have formed since I left London a month ago is of the strength of this African national consciousness. In different places it takes different forms, but it is happening everywhere. The wind of change is blowing through this continent, and, whether we like it or not, this growth of national consciousness is a political fact. We must all accept it as a fact, and our national policies must take account of it.

\*     \*     \*

In 1958 Professor C. Northcote Parkinson, a historian of the British Empire and author of the definitive study, *British Intervention in Malaya 1867–1877*, published a book, *Parkinson's Law*, which was partly inspired by recent developments in the Colonial Office. He found that during a period of imperial decline the staff in London rose from a total of 372 in 1935 to 1,661 in 1954. From this and similar statistics concerning the Admiralty, he evolved the theory that work expands to fill the time available for its completion.

The book was a satire, but the figures were true. The Colonial Office expanded because, after some two hundred years as a small department that let the Colonial Governors run their territories with the minimum of interference, the Government had decided that initiatives from London were needed. Strikes and political violence in the West Indies over several years had led to the setting-up of a Royal Commission with Lord Moyne as Chairman, which reported in 1939. It found serious social unrest attributable largely to neglect by the British Government:

> Demonstrations of unemployed are the cause of growing concern . . .
> Nothing in the way of long-range policy to deal with the problem . . .
> Serious to the point of desperation . . . unofficial element adopt a consistently hostile attitude towards Government.

To avoid the adverse reaction this information would have caused in the United States, whose alliance Britain was then seeking, the report was kept unpublished until 1945. But within the Colonial Office it generated a new spirit. The Empire was converted to economic and social planning. In 1940 Parliament passed a Colonial Development and Welfare Act, setting aside millions of pounds for investment in the colonies. Even if Conservatives thought this was largely propaganda to impress the Americans, officials in the Colonial Office took it seriously. British policy had been that each colony must finance itself and have no more public facilities than the Governor could induce local taxpayers to provide. As a result, most colonies were tumbledown and without social services. The new wartime spirit meant a departmental revolution. Inspired by a new head of economic planning, Sir Sydney Caine, the Colonial Office for the first time assumed the role of driving force.

The Labour Government that came to power in 1945 adopted the new policy with enthusiasm. To the Treasury the investment could be justified as the way to make the colonies more profitable; building roads, harbours, irrigation and electricity dams would help Britain meet its wartime debts. To the new Colonial Secretary, Arthur Creech Jones, the purpose was equally to bring economic benefits to the colonised people and set them on the road towards political advance. Herbert Morrison, Labour's deputy leader, had said that to give African colonies independence would be 'like giving a child of ten a latch-key, a bank account and a shotgun'. Creech Jones, the minister responsible, was more realistic. He thought that not to give these particular children a latch-key would drive them into bad company on the streets.

The new sense of purpose in the Colonial Office and the vast increase in its staff meant that it needed new accommodation. It moved out of its old offices in Downing Street and into temporary quarters in Great Smith Street, rented from the Church of England. When Churchill returned to power in 1951 he and his new Colonial Secretary, Oliver Lyttelton, decided that this was not good enough: the time had come to build a new Colonial Office. Wartime bombing had left vacant a huge site just across Parliament Square from the Palace of Westminster, the perfect spot for the administrative headquarters of an increasingly busy, modernising Empire. Architects were engaged, plans drawn up and a model made for a grand, appropriate Colonial Office building. Churchill took particular interest in the design, stressing the need for an imposing audience chamber in which the Secretary of State for the Colonies could receive the prime ministers and chiefs, princes and emirs of the Empire, together with their usually considerable retinues.

It was never built. The Colonial Office remained in Church House, occupying, as the 1960s advanced, a diminishing number of rented rooms. In 1967 it was closed down, to be absorbed into the Commonwealth Office and then, like a minor administrative inconvenience, tucked away in a remote part of the Commonwealth section of the Foreign Office.

# CHAPTER 1

# India

'The Jewel in the Crown' is a phrase often used to describe India's position in the British Empire. No term could be less appropriate. A jewel is a small object. India is the largest and most populous territory ever to have been possessed by an imperial power. A jewel is of great value relative to its size. The Indian subcontinent is, man for man and mile for mile, one of the poorest areas in the world.

India was never treasure-trove for Britain with galleons bringing home gold as they did from South America to Spain. Yet India was unquestionably the most important imperial possession of all time: it was India that made the British Empire unique. Like Rome in Egypt, Britain acquired in India a monarchy which expressed its magnificence in buildings that still startle and overwhelm. Like Rome in Egypt, Britain became the overlord in India of religions and artistries, skills and traditions running back to the days of the first civilisations, to times when Rome and London were not yet even primitive villages but the Nile and the Indus were already sophisticated trade-routes with large towns on their banks administered by the literate clerks of affluent rulers. Like Rome in Egypt, Britain acquired in India a large cowed population who, in the fertile parts of the country, could grow and sell enough to pay taxes, enabling the rulers to build their palaces and tombs. At first what mattered most to Britain was trade. By the 1914–18 war, what mattered most, what made India exceed Egypt or any other imperial possession in history, was the provision of men: India sent – and paid for – a million men to fight for Britain in the 1914–18 war; India sent two million men to fight for Britain in the 1939–45 war. India provided the muscle that sustained the British Empire: not so much a jewel, more a gigantic engine of war.

India started as an imperial possession and became a second pole of the Empire with decisions made in Delhi shaping both British and imperial policy. It was in India that the decisions were taken to colonise Singapore (in the face of fierce resistance from London), to colonise Aden, to establish hegemony over the Persian Gulf, to conquer Burma and to attempt to conquer Afghanistan. Both in Persia (Iran) and in what later became Saudi Arabia, the government of British India had its own representatives and policies which were largely independent of those of the United Kingdom.

Had Britain lost the 1914–18 war, an empire based on India might well have continued, just as an empire based on Constantinople survived the sack of Rome.


## The Second Choice, 1497–1906

The British who first sailed there were not looking for India at all. The story begins in the days of Queen Elizabeth I. The Portuguese Vasco da Gama had sailed round the southern tip of Africa and on to India in 1497. His voyage, like that of Columbus five years earlier, changed the shape of the world as known to Europeans. Till then the eastern Mediterranean had been the main highway of Europe's foreign trade. Goods from India and China had passed from market to market overland to Syria (the Levant) and thence by sea to Italy, particularly Venice, for forwarding on horses and donkeys to northern and western Europe. Da Gama revealed that sailing ships could cross the huge unenclosed oceans, reaching India and China with no need to hump the cargoes onto caravans of camels, no need to pay taxes and profit to Turks and Persians on the way. Until da Gama, Europe's trade via southern and eastern Europe went in oared galleys across the Mediterranean. After him, Europe's main traders came to be the men who sailed, without oarsmen, from the northern and western coasts of Portugal, Holland, England and France, out onto the ocean. The ships these men built, strong enough to face Atlantic gales, were also strong enough to fire iron cannon.

The British soon tried to follow where the Portuguese had led. The destination was 'the Indies', but not India. The fabled lands were the spice islands, the purpose to displace Arabs, Persians, Turks, Venetians and Genoese – the masters of the Mediterranean and overland routes – in supplying the spices that improved the flavour of meat in the European winter. Spices were needed because most livestock had to be slaughtered each autumn, as the barren fields of winter could not feed them and the storage of winter fodder had not been developed. So farmers would, like Noah, keep a male and a female of each species in the house for breeding next spring and would dry, salt or pickle the rest. After a month or so, everyone wanted spices: a small quantity of cloves or ginger, nutmeg or mace, pepper or cinnamon could disguise the flavour of imperfectly preserved meat. The demand was high and the goods weighed little. They came above all from the Moluccas, small islands to the east of Borneo.

The Portuguese, firmly established in the spice islands, kept out all rivals with their cannon. Then the Dutch displaced them, and proved equally monopoly-minded. The British East India Company, founded by royal charter in 1600, tried to break into the trade; its merchants (and juniors called 'factors') set up a warehouse (or 'factory') on Amboyna, a small island in the Moluccas. The Dutch reacted violently. In 1623 they seized the factory and killed all the inhabitants in what became known in England as the massacre of Amboyna. The British decided to pursue their trading in lands less profitable, but safer. They turned to India as a second best.

Here were few spices and no prospect of securing a monopoly in those there were. The chief products – textiles, saltpetre and sugar – were bulkier and so less precious. And instead of the few innocent natives of the Moluccas whom the Dutch dominated, in India the British found towns with rich businessmen and strong rulers, many of them independent, the majority owing allegiance to the Mughal Empire. In 1615 its Emperor Jahangir received the embassy of Sir Thomas Roe and granted the East India Company the right to trade. The Mughal Empire was strong enough to put down disorders throughout northern and central India, enabling the Company and thousands of Indian merchants to travel safely with their goods. India had the more sophisticated economy of the two: while Britain wanted Indian products, the Indian traders did not want to buy much of Britain's tin, lead and quicksilver, so the Company regularly had to bridge the gap with silver bullion imported from London. Compared to the 2,500 per cent profit made by the first Dutch 'clove' ship, the trade with India was not spectacular; but profits were steady and high: once in the late seventeenth century the East India Company's dividend was 50 per cent in cash plus 100 per cent in bonus shares for every share held.

The Mughals had never controlled the whole of India. Turkish in origin with a Persian cultural veneer, they had swept down through the Khyber Pass to conquer northern and central India. They were the last of a succession of conquerors from the north-west and the most successful, seizing more of the subcontinent than either Alexander the Great or Tamburlaine. And they lasted far longer than their predecessors, dominating India from 1526 (the accession of Babur) to 1707 (the death of Aurangzeb). Where they did not rule directly, they held sway over princes who deferred to them rather than risk being attacked.

From the hundred and eighty years of effective Mughal rule, the clearest evidence of their power lies in the conversion of a quarter of all the people of India to their religion, Islam, and in their extraordinary monuments. The Taj Mahal at Agra – a tomb of white marble inlaid with floral and abstract designs in precious and semi-precious stones, built in a formal, walled garden by Emperor Shah Jahan for his wife Mumtaz Mahal – is the culmination of a great tradition. Throughout northern India, notably in Delhi and Lahore, earlier Mughals had built such tombs, subtly varying the Persian pattern, so that the narrow gateway frames the view of the onion-domed mausoleum far away beyond pools in which it is reflected; so that a tranquil, shaded garden, symmetrically laid out, offers both quiet protection from the sun and marvellously contrived and varied vistas. Each of these monuments, as vast as the pyramids, required thousands of slaves to labour for many years, carrying out with precision the orders of architect and emperor. Such control and discipline also produced victorious armies. Yet, as ambassador Sir Thomas Roe noted, while the court of the great Mughal was more gorgeous, more vast and more richly supplied with every known luxury than any court in Europe, most of the people of India were abjectly poor, toiling on the land, barely surviving, paying each year to the Mughal tax farmer a third or more of all they earned. Nothing like such high taxation was paid anywhere in Europe at that time.

By the beginning of the eighteenth century the Mughal Empire was no longer able to protect trade – even to protect itself. The Empire split in two with the Nizam of Hyderabad becoming the most powerful ruler in central India. In the north, Persian armies, following the route the Mughals had earlier taken, marched down from the mountains in 1738, sacked Delhi and carried the Mughal's peacock throne back to Tehran. After they withdrew, another invading army from the north-west, the Afghans, destroyed the greatest army India could muster – at the battle of Panipat in 1760. The Afghans then also withdrew, leaving a power gap in northern India which nobody succeeded in filling for forty years.

Britain was at war with France for most of the years 1740 to 1763. Consequently the British and French East India Companies, long commercial rivals, became obliged to make war on each other, adding to the anarchic conflicts of the Indian princes. At first the French in India had the upper hand, but they were stopped by a military genius.

Robert Clive, a young Englishman of no established distinction, the son of a country lawyer, was sent to India as a clerk (or 'writer', one step below a factor). Twenty-two years old, bored and homesick, dreaming of Manchester, 'the centre of all my wishes', he volunteered to be a soldier to escape from his ledgers. A fellow writer described him as 'short, inclined to be corpulent, awkward and unmannerly, his aspect gloomy, his temper morose and untractable'. When Clive came on the scene the English and French were fighting each other only as auxiliaries of native princes. One of these seemed to have fulfilled his own ambitions and those of the French by becoming master of the region centred on Arcot, a town of about 100,000 inhabitants. This success encircled and threatened to strangle the British east-coast trading town of Madras. In September 1751 Clive, aged twenty-six, leading two hundred European troops with six hundred Indians and three field guns, took the fort of Arcot. He then held its mile-long perimeter for fifty days, against a besieging force of ten thousand, half of them well-trained and disciplined soldiers. His holding out for so long against such impossible odds until he was finally relieved is generally regarded as one of the greatest feats of British imperial warfare. It turned the war. The princes backed by the French were defeated.

Until the 1740s, the French and British Companies had both behaved subserviently towards Indian rulers and their local agents. The Anglo-French conflicts around Madras revealed that such conduct was ridiculous: the rulers were now incapable of giving the European traders protection and were themselves ready to turn servile when faced with the Companies' military force. Consequently the French could put their own candidate into

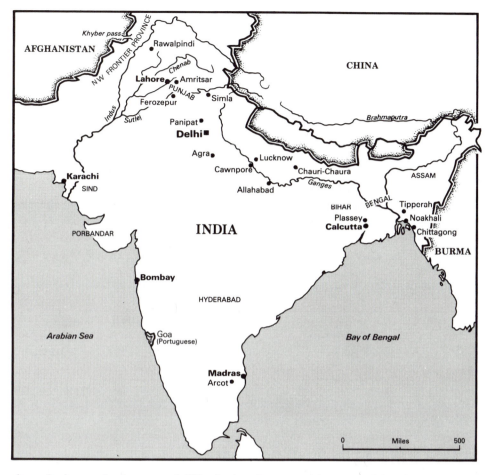

the ruler's seat in Arcot and Clive's tiny force could remove him. Most of the Indian states, eager for peace, were actively seeking a conqueror to protect them.

Before Clive could complete the destruction of the French and their one remaining ally in south India, the Company sent him north to Bengal where the Nawab, Siraj-ud-daula, had driven the British from the small town they had built at Calcutta. The Mughals had granted the British the right to trade, to pay agreed taxes and to fortify their Calcutta factory. When Siraj-ud-daula, nominally a Mughal agent, had tried to increase the taxes and to forbid the fortifications, the British appealed to the Mughal Emperor in Delhi to enforce the rights his authority had granted. Siraj-ud-daula ignored the Emperor and resorted to force. The fortifications at Calcutta were negligible and in the course of overrunning them in June 1756 Siraj-ud-daula's men treated many British cruelly. According to reports that soon appeared in Britain, 146 men, women and children were locked in a cell eighteen feet long by fourteen feet nine inches wide, so that in one night 123 died of heat and suffocation. This was the famous Black Hole. Later some of those named as dead were found to be alive, casting doubt on the whole story, but the fact that fewer than 123 died and that the exact number who did was uncertain did nothing to diminish the power of this episode as an imperial myth.

Clive was diverted north to recover Calcutta. With naval assistance, he recaptured the town and went on to show Siraj-ud-daula that interfering with the Company's trading concession and murdering its people would be avenged. His campaign consisted mostly of tortuous intrigue punctuated by sabre-rattling. Eventually a small army led by Clive met a large army led by Siraj-ud-daula at Plassey in June 1757. Battle was never joined. Artillery fire led Clive to withdraw his troops behind the brow of a hill and to reply with his own artillery, causing severe losses among Siraj-ud-daula's troops, who were in an exposed position. Skirmishes followed, at which point Siraj-ud-daula and his army fled. This confused incident is generally held to be the most decisive battle in Britain's conquest of India. Clive installed a pliant new Nawab of Bengal and formally asked the Mughal Emperor in Delhi to legitimise him. Clive wrote, 'I have 25,000 matchless sepoys [soldiers]'. The Emperor granted the new Nawab his recognition. The British had made their first appearance as a major power on the Indian political stage.

Unfortunately the victors were not just Clive and his men but the entire Calcutta coterie of British traders, who could now force the new Nawab to make laws to suit them. The result was that Bengal, which Clive described as 'an inexhaustible fund of riches', was all but bled dry. The traders and soldiers, following the accepted conventions of the eighteenth century, gathered profits, bribes, presents, monopolies and taxes as fast as they could. Clive was more scrupulous than many; all the same he soon returned to England a millionaire. Every conquering army plunders and rapes: the moment of victory is irresistible but is usually soon over. In Bengal the British traders, following the army, were exceptionally determined plunderers and kept at it for years. They brought misery to the people of the province and, far more important for the court of the East India Company in London, they made money for themselves rather than for the shareholders; further, their conduct provoked a new and less pliant Nawab to attack the Company and inflict a serious defeat on its forces. So in 1765 Lord Clive of Plassey (he had been created an Irish peer in 1762) was appointed Governor-General of Bengal and Commander-in-Chief in order to save the Company's possessions in Bengal from anarchy and consequent loss. 'Oh, my dear sir', said Horace Walpole. 'We have outdone the Spaniards in Peru . . . We shall lose the east.'

Clive returned to Bengal as poacher turned gamekeeper. The military position had been retrieved before his arrival and soon he became unpopular with the Company's servants as he tried to stop their worst excesses. Until now the Company had been a trading organisation that defended its factories with guards and guns and occasionally, when threatened by aggression or chaos, used military force. Now Clive obtained from the Mughal Emperor the *diwani* or revenue-collecting authority in Bengal. The Company thus became part of the Indian political system.

Clive was not the administrator to complete the process he had set in train. He returned to London to his seat in the House of Commons, where a select committee in 1773 censured him for acquiring his Indian fortune. James Boswell wrote: 'Capability Brown told me that he was once at the seat of Lord Clive, who had returned from India with great wealth, and that he showed him at the door of his bed-chamber a large chest, which he said he had once had full of gold.' For months Clive was publicly assailed, in his own words, 'more like a sheep-stealer than a member of this House'. Eventually, although the Prime Minister, Lord North, voted against him, the censure was not pressed home; but the months of public criticism no doubt contributed to Clive's suicide a year later at the age of forty-nine.

Drastic reorganisation was now needed. The East India Company was no longer a mere body of traders: it was a government, collecting huge tax revenues, making wars, negotiating with princes. Committees of get-rich-quick traders in the three Company trading posts at Calcutta, Madras and Bombay could not be left in charge. So Parliament, in the Regulating Act of 1773, made Calcutta supreme over Madras and Bombay and, to sort out the mess, the Government appointed as the first Governor-General of all Britain's possessions in India a long-standing Company official in Bengal named Warren Hastings. For the first time someone represented the King and the British Government throughout India. His salary, however, was paid by the Company which he had to make profitable, and he had to work through the Company's men, whose principal purpose remained the quick accumulation of at least one fortune.

Warren Hastings was a subtle and scholarly man. Governor-General for fourteen years, he determined by his reforms the character of future British rule in India. He created the 'collector', the British official in charge of a district who gathered the revenue from local Indian subordinates. He abolished the free passes that had released Company servants from payment of taxes and dues. He established the supremacy of his office in the face of sometimes savage opposition. He stabilised and regularised government, so that a reliable defence could be locally financed and maintained. Where Clive had conquered, Hastings consolidated. Inevitably, he had to trim and compromise to carry through his policies. To create an administrative and defence system with fortune-hunters for colleagues was an amazing achievement and some of his actions were harsh. Like Clive, he made enemies. After he returned to England, Edmund Burke, Charles James Fox and Richard Brinsley Sheridan led a grand impeachment of him in Westminster Hall. The trial lasted 142 days, spread over seven years, from 1788 to 1795. It was at times the best entertainment in London, with Sheridan making brilliant speeches before a fashionable and rich audience. He called Hastings 'a man holding in one hand a bloody sceptre, while with the other he was picking pockets'. Edward Gibbon was there and described the speech as 'a display of genius', but added, 'what an actor!' Burke called Hastings 'a rat', 'a weazel', 'a keeper of a pig-stye, wallowing in corruption', 'gangrened to the very core'. Said Burke: 'He never corrupts without he is cruel. He never dines without creating a famine.' Many swindlers and profiteers had been pounced on by Hastings. Now their tales against him brought revenge.

In 1791 he began his defence and gradually the charges were rebutted. Witnesses of attested honesty revealed the unexpected truth that Hastings was in no way corrupt: every gift he had received had been recorded and made over to the Company. Eventually he was acquitted on every charge, but the trial had taken the spirit out of him and he retired from public life.

Although Edmund Burke and his colleagues had deployed tittle-tattle based on malice, some honourable motives lay behind the impeachment. Burke had seen that the Indian administration was fundamentally unsound as soon as Clive had conquered Bengal. The problem was as much in London as in India: the East India Company was, after the Bank of England, the biggest thing in the city; it was a major bank, making loans and taking deposits. When it failed to make profits because of the greed of its servants in India or the cost of a war, the entire London money market was shaken and investors were ruined. So Burke was determined to put a stop to 'nabobs' stuffing their pockets at the Company's expense. He had been the leading critic in the House of Commons of the recent use of force against the American colonies. He had seen King George III and Lord North ignore his views and attempt to bludgeon the settlers. Now, in the immediate aftermath of their failure and of the colonies' declaring themselves independent, he was beginning to develop a theory of trusteeship, insisting that unrestrained exploitation of colonies would merely lead to conflict. He told the House of Commons:

> England has erected no churches, no hospitals, no palaces, no schools; England has built no bridges, made no high roads, cut no navigations, dug no reservoirs . . . If we were to be driven out of India this day, nothing would remain to tell that it had been possessed, during the inglorious period of our dominion, by anything better than the orang outang and the tiger.

Burke was determined to devise a system of government for the Company that would make it publicly responsible in London for honourable government in India without making it into yet another source of patronage for the King and his ministers. To this end he drafted successive India bills whose purpose was to create something like the modern public corporation – a body independent of government, but bound by statute to serve the public interest. His efforts, both in the unjustified impeachment of Warren Hastings and in the India Act of 1783, helped shape the form of British control over India for the next seventy years. The home government gained a general power of supervision through a Board of Control, and a new breed of imperial administrator evolved, aware of the risk of scrutiny by Parliament and of Burke's argument that the Government's interest lay in advancing the welfare of the people it ruled.

*Edmund Burke, once respected by the House of Commons, was seized by a near maniacal obsession about India. Pitt and Fox urged him to drop the matter, but he persisted, maintaining that the British in India were everywhere guilty of rape.*

The Company's service was split in two, the commercial and the political: merchants could still deal on their own account but administrators were paid a high salary to govern honestly. Independent courts were introduced, before which officers of the Government could be tried, with a criminal code more humane than that of contemporary England. This thin top crust of honest administration, like the tomb-building of the Mughals, had little effect on most Indians, who continued in their villages to till the soil and pay taxes. But in the Indian political structure it became decisive. A well-administered state with a well-paid and well-organised army first became efficient at repelling the attacks of neighbouring princes, then at ensuring that its neighbours were friendly. Those who were not were liable to have their territory annexed; sometimes their thrones were guaranteed by the Company's stationing a force of its troops in their capital, paid for by the local ruler but under the control of a British Resident. When such a prince fell out with the Company, he found the Company's hand already at his heart. Thus most of India came in time to be ruled by the Company, directly or indirectly.

The Company continued to expand in this way because it was profitable for it to do so: only in secure, orderly states could traders – both Indian and British – flourish. The Company's profits from the trade with Europe were largely used up by the costs of expansion and administration; the big money came from trading to China, where East India Company merchants sold Indian-grown opium and bought tea for sale in Britain.

After Clive other governors-general, notably Wellesley, enlarged the area under British control, nearly always against strong opposition from the

Court of Directors and Board of Control in London. After Warren Hastings others, notably Cornwallis, made improvements in the administration. But British rule in India brought more than pacification and sound administration in the interests of profit. Once those objectives were achieved – and they were the chief concern of every governor-general – some of the British, imbued with a missionary spirit, tried to spread western moral ideas among Indians and thereby to change their habits. The Governor-General most notable for this evangelical approach was Lord William Bentinck, who ruled from 1828 to 1835.

The abolition of suttee is the reform for which Bentinck is chiefly remembered. When a married Hindu died, his widow could show that she was suttee, or devoted, by throwing herself on the flames of his funeral pyre. The action was supposed to be voluntary and often was – a complete act of selflessness and devotion. But many terrified widows were strapped to the pyre by their relatives for motives that included greed for property and shortage of food. Many British were outraged by the practice, but interference with the religious rites of others had caused much bloodshed. So Bentinck's predecessors did nothing. He acknowledged that to ban suttee would 'inspire extensive dissatisfaction', but he banned it nonetheless because, he wrote, of 'the moral goodness of the act and our power to enforce it'. He caused the law to be amended to define the act of assisting suttee as murder and he required the police to prosecute.

Bentinck next set out to suppress thuggee. This was another practice defended by quotation from Hindu scripture. Gangs of bandits, calling themselves thugs, would join a group of travellers, become friendly with them and then, in honour of the goddess Kali, would ritually strangle with a silk cord those they robbed. Bentinck created the office of Superintendent of Thuggee to scour the country, using informers, the most modern police methods and passionate moral dedication to wipe out this terrifying cult. He also, with the help of the law member of his council, Thomas Babington Macaulay, gave government backing to English education in India, promoting English schools and the study of western science. He made English, instead of Persian, the official state language, both in government and in the higher courts of law. He was the model of the interfering do-gooder Englishman, hated by the British officers of the army in India (whose pay he docked on the instructions of an economy-minded board in London), but warmly applauded by a new class of modernising Indians.

Bentinck was not the only radical Englishman to push India towards British ideas and institutions. Macaulay wrote, 'By good government we may educate our subjects [so] that they may in some future age demand European institutions. Whenever such a day comes, it will be the proudest day in English history.' The Governor of Bombay from 1819 to 1824, Mountstuart Elphinstone, wrote, 'We must not dream of perpetual possession, but must apply ourselves to bring the natives to a state that will admit of their governing themselves in a manner that may be beneficial to our interests as well as their own.' Such views were expressed in private letters and minutes more than in public. They reveal both Burke's spirit of trusteeship and the confidence of imperial rulers who now felt secure, ready to punish and eventually wipe out further un-British customs, like infanticide of daughters and the burying alive of lepers, to organise the construction of roads, railways and irrigation canals and to plan schools and universities. They even told their pensioner, the Mughal King in his great red fort at Delhi, nominally still sovereign of most of India, that on his death his title would lapse.

To this settled and self-confident authority, the mutiny of 1857 came as an earthquake. In 1856 the sepoys in the Indian army were told that all future recruits must go overseas to serve Britain whenever they were so ordered. India was, in Lord Salisbury's words, 'an oriental barracks in an eastern sea', and naturally its men must go where they were told to. That upset many Hindu sepoys who wanted their sons to follow them in the army and whose religion forbade travel over the sea. In an earlier period the army's British officers had lived in close touch with their Indian men, but recently increasing numbers of officers' wives had settled in India, creating an isolated British social circle. The immediate cause of the soldiers' mutiny was the issue of new cartridges said to be greased with cow or pig fat, defiling to Hindu or Muslim. The deeper cause was that the Indian soldiers in the Bengal regiments felt things were changing in a dangerous way: laws of inheritance had been changed; Indian values were being trampled on.

The British army in India at this time comprised 34,000 European soldiers and 257,000 Indians. So the Indians could have overwhelmed the British if they had wanted to. And in some places they did. At Cawnpore, a group of British soldiers, women and children, under safe conduct from a Hindu prince, were massacred in the Ganges river. At Lucknow, some 1,700 men, half of them sepoys, were besieged with as many women and children in the British residency. After 150 days, more than half of them were dead, the huge residency, pounded by gunfire, was a ruin, medicines were exhausted and food was scarce; but the Union Jack flew until the relieving force arrived.

Had the rebel soldiers been united or possessed any political leadership, they could easily have crushed the British. But only the Bengal regiments revolted (and even many of them spared their officers) while the regiments of Madras and Bombay stood aloof. Nearly all the princes, powerful within their various states, helped the British, who sustained them in great dignity while the rebel soldiers' purposes and trustworthiness were doubtful. As for supreme political leadership, the mutineers captured the Mughal Emperor in Delhi and declared him their leader. But he, despite the British announcement that his dynasty was at an end, had no taste for fighting the British, preferring to write erotic poems and relax in his beautiful gardens. So, within eighteen months, the disorderly mutiny was crushed.

The British shot and slashed their way back into full control and then wrought a bloodthirsty vengeance on the mutineers, both proved and suspected. The Governor-General, 'clemency' Canning, tried to restrain the excesses of retribution, but he could not subdue the anger of his men. Nobody knows how many Indians were hanged, run through, shot or disembowelled, how many villages were burned, how many temples desecrated, or how much was looted from innocent Indians. The punishment for those found guilty by court martial of rebellion was to be tied over the barrel of a cannon and, to the beat of drums, blown to pieces. The Indian army was never again to rise in force against the British.

The mutiny caused British officers to seek a renewed intimacy with their Sikh, Muslim, Gurkha and Rajput soldiers. Indian army officers became a caste apart from other Britons: the mutiny had shown this to be essential. The same need to be aware of the feelings of Indians was recognised in civil government. By the 1850s the East India Company had ceased to trade and had become the instrument through which London governed India. In 1858, immediately after the mutiny, it was abolished. Victoria became Queen and later (in 1876) Empress of India, beginning a strangely warm relationship with a possession she was never to visit (she employed an Indian accountant, who gave her lessons in Hindi, and several Indian servants, including one, Munshi Abdul Karim, who became her inseparable companion); the Governor-General was given the extra title of Viceroy, personal representative of the monarch; and, most important, the formerly all-British legislative council which advised the Governor-General was reinforced by the addition of its first Indian members – a chosen few who could keep the Viceroy informed about the thinking of the commercial and educated classes, while getting a taste for the British method of government.

The main lesson the British learned from the mutiny was that to force western moral ideas on India was liable to inspire the 'extensive dissatisfaction' Bentinck had risked when he abolished suttee. From now on the British rulers reduced their evangelism and concentrated on supplying the kind of benefits Rome had brought to its colonies – not only the roads, railways, canals, bridges and irrigation works of earlier years, but also new industries like coal-mining and jute (mostly British-owned) and iron-smelting and cotton (mostly Indian-owned). These practical innovations did not offend, at least not to the same extent (though high-caste Hindus were outraged, in railway carriages, at having to suffer the defiling presence of Muslims and untouchables).

The only major reversion to Bentinck-like ideas came when William Ewart Gladstone, another Christian radical, was Prime Minister. He sent Lord Ripon out as Viceroy in 1880 'to give to India the benefits and blessings of free institutions', and Ripon soon introduced a general system of local self-government for the explicit purpose not of improving efficiency but of training Indians in the subtleties of democracy. He also tried to remove the rule that an Englishman could be tried only before another Englishman. But the British community in India would not allow their errant members to

appear before an Indian judge, so Ripon backed down, vilified by his fellow Britons, notably in Frank Bignold's lines:

> Woe to the blinded statesman
> Who truckles to the base
> And sets above the nobler
> The feebler falser race.

Bignold's view was widespread, both among clever civil servants like himself and among the British traders, who were more likely to be brought to court. But the Bentinck–Ripon spirit could not be suppressed. Immediately after the British in India had defeated Ripon in 1883–4 on the issue of Indian judges, a retired British official, Allan Octavian Hume, founded the Indian National Congress, to channel the counter-surge of educated Indian feeling. Hume had nearly been appointed to the Viceroy's council in 1877, but he was turned down because, although able, he had 'obvious faults'. One Englishman did not need to explain to another what these were: he was an interfering busybody, prone to taking the side of the Indians against the administration. So he retired from the service, but, unusually, stayed on in India. When Ripon came out as Viceroy he was pleased to accept Hume's advice on Indian aspirations and Hume appointed himself the two-way conduit between the Viceroy and a small group of politically conscious, English-speaking Indians eager to benefit from Ripon's reforms.

When Ripon retired in December 1884, Hume was active in organising the biggest ovation from Indians ever accorded to a Viceroy, before or since, until Mountbatten ended British rule. Hume followed this success by organising his Indian political associates into the Congress, which in 1885 held its first meeting in Bombay; 72 English-speaking Indians were present. In 1886 in Calcutta 434 delegates attended; in 1887 in Madras 607; in 1888 at Allahabad more than 1,200 – an annual gathering of Indian lawyers and other wealthy men to discuss in English matters of common concern on which they could pass resolutions and hope to influence the government. At the first meeting the chairman, W. C. Bonnerjee, described the object of the Congress as to promote 'those sentiments of national unity which had their origin in our beloved Lord Ripon'. When Congress demanded representative institutions, they wanted the voters to be men of education and property. When Congress raised money, their first purpose was to set up an office in London, so as to influence opinion in Britain and to try to secure the election of an Indian to the House of Commons. In this they succeeded when, with Gladstone's support, Dadabhai Naoroji was elected for Central Finsbury in 1892 (at the time, of course, no Indian could be elected to a comparable position in India). Hume took total charge of all Congress affairs; he was general secretary for twenty-three years from 1885 to 1908, making arrangements for the annual session every Christmas, fixing the agenda, arranging publication of the report afterwards and travelling to London to join Naoroji in lobbying at Westminster.

At first the Viceroy took a sympathetic interest in what appeared to be the development of a loyal opposition and encouraged these Anglophile Indians, attracted by the qualities of British administration, literature and law – quite apart from the sheer fact of British power. Hume believed responsible complaint and criticism had won Gladstone over to home rule for Ireland, and Congressmen shared his belief that the British would listen to reason – after all the Congress were asking only for representative government in India, not for independence. But, after winning some concessions in the 1880s and 1890s, the Congress began to want more and to want it quickly while the British administration increasingly sought to restrain their demands and to impose delay. Conflict developed.

The Congress were the first body of Indians since the Emperor Asoka, two thousand years before, to take an all-India view. India contained hundreds of rulers, each nominally sovereign, scores of languages written in almost as many scripts, wide diversities of race and religion, of climate and food; the concept of the whole subcontinent as a single nation had simply vanished from memory. Asoka himself did not really become known until inscriptions naming him were identified in 1915. Indians during most of the British period thought of themselves as belonging to their village; even merchants who travelled widely felt they were members of a caste or a family rather than a nation. This was not surprising. After all, nationalism developed in Europe only in the nineteenth century. So the Congress members, to strengthen their attempt at developing an India-wide response to the India-wide rule of the British, invented the idea of an ancient 'mother India' to which all Indians had once owed allegiance. It was a useful historical fabrication.

Yet from the beginning it was challenged. The Congress in its earliest years was particularly concerned to advance the opportunities for Indians in the Civil Service and public life generally. The principle of Indian access to posts in the highest grade of the Civil Service had by now been conceded, but in practice the competitive examinations for entry were held for candidates aged nineteen in London. This effectively excluded Indians, unless they had been to school in England. The Congress pressed for the exams to be held in India as well as in England and for the age at entry to be raised to twenty-three in order to give young Indians time to achieve the necessary standard in English. Such demands were popular among middle-class Hindus, particularly in Bengal, whose sons were doing well in English education and were likely to succeed in open exams. The Muslims, by contrast, were badly placed to compete. Until Bentinck's reforms, the Indian courts had worked in Persian, as had the old Mughal administration. Muslim schools still taught in Persian, so its replacement by English, intended merely as an efficient act of westernisation, had in fact discriminated between one Indian group and another. When the Congress won easier access for Indians to the Civil Service, many Muslims feared that the beneficiaries would be Hindus only. They preferred British administrators.

From the launching of the Congress in 1885, Muslim dissent was to accompany it like a shadow. Congress leaders tried hard to avert this danger. Badruddin Tyabji, a Muslim lawyer from Bombay, presided over the third annual meeting of Congress. He told the delegates that, while some general questions affected India as a whole, India was in no sense one nation. He tried to persuade Congress to modify its claims so as to attract Muslim members. But Muslim fears spread quickly. Most middle-class Muslims lacked Tyabji's self-confidence. Within a year of the first Congress, rival Muslim organisations sprang up to oppose the dangerous idea of a single voice for Indian interests.

Some Hindus in the Congress wanted to destroy their British rulers, not to join them. The leader of this group, Bal Gangadhar Tilak, a great Sanskrit scholar and an orthodox Hindu, tacitly encouraged the murder of British officials – and was sent to prison. Most members of Congress supported his rival, Gopal Krishna Gokhale, a westernised, urbane conciliator who, recognising that British rule was too powerful to be destroyed, restricted his aim to self-rule under a liberal constitution, with British overlordship. Gokhale and the Congress majority were equally motivated by the desire to secure British institutions permanently for their country.

The apex of this admired British system was the Indian Civil Service (ICS), whose 1,200 members – almost all British, though the first Indians were appointed in 1869 – were commonly known as 'the heaven born'. When scholars of administration write essays on the finest civil service ever created, they consider the Chinese mandarinate at its peak and the ICS. The assistant magistrates and collectors were – and knew they were – an élite among élites. The reason the British created a service so exceptionally fine in India, long before anything comparable had been developed at home, goes back to the days of Clive. The rapacity of the early administration was so disgraceful that it had to be totally purged if British government in India was to survive. Where the early administrators took bribes and presents, and Clive even defended in the House of Commons his action in accepting them – 'I walked through vaults piled with gold and jewels. I stand astonished at my own moderation' – among ICS members corruption was unknown.

The young men who joined were usually able, for amusement, to write to each other in Latin or classical Greek. The most famous Latin joke of British India came not from an ICS man but a general; as so often, he had orders not to conquer, but nevertheless had done so, his victim being the princely state of Sind. His report was a one-word cable in Latin: 'Peccavi' (I have sinned). Young ICS men always, as a matter of course, learned the local Indian language of the area, in which they might well find themselves, at the age of twenty-two, ruling a million people. They were Plato's guardians – a caste apart, bred and trained to be superior. Two anecdotes about a notable ICS man, Lord Hailey, help convey the flavour of the service. When he was Chief Commissioner of Delhi, Hailey showed the ability to let another man do his own job with the following instruction to a District Magistrate: 'You will have a trying day tomorrow. You will probably have a riot. But I have discussed all your arrangements and I approve of them. One embarrassment at least you shall be spared. I am going fishing.' When Governor of the Punjab, he escaped one day from after-dinner drinks for a walk with his dog in the pouring rain, taking no mackintosh because it was too hot. He saw a procession pass, shouting slogans, and wondered how the police dealt with such events. So he joined. Nothing happened, but he sent next morning for a copy of the police report and read with delight that the procession had been joined 'by a disreputable European with a dog'. These clever men were not motivated by sympathy for Indians or by altruism: such soft feelings were despised. They were motivated rather by proud ideals like fair and open justice, efficient, properly recorded administration and the possibility and duty of making improvements. Their English public schools and universities had imbued them with a contempt for money-making and the hustle and corruption that inevitably go with it.

At their head was the Viceroy, but he was never drawn from the ICS, because members of the Service had the unfortunate habit of identifying with their charges: 'I'm a Hindu', one would say, or, 'I'm a Punjabi'. This was the other aspect of their high quality: they were given great freedom to implement policies of their own and often devoted a lifetime to pursuing works of local improvement – road building, tree planting, sewage, schools or medical centres – whatever they believed 'their' people needed. It required a man trusted in Downing Street to preside over such officers. In 1898, George Nathaniel Curzon was appointed Viceroy. He had the brains

of an ICS man and an enormous sense of his own importance. Of the impeccable memo-writing and file-shuffling of the men who ruled India, he wrote: 'Round and round like the diurnal revolutions of the earth went the file, stately, solemn, sure and slow; and now, in due season, it has completed its orbit and I am invited to register the concluding stage.' In 1903 he held a great durbar: he transported thousands of people from the British capital, Calcutta, to the elegant buildings of the old Mughal court at Delhi, surrounding himself there with all the princes, armies, jewellery and pomp that might occupy a child's dream of the Arabian Nights to proclaim the succession of the new King, Edward VII; and at the centre of it all, lording it even over the King's brother the Duke of Connaught, was the Viceroy on his bejewelled elephant, entitled to precedence over everyone except the King himself.

Curzon was a stickler for detail and rejected the hymn 'Onward Christian Soldiers' when it was suggested for church services during the durbar, not, as might have been supposed, because most of the King's soldiers and subjects in India were not Christian, but because of the line, 'Crowns and thrones may perish, kingdoms rise and wane', which hinted at the unthinkable. Curzon's durbar was not the last nor even the most spectacular assertion of the inevitability of Europeans for ever ruling Asiatics, but of the glorification of the office of Viceroy it was the apogee.

Eight years later, in 1911, another reign had begun and King George V

*Curzon makes his entrance to the durbar in Delhi.*

insisted on visiting India. His ministers tried to dissuade him. They thought he could bring nothing but trouble. His durbar, of course, had to be even more splendid than Curzon's. It was to be the only visit to the greatest imperial possession by a reigning British King and Emperor of India – 'Ind. Imp', as all the coins of Britain and the colonies proclaimed him. To top the bill at the end of the durbar George V suggested a spectacular climax: he would be crowned Emperor of India. The Archbishop of Canterbury objected, on the grounds that the coronation was an act of Christian worship, ill-suited to a land of Hindus and Muslims. So the King announced that he would put the crown on himself, in his tent, and emerge wearing it. The question then arose, which crown? The state crowns could not lawfully leave England. The crown jewellers, Garrard, said a new one would cost £60,000, which ministers said was too expensive to be paid from British taxes. The Government proposed that the cost be met from the gifts of precious stones which the King might expect to receive from India's ruling princes, but this was turned down by the Viceroy. If it became known, it would offend the princes and diminish the Crown in their eyes. The next scheme, that the London jewellers Garrard make it, hire it to the King for the durbar for £4,400, then unmake it on his return, was also turned down: undignified. So in the end the Indian taxpayer footed the bill for the

*Indian princes pay homage to King George V at his durbar.*

spectacular bauble, which was promptly removed from India and placed in the Tower of London, where it remains to this day.

## Fancy Franchises, 1906–1939

Between the two durbars of Curzon in 1903 and of George V in 1911 came the turning-point, the beginning of the end of British rule. In Britain a Liberal Government was elected in 1906 and, like previous Liberal governments, introduced reforms in India. However, where Lord Bentinck's evangelical radicalism and Lord Ripon's Gladstonian Liberalism had hit the British in India like passing earth tremors whose damage subsequent Viceroys could contain, the Morley–Minto reforms of 1909 – Morley was Secretary of State for India, Minto was Viceroy – opened the way to an unstoppable process. Needless to say, this was not their intention.

The content of the reforms looks undramatic. Some elected Indians were to sit on provincial legislative councils ('legcos') and the number of appointed Indians on the central legco was substantially increased. The new Liberal Government believed in this sort of thing, just as Gladstone had done. The reason the Morley–Minto reforms led inevitably onwards, where by comparison the Ripon reforms were static, was the creation in the meantime of the Congress. Ripon, wanting to talk to educated Indians and involve them in the processes of government, had found no spokesman available and so talked to Allan Octavian Hume. Minto not merely was able to consult a spokesman of progressive Indian opinion, Gokhale, he had to. Tilak's wing of Congress had begun a terror campaign, mainly in Bengal, and both Morley and Minto realised that to repress this movement, while necessary, was not enough. So the reforms were shaped in consultation with the Congress moderates and Gokhale became a member of the enlarged legislative council, thus acquiring a splendid platform from which to demand further reforms. Morley and Minto even insisted in March 1909 on appointing the first ever Indian to the Viceroy's Council, the nearest thing India had to a Cabinet. He was a Hindu lawyer, Satyendra Prassano Sinha (later Lord Sinha and a member of the Judicial Committee of the Privy Council). Morley wrote to King Edward VII that the appointment was necessary and expedient 'for the contentment of Your Majesty's Indian dominions'. Edward replied: 'The King has thought it over quite as much as Lord Morley has. He remains of opinion that the proposed step is fraught with the greatest danger to the maintenance of the British empire under British rule ... As Lord Morley as well as the Viceroy recommend Mr Sinha, the King has no alternative but to agree to his appointment.' He later wrote: 'Morley knows how strong my views are on [this] subject and so does Minto, but they don't care what I say'.

One feature of the Morley–Minto reforms was to remain the subject of controversy till long after independence. In the elections to the larger provincial assemblies, constituencies of the British type were not thought suitable: the numbers to be elected were too small and the voters too excitable. So appropriate groups were invited to choose representatives: universities, chambers of commerce, municipal boards, landowners and – the contentious case – minority religious groups. Minto accepted the argument that in the few elections hitherto held in India – following Ripon's act and some others – the Muslims had done badly: not only did Hindus greatly outnumber them but a larger proportion of the Hindus were rich and therefore qualified to vote and Hindus usually got elected; so it followed that the Muslims must have reserved seats. Because of this decision Minto was charged by Hindus with attempting to divide the communities of India so that Britain could continue to rule. The evidence suggests that he was not so Machiavellian. He simply wanted to get on with the job of manning the assemblies. Nevertheless 1906, the year in which he conceded separate electorates, was also the year in which the Muslim League was set up. It marked the creation of a political career structure in which success was to be achieved by encouraging sectarianism, something Parliament would never have allowed in England. Among those opposed to separate electorates was a young Muslim Congressman, Mohammed Ali Jinnah.

At first the Morley–Minto reforms were successful: Tilak's terror squads did not cease their activities, but the Government won the active co-operation of the moderate majority in Congress and of the politically active Muslims, thus rendering the extremists containable. Tilak himself was sent to prison in Burma. When the 1914–18 war began, the German Government expected that trouble in India would greatly weaken the British. But trouble never came. Indians supported the war effort in vast numbers, more than a million eventually volunteering and fighting in Egypt and the Sudan, in Aden, Africa and Mesopotamia and in the freezing trenches of France and Belgium. King George V, visiting his troops on the western front, was concerned for the welfare of the Indians. He wrote to the Viceroy, 'The accommodation did not seem to me at all suitable. I spoke to Lord Kitchener [the War Minister] about it and he has appointed a special commissioner to look after the Indian wounded.' Not only did India provide men, it also paid for them and provided rations. In 1918 Tilak, the philosopher of anti-British terrorism, released from prison, joined M. K. Gandhi, a new Congress leader, in recruiting men to assist the war effort of the British Empire. They believed that the Empire would give India home rule and the Empire must therefore be saved. Gandhi wrote: 'The gateway to our freedom is situated on French soil . . . If we could but crowd the battlefields of France with an indomitable army of Home Rulers fighting for victory for the cause of the allies, it would also be a fight for our own cause.'

Their belief was based on the words of the Secretary of State for India, Edwin Montagu, in the House of Commons in 1917: 'The policy of H. M. Government is the gradual development of self-governing institutions, with a view to the progressive realisation of responsible government in India as part of the Empire.' He meant a status rather like that enjoyed by Canada, Australia, New Zealand and South Africa: attachment to the crown and to the highest court of appeal (the judicial committee of the Privy Council), but freedom otherwise for the Government to act independently. It had been conceded in response to pressure in India, from extremists and moderates alike, at a time when Britain desperately needed Indian recruitment for the war; and within two years it began to be put into effect with the first of an amazing series of fancy franchises and confusing constitutions that were to make the final stages of the British Empire a paradise for lawyers. The special ingredient in the 1919 package was 'dyarchy', meaning government by two rulers or two systems. In each province of India the Governor was now to have two distinct roles: in respect of subjects like policing and finance he was to be the old-fashioned colonial Governor with a small executive council of British officials and absolute power; in respect of other subjects, like education, health, public works and agriculture, he was to be a constitutional sub-monarch, bound to accept the advice of Indian ministers who were themselves answerable to elected assemblies.

This subtle bargain looked as though it would suit both the Congress, who saw in it a path to increasing power, and the Government, who saw in it the mechanism to secure authority over the things that really mattered. But the prospect of consent was suddenly shattered. Public protests against the Government had erupted when some repressive laws known as the Rowlatt Acts were introduced. They became worse when Britain and her allies dethroned the Caliph in Istanbul (the chief ruler of Islam, successor to the prophet), an act that aroused far more anger among Indians, both Hindu and Muslim, than it did among Turks. An English general, R. E. H. Dyer, decided to put down a small town's unruly and dangerous protesters by a procedure without which no empire could survive and which had been much used in recent years by the Ottomans: a massacre.

One day in April 1919 a mob in Amritsar, a town in the Punjab in north India, ran wild, killing three Englishmen, violently assaulting two English-women, burning shops and banks and looting widely. The Deputy Commissioner, unable to control his area, handed over his powers to Dyer, the local Commanding Officer of the army, to restore order. Three days later, on the morning of Sunday, 13 April, Dyer and a large column of British and Indian soldiers toured Amritsar for two hours, accompanied by drummers and the town crier who, at nineteen places in the city, read a proclamation in Urdu and Punjabi. This ended with the words: 'Any . . . processions or gatherings of four men will be . . . treated as an unlawful assembly and dispersed by force of arms if necessary.' The proclamation must have become generally known, but it was not read out anywhere within a third of a mile of the Jallianwala Bagh, a principal meeting place in Amritsar, even though the general was told that a meeting was due to be held there late that afternoon.

The meeting was held to protest at some recent arrests, but the crowd in the Jallianwala Bagh, variously estimated at between 15,000 and 50,000, were not all there for politics. Sunday, 13 April was Baisakhi, the start of a religious festival that attracted many Sikh pilgrims to Amritsar's Golden Temple, visible over the nearby houses. Others came for the horse and cattle fairs. Many were prepared to sleep wrapped in blankets near the Jallianwala Bagh's large drinking well. Dyer did not order the crowd to disperse. He did not warn them in any way. He simply marched his fifty riflemen to a raised bank and ordered them to kneel and fire. The Bagh is sunk below the level of the surrounding streets and the huge crowd were trapped. Some tried to climb the enclosing walls, only to find that to do so made them easier targets for the riflemen. Others tried to run through the three narrow lanes out of the square, but in the crush the lanes were impassable. The soldiers went on loading, firing, reloading, firing – with Dyer directing where they should shoot – until they had used, on average, thirty-three rounds each. It took them, in all, about six minutes. They aimed particularly at the gates, so that the dead and wounded were soon piled high where some had trodden on the fallen in their efforts to escape and had themselves been shot. Many hundreds lay bleeding, as Dyer marched his men away.

From the surrounding narrow alleys of Amritsar, some came that night to seek their relatives. Others, knowing of the shooting and the curfew Dyer had imposed, were too frightened to come. So the wounded lay among the dead as vultures scavenged. Dyer reported to his superior officer: 'I entered the Jallianwala Bagh by a very narrow lane . . . On entering I saw a dense crowd . . . [and] a man on a raised platform addressing the audience and making gesticulations with his hands. I realised my force was small and to hesitate might induce attack. I immediately opened fire and dispersed the mob. I estimated that between 200 and 300 of the crowd were killed. My party fired 1650 rounds.'

Dyer had not finished. He next imposed what became known as his 'crawling order'. At the spot where, a few days earlier, an English missionary teacher, a woman, had been attacked by a mob and left for dead, Dyer posted soldiers to make sure that any Indian who passed would crawl on his stomach. According to the official committee of inquiry chaired by Lord Hunter, a senior lawyer from Scotland, some fifty people were made to do so.

Until his death eight years later, Dyer continued to maintain that his action was right: the British in the Punjab would, but for him, have been swept aside by ungovernable violence. British opinion was divided. Dyer was told by his superior officers that he must resign his command, but when his ship left for England a vast crowd cheered him as a hero. While he was still at sea, a *Daily Mail* reporter came aboard for an exclusive interview with the great man. The British Cabinet backed the decision of the Viceroy's Council in India, that Dyer should resign and be offered no further job. Winston Churchill, the Secretary of State for War, had trouble persuading the Army Council in London to implement the decision of both Delhi and Downing Street: the Chief of the Imperial General Staff, Field Marshal Sir Henry Wilson, insisted on Dyer's right, in spite of the report of the

*General R. E. H. Dyer had been brought up in a world where empires were expected to sustain themselves by the occasional massacre.*

committee of inquiry, to state his case. Edwin Montagu, Secretary of State for India, told the House of Commons that Dyer's actions amounted to 'terrorism, racial humiliation and frightfulness'. Sir Edward Carson, former Attorney-General, replied that Dyer's action 'might have saved a most bloody outbreak, which might have caused the loss of thousands of lives'. The *Morning Post* appealed for funds for 'The Man who Saved India' and eventually raised more than £26,000. The House of Lords passed a motion deploring the Government's conduct towards Dyer 'as unjust to that officer'. With so substantial a part of the nation against it, the Government nevertheless stood by its policy: massacre was not to be British practice towards colonial peoples.

The massacre and the widespread British support for its perpetrator were the main reasons Gandhi and the Congress ceased to trust the British. Previously Gokhale and Gandhi had believed that the fairminded law-bringers, the honest guardians who had given India better government than it ever had before, would with some prodding act on their professed beliefs in democracy, the rights of man and racial equality; they would deliver the self-government that Edwin Montagu had promised in 1917. Dyer's massacre in 1919 showed the opposite: contempt for Indians and indifference to their rights. If these were ultimately the dominant traits in the British, then they were not to be trusted: dyarchy would have to be recognised for what it was, not a step towards self-government but a steely demonstration that the guns and the decisions about when to use them would stay in British hands for ever. Nobody can say that, but for Dyer, co-operation and steady constitutional progress would have occurred. What can be said is that after Dyer co-operation could never again be relied upon. Thousands of Indian clerks and soldiers remained at their posts, but the political leadership of the Congress was seized by a new spirit: that of Gandhi, who during the war was recruiting Indians to fight for Britain in the trenches of France, but who by 1920 was demanding that Indians confront the British with civil disobedience, with what George Orwell called 'a sort of non-violent warfare'.

Gandhi more than any other person embodied the see-saw of Indian feelings about the British Empire. The son of the chief minister of a tiny Indian state, Porbandar on the Arabian Sea, Gandhi decided in 1888 when he was eighteen that he must qualify as a lawyer in England – at exactly the time when the newly-founded Congress was seeking to ensure that Indians with such qualifications would receive a growing share of power. Gandhi's caste were not permitted to make a sea voyage: elders of his community warned him that if he went he would be an outcaste. But he was adamant and sailed to London, where he not only qualified as a barrister but also took dancing lessons. When he returned to practise he had little success in the Bombay courts and so it was convenient for him that a big case in South Africa cropped up: an Indian company there needed a lawyer and Gandhi was recommended. He again crossed the sea, initially on a year's contract. In South Africa he met vicious racial discrimination for the first time. Travelling first class on a train, as was his wont, he found himself ordered out of the compartment and then, when he showed his ticket as proof of his right to be there, he was thrown off the train. As a result he became involved with the political rights of the Indian community in Natal, which were under threat. The Natal Indians found that this clever young lawyer from Bombay with the confidence of a prime minister's son had more idea than any of them how to resist the Government. His technique was based on naive faith in the British, whom he relied on not to shoot when he led South African Indians in burning their passes or obstructing essential routes by organised sit-ins. He turned out to be right. Rather than shoot, the British-educated rulers of Natal arrested him. He offered no resistance. He merely made sure foreign newspapermen were at hand to witness what was happening. When he came to court, he pleaded guilty, offered evidence against himself and asked for the maximum sentence. He believed that the local regime was acting against the British imperial ideal so that when reports of his conduct reached England and India, public outrage would make sure that the Government backed down. Again he was right. The Viceroy of India exerted pressure on behalf of the South African Indians; so did the Secretary of State for India in London. The necessary concessions were made and Gandhi was released. He became something of a hero, especially in India. His technique of non-violence was not entirely original; his caste in Porbandar had links with the Jains, an unusual Hindu sect for whom non-violence was a principle; but he turned it into a unique weapon: his adversaries, the British, were almost certainly the only imperialists in history who could have been *embarrassed* into retreating; in spite of the British reputation for pragmatism, members of the ICS believed in the principles they professed and were, particularly when visible to newspaper reporters and therefore Parliament, prepared to act on them, even against the interests of fellow Britons.

Gandhi returned to India in 1915 after more than twenty years in South Africa, still a believer in the British Empire and its willingness to teach Indians self-government. When, in the course of re-learning about India, he wrote a report to the Viceroy on the appalling conditions on the indigo plantations in Bihar, his every recommendation was accepted and implemented. He joined a committee set up by the government of Bombay to deal with the problem of professional beggary. Montagu, the Secretary of State, who met Gandhi in Delhi in 1917, described him as 'my friend'.

After Amritsar, as he turned against the British, Gandhi showed the bitterness, the vengefulness and also the inconsistency of a rejected lover. He had given the British Empire his energy and trust – even his love – and Dyer was the reply. He began to use the techniques he had developed in South Africa to expose the weaknesses of the British administration. He had abandoned the black tailcoat and striped trousers of the lawyer and adopted instead a style like that of a poor Indian peasant, a dhoti (or long loincloth) and a shawl of simple cotton. These helped him on his return to India, when he was shocked by the poverty of his fellow countrymen, to win their support. Further, he insisted that his clothes be made of hand-spun cotton – *khaddar* – which was formerly common throughout India, but had been totally displaced by cheap British, Japanese and later Indian factory cloth. He wanted to resurrect village industries, to show that traditional Indian methods could overwhelm the modern western. His lead was followed by other senior Congressmen, who put British clothes on bonfires and under- took to wear *khaddar* in future. It became almost a uniform. In a single brilliant gesture Gandhi symbolised Congress's turning away from its English, educated origins and identifying itself with the village traditions of the Indian masses.

The leading Congress moderate at this time was a rich lawyer, Motilal Nehru. His son, Jawaharlal, a timid, pleasure-loving science graduate from Cambridge who like Gandhi had qualified as a barrister at the Inner Temple in London, was appointed an assistant to the Congress committee that investigated Dyer's actions in Amritsar. The experience opened young Nehru's eyes to the side of British rule that affected Indians less fortunate than himself and brought him into close contact with Gandhi, who was eventually to become almost his second father. Within a few years Gandhi, with the young Nehru always close behind him, had succeeded in changing the Congress from a predominantly Anglophile, middle-class debating society into a political force that could bring Indians in their millions onto the streets. Gokhale and Tilak had played their part in this evolution, but Gandhi was decisive – and General Dyer helped in ways he would never understand.

Thus from 1920 on, India became intermittently ungovernable. Gandhi's response to the Amritsar massacre had been to say 'co-operation in any shape or form with this satanic government is sinful'. He won support for a demand that members of Congress resign government office, withdraw from government schools and colleges and boycott the elections to the provincial councils. One Congress poster read: 'There is no atrocity if a thousand men refuse to pay taxes; but to pay taxes to a Government which commits atrocities is to support such rule and thus encourage atrocities.' Gandhi's call struck a chord among Indians throughout the subcontinent. Whether the reason was the attraction of withholding taxes in company with thousands of others and claiming it as a patriotic duty, the dazzling hope inspired by the Russian revolution, US President Woodrow Wilson's commitment to self-determination, a succession of local grievances or a mixture of all of these, Gandhi's anger at the British exactly matched the feelings of the mass of politically responsive Indians; his tactic of *satyagraha* – soul-force – loosely translated as 'civil disobedience', equally matched their mood. Crowds of peaceful but disobedient Indians in the streets repeatedly reduced police and government to a state of flustered impotence.

For the next twenty-seven years relations between the British Government and the Indian National Congress were on a continual zig-zag: Gandhi was frequently suspicious of the British but often trusted them, while they were alternately exasperated and impressed by him. The British had proclaimed self-government as their objective for India and Gandhi believed many individual Britons – particularly Lord Irwin, Viceroy from 1926 to 1931 – to be sincere in their pursuit of this aim. But repeatedly, when his confidence had been gained, it was shattered as he became convinced that many of the British in authority were prepared to concede enough, but only just enough, to silence Indian protest, in order to win over the Congress moderates and thus to maintain effective power. So Gandhi launched campaigns of non-cooperation with the Government between 1920 and 1922, between 1930 and 1934 and again in 1942. During each of these periods he aroused civil disobedience on a massive scale. In the first two campaigns he openly disobeyed what he considered unjust laws, toured the country urging others to follow his example and then, when he was arrested, asked for the maximum sentence. But when his civil disobedience campaigns were turned by others to violence, he became deeply distressed. This first happened in 1922 when villagers at Chauri-Chaura in the United Provinces, taking Gandhi's inspiration substantially farther than he intended, set fire to a police station in which twenty-two policemen were burnt to death. Gandhi immediately suspended the campaign. But violence had by then been spreading for some time and Gandhi was arrested and charged with inciting it. This, his first arrest in India, produced from the young judge, Mr C. N. Broomfield, a memorable statement:

Mr Gandhi, you have made my task easy in one way by pleading guilty to the charge. Nevertheless, what remains, namely the determination of a just sentence, is perhaps as difficult a proposition as a judge in this country could have to face . . . You are in a different category from any person I have ever tried or am likely to have to try . . . In the eyes of millions of your countrymen, you are a great patriot and a great leader. Even those who differ from you in politics look upon you as a man of high ideals and of noble and even saintly life. It is my duty to judge you as a man subject to the law who has, by his own admission, broken the law and committed what to an ordinary man must appear to be grave offences against the state. I do not forget that you have constantly preached against violence and that you have . . . done much to prevent violence.

Broomfield then sentenced him to six years' imprisonment, and added,

If the course of events in India should make it possible for the Government to reduce the period and release you, no one will be better pleased than I.

The British did soon release him. He was more effective than all their police and arms in maintaining British rule. In 1922, when he was putting an end to violence after Chauri Chaura, a small group of nationalists in Ireland expelled the British. Had Gandhi not stopped violence, a much larger group in India would almost certainly have swept them out there too. To forestall this danger, the Government of India began introducing liberal reforms. It decided that the army would henceforth include Indian officers and set the objective of equalising the number of British and Indian members of the ICS.

Even over finance the British proved accommodating. In the 1914–18 war India had, in effect, paid the cost of providing a million men to fight for Britain. This meant substantial rises in Indian taxation which were, inevitably, unpopular. After the war, the British Government tried to impose on India the obligation to provide the men and money to secure Britain's newly-conquered possessions in the Middle East, filling the gap left by British troops who had been demobilised. The Viceroy pointed out that this policy would cause severe political problems in India: the central legislative assembly would almost certainly refuse to vote any new taxes and Indian members of the Viceroy's Executive Council would resign. So, after battles in the British Cabinet between the India Office on the one hand and the War Office and the Treasury on the other, the British Government gave up many of the rights it had been exercising; in future, the Cabinet stipulated, the Indian army was to defend India and, except in the gravest emergency, should be employed outside the Indian empire only after consultation with the Viceroy and his council, the whole cost, direct and indirect, to be borne by the Government in London or by the colony requiring armed assistance.

Policy on customs duties evolved in much the same way. Although in the nineteenth century India had been a captive market for British goods, notably cotton and steel, by the 1920s, despite attempts by Lancashire MPs to remove import duties imposed by the Indian Government on British cotton exports, the pressure of Indian manufacturers proved decisive. The duties were repeatedly raised, with damaging consequences for the British industry. And the excise duty on Indian cotton goods was abolished. In this the Indian cotton interests overrode the British Cabinet. By 1931 the Government in London had accepted that the use of tariffs as a method of maintaining a British commercial advantage was closed to it. When, following the great crash of the world's economies in 1929–31, Britain tried to set up a system of imperial preference through a conference in Ottawa, an Indian Government delegation attended only to establish 'whether or not it will be in India's economic interests to give and receive tariff preferences'.

In monetary and exchange rate policy, British Governments did not so readily agree to the transfer of substantial functions. The reason was not, as some have supposed, the desire to keep India down. It was the fear that, were these matters transferred to Indian ministers, the British taxpayer would have to pay for India's debts. These consisted first of the 'home charges', items that had to be paid in sterling in England, including the pensions of retired Indian civil servants and army officers, the cost of the India Office in London, leave allowances and training in England for Indian government service. A second element was the large sums borrowed in London to build India's railways and to finance irrigation and public works schemes. British Treasury ministers believed that full payments were essential. If the rupee were allowed to fall in value and the sums paid in sterling were consequently reduced, the pensioners would have been disgracefully treated, unless the British Treasury made up the difference. If a finance minister of India were to win popularity by repudiating part of the debt (thus lowering Indian taxes), the Treasury would have to pay the interest on the debt to enable India to borrow in future. Thus, over vast areas of financial policy, Britain bowed to the facts of Indian political life, even at the cost of imperial defence and British industry, drawing the line only at charging the British taxpayer for what it considered services to India.

However liberal many of these policies may have been in substance, the British still had a knack of offending Congress leaders. The first step to follow dyarchy had been laid down in 1919: a commission was to be appointed after ten years to recommend how to proceed. It was appointed early, and this action, intended to forestall a more radical commission being set up should Labour win the next election, was represented to Indians as a conciliatory gesture; but the possible benefits of such a gesture were entirely undone by the Government's appointing to the commission not a single Indian. Gandhi and the Congress responded by boycotting its hearings, except for black-flag processions and demonstrations. Consequently the commission's report – an enormous, detailed study of how India had been governed under dyarchy and should be thereafter – did nothing to improve relations with India's most effective political leaders, which was exactly the step that needed to be taken if progress from dyarchy was to be made. Indeed, the commission would have vanished from the pages of history but for one quiet, hardworking member, the backbench Labour MP, C. R. Attlee. The commission's two visits, the second lasting six months, provided him with first-hand knowledge of every province of India, which was decisively to affect his conduct when, fifteen years later, he became Prime Minister and personally took charge of India policy.

The Congress boycott of the commission did produce a response. The Viceroy, Lord Irwin, announced before the commission had even finished its report that dominion status was the Government's objective for the subcontinent and that a round-table conference of British and Indians would be held to consider the next step. This was what Gandhi and the new young leaders of Congress, Jawaharlal Nehru and Subhas Chandra Bose, had been demanding. But Nehru and Bose had by now raised their demand to complete independence, and Gandhi, although disposed to accept Lord Irwin's offer, did not wish to be outflanked on the left by his young colleagues. So he created a series of distractions, culminating in his famous salt march. This was nothing more than a political publicity stunt. Because of the tax on salt, its unlicensed manufacture was illegal, so in March 1930 Gandhi led a procession to the sea to break the law by boiling sea water in the presence of all available journalists and newsreel cameramen. The Government tried to look the other way, but Gandhi's instinct for rousing popular feeling once again led quickly from the civil disobedience he encouraged to the violence he deplored. He and many thousands of others were imprisoned, some for illegally making salt, others for their part in riots and bloodshed.

Gandhi's tactic caused more damage than was necessary, but it worked. His own dominance over the Indian masses was reasserted and the opposition of the young Congress leaders could now be contained. Viceroy Irwin released Gandhi from prison. Gandhi wrote to Irwin, proposing that they talk. Irwin agreed and invited Gandhi to his residence, larger than Louis XIV's palace at Versailles, in the new capital at Delhi that Edward Lutyens was then completing. The Irwin–Gandhi talks were regarded by Indians as a great breakthrough, with Gandhi treated (in the words of the next Viceroy, Lord Willingdon) as a 'plenipotentiary on equal terms with the Viceroy' and 'practically the head of a parallel government'. Winston Churchill was appalled and spoke of 'the nauseating and humiliating spectacle of this one-time Inner Temple lawyer, now turned seditious fakir, striding half-naked up the steps of the Viceroy's palace . . . to parley on equal terms with the representative of the King Emperor.'

Churchill, formerly a Cabinet minister, was at this time far removed from the centre of British politics. So was his view of India. Irwin was a close friend of the Conservative Prime Minister from 1924 to 1929, Stanley Baldwin, and convinced him that major constitutional advances and compromises with the Congress leaders were essential. Baldwin was prepared to risk his leadership of the Conservative party to back his and Irwin's judgment. Likewise Ramsay MacDonald, Labour Prime Minister from 1929 to 1931, himself presided over the round-table conference of Britons and Indians in London. The two Prime Ministers stood firm against Churchill and his small band of imperialist friends, who argued that to grant self-government and dominion status would mean the end of British rule in India and, soon after, the end of the Empire.

Baldwin and MacDonald were equally firm in rejecting the views of MacDonald's left wing, the Independent Labour Party, which backed the Congress left's demand for immediate independence. Baldwin, according to his biographers, decided 'India was to be his great mission' and won his party over to immediate responsible government. The two Prime Ministers hoped that, in return for this substantial concession, the Indian political leaders would stop demanding independence and take steps to calm their volatile followers. Gandhi eventually came to London for the second session of the round-table conference where he made a great popular impact. King George V invited him to tea in Buckingham Palace and a small part of what was said is on record. As Gandhi was leaving, the King said, 'Remember Mr Gandhi, I won't have any attacks on my Empire.' Gandhi replied, 'I must not be drawn into political argument in Your Majesty's palace after receiving Your Majesty's hospitality.' Afterwards reporters asked Gandhi why he visited the King so underdressed. He answered, 'The King wore enough for both of us.'

Gandhi after lengthy wavering secured Congress's grudging co-operation with the measures of Baldwin and MacDonald. These were eventually embodied in the India Act of 1935, which gave each of India's eleven provinces an autonomous government responsible to a parliamentary assembly elected on a qualified franchise.

The British Governor of each province was now to be little more than a constitutional monarch, though with substantial reserve powers in case of emergencies (the 'section 93' powers). Nehru wanted to boycott the elections; he said, 'It would be a fatal error to accept office. That would involve co-operation with British imperialism.' Nevertheless the Congress decided to participate and, with their allies, seeking the votes of an electorate raised from seven to more than thirty million, won in eight of the eleven provinces. After much heart-searching they decided to accept the Governors' invitations to form the governments, so effectively taking power over a large part of the subcontinent.

If the arrangements for governing the provinces had been the whole story, the 1935 Act would have been a success for both Britain and Congress and a clear step towards complete independence. But they were not and the rest went wrong. The 1935 Act set out a scheme for a federal legislature and system of government in Delhi that never came into being. What blocked it was the mistrust of the princes, India's elephant-riding, tiger-shooting super-landowners, combined with the British Government's scrupulous concern to push them only gently. More than a third of the land of India was made up of princely states, whose rulers had allied themselves with the

British in the eighteenth and nineteenth centuries and who had consequently never been conquered. Each had his own separate treaty with the British crown, under which, by and large, the Prince gave up power over foreign affairs and defence while retaining effective autonomy in his state's internal affairs, helped, advised and watched by a British Resident. While all the princes governed autocratically, those who were scandalously brutal or incompetent were sacked by the British and replaced. Thus the princes became in practice increasingly weak. Yet legally their position was inviolable: they were voluntary allies of the British crown, entitled to refuse to deal with the Governor-General in Council (the Government of India) and to treat only with the Viceroy (the Governor-General wearing the hat of personal representative of the monarch); they had nearly all sided with the British against the mutiny of 1857, thus decisively reinforcing British power at the moment it was most threatened, and many of them had voluntarily raised troops, at their own expense, to fight for the British in the 1914–18 war. So Britain, in seeking to advance India towards self-government and dominion status, felt that to act against the princes' will would be a breach of faith.

The Chamber of Princes, their mutual protection society, put forward the key proposal of the 1935 Act: the creation of a federal legislature at the centre to represent both the provinces and the princely states. This idea seemed to British lawyers to overcome the problem of the princes' formal autonomy. It also appealed to British political caution. Most of the princes had banned the Congress and other political parties in their states and had thus maintained a façade of political stability; their over-representation in the central legislature (a third of the seats though they had only a quarter of the population) promised a conservative, restraining counterweight to the Congress radicals, who might otherwise predominate.

The Congress, despite the objections of Jawaharlal Nehru to these patently unfair terms, agreed to take part in the 1935 scheme. To most Congressmen effective autonomy in the provinces was a gain worth having, even at the price of an over-princely centre. But having proposed the federal scheme, the princes now scuppered it. Winston Churchill, in his savage opposition to the measure as a step that would inevitably lead to complete independence under Congress rule, urged the princes 'to stand out of it'. The way the scheme was written gave their highnesses a moment of unwonted power over the British and all India: the federation could not start to function, the Act said, until half the princes acceded to it.

A new Viceroy, Lord Linlithgow, was sent out to Delhi to put the new constitution into effect. He tried to convey to the princes that if they did not accede to the federation they would almost certainly face some less attractive option later. He laid before each of them legal documents setting out their own status. He sent a trio of officials round India to explain the Act to them. But where in Congress he had a skilful, powerful and discreet ally in Gandhi, among the princes no comparably strong leader emerged. Churchill's depiction of Congress as a tyrannical Hindu priesthood greedy for power reinforced the princes' own fears, so they failed to agree to an arrangement that could have been their best defence for the future.

The result was that, at the end of the 1930s, the government of India was in a peculiar state. In most of the provinces Congress governments ruled. Many of their ministers, encouraged by Nehru, believed they had assumed office in order to destroy from within a British trick and deception. But once in office they found that the Governors of their provinces did not obstruct them and that the British civil servants obeyed their orders. In the provinces at least, the British handover of power was genuine. In the centre, by contrast, the new constitution simply did not take effect. The 1935 Act provided that dyarchy, now removed from the provinces, would apply in Delhi; this would have meant an executive council responsible to a central legislature for most internal matters, including finance, with the Viceroy retaining personal charge of defence and external affairs. The failure to introduce this system left the Viceroy, advised by his council, in sole charge of all central policy – an arrangement that many Britons found perfectly satisfactory.

Even in the provinces the success of the 1935 Act was not unblemished. The first elections under its provisions, held in 1937, left the Muslims with a grievance which was to fester dangerously in the years ahead. The Muslims made up a quarter of India's population. Before the British came they had ruled India, but they were slower than the Hindus to adapt to British ways. Even in those provinces, notably Bengal and the Punjab, where Muslims were the majority, many of the biggest landowners and businessmen were non-Muslim. Many Hindus had mastered British institutions like the civil service and the law courts. Few Muslims did. Even where Hindus and Muslims lived together in villages, they mixed little. Hindus worshipped the cow, Muslims ate it. They did not study together: Muslims turned to the Koran in Arabic, which to the Hindus was infidel. Railway servants offered 'Mussulman water' and 'Hindu water' for passengers to drink. Years later Mian Mumtaz Daultana, a Muslim League politician, described what it was like:

> We were so far apart that, although we lived next door to each other, we didn't intermarry, we didn't eat together, we were not called to each other's ceremonies. The heroes of one were the villains of the other. So we became quite distinct. It was an ambiguous situation because for seven hundred years the Muslims ruled, and so a Muslim in India did not really quite know whether he was basically a Muslim or an Indian.

Where the Muslims were in a minority, they had extra seats to compensate, and Viceroy Linlithgow instructed all the Governors, when inviting elected members to form the new governments, to attempt to include members of important minority communities. However the Congress's overwhelming majorities in most provinces enabled its leaders to point out that, under

*A wise oracle in 1931 would have said, 'This map foretells the future of the subcontinent.'*

Map labels:

NORTHWEST FRONTIER PROVINCE 91.8

JAMMU & KASHMIR 77.3

PUNJAB 55.7

PUNJAB STATES AGENCY 34.8

BALUCHISTAN 91.8

DELHI 32.5

RAJPUTANA 9.5

SIND (Bombay province) 72.7

AJMER-MERWARA 17.3

GWALIOR 5.8

UNITED PROVINCES 15.0

SIKKIM 0.1

ASSAM 30.1

BIHAR AND ORISSA 10.1

BENGAL 54.4

WESTERN INDIA STATES AGENCY 13.6

CENTRAL INDIA AGENCY 5.7

CENTRAL PROVINCES AND BERAR 3.9

CALCUTTA 25 (estimated)

BARODA 7.5

HYDERABAD 10.6

BOMBAY 8.8

MADRAS 7.1

MYSORE 6.1

COORG 8.4

COCHIN 7.3

TRAVANCORE 6.9

Muslims as % of total population, 1931 (by major administrative regions)

- Over 60%
- 40-60%
- 20-40%
- 10-20%
- 0-10%

Source: 'A Historical Atlas of South Asia', University of Chicago Press

British electoral rules, winner takes all. Many Muslims had stood as Congress candidates, many Muslims had voted for the Congress, therefore Congress ministries would include only Congress Muslims. The party thus reasserted its claim to represent all Indians. The only India-wide Muslim party, the Muslim League, was particularly angry at being shut out in this way and its leader, Mohammed Ali Jinnah, hitherto in favour of co-operation with the Congress, set about building an effective political counter-force.

Jinnah was no Muslim fundamentalist. He was an ambitious lawyer. Muslim and Hindu fanaticism were alike distasteful to him. When a young man, he openly favoured Muslim–Hindu marriages and himself married a Parsee girl. He drank whisky. He wore a stiff white collar even in the hottest weather and when making a speech he would fix his monocle to his eye to add emphasis to a pause. He had been an active lieutenant of the Congress moderate Gokhale and in the 1920s he was described as the ambassador of Hindu–Muslim unity. But as the 1920s advanced and Gandhi's campaigns brought the Congress widespread mass support, Jinnah found himself displaced. His fastidious taste was offended by the organisation's changing tone: he was better at studying a brief and drafting an opinion than at responding to popular moods. Furthermore, he became convinced that the change in Congress from a middle-class pressure group into a mass party marked also its evolution into an engine of Hindu fanatical power. Jinnah tried to persuade Gandhi and the Congress to make concessions that might have calmed Muslim fears. When he failed, he at first quit both politics and India, settling down in 1931 to a successful practice as a barrister in London.

Two years later a Muslim landowner, Liaqat Ali Khan, came to London to persuade him that the Muslim League needed him back in India as their leader. In 1934 he returned, still hoping for co-operation with the Congress. After the 1937 provincial elections he expected the Muslim League – following the Viceroy's instruction to the Governors – to be given a share in the government of most provinces. But the League had won less than five per cent of the *Muslim* vote, so the Congress gave it nothing.

Till his dying day Jawaharlal Nehru maintained that the 1937 decision was right: a non-communal nationalist party had no need to share power with a Muslim League that was so patently without popular support. Justifiable though it was in terms of British constitutional practice, however, the 1937 decision had damaging consequences. The triumphant Congress ministries in the provinces included Hindu extremists. Some tried to require the use of Hindi and the Devnagri script instead of Urdu and the Persian script. Some demanded deference to Hindu symbols. The Viceroy looked into the many complaints and found that none was substantial; but to a great many Muslims it seemed that a Hindu raj might take complete control. Nehru said in March 1937, 'There are only two forces in India today, British imperialism and Indian nationalism as represented by the Congress.' He hoped that once the Muslim League and the provincial Muslim parties had learned that they could not beat Congress they would join it. This was partly an attempt by Nehru to keep Congress to its original non-sectarian character and partly it was a calculation in power politics: that firmness rather than conciliation was the way to win unified support. The calculation seemed sensible at the time, but it proved a fatal mistake – in the literal sense of the term – because of one man.

Mohammed Ali Jinnah, having reluctantly agreed to lead a Muslim communal movement, was not prepared to be slighted. He set about the uphill task of building mass support for the Muslim League. Gandhi and Nehru had insulted a man whose iron will more than equalled that of Robert Clive, who, 180 years earlier, had held out at Arcot for fifty days.

## The Emergence of Mr Jinnah, 1939–March 1947

In September 1939 Viceroy Linlithgow proclaimed that, war having broken out between Britain and Germany, India too was at war. No Indian was consulted. Yet the legislatures of Canada, Australia, New Zealand and South Africa were entitled to decide whether to go to war. This reminder of

the contrast with their own position was offensive to Indian politicians, particularly in the Congress.

A brief spell of bargaining followed. Gandhi, while a pacifist, favoured the British against the Germans and was disposed to offer unconditional moral support to Britain during the war. Nehru, equally pro-British and passionately anti-fascist, wanted to know what were Britain's war aims in respect of India. The British Cabinet would not let the Viceroy offer anything firm. So the Congress high command demanded immediate independence and, when that was rejected, caused all the Congress provincial governments to resign. Thus the high command, the working committee of the Congress at the centre, demonstrated its power. Many of the ministers in the provincial governments were enjoying office and saw no reason to give it up but one by one their ministries resigned and the provincial Governors, Britons to a man, resumed all powers – under section 93 of the 1935 Act.

This withdrawal of Congress co-operation was important. India was eventually to provide two million men to fight for Britain in the 1939–45 war, sharing in General Wavell's spectacular defeat of the Italians in North Africa, fighting under Auchinleck and Montgomery in the desert campaigns, invading Iraq and defeating a pro-German regime – also in Syria, Persia, Malaya and Burma. Most of these men had to volunteer and had to be trained, equipped and transported, functions that required yet more Indians to perform supporting tasks. Effective opposition or non-cooperation by the Congress might have disrupted these efforts. So the

*Gandhi in Delhi in October 1939 on his way to talk to the Viceroy about India's role in the war.*

British Government made three attempts to persuade the Congress that helping the British win the war would bring its reward – just as, it could be argued, India's helping Britain in the 1914–18 war had brought Edwin Montagu's promises of 1917 and their progressive implementation. The first efforts this time were made by the Viceroy, Linlithgow, but Churchill would not let him offer enough to win over the Congress.

Linlithgow was a Scottish landowner and Conservative Party worthy to whom Baldwin had offered the choice of joining the Cabinet as Secretary of State for India or becoming Viceroy. Now, working with his formal superior, the Secretary of State Leopold Amery, he spent some months in 1940 preparing a declaration that promised an immediate expansion of the Viceroy's Council to include more representative Indians and dominion status to India – i.e. full independence with the British monarch as constitutional head of state – within a year of the war's end. When the Viceroy and he had reached agreement, Amery put their proposal to the Cabinet. Churchill immediately cabled the Viceroy: 'Secretary of State has shown me the telegrams and for the first time I realise what has been going on . . . You must remember that we are here facing the constant threat of invasion . . . In these circumstances immense constitutional departures cannot be effectively discussed in Parliament and only by the Cabinet to the detriment of matters touching the final life and safety of the State. I am sure that I can count upon you to help us to the utmost of your power.' Thus Churchill crushed the attempt by the men primarily responsible for the government of India to win Indian co-operation. The grudging offer the Viceroy was allowed to make to the Indian leaders in August 1940 was predictably rejected by them.

In the aftermath of the Japanese destroying the American fleet at Pearl Harbor in December 1941 and capturing Singapore in February 1942 and Rangoon the following March, the need for wholehearted Indian support in the war became urgent. The Japanese army was just over the Burmese border; the British navy, driven from the South China seas, could no longer protect India's east coast; people were beginning to flee from Calcutta. Churchill's coalition partners, the Labour Party and the Liberals, both favoured a generous offer to the political leaders of India. President Roosevelt, now in the war as Churchill's most powerful ally, did not want to find himself fighting for the restoration of that very British imperial power which the United States had been the first to reject. He urged Churchill to make a liberal statement of Britain's war aims for India, as did General Chiang Kai-shek, the ruler of China who paid a brief visit to Delhi in February 1942.

Under this pressure, Churchill reluctantly agreed that something would have to be done. He accepted the proposals of the Cabinet's India committee chaired by his deputy Prime Minister, Clement Attlee, which in effect offered India independence after the war in return for co-operation now. And he sent Sir Stafford Cripps, a senior member of the coalition Cabinet, to persuade the Indian political leaders to accept this package. Cripps, the Leader of the House of Commons, was an austere, intellectual lawyer and a vegetarian who had invited Nehru to his house in the Cotswolds with Attlee in 1938, to try to ensure that the British Labour Party and the Congress were at one over India's future.

Churchill wanted Cripps to fail. He did not want to be bullied by the Americans or the Labour Party or Chiang Kai-shek; he did not want Indians in the government meddling in the running of the war; and he certainly did not want to hand India to the Indians when the war was over. For him the purpose of the war was to save the Empire, not to give it away. Linlithgow's manner of announcing that India was at war was constitutionally correct and seemed to Churchill the right way to go on. To him the Cripps mission was useful in that it would show the Americans and the Labour Party that every effort had been made to please Congress and that now the war must be prosecuted firmly, with one person in charge and Indian political troublemakers kept out of the way for the duration.

Cripps was sincere. He thought he enjoyed the trust of the Congress leaders, particularly Nehru, and that he could therefore bring them to co-operate with Britain's war effort where others could not. He had two things to offer: a promise that after the war India could frame her own constitution for independence and Britain would accept it, and an immediate invitation to the big Indian parties to join the Viceroy's Executive Council to help run the war. Congress, however, wanted more than this; in particular they wanted India to be handed over at once to a government largely of Indians, who would then back the British war effort and wholeheartedly fight to protect India from the Japanese. Cripps tried to make the Congress leaders feel that the offer he was bringing met them more than half way. In a press conference in Delhi on 19 March 1942 he said it was possible to 'turn the Executive Council into a Cabinet'. The Congress leaders pressed him on this idea and Cripps tried in turn to persuade Linlithgow that he could run his executive council in a way that could satisfy their demands while not weakening the Viceroy's ultimate authority.

Cripps was an exceptionally clever lawyer and he knew he lacked the authority to offer changes in the constitution. He therefore tried to make the Congress leaders understand that a representative majority of Indians on the Viceroy's Council would, like a responsible cabinet, be in a strong position, almost impossible for the Viceroy to overrule. But in his enthusiasm to persuade the Congress he got out of step with the Viceroy. Linlithgow complained that Cripps was 'baiting the trap with my cheese' and with Churchill's encouragement began to send secret reports to 10 Downing Street. By now President Roosevelt had sent a personal representative, Colonel Louis A. Johnson, to Delhi, and Johnson was helping Cripps to win over the Congress. Cripps's great negotiating skill and transparently genuine commitment to India's rapid advance to independence combined with Johnson's powerful advocacy to leave Linlithgow feeling isolated.

Neither he nor Churchill liked American interference. Nor did they want a substantial Congress voice in the Indian Government.

Behind Cripps's back Prime Minister and Viceroy exchanged messages and persuaded the Cabinet in London that Cripps had exceeded his authority. The charge was false. He had merely tried to devise a way for the Viceroy to run his Executive Council, while retaining full reserve powers, which could have met both Britain's wartime needs and Congress's immediate aspirations. But the Churchill–Linlithgow alliance won the day: Churchill took the chair at a meeting of the Cabinet India committee (displacing Attlee) and laid down the policy: Cripps had no power to negotiate, only to present the Government's proposal; a cable was sent to Linlithgow: 'There can be no question of any convention limiting in any way your powers under the existing constitution ... If Congress leaders have gathered the impression that such a new convention is now possible this impression should be definitely removed.' Cripps was sent a copy.

That was the *coup de grâce*. Cripps already knew that mistrust of him was building up in London and he had therefore felt bound to point out to the Congress leaders the extent to which the offer fell short of their hopes. So his imaginative attempt to reconcile the two sides was turned down by both, the Congress in the following words: 'You ... referred both privately and ... in public ... to a ... Cabinet consisting of Ministers ... We had imagined that the new Government would function with full powers as a Cabinet with the Viceroy as constitutional head ... We did not ask for any legal changes but we did ask for definite assurances and conventions ...' Gandhi was said to have described the offer of post-war independence as 'a post-dated cheque on a crashing bank'. That was the end of the Cripps mission and Churchill did not attempt to conceal his delight. Cripps realised he had been used for the Prime Minister's propaganda to the Americans and dutifully kept his resentment to himself. Churchill and Linlithgow in schoolboy celebration of their victory over the Cabinet's emissary privately referred to him as 'Sir Stifford Crapps'.

The effect in India was dangerous. The Congress felt cheated. Some of its members, led by Subhas Chandra Bose, a former President, had always believed that Britain, in spite of liberal promises, was determined to hold on to power as long as possible. The only way to get rid of the British, therefore, was to side with Britain's enemies, first Germany, then, when she entered the war, Japan. Bose had travelled to Berlin and broadcast on 'Free India' radio, telling thousands of Indian listeners that Britain was doomed and that her enemies would be the bringers of Indian freedom. Bose then went on to Tokyo and met the Japanese Prime Minister Tojo.

From the many thousands of Indian troops captured at Singapore, Tojo arranged that Bose should take charge of an Indian National Army, which would assist in the forthcoming conquest of India. Bose had won a high place in the ICS examinations but had then turned down the proffered job. Twenty years later he won a second term as Congress President in the face of the opposition of Gandhi. He was no Japanese puppet. Had many Indians joined him in defecting to the Japanese, the situation facing the British could have been desperate.

Gandhi and Nehru knew that Churchill was the principal opponent of any constitutional advance for India and that if he won the war the prospects for Indian independence would be bleak. Yet they could not bring themselves to side with Britain's enemies. Both were trained in English law and felt profound affection for Britain. Gandhi said he could not bear the thought of St Paul's being bombed; Nehru, when the British repeatedly put him in prison, kept a picture of his old school, Harrow, in his cell. His socialism, though sympathetic to that of Russia, was mainly a mixture of Marx and the British Labour Party, in which he had many friends. Both Gandhi and Nehru detested Hitler's Nazism and wanted to see it crushed.

As usual when the Congress faced such dilemmas, Gandhi produced the slogan around which the mass of Indians proved ready to unite: a demand that the British should immediately 'Quit India'. It was never clear – probably not even to Gandhi – where exactly he expected the Quit India campaign to lead. He said he wanted the British to leave India to the hands of God – not to hand over power to an Indian government, but simply to go.

Asked if this would not cause anarchy, the bloodshed of millions and an easy victory for the Japanese, he replied that the resulting anarchy might lead to domestic warfare and the loss of several million lives, and if the Japanese came a non-violent response would 'sterilise' them. In part this reflected his fear that a Japanese victory was now likely, in which case India must not appear to be Japan's enemy; but in part 'Quit India' was a retreat by Gandhi from complex problems into the impractical. It was not a proposal of Gandhi the tough and wily political negotiator, but of Gandhi the leader of popular Indian mass movements. For him a united demonstration of the people's will was an end in itself because it helped preserve the strength of the nationalist movement.

Gandhi's demand for a non-violent mass movement in support of a simple, grand objective soon led to violence. He knew that this was likely and even urged his followers to be willing to 'Do or die'. The day Gandhi launched 'Quit India' the Viceroy had him and the other leading Congress members imprisoned and prepared the police and the army for the widespread violence that must follow. It amounted to the biggest threat to British control of India since the mutiny. The railway line between Delhi and Calcutta – the main artery of the government – was blown up in Bihar, where, for more than two weeks, the British completely lost control and so could not organise repair teams. Supplies could not be sent to the Burmese front, where a Japanese invasion was feared. In many parts of the country police stations were burnt, policemen killed, British people on the roads stopped by gangs and beaten up, telegraph wires cut: in all about a thousand people, almost all Indians, were killed. The Government did all it could to suppress news of what was happening in order to preserve morale in both

India and Britain. For a week or more it was unclear whether the British would be able to reassert control. But Linlithgow, the Viceroy, had not been idle. He had enlarged his Executive Council to fourteen, eleven Indians (but none representing a political party) and three British officials, to demonstrate that the Government was responding to Indian feelings. This helped secure the support of the bulk of the commercial and professional classes. The army, the police and the administration stood firm. Gradually the violence subsided. The British and their many Indian collaborators once more dragged India back under imperial control. Army recruiting officers proceeded steadily with their work.

Churchill now got his way. The passing of the Quit India resolution provided the excuse he had wanted for locking up the Congress leaders, banning all the Congress committees and forgetting about India's political aspirations. These were not, however, politically neutral acts. Many non-Congressmen now found that they could share in the running of the war, gain experience in the Viceroy's executive and the provincial cabinets and cause benefits to flow to their own supporters. The principal beneficiary of the banning of Congress from the Indian political scene was the Muslim League, whose members were over the next few months invited to form governments in Sind, Assam, Bengal and the North-West Frontier Province.

Since the 1937 elections Jinnah had redoubled his efforts to make the Muslim League into the mass party of the Muslims. In this he could not show much early success. In provinces where the Muslims were a small minority and Congress had ministries Muslims were frightened, which boosted Jinnah's campaign for mass recruitment. But in the Punjab and Bengal, where most of India's 100 million Muslims lived, the Hindus and Muslims were both represented in governments of inter-communal coalition. The Muslim League's cry that the Muslims were a separate nation in India, endangered by Hindu extremism and therefore required to fight without quarter against the Congress, had limited appeal in the Punjab, where a Muslim, Sir Sikander Hyat Khan, was leader of the governing party, an alliance of Muslims, Hindus and Sikhs, or in Bengal, where in the early part of the war another non-League Muslim, Fazlul Haq, led a coalition government. To get the majority of all Muslims throughout India to support the Muslim League, Jinnah needed a touch of the Gandhi magic – something like the salt march – to capture their interest and fire their enthusiasm.

He found it in a scheme dreamed up by a group of Muslim students at Cambridge in 1932–3. Characteristically for a student initiative, it was stronger on verbal dexterity than political realism. 'Pak' in Urdu means pure and 'stan' means land, so Pakistan means 'land of the pure'. It also forms a mnemonic of the main Muslim-majority areas of north-west India; P for the Punjab, A for Afghania (the North-West Frontier province), K for Kashmir, S for Sind and TAN for BaluchisTAN. Chaudhari Rahmat Ali, the Cambridge student principally responsible for the idea, explained it as calling for a federation of Muslim Indian states totally separate from the rest of India. Ironically, the Muslim League, in evidence to a joint parliamentary committee in London on Indian constitutional reform, had promptly dismissed the idea of Pakistan as 'chimerical and impracticable'.

By 1940, however, Jinnah recognised it as his equivalent of one of Gandhi's popular slogans like *swaraj* (independence). To the five provinces specified in 'Pakistan' were added two more, Bengal and Assam, the Muslim regions of North-East India; and the scheme was clothed in dry, legal jargon:

> Resolved that it is the considered view of this session of the All-India Muslim League that no constitutional plan would be workable in this country or acceptable to the Muslims unless it is designed on the following basic principles, viz; that geographically contiguous units are demarcated into regions which should be so constituted, with such territorial adjustments as may be necessary, that the areas in which the Muslims are numerically in a majority, as in the North-Western and Eastern zones of India, should be grouped to constitute 'Independent States' in which the constituent units shall be autonomous and sovereign.

This was the famous Lahore resolution, understandably more often referred to than read, but powerful in conveying a simple idea: the Muslims of India were a single nation, however dispersed, and must have a single state: Pakistan. Jinnah knew that any more precise definition would immediately have led to quarrels within the Muslim communities.

Although the Lahore resolution and the growing effectiveness of Jinnah's campaign brought new strength to the Muslim League, it still had some way to go to achieve real political effectiveness when in 1942 it received a major

*The crossword-puzzle on a map that framed the idea of Pakistan.*

and unexpected bonus. Sir Stafford Cripps, in the draft declaration which spelled out the British Cabinet's definition of his mission, announced that after the war any province could stay out of the proposed independent Indian Union and form its own government. This meant that if the Muslim League could persuade the governments or voters of the seven provinces, they could set up Pakistan. Nobody thought they could do it, but this was a major concession and came as a surprise. Jinnah had expected a long struggle, with both the British and the Congress determined to keep India united, and he had begun to press for the creation of Pakistan through friendly Members of Parliament in London. His pressure was a principal reason for the setting-up in February 1942 of the Cabinet's India committee which drafted Cripps's instructions. Once the mission's terms were published, Jinnah could claim to wavering Muslims that, the principle having been conceded, he was home and dry as far as the British were concerned.

The British Cabinet's India committee did not realise that the concession might be used in this way. They were mainly responding to what they saw as the genuine fear among the minorities, particularly the Muslims, of growing Hindu domination. They were also shaping their proposals to avoid the gales that might capsize them from the office of that great India expert, the Prime Minister. Churchill had served in the army in India and as a war reporter in the North-West frontier in the 1890s. He had become convinced by the 1930s that the Congress were an unrepresentative party financed by rich Hindus for their own anti-British purposes while the Muslims were good soldiers, akin to Christians. The opt-out clauses in Cripps's declaration pleased Churchill because he wanted both to upset Congress and to encourage the loyalty to Britain of Muslim soldiers. Both Linlithgow, the Viceroy, and Sir Archibald Wavell, the Commander-in-Chief in India, had said they were uneasy about the opt-out provisions. They warned of the danger of encouraging communalism and separatism. But some offer of reassurance to the minorities was unavoidable.

Within four years Jinnah had established himself. In 1940 he had been the leader of a Muslim League that had failed to win a substantial share of the Muslim vote and had just adopted the apparently chimerical and impracticable policy – opposed both by the British and the Congress – of a separate Muslim state of Pakistan. By 1944 his Pakistan policy was winning him mass support among Muslims and had been conceded in principle by the British; his star seemed to be rising while the leaders of Congress, formerly determined to make him look insignificant, were now themselves locked out of sight.

Increasingly Jinnah asserted that he was the leader not only of the Muslim League but of all the Indian Muslims. And he got away with it. When the Viceroy in July 1941 formed a National Defence Council, the Muslim Chief Ministers of Punjab, Assam and Bengal agreed to join. Jinnah ordered them to resign, and they all did, afraid that he would appeal over their heads to the

Muslim voters in their provinces. Fazlul Haq, Chief Minister of Bengal, protested against Jinnah's 'arrogant and dictatorial line'. Sir Sikander Hyat Khan, Chief Minister of the Punjab, told Penderel Moon, then secretary to the Governor, that 'Pakistan would be an invitation to the Punjabi Muslims to cut the throat of every Hindu *bania* [moneylender] . . . Pakistan would mean a massacre.' He told the Punjab legislative assembly: 'We do not ask for freedom, that there may be a Muslim raj here and a Hindu raj elsewhere. If that is what Pakistan means I will have nothing to do with it.' But when Jinnah cracked the whip, he obeyed. He judged the enthusiasm among young Muslims for Pakistan and its prophet to be too strong for him to resist openly. When, soon afterwards, Fazlul Haq reorganised the Cabinet in Bengal in defiance of the League, Jinnah put pressure on Muslim politicians and forced Haq to resign.

Jinnah's assertion of his own primacy paid off equally with the British. Linlithgow turned to him as the all-India leader of the Muslims, even though the League did not yet have anything like the authority over its provincial ministries that the Congress had exercised. Similarly Cripps turned primarily to Jinnah for a Muslim view of his draft scheme. This was partly because, as one successful practising lawyer to another, he could talk to Jinnah. It was also because the British believed their greatest gift to India was unity, and that meant dealing with political leaders, Hindu and Muslim alike, who had the ability to create unity. Further, the Muslims were disproportionately heavily represented in the armed forces and it therefore seemed prudent to do nothing during the war that might antagonise their only national political leader. Jinnah used every advance he made with the British to strengthen his position with Muslims in general and the Muslim provincial ministers in particular. Like Gandhi, he avoided ministerial office, with its debilitating requirement to make decisions adverse to some supporters. Like Gandhi, he adopted public positions more anti-British than his own judgments, to maintain popular enthusiasm. Skilfully he climbed his way into the key role.

The time came for a change of Viceroy. Churchill as Prime Minister had been happy with Linlithgow and wanted a successor who would continue to keep the Congress leaders in detention and concentrate on recruitment, production and organisation for war. His choice fell on the apparently safe Lord Wavell, who as Commander-in-Chief in India had helped frame many of Linlithgow's policies. He was one-eyed, taciturn and notably bad with politicians. In his recent appointment as C-in-C Middle East, he had won a heroic reputation for sweeping the Italians from north Africa, but he was relieved of his command and brought back to London because he refused to send troops to Iraq when Churchill needed them. An unemployed warrior in the midst of war, his presence aroused speculation. Packing him off to India as Viceroy put a stop to it. But Churchill did not get what he had bargained for. It was September 1943, the war was going well for Britain and her allies, and Wavell, before taking up the Viceroyalty, said that now was the time for an initiative: the reconstruction of the Viceroy's Executive Council to represent the major political parties. The Cabinet's India committee was sympathetic but Churchill turned the proposal down flat. Nevertheless Wavell returned to India as Viceroy clear in his mind that, now India's war machinery was working well, his principal task must be to prepare for rapid constitutional advance and independence after the war. In this purpose he had two main enemies: in London Churchill, who wanted none of it, and in India Mohammed Ali Jinnah, who was determined to have it, but only on his own terms.

In May 1944 Wavell released Gandhi from detention on humanitarian grounds: he had malaria and his wife had died. Wavell wanted to talk to Gandhi about India's political future but received orders from London not to do so (not surprisingly in view of Churchill's opinion of the Gandhi–Irwin talks twelve years earlier). So Gandhi came out of detention to a strangely altered political scene: the Viceroy, to whom he had written, would not meet him; the Congress, which he had led and inspired, seemed semi-moribund, no longer holding office, nor possessing provincial or national committees, its other leaders still detained; the Muslim League, which a few years earlier had seemed a mere irritant, now occupied the centre of the political stage; and the topic which was inspiring millions and was the talking-point of political India was not one of Gandhi's great protests, but Jinnah's campaign for Pakistan.

Gandhi suggested that he and Jinnah should meet, which they did in September 1944 at Jinnah's house in Bombay. It was a remarkable mistake by Gandhi. He put forward a proposal drafted by the Madras Congress moderate, C. Rajagopalachari, accepting much of the Lahore resolution and proposing a federation from which provinces that so voted could opt out. Jinnah responded in a way that was to become familiar: having received an offer of enormous gains, he rejected it as grossly inadequate. In this case his gains were, first, to be treated by Gandhi as an equal and, second, to receive a Congress offer of the right of Muslim provinces to opt out of substantial parts of the forthcoming political union. He rejected Gandhi's proposal on the grounds that it fell short of a fully independent Pakistan.

Wavell saw Jinnah's growing intransigence as proof that he had been right about the need for a political initiative by Britain. The Governors of all the eleven provinces agreed with him, so he wrote to London proposing to try again. But the Cabinet's India committee were reluctant even to renew the Cripps offer of major party representatives on the Viceroy's Executive Council. At first they refused to let Wavell come to London to discuss the proposal and then, when they eventually allowed him to come, they were slow to be persuaded. Wavell spent ten weeks waiting about. Plainly progress towards independence in India was low on the Cabinet's agenda. It was not until May 1945 that Wavell finally got permission to bring Congress and League representatives (instead of individuals chosen personally by the Viceroy, as hitherto) onto his Executive Council. The Cabinet's resistance is remarkable in the light of Wavell's letter to Churchill of October 1944 in which he raised the issue:

> . . . the future of India is the problem on which the British Commonwealth and the British reputation will stand or fall in the post-war period . . . Our prestige and prospects in Burma, Malaya, China and the Far East generally are entirely subject to what happens in India. If we can secure India as a friendly partner in the British Commonwealth our predominant influence in these countries will, I think, be assured; with a lost and hostile India, we are likely to be reduced in the East to the position of commercial bag-men.

Wavell argued that, whether Montagu's 1917 promise of responsible government had been right or wrong, it had been made and confirmed by Cripps in 1942: 'We cannot now withdraw.' Early independence was unavoidable. The only alternative was repression but, after a long, debilitating war, British soldiers could not be brought to India for such a purpose. The Viceroy's Council was now dominated by Indians. Of the 950 ICS men, more than half were now Indians and the British in senior positions no longer had the will to dominate: they were older than their Indian colleagues, many were near retirement, and they agreed with Wavell that a British initiative to advance India towards independence was urgently needed. So did Sir Claude Auchinleck, the Commander-in-Chief.

For seven months after Wavell wrote renewing his proposal for an initiative, Churchill refused to permit action. Then the Viceroy was allowed to go ahead. The timing is significant. By May 1945 Germany had surrendered, the war in Europe was over, Labour had left the Government and a general election was imminent. Wavell had lost face both in London and in India. He was angry at the way he had been treated. His proposal was known to the Labour Party leaders (it had been put forward while they were still in the Government) and, if Churchill did not agree to it, might become an issue in the election. Some Conservatives feared Wavell might resign; others, including the Secretary of State for India, Leopold Amery, now spoke up in support of his policy. So Churchill at last gave in.

Wavell returned to India and immediately released the Congress leaders, including Nehru, from detention. He then called a conference at Simla of the twenty-one main leaders of all parties to agree on the membership of an Executive Council, all of whom, apart from himself and the Commander-in-Chief, would be Indian, to help him preside over the advance to independence. The proposal Wavell put to the Simla conference was generous to the Muslims: the Executive Council was to contain equal numbers of Muslims and Hindus, although the 100 million Muslims comprised only a quarter of the total population. This proposal was accepted by the Congress leaders in the hope of getting their hands on the levers of power, but Jinnah rejected it as not giving enough. What he demanded in addition was audacious and arrogant: that only the Muslim League should be allowed to nominate the Muslim representatives. Since the President of the Congress at that time, Maulana Abul Kalam Azad, was a Muslim and since the Congress insisted that it was not a communal Hindu party, its assertion that it must be allowed to include people of any religion among its nominees was understandable. Wavell was equally influenced by the position of the Punjab Unionists. The Punjab was India's key province in the war (in which Japan was not yet defeated); Punjabis made up almost half the Indian army and the Punjab produced a huge surplus of wheat. The Muslim-led Unionist government of the Punjab was helping the war effort. To leave them out of the executive in favour of a Muslim Leaguer would cause trouble. So Wavell turned Jinnah down. In that case, Jinnah replied, the Muslim League would not co-operate in the Council.

This was a daring bluff but one which the Viceroy did not feel able to call. To do so Wavell would have had to form an Executive Council dominated by the Congress and, with Churchill Prime Minister and expected to win the imminent general election, such a proposal seemed certain to be overruled. The Viceroy could not form a politically representative council with the League in it nor an unrepresentative council with the Muslim League left out. After months persuading the Cabinet in London to permit his initiative and after proudly announcing it over the radio to the people of India, Wavell now chose publicly to take all the blame for its failure. Though Jinnah was only a minority leader and had never won an election, his judgement of the political options facing all parties had proved better than that of the Viceroy, the British Cabinet or the Congress leaders. He had effectively exercised his veto, and from now on was increasingly the decisive force.

Suddenly the scene changed. The dropping of atom bombs on Hiroshima and Nagasaki ended the war against Japan far sooner than had been expected, a mere fortnight after the election of a Labour Government in Britain had replaced Churchill's Prime Ministerial determination to procrastinate over India with Attlee's brisk will to get on with it and get out. Attlee wanted Indian elections held at once and the newly elected assembly members organised into a constitution-making body to agree the post-independence arrangements. He was against constitutional talks with anybody unless they had the legitimising power of electoral victory behind them.

Elections were held at the end of 1945 for legislative assemblies at the centre and in the provinces. The Congress won the overwhelming majority of the unreserved seats; in the Muslim seats the League majority was almost of the same proportion. The anti-League Muslims, notably the Unionist Party which had formed the government of the Punjab since 1920, were decimated. At last Jinnah's claim to speak for the Muslims was backed by the evidence of the ballot box: it was not to diminish his imperiousness.

Attlee considered that Wavell lacked the political nous to persuade the Congress and the League to set aside their rivalry and agree a formula for independence so he sent three senior ministers – the 'Cabinet mission' – to help the Indians to sort themselves out. The mission's principal instruction was to get the Indian leaders to agree on the constitution-making machinery for independence, whether of a united or a divided India. The Prime Minister hoped India would stay in the Commonwealth but made it clear she must be free to leave. He hoped a defence treaty would be signed with Britain but likewise did not require it. None of Britain's needs was to be treated as essential. Attlee knew it would be difficult to get the Congress and the League to agree to anything and therefore withdrew all the preconditions he felt he could. All that the Cabinet mission's instructions required was protection for minorities, a clean end to Britain's treaty relations with the princes, arrangements by which India could protect herself and the Indian Ocean area and a satisfactory financial settlement. If Hindu–Muslim violence erupted widely – and it seemed likely in view of Jinnah's insistence on dividing the subcontinent – Britain no longer had the power to suppress it. The Viceroy was running a lame-duck administration. When his government began to conduct trials of the traitors who had fought in Bose's Indian National Army, supporting the Japanese in their attempt to invade India, public feeling erupted, hailing the accused as patriots. They were undoubtedly guilty of 'waging war against the King-Emperor', an offence punishable by death under the Indian Penal Code; but to millions of Indians they had risked their lives for the freedom of the motherland. The British could not go on with the trials. English law had to be set aside in face of Indian feelings. In the Indian army itself the number of Indian commissioned officers had greatly increased during the war. The preponderance of British officers could not now be restored; the actual number was down from eleven thousand before the war to four thousand after. The British were not yet on the run, but they did not have long to go. The Cabinet mission's task, to obtain an agreement between Congress and the League that would enable the British to leave, was urgent.

The mission consisted of three men: Cripps, the brilliant lawyer who had failed in 1942; Lord Pethick-Lawrence, whom Attlee had made Secretary of State for India because of his many Indian friends but who came to be widely known in India as 'pathetic Lawrence'; and A. V. Alexander, First Lord of the Admiralty, affable, direct and a great man for singing at the piano. They arrived in India in March 1946, soon after Jinnah's triumph in the elections. Muslim politicians were now flocking to Jinnah, even some who had long considered the Pakistan proposal a recipe for massacre and disaster. He was now demanding the areas adjacent to those with Muslim majorities, to ensure Pakistan's economic viability.

The Cabinet mission had to secure agreement between parties which had drifted into irreconcilable positions. The British ministers scurried from side to side, offering suggestions, carrying messages, giving and receiving lectures. But they had no power to impose a settlement. Jinnah listened politely and said he would consider whatever was put to him; not even his closest colleagues knew exactly what he was seeking; they trusted him as a litigant

*The Cabinet mission with the Viceroy. Left to right: Sir Stafford Cripps, Lord Pethick-Lawrence, Lord Wavell and A. V. Alexander.*

trusts his barrister to secure the best verdict from the court. The position on the Congress side was more complicated. There the Cabinet mission never quite knew whom they should be dealing with. The Congress president at the time was Maulana Azad, who was not the most powerful figure in Congress but was their nominated spokesman to the mission. Cripps, who thought that one reason why his 1942 mission had failed was that he did not pay enough attention to Gandhi, was determined that this time Gandhi would be on his side and fully involved. Gandhi, however, said that he held no office in Congress now, he was no longer even a member: the key figure for the mission to consult was Nehru. Others held that the strong man of Congress was Vallabhbhai Patel; certainly Nehru and Patel were more powerful than Azad; but was Gandhi more decisive than either? And could any of them persuade the Congress working committee to concede enough of Pakistan to prevent Jinnah's seemingly inevitable veto?

Nor was that the end of the Cabinet mission's problems. The 'scheduled castes', as the untouchables were supposed to be called, the 60 million whose presence could pollute caste Hindus, were represented by Dr B. R. Ambedkar, who held that they were a separate religious minority like the Muslims and therefore needed separate electoral representation (a scheme Gandhi passionately opposed). An alternative spokesman, Jagjivan Ram, explained that the scheduled castes were really Hindus who needed help to raise them up within Hindu society. And then came the Sikhs. They were the descendants of a breakaway group of sixteenth-century Hindus who happened to live in the middle of the Punjab, many of them in and around Lahore, where they were a substantial and largely prosperous minority in one of the Muslim areas most likely to go to Pakistan if Jinnah had his way. So long as the Unionist party had won the votes of most of the Punjab Muslims, the Sikhs had been secure and were not a problem. But the 1946 election showed that the majority of Punjab Muslims now supported Jinnah's demand for Pakistan, raising the spectre of the massacre that the former Unionist party leader Sir Sikander Hyat Khan had warned of. The Sikhs in the Punjab were afraid. They came to the Cabinet mission to demand a separate Sikh state or special protection or special electoral arrangements. They did not know what they wanted, but they were alarmed. The Cabinet mission did not take the Sikh fears seriously.

To resolve the Congress-League conflict the mission cooked up a kind of three-tier cake of a constitution. The eleven provinces (the bottom tier) were to be allowed to form themselves into groups (the middle tier), thus enabling the Muslim provinces to club together into a kind of Pakistan-without-sovereignty. The all-India federal government (the top tier) would have responsibility for foreign policy, defence and communications. The trouble with this scheme soon became clear. It was acceptable to Jinnah and the League so long as the second tier groups were formed first and were free to bargain about the powers to be handed to the top tier. But it was acceptable to the Congress only so long as the top tier, the all-India Union, was formed first and selected the powers to be devolved downwards.

Sometimes Jinnah said yes, only to add that he nevertheless kept his options open; sometimes he said yes, only to add that he must obtain the consent of the League's working committee. When the mission invited Congress and League leaders to Simla for a conference, Jinnah kept them all waiting three days because, he said, he was busy in Delhi. (Arriving late for appointments with the Viceroy was one of his habits.) Sometimes Gandhi said yes, only to send a note later saying something much more complicated and elusive. Once he came to meet the mission only to pass them an envelope on the back of which he had written: 'Please go on. It is my day of silence.' He was always punctual. The Viceroy considered the Cabinet mission far too pro-Congress. The Cabinet mission considered the Viceroy, who sat with them in their deliberations, far too hasty and unsubtle a negotiator.

In the end Jinnah and the Muslim League Council accepted the Cabinet mission's three-tier plan, with all its associated short-term arrangements. They thus agreed to less than a fully independent Pakistan, convinced that self-governing status within an Indian federal union was not only the best they could get but a reasonable assurance of protection for the Muslims throughout India. In abandoning the notion of a sovereign Pakistan in this way, Jinnah revealed his consummate political and negotiating skill and almost certainly his real purpose. He had used the notion of Pakistan as the rallying-cry to build up mass support; he had used it to veto schemes for the future of India which he found unsatisfactory. Now, when the British were plainly determined to quit, he abandoned his tough bargaining stance in order to secure both power for the League in the Muslim areas and a substantial position for himself in the government of the whole of India. This offered him and the League a lever with which to seek to protect the many millions of Muslims scattered throughout the Hindu-majority areas. Jinnah's acceptance of the Cabinet mission scheme suggests that what he was really seeking was a major role in a united India, rather than the creation of a separate Islamic state of Pakistan. This view is supported by the origins of both Jinnah and his principal lieutenant, Liaqat Ali Khan: they came from Muslim minority areas; both lacked local power bases in Muslim majority areas and could expect, if Pakistan ever came into existence, serious trouble from the political leaders of Bengal and the Punjab. So Jinnah, Liaqat and the Muslim League dropped their demand for Pakistan and perhaps Jinnah, at least, had never really wanted it. The decisive step that at this stage led on towards the creation of Pakistan must be attributed not to Jinnah but to the leaders of Congress. They quickly realised that Jinnah had won from the Cabinet mission both a disproportionately large share in the proposed distribution of power and a centre so weak that their own ambition to rule an effective government of a united India would be frustrated.

On 6 June 1946, when the Cabinet mission, as the climax to its patient negotiation and its interviews with 472 political leaders, secured Muslim League acceptance of an all-India federation, the Congress raised a series of quibbles about a subordinate part of the scheme, the exact composition of the interim government. On offer was a chance to secure a minimal union of all-India. A year later this was to look like a great opportunity lost. The side that was intransigent at that moment was the Congress.

So the Cabinet mission failed to secure agreement either on the final form of a constitution for independent India or on the immediate steps: designating a constitution-making body to take over the task and itself to draw up the details, and designating an interim government to run India while constitutional arrangements for independence were worked out. On all three matters – the three-tier constitution, the rules for the constituent assembly and the composition of the interim government – the mission left behind proposals and Wavell had to try to make them work. But uncertainty over the Congress position on each item made his task near-impossible. The mission looks in retrospect like a waste of three months. But these months convinced everybody in India that the British were now really determined to go. Attlee, back in London, closely supervised the mission's efforts and learned from them that a more telling form of persuasion was needed to make the Indians get their house (or houses) in enough order for the British to leave.

It was not the British, however, but Jinnah who introduced a new form of persuasion: a deliberate provocation of violence. He complained that the Congress had dishonestly backed away from the Cabinet mission compromise because they wanted complete power at the centre, without even the concession of groups of Muslim provinces allowed to federate beneath the all-India umbrella. He also thought he was misled over events following the Cabinet mission's departure. The Viceroy formed a short-term interim government of officials only, where Jinnah thought that the League, having accepted the mission's proposals, would be included in a government of political leaders. Then Nehru, newly appointed as Congress President, announced that in the forthcoming constituent assembly, the constitution-making body, the Congress would not consider itself bound by any prior agreements, even though the League had agreed to take part in the assembly only if all parties were bound by agreements they had reached with the Cabinet mission. Nehru's statement was later described by Azad as 'one of those unfortunate events which change the course of history'.

To Jinnah and the League it appeared that the British and the Congress were slipping back into the belief that they could together settle the future of India without concessions to the Muslims. The League therefore turned to 'direct action'. Both the British and the Congress, Jinnah explained, had held pistols at his head: 'Today we also have forged a pistol and are in a position to use it . . . This day we bid goodbye to constitutional methods.' 16 August 1946 was fixed by the League as 'Direct Action Day'.

In most of India it passed off without violence. But the Muslim League government in Bengal, led by H. S. Suhrawardy, declared 16 August a public holiday. Bengal had been India's principal centre of political violence for decades. No sane government, knowing the widespread sense of outrage that Jinnah and the League had stimulated among Muslims at the notion that Congress had double-crossed them in an effort to secure a Hindu raj, could have doubted that to make the League's direct action day a public holiday in Bengal was to invite trouble – an opportunity for Muslims to show that they were not to be trifled with. But Suhrawardy and his League colleagues cannot have begun to guess how much trouble their decision would release. There started in Calcutta that day an uncontainable mass slaughter that spread across most of northern India and lasted for the next sixteen months.

It began with the Calcutta killings, three days of murder, unleashed by a Muslim initiative but soon overwhelmed by massive retaliatory Hindu onslaughts, reinforced by a cavalry of local Sikh taxi and lorry drivers. When it was over, corpses were strewn about the streets, putrefying in the damp heat of the monsoon. Informed estimates of the number killed range between four and five thousand. Many more were wounded and more still were made homeless by mobs setting fire to their dwellings. When the army were brought in and, after three days, stopped the looting and murder, corpses were piled high on waste plots. A week later the stink of putrefaction still permeated the city, from bodies shoved down drains or ignored in burnt-out houses.

Wavell visited Calcutta and grasped its warning: unless a Congress-League settlement was reached quickly, the killings were likely to spread. He tried to persuade the Congress leaders to take part in a coalition government with the League, as proposed by the Cabinet mission, but Gandhi and Nehru disliked what they considered his 'minatory' approach, and he was ordered from London not to risk a breach with the Congress. So, instead of a Congress-League coalition, Wavell was stuck with Nehru presiding over the first all-India government led by an Indian, but with no League members. The conflict between Wavell and the British Cabinet was simple. Wavell considered that the terms laid down by the Cabinet mission for the interim government and constituent assembly, having been accepted albeit with reservations by Congress and League, must be adhered to. Attlee and Pethick-Lawrence considered that they must respond to Congress's determination to vary the terms. While an angry, dissatisfied Muslim League was unfortunate, they believed an angry, dissatisfied Congress would be a disaster. Congress had the majority, in numbers, in wealth, in skill at running government; they could take over in Delhi a machine that worked and that they could continue to run. They moralised too much and postured and raised silly legal quibbles and repeatedly failed to seize an opportunity when it was handed to them – tactically they were inept – but their majority position was decisive. Attlee was an English democrat and to him majorities mattered.

The interim government and the constituent assembly both faced the prospect of being dominated by Congress and boycotted by the Muslim League. It was an ugly time. The flame lit by the Calcutta riots spread. Muslims at Noakhali and Tipperah in East Bengal murdered Hindus and burned their shops and houses. Fleeing Hindus arrived in Bihar, where their descriptions of the horrors they and their co-religionists had suffered provoked Bihari Hindus to a mass slaughter of Muslims. Some political leaders, unable to contain their rage, encouraged their followers to seek revenge. Across northern India minorities who had lived safely in their villages for generations were suddenly at risk. When outbreaks occurred, the police were no longer effective: many policemen were reluctant to arrest men of their own religion and afraid to tackle aggressive groups of the rival religion. When murder and arson occurred in a big city like Calcutta, the army was able to restore order. The soldiers were of all religious groups and held together, obeying their officers, continuing to act impartially. When the violence was in scattered villages, as at Noakhali and in Bihar, the army was less effective: there were not enough soldiers to protect minority-dwellers in all the endangered villages.

Lord Wavell responded to the spread of violence with a withdrawal plan which he sent to London: if things got worse and the British could not govern, they should simply go, first turning over the southern provinces, where the Muslims were few and violence had not erupted, to their provincial governments, then evacuating the British women and children and concentrating the army in the troubled northern provinces before a final departure. To Attlee the plan smelt of scuttle, a military withdrawal without finding a political solution; it showed that Wavell had become defeatist and himself must go.

## Divide and Quit, March–August 1947

Wavell's successor was an Attlee-Cripps inspiration – Lord Louis Mountbatten. The choice was thought remarkable – he was regarded primarily as a member of the royal family, a leading naval officer and a socialite – but Attlee's dealings with him over Burma help to explain the decision. Mountbatten had been Supreme Commander of all allied forces in south-east Asia from 1943 till 1946. This meant that he was responsible for driving the Japanese out of the territories they had conquered. The first of these was Burma, immediately north-east of India. The military story of the reconquest of Burma has been told often, but the Supreme Commander was particularly responsible for the political decisions. In a difficult campaign, and knowing nothing of the plan to drop atom bombs on Japan, he needed Burmese allies and decided that the most effective Burmese leader was Aung San, formerly head of an anti-British revolutionary party and subsequently the ally of the Japanese when they conquered Burma. By the latter stages of the war, Aung San had moved over to lead an anti-Japanese resistance movement and Mountbatten, needing his help, was prepared to give him in exchange political backing in his demand for immediate independence. The returned British Governor, Sir Reginald Dorman-Smith, did not agree. He supported the policy of the wartime coalition in London, namely that the British owed something to those who had helped them run Burma in the years before the war and who had not sided with the Japanese invaders.

When Attlee began to take a decisive interest in Burma, Dorman-Smith's efforts were keeping Aung San and his popular nationalist party out of the government. Aung San responded by calling for 'a full scale battle for freedom . . . civil disobedience or a parallel government'. Attlee could see the risk of violent conflict and telephoned Mountbatten, who had just returned to London. They saw each other every few weeks to discuss Burma and Mountbatten's advice was that Attlee should consult Brigadier Sir Hubert Rance who had been his own chief adviser on civilian affairs in Burma and who had recommended full military co-operation with Aung San. Attlee summoned Rance to Downing Street, cross-examined him in his usual monosyllabic way, puffing at his pipe and, satisfied that Rance favoured prompt Burmese independence, within the hour appointed him Governor. Britain's policy towards Burma changed in that hour from trying to delay independence by keeping Aung San out of government to welcoming independence by bringing him in. Mountbatten was amazed by the speed of the decision.

Attlee found that Mountbatten's advice was sound. Burma quickly ceased to be a dangerous country close to war with Britain and became a willing partner advancing to independence. Aung San came to London and Attlee considered his delegation 'a very pleasant lot'. Churchill denounced the policy as scuttle and humiliating abasement before an ally of the Japanese, but Attlee knew Britain had not the resources to suppress Aung San's

*The outgoing Viceroy, watched by Lady Wavell, greets his successor, Lord Mountbatten.*

movement and therefore made no fuss about doing a deal with him. The replacement of Dorman-Smith by Mountbatten's man, Rance, was a trial run for the replacement of Wavell by Mountbatten. (Aung San and all his ministers were shot dead by agents of a rival, U Saw, in July 1947, but Attlee and Rance stuck to their policy, transferring power to other leaders of Aung San's party a few months later.)

Mountbatten's appointment as Viceroy of India did not go altogether smoothly. As Supreme Commander he had been briefed by the two previous Viceroys, Linlithgow and Wavell, and he knew something of their difficulties. Recognising the risk of failure, he laid down extraordinary conditions: first, he must consult his cousin the King (which Attlee had already done); second, in announcing his appointment, the Government must also announce that British rule in India was to end by June 1948 – he would assume office only with the public promise that he was the last Viceroy; third, he required a substantial say in drafting the statement announcing his appointment and defining his task; finally, he required to be allowed to complete the job without interference from the Secretary of State for India or the Cabinet. Mountbatten was only forty-six. He had achieved spectacular seniority during the war. Now he was asking for more power than any modern British peacetime government had ever granted an individual.

Attlee had wanted Mountbatten as a new man to bring renewed energy to a basically unchanged policy. But Mountbatten, by his demand over timing, in effect changed the policy, although this was not generally realised at the time. By announcing a date by which they would go, come what may, the British Government was effectively announcing something else: that if no agreement was reached between Congress and the League, the British would hand over to the existing provincial governments. Jinnah, having lost the powerful role in a united India that the Cabinet mission had almost secured for him, was likely to have to accept those provinces that opted to join Pakistan. Mountbatten's purpose in asking for a definite, final date had been to concentrate the minds of the Indians and make them get on with it. The granting of his request made the creation of Pakistan inevitable if the negotiations broke down.

Mountbatten arrived in Delhi on 22 March 1947. By then an interim government of sorts was functioning: Wavell was trying to get Congress and League to work together as colleagues; the Congress members were trying to dominate and the League members were using office mainly to show how much trouble they could cause. Of the three, the League were the most successful. Their principal representative in the government, Liaqat Ali Khan, was Finance Minister, and was doing all he could to damage Congress's ministers and business supporters. Abul Kalam Azad later wrote, 'Whatever proposal [Patel, the Home Minister] made was either rejected or modified beyond recognition by Liaqat Ali . . . internal dissensions broke out within the government and went on increasing.' An ICS man, K. B. Lall, later recalled:

> The Muslim League Minister, Abdur Rab Nishtar, was in charge of communications. Naturally he wanted to be informed of what was going on inside the Congress Party. The easiest way was for him to organise bugging at the telephone exchange. He got all the telephones of all the Congress ministers bugged, and I'm not sure whether even the Viceroy's telephone was not bugged by him.

Patel, who was number two to Nehru of the Congress ministers, became convinced by the Muslim League's tactics in the interim government that co-operation after independence would be impossible. He took the lead in persuading Congress that the League must be ejected. In effect he had decided to support the creation of Pakistan. But it was to be a minimal Pakistan. The Congress Working Committee resolved early in March 1947, just before Mountbatten's arrival, that both the Punjab and Bengal must be partitioned. That way the warring Muslims would be removed from the Indian union but they would not take too much of India with them. 'When you get gangrene in your leg,' Morarji Desai, a Gandhian Congressman in the 1940s and Prime Minister of India in the 1970s, explained, 'you have to cut it off. If you allow it to remain the whole body gives in.'

But Mountbatten's instructions did not go this far. Attlee and his colleagues in London were still committed to the Cabinet mission plan for a constituent assembly that would create a unitary government acceptable to all Indian parties, and Mountbatten was instructed to pursue this objective to the utmost of his power. Only if by October 1947 he found it to be impossible was he to consider alternatives. He thus arrived to find his instructions overtaken. The Cabinet still required him to spend seven months fighting for a unitary state when the Congress, supposedly a prime beneficiary of this policy, had given up the struggle.

Mountbatten introduced a new procedure. He decided to resolve the Indian problem by establishing relationships of understanding and trust with the five key Indian leaders, Gandhi, Nehru, Jinnah, Liaqat and Patel. He began with grand entertainments. More Indians were invited to Viceroy's House than ever before. Mountbatten put his all into making them feel welcome. He was a sparkling socialiser and this part of his task came easily to him. He put on his uniforms and all his medals and quickly won personal credit not only with the princes, who had been accustomed to come to the Viceroy's palace, but with political, social, administrative and industrial leaders. Many years later Countess Mountbatten's lady-in-waiting, Jaya Thadani, remembered this last Viceroyalty:

> Everything moved so well because they themselves were both very proficient. He had the German quality of extreme discipline and everything had to be perfect. It was a very social household. There were dinner parties and drinks parties. Everybody in that house knew that it was the end of an era, that when Mountbatten left there was going to be prohibition. So everybody was determined to drink the Viceroy's cellar dry. That didn't make for a clear head early in the morning, except that Lord Louis, as we called him, and Lady Louis always were clear-headed and knew exactly what they were going to do with the rest of the day. We would follow rather bleary-eyed and often muddled along as best we could. He was very vain. He was extremely good-looking: he had only to walk into a room and every female heart fluttered. He knew that and he would stand there with a very 'look at me' sort of attitude and charm everybody in the room. He enjoyed the way he looked and the ADC who walked behind him would generally carry a comb so that when Lord Louis stepped out of a plane or a car he could see that his hair was in place. In sharp contrast, she never really cared how she looked. She didn't care whether her hair looked right or her make-up. Often friends of hers who came out from England would say, 'You have only got two dresses, don't you think you ought to have a few more?' She never cared about that sort of thing and that too was very endearing.

Mountbatten saw each of the Indian leaders alone and devoted his first meetings to relaxed discussion about the past, their shared interests and cultural and personal matters. They always sat in armchairs, in as informal and friendly an arrangement as he could devise. The only major Indian leader he had met before and the first to join him in Delhi was Nehru, whom he had got to know in 1946 in Singapore, when Mountbatten was Supreme Commander and Nehru a visiting Indian politician fresh out of prison. Officials had then advised against his seeing Nehru but Mountbatten was sympathetic to nationalists and arranged a meeting. The two men at once got on, as did Nehru, a widower, with Lady Mountbatten. They were all rich patricians with radical ideas, quick talking, quick thinking and widely cultured. Mrs Indira Gandhi, Nehru's daughter and later Prime Minister of India, said of the relationship:

My father was rather starved. When you have a rich, many-sided personality, you need a number of different relationships in order to feel fully alive. I think he was missing the type of conversation he got with the Mountbattens and the close touch with new ideas from the western world.

Mrs Vijaya Lakshmi Pandit, Nehru's sister, commented:

My brother's colleagues, men who were identified with him in spirit, loyalty and love, nevertheless spoke a different language. And here was this Englishman who was closer to him in background and knew just how far to go with Nehru.

For the new Viceroy, Nehru was the key. Not only was he the leader of the interim government and Gandhi's chosen successor to lead Congress; he became a close personal friend of Lady Mountbatten in a relationship that transcended their families' political business. Richard Hough, author of books on naval history and on the Mountbattens, writes in *Edwina*, his biography of Countess Mountbatten, that Nehru was 'Edwina's first and only great love'. Between the two men the close understanding and trust that developed were not unparalleled among last British rulers and their nationalist successors, but nowhere else did a British proconsul need so quickly to establish a firm rapport with a nationalist leader. Mountbatten and Nehru liked and respected each other and frankly surveyed the problems and personalities of pre-partition India.

Mountbatten next saw Liaqat Ali Khan, Jinnah's number two, and then, benefiting from Nehru's advice, he saw Gandhi. Again Lady Mountbatten helped to win the affection and trust of a key figure. It was Gandhi's habit to walk with his hands resting on the shoulders of two young woman disciples. He felt sufficiently warm towards the Mountbattens to walk through the gardens of Viceroy's House with his hands resting on their shoulders instead.

Then came Jinnah. Mountbatten did not like him and said he was 'a psychopathic case', but he won unusually warm tributes from the Muslim leader. To do so took all his seductive skill. He told Jinnah that they must get to know each other before discussing business and spent their first and second meetings trying to break through the barrier of Jinnah's reserve. The conversations began with Mountbatten voluble, Jinnah taciturn and embarrassed, ill-equipped to respond. He had come to the Viceroy to discuss matters of state and could not bring himself to indulge in what he considered small talk. But Mountbatten spoke critically of the Congress leaders and their unwillingness to accept fair terms. That was a theme to which Jinnah warmed. Gradually the Viceroy worked his way into the trust of this cold, pedantic, rational but obsessively mistrustful man and only after these preliminaries did Mountbatten get down, in subsequent meetings, to talking business. Each session with an Indian leader lasted about an hour; he then spent fifteen minutes dictating a note, which was usually circulated to his staff.

Gandhi had not been consulted about the Congress decision to accept a truncated Pakistan, partly because he was at the time in Bihar, trying to persuade Hindu and Muslim leaders to stop their extremists from murdering people of the rival community. He cared passionately for Indian unity. If he resisted the Congress decision by appealing to the Hindu masses to oppose the creation of Pakistan, he could rouse them as he had so often done before.

Mountbatten regarded Gandhi as peripheral. His principal negotiations would be with Nehru and Patel for the Congress and with Jinnah and Liaqat Ali Khan for the League. They could talk terms and settle. Gandhi had to be placated and prevented from causing trouble. His genius for inspiring India-wide resistance had to be propitiated by due deference, but he was not a man to deal with because he did not care for carrying complicated messages from one group to another. Nevertheless Gandhi quickly showed that he had accepted the creation of Pakistan as inevitable. At his first meeting with Mountbatten he proposed that Jinnah be asked to form the interim government; he must have already given up any hope of keeping India united, for there was no chance of the Congress's agreeing to such a proposal. Gandhi soon admitted as much and conceded that partition might have to come. With riots and murders continuing, any attempt by him to rouse the masses would only make for increased violence. He therefore devoted himself to peace missions in areas of extreme bloodshed. He remained the most revered Congress leader, beloved throughout India, and the Mountbattens developed an affectionate personal relationship with him. But he was not to be central to the events of 1947.

Not only was Gandhi by now in a mood of acquiescence; so was Jinnah. When he met Mountbatten he still argued relentlessly for a big Pakistan – all the Muslim majority provinces undivided, including many millions of Hindus – but two decisive things had changed since Wavell's conference at Simla and the Cabinet mission: Mountbatten had a timetable for departure and he was no longer limited to persuading the parties to agree. He had the final authority to make an award. While Jinnah was certain, therefore, that by delaying tactics he could secure a sovereign Pakistan, he was reduced to *begging* Mountbatten not to make it so small that it would be, in Jinnah's own words, 'moth-eaten'. Furthermore Jinnah had by now unleashed his only weapon, direct action leading to murder, arson and looting on a vast scale. It had worked. It had led to prompt Congress capitulation. But in northern India Muslims were suffering as badly as Hindus. Any extension of the violence would inflame areas where Muslims were a small minority and would be the main victims. So, although Jinnah continued to argue toughly, Mountbatten knew from their first meeting what the outcome must be. He did his best to sell the Cabinet mission scheme; that was his instruction and he obeyed it. But the further instruction to go on pressing it until October 1947 made no sense. Jinnah pointed out that the Congress working committee had accepted the principle of the creation of Pakistan: anything less was not worth discussing. Mountbatten tried, even so, pointing out that within an all-India union the Muslim-majority provinces would be almost independent, would be able to group themselves in their own federal system – the middle tier – and could be expected to include the whole of the Punjab and the whole of Bengal. Thus Jinnah would obtain all the territories he was demanding and substantial powers. He had accepted this when the Cabinet mission were in India, why not now? Jinnah replied that the instant he had given his agreement the Congress had gone back on theirs; it was they, not he, who were the enemy of compromise. They had shown that what they were really after was complete Hindu raj. To protect the Muslims against this he had only one recourse: to insist on a sovereign Pakistan. Only total separation from the Hindu state could guarantee the Muslims the protection they needed. When Mountbatten put it to him that his insistence on sovereignty for Pakistan would mean dividing the Punjab and Bengal and leaving the non-Muslim halves of both provinces outside Pakistan, Jinnah was trumped: he had no more cards in his hand with which to bluff or bargain.

The issue turned substantially on the army. In the all-India union, defence would be handled by the top tier, where the Muslim view would not predominate. Jinnah was attracted by Gandhi's proposal that he should head the all-India government, but he knew that it could not last: after independence the Congress would quickly replace him. Thus, before long the federal scheme was certain to place power over the army in the hands of non-Muslims or, in Jinnah's view, anti-Muslims. Therefore the Muslims must have their own army to protect them, which meant their own state. By early April 1947 it was clear that partition was inevitable. Liaqat Ali Khan wrote to the Viceroy proposing a reorganisation of the armed forces so that they could be readily divided at independence.

For Mountbatten and the British this was a shock. The question had not been seriously considered. The all-India army was an instrument the British were proud to have created. It had kept peace throughout the subcontinent for 150 years; men of all religions served in most regiments. The Commander-in-Chief, Field Marshal Auchinleck, had worked out a scheme for 'nationalising' the army – removing the British officers in such a way that the effectiveness of the entire force would not be undermined. To add to that complicated and inevitably disruptive change the splitting of the army to form Muslim and non-Muslim units was, many officers believed, asking for trouble. First the soldiers – strong, armed young men who had hitherto been held by military discipline above the discord – might at the break-up of their units join in the inter-communal slaughter. Second, the Viceroy might find the one instrument of control that had continued to function reliably weakened at his moment of greatest need. Third, given that most of the senior officers were Hindus, it might be impossible adequately to officer the army in Pakistan, the area where most disruption of the community was likely to occur. Finally, splitting the Indian army must mean severely reducing its ability to defend the subcontinent. In the political disorder that might well follow Britain's departure, a strong, united army was one way to keep out foreigners. Communist expansion in Europe was already worrying the British Government and its allies. The supposed threat of Russian expansion into India had long been a British obsession. Almost anything seemed better than dividing the Indian army.

Within a month of becoming Viceroy, Mountbatten decided that the partition of India into two sovereign states was inevitable. He sent a draft plan to London. But Liaqat Ali Khan's proposal that a plan for the division of the army be prepared was opposed by Auchinleck and by Baldev Singh, a Sikh who was the Defence Minister in the interim government. Mountbatten himself did not like the idea. The principal adviser he had brought with him from England, Lord Ismay, a former Indian army man, did not like it either. The logic of dividing the subcontinent pointed inevitably to dividing the army, but it went deeply against the grain. For years only the top men passing out from the Royal Military Academy, Sandhurst, had been admitted to the Indian army. Many had devoted their lives to maintaining it as an integrated force. After the mutiny of 1857, they developed the tradition of living close to their men and, after 1920, to their Indian fellow-officers. Civilians might mock the sentimental attachment of British officers to the Indian army, with its funny words and apparently outdated traditions, but Indian regiments had fought for Britain as well as any British regiment and Indian soldiers had died heroically. Rudyard Kipling's description of an Indian military orderly, 'You're a better man than I am, Gunga Din,' moved British officers to tears. These are among the strange reasons why no plan to divide the army was drawn up. The Muslims complained that the cause was the British Labour Government, showing, as usual, pro-Congress prejudice.

The two decisions, first, to divide the subcontinent and second, how to do it, had to be agreed by the Viceroy, the Government in London and the major parties in India. London was no great problem; the Cabinet's insistence that Mountbatten try for seven months to sell the Cabinet mission's scheme was readily abandoned. But Mountbatten continued to hope that, once the principle of partition had been conceded, Jinnah would agree to a supreme defence council in which control over the Indian army would be shared by the two new states.

Mountbatten's first draft of the agreement for independence unexpectedly proved a failure, because it suddenly brought home to Nehru the possible impact of the opt-out clause. After it had been accepted (with minor amendments) by the Cabinet in London, Mountbatten showed it privately to Nehru, who reacted violently. The Viceroy was amazed at what he called 'Nehru's bombshell', as he thought the plan was largely based on his own conversations with Nehru and Patel. But Mountbatten and the British Cabinet had undoubtedly made a dangerous error. Nehru told him that the Congress would certainly turn down the plan, which had totally failed to meet the vital needs of the successor states. Had Congress turned it down after the Cabinet in London had approved it, Britain's chance of extricating herself from India without disaster would have been at an end.

The flaw Nehru found was the provision that any province or princely state, and even sub-provinces in the case of those whose legislatures opted for their division, could enjoy the full right of self-determination. The principle of self-determination had since 1942 been conceded by the British Government to provinces that might wish to opt out, so this seemed to Mountbatten nothing new; and once a final departure date had been announced, succession by the provincial governments would be inevitable if no agreement concerning the centre had been reached. But Nehru wrote to Mountbatten on 11 May 1947, the day after he was shown the proposal, that the British Government was now accepting the theory of 'provinces being initially independent successor states' with 'sovereignty to the provinces' and central authority merely 'a later step'. This, he wrote, would be 'Balkanisation' and would lead to 'civil conflict . . . violence . . . disorder . . . the breakdown of the central authority . . . chaos and . . . demoralisation.'

The explanation least charitable to Mountbatten is that when it came to drawing up constitutional documents – or sometimes even reading them – he was not at his best. Lord Ismay, who had been Churchill's Chief of Staff throughout the war, Attlee's afterwards and was now Mountbatten's principal adviser, wrote to his wife on 23 April 1947: 'We have made innumerable drafts . . . but it is impossible to get Dickie to go through them methodically. He's a grand chap in a thousand ways, but clarity of thought and writing is not his strong suit.'

An alternative explanation is that the India Office, the British Cabinet, the Viceroy's staff and the Indian political leaders had all failed to recognise where they were heading. Churchill's attitude to India in 1942 – in effect that if the Congress ever obtained independence, any province wanting to opt out should be encouraged – had started a headlong movement. Attlee pushed it farther, with his principled belief that peoples had a right to self-determination, particularly if their wishes had been tested in a free vote. And Jinnah seized every such concession, determined not to let a syllable slip. Consequently this had become one of those extraordinary areas of policy where sensible men know they must not ask intelligent questions: whatever had been agreed by Churchill, Attlee and Cripps, Nehru and Jinnah must not be reopened, because it had probably taken months of painful arguing and a few hundred deaths to get top-level acquiescence. Everyone had assumed that the provinces, given the option, would choose either India or Pakistan. Nobody had taken account of the fact that Bengal, to name but one, was likely to opt for sovereign independence. It was – like the emperor's nakedness in the Hans Andersen story – obvious but unmentionable. So each successive plan for the transfer of power had contained provisions that kept open the possibility of Balkanisation and nobody had complained. A solicitor, transferring title to a house for his client, would be rightly sued for negligence if he produced a deed as vulnerable at the moment of transfer as Mountbatten's and the Cabinet's agreed plan.

Nehru's demand that the plan be scrapped was a severe blow to the Viceroy, but his powers of recovery were amazing. He immediately cabled the Cabinet to cancel it. This threw the India committee into some confusion: apparently they again had a Viceroy who lacked the political nous to handle the problem. They considered sending out a minister 'to settle matters there with full powers'. Attlee was even urged to go himself as his 'leadership would count for everything'. But Attlee did his best to support Mountbatten and merely recalled him to London for consultation. He was back in London within a week and had by now swung over to a significantly different plan. One of his principal objectives was to try to ensure that the successor states remained on the best possible terms with Britain. His favoured route to this destination was to get them to stay in the Commonwealth, but he knew that to press the Congress to do so would be counter-productive: they would see it as a fresh instance of British imperialism. So he exercised his considerable talent as a diplomat to cause Congress itself to press for Commonwealth membership, which was then a more substantial matter than it has since become. The principal members – Canada, Australia, New Zealand, South Africa and Britain – had all recently chosen to fight as allies in war. A close relationship was therefore thought to exist between Commonwealth membership and access to British military training and supplies.

Jinnah had said he would want Pakistan to be a member of the Commonwealth. Mountbatten used Jinnah's statement as a threat to the Congress leaders, suggesting that Pakistan might thereby acquire a military advantage. The tactic worked. The Congress leaders, seeing little prospect of agreement on arrangements for the succession, put forward a solution of their own: that the existing government in India should be accorded immediate dominion status, with final details about the possible division of the country and the precise constitutional arrangements, including possible withdrawal from the Commonwealth, to follow by June 1948. This proposal would have made the existing, Congress-led government the effective ruler of independent India, which would have breached undertakings repeatedly given since 1942 to the Muslims and the League. Nevertheless Mountbatten took up the scheme and, after amending it to meet Muslim requirements, pressed it upon the Cabinet. It became the basis for the final settlement.

Mountbatten's constitutional adviser was an Indian, V. P. Menon. He was the only non-Briton in a senior role on the Viceroy's staff and had been effectively excluded from Mountbatten's early counsels because he was known to be close to the Congress leaders, particularly Patel. He now came into his own. Menon had long favoured the maintenance of the Commonwealth link as of value to both Britain and India, but Nehru had ruled it out, writing, 'Under no conceivable circumstances is India going to remain in the British Commonwealth . . . Any attempt to remain in the Commonwealth will sweep aside those who propose it.' Patel, facing the prospect that June 1948 might come with no constitutional agreement in sight, worked out with V. P. Menon a neat bargain: if the British would transfer power at once, by simply declaring the existing Indian Government an independent dominion within the Commonwealth, then the Congress would do its best to make sure that India would remain in the Commonwealth. After all the labours of Simla and the Cabinet mission and the constituent assembly, it was a back-of-an-envelope kind of deal. Indeed it was a mess: the provinces were governed under the 1935 Act; but the provisions of that act concerning the central government had never come into force. So Delhi was still operating under the largely autocratic provisions of Montagu's Act of 1919. The proposal had little to be said for it, except that Congress would accept it, that it would probably keep India in the Commonwealth and that it would enable the British to get out quickly; also that, after the collapse of Mountbatten's last plan, it appeared to offer a way forward. Immediately after receiving Nehru's 'bombshell', Mountbatten asked V. P. Menon to write up this new scheme as a workable proposal. It took Menon six hours. Mountbatten quickly obtained the approval of Congress and the League and then brought the document to London. Within days it had become the British Government's policy. On 4 June 1947 Mountbatten, back in India, told a press conference that the date for independence had been changed. No longer was it to be June 1948, as Attlee had announced, but midnight on 14–15 August next, a mere two months away. And no longer was independence to be on the basis of constitutional plans worked out by Indians themselves in a constituent assembly. The government of British India, with all its British characteristics, would simply be sliced in two and handed over. A series of committees was hastily set up to divide the army, the civil service and the two great provinces of Bengal and the Punjab.

No part of the process was easy, but none was harder than the division of these two provinces. Bengal was culturally united. Its people, both Hindu and Muslim, were recognisably different from other Indians, sharing a distinctive culture, language and script. Their main city, Calcutta, had until recently been the capital of British India and was India's greatest industrial and commercial centre. Coalition governments of Hindus and Muslims had ruled Bengal since the 1919 Act and Bengalis were politically more sophisticated than other Indians. The most ferocious anti-British movements had sprung up there. The Muslim Prime Minister who led the Bengali coalition government, H. S. Suhrawardy, had been pressing the demand for Bengal to become independent as a single, united state. Under Mountbatten's earlier plan he might have got away with it. But the new plan offered the Bengal legislature no such option. Its members had now to choose to join India or Pakistan or to be divided with half joining each. They voted for division.

The Punjab had never been really united. Until the late 1840s a Sikh ruler dominated its largely Muslim population. Then the British took over and built the most spectacular irrigation schemes in India. The Punjab's five great rivers, all tributaries of the Indus, were used to create a huge area of grain production. The Muslims, Sikhs and Hindus of the province worked together because the irrigation made them wealthy. The Muslim League won more seats than any other party in the 1946 election in the Punjab, but the defeated Unionist party clung to power, in coalition with the Hindus and Sikhs. Before long they fell, no party could form a government, and the state had to be ruled by the Governor under section 93, at a time when a representative form of government was desperately needed. By May 1947 the killings which had begun in Calcutta and had subsided there had spread across northern India into the Punjab.

Here it was not just Hindu against Muslim. The Sikhs, sword-carrying, turban-wearing and warlike, formed a minority of some six million, many of them living as landlords or businessmen in the Muslim areas. In rural Rawalpindi more than two thousand of the small Sikh and Hindu community were murdered. In Amritsar and Lahore mobs ran wild, killing and burning. A senior British police officer in Lahore, the capital of the Punjab, superintendent Jack Morton, said of those days:

> I was almost at the end of my tether. We'd had rioting since November 1946, there was practically no rest and no sleep. My Sikh and Hindu police were being singled out by the Muslim mobs for violence. The Muslims came along to me saying, 'You British and your Muslim police can do what they like to us, but we're not going to have your Hindus and Sikhs. We won't answer for the consequences.' So it was a very worrying situation because the police were a thoroughly integrated force.

Another senior British police officer in Lahore, superintendent Gerald Savage, remembered:

> The Muslims and Sikhs got up on their roofs and they were shouting to each other across the roof-tops the Urdu words for 'Beware', *Khabadar, Khabadar*, and this sounded almost like a pack of jackals. People were simply scared to death. People who had been living quite peacefully for many years, Muslims at one end of the street, Hindus or Sikhs at the other, suddenly found that they couldn't trust their neighbours. They were terrified of being bombed or shot or having their house set fire to. There was a sort of snowball effect of fear, spreading right through the city of Lahore. It was awful to watch it happening.

The fear had been growing since it was expressed to the Cabinet mission in March 1946. The killing in the Punjab began early in 1947. From the day Mountbatten announced the partition plan, murder spread like fire. Near Lahore, Muslims killed Sikhs and Hindus. Near Amritsar, the Sikhs went on organised rampages of revenge, killing Muslims. The weakened Government could do little about it, unable even to enforce its own ban on the use of uniformed guards by the League. A Punjab Boundary Force began to function on 1 August, with a British commander assisted by two brigadiers, one an Indian, the other a future Pakistani. Although the force rapidly grew to more than 50,000 men, 'about the largest force ever concentrated in one place in time of peace', according to Mountbatten, it could not stop the knifings and burnings and bombings which replaced the earlier mob violence. Sir Evan Jenkins, Governor of the Punjab, explained to the Viceroy: 'We are faced not with an ordinary exhibition of political or communal violence, but with a struggle between the communities for power which we are shortly to abandon.' It was a struggle also for property: the Muslims wanted Sikhs and Hindus, particularly those with large properties, removed from Lahore and Rawalpindi and the remainder of what would soon be Pakistan; the Sikhs, in revenge, drove Muslims from Amritsar and the rest of east Punjab. Jenkins accused political leaders, including Vallabhbhai Patel for Congress and Liaqat Ali Khan for the League, of encouraging the expulsions.

Into this situation of growing violence the partition plan thrust a new instrument: a boundary commission to divide Bengal and the Punjab, as well as part of the province of Assam. A leading lawyer at the English Bar, Sir Cyril Radcliffe, a fellow of All Souls, was given the job of carving villages, rivers, hydro-electric cables, irrigation canals, railway lines, even cities, on the basis of 'ascertaining the contiguous majority areas of Muslims and non-Muslims'. He was allowed to take into account 'other factors', which were not specified. He had never before been to India and was therefore equipped with judicial ignorance. Mountbatten avoided contact with him, to stifle the inevitable accusation of influencing his decisions. All parties agreed to accept his awards and to enforce them.

It was a curious task. Where thousands of British officers had tramped the hills and valleys of India, producing maps of the entire subcontinent, Sir Cyril sat in a house on the viceregal estate, with little time to go out and tour Delhi and less to inspect the heavily populated areas whose borders he was defining. He had commissioners, mostly Indian high court judges, sitting simultaneously in Calcutta and Lahore. As he could not sit with both groups he sat with neither. Instead he studied the written evidence submitted to them and the transcripts of the hearings. The commissioners, selected from the rival communities, predictably disagreed. Therefore Radcliffe made the final awards himself, sitting alone in Delhi, poring over old maps and census data and the claims of residents. He had to decide whether the most populous city in the empire, Calcutta, should go to India or Pakistan. The majority of the population were Hindu, but East Bengal's only source of foreign exchange was jute and all the mills that processed it were in Calcutta. Without the mills, the Muslims of East Bengal argued, they would be throttled, their territory left a 'rural slum'. Calcutta went to India. To the east of Bengal lie the Chittagong hill-tracts, with a population almost entirely of primitive tribespeople, few Muslims, but with easy access only to the Muslim areas of East Bengal. Vallabhbhai Patel learned from a deputation of tribespeople that they feared their area was to go to Pakistan and he wrote to the Viceroy that he had told the hill people that Radcliffe's ignoring local opinion in this way 'was so monstrous they would be justified in resisting to the utmost and [could] count on our maximum support'. The hill tracts went to Pakistan.

It was to be in the Punjab that the worst effects of partition would fall. Mountbatten knew of the growing violence there and that, whatever the details of Radcliffe's award, many would be disappointed and possibly vengeful. Radcliffe had consulted the Congress and League leaders and explained that, if they required him to deliver the awards by 15 August, the result would inevitably be rough justice. They all insisted that the date must be met. Mountbatten, on the other hand, did not want the awards announced until after 15 August, in case the reaction to them marred Independence Day. Radcliffe had said he would deliver them to the Viceroy by 13 August. Mountbatten conveniently arranged to leave Delhi that afternoon for Karachi, staying away until too late on the 14th to read the awards. The 15th was the day of celebration, so the awards were kept from the political leaders of the new states until the 16th and from the public until the 17th. On Independence Day millions did not know which country they were in. Soon Pakistanis were complaining bitterly that Radcliffe had been partial, above all that in awarding the *tahsil* (district) of Gurdaspur in the Punjab to India he had deliberately wounded Pakistan by keeping open the only passage along which India might build a road to Kashmir. But by then British rule was over.

By comparison with the two great provinces, partition of the army and the civil service was easy, though by any other standard it was difficult, wasteful and destructive. The army could scarcely believe in the division. Officers received a duplicated form on which to record their choice. Most Hindus and Sikhs had no option. Pakistan would not have them. But for those Muslims whose homes lay in what was to be India, opting for Pakistan could mean leaving parents, property, all they had known. Most opted for Pakistan, but many Muslims, convinced of the need for a secular army in a secular state, chose India. At their farewell parties, the divided comrades swore to be dining together and playing polo again soon and dismissed as ridiculous the idea that they might shortly face each other in war.

The men were transferred in their units. Regiments of Sikh and Hindu soldiers from the north-west frontier had to make their way through Muslim territory to get out of what was to be Pakistan. Many faced tribesmen, angered by tales of massacres of Muslims; battles on the way included one in which 24 soldiers and 94 tribesmen were killed. Units composed mainly of Muslims were sent by lorry and train across India into Pakistan, with the non-Muslims encouraged to desert *en route*. The regiments took their equipment with them. The bulk of the stores and all the ordnance factories were in India. Pakistan received far less than her share of equipment and none of the ordnance factories.

Much the same applied to the civil service and its possessions. Most Muslims opted for Pakistan, but the bulk of the files, typewriters, chairs, desks and in- and out-trays stayed in India. This was not British policy. The partition plans assumed good will and the readiness of the Indian Government to hand over what Pakistan was allotted. But most of the central Government's records and goods were in Delhi and could be removed only

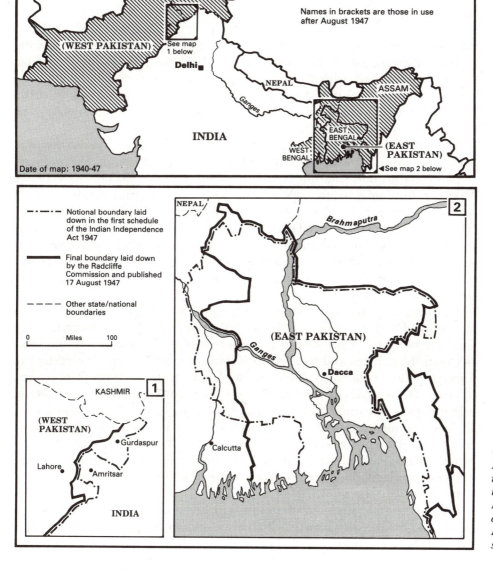

*On 19 July 1947 the Indian Independence Act was passed. It appeared to define the borders of Pakistan. But less than a month later Radcliffe's award made substantial changes.*

with the approval of the Congress. Bureaucrats skilled at obstruction came into their own. A dozen good reasons could always be found for not handing over a particular item. India acquired in Delhi a governing machine in good order, with competent people in the appropriate offices and the equipment to get on with the job; Pakistan had few of the top civil servants and inherited at Karachi no government structure and the fag-end of the equipment.

Not until the partition plan was announced and the decision taken to set up all the committees dealing with the carve-ups did Mountbatten turn his mind to the princes. Indeed he complained that nobody had told him the princes were likely to be awkward: 'I had been given no inkling,' he later wrote, 'that this was going to be as hard to solve as British India, if not harder.' One of the reasons for his appointment was that, as a member of the royal family, he would have extra pull with the princes: he had visited India with his cousin the Prince of Wales (later King Edward VIII) in 1922 and had then been the guest of many princes, hunting tiger on their elephants, courting Edwina in their company; his friendship with several went back far longer than his link with Nehru. Late in his short viceroyalty he gave his mind to the political threat presented by this group who had stopped the implementation at the centre of the 1935 Act and now endangered the transfer of power itself.

Mountbatten's first plan was welcomed by the princes: sovereignty over their own states. A third of the land of the subcontinent would be transferred to them on the understanding that they would probably elect to join India or Pakistan, but remained free to stand out and resume full independence. This was a large part of what Nehru meant when he rejected the plan as 'Balkanisation'. The British Government did not intend anything so damaging: knowing that most princes lacked the means to exercise sovereignty, it assumed that they would come to sensible agreements with the two successor states, a reasonable view so long as the lead in opting out was not given by some of the big provinces.

An obstacle to disposing of the problem was Sir Conrad Corfield, head of the Political Service. He was in charge of the residents and advisers who were formally not part of the British government of India but merely the links between the princes and the British Crown, personally represented by the Viceroy. Many residents came to like and sympathise with the princes they advised. If the resident tried to interest the prince in modern methods of administration or improved agriculture, the prince, often grateful and keen to learn, would try to interest the resident in hunting and the ancient traditions of the state. Each liked to prove that he was well versed in the other's field. This had been an effective mechanism for ensuring that the princes remained allies of the Crown in the nineteenth century.

Corfield was the guardian of a peculiar doctrine, 'paramountcy'. The princes were independent rulers but had given over defence and foreign policy to the British Crown, which was their protector and friend. The Political Service had persuaded them to keep British troops garrisoned on their land, to have railways and telegraph wires and irrigation canals cross wherever the interests of India as a whole, i.e. British India, had dictated.

The Political Service had long held that the British could not transfer paramountcy to the successor states. The Crown had, in effect, been accepted by the princes as trustees of their interests and it could not hand on the trust without their consent. Corfield went farther: he thought it right to help the princes to get into as strong a position as possible to bargain for good terms. It all boiled down to a single issue: the timing of accession. Corfield thought the princes should delay signing their instruments of accession to India or Pakistan until after independence. Mountbatten, once he had become converted to Nehru's view on the danger of 'Balkanisation', undertook to persuade or bully the princes into signing before.

Nehru threatened the princes with a Congress-led rising of their peoples against them if they did not accede. Mountbatten reprimanded him. That was not the way to secure compliance. On the contrary, it was likely to make many princes resist (which some of them had the armies as well as the will to do). The solution to the problem came, once again, from an alliance of Vallabhbhai Patel, the leading fixer in Congress, and V. P. Menon, who had by now established himself as the most important member of Mountbatten's staff. Menon devised the scheme: the princes would be invited to accede to India or Pakistan for foreign policy, defence and communications only; in internal matters, including finance, they would retain all power. Patel persuaded Congress to agree, subject to Mountbatten's whipping in all the princes before 15 August.

Many Congressmen regarded the princely states as reactionary, corrupt, undemocratic and ripe for revolution, and Corfield and his department as the protectors of the princes, a view which was confirmed when Corfield's men began burning papers. Nehru protested that the papers belonged to the successor governments, but Corfield explained to Mountbatten that they contained only secret reports on the behaviour of the maharajahs, including their sexual habits; it was not for the British Government to hand over such documents to people who might wish to make them public or use them for blackmail (the fact that the British Government had gathered them partly for use as blackmail in no way weakened this argument). Mountbatten understood at once and urged Corfield to continue the burning, but discreetly. However, he also agreed to Patel's demand for the dismemberment of Corfield's department. To replace it a States Department of the Government of India was set up, with Patel as minister, Menon as chief official and Mountbatten himself as chief diplomat and whipper-in. This triumvirate now handled, with spectacular flair, the group who had defeated Linlithgow in 1935–40. Sir Conrad Corfield retired early to Britain.

Mountbatten's persuasion of the majority of the princes was a diplomatic coup even though he failed with the rulers of two of the largest states. Congress had agreed to the Menon scheme only if it provided, in Patel's words, 'a full basket of apples'; that meant 565 apples, voluntary accession by all the princely states. Mountbatten told Patel he would try to secure 560. If many of the larger princely states opted for independence, the transfer of power could still lead to Balkanisation or civil war. Although the provinces of British India no longer had the right to opt out, the princes could do almost as much damage.

The vast majority of the 565 states were within what would become independent India. Jinnah and Liaqat Ali Khan did their best to persuade the fourteen that shared borders with Pakistan to join it, declaring that sovereignty was the legitimate goal of all. Several princes had thought of this for themselves, including the Muslim Nizam of Hyderabad, ruler of the largest state, in the centre of the subcontinent, with a mainly Hindu population of sixteen million (more than Canada, South Africa or Australia) and a land area as large as France. The Nizam employed as legal and political adviser Sir Walter Monckton, who had advised King Edward VIII during the abdication crisis and was a friend of Churchill. Monckton involved Lord Ismay, Mountbatten's most senior adviser, and R. A. Butler, a former Conservative minister who had been on the Cabinet's India committee throughout the war, in drafting a parliamentary question designed to keep open the possibility of relations with Britain and even dominion status for states that opted to join neither India nor Pakistan. The question was shown to officials in London and an answer drafted: His Majesty's Government would not refuse direct relations with states that opted for autonomy. That answer alone, if published, would have been enough to defeat Mountbatten's effort to secure his 560 apples.

Mountbatten addressed the Chamber of Princes. He told them that 'his' scheme, by which they could retain complete internal sovereignty if they relinquished their powers over foreign policy, defence and communications, was available only if they all acceded before 15 August. After that, the new Indian Government would offer less favourable terms, both financially and in respect of other encroachments on the states' rights. He employed what V. P. Menon described as 'the apogee of persuasion' on the majority of rulers, the smallness of whose states afforded them no real prospect of independence. He calculated that they would then persuade the rulers of larger states that the guarantees concerning finance and autonomy should be seized while they were on offer, that once British overlordship was gone the states would be on their own against the Congress unless they had signed the deal. Jinnah regarded Mountbatten's performance as blatantly helping India bully the princes into acquiescence. Corfield regarded it as deception of the princes to lead them to act against their own best interests. But Monckton became convinced by Mountbatten's argument that to fail with the princes now could destroy the transfer settlement, with consequences too horrifying to contemplate. So Monckton made sure that his parliamentary question with its potentially disruptive draft answer was never asked, and bent his efforts instead to persuading the Nizam to accede to India. He did not succeed.

In dealing with the princes Mountbatten enjoyed many advantages over Linlithgow. One was the changed position of Churchill. Ten years earlier Churchill's powerful encouragement had fired the princes to resist the 1935 Act. Now Churchill was quelled. He did not like Britain's giving independence to India, but his colleagues, including R. A. Butler and Anthony Eden, recognised that his wartime dominance of Indian policy had frequently gone directly against the opinion of the Viceroy and the Governors of all the Indian provinces: he did not want to know the facts about the political needs of India; he just wanted it kept British. Now they persuaded him that the Indian Independence Bill had to be hurried through the House of Commons unopposed if Mountbatten's deadline of 15 August was to be met; otherwise Britain would be responsible for a disaster. 'Why call it independence?', Churchill asked. Attlee insisted. Churchill reluctantly acquiesced. Philip Noel-Baker, Secretary of State for Commonwealth Relations, piloted the Bill on its brisk, perfunctory passage through the Commons, because Listowel, Secretary of State for India, was in the Lords.

> Anthony Eden's job was to keep Churchill away from the House while the Bill went through [Noel-Baker recalled] because if he came into the chamber he might be unable to stop himself from speaking against. One day he came in and I thought trouble was in store. But he just glared at me and went away.

With Churchill neutralised and Monckton, the Nizam's adviser, won over by Mountbatten, the princes lacked those who might have been their key allies in resisting accession. On the other side, Mountbatten, Patel and Menon promised the princes that they would not only retain their powers if they acceded, they would strengthen the Congress right wing and thus help secure a sympathetic post-independence government of India. Patel, as the leading Congress right-winger, was well placed to advance this argument with force.

Nobody knew whether the princes had any real political fight left in them, although those who had sent troops to serve Britain in the war and still had armies under their command seemed a real danger. Linlithgow had believed that if he had tried to bully them they would have resisted. Mountbatten treated them with the courtesy due to a powerful ally and they crumbled like the relics of the past in fancy uniforms that they really were. The extent of their capitulation, only three refusing to accede before 15 August, was a surprise to be repeated throughout the closing years of the Empire: the traditional rulers whom the British had propped up proved almost everywhere unable to revive their power.

Mountbatten had assumed, as he faced the inevitability of partition, that India would leave the Commonwealth on independence and that he would promptly return to England, not much lamented in India. His second partition plan changed these prospects. By retaining dominion status immediately on becoming independent, India and Pakistan were committed, for an interim period at least, to remaining in the Commonwealth; and by advancing the date of independence so sharply, Mountbatten and the British Government left too little time for the division of assets and, above all, of the armed forces, to be completed under British rule. Nehru therefore suggested that the two new nations should at first have a common Governor-General. Plainly the only man for this task was Mountbatten himself, well qualified to mediate the inevitable disputes and conflicts that partition would throw up: he would no longer have the executive authority of Viceroy but could guide both governments in a way that would minimise clashes. Once the idea had been approved in London, Mountbatten took it up with enthusiasm. It was, of course, flattering, and nobody denies that he was a vain man; more important it was the only way to make sure that smoothing the transition impartially was the concern of the highest officer of each of the new states.

Mountbatten's vanity, however, now clashed with Jinnah's. The Muslim League leader was determined to be the first Governor-General of Pakistan. Mountbatten tried desperately to persuade him to accept the office of Prime Minister, where, he argued, the real power would lie, but Jinnah was rigid. Mountbatten's note of their final conversation on this subject reveals his pique:

*The meeting at which all parties agreed to the partition scheme. Left to right: Jawarharlal Nehru, Lord Ismay, Lord Mountbatten, Mohammed Ali Jinnah.*

I asked him, 'Do you realise what this will cost you?' He said sadly, 'It may cost me several crores of rupees in assets', to which I replied somewhat acidly, 'It may well cost you the whole of your assets and the future of Pakistan.' I then got up and left the room.

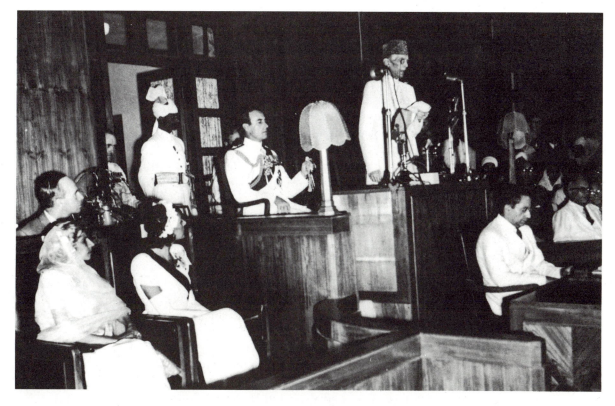

Jinnah, as usual, explained himself to nobody, but he had good reasons. He knew, as only his doctor and his sister knew, that he was dying of tuberculosis: he therefore needed to get Liaqat Ali Khan established as head of the Government as quickly as possible. At the same time he considered that the securing of Pakistan had needed and would continue to need himself as both figurehead and chief executive. Muslim politicians in Sind, the North-West Frontier, Bengal and the Punjab, many of them men he despised, would be out for what they could get and he felt he needed supreme status to secure his authority over them. Both Jinnah and Mountbatten were driven by honourable concerns of state as well as a dash of pettiness.

Mountbatten was appointed Governor-General of India only. This meant that his hopes for a supreme defence council and for other mechanisms of co-operation between India and Pakistan – all of which had come to depend on his role as shared head of state – were destroyed. His relations with the Congress leaders continued to improve during the final weeks of British rule, while those with the Muslim League leaders at best remained stable. The difference in tone between his speeches at the inception of the two states was marked. On 14 August in Karachi, at the ceremony marking the birth of Pakistan, the most populous Muslim nation in the world, he said: 'I would like to express my tribute to Mr Jinnah. Our close personal contact and the mutual trust and understanding that have grown out of it are I feel the best omens for future good relations. He has my sincere good wishes as your new Governor-General.' The next day, in Delhi, he said: 'In your first Prime

*The birth of Pakistan. Jinnah reads his speech immediately after Mountbatten has formally handed over his powers.*

Minister, Pandit Jawaharlal Nehru, you have a world-renowned leader of courage and vision. His trust and friendship have helped me beyond measure in my task. Under his able guidance . . . India will now attain a position of strength and influence and take her rightful place in the comity of nations'. Of his own role as Governor-General, he said: 'I would ask you to regard me as one of yourselves, devoted wholly to the furtherance of India's interests.'

While in part this contrast in tone reflected Mountbatten's resentment at not being invited to become Governor-General of Pakistan, more fundamentally it reflected his profound view, shared by Attlee and Cripps and most of the British, that the creation of Pakistan was a mistake. Whether he blamed those Congress leaders who repeatedly aroused Muslim fears and thus strengthened the League's determination to have a separate state, or Churchill's 1942 Cabinet for providing the provincial opt-out clause which was the irreversible opening the Pakistan campaigners needed, or Jinnah for the ruthlessness with which he fought for power, Mountbatten was saddened by Britain's failure to hand on a united India.

That sadness did not show itself on 15 August 1947. The size and enthusiasm of the crowds were overwhelming. Mountbatten, in his 'Report on the last Viceroyalty', submitted to the British Government in September 1948, included a description written the day after independence. The crowd was so much larger than expected that the planned ceremonial had to be abandoned. The bands could not play. Mountbatten could not leave his gilded carriage to mount the stand. So he signalled from the carriage for India's flag to be raised and the crowd let out a long powerful roar of delight.

> Danger of a large-scale accident was becoming so great [Mountbatten wrote] that we decided the only thing to do was to move the state coach on and draw the crowd with us. For this reason I invited Nehru to stay in the coach, which he did, sitting like a schoolboy on the front hood above the seats. Meanwhile refugees who had fainted or had been almost crushed under the wheels were pulled on board and we ended with four Indian ladies with their children, the Polish wife of a British officer and an Indian pressman who crawled up behind. The bodyguard gradually opened a way through the crowd and then the whole throng began to follow us. Hundreds of thousands of people all running together is an impressive sight; several thousand ran the whole three miles back alongside the coach and behind it, being stopped finally by the police only at the gates of Government House.

Years later Khushwant Singh, a journalist, remembered that day:

> I happened to be outside the Parliament House when Nehru made his famous 'tryst with destiny' speech [see p. 3]. It was an enormous crowd and somehow one had forgotten all about what we'd been through and the killings and the riots. One felt very elated: at long last the country was free

and we could manage our own affairs. Next morning near Princes Place where the Mountbattens went in their horse drawn carriage to the Red Fort, I couldn't believe it, the crowd took the horses away and dragged his carriage themselves, cheering the British. Staid, stiff British officers in uniforms were lifted shoulder high and cheered. It seemed that a hundred and fifty years of bitterness, the massacre at Amritsar, all the civil disobedience movements and all the anti-British feelings had totally vanished and this nation had become more pro-British than it had ever been since the British came.

It was a day of elation, of speeches to vast crowds who were easily moved, of parties, of compliments. Dickie had pulled off an extraordinary triumph. But the details of the partition, the Radcliffe awards, could not be delayed much longer. Even on Independence Day the Punjab was principally occupied with what may well have been the most savage mass killing of all time. Gandhi, after the terrible Calcutta killings of the previous autumn and the follow-up killings in the Bengal countryside, decided that his base must be there, to seek to serve as a one-man boundary force, calming communal passions when the awards were announced. His presence, accompanied by the Muslim Chief Minister of Bengal, H. S. Suhrawardy, was a major reason – probably the main reason – for Bengal's relative calm. When the killing was resumed Gandhi started a fast unto death. All the Bengali political leaders tried desperately to forestall his dying; youths who had murdered came to his bedside to apologise and only when he was persuaded that the

*Gandhi, a few days after independence, visits a camp in Delhi where Muslims at risk are assembled before being sent to Pakistan.*

violence around Calcutta had totally stopped did he consent to take food. Thus Bengal, often the most inflammable and violent area in Indian politics, calmed down – to be outdone by the normally more stable Punjab.

There the terror went through three stages. It had begun early in 1947 with demonstrations that regularly turned violent; it then changed character into thousands of quiet killings in alleys and at night; and in the days after 15 August it reached its worst phase: two extermination campaigns leading to mass migrations in opposite directions, the helpless migrants prey to bands of organised killers. Sikh leaders, particularly Master Tara Singh, had been inciting their followers to carry out organised attacks on Muslims; Nehru admitted as much to Mountbatten. Now, with partition, the Punjab was left with no effective police force to exert control. Policemen were as anxious as other citizens to move with their families to safety on their own side of the border; thousands simply deserted their posts, as did many officials. So a process which government and police had been unable to control before 15 August now ran wild, with two new provincial governments and police forces not yet sufficiently established to make even a serious attempt at control. The two new Prime Ministers, Nehru and Liaqat Ali Khan, met in the Punjab to try to organise a joint effort to stop the killing and help the refugees, but there was little they could do. Tara Singh and other Sikh leaders agreed to tour East Punjab in military vehicles, urging their followers to cease all acts of violence, but what they had started they could not stop.

The migrants were easy victims: tired after walking scores of miles through the dusty humidity and blazing heat of the Punjab in August; burdened with children, cooking pans, bed rolls, everything they possessed; slowed by aged parents and the inevitable wounds of walking, mostly barefoot, farther than they had ever walked before; they had neither the strength nor the will to fight when bands of youths attacked them with swords or stones. Day after day the columns of migrants trudged, Muslims in one direction, Sikhs and Hindus in the other, seemingly endless crocodiles of people, some more than fifty miles long. The Sikhs going east appeared to be in the better order, with their flocks and many bullock carts moving in fairly tight formation. The Muslim columns moving west usually looked more panic-stricken and disorganised, with fewer bullock carts and animals, walking in more of a straggle. At this stage it was above all the Muslim columns that were the victims. Wynford Vaughan Thomas was reporting for the BBC:

> I had a small portable recorder and a jeep. Again and again I used to see these massacres taking place on the Grand Trunk Road. People tried to cut people down, I'd lift up the microphone and say 'The BBC is watching you', and they'd stop. It was most extraordinary, in the middle of all these scenes, that nobody for a moment touched me or any European. The English were untouchables in the nicest possible way.

Mustapha Khaled, a journalist in 1947, remembered:

One afternoon there was a convoy which came across from Ferozepur in India. These refugees were in a very miserable condition: as many as two hundred men, women and children coming along stark naked without a stitch of clothing on them. They were horribly mutilated, some of them had broken limbs, and the women had their breasts cut off. There were children carrying dead children just for the sake of burying them in the soil of Pakistan. All told it was not a very pretty sight.

Gerald Savage, the Lahore police superintendent

. . . personally saw a lorry load of corpses. They were women who had been stripped naked, appallingly mutilated, and left on the side of the road in Lahore city. Since they were Muslim women I can only assume that they had been murdered by Sikhs or Hindus.

The luckier families could afford to go by train. But even the trains were attacked, as Wynford Vaughan Thomas saw:

The trains ran a serious risk. Anglo-Indian drivers would shunt into a siding and go off to water the engine. That would give the Sikh bands a chance to come in and they would go right through the train and kill everybody. And the train would then shunt on to Lahore where in a siding they'd have to take the dead out. They were a terrible sight. I don't want to think over it. You could see them coming with the fly swarms around them. And when the bodies were taken out and laid down, there would be

*To Pakistan or death. Muslim refugees crowd aboard a train at Delhi.*

about two thousand at a time. One station official turned to me, he'd obviously been used to order – the pride of British India was the railways, it was a tremendous system – and in a voice I will never forget, he said, 'Sire, it is hardly worth issuing tickets anymore.' A good man horrified by the collapse of order.

A Pakistani who was formerly a minister in the Punjab Government, Sardar Shaukat Hyat Khan, recalled:

We were taking these trains to the Walton railway station because otherwise people were getting worked up in Lahore. There you saw bodies of women, some suckling their babies, and lances straight through the babies and the mothers. Bloated bodies; pulling them out, you couldn't get to those compartments on account of the smell. And then to look at the bodies – no human being could stand the sight of women in such a condition.

D. C. Mehra, a hotel owner, was at the railway station in Amritsar:

The local people got hold of a boy and, when his pants were taken off, he was found to be circumcised and they said, 'You are a Muslim'. He begged of them that he was not Muslim. His mother cried, and she said, 'We are Hindu and he is not a Muslim boy'. But because of the circumcision he was killed right in the station. I have never seen such a ghastly scene in my life.

The Sikh killing of Muslims dominated the eastern Punjab. But in Lahore, the greatest city of the province, the Muslim majority was determined to drive out every last remnant of the formerly dominant Sikh and Hindu commercial class. Even in Amritsar many Sikhs were afraid and the impact on one such family was described by Mrs Iqbal Kaur, who in 1947 was a schoolgirl in Amritsar:

Our parents made us stay together in one room and locked us in and brought kerosene oil for us. And they said, 'If there is a raid by the Muslim people we will burn you up there.' And we girls were prepared for that. We preferred that to disgrace at that time. My sister-in-law was stabbed by her own husband, because she was being removed by the Muslim people. So he just killed her there, right in her own house.

The Punjab Boundary Force could do little to stop the killing, though they made some brave efforts. Major-General T. W. Rees, their commanding officer, in his final report, mentioned one case, a Sikh major who was commanding the escort party of a train full of Muslim refugees: 'He suffered three gunshot wounds and six spear wounds in repelling attacks on the train by people of his own religion.' But against a tidal wave of killing, the Force could do little more than send daily reports on the numbers killed. Lt-Col. Philip Mitchison, recalled:

The situation reports were made up and sent in quintuplicate. One copy went to the Cabinet, I know, two or three copies were retained in India, and one, we were told, always went to Churchill. These situation reports went in every day with an assessment of casualties, made up from reports from all over this very large area. It is true that they were difficult to assess, but based on what one saw oneself, there is reason to think that something in the order of a million men, women and children, civilians, was by no means unlikely for the total killed. It's always been my own view, and one which I have not departed from.

Officially the Governments put the number killed in the Punjab at about two hundred and fifty thousand. No exact figure will ever be worked out. Wynford Vaughan Thomas, whose job was to try to establish the facts for his BBC reports, believes that the massacre total has been seriously under-estimated:

> I know a figure of a quarter of a million has been suggested and almost officially accepted; you couldn't possibly make an accurate account because these massacres were taking place in lonely places, in all sorts of villages, little towns all through the Punjab and in Sikhistan. But I think I would go on record, stick my neck out and say nearly a million killed.

At the end of August 1947 the Punjab Boundary Force was wound up, not because the killings had stopped – they continued through September and October and began to peter out only in November – but because both Indian and Pakistani ministers blamed the Force for failing to protect their people and for alleged partiality to the other side. The British officers of the force were grateful to be relieved of a horrible task in which they were largely ineffective. The senior Muslim Officer, Brigadier Mohammed Ayub Khan, later President of Pakistan, explained its impotence:

> The Force could only rush to a place that was being attacked, and by the time the troops arrived it was looted, burnt and the Muslim inhabitants massacred. In the end all that this Force could do was to try and keep the roads clear for the refugees. This was done by patrolling the main thoroughfares and the railway lines.

Early in September 1947 the wave of murder in the Punjab swept back to engulf Delhi itself, both New Delhi, the British capital so recently completed with its broad, long avenues, and old Delhi, the city of the Mughals, with its crowded bazaars and tiny alleyways. Nehru himself saw Sikh and Hindu youths murdering Muslim shopkeepers. He howled at them and hit them. But that was not enough to stop the contagion. Many of the Delhi police were Muslims and had deserted. The killing of Muslims spread round the capital, from the smart shopping areas to the residential suburbs and the poorer districts. If the new capital of India went the way of the Punjab, as it was beginning to do, the state might collapse within a month of its foundation. The horrified Congress ministers, with years of experience in prison behind them but none of running a government in an emergency, asked Mount-batten, newly installed as constitutional head of state, to resume total control to deal with the crisis. He tactfully refused, but agreed to head an emergency committee subordinate to the Cabinet. Nehru and Patel promptly joined his committee, acting as his assistants.

Mountbatten set up a military response to the violence, first sending out spotter planes and reconnaissance teams to report where the migrant columns in the Punjab were, where the outbreaks in Delhi were occurring, then using every official of every department of the new state, from Nehru and Patel down – removing them from whatever business they were doing – to convey information, food, medicines, water and, above all, reassurance, to the areas under threat. The purpose was both to bring relief and to demonstrate that the Indian Government was in charge and able to concentrate resources in areas of anarchy so as to suppress it. The return of executive power to the former Viceroy so soon after independence was kept secret for many years, in case it should damage the standing with the Indian electorate of Nehru and Patel.

*     *     *

The villain in the long saga of the end of British rule in India was Winston Churchill. His encouraging the princes to stand out from the arrangements of the 1935 Act was a major reason for Indians' not acquiring responsible government in Delhi before the 1939–45 war. Whether Churchill's motive was genuine political conviction about India or determination to use any convenient stick with which to beat his despised rival Stanley Baldwin, the effect was to kill a complicated compromise that had proved just acceptable to Congress, the princes, the Muslim League and both major parties in the British Parliament. The Viceroy, Linlithgow, believed he could talk the princes into participating. The Congress, after their satisfactory experience in running the provinces, found the prospect of office at the centre attractive. Gandhi helped the Viceroy smooth the way; Nehru, initally opposed, had acquiesced; Churchill was the chief wrecker.

When the war came, he continued to play the same role. The offer that the Viceroy and the Secretary of State for India worked out early in the war seemed at that time to be enough to buy Congress co-operation. Churchill vetoed it. When, in 1942, he was forced by Roosevelt and the Labour members of his Cabinet to let a similar offer be taken to Delhi by Sir Stafford Cripps, he and the Viceroy corresponded behind Cripps's back in order to destroy the deal. Gandhi, in spite of his pacifism, stood back to allow the negotiations to succeed and Nehru was doing all he could to bring Congress into the government in support of the war. Naturally the Viceroy was piqued at having a minister brought to India over his head and clearly Cripps was wrong to let Linlithgow feel that he had been excluded from the negotiations, but for the Prime Minister to encourage the Viceroy in undermining the Cabinet's emissary was, again, the action of a wrecker.

Wavell's diaries offer repeated evidence of Churchill's determination to prevent Indians sharing in constitutional progress which everyone else –

Viceroy, provincial Governors, Commander-in-Chief, Secretary of State, the entire weight of British official opinion in India – considered inevitable. Wavell's straightforwardness and honesty are universally acknowledged: he was not a radical with Bentinck- or Ripon-like inclinations but a cautious Viceroy who recognised that the Congress, as India's government-in-waiting, must be given some practice at the helm if the transition was to be handled successfully. Churchill refused to listen. He wanted the Congress leaders kept in prison and all considerations of constitutional advance avoided. He would not allow Wavell even to meet Gandhi. Attlee, Amery and other members of the Cabinet's India committee disagreed, but they followed Churchill's policy because they had learned from the Cripps mission that on Indian policy he was irrational and intransigent. Since he was the leader who was winning the war, they felt they could not oppose him. At the end of the Simla conference the fact that Churchill was Prime Minister was a principal reason why Jinnah was able to hold out, thus destroying Wavell's plans for an interim government. Under any other Prime Minister, Wavell could have outbluffed Jinnah with the threat of an all-Congress government. Churchill's hatred of Congress was so pathological that he rendered the Viceroy impotent.

These repeated wrecking tactics had enormous effect. If a representative government of Indians had been formed before the war, or in 1940, or in 1942, or when Wavell begged to be allowed to form one in 1943–44, or even after Simla in 1945, Congress and the Muslim League could have exercised power for a useful period before the final transfer. Some, at least, of the disasters of 1947 would thereby have been avoided.

## After Independence

If India and Pakistan are to be judged by the thirty-seven years following 1947, then India is a success, Pakistan a failure. India in those years succeeded in holding all the territory left to it by the British, while Pakistan lost its more populous half, East Bengal, to a secessionist movement in 1971. India was governed by a form of parliamentary democracy, with regular elections and governments peacefully relinquishing office in 1977 and 1980, while Pakistan's efforts to maintain democratic forms repeatedly failed, to be replaced by military rule. In India the courts remained by and large independent of government, while in Pakistan the military regimes – notably that of President Zia ul Haq after 1977 – seriously weakened judicial independence and even hanged an ex-Prime Minister, Zulfiqar Ali Bhutto.

Things went wrong in Pakistan from the start. Mohammed Ali Jinnah, the creator of the nation and its first Governor-General, died on 11 September 1948, just a year and a month after independence. Liaqat Ali Khan, the first Prime Minister, was assassinated in 1951. Pakistan thus lost the two men who seemed most likely to prevent local and self-interested factionalism among the political élite.

India by contrast was lucky. Jawaharlal Nehru remained Prime Minister from independence until 1964, more than sixteen years. His leadership provided time for the powerful interest groups to learn to mediate their conflicts through the centre, by procedures patterned on those of the British Parliament. This was one of Nehru's principal achievements, secured in the face of much opposition. Many of Gandhi's followers wanted an end to western inheritances like the civil service, industrialisation and British parliamentary methods. Gandhi had long practised the ancient Indian craft of hand-spinning cotton and consequently the spinning wheel became the centrepiece of the Congress flag. It symbolised the return not only to village crafts but to the traditional Indian village system. Gandhi was murdered by a Hindu extremist less than a year after independence, but his followers continued to press for the replacement of the western system of government by *panchayati raj*, a system based on the ancient village council or *panchayat*. Since the vast majority of Indians still lived in villages Gandhi's followers wanted to make the village the basic unit of government. They were inspired by a simple idea that has much in common with Rousseau's idealisation of the Swiss canton and the Greek city state: everybody could come together in a village meeting and decide matters democratically.

Nehru would have none of it. He valued the superb ICS, the impartial legal system, the freedoms conferred by the democratic state and – though he knew how to manipulate it to secure virtually absolute power for himself – the parliamentary system. Critical as he had been of the British in the 1930s, he was determined that institutions brought by the British should continue to run the new India. In this he followed the early Congress tradition from Hume to Gokhale and Jinnah, and rejected the ideas of Gandhi, his own mentor.

Nehru was equally tough in rejecting communalism. Many Indians wanted to eject the thirty million or so Muslims who remained in India. With an estimated five million Hindu and Sikh refugees from Pakistan – many of whom had suffered horribly and all of whom needed help – popular feeling against the Muslims was powerful and infected even Nehru's Cabinet. Nehru fought it. He insisted that India must be a secular state, with all minorities enjoying the full protection of the law. In 1950 a supporter of Hindu raj, P. D. Tandon, was elected Congress President with the backing of Vallabhbhai Patel, long Nehru's rival within Congress and after independence his deputy Prime Minister. The following year Nehru arranged to have himself elected to the Congress presidency, an office he did not want in addition to those of Prime Minister and Foreign Minister, but felt he must retain to protect himself.

His success is visible in the constitution, in which Nehru caused India to be proclaimed a secular, democratic republic with no state religion, no religious instruction in state schools, no taxes to go to any religion, and religious liberty guaranteed to individuals and groups. Nehru had allies in his battles against communalism, notably lawyers and civil servants, but the secularism of India was his personal triumph. He symbolically underscored it by having a Muslim elected President of the Indian Republic.

When Nehru died in office, the regional bosses and power-seekers in Congress did not want a second strong man to dominate them as he had done. His immediate successor was Lal Bahadur Shastri, who died only two years later, and Congress chose to succeed him a woman who had less than two years' experience of parliament and Cabinet office – their own instrument, as they thought.

The instrument had one principal qualification: she was Indira Gandhi, Nehru's daughter, and could therefore be expected to win her backers the votes of the masses. Unexpectedly she soon routed the Congress bosses who had brought her to power. From 1966 until October 1984 she dominated Indian politics. She lacked the intellectual originality and charm of her father and she did not become a world figure in her own right, as he had done. In 1975 she nearly steered India into the abyss when she declared a state of emergency, arrested many thousands, including thirty-three members of parliament, suppressed basic freedoms and seemed about to put an end to parliamentary democracy. Two years later, confident of popular support for her increasingly dictatorial government, she called an election and was ejected from office. The alliance that defeated her stayed in power for three years, just long enough to re-establish the standing in India of the liberal democratic system. It too then called an election and lost, bringing Mrs Gandhi and her family, the heirs of Nehru, back to power.

Nehru was the key figure in a number of international political movements. The British and many Americans had assumed that, on independence, India would become part of the western alliance against Communism. Nehru quickly invented an alternative position, non-alignment, asserting that India was a member neither of the western nor the Communist bloc. Along with President Nasser of Egypt and President Tito of Yugoslavia he led a world movement of countries determined to keep the great powers from dominating them. This position was not, however, solely negative. Nehru pushed the non-aligned group of countries into playing a persistent anti-colonial role, opposing the French, British, Dutch, Belgian and Portuguese empires in nearly all their attempts to retain colonies. Governments of Pakistan, by contrast, were generally much more committed to the western alliance, much less ready to criticise British or American policy. Perhaps most remarkably in these circumstances, Nehru was the decisive figure in causing the British Commonwealth of Nations to survive. This small club of white nations which Nehru had been determined to quit was transformed, largely by his decision that India should remain a member, into a free association of states of all races. Their common characteristic was that they had been ruled by Britain, but as more states joined on becoming independent the club changed into a forward-looking and remarkable body, helping lawyers, civil servants, doctors, accountants and the armed forces in member-countries to maintain precisely those standards which Nehru was determined India should preserve from its British experience. The Commonwealth also influenced Britain in its conduct of overseas and colonial policy, notably over Rhodesia (see Chapter 10).

In the twenty years after independence India and Pakistan were constantly on the brink of war. The trouble began over Kashmir, a mountainous princely state in the Himalayas, where lakes and glaciers provide a cool Switzerland of retreat from the summer heat of the plains. Kashmir was the ancestral homeland of the Nehru family, but eighty per cent of its citizens were Muslims and its principal rivers and roads run into Pakistan. Therefore in 1947, when its ruler was one of the three princes who refused to sign an accession agreement, he was thought likely to join Pakistan. But the Maharajah of Kashmir was a Hindu and after three months' dithering chose, as he was entitled under the Indian Independence Act to do, to join his state to India. Pakistani tribesmen promptly invaded.

Here was a model issue for the United Nations: should the majority will of the citizens of Kashmir or the legal act of the ruler prevail? India promised to test the will of the citizens in a referendum, but conveniently neglected to hold it, flying in troops instead to crush the Muslim tribesmen. To Pakistan, India's conduct over Kashmir was evidence that the rulers in Delhi would never be satisfied until they had destroyed the Muslim state. So in 1965 Pakistan's President, General Ayub Khan, driven forward by his foreign minister, Zulfiqar Ali Bhutto, sent Muslim infiltrators into the Vale of Kashmir to try to stir the Muslims there into rising against India. The Indian Government retaliated by moving its armies across the international border in the Punjab to within shooting distance of Lahore, Pakistan's finest city. Pakistani soldiers and airmen fought back bravely, but India was the bigger country and had more military clout. Bhutto told the United Nations: 'We will wage war for a thousand years . . . the ghettoes of Kashmir are stinking to high heavens with human flesh ripped asunder by a monstrous and habitual aggressor determined to destroy like a bloodthirsty barbarian . . .' Diplomats in New York and commentators throughout the world thought Bhutto's language excessive but in Pakistan, particularly in the Punjab, his words matched the public mood. He became a hero. India, by her invasion, had closed the Kashmir issue, but millions of Pakistanis, inspired by Bhutto, refused to believe it.

The binding of Kashmir to India by force, concluded by the 1965 invasion of West Punjab shortly after Jawaharlal Nehru's death, illustrates a side of India's politics that he constantly tried, but failed, to suppress. Nehru, devoted follower of Gandhi, was genuinely opposed to the use of force. He took little interest in India's army, which he intended, by means of a subtle and conciliatory foreign policy, to avoid using. However in parliament, the press and public meetings – and even in his Cabinet – Nehru repeatedly found his peaceful intentions challenged and overwhelmed. As a result many, particularly in the United States and in Pakistan, considered him a humbug. He was for ever preaching morality in international politics, stating that he was opposed to the use of force and thus winning the approval of those in Britain who had on moral grounds backed India's demand for independence. As head of government, however, he used his armies to invade neighbouring territories more often than any contemporary ruler.

While he enforced the right of the Maharajah of Kashmir to opt for India, he conceded no such right to the rulers of Hyderabad, the largest princely state, or of tiny Junagadh. These rulers were Muslims, though with Hindu majorities, and he promptly settled the issue of their failure to accede before independence by invading them. In 1961 he allowed himself to be hustled into invading Goa, the ancient and defenceless Portuguese enclave, with much bragging by his Cabinet colleagues about the triumph of the Indian army and threats to teach a similar lesson to China. His government then went on to provoke a war with China in 1962 by asserting repeatedly that the Chinese were invading Indian territory high in the Himalayas when in fact Indian troops were pursuing a 'forward policy' (Nehru's words) in unde-fined border areas. The Chinese put up with this mixture of pinpricks and bombast for many months. Yet Nehru himself was determined to maintain good relations with China, had angered the United States by recognising China's new Communist government in 1949 and made great efforts to persuade the new rulers of China to join India in securing the non-alignment of Asia. He did not realise that putting some fifty manned guard posts into territories which China thought its own and publicly announcing that he had ordered the army to turn the Chinese out of 'Indian territory' must bring retaliation. Eventually China sent her armies sweeping down from the Himalayas into Assam, humiliating the Indian defence forces. When they had made their point, the Chinese withdrew. Nehru's many supporters in the west blamed China for aggression. Later, impartial western scholars found that on the matter at issue – the details in some old treaties – the Chinese were entirely in the right. By this action Nehru added the Chinese to the ranks of those who thought him a humbug.

His daughter, Indira, was similarly driven to attack, achieving a spectacu-lar success in 1971 when she used Indian troops to secure the dismember-ment of Pakistan. India's principal ally in this achievement was the amazing incompetence of successive governments of Pakistan. East and West Pakistan were difficult to weld together, united only by Islam and Jinnah. They differed in race, the West Pakistanis being mostly tall, pale, hook-nosed Turco-Persian types, invaders of India from the north-west, the East Bengalis more like the original Dravidian inhabitants of the subcontinent, short, dark, with short, straight noses; they differed in what they ate, the West Pakistanis eating meat and bread where the Bengalis ate fish and rice; they differed in temperament, the West Pakistanis being people of the hills and deserts, accustomed to a sparse life, obliged to irrigate much of their land, whereas East Bengal is one of the most lush, fertile areas on earth, always wet and green, regularly flooded by the Ganges with its deposits of rich silt; they differed in lifestyle, many West Pakistanis living like the people of the Middle East with their camels, the East Bengalis densely crowded together, living like the people of south-east Asia with their boats; and they spoke mutually incomprehensible languages, in the West mostly Urdu, Punjabi and Pushto written in the Persian script, in the East, Bengali, written in its own Sanskrit-based script. The dominant population of West Pakistan, the Punjabis, professed an unaccountable contempt for the East Bengalis, whom they were always describing as lazy, dirty, non-military and incompetent; and separated by over a thousand miles of Indian territory, through which Indian governments intermittently forbade them to travel or communicate, East and West Pakistan had to exchange goods by ship, via Ceylon (later Sri Lanka) or expensively by air. It would have needed all the political skill of Jinnah or Liaqat Ali Khan applied over many years to unite these two territories into a single nation. Instead leading Punjabis exacerbated the resentments of the East Bengalis by taking the income from Bengal's jute exports for investment in West Pakistan and billeting on the Bengalis arrogant regiments of Punjabi soldiers whose conduct made the Bengalis feel more like a colonial fiefdom than they had under the British.

When the East Bengalis, led by Sheikh Mujibur Rahman, asked in 1970 for a fair share in the government and assets of the country, West Pakistan's leading politican, Zulfiqar Ali Bhutto, the UN performer, turned them down flat. The country had just held the first nation-wide general election in its twenty-three years' history, and the Bengalis, who were the majority of the total population, demanded a proportionate share of power, backing their claim by near-unanimous support for Sheikh Mujib (whose party won 167 out of 169 East Pakistan seats). Bhutto, whose electoral success in West Pakistan was impressive but not quite so overwhelming, was not prepared to play second fiddle. By refusing to compromise he encouraged the military government of Pakistan to arrest the Bengali leader and to impose a savage military clampdown, Pakistani soldiers murdering many prominent Bengalis. But the election result, following twenty years of growing resentment, had bred in East Bengal an endless stream of replacements. India could provide the Bengalis with weapons and reinforcements more efficiently than Pakistan could supply its own army. After a brief war the new state of Bangladesh was founded; Pakistan lost more than half its population, and Indira Gandhi's government smiled like a Bengal tiger that has eaten the evidence.

The break-up of Pakistan illustrates by contrast the skill with which India's central institutions were managed. India underwent a dozen episodes that were potentially as dangerous to its unity. The attempt to impose Hindi, the *lingua franca* of north India, as the single unifying language of the whole nation led several southern states to demand secession: they did not speak Hindi and insisted on the retention of English as the common language of law and administration. West Bengal, always a centre of Marxism and political dissent, became ungovernable. Communists won power in the southern state of Kerala. Old India hands constantly produced articles, lectures and television programmes on the theme, 'Is India about to disintegrate?' But Nehru and his daughter did not once imprison a local leader whose power-base was so strong that he had to be conciliated. Several times they imposed 'presidential rule' (article 93 of the 1935 Act still applied), displacing the elected government of a state by their own nominee. But, after accidentally helping to create Pakistan in 1947, the Congress leaders did not make the same mistakes again. On the contrary they were strikingly successful in holding their country together through its most dangerous early years

The only yardstick against which India can be measured is China. With independence in 1947 and the arrival of the Communist regime in 1949 as their respective starting points, it is possible to compare the progress of the two most populous countries in the world, in per capita consumption of steel, electricity and food and, above all, in life expectancy. The results show surprisingly steady progress in both countries, with famines becoming less frequent, infant mortality declining, output from both agriculture and industry rising impressively. The comparison does not support the case for the clear superiority of the capitalist over the communist system, or vice versa. Nor does it support the view of those who, allowed easy access to her poor and shocked by what they see, deride India as a cesspit of degradation. The poverty and the cow-worship, the caste system and the bejewelled minority, the smell of burning cow-dung and the spitting of betel-juice, above all the hundreds of thousands of dusty villages, remain after the end of British rule much as they were before the British arrived. But in justice and nuclear physics, in free speech and the manufacture of aircraft, India approaches the 1990s ahead of China. Many Britons take pride in these facts.

# CHAPTER 2

# Palestine

For Britain the colonisation of Palestine was a disaster from start to finish. No other mistakes – not even the mismanagement by King George III and Lord North of the American Colonies – brought such total humiliation for such total absence of gain. Britain would have been in every way better off if General Edmund Allenby had never made his triumphal entry into Jerusalem in December 1917, dismounting, like a good Christian, to walk humbly through the Jaffa Gate.

The world's two most ancient civilisations, those of Egypt and Mesopotamia (now called Iraq), flourished simultaneously 3,500 years ago. They were separated by the desert of north Arabia, as difficult to cross as the most hostile sea. The only route between them was round the northern fringe of the desert where some hills brought rainfall and rivers, producing what has been known throughout recorded history as 'the fertile crescent'. From Egypt the first step into the fertile crescent, after crossing the Sinai, was Palestine, and that strip between the sea and the desert has always been a passage for traders, usually controlled by the most powerful state in the Middle East, in turn Persia, Egypt, Rome, Byzantium, the Arabs.

Palestine was not a land of milk and honey, except in the judgment of those who had just walked across the Sinai desert. In crops and animals it was only moderately fertile. But it has proved the most fertile spot on earth for religions. Not only did the Jews go there from Mesopotamia to evolve their one-god theology and write their Bible, the first written history of a people so far as we know, but two daughter religions, Christianity and Islam, both similarly reverential towards the early Jewish heroes, flowered in Palestine. The founder of Christianity, Jesus Christ, was born and died there and the founder of Islam, Mahomet, also a frequenter of trading towns, allegedly leaped to paradise on his Arab horse from a rock in Palestine's chief city, Jerusalem.

This first comfortable resting place to the north of Egypt was inevitably fought over. But it was not merely a case of local powers fighting over a commercial asset in the way Macchiavelli or any dynastic ruler would approve, with religion writ large on the banner mainly to win support. Both the Christians and the Jews travelled many thousands of miles and overcame obstacles they should have considered insurmountable, the Christians in the

Crusades and the Jews in the Zionist movement, to recover this rocky land. No territory on earth has aroused such passion.

In the four hundred years that ended in 1917, the most powerful state in the Middle East and therefore the ruler of Palestine was the Ottoman Empire. Under its rule Muslims, Jews and Christians lived peacefully in Palestine which was administered as the Damascus–Egypt roadway, a route worth protecting. The tolerant agents of Constantinople would have been surprised to learn that acquiring this small territory would prove of any importance for their British successors and amazed that it should turn out to be a serious mistake.

## Careless Promises, 1915–1939

Trouble was beginning before the British arrived. And their first actions concerning Palestine, before they had even conquered the land, were to make disaster certain: they allowed two rival suitors to believe they had been promised the bride. The idea of nationalism, spreading throughout the nineteenth century, had led to the independence of Greece and then other Balkan states from Ottoman-Turkish rule. Such developments at the European end of the Sultan's empire inspired similar ambitions at the Arab end. When Turkey sided with Germany during the 1914–18 war, Arab leaders were promised that the British Empire would help them to secure independence if in return they would fight alongside the British. Sir Henry MacMahon, British High Commissioner in Egypt, wrote to Hussein, Sharif of Mecca, promising independence to all Arab-populated areas of the Turkish Empire except 'the portions of Syria lying to the west of the districts of Damascus, Homs, Hama and Aleppo'. These words exclude only Lebanon, which Britain had promised to France, and parts of what is now Syria. Palestine lies farther south and therefore appears to the reader who glances at the map (p. 108) to have been promised to the Arabs. However, Sharif Hussein showed no interest in Palestine. The agreement was made in wartime: its fine print did not concern him.

The British, in their anxiety to win the war, made another promise, offering part of this land they had not yet conquered to a second party, the Jews. This offer came in a letter, dated 2 November 1917 from Arthur James Balfour, Britain's Foreign Secretary, to Lord Rothschild, a leading British Zionist, stating, 'His Majesty's Government view with favour the establishment in Palestine of a national home for the Jewish people, and will use their best endeavours to facilitate the achievement of this object.' This – the Balfour Declaration – was made because the British wanted to escape from yet another promise they had made – to France – that Palestine would be placed under international control. American control had also been considered. But British officials, looking back on the rapid Turkish advance in 1914 through Palestine to the Suez canal, decided that this narrow roadway was too vital to British imperial interests to be left in international hands or those of foreigners. A way had to be found to escape from the various undertakings and to keep Palestine British. To this end the Zionist movement proved convenient. The Zionists wanted a home, the British wanted a defence post astride the road to Suez.

The British-Zionist package was tied together by a remarkable string: Dr Chaim Weizmann. He was a chemist at Manchester University who met newspaper editors and Cabinet ministers at parties and within hours won them over to Zionism. His research happened to lead to his inventing a way to make synthetic acetone – a vital ingredient in gunpowder. This became so important during the 1914–18 war that he was brought to work for the Admiralty in London. His success in developing his invention for large-scale manufacture led him to meet the First Lords of the Admiralty, in succession Winston Churchill and A. J. Balfour, and the Minister for Munitions, David Lloyd-George. They became three of the leading figures in the British Government towards the end of the war and were looking for a way to justify breaking Britain's promise to France so as to secure Palestine for the Empire. He was looking for a powerful patron for Zionism. The British Empire turned Zionist. Abba Eban, later Foreign Minister of Israel, summed it up:

> The Zionists were lobbying all over the world – in the Versailles Peace Conference and everywhere else – to see that Britain did get this charge. So there was a contract: we would help Britain become the ruling power and Britain would help us to develop the Jewish National Home.

Precise British officials were later to deny that they had double-crossed the Arabs: they said Sharif Hussein knew Palestine was not included in the Arab lands to receive independence and that Balfour's letter referred only to 'the establishment *in* Palestine of a national home', which could be quite a modest proposal given the insistence later in the same letter that 'nothing shall be done which may prejudice the civil and religious rights of existing non-Jewish communities in Palestine'. But to most Jews and Arabs these reservations carried no weight. Arabs thought they had been offered independence throughout the Turkish-ruled lands they inhabited, including Palestine. Jews, especially Zionists, thought they had been offered a national home in the place to which they had prayed to return since their expulsion two thousand years earlier.

The British were not stupid. They had reason to believe that the Jewish and Arab leaders would co-operate. Sharif Hussein led the Arabs who sided with Britain in the war; his son, the Emir Feisal, met Weizmann in London in January 1919 and they agreed that Jewish immigration to Palestine could do much to improve the lot of the Arab population. Philip Noel-Baker, a leading Labour Party international specialist and later a Cabinet minister, was a young member of the British delegation to the Versailles peace conference in 1919 and to the subsequent League of Nations conference at Geneva. He recalled:

I did not believe the Arabs would accept a Jewish national home in Palestine, but one of my colleagues took me to see the Emir Feisal in Geneva. T. E. Lawrence, the great friend of the Arab leaders, was with him and Feisal said that the arrival of European Jews with their energy and enterprise and modern scientific skills would be good for Palestine and good for the Arabs. It was that conversation which converted me to Zionism.

*Anglo-Zionist cooperation: Dr Chaim Weizmann (left in white hat) beside General Allenby in Jerusalem, May 1918.*

Feisal said these things to oblige his powerful British allies. If they wanted Palestine for their own purposes and needed Zionist support to secure it, he was not the man to stand in their way.

Such attitudes led to the drafting of a remarkable document, the League of Nations' Mandate for Palestine. The President of the United States, Woodrow Wilson, disapproved of empires. He did not want to see the British Empire enlarged, but he could not remove from his victorious allies the fruits of their triumph. So he was the driving force behind the creation of the mandates system, by which the League of Nations entrusted territories captured from Turkey and Germany to the temporary care of a 'mandatory', whose nominal task was to secure the advancement and welfare of the conquered people. Britain thus acquired mandates over Iraq, Tanganyika, South-West Africa and Papua-New Guinea, as well as Palestine. Whether these mandates were really to be trusts for the inhabitants, as Woodrow Wilson intended, or colonies by another name, as most of the British assumed, the mandate documents all placed first emphasis on leading the inhabitants towards self-government – all, that is, except the mandate for Palestine. This gave first priority to 'the establishment of the Jewish national

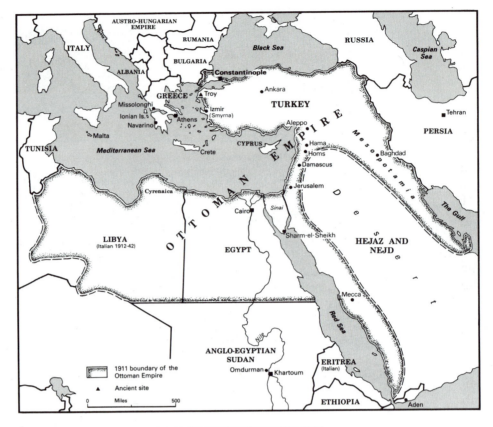

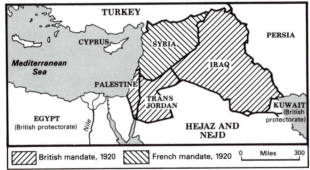

home' and instructed the British Government to 'facilitate Jewish immigration . . . and . . . encourage . . . close settlement by Jews on the land.'

The League of Nations did not issue the mandate until 1922. By then British administrators in Palestine were reporting that the creation of any sort of Jewish government would lead to an Arab uprising. Previously the views of the Arabs in Palestine had not been considered a serious obstacle since Britain's ally, Hussein the Sharif of Mecca, was doing well out of the peace settlement and was assumed, as guardian of their most holy city, to speak for Arabs as a whole. His son, the Emir Feisal, was given the most important of the ex-Turkish *vilayets* (provinces), Syria, with its capital city of Damascus the centre of the Arab nationalist revival. However, careless promises had been made about Syria as well as Palestine. Britain had agreed that in this area France would be the sole supplier of 'advisers or foreign functionaries' but led Feisal to believe his government would be fully independent. Feisal was king for twenty months. Then French troops unceremoniously threw him out.

So the British gave Mesopotamia, renamed Iraq, as a kind of consolation prize to Feisal. He was to be its king, with British civil servants, largely from India, to help him build up an efficient administration. Naturally the British had a base there, the latest thing, a large installation for the Royal Air Force at Habbaniya. In 1921, further to secure the alliance of the Arab nationalist leaders, Britain's Colonial Secretary, Winston Churchill, created a second new realm to be ruled by a son of Sharif Hussein. It was a matter of marking lines on a map: to a vacant lot in the north Arabian desert Churchill added a narrow slice of territory adjacent to Palestine and east of the Jordan river; the capital of this new state was to be a former Roman city now reduced to a village named Amman and the state itself was called Transjordan. Here too the British set up the administration and secured military rights, in the form of a small army with a British commander and British officers. The new ruler, Abdullah, told Churchill he would accept the Jewish national home in Palestine. In this way a new British imperial structure was created in the Middle East, with Colonial Office rule in Aden, Cyprus and Palestine and subordinate states, apparently not unlike the Indian princely states, in (in declining order of British influence) Transjordan, Iraq, Egypt and Persia. Given such vast matters to be arranged, Britain's Middle East experts were too busy to seek out the worries of a mere handful of Palestinian Arabs about a plan which might in due course greatly enrich some of them. In the words of the 1937 British Royal Commission on Palestine, chaired by Lord Peel (grandson of Sir Robert, the nineteenth-century Prime Minister):

> It was assumed that the establishment of the National Home would mean a great increase of prosperity for all Palestine. It was an essential part of the Zionist mission to revivify the country, to repair by Jewish labour, skill and capital the damage it had suffered from centuries of neglect. Arabs would benefit therefrom as well as Jews. They would find the country they had known so long as poor and backward rapidly acquiring the material blessings of western civilisation. On that account it was assumed that Arab fears and prejudices would gradually be overcome.

Nothing pleases a politician better than a coincidence of morality and interest. Many British politicans were persuaded that the thousand years of Jew-baiting and Jew-slaughter by Christians was an evil for which restitution should be paid. In the previous generation thousands of Jews had fled from pogroms in Russia. Many settled in Britain, where anti-semitism and the predictable fear of newcomers had at the turn of the century led the Government to limit the admissions. The United States, which had received hundreds of thousands, was also keen to direct some of the next exodus to an

alternative destination and in 1922 introduced a quota system banning
eastern European immigrants. For the first time the wandering Jews had
nowhere to wander. To Britain Zionism offered an additional attraction,
much emphasised by Weizmann: to settle an advanced, industrious, techni-
cally skilled people in Palestine should provide a reliable ally in an area
otherwise backward and volatile.

The trouble began for Britain with the launching of the practical application of the policy: Jewish immigration. During the previous thirty years
the Zionist movement had raised money to buy land in Palestine and by 1918
some 70,000 Jews were living there. After the war the pace of immigration
increased and the Arab backlash began. In one riot in May 1921 in Jaffa
forty-seven Jews were killed. The British security forces, in clamping down,
killed forty-eight Arabs.

Shortly afterwards the Colonial Secretary, Winston Churchill, visited
Palestine. He reported to the House of Commons in June:

> The Arabs believe that in the next few years they are going to be swamped
> by scores of thousands of immigrants. There is really nothing for the Arabs
> to be frightened about. All the Jewish immigration is being very carefully
> watched and controlled both from the point of view of numbers and
> character. No Jew will be brought in beyond the number who can be
> provided for by the expanding wealth and development of the resources of
> the country. There is no doubt whatever that at the present time the
> country is greatly underpopulated. Anyone who has seen the work of the
> Jewish colonies which have been established during the last twenty or
> thirty years in Palestine will be struck by the enormous productive results
> which they have achieved. I had the opportunity of visiting the colony of
> Rishon le Zion about twelve miles from Jaffa, and there, from the most
> inhospitable soil, surrounded on every side by barrenness and the most
> miserable form of cultivation, I was driven into a fertile and thriving
> country estate, where the scanty soil gave place to good crops and good
> cultivation, and then to vineyards and finally to the most beautiful,
> luxuriant orange groves, all created in twenty or thirty years by the
> exertions of the Jewish community who live there. I defy anybody, after
> seeing work of this kind, achieved by so much labour, effort and skill, to
> say that the British Government, having taken up the position it has,
> could cast it all aside and leave it to be rudely and brutally overturned by
> the incursion of a fanatical attack by the Arab population.

It was particularly satisfying for the British Government that the new
colonies being established for Jewish settlers were financed entirely by the
international Zionist organisation, without a penny from the British taxpayer, on land bought from willing Arab sellers on a rising market. They
approved also of the Zionists' raising money for the Hebrew University, the
foundation stone of which had already been laid. A scheme that promised to
stop too many Jews demanding entry into London and New York while at

the same time fertilising, watering and educating a backward area of the Middle East and securing an ally there – all at no cost to the British taxpayer – seemed too good to be true. And it was.

Between 1922 and 1926, 75,000 Jews settled in Palestine, including 33,801 in 1925 alone. Although the principle governing their entry was, as Churchill had stated, that the numbers should not exceed the economic absorptive capacity of the country, and although many who came were doctors, willing to offer their services to Arabs, scholars willing to teach them and above all pioneers eager to dig for water and make arid land fertile, others were less altruistic. To the Palestinian Arabs they were all a threat. Often the land sold by an absentee Arab landlord was the only livelihood of his tenants, whom the Jews now displaced in their eagerness to till the soil themselves. Many British officials had the distasteful task of evicting landless Arabs, after Jewish purchasers had obtained court orders giving them vacant possession of land they had bought. Often the immigrant Jewish worker would get a job in an expanding Jewish enterprise which an unemployed Palestinian could have filled. To the Arabs it was ominous that the first Governor appointed by Britain was a Jew and a Zionist, Sir Herbert Samuel. It made no difference to them that he was a former Liberal Home Secretary; their suspicions were aroused by his easy and sympathetic understanding with leading Zionists.

One of Samuel's early acts was to try to set up, as the British usually did, a council representative of the local population, the Palestinian Arabs. When they refused to take part, he turned to an existing body, the Supreme Muslim Council, to perform a similar function. As President he chose Haj Amin al-Husseini, later to become famous as the Mufti of Jerusalem. The Mufti has been blackened as a suave Muslim religious leader who encouraged terrorism and fascism. The criticisms contain much truth. Murder of political opponents and intimidation of the uncommitted became the normal tools of his trade in the 1930s. The Mufti's hatred of the Jews and his tactics need, however, to be seen in context. The British Empire was imposing upon his people a large number of aliens. This was done, as the mandate required, in consultation with an agency representative of the Jews. The Palestinian Arabs opposed this policy and therefore no agency representing them could be allowed any say over immigration into their country. Worse, they saw Zionists enjoying effective local self-government through the Jewish Agency. Partly this was because of the requirement of the mandate, partly it was because the local Jewish leaders were sophisticated and competent. The effect, combined with the land sales to Jewish organisations, was to make the Palestinian Arabs frightened and angry.

The Mufti and his supporters felt that they were being swamped by the Jewish immigration. He encouraged the anti-Jewish feeling that led in August 1929 to riots, mob frenzy and the murder of 133 Jews. He refused to take part with British and Jewish representatives in joint bodies to help run the country because these would have over-represented the Jews and under-represented his own people and, more fundamentally, because he did not recognise the mandate, with its insistence on Jewish immigration and its lack of even a single mention of the Arabs. British administrators became increasingly worried; they pressed both privately and in published reports for severe restrictions on Jewish immigration, and in 1931 the Labour Colonial Secretary, Sidney Webb, was persuaded. A white paper, the agreed view of the Cabinet, proclaimed the new policy. The Prime Minister, Ramsay MacDonald, subjected to a barrage of pressure and argument, overruled it. Zionism was confirmed as the policy of the British Government.

Following Hitler's coming to power in Germany in 1933, a brutal and systematic persecution of Jews spread across central Europe. Thousands fled and sought sanctuary in Palestine. In 1935 alone some 60,000 Jewish immigrants arrived, a number the British High Commissioner concluded was 'beyond the absorptive capacity of the country'. Arabs saw this influx as confirmation of their fear that the British and the Zionists were conspiring to reduce them to a minority in their own land. At the same time, the military threat posed by Hitler's regime caused Britain to need as allies the Arab states it had helped create. Britain's embassies in the Middle East all sent the same message to London: an essential step towards winning the support of the Arab nations in the imminent war against Hitler's Germany was to prevent Jewish refugees from dispossessing the Arabs in Palestine.

The dilemma was particularly acute for Malcom MacDonald, who in

*Arabs rioting in Jerusalem, 1937.*

1931 had helped influence his father's decision to overrule Sidney Webb and hold to the policy of immigration to establish a Jewish national home. Newly out of Oxford, Malcolm was impressed by one of his tutors, Lewis Namier, the historian and Zionist, through whom he met Chaim Weizmann. Their arguments encouraged the Prime Minister to take the unusual step of reversing a Cabinet colleague's policy after it had been published in a white paper. Britain's Arab friends were shocked by this action, showing, as it did, that the Jews had backstairs influence at the top, and Malcolm MacDonald became a trusted ally of the central group of British Zionists.

In 1938, at the age of 36, he was made Colonial Secretary in the government headed by Neville Chamberlain. The Palestine policy of his father and of his Jewish friends had been somewhat modified in the face of growing Arab violence, mostly directed against Arab 'traitors', secondly against Jews but increasingly after 1936 taking its toll of British soldiers. This 'Arab Rebellion' lasted from 1936 to 1939 and caused some five thousand deaths, mostly Arabs. The Royal Commission under Lord Peel, appointed as the rebellion began, recommended that the British should get out, leaving the northern part of the country as a small Jewish state (by 1936 the number of Jews had risen to some 400,000, roughly a third of the population), the centre and south as an Arab state and retaining only an enclave including Jerusalem under British rule. The Government accepted the proposal with relief, but leaders of the Palestinian Arabs would not agree to having a third of their country hived off as a Jewish state and continued the rebellion. The mood of their supporters left no doubt that they required the whole territory for an Arab Palestinian state which would soon dispose of the Jewish minority. The British Government could not partition the country into two states, with the possible need to move large numbers of Arabs compulsorily, in the face of violent Arab resistance. They needed a new policy.

Malcolm MacDonald, welcomed in office by the Zionists, soon faced his moment of decision. The Arab leaders were demanding an immediate stop to Jewish immigration. Restricting the numbers entering Palestine would anger the Jews but do no harm to Britain's war preparation. Whatever the Government did, the Jews would be bound to help Britain against Hitler. MacDonald told the Cabinet that 'from the defence point of view it was literally out of the question that we should antagonise either the Muslims within the Empire or the Arab kingdoms of the Near East.' The vital issues were the route to India and oil. If war came, India was likely, as in the First World War, to provide Britain's largest single military recruiting ground; so the way to India had to be kept open for ships through the Suez canal, for aircraft via Palestine and Iraq and for a variety of overland and undersea cables. Cutting these lifelines was bound to be a high German priority. Within a year, the Mufti began encouraging anti-British feeling in Iraq and Syria. Britain risked being cut off from the Iraqi and Persian oil which was essential to keep tanks, aircraft and the entire British economy working. So

MacDonald helped to persuade the Cabinet to reverse his father's policy. The Arabs were told that Jewish immigration would be restricted and the Jewish population of Palestine would never exceed 40 per cent of the total; after a five-year period during which immigration would be held to 75,000, any future Jewish immigration would be subject to Arab acquiesence. For the Zionists, who had relied utterly on Britain and in particular on Malcolm MacDonald, this was an act of treachery. Many of them never trusted the British again.

The creation of a Jewish state in Palestine had always been the aim of most Zionists. They had denied it in public and tried to keep it out of their writings because in this the British did not support them. So British ministers had been able to promise, and perhaps in some cases even to believe, that immigration leading to the creation of a Jewish national home did not mean depriving Palestinian Arabs of the right to rule themselves. The Peel Commission's partition proposal had brought the Zionists into the open: it offered them a state in part of Palestine and the principal leaders seized it gratefully. Weizmann said, 'The Jews would be fools not to accept [a state] even if it were the size of a tablecloth.' The approach of war and the intransigent rejection of partition by the Arabs not only caused the offer to be withdrawn; MacDonald's 1939 white paper promised to restrict the Jews in Palestine to minority status for ever. The Zionists were trapped. The leader of the Jews in Palestine, David Ben Gurion, said: 'We shall fight with Great Britain in this war as if there was no white paper and we shall fight the white paper as if there was no war.'

## The Wasps' Nest, 1939–1948

The British Government's new policy was debated in the House of Commons in May 1939, when the British establishment's most outspoken Zionist, Winston Churchill, now a Conservative dissident, excoriated the Government for breaking its word. Speaking as one who was in the Cabinet at the time, he said that the Balfour Declaration in 1917 and the League of Nations mandate in 1922 had both made it clear that Britain's first duty in Palestine was to establish a Jewish national home:

> This pledge of a home of refuge, of an asylum, was not made to the Jews in Palestine but to . . . that vast, unhappy mass of scattered, persecuted, wandering Jews, whose intense, unchanging, unconquerable desire has been for a national home . . . That is the pledge which was given and that is the pledge which we are now asked to break, for how can this pledge be kept, I want to know, if in five years' time the national home is to be barred and no more Jews are to be allowed in without the permission of thé Arabs? . . . We are asked to submit to an agitation which is fed with foreign money and inflamed by Nazi and Fascist propaganda.

In spite of Churchill's speech the Government's policy was accepted by the House.

A year later, in May 1940, the Zionists had cause to celebrate. Chamberlain's Government fell, MacDonald was removed as Colonial Secretary and the new Prime Minister was Winston Churchill. Over India he was to prove true to the policies he had supported in opposition. Over Palestine his public commitment was equally firm, but he decided that to back his beliefs and his friends would be dangerous: to allow Jews fleeing from Hitler to enter Palestine would mean admitting vast numbers; that would promptly swing the Arab states onto Hitler's side and might lose Britain the Middle East and possibly, therefore, the war. He concluded that his Zionism must be subordinated.

Eighteen months after Churchill took power in Downing Street, a passenger ship called the *Struma* set sail for Palestine from the Rumanian Black Sea port of Constanza. Her passengers on 12 December 1941 were Rumanian Jews who for a year had witnessed the effects of Hitler's policies in their country: officially sponsored anti-Jewish riots which, according to the American minister in Bucharest, regularly ended with Jewish corpses displayed on butchers' hooks. Surviving Jews were therefore relieved to read advertisements offering passages to Palestine, some stating that the British authorities would welcome Jewish immigrants, others admitting that entry would be illegal.

The *Struma* was designed to carry no more than a hundred passengers, but she left Constanza with 769 aboard. They are reported to have paid more than US $1,000 each for their places. Just before departure, Rumanian officials came aboard and confiscated passengers' valuables. The ship's engines were defective and after four days' limping through the Black Sea she reached Istanbul. The Turkish authorities considered the *Struma* unseaworthy. Once past Istanbul she would enter the Sea of Marmara, a waterway entirely surrounded by Turkey, and if she foundered there the rescued passengers would be Turkey's responsibility. The local authorities therefore asked the British ambassador to confirm their view that it was pointless to let the ship proceed because even if she reached Palestine the passengers would all be turned away. The Turks' solution was to send her back to the Black Sea, where, whether she sank or managed to return to Constanza, she would not be Turkey's or Britain's affair.

The British ambassador, Hugh Knatchbull-Hugessen, was moved by compassion. Reluctant to have the ship returned to the Black Sea, he told the Turks that, if the passengers reached Palestine, 'they might despite their illegality receive humane treatment'. When his report of the advice he had given reached London, contempt was heaped on him. Colonial Office officials wrote that he had muffed 'a heaven-sent opportunity of getting these people stopped and sent back to Constanza'; with the Palestine administration already facing the problem of hundreds of illegal immigrants, the arrival of the *Struma* 'will have a deplorable effect throughout the Balkans in encouraging further Jews to embark'. German encouragement of refugee ships damaged Britain whatever happened: if the Jews were admitted, Arab anger was whipped up, making the Arab states more likely to ally with Germany; if the Jews were turned away, the Jewish lobby in the United States bellowed complaints of Britain's inhumanity. British policy, therefore, was to stop refugee ships getting anywhere near Palestine. Knatchbull-Hugessen was told to withdraw his advice and make it clear to the Turks that the refugees would not be admitted.

The Turks promptly ordered the *Struma* back into the Black Sea. By now, however, her engines would not work. A Jewish relief committee and the Red Cross did their best to provide the passengers with food and water. New Year passed with no heating on the ship, sanitation inadequate and no country willing to admit the passengers. By February, British official consciences were troubled. Prompted by the Prime Minister's frustrated Zionism, the British Government decided to admit children under sixteen from the *Struma* into Palestine. But the Turks would not allow them to travel overland and the British would not provide a ship. So, on 24 February 1942, a Turkish tug towed the *Struma* into the Black Sea and left her drifting outside Turkish territorial waters. Soon afterwards an unexplained explosion sank her. Of the 769 Jewish refugees aboard, only two were saved. They were admitted to Palestine 'as an act of clemency'.

For the previous twenty-five years friendship with Britain had proved the Zionists' best strategy. Chaim Weizmann had married the Zionist movement to the British Empire and the Zionists had done well out of the relationship. Now Malcolm MacDonald and Churchill, both good friends of the cause, had let Weizmann down. The Jews in Palestine grew bitter, particularly as they saw the British turn away boatloads of immigrants – the *Struma* being only the most dramatic case of many. The British Empire seemed to have become Zionism's enemy. Weizmann lost his hold over the Zionists. Some of them even turned to what Weizmann considered the insane policy of making war on Britain.

During the pre-war Arab rebellion, the British had helped the Jewish self-defence organisation which assumed part of the burden of protecting Jewish settlements. Some of the arms put into Jewish hands by the British were passed on to the Haganah, the Zionists' private army. At first the British winked at this: the Haganah, though illegal, were no threat. But following Malcolm MacDonald's change of policy, British officials thought the Haganah might turn on them.

The first aim of British policy was now to avoid upsetting the Arabs, some of whom in the final phase of the rebellion were still being hanged for carrying arms, so the British put on a show of even-handedness. When, in October 1939, the young Moshe Dayan, later Israel's Defence Minister, and forty-two other Haganah men were caught parading with arms, they were arrested and faced the death penalty. Their defence was that they were preparing to fight against Britain's enemy Nazi Germany. The court did not condemn them to death, but they all received long prison sentences. Jews in Palestine were further encouraged to turn away from Weizmann's policy and towards a clash with Britain.

For a while British policy on arming the Jews was schizophrenic. The Palestine Government insisted the Haganah was an illegal organisation whose members should be arrested, but intelligence officers of the British army sought Haganah help. Jewish refugees from Germany, Poland and Rumania often had valuable local knowledge. To interrogate them the Haganah supplied Jews who had themselves fled earlier from these countries. They thus obtained the information fast and reliably, and British army units gave the Haganah arms and assistance in return. The Haganah's eagerness to help the British again proved useful following the fall of France to Germany, when Arabic-speaking Jews, including the same Moshe Dayan, helped guide British troops from Palestine into the French territories of Syria and Lebanon, where they replaced the pro-German governor by a Gaullist.

Through the first four years of the war the British policy was successful. Although Iraq wobbled near enough to joining the German side in the war to justify the Cabinet's view that unrestricted Jewish immigration to Palestine would have toppled it irretrievably over, the Middle East stayed on the British side. So did the Jews, but only just. David Ben Gurion, the leader of the Palestine Jews, was convinced that the British no longer backed a national home for the Jews. Two small military groups went farther. The Stern Gang (named after an early leader who was killed in a gunfight with British police) was a tiny group of out-and-out terrorists who believed in murdering the British. They thought that the terrorism of the Arab rebellion had won concessions and that they could do the same. They chose individual Britons and, one at a time, killed them. One of their leaders, Itzhak Shamir, was Prime Minister of Israel from 1983 to 1984.

The other violent dissidents from Weizmann's pro-British line were a larger terrorist group named Irgun Zvai Leumi. From the late 1930s the Irgun hit at Arabs in Palestine, on the basis that if Arabs murder Jews then Jews had better murder Arabs. They received arms and training from the right-wing anti-semitic government of Poland, which wanted to see as many Jews as possible removed from Poland to Palestine and therefore wanted the Arabs intimidated or driven out. This accounts for Irgun's predominantly Polish composition.

In 1942 a Polish Zionist named Menachim Begin (Prime Minister of Israel 1977–83) reached Palestine and soon became head of the Irgun. He was convinced that Britain and the United States were Hitler's accomplices in murdering Europe's Jews. He rejected the well-meaning but complicated reasoning of people like MacDonald and Churchill. For Begin the issue was simple: the British and Americans could have saved the Jews of Central Europe but did not because they wanted the Jews not to be saved. Coming from Poland, where the thirty thousand Jews of his home town, Brest-Litovsk, were by 1944 reduced to only ten, where he had served as a private soldier in a Polish army whose leaders hated and used the Jews, his view was understandably different from that of the cosmopolitan, well-connected Weizmann.

In February 1944, Begin declared war on Britain. He set the Irgun on a new path. Instead of killing Arabs, their main task now was to attack the bastions of British rule in Palestine. Begin did not have individual Britons shot in the streets as the Stern Gang did, nor – so long as the war against the Nazis continued – did he allow the Irgun to attack the British military. He directed Irgun's bombs at immigration offices, police stations and Palestine Government buildings: these were engaged in the conspiracy, as he saw it, to bring about the slaughter of the Jews of Europe. When, in March 1944, Irgun bombs killed six British policemen, Weizmann was horrified. He feared that murders and bombings of the British by the Stern Gang and Begin's Irgun could turn Churchill himself against the Jews. The Jewish Agency, the body the British dealt with as a representative of the Jews in Palestine, dissociated itself from the murders and publicly condemned them.

In 1944, the United States entered the story. It was to prove a decisive force. 1944 was an election year and presidential candidates wanted the Jewish vote. President Franklin D. Roosevelt wrote: 'I know how long and ardently the Jewish people have worked and prayed for the establishment of Palestine as a free and democratic Jewish commonwealth. I am convinced that the American people give their support to this aim and if re-elected I shall help to bring about its realisation.' The millions of Jews who had enjoyed free access to the United States until 1922 and the thousands who were granted admission thereafter had grown into an important political group. In American presidential elections the largest vote in the electoral college then belonged to the state of New York, where the influence of the Jewish community was held to be decisive. But the link between Zionism and American politics was not simply one of calculation and vote-getting. The United States contained the largest Jewish community in the world, many from Eastern Europe. US newspapers and radio, therefore, took more interest in the plight of the European Jews than did the media in other countries. As the war proceeded the scenes of horror reported by Christians, agnostics, US Government officials, newspapermen and impartial by-standers built up an overwhelming conviction amongst Americans of all religions that Hitler's 'final solution' of the Jewish problem was the most terrible crime in human history. President Roosevelt did his best to stand by the policy that the British Foreign Office had convinced the US State Department was necessary to prevent trouble in the Middle East during the war, namely continued tight limits on Jewish immigration to Palestine, but he faced growing sympathy throughout the United States for the Jewish cause.

By 1944 the war was going well for the Anglo-American-Russian alliance. The fear of the Middle East's swinging to the Germans was past. Churchill had long favoured the creation of a Jewish army to fight alongside the Allies, but had allowed the Colonial Office and the Foreign Office to overrule him with the argument that it would boost Arab opposition and terrorism. Jewish co-operation in the war effort was therefore minimised and censored from the Palestine press. But, just as India's nationalist leaders wanted to recruit for Britain in the 1914–18 war, Weizmann and his colleagues kept begging Churchill to allow a Jewish force to fight alongside the Allies, like the Free French, the Poles and the Czechs. The Colonial Office now warned that, given the activities of Irgun and the Stern Gang, arms and training given to Jews might soon be used against the British, but Churchill preferred to rely on his long understanding with Weizmann. Some 27,000 Palestinian Jews served in the British army, and in September 1944 the Jewish Brigade Group was formed from among them. It took the field with its own insignia bearing the star of David: an important step, Zionist leaders thought, towards the establishment of a Jewish state.

However, Weizmann's success with the Jewish brigade did not lead to the wholehearted Churchillian support he still hoped for. On 6 November 1944 in Cairo the Stern Gang murdered Lord Moyne, Churchill's Minister of State for Middle East affairs who was also his close friend, ending for the rest of the war the Prime Minister's commitment to Zionism. The Jewish Agency and the Haganah immediately demonstrated their abhorrence of such terror tactics. They launched what became known as the *saison* (the hunting season) against both the Stern Gang and the Irgun. They captured, beat up and tortured hundreds of members of the two organisations and handed many over to the British. The Zionist leadership announced that the Jews of Palestine were 'required to spew up all members of this destructive and ruinous gang, to deny them shelter and refuge, not to give in to their threats and to grant the authorities all the aid required to prevent the acts of terror'. For the final months of the war anti-British terrorism was thus prevented.

In 1945 the advancing Allied armies found Hitler's extermination and concentration camps: Auschwitz, Belsen, Buchenwald head a long list of places where Jews and others were brought to be efficiently murdered. In all about six million Jews were wiped out by the Nazis. Film reinforced by the soldiers' harrowing reports proved to the most sceptical the truth about Hitler's policy towards the Jews. Those who survived and who clamoured to escape from the horrors of Europe to a land where Jews would rule themselves had now, more than ever, a claim on the sympathy of the victorious Allies. But the British, who had the direct responsibility, were not prepared to meet that claim. Churchill's previously helpful and encouraging responses to Weizmann's approaches had by now ceased. Following the murder of Lord Moyne he acquiesced in the judgment of his Foreign Secretary, Anthony Eden: 'If we lose Arab goodwill, the Americans and the Russians will be on hand to profit from our mistakes.'

The British general election in July 1945 gave Weizmann's tactics a last brief moment of hope. The election victors, the Labour Party, had promised in 1944 to let Jews enter Palestine in such numbers as to become a majority.

*The Mufti inspects a Muslim unit of the German army, January 1944.*

Furthermore the leader of the Palestinian Arabs, the Mufti of Jerusalem, had spent the war recruiting Arabs to fight for Germany, broadcasting from Berlin, doing all he could to help Hitler. He was ill-placed to stand between Labour in Britain, the Democrats in the United States and their joint desire to reward an ally whose people had suffered so appallingly. Surely Weizmann's moment had come.

Still it did not happen. The British ambassadors to all the Arab countries argued, as they had done in 1938–9, that a major concession to the Jews in Palestine would undermine Britain's position in the Middle East. The success of war had now to be consolidated. Friendly regimes in Iraq and Egypt and Transjordan must not be weakened by Britain's taking action in Palestine that would outrage Arab nationalists. King Ibn Saud of Saudi Arabia told both the British and American Governments that the friendship of his state and of the millions of Muslims whose holy places his state contained depended on the interests of the Palestinian Arabs being placed above those of the Jews.

In July 1945 Ernest Bevin was appointed Labour's Foreign Secretary and took control of Britain's Palestine policy. Bevin was a giant. He had built up the Transport and General Workers' Union into the largest trade union in the world; he had made the decisive speech at the Labour party conference in 1935, in which he contemptuously dismissed the then party leader George Lansbury for his pacifist unwillingness to support rearmament against the European Fascists, thus bringing about Lansbury's resignation and Attlee's election as leader; and during the Second World War he had taken on the huge job of Cabinet minister responsible for mobilising the entire British labour force, in which role he overrode his fellow union leaders, Cabinet members and even, on occasion, Churchill himself. Of the top men in the Labour Party, Bevin despised quite a few, including Herbert Morrison.

When it was put to him that, 'Herbert is his own worst enemy,' Bevin replied, 'Not while I'm alive, 'e ain't.' Bevin considered that, with his trade union experience, he could get Jews and Arabs to hammer out a compromise. He said he would stake his 'political future' on solving the problem.

Like most Labour Party members, Bevin had been a Zionist. Along with Malcolm MacDonald he had intervened to oppose Sidney Webb's 1930 white paper on Palestine. Faced by a clear division between the views of the Foreign Office and the Labour Party, he set about mastering the brief. According to Attlee's biographer, Kenneth Harris, Bevin went to the Prime Minister and said: 'Clem, about Palestine. According to my lads in the office we've got it wrong. We've got to think again.' Within a few weeks, having read all the arguments, he concluded that the Labour Party had indeed been wrong: it was not in Britain's interest to send the Jews of Europe to Palestine because of the damage it would cause to Britain's position throughout the Middle East. It was also the wrong policy, he decided, from the point of view of the Jews: those who survived in Germany and Central Europe should be helped to re-establish themselves *there*: to move all the Jewish refugees to Palestine, where they would immediately face violent confrontation from the Arabs, would be to take them from the frying pan into the fire; it was Europe, not the Arabs, that owed the Jews restitution. Further, the Allies had fought the war to rid Europe of racism, not, after victory, to give in to it. Bevin rapidly persuaded his overwhelmingly pro-Zionist Cabinet colleagues that the best Britain could do for the Jews over the next few months was to continue the 1939 policy of permitting immigration to Palestine at the rate of 1,500 a month. Even this concession now required Arab acquiescence if it was to be extended.

On the day Labour came to power, the new Prime Minister, Clement Attlee, received a letter about Palestine from the new American President following Roosevelt's death, Harry Truman. It stated: 'I hope that the British Government may find it possible without delay to take steps to lift the restrictions on Jewish immigration.' A month later Truman wrote again, pressing Britain to admit 100,000 Jews from Europe: 'No claim is more meritorious,' he wrote, 'than that of the groups who for so many years have known persecution and enslavement.' In mid-September Attlee replied, setting out the case with which Bevin had convinced the Cabinet: to ship the refugees to Palestine was certain to cause conflict with the Arabs and would probably render the territory ungovernable; an alternative policy for the Jews in Europe must be worked out, to take account of their needs, of the rights of the Jews and Arabs already in Palestine and, not least, of the British and American need for continuing good relations with the Arab Middle East. Working out such a policy would take time.

President Truman and the international Zionist movement had no time. The displaced persons (DP) camps of Europe contained thousands of Jews who had been deprived of their homes, their work, their families and their community and who urgently needed somewhere to go. So Truman told a group of journalists about his letter to Attlee and had Attlee's reply leaked to a senator, causing Bevin and Attlee to explode with anger. They were asking American help calmly to work out the appropriate policy to deal with a complex problem and the White House deliberately scuppered their efforts. They thought Truman's conduct irresponsible and disloyal.

Its immediate consequence was certainly troublesome for Britain. Weizmann and the moderate Zionists had sensed the way the wind was blowing. The refusal of British ministers to meet them or to reply to their letters had already suggested that Weizmann's hopes of the Labour Government were to be disappointed. The confirmation from America concluded the matter. Weizmann had with difficulty managed to restrain the Jews of Palestine in their growing desire to launch anti-British violence; now his ability to reassure them that the British would keep their promises was at an end. David Ben Gurion, less scholarly and eloquent than Weizmann but more the practical politician, increasingly emerged as the principal Zionist leader.

In July 1945 in New York Ben Gurion had met seventeen Jewish millionaires. Soon afterwards a company was set up, ostensibly to deal in agricultural and medical goods, actually to buy military equipment which was becoming available at bargain prices following the end of the war. At first these arms had been intended for protection against Arab attacks, but the revelation of the Labour Government's policy changed Ben Gurion's mind. Already he had cancelled the *saison*, because Haganah units were reluctant, in the changing political climate, to continue it. Now the policy of the *saison* was totally reversed. The Haganah, the Stern Gang and Irgun Zvai Leumi combined their efforts to force the British to concede or quit. In the words of Golda Meir, later Prime Minister of Israel 1969–74, 'We kept hearing the argument, "The Arabs can create so much trouble, therefore you have to give in." So in the end we decided, very well, *we'll* create trouble.' The first big instalment took the form of several hundred co-ordinated explosions throughout Palestine on 31 October 1945, causing more than 150 breaks in the railway network and blowing up locomotives, a train and three police launches on the Mediterranean (used to track ships bringing in illegal immigrants). Compared to the Arab rebellion, this was a highly professional military operation, the result of the planned and timed effort of hundreds of skilled people. The morale of Jews in Palestine and Europe was boosted: at last the Zionist movement was united in fighting the British.

Bevin, already angered by the mischievous behaviour, as he saw it, of Truman, was outraged by the launching of Jewish terrorism. He had thought he was pursuing the best interest of all, including the Jews, and that he had been honestly negotiating with their leaders. Now, apparently, he was at war with them. To prevent total loss of control, he decided that Britain must drag the United States into sharing responsibility for Palestine: once Truman was made to deal with the consequences of his pleas, he would stop pestering the British Government to take self-defeating steps. Bevin devised a clever way to secure American involvement: the two governments appointed an independent committee led by two judges to advise them. During its inquiry, Truman was prevented from making public pronouncements about the issue. Bevin had at least won himself some time.

On the ground in Palestine it did not seem a useful gain. The Haganah, Stern Gang and Irgun stepped up their violence. The Haganah had by now grown from a home guard into a part-time conscript army which included every Jew in Palestine, male and female, who was capable of bearing arms. They had learned from the Arab rebellion and from military service with the British how to run an urban guerilla movement.

The Nazi atrocities against the Jews had created a political will that was rising like the sea around a sandcastle. Bevin thought the Jews in the DP camps would prefer to stay in Europe. He was told that they said they wanted to go to Palestine only because Zionists visited the camps and put pressure on them. The Anglo-American committee, however, reported that the Jews in the camps regarded Europe as a crematorium from which they must escape. Most would have preferred to go to the United States or Britain, but since neither would admit them, Palestine was the place they chose. Bevin and the Foreign Office believed that the Jews in Palestine would calm down, that the growing violence was the work of some extremists who could be removed. But, as Richard Crossman MP, a member of the Anglo-American committee, told the House of Commons, the whole Jewish community in Palestine was backing the Haganah and the extremist gangs which it was now impossible for the British to defeat, even if they arrested thousands. Finally, and decisively, the rising sea of Zionism was pumped up further by Harry Truman.

President Roosevelt had trodden a tightrope of ambiguity over Palestine. Publicly he said what he considered necessary to win elections, privately he followed the State Department line and was careful not to embarrass the British. In contrast, Truman from 1945 to 1948 was an unelected and unpopular President, widely thought not up to the job. When a group of US diplomats based in Arab countries told him in October 1945 that to support Zionism would damage American interests throughout the Middle East he is reported to have told them, 'I'm sorry, gentlemen, but I have to answer to hundreds of thousands who are anxious for the success of Zionism; I do not have hundreds of thousands of Arabs among my constituents.' Truman showed contempt for 'the striped pants boys' of the State Department and they in return thought him a small-town machine politician who had got into the Senate merely as front man for Tom Prendergast, saloon keeper, cement dealer and political boss of Kansas City. The Foreign Service professionals resented their exclusion from policy-making over Palestine. At first they told their British colleagues that they hoped to get Truman into line. Their anger increased as they saw the President make decisions on Palestine according to the needs of election campaigns not only for Congress but even for the Mayoralty of New York. The State Department sent Truman a warning that, if a policy for Palestine was not carefully worked out with all parties concerned, the result would be 'years of political instability in Palestine and the Near East'. No record exists to show whether Truman, the darling of the historians, read the warning. He certainly took no notice of it.

Good relations with the United States were the foundation of Bevin's foreign policy. Immediately on taking office in August 1945, he went to the Potsdam conference and saw that the wartime co-operation of the Russians was now likely to cease. Both the defence and the economic recovery of Europe required him to obtain from the United States more than its previously isolationist electorate had ever granted. Public disagreements with the US President were therefore particularly unwelcome, but over Palestine they persisted.

The joint committee of inquiry recommended that 100,000 Jews be admitted. Bevin and his officials believed the recommendation, if implemented, would lead to an Arab rising in Palestine and trouble elsewhere in the Middle East. Nevertheless Bevin and Attlee did not reject the report, as they found its other provisions more acceptable. It stated that Palestine should be 'neither a Jewish state nor an Arab state' and called on the Zionist leaders to help the authorities suppress both terrorism and illegal immigration; most important from Bevin's point of view, it said that Palestine alone could not solve the Jewish refugee problem. That meant that the United States and other countries should help find a solution. Bevin's plan seemed to be working after all and he urged the Americans to say nothing until the two governments had consulted.

Truman, however, took 'the plum out of the pudding' (in Dean Acheson's words) by publicly accepting the recommendation that 100,000 be admitted, while giving no hint of his attitude to the report's other nine recommendations. Once again Truman was out to win Zionist votes in the US, and had no desire to know if this made problems on the ground more difficult. Bevin and Attlee were outraged, a Cabinet meeting was held for the sole purpose of working out a response and Attlee made a statement in the House of Commons which amounted to a public rebuke for Truman. He said that the report was addressed to both governments, which must consult, that it must be considered as a whole, that the practical difficulties of admitting 100,000 immigrants 'would obviously be very great' and that the British Government wanted to know 'to what extent the Government of the United States would be prepared to share the resulting military and financial responsibilities'.

Attlee and Bevin remained determined to inveigle the United States into sharing the burden both of resettling the homeless Jews of Europe, which was bound to be expensive, and of keeping the peace in Palestine, which promised to be not only expensive but also militarily and politically difficult. Truman saw little benefit in getting involved. Dean Acheson, who as Under Secretary of State was the official most closely involved with him in dealing with Palestine, describes Truman's view in 1945–6 as 'centred exclusively upon two points: first, immediate immigration of one hundred thousand;

second, determination to assume no political or military responsibility for this decision'. Bevin, whose trade union experience might have been expected to give him some insight into Truman's need to win votes, gave vent to his frustration with US policy in a speech he made at the Labour Party conference in June 1946. He said the Americans demanded Jewish immigration to Palestine only because 'they did not want too many Jews in New York'. It may have been true, but it was tactless. Truman, in his memoirs *Years of Trial and Hope*, complains of Bevin's rudeness over Palestine, at one point describing him as 'very undiplomatic' and 'almost hostile', and commenting, 'I was outraged by Bevin's charge.'

An Arab comment on Truman's policy was made by the Iraqi parliament in Baghdad, where a bill was introduced in parody of the Balfour Declaration, calling for the establishment of a national home for the Arab people in California.

One of the reasons for the refusal by Bevin and Attlee to do what the President asked was that both the army and the Colonial Office thought a major outbreak of Arab violence would be more dangerous than anything the Jews could do. In this they were now to be proved wrong. The apparent British indifference to the fate of the Jews in Europe antagonised even those like Weizmann who had trusted the Labour Party. Most Jews had come to regard Bevin as an anti-semite and a remark he made about their wanting 'to get too much at the head of the queue' to escape from the DP camps was offered as proof. A cartoon was published showing skeletal Jews from the camps lining up with Bevin's words as the caption. He made matters worse by saying publicly that if 100,000 Jews entered Palestine immediately, he would have to send another division of troops to keep the peace and this he was not prepared to do.

The alliance of the Haganah, Irgun and the Stern Gang was by now proving its effectiveness. The British security force was built up to 100,000 (80,000 troops and 20,000 police) to deal with a Jewish population in Palestine of barely 600,000. The Jewish terrorists were blowing up bridges, raiding military camps, destroying railways, killing soldiers, and the campaign took growing numbers of British lives. The British tried to hit back in a civilised way, by searches and arrests, without being too illiberal. But the five thousand or so terrorists vanished in the Jewish population. When, at the end of June 1946, the British seized the Zionist headquarters in Jerusalem and arrested 2,700, including most of the leaders of the Jewish Agency, they still failed to remove the terrorist leadership.

All they achieved was to stimulate an extreme act of revenge. On 22 July at midday a small Irgun gang, all dressed as Arabs, delivered seven milk churns full of explosives to the basement kitchen of the King David Hotel, Jerusalem, the main social centre of the city, of which 'Chips' Channon, the millionaire Conservative MP, wrote, 'Next to the Ritz in Paris, it surely is the world's best hotel.' In 1946 its southern wing contained the headquarters of the British Government and forces in Palestine. Weizmann, the aged Zionist

*The King David Hotel after the explosion.*

leader, knew that some big terrorist act was planned, but not what it was. He used the last reserves of his authority as President of the movement to order that it be called off: the Zionist movement must avoid all-out war with Britain. This operation, however, was controlled by Menachem Begin, the leader of Irgun, who did not recognise the authority of Weizmann. At 12.37 pm the milk churns exploded underneath the southern wing of the hotel. The entire six-storey wing collapsed into a heap of rubble, killing ninety-one (41 Arabs, 28 British, 17 Jews, 5 others), mostly clerks, typists, messengers and junior staff of the hotel and secretariat, but including a few senior British officials.

Britain was horrified. So was the Zionist movement. The movement's own army, the Haganah, always made sure a warning was given before explosions, so people could escape. Although Begin claimed the Irgun were equally meticulous, clearly they were not. A warning was telephoned, but to the hotel switchboard not the British, in a manner that left some uncertainty as to its genuineness and probably too late for evacuation to be possible. The British officers in charge, who happened to be in another wing of the building, received no direct or clear warning.

The King David Hotel explosion threw all parties into confusion. Weizmann did not believe the protestation of the leader of the Haganah that he had known nothing about the plan and insisted on his resignation. The British Commander-in-Chief in Palestine, General Sir Evelyn Barker, whose office was in the King David Hotel though not in the south wing, was shocked by the horror he witnessed and immediately wrote an instruction to his troops forbidding 'any social intercourse with any Jew' as a means of 'punishing the Jews in a way the race dislikes . . . by striking at their pockets and showing our contempt for them'. The order soon fell into the hands of the Zionists, who ensured that it received wide publicity, counteracting some of the anti-Jewish feeling aroused by the explosion. The Zionists demanded Barker's removal.

Officials in Palestine wanted to back Barker and take punitive measures against the Jews, such as a large collective fine and a complete end to Jewish immigration. The Cabinet in London, however, was engaged in talks with the United States Government about co-operation following the joint committee's report. Anything likely to worsen relations with the Jews was therefore ruled out. The British even agreed, during the course of these talks, to admit the 100,000 as part of a comprehensive settlement but, as usual, the American President found domestic political advantage, this time in a forthcoming congressional election, more important than a deal with the British. The Zionists feared that the deal, which proposed autonomous provinces for Jews and Arabs under British trusteeship, might kill the chance of obtaining a Jewish state. They therefore pressed Truman to reject the plan even though it had been agreed between his own representatives and the British and included admission of the 100,000. Attlee once more expressed his dismay.

*Two ministers from the Transport and General Workers' Union, Arthur Creech Jones, Colonial Secretary (left), and Ernest Bevin, Foreign Secretary, at a conference on Palestine, January 1947.*

This repeated pattern of presidential eruptions over Palestine was yet to reach its climax. In October 1946 British ministers began meetings with Zionist leaders. After the growing mistrust of recent months this was an important step: the Zionist council condemned terrorism and the admission of the 100,000 was on offer if it stopped. The 2,700 arrested in June were released. Bevin hoped that his scheme for autonomous provinces – which could ultimately lead either to a single Jewish–Arab state or to partition – might be reluctantly accepted by both sides. But elections in New York overruled all that. A statement was prepared for Truman, again insisting on immediate admission of the 100,000 and favouring a Jewish Agency plan for a 'viable' Jewish state. Before publication it was sent to London. Attlee immediately cabled:

> Dear Mr President, I have been shown a copy of your proposed statement on Palestine . . . You are, I am sure, aware that we are in consultation [with the Zionist leaders]. I would therefore earnestly request you to postpone making your statement, at least for the time necessary for me to communicate with Mr Bevin in Paris.

Attlee considered that Truman's statement was certain to preclude the Zionists making any concession in the negotiations, thus reducing the slim chance of compromise to zero. But Truman had been told the content of a speech on Palestine by Thomas Dewey, a leading Republican, calculated to outbid him for the Jewish vote in New York. He felt he had to get in first and therefore went ahead with the release. Attlee cabled him:

> I . . . regret . . . your refusing even a few hours' grace to the Prime Minister of the country which has responsibility for the government of Palestine, in order that he may acquaint you with the actual situation and the probable results of your action . . . I am astonished that you did not wait . . . I shall await with interest to learn what were the imperative reasons which compelled this precipitancy.

Truman's statement was, for Attlee and Bevin, very nearly the last straw. As they had predicted, the Zionists promptly became inflexible in their demand for a 'viable' Jewish state, i.e. the partition of Palestine. Bevin, thanks to his tough approach to Russia, was used to warm receptions in the United States, but he experienced the intensity of American feeling on the Palestine issue during a visit in November 1946. The newspapers were reporting 'British atrocities', Ben Hecht's anti-British play *A Flag is Born* was drawing full houses on Broadway and the Foreign Secretary was himself pelted with eggs. He told Jewish leaders in New York that if he could not get a permanent solution to the Palestine problem soon, Britain would give up the mandate. Churchill had already recommended such a policy in the House of Commons and Bevin placed it before the Cabinet as an option.

He was not yet ready to give up, however, and produced an unexpected initiative. Many of his Cabinet colleagues were still Zionists and unhappy with his policies. They now pressed for the proposal American Zionists had persuaded Truman to support – partition and a Jewish state. In February 1947 Bevin attempted to forestall this demand by asking the United Nations for an advisory opinion, which he expected would support his own even-handed approach. He warned the Zionists that the reference to the UN would do them no good.

In Palestine the Stern Gang and the Irgun stepped up terrorism. Many years later, Clare Hollingworth, defence correspondent in turn of the *Guardian* and the *Daily Telegraph*, asked how she had the nerve to report from the midst of urban guerilla-wars in Algiers, Aden, Cyprus and Northern Ireland, replied: 'They were all fairly quiet really, compared to Palestine once the Jews got going. That was the only place where the ruling power became frightened to walk along the street.' The British Government withdrew non-essential staff; some two thousand men, women and children were evacuated in January 1947; the main post office, police headquarters and other government buildings were enclosed within a wire security compound which the Jews called Bevingrad. The Government of Palestine was besieged. In March 1947 martial law was imposed in parts of Tel Aviv and Jerusalem to enable the military to stop all movement and catch the terrorists who were continuing to kill and sabotage, seemingly at will. The High Commissioner, Sir Alan Cunningham, wrote: 'I have recently been greatly concerned by the apparent inability of the army to protect even themselves.'

After two weeks, martial law was abandoned. The army had not enough troops to carry it out efficiently and it had failed to catch terrorists. A policy of counter-terrorism – appointing select squads to mix with Stern Gang and Irgun members with a view to eliminating them – was briefly adopted by the Palestine police, but the outcry when on 6 May 1947 the first Stern Ganger 'vanished' (he was a seventeen-year-old youth allegedly tortured to death) reminded the British that to allow themselves to be reduced to lawlessness was both a confession of defeat and certain to be self-defeating.

In December 1946 two Irgun youths were sentenced to prison and eighteen lashes for carrying guns. The Irgun announced, 'If you whip us we shall whip you.' The British whipped the first youth. The Irgun captured a British major and three non-commissioned officers, gave each eighteen lashes and set them free. The second Irgun youth was spared the whip, and for the remainder of their rule in Palestine the British flogged no more Jews or Arabs. When three Irgun men were sentenced to hang for their part in blowing a hole in the massive stone wall of Acre fortress, a medieval prison, releasing 251 prisoners including 29 key Irgun men, the Irgun again looked for retribution. By now the British in Palestine were going out only with armed escorts in groups of four. Nevertheless the Irgun managed to capture two sergeants, Clifford Martin and Mervyn Paice, as they were walking home from a café, unarmed, after permitted hours. A test of nerves began. The three Irgun men had been duly sentenced by law. The Government's 'softness' in dealing with the Jews in Palestine had been criticised by many, notably the Chief of the Imperial General Staff, Field Marshal Sir Bernard Montgomery, who had argued that a firm hand would put a stop to the trouble. Soldiers in Palestine could not understand why the Government failed to clamp down on the population whose support kept the terrorists going. In the face of such criticism the three Irgun terrorists had to be hanged.

The Zionist leaders publicly begged the Irgun not to commit 'a blood-thirsty deed contrary to all human standards', but the Irgun leadership had made up their minds. The sergeants had been kept in a tiny cell beneath a diamond factory. They were brought out and hanged in the factory. Their bodies were hung from two eucalyptus trees in a government forestry station, with a mine in the earth below so that their finders too should suffer.

Soldiers and policemen in Palestine went uncontrollably on the rampage, assaulting Jews and smashing their property; five Jews were killed. Anti-semitic riots broke out in Liverpool, Manchester, Glasgow and London. With Palestine reducing the British army, police and public to such a condition, the pressure grew for Britain simply to throw in the towel.

What reason was there to stay? In 1945 Attlee had seriously contemplated clearing out of the whole of the Middle East, on the grounds that Britain could not afford to defend the area and that popular Arab feeling against British bases was certain to lead to trouble and perhaps, before long, to the need to evacuate under pressure. This was already beginning to happen in Egypt, which had been crowded with British equipment and staff during the war; afterwards leading Egyptians demanded their removal. Bevin quickly persuaded Attlee that total evacuation of the Middle East was out of the question. If Russia under Stalin tried to expand in Europe, Britain's bases in the Middle East would be the only place from which to bomb the advancing Red Army. Therefore the military equipment and manpower removed from Egypt must be kept in the region. In the event of war, a local base required a good port, plentiful supplies of safe water and a population with the skill to provide some technical services. What better location could there be than Palestine? Without consideration of the political problems there, the War Office had set about ferrying its equipment to Haifa. It continued busily to do so until Bevin's change of policy caught it on the hop. But the Chancellor of the Exchequer, Hugh Dalton, one of the Cabinet's leading Zionists, had seen faster than the soldiers why the military argument for staying in Palestine was not valid: as he wrote in a memorandum to Attlee, 'You cannot have a secure base on top of a wasps' nest.'

The arguments for Britain to get out were reinforced by the immigrants' ships. Like the *Struma* in 1941, these sailed with mixed motives. Most of the Jews on board simply wanted to reach Palestine, but some of their organisers were more interested in showing the British in a bad light. The Cabinet's decision not to allow large-scale Jewish immigration to Palestine meant stopping any admissions above the decreed 1,500 per month. Immediately after the war this was done by interning excess arrivals in a camp in Palestine and filtering them into the country as certificates from the monthly quota became available. But soon the numbers arriving grew, so additional and larger camps were set up in Cyprus. A ship would approach Palestine carrying refugees, the Royal Navy would board it, check the passengers and, if they did not have immigration certificates, put them onto a British ship for Cyprus. This was often a nasty business. Many of the refugees had been in Nazi camps in Europe. They knew that, if only they could land in Palestine, fellow Jews would hide them from the British authorities. So Royal Naval officers were trained (at special courses in Malta) in the humane capture, searching and removing of people who, though they resisted fiercely, must if possible not be hurt. The captains of the refugee ships, which were mostly ready to be scrapped, achieved their greatest success if they evaded the British patrols and beached in some obscure inlet where the Zionists could find the passengers before the police did.

In theory the refugees who were sent to camps in Cyprus joined the queue for certificates, but by mid-1947 the camps were so crowded that their inmates saw no hope. Utterly demoralised they refused to work or make their accommodation comfortable: all they wanted was to be let into Palestine and all they could grasp about British policy was that it imprisoned them.

Between the end of the war and May 1948, the Zionist movement sent some 70,000 Jewish illegal immigrants, of whom more than 50,000 were intercepted by the Royal Navy. Small boats containing a dozen or fewer often got through. Of the 63 larger ships the vast majority were spotted from British aircraft and stopped; only five evaded the blockade. The largest immigrant ship came in July 1947. She was a ferry-boat that had sailed for years in the sheltered waters of Chesapeake Bay in the United States. The Zionists bought her and named her *Exodus*. The 4,500 would-be immigrants who travelled in her were used by both the Zionists and the British in one of the most ruthless propaganda battles in history.

The Zionists had the ferry adapted to carry its cargo in spaces so narrow and shallow (eighteen inches wide, two feet high) that they are more appropriately called shelves than bunks. Her certificate of seaworthiness described her as fit to sail only in coastal waters without passengers. The First Lord of the Admiralty said in April 1947 that the immigrants were – at three persons per gross ton of shipping – generally as overcrowded as those on old slaving ships (the Royal Navy in its time had the job of arresting both, see chapter 8, p. 357). The *Exodus* was much more crowded even than the average immigrant ship. From camps in Germany the hopeful came to board her in Southern France at the small port of Sète, near Marseilles. On 12 July 1947 they set sail and were soon spotted by the British, who provided a military escort for the journey across the Mediterranean. Once the *Exodus* was inside the territorial waters of Palestine, the British could legally arrest her.

Meanwhile Britain's decision to seek the opinion of the UN had led to the

creation of the United Nations Special Committee on Palestine (UNSCOP),
a body whose purpose was to advise the UN how to advise the British. They
were in Palestine pursuing their inquiries as the *Exodus* approached. For the
Zionists it was a crucial moment.

The captain, crew and refugees aboard the *Exodus* had fought the British
marines who leapt aboard while the vessel was still out on the open sea and
had prevented them from getting control of the ship's steering. They were
therefore still in a position to make a run for a beach, as her flat bottom and
the hopes of the 4,500 aboard suggested. But the captain accepted the orders
of his Zionist superiors to make a show of pitiful weakness and hand over

*The* Exodus *brought
into Haifa by the Royal
Navy, July 1947. The
battered objects over the
side are life-rafts.*

control to the British while, on their own radio, the crew and immigrants transmitted blow-by-blow commentaries that were heard in Palestine and passed round the world. UNSCOP members saw the *Exodus* arrive at Haifa and British soldiers transfer the immigrants to three British transport ships which promptly removed them from Palestine.

They were expected to go to Cyprus, but did not. The camps were full. Bevin used the occasion to proclaim a policy of returning would-be immigrants to the countries from which they had set sail. The British ambassador to France warned that the French authorities would not help with the forcible eviction of the Jews from the ships onto French soil, because such action would be too reminiscent of the recently departed Nazis. Bevin, at the end of his tether, informed the ambassador: 'Guards have been instructed to use whatever force may be required to deliver immigrants into French hands.' He had reports that thousands more illegal immigrants were ready to travel and he could admit them neither to Palestine, for fear of the Arab reaction, nor to Cyprus. So the British tried to use the *Exodus* in 1947 like the *Struma* in 1941 as a warning to others not to attempt the journey.

Bevin's policy required that the country from which the immigrants sailed should let them return. He explained this to the French Foreign Minister, Georges Bidault, who agreed. But Bevin made a mistake. Bidault agreed to let the 4,500 Jews live in France. Nothing was agreed about how to handle them at their port of entry. As the three ships approached France, another French Minister, François Mitterand, added a rider: France would not be a party to measures of force to compel the immigrants to land.

Still Bevin hoped his tactic might work. Given the choice of settling immediately in France or continuing their journey to an unknown destination, the 4,500 might well choose France. Thirty-one did. But French Zionists in small boats came alongside the three transports, urging the passengers not to come ashore and a united Zionist spirit seized the overwhelming majority, so that waverers needed courage to leave. The three British ships at the French port became a focus of world attention and the French Communist newspaper *Humanité* described them as 'a floating Auschwitz'. For over three weeks they waited, the British trying to persuade the passengers to land and Zionists urging them to stay aboard. The French authorities were reported to have derived some satisfaction from the British embarrassment.

At this moment the two sergeants were hanged in Palestine, to the outrage of the British people. The Cabinet decided to return the three shiploads whence they had originally come – back to camps in Germany. This inhuman and stupid decision was reached by rational administrative steps. To admit the 4,500 into Cyprus or Palestine would be a humiliation for Britain, would encourage thousands more to make similar journeys and would anger the Arabs; no British colony was equipped to accommodate and feed 4,500 at short notice; no other country would admit them; if admitting them to Britain itself had ever been a possibility, it was ruled out by the anti-

semitic riots started by the hanging of the sergeants; and in the zone of Germany that was under British military administration refugee camps were available. So the three shiploads of Jews were told they would be forcibly returned to Germany. Bevin hoped that this prospect would cause the Zionists to advise them to settle in France. For the Zionists, Golda Meir replied that no Jew could advise another Jew to go anywhere but Palestine. If the British were determined to translate what was already a major propaganda victory for Zionism into a triumph beyond their wildest hopes, why should the Zionists stand in their way?

The refugees allowed themselves to be taken back to Hamburg and there put in trains to Poppendorf camp near Lübeck. Some resisted and British soldiers were ordered to drag or carry them. Reporters and photographers sent such incidents round the world, suggesting that the British Government had either gone mad or turned viciously anti-semitic. The cause of the Zionists was further strengthened.

Soon after, in September 1947, UNSCOP recommended that the British mandate should be ended as soon as possible and Palestine be partitioned into an Arab and a Jewish state. The UNSCOP members had been impressed by Jewish evidence and by the refusal of the Palestinian Arabs to talk to them, on the grounds that they were known to be pro-Zionist. Their partition scheme proposed to give more of Palestine to the Jews than did previous schemes which the Arabs had rejected; it proposed dividing the tiny area into seven segments, three for the Arabs, three for the Jews and an international (map p. 139) Jerusalem. The British Cabinet saw the scheme as unfair to the Arabs and impossible to impose except by the overwhelming use of force, which they were neither willing nor financially able to employ (1947 was the worst point in Britain's post-war teetering on the edge of bankruptcy). So the Cabinet made two decisions. First, it accepted the recommendation that the mandate should end and agreed to withdraw from Palestine; second, it announced that it would not implement any policy that was unacceptable to either Arabs or Jews.

The main reason for this unworldly announcement was the usual one: the need to maintain good relations with the Arabs. During 1947 Bevin was negotiating to remove British troops from most of Egypt but to retain a defence arrangement covering the Suez canal zone; he was also engaged in talks to protect Britain's RAF base and oil concessions in Iraq. Both were too important to be set at risk by performing a boy scout act in Palestine, as the agent of an indifferent international community. Furthermore, the House of Commons, following the *Exodus* episode and the hanging of the two sergeants, was anxious to remove British soldiers and sailors from tasks they could not master and that caused them to be needlessly exposed.

No doubt reasons of state were decisive, but the British view of the UN committee's recommendation as unfair was genuine; Bevin called it 'manifestly unjust to the Arabs': the Jews were roughly a third of the population yet they were allotted half the land. The British were also nagged by a more profound sense of injustice: it was their claim throughout the Empire that they treated all colonised people fairly, but they had themselves been less than fair to the Palestinian Arabs. Partly this was because of the original deal, under which the British chose to ignore the views of the Palestinians in order to win Jewish help to secure the territory. Partly it was because of the contrast in political skill between Jews and Arabs; as Christopher Mayhew, Parliamentary Secretary to Bevin at the Foreign Office in 1945–7 and dealing with Palestinian affairs, recalled:

> The Arabs were separated by the totally different culture and procedures and politics of their countries and ours. If they did make some kind of submission in writing it would be wrongly worded, the arguments would be all wrong and it would be sent to the wrong person. On the other hand there were Zionists so close to the Cabinet that there had been instances where Cabinet ministers actually telephoned the result of a Cabinet meeting straight to the Zionist concerned.

Much as the Colonial Service officers on the spot tried to be fair to the Arabs, the pull of Zionist influence in London and Washington constantly overrode them. Nor did the Palestinians' own leadership help. So divided that they devoted more time to injuring one another than to damaging the Jews or the British, the Palestinian leaders were tactically incompetent. The 1939 white paper offered them practically all they asked. Had the Mufti and the group around him been politically skilful they would have seized it. But the Mufti insisted on all or nothing – and got nothing. His active support for Hitler during the war led the British to feel little warmth for him, but he continued from Cairo to dominate Palestinian politics, preventing the emergence of an effective leadership in touch with local feeling. This he managed partly through his high status as a religious leader, with control over religious funds, partly by assassination and violence. Knowledgeable Britons felt it was hardly fair on the Palestinians to be saddled not only with the most able of opponents but also with a leadership of such poor quality.

In its role as patron of Arab interests Britain had encouraged the creation in 1944–5 of the Arab League, to co-ordinate the policies of the independent Arab states. Immediately the new organisation had to prove to Arab opinion that it was not a British tool. Palestine was the perfect issue: the League's members could express suitably anti-British, anti-Zionist and anti-imperialist sentiments on Palestine without impairing their ability to deal with Britain on matters that concerned them more directly. The Mufti, ill-placed to keep in touch with Palestinians, thought he could secure a powerful impact in Palestine by means of pressure from the League states on the British Foreign Office. Thus the Governments of Egypt, Iraq, Saudi Arabia, Yemen, Lebanon, Syria and Transjordan gradually acquired standing in the Palestine issue and were invited to London in 1946 to give their views. They told Bevin and Attlee that partition would merely be used by the Jews as a first step to expansion, that 'the Arabs of Palestine could not be restrained from adopting violent means to check Jewish expansion' and that such means would be backed by the Arab Governments. This often repeated warning made the British Cabinet unwilling to impose the 1947 UN partition plan by force. If a war was inevitable, Britain did not want to be involved in it. Britain had nothing to gain.

The UNSCOP partition plan was put to the vote in the United Nations General Assembly on 29 November 1947, in accordance with the UN's role as successor to the League of Nations in respect of mandated territories. In the months beforehand it was widely expected that the plan would fail to secure the two-thirds majority needed for implementation. In April, when the Arab states had proposed the termination of the mandate and the declaration of an independent Palestine state with an Arab majority, the vote was lost by twenty-four to fifteen with ten abstentions. The British Government doubted whether the vote for partition would be much more favourable. The American Secretary of State, George Marshall, in a preliminary UN session in September, avoided committing his government on the issue. He expected the Soviet Union to vote against partition, because of its need for allies among its southern neighbours, the Arab states. The US delegation, in other words, hoped by saying little to avoid losing the President Jewish votes, while quietly allowing the policy to go under. Marshall believed that Britain would refuse to implement partition if it were approved and that American support for the measure would therefore require the President to send troops to Palestine to enforce it – a policy Truman had explicitly ruled out.

A month before the vote, however, Truman overruled his Secretary of State and had his representative at the UN announce that the United States would vote for partition. He later wrote, 'I do not think I ever had as much pressure and propaganda aimed at the White House as I had in this instance.' Truman knew the Bible well and was moved by the holocaust and the plight of the Jewish refugees; but belief in the cause was for him a secondary motive; he was late coming to support the creation of a Jewish state. For him the issue was an American domestic one: in the key period, September–October 1947, the US Postmaster General Robert E. Hannegan, who was also chairman of the Democratic National Committee, twice spoke in Cabinet of the 'very great influence' support for Zionism had on fund-raising for the party. Truman remained vulnerable to electoral arguments: 1948 was to be a presidential election year and, having bought Jewish votes for mayors, congressmen and senators, it hardly seemed sensible in November 1947 to refuse to pay the last instalment.

Soon after Truman's decision had been announced Chaim Weizmann arrived in Washington. He was described by Sir Charles Webster in *The Art and Practice of Diplomacy* as one of the supreme diplomatists of his time and he quickly showed his skill. A UN committee was working out the details of partition in case it should be passed, and the US representatives on this committee had been instructed to vote for the Negev, the southern Palestinian desert, to be in the Arab area. Weizmann, with his mastery of scientific argument, described to Truman the work done by Jewish scientists in Palestine on desalination of the brackish desert water and the successes already achieved by irrigation in growing carrots, potatoes and bananas in an area where, Weizmann maintained, 'there has not been a blade of grass for a thousand years'. He argued further that Egypt might well deny the Jewish state use of the Suez canal, in which case access to the eastern seas by way of Negev's southern tip at the bay of Aqaba – at the time a useless, silted desert place – would be essential. Truman was convinced and instructed his UN delegates to reverse their instruction.

Even after the United States and – to widespread surprise – the Soviet Union had announced that they would vote for partition, the issue remained in doubt. Three days before the final vote it seemed that the Zionists would fail to get the two-thirds majority they needed. At this point they pulled every string. They had yet more party pressures applied to Truman, who, having instructed the US delegation at the UN not to twist any arms in favour of partition, now gave his White House staff overriding orders to the contrary. The last-minute alliance of Zionists and White House was decisive. They caused Supreme Court Justices (who happened to be Jewish) to press the Philippines to reverse policy and vote for partition. They had the Firestone Rubber Company threaten Liberia with a loss of investment if it did not reverse its vote. Some Latin American votes, it was later alleged, were bought for cash, some by threats. Delegates with no interest in the Middle East from countries at the other end of the earth now determined the fate of Palestine. Twice the vote was adjourned, first at the behest of the Zionists, desperate for an extra day to apply pressure to governments and delegations, then at the request of the Arabs, seeking time to retaliate. Dean Rusk, Director of UN Affairs in the State Department in 1947–8, remembered:

> We were working very hard, under the direct personal instructions of President Truman, to get a successful vote on that. We used all the persuasion we could with delegates in New York. We went to many capitals to try to get their governments to be sure they had the instructions to work with us on this matter.

Sir Frank Roberts, Bevin's private secretary at the Foreign Office, explained his minister's view:

> Bevin said, 'Well alright, the United Nations has a plan; we are not going to oppose it, but we don't think it will work; it will cause too much trouble between the Arabs and Jews and we are not going to take the responsibility of executing it.' We had been forced into this policy which we would not have chosen ourselves. But the policies we had wanted to follow had not been acceptable to other people. So we washed our hands of it.

Bevin told the House of Commons: 'I do not want the Arabs to be dismissed as if they were nobody.' General Sir Gordon Macmillan, the officer commanding British forces in Palestine, said:

> If we tried to impose partition we would at once alienate the Arabs and probably start a war with them. The Arabs would then possibly gravitate to be friends with the Russians. And we would be involved in a futile war fighting Arabs who were our friends on behalf of the Jews, who you could hardly say were our friends at the time.

When the vote was finally taken on Saturday, 29 November 1947, Jews in Palestine clustered round radio sets, noting each delegate's response: Argentina, abstain; Afghanistan, no; Australia, yes; Belgium, yes; Bolivia, yes; Byelorussia, yes . . . France, expected to abstain or support the Arabs, voted yes; the United Kingdom abstained. The result was 33 for, 13 against, ten abstentions. The representatives of Syria, Lebanon, Iraq, Saudi Arabia, Yemen and Egypt rose and filed out. The vote recommended the setting-up of Jewish and Arab states in Palestine and outlined their boundaries. Britain, nominally administering Palestine on behalf of the UN, made plain its determination to do nothing to implement the resolution and not to allow UN representatives or forces or anyone else's to enter the territory to implement it – or even to keep the peace – until a time of the Cabinet's own choosing when British administrators and soldiers had withdrawn in safety and good order.

Thus Britain ducked out. Although thirty more British policemen were killed before the final departure, the British were no longer the principal

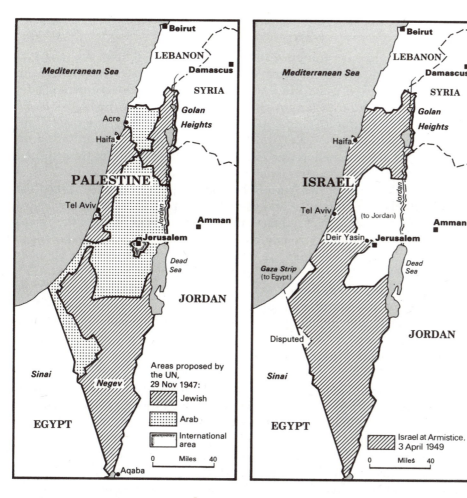

*The partition of Palestine – as proposed by the UN and as accomplished by war.*

Map legend (left map):

Areas proposed by the UN, 29 Nov 1947:
- Jewish
- Arab
- International area

0    Miles    40

Map legend (right map):

Israel at Armistice, 3 April 1949

0    Miles    40

target: Arabs and Jews now faced each other, with no effective force to separate them. Britain refused even to keep the peace. The High Commissioner, Sir Alan Cunningham, repeatedly begged to be allowed to bring in extra police, particularly to Jerusalem, to stop bloodshed. But the Cabinet forbade it.

At first it was not clear that a war was to break out. The enthusiastic celebration by the Jews in Palestine of their victory in the UN vote was followed by Arab rioting and the burning of the Jewish commercial centre of Jerusalem. Within a week the violence spread through the rest of Palestine. The Zionist leadership were afraid the United Nations would reverse the partition resolution if they saw the Jews crowing over their triumph or behaving aggressively. So the leading Jews prepared to resist attack, rather than launch it. The Palestinian Arabs took the initiative. At first neither side really believed the British would leave (their date of departure was not decided by the Cabinet until 4 December) and neither thought it possible that the British would cease to maintain law and order.

Most observers expected that the Palestinian Arabs would hold their own until, by the time of the promised British withdrawal the following May, the

Arab states would have equipped the Palestinians to fall upon the Jews and destroy them. However the Mufti found the Arab League less helpful than he had hoped. He asked it to form a temporary Palestine Government on the British departure, to transfer power in areas evacuated by the British to his own High Arab Committee, to appoint a Palestinian to its general staff, to finance the setting-up of an Arab administration in Palestine and to compensate Palestinians for war damage. All these requests were turned down. The Mufti's supporters knew how to shoot and to organise acts of destruction like those of the Arab Rebellion in 1936–9 but they lacked the ability of the Haganah to plan and co-ordinate operations, and they lacked both money and arms. Nevertheless in the early weeks of 1948 the Arabs dictated the pattern of the struggle, as they blockaded or ambushed roads to isolated Jewish positions and set off bombs in the towns. The Zionists responded in kind. The two communities were sizing each other up, waiting for 15 May 1948, when, if they were true to their word, the armies of the neighbouring Arab states would invade. Until then the British would be obliged to resist any invading army, an eventuality neither they nor the Arabs wanted.

One Arab army was powerful: the Arab Legion, the army of King Abdullah of Transjordan (the Amir having been promoted King by the British in return for his loyal support through the 1939–45 war). Transjordan remained a British dependency, even though it had become a nominally independent kingdom. It was not economically viable and was therefore able to sustain a well-trained army under the command of a British officer, Sir John Glubb, known as Glubb Pasha, only at Britain's expense. The cost was justified in a single action, when in 1941 Glubb marched part of the army into Iraq to put down a pro-German coup there – one of the turning points in the 1939–45 war. By 1948, the Arab Legion numbered fourteen thousand and was the best army of any Arab state.

Abdullah's intentions were therefore crucial. They were clear: he wanted a substantial slice of Palestine, partly to make his kingdom more nearly viable, partly to keep out the Mufti, whom Abdullah feared and disliked. Further, he was privately tolerant towards the creation of a Jewish state and negotiated to that effect with a Zionist representative, Golda Meir, who visited him secretly, in Arab dress. He did not want to fight the Jews but as peacefully as possible to secure control of the areas of Palestine allotted to the Arabs under the UN partition plan. He sent his Prime Minister to explain his intentions to Bevin, who (according to Glubb, who was present) replied, 'It seems the obvious thing to do. But don't go and invade the areas allotted to the Jews.'

Abdullah's acquiescence in a Jewish state, like his brother Feisal's acquiescence in a Jewish national home in 1919, made him the ideal ally of the British. If he could integrate the majority of the Palestinians into Transjordan, he might forestall the Arab–Jewish war that otherwise threatened. Abdullah's ambitions matched Britain's need. Transjordan, though poor, occupied a convenient position in the centre of the Arab heartlands where the King would continue to allow Britain to maintain military facilities.

As the British forces withdrew, usually without notice, from town after town, the Haganah was quick to step in with a Jewish army, police force and administration. In the areas allotted to the Jewish state, this was to be expected. But some Jewish settlements were in parts of the country allotted to the Arabs. If the Haganah was to defend these, they had to march into Arab areas. They found their justification for doing so in the Arab rejection of partition. As Yigael Yadin, chief of staff of the Haganah in 1947–9, remembered:

> The Arabs made their major mistake. If they would have accepted at that time the United Nations resolution, the Jewish state would have been perhaps as based on that partition. Once they broke the rules of the game, then there was no game.

A further justification for entering areas allotted to the Arabs was to secure strategic points which dominated Jewish areas – or might do so. Thus while the Arabs let off bombs and murdered Jews in the areas allotted to the Jewish state, their actions were mostly disorganised; the Jewish actions, by contrast, were comparatively well planned. Only one group of Jewish settlements, the Etzion block, was taken by the Arabs – and it was in an Arab area. Many Arab villages were conquered by the Jews.

In Jerusalem, defined by the UN as part of an international zone, a Jewish population of 100,000 was besieged. Jewish convoys bringing supplies up the

*Jewish inhabitants of Ben Yehuda Street, Jerusalem, flee from an explosion in February 1948 that killed fifty-one of them. The Jews blamed British soldiers, but Arabs later claimed responsibility.*

winding road from Tel Aviv were regularly ambushed. The Zionists decided they must secure the Arab villages that controlled the road. The Haganah were successfully completing this process when the Irgun and Stern Gang volunteered to capture a village near Jerusalem that was strategically less important, that had made a non-aggression pact with the Haganah and had abided by it strictly: its name was Deir Yassin. With Haganah approval, the Irgun and the Stern Gang captured Deir Yassin on 9 April 1948.

> Jerusalem [Yigael Yadin recalled] was one area in which there was co-operation between the Irgun and Haganah. The Haganah commander of Jerusalem was given latitude to work with the Irgun.

The Irgun, however, went farther than the Haganah commander can have thought possible. After capturing the village and reducing all resistance ruthlessly and indiscriminately, they paraded many of the inhabitants through the streets of Jerusalem, then took them back to Deir Yassin and murdered them. Those massacred included old men, women and children, in all some two hundred and fifty. The British commander, General Macmillan, was sufficiently shocked to contemplate breaking his own instructions to his troops by intervening, but refrained when the Haganah told him that they had taken over the village.

Already Arabs had begun to flee in fear from the areas allotted to the Jews. After Deir Yassin the exodus became a flood. Whatever else drove 750,000 Palestinian Arabs to flee from their homes – guns and radio broadcasts and the dynamiting of their houses – the terror inspired by Deir Yassin gave the strongest push. The scholarly Dr Weizmann later described the exodus of the Palestinians as voluntary and 'a miraculous simplification of Israel's tasks'.

Amidst the violence and the spreading chaos the British concentrated on leaving. They did their best to remove the vast quantity of military stores that over the past two years they had been busily ferrying into Palestine; inevitably some were illegally sold to one side or the other, according to the sympathies of a guard or the price offered. One group of British army lorries was parked in a Jewish area when bombs concealed inside were exploded, killing more than fifty. Nobody was prosecuted. In supposed retaliation for Deir Yassin, Arabs massacred a convoy of Jewish doctors and nurses on their way to Jerusalem.

British women and children were shipped out in February 1947; the officials followed early in 1948. Finally the British forces, concentrated at Haifa, gave all their attention to protecting themselves and preparing to depart. In May 1948 a small United Nations commission was admitted, nominally to oversee the succession and ensure that partition was carried through as the vote in the General Assembly had specified. But the UN commission had no arms.

> On 12 May 1948 [Yigael Yadin recalled] I was summoned by Ben Gurion to an emergency meeting of the temporary government of Israel. Ben

*David Ben Gurion reading the proclamation of the State of Israel, 20 May 1948.*

Gurion said to me, 'We are about to decide to declare the state of Israel, the moment the British quit on the 15th, but members here would like to know from you, as objectively as you can, without expressing your own feelings, whether a state should be declared or not. What are the chances of us defending this future state if the British leave and the Arabs invade the country?' I must say that this was the most difficult answer I've ever had to give. The gist of the answer was fifty-fifty; the whole thing was based on one hope. On 12 May we didn't have one piece of artillery, but some were on the way, and I said, 'If we manage to break through the British embargo and get the artillery pieces after 15 May, then I believe that the chances are even.'

In their final days in Palestine the British policy of even-handed inactivity was successful in its purpose. The last British were ignored and escaped without damage. The High Commissioner, General Sir Alan Cunningham, drove to the docks at Haifa in a car with inch-thick bullet-proof windows built to protect King George VI during the German bombing of London. All that he and his staff could do at the end was keep out of sight and seek to inform London what might follow their departure. Some reported that the Arabs would destroy the Jewish state before it was born. Others predicted that the Jews could look after themselves. The British left them to it.

The Government that in 1947–8 decided to cease operating and withdraw has been blamed for ignominiously abandoning its responsibility. The departure was not one of which the British could feel proud. But Bevin, Attlee and the Labour Cabinet were driven by Truman and the Zionists into facing facts which Eden, Macmillan and the Conservative Cabinet were to refuse to face eight years later when they invaded Suez: a moment comes when the wisest policy is to go quietly.

*On the quayside at Haifa the flag of the British rulers is lowered for the last time before they take to the boats.*

## After Independence

The British departure marked the start of a war which, almost forty years later, is still going on. Periods of non-violence have intervened; some speak of five wars, those of 1948–9 (post partition), 1956 (Suez), 1967 (the six-day war ending with the most dramatic Israeli expansion), 1973 (the Yom Kippur war, Egypt's attempt at recovery) and 1983 (the crushing of the Palestine Liberation Organisation in Lebanon). In the long view of history, however, these were not separate wars but merely the big bangs, the climaxes, in an unfinished saga which may yet prove to be a second hundred years' war.

The 1948–9 outbreak had two victors: the new state of Israel defeated the armies of Egypt, Lebanon, Iraq and Syria, thereby acquiring 77 per cent of the land area of Palestine instead of the 56 per cent the United Nations had allotted; and the Kingdom of Transjordan captured east Jerusalem and an area to the west of the Jordan River that had been allocated to the Arabs under the UN partition plan. The principal losers in this and the next thirty-five years of war were the Palestinian Arabs, who replaced the Jews as the dispossessed people who, insofar as mankind may be said to have a conscience, troubled it. Some 750,000 of them fled in 1947–8 from the emerging state of Israel, driven out first by the terrorism of the Irgun and the

Stern Gang, of which the official Zionist leadership claimed total innocence, and later by the actions of the Israeli army.

The Arab refugees rapidly acquired several of the characteristics of the Jews. Their experience in thirty years under British rule, during which many of them had benefited from living in a thriving Zionist economy, helped to make them the most sophisticated Arab workforce in the Middle East; the priority given to secondary and vocational education by the UN officials who ran the refugee camps increased their skills. Many Palestinians made their way to the Gulf states and Saudi Arabia. Like all immigrants, they had to use their wits and build their own success. Most of those who left in 1947–8 and in the subsequent explosive phases of the war were, however, trapped in refugee camps in Jordan (as Transjordan was soon renamed), Syria, Gaza and Lebanon; their misery was used by the Arab states as an advertisement of the iniquity of the Zionists, much as the DP camp inmates and the immigrant shiploads had been used by the Zionists themselves. All the Palestinians suffered political discrimination, as the Arab states, with the exception of Jordan, refused to grant them full rights of citizenship. The 100,000 or so who stayed in their homes and the 60,000 who, having fled, returned and lived under Israeli rule enjoyed the economic benefits of a western type of state. They also gained the vote and a few of them usually sat in the Israeli parliament; but even though they enjoyed more democratic rights than most citizens of Arab states, they were still second-class citizens

*Two Presidents, Harry Truman and Chaim Weizmann, May 1948. Truman is holding a Torah, a hand-written scroll of the five books of Moses in Hebrew, that Weizmann has given him.*

in their own homeland. These Israeli Palestinians and those who escaped to the Gulf states and Saudi Arabia were – along with the moneyed minority in Beirut and Amman – the best off. The majority, almost a million virtually imprisoned in camps, fed and housed by the UN, were filled with hatred for Israel, which would not let them return to their homes until, its Government said, the Arab states would agree to sign a peace treaty. They felt almost as bitter towards the Arab states, which had let them down in 1947–8 and refused as adamantly as the Israelis to allow them to settle in places where work and a normal life would be possible.

The conduct of the Arab states towards the Palestinians continued to be ambiguous. Outrage at the behaviour of the Zionists and their western allies remained the strongest feeling widely shared among Arabs. In the great cities of Baghdad, Cairo and Damascus, political leaders demanding justice for the Palestinians drew excited crowds and channelled popular energies that might otherwise have been troublesome. For most of the Arab governments, however, the Palestinian cause was not a high priority.

From time to time it was taken up vigorously by one of the Arab states, when its ruler decided to seek the leadership of the 'Arab nation' by proving his credentials over Palestine. Gamal Abdul Nasser had in 1948 fought in the ineffective Egyptian army of which Chaim Weizmann said 'its soldiers are too lean and its officers too fat'. Seven years later, when he had become President of Egypt, the Palestine refugees bottled up under Egyptian control in the Gaza strip gave Nasser his occasion. They had been conducting small raids into Israel, to which the Israeli army regularly responded with larger counter-raids. Nasser escalated this pattern, training *fedayeen*, saboteurs, mostly Palestinians but sometimes Egyptians, who in 1955 began to penetrate deep into Israel, blowing up installations, sometimes killing people. The raids were frequent and effective and widely known to be backed by the Egyptian Government. To Nasser's surprise Israel retaliated with an invasion across the Sinai launched in collusion with the British and French Governments.

The Zionist-imperialist conspiracy to invade Egypt in October 1956 (see chapter 5, p. 271) increased still further Nasser's standing among the Arabs and his commitment to back the Palestinians. Syria asked him to become its ruler in a joint state (a short-lived affair). In 1967 he again took the lead in provoking Israel to a war he did not expect, this time by ordering out the UN peace-keeping force that had been installed in 1956, advancing his army to Israel's frontier and closing off Israel's sea access to the south by placing guns at the Straits of Tiran. The other Arab states followed Egypt's lead in mobilising and Israel then launched what was seen world-wide as a pre-emptive air strike which destroyed the Egyptian, Syrian, Jordanian and Iraqi air forces on the ground and rapidly led to Israel's taking Sinai and the Gaza strip from Egypt, the Arab territories on the west bank of the Jordan river from Jordan and the Golan Heights from Syria. For the third time, the actions of the Arab states had led not to the Palestinians' getting their land back, but to Israel's acquiring more. This, the moment of Israel's greatest military triumph, was the time when magnanimity might have won peace. The Government of Israel chose not to be magnanimous. It thereby provoked a new body, the Palestine Liberation Organisation (PLO), founded a few years earlier as a tool of first Egypt and then Syria, into the same mixture of propaganda campaigns, extortion of funds, diplomacy and terrorism that the Zionists had used a few years earlier.

Publicly the Arab leaders swore to support the PLO – the hyperbole of many of their speeches on this subject is incandescent – but some of them found it necessary in practice to do the opposite. In Jordan in 1970 and in Lebanon in 1982 the principal purpose of the most powerful people in each state was to crush the Organisation. In each case the PLO had tried to use the country as the launching-pad to reconquer Palestine. But neither King Hussein of Jordan in 1968–70 nor the Government of Lebanon in 1978–83 wanted war with Israel. So the Palestinians formed alliances with radical Jordanians and later Lebanese to overthrow their governments. Each time a bloody civil war followed, the Palestinian fighters almost destroying the state before themselves being defeated and ejected. In the Lebanese case the main force that drove out the PLO in 1982 was the army of Israel, but the final blow came from a supposed friend, and the episode revealed the Organisation's fundamental weakness. Syria had long claimed to be the state most committed to the Palestinian cause, but after the PLO had been battered by the Israeli army the *coup de grâce* was administered by a Syrian-controlled wing of the PLO, which forced the Organisation's principal leader, Yasser Arafat, to relinquish his last foothold within striking distance of Palestine and flee by boat. Syria's President, Hafiz Assad, wanted a tame Palestine Liberation Organisation; it must not drag him into war with Israel at a time of the Palestinians' choosing. Like Jordan and Egypt, Syria wanted to use the Palestinian claim for its own purposes.

The abused Palestinians were thus in reality friendless. The oratory, the brotherhood of all Arabs, the warm embraces at airports and wherever cameramen were in attendance, served principally to conceal reality from militant young Arabs.

The Jews came to Israel with a reputation for scholarship, commercial skill and cosmopolitan worldliness, but not for ability in war. It was a surprise, therefore, when the Israel Defence Force proved itself to be more powerful than all the Arab forces. In the first thirty-five years of the new state it won repeated victories against apparently overwhelming odds. Each time the tally of military aircraft, tanks and manpower ranged against Israel suggested its imminent destruction. Each time daring tactics, outstanding intelligence and determination – and the disunity of its enemies – carried it through. The tiny state began regularly to supply Soviet guns, tanks and even aircraft captured in its battles against neighbouring Arab countries to the United States Defence Department, which thus acquired priceless exhibits and information.

Politically and economically Israel's progress was less spectacular but nonetheless impressive. Money raised from the diaspora – Jews throughout the rest of the world – helped to keep Israel solvent and the United States remained, except briefly under President Eisenhower, a generous ally, supplying vast quantities of military and economic aid. Nevertheless the bustling economy was permanently in debt, buying more western goods than Israel's exports could match. Politically Israel remained a democracy, with a free press, vocal and sometimes savage opposition freely expressed in Parliament and open, respected courts. When Palestinian Arabs were massacred by Lebanese Christians in the Sabra and Chatilla camps in Beirut in September 1982 in an area temporarily under the control of the Israeli army, a judicial inquiry was promptly demanded and held in Israel to establish the culpability of Israeli ministers and the Defence Minister was forced to resign. Few countries would have held such an inquiry in wartime.

In November 1977 President Anwar Sadat of Egypt flew to Jerusalem, met Prime Minister Menachem Begin and began a process which led to an Israeli–Egyptian peace treaty. In return Egypt received back all the Egyptian territory Israel had conquered. Thus thirty years after the British departure the first of the neighbouring Arab states formally recognised Israel's existence. This meant that in any future military confrontation with Israel, the Arab side was likely to lack its most powerful member. The other Arab states showed less will thereafter to resume active warfare. Arab governments continued to declare themselves the champions of the Palestinians but the plight of the dispossessed living in the camps, by now numbering well over a million, remained unresolved.

The story of Palestine from 1917 to 1985 is the story of two nationalisms provoked by the British. The Zionists until 1948 and the PLO from 1967 onwards were in many ways alike, each with its terrorists and its democrats, each with the heartrending appeal of its dispossessed people, each dependent on the self-interested support of distant governments. The Zionists, by chance, were twice useful to a major power: to the British to help secure the road to Suez in 1917–22 and to the American President to help win some elections in 1946–8. Those were the decisive moments in which the Zionists won their state. The Palestinians from 1947 onwards, by contrast, were merely used as a tool by the Arab states and Russia; they did not enjoy the extraordinary opportunity that twice came to the Zionists – to be needed by the most powerful.

# CHAPTER 3

# Malaya

It is said that Britain acquired many of its colonies in a fit of absentminded-ness. Of nowhere was this more true than Malaya. Thanks to the rubber tree, brought from Kew Gardens, the Malayan jungles were to prove the most profitable patch in the Empire. But at first the British did not want them. While south-east Asia contained many rich and desirable lands – the spice islands of Indonesia, the ancient empires of Cambodia and Thailand – the mainland of Malaya was regarded by the British as impenetrable jungle, definitely not worth possessing. All Britain wanted in the area was to maintain naval and commercial bases in the Malacca Straits, from which to dominate the substantial trade that passed through. When, in 1874, traders in the Straits Settlements clamoured for British protection in the Malay interior (where tin was beginning to be mined), governments in London, both Liberal and Conservative, refused to allow any money to be spent on so fruitless a venture. The Governor of the settlements, Sir Andrew Clarke, found a way to protect the traders on the cheap, by sending 'Residents' to the 'courts' of the petty-robber-baron Malay sultans. Thus, unknown to London, control over Malaya was acquired.

## Raffles, Rubber, etc., 1511–1945

The British Empire specialised in controlling the key bottlenecks of the world's sea-borne trade. Malaya lies between India and China, and the narrow sea along its western coastline, the Straits of Malacca, has been one of the principal such bottlenecks throughout recorded history. Trade between the Roman and Chinese empires went by way of the Malacca Straits as early as 160 AD. Overland caravans had followed the silk route from China to the Mediterranean for two thousand years and were regularly plundered by the many rulers and brigands through whose territory they passed. The sea route was vulnerable to piracy at fewer points, and by the sixteenth century European mariners, with their superior seamanship and guns, came to dominate these narrows.

The European colonial era in south-east Asia began in 1511 when the Portuguese besieged and captured the town of Malacca, strongpoint of the straits. For the next hundred years the Portuguese, with trading colonies at Goa in India, Macao in China and Malacca in between, dominated the eastern trade, particularly the spice trade. Then, in 1641, the Dutch captured Malacca from the Portuguese; they also secured control of most of what is now Indonesia.

Dutch domination of the Straits ended with the Napoleonic wars, when Holland fell to the French, making Dutch territory overseas fair game for Britain. By now the great competition for imperial power was between Britain and France. Napoleon tried to secure the shortest route from Europe to the east by taking Egypt, but was stopped by Nelson at the battle of the Nile. At the same time, Napoleonic vision was exercised on the British side by an obscure official of the East India Company, Thomas Stamford Raffles, Assistant Secretary to the Government of Penang, an island in the Malacca Strait which the British had taken in 1786 for use as a naval base (a role for which it was quite unfit). Raffles thought it vital for Britain to displace both the Dutch and the French in the trade with China and the spice islands. But the Dutch were Britain's allies against Napoleon and the needs of the alliance in Europe came first. When British forces took Dutch territories to keep out the French, as they took Malacca and Java, the Government in London promised that after the war all would be returned to Holland. Meanwhile Raffles, put in charge of the temporary wartime administration of Java, wrote long memoranda to his immediate superior, the Governor-General of India, explaining how essential was an enlargement of Britain's role in the area. His arguments failed to convince the East India Company's Court of Directors in London, and he was relieved of his post.

After the defeat of Napoleon in 1815, the Dutch were given back Malacca, Java and other colonies and signed treaties with the Malay sultans to make sure that British traders were kept out. To Raffles, it seemed that everything Britain had gained and he had dreamed of was being thrown away. He

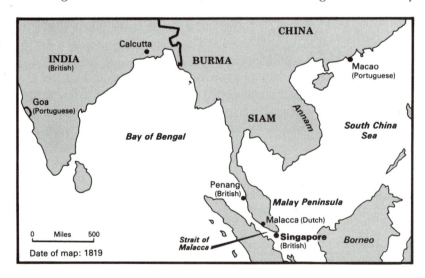

*Why Raffles chose Singapore.*

*Raffles – imperialist and renaissance man.*

returned to London where his scholarly interests had won him powerful friends. In Java he had collected manuscripts, carvings, textiles, plants, stuffed animals, insects and folk art, and he shipped home two hundred cases weighing more than thirty tons. His detailed work on his collection impressed the Royal Society, which elected him a Fellow. He wrote an encyclopaedic history of Java, which was published to great acclaim. He also sent home live animals from the Indies to be kept until a zoo could be opened and eventually became founder and first President of the London zoo (where his bust stood in the lion house until 1975). His celebrity led to his being taken up by the Prince Regent, who in May 1817 knighted him, much to the annoyance of the Court of Directors. Now, when he wrote to the Governor-General of India, Lord Hastings, he could not be ignored. On the contrary, he was invited to Calcutta, where he persuaded Hastings to pay for an expedition to the Malacca Straits, 'for permanently establishing British interests' over the China trade by developing a station on one of the islands. Raffles' letter of instruction said that he must 'abstain from all negotiation and collision' if the Dutch were established. Hastings reported this initiative to London and the East India Company's board immediately sent an instruction to Calcutta forbidding Raffles' mission: both cost and risk must be avoided. But it came too late.

The small island on which Raffles chose to establish his station was one where, until the fifteenth century, a walled city known as Singapura had stood. Scholars do not know whether Singapura was a city concerned in the

China trade or even who ruled it, and by the time Raffles arrived there in January 1819 almost all remains had vanished. The island had few inhabitants. It belonged to the Sultan of Johore, but the succession to that title was disputed. Raffles took a chance.

Governor-General Hastings had, under Raffles' persuasion, exceeded his orders in authorising the expedition. Raffles now exceeded even Hastings' order. One of the claimants to the disputed sultanate was already ruling the island, recognised by the Dutch and also implicitly recognised in some previous dealings by the British; he would never cede Singapura to Britain. So Raffles sent for the possessor's brother, who came to the island and nervously agreed – in return for promises of British protection and 5,000 Spanish dollars a year – that he was now the Sultan. He then granted the East India Company the right to maintain what was henceforward to be the British colony of Singapore. To mark the occasion, Raffles organised as splendid a ceremony as he could, with artillery salutes fired by sepoys and the union flag raised.

Since the Government in London had assured the Dutch that Raffles had no authority to make political settlements, and the new Sultan assured his dispossessed brother and the Dutch most humbly that he had signed his agreement with Raffles only under duress, the visionary's coup was vulnerable. But Raffles left a reliable officer in charge in Singapore with 340 soldiers and ten big guns and the Dutch decided it would be risky to attack him or the new Sultan he was protecting. The other arrangements that Raffles rapidly made won his imperial acquisition important new allies. He drew a plan of how the town was to be laid out, sought to encourage trade by making it duty-free and safe and had small traders recruited from nearby centres to serve the needs of the merchants and their agents from Calcutta and Canton. These men profited and gave the new colony their backing. The *Calcutta Journal* hoped the settlement at Singapore would receive the fullest support of government. Governor-General Hastings was faced, on the one hand, with orders from London to disown Raffles' treaty and, on the other, with evidence that the Dutch were not willing to fight and that British merchants welcomed the foundation. He decided he had been right to back Raffles and stood by his earlier decision.

Shortly afterwards, in 1824, the Dutch ceded Malacca to Britain and agreed to seek no territory or base in the Malay peninsula; in return, their hold on Java, Sumatra and the rest of the spice islands was reaffirmed. Thus in forty years Britain had acquired a useless island naval base (Penang), a well-fortified trading town whose harbour was to prove too shallow for the big ships of the nineteenth century (Malacca) and an island with deep water harbours at the narrowest point of the Straits (Singapore). These three places, ruled at first from Calcutta, were later removed from the Government of India and administered from London as a single colony, known as the Straits Settlements.

While the Straits were important, the hinterland of Malaya was valueless, permanently hot and wet, overgrown, impassable: a green wilderness with few inhabitants. The petty sultans and their few subjects, Muslims to a man, could not contact one another through the interior. Each sultan was the religious as well as the secular ruler of a primitive people and they had all established themselves astride rivers, over the control of which they squabbled and fought. There was little there to profit the British.

Since labour was scarce throughout Malaya, Raffles encouraged Chinese to settle in Singapore, which rapidly developed into one of the great ports of the world – a town of sailors and prostitutes, warehouses and traders, ship repairers and gamblers, mostly run by Chinese but under the law of Britain. Malacca and Penang prospered as lesser trading cities. And it was the traders, both Chinese and British, who asked for British intervention in the Malay sultanates, because their endemic disorder endangered trade. Tin had been discovered in many parts of Malaya and during the nineteenth century Chinese flocked into the country to mine it. This provided some lucky sultans with a new source of income and the others with new reasons for making war. Requests by Singapore merchants for British intervention to secure peace and, more especially, protection for themselves, redoubled. Governments in London refused either to act or to permit action, since pacifying the interior of Malaya promised expense without reward. Governors of the Straits Settlements were ordered to do no more than 'use influence' to bring peace. Then in 1874, when yet another merchant under British protection was the victim of river piracy in one of the Malay states, the Governor of the Straits Settlements, Sir Andrew Clarke, called the west-coast sultans to a conference and made them agree to accept British Residents at their courts whose 'advice must be asked for and acted upon in all questions other than those touching Malay religion and custom'. London found itself unwillingly assuming control.

Although the sultans remained formally in charge of their states, they were compelled to follow 'advice', which soon led to British officials running their revenue systems, customs, police, defence and development. In 1895 the four central states, Perak, Selangor, Negri Sembilan and Pahang, were formed into a federation under a unified administration presided over by a British High Commissioner, who was also Governor of the Straits Settlements. These four 'Federated Malay States' were now effectively run as colonies, and the remaining five sultanates soon followed, except that they were collectively known as the 'Unfederated Malay States' and the Englishmen whom their rulers had to consult were called Advisers instead of Residents.

The confusion of this arrangement at the formal level did not cause problems on the ground. Alan Lennox-Boyd, Colonial Secretary when Malaya became independent, recalled a conversation with Tunku Abdul Rahman, Malaya's first Prime Minister:

I said, 'You weren't a colony. Your brother the sultan of Kedah was an independent ruler in a treaty relationship with us.' The Tunku answered, 'That didn't stop you treating us like a colony.'

Mainland Malaya's second major source of wealth, following tin, was rubber. Seeds of the rubber tree were brought from Brazil and grown in the tropical-plant house at Kew Gardens in south London. From there they were brought to Malaya by Sir Hugh Low in 1877. The conditions were just like those in the tropical rain forests of Brazil. Plantations were hacked out of the jungle, and Malayan rubber came onto the market at the start of the twentieth century, just in time to provide tyres for early motor cars. Rubber was eventually to make Malaya rich. But it also brought problems. Clearing jungle was a huge task. Malay peasants were few in number and, given the ease with which they could grow food on their plots, little inclined to work for wages. So immigrant labourers had to be brought in to clear and later tend the plantations. From China shiploads arrived; Chinese labour-brokers paid their fares; in return these 'coolies' had to work for any employer chosen by the brokers. Workers came in equal numbers from India but, by agreement with the British Government of India, they were mostly repatriated after fixed terms of service. Malays too came into the peninsula, from Sumatra across the Straits. Between 1900 and the 1939–45 war, with the exception of a few years of slump, Malaya's expanding tin and rubber industries, combined with the growing trade and industry of the Straits Settlements, especially Singapore, attracted immigrants in a constant flow.

A Malay walking down the main street of Kuala Lumpur, the administrative centre of the Federated States, or any other Malay town, saw shops and banks entirely dominated by Chinese. The same was true of tin mines, of the few factories and even of some rubber estates. In any competition calling for modern skills or professionalism, the Chinese rapidly outpaced the Malays. The rural Malays were the kind of people who might have needed protection anywhere in the world; their leaders learned of the fate of the north American Indians and dreaded it. One British administrator described his role idiosyncratically as that of curator of a 'Malay museum'. Whether peasants or fishermen, the Malays expected periods of inactivity in the year, for sport, religion and social life; they placed little value on individual initiative or the competitive ethic. The overseas Chinese, by contrast, were among the most forceful, ambitious, mutually supportive and fast-moving immigrants on earth. Many Chinese arrived in Malaya poor, worked ceaselessly and saved and drove themselves and their families until they became millionaires. Malays did no such thing. And while the Indians were mostly shipped back to India, too many Chinese, so far as the Malays were concerned, stayed in Malaya. By the end of the Second World War, of a total population in Malaya (excluding Singapore) of five million, more than 38 per cent were Chinese; 50 per cent Malay; 11 per cent Indian. To the Malays, the Chinese seemed to be taking over the country.

The Malays' resistance to this threat was built round their traditional

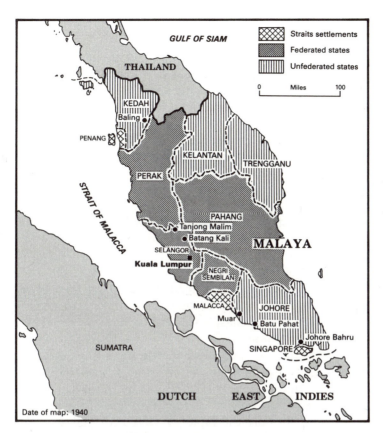

GULF OF SIAM

THAILAND

KEDAH
Baling

PENANG

KELANTAN

TRENGGANU

PERAK

PAHANG

Tanjong Malim
Batang Kali

MALAYA

SELANGOR
Kuala Lumpur

NEGRI
SEMBILAN

STRAIT OF MALACCA

MALACCA

JOHORE

Muar
Batu Pahat

Johore Bahru

SUMATRA

SINGAPORE

DUTCH    EAST    INDIES

Date of map: 1940

0    Miles    100

*The administrative jumble that was British Malaya, until the Japanese arrived in 1941.*

Islamic political structure. The Sultans were their protectors, making sure that jobs in government service went to them and not to Chinese, making sure that citizenship was their automatic right but denied to non-Malays and non-Muslims, preserving land ownership rights for Malays only. And until the 1939–45 war British colonial policy supported these conservative tendencies, designed to protect both the Malay way of life and the Malay political structure. That, the British considered, was the way to avoid trouble.

Malaya was the colony celebrated by Joseph Conrad and Somerset Maugham, its European plantation managers and their wives compelled, so they said, to live in enormous bungalows because, just north of the equator, space was essential to let the air circulate; compelled to follow a slow, fixed, daily routine, with lots of drink, because in such heat and humidity it was the only way to survive; compelled to have lots of Chinese servants, because the place was simply too enervating for a white man to fend for himself; and fortunate to have the Chinese because, though inscrutable and sometimes unnerving, they were the cleverest and most efficient servants and, when one suddenly decided to invite a few friends home for dinner after tennis at the club, one's Chinese cook could instantly perform wonders.

The British built at Singapore a great naval dockyard, the biggest single item of expenditure by the British Government between the two world wars, a rock-solid guarantee, it was thought, of the security of the area. When the war started in Europe in 1939, Singapore, eight thousand miles away, felt itself impregnable. Business continued as usual, loading rubber and tin into the cargo ships at Singapore, playing music for the dancers at Raffles Hotel, servicing the sailors and the commerce. When two great British capital ships, the *Prince of Wales* and the *Repulse*, reached Singapore late in 1941, they symbolised the certainty of British protection. The *Prince of Wales*, the latest British battleship to be completed, had been selected by Prime Minister Winston Churchill himself to take him to Newfoundland to meet President Roosevelt and sign the Atlantic Charter. What greater assurance could be given?

But a shock was in store for all the people of Malaya. In December 1941 Japan launched simultaneous bombing raids on the United States Pacific fleet in Pearl Harbor and on the British Far Eastern naval bastion of Singapore. That same night Japanese boats approached the Malayan east coast and landed the first small spearhead of an invasion force. The two great British ships set out majestically at night to put a stop to this impudence. Together they sailed up the coast towards Thailand, where they were seen from Japanese spotter planes.

The theory of that time was that a battleship's guns would see off an attacking aircraft, that most of the bombs and torpedoes dropped would miss and those few that hit would be deflected by the ship's armour-plating or else the damage would be contained within one of the great watertight compartments. Furthermore the Japanese were little yellow men who wore glasses and could not pilot a plane properly, let alone dive-bomb. So Malaya should have been safe. But the theories proved false, as did the British promise to protect the peoples of Malaya. Both great ships were sunk in a single day, the Japanese landed with ease on the Malayan mainland and swept down within seven weeks from north to south, defeating the British, Australian and Indian troops who tried to stop them until, on 15 February 1942, they reached Singapore, where 130,000 British Empire troops surrendered to 50,000 Japanese. Prime Minister Winston Churchill described it as: 'The greatest disaster and worst capitulation in the history of the British Empire.'

For the next three years, the Japanese ruled Malaya. The Malays could hardly be blamed for co-operating with them. The Japanese in 1941–2 defeated the British, the Americans, the French and the Dutch, removing in little over four months all the colonial empires in south-east Asia which had taken nearly four hundred years to build up. This confirmed what their defeat of Russia in 1905 had suggested, that they were the new great power throughout Asia: what point resisting them? The Chinese in Malaya had even less choice. Japan had entered the world war primarily to complete its conquest of China, ruthlessly and cruelly pursued since 1935. Through Burma the United States Government was sending supplies to China, and these the Japanese had to stop. Malaya was therefore conquered principally as a strategic necessity to enable Japan to cut off the back door to China. To

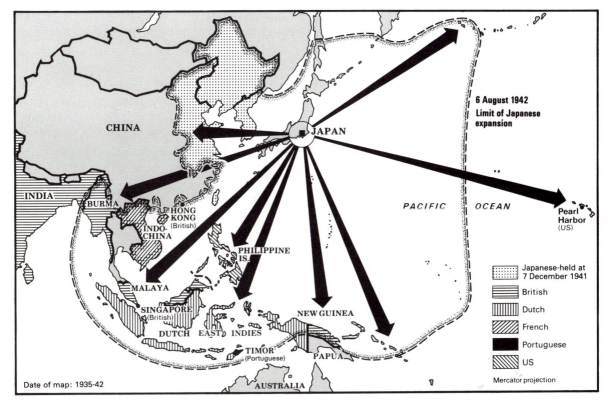

Date of map: 1935-42

CHINA

INDIA

BURMA

HONG KONG (British)

INDO-CHINA

MALAYA

SINGAPORE (British)

DUTCH EAST INDIES

TIMOR (Portuguese)

PAPUA

AUSTRALIA

JAPAN

PHILIPPINE IS.

NEW GUINEA

PACIFIC OCEAN

Pearl Harbor (US)

6 August 1942
Limit of Japanese expansion

Japanese-held at 7 December 1941

British

Dutch

French

Portuguese

US

Mercator projection

Japan, every Chinese was a potential enemy. The atrocities committed by Japanese against the Chinese in Malaya were among the greatest horrors of the Second World War, greatly exceeding even those they committed against Indian and British prisoners of war who worked for them as slave labour. For the Malays, however, the Japanese Co-Prosperity Sphere offered promise: Japan had plans to create a unified state comprising most of Malaya and Sumatra, uniting peoples of the Malay race from both the British and Dutch colonies. Only as the war advanced and the Japanese failed to keep their promises did the Malays become disillusioned.

Japan's victories over the European empires encouraged a determination among almost all the peoples they ruled to be rid of their western masters as soon as the war ended. In Indonesia, Malaya's immediate neighbour, the Dutch were never allowed to re-establish themselves. In Vietnam the French made more determined efforts than the Dutch to reassert their authority, but Ho Chi Minh and his comrades resisted fiercely and finally the French surrendered at Dien Bien Phu in 1954. In Burma, Malaya's north-western neighbour, the nationalists who had joined forces with the Japanese demanded immediate independence and separation from the Commonwealth, and Attlee, Britain's post-war Labour Prime Minister, recognised that their demand must be met, even though others in the British Government disagreed. Thus, partly inspired by the Japanese, the countries of south-east Asia rejected colonialism. The only country in the region where the former colonial masters were welcomed back, with spontaneous and enthusiastic

*Almost four hundred years of western empires were conquered by Japan in four months.*

demonstrations, the only country where the Europeans settled securely to their old desks, as Governors and Residents, Departmental Secretaries and District Magistrates, was Malaya. No clearer evidence could be produced that British rule was genuinely acceptable to most Malays, if only because the British protected them from being politically as well as economically dominated by the Chinese. Likewise British rule was genuinely acceptable to most Chinese in Malaya, because the British protected their wealth and enterprise from the resentment and intermittent violence of the Malays. The small Malay nationalist party demanding that, like the Dutch, the British should be ejected was easily suppressed.

## The Red Menace, 1945–1960

Throughout the British Empire's declining years the great threat to its survival was widely thought to be the international Communist movement. White settlers on their farms in Kenya and Rhodesia, Nyasaland and Tanganyika, white officials in Cyprus and Aden, the Gold Coast and British Guiana, declared whenever things went badly wrong that there was a red under the bed. A nationalist leader had only to show a mild interest in Marx or Moscow to be at once branded a Communist. British newspapers like the *Daily Express* and the *Daily Telegraph* continued to declare, year in year out, that the Empire was under siege by Communists. A noisy section of the Conservative Party at Westminster professed the same view.

The Empire did indeed appear an obvious target for international Communism. Not only was Britain the original centre of industrial capitalism; the Empire was Lenin's prime model of the exploitation and oppression of subject peoples for the benefit of a distant, acquisitive ruling class. If Communist theory was right, the colonies should have fallen in rapid succession, like rotten fruit, to the forces of progress. Stalin knew well, from his membership of the wartime triumvirate, that the Empire had been greatly overstretched, that Churchill was desperately dependent on Roosevelt's support, both military and economic, and that Britain would have difficulty, after the war, in reasserting its imperial authority. Here was the opportunity for him and for the monolithic international movement he was supposed to control.

It was to be expected, therefore, that as the Communists continued to spread revolution worldwide, they would choose at least one area of imperial weakness to attack. Russia's enormous post-war gains in eastern Europe, with Communist regimes newly established by 1948 in East Germany, Poland, Rumania, Bulgaria, Hungary, Czechoslovakia, Yugoslavia and Albania, seemed about to be matched in Asia. By 1948 many governments in Asia and the Communists there thought the moment of confrontation had come. British colonial administrators were significantly less corrupt, inefficient and cruel than other regimes in the area, but the mere fact that they were European colonialists seemed to place them in the path of historical inevitability. The Communists appeared to be making impressive advances in China, Indonesia, the Philippines and Vietnam. They were not alone in thinking that victory was likely. The United States Senator Joe McCarthy claimed that the Communists had gone so far as to take control of vital aspects of the Government in Washington – and for a while many Americans seemed to believe him.

If a co-ordinated Communist policy had been at work, Malaya would have been a good target from the Soviet point of view. It was far and away Britain's most profitable colony. In the late 1940s and 1950s, Malaya was the source of nearly a third of the world's natural rubber and tin, providing in both cases the most sought-after grades. These commodities brought huge export earnings, particularly US dollars, which Britain desperately needed after the war. A successful Communist thrust in Malaya threatened a vital British interest.

The Malayan Communist Party (the MCP) had few Malay members. Its supporters came almost entirely from among poor, immigrant Chinese. It was to prove a dangerous, ruthless enemy, although its early history suggested no great menace. In the 1920s and 1930s Communist emissaries from Russia, China and Vietnam made repeated efforts first to set up, then to strengthen the MCP, but the British police seemed to know most of what was afoot and usually forestalled serious trouble. The Secretary-General of the MCP from 1936 to 1947, Lai Tek, although he built up a highly efficient cell system throughout Malaya, is reported by the most authoritative historian of the subject, Anthony Short, to have been an agent of both the British and the Japanese – whichever was in power. His appointment is described as a 'brilliant success' for the British police special branch in Singapore. He enjoyed surprising escapes. On two occasions secret meetings of the top officers of the party were raided and his colleagues were arrested, while he was spared through being unavoidably late. During the wartime occupation he used to drive in a Japanese car from Singapore over the causeway to mainland Malaya to meet Communist colleagues who were running a jungle-based resistance movement against the Japanese. And when eventually the party's central committee started asking awkward questions about him, he conveniently vanished (possibly to Hong Kong and then Thailand). The party's subsequent report accused him not only of treachery but of embezzling funds.

In 1941 the small, well-organised MCP, nominally the enemy of the British Empire but efficiently penetrated by its agents, offered to join the war on the side of the English-speaking imperialists. Until then the Hitler–Stalin pact had caused Communists throughout the world to side with the Germans. But when Hitler invaded Russia, Moscow ordered Lai Tek and his party to help fight Hitler's allies, the Japanese. Early in 1942, the British took up the offer. With Japanese forces sweeping through Malaya, British officers gave hurried training to some two hundred Communists who were to

set up jungle camps from which they would disrupt Japanese communications. Over the next three years this guerilla force grew to 7,000 men, armed
by the British and trained and advised by a small team of Britons who lived
with them in the jungle.

One of this tiny group of jungle-dwelling British guerillas was later to
become famous throughout Malaya. John Davis had been a Malayan police
recruit before the war and was made a Captain in the Special Operations
Executive. Later he described what happened:

> During the Malayan campaign the Communists, who were an illegal
> party in Malaya, offered their services to the Government because now we
> were all in the same battle. They suggested that they had a number of
> young Chinese who might be very useful fighting as guerillas or as
> resistance forces.
>
> I was seconded to help in their organisation. We took bands of young
> Communists who had been trained by British instructors in Singapore
> and put them up as close as we could to the Japanese lines, in order that
> shortly afterwards, with the Japanese coming down, they would be
> overrun. They were hiding in the jungle, and then they could start
> fomenting the resistance movement behind.
>
> In April 1942, we arrived in India. No information had been received
> from Malaya whatsoever after it fell to the Japanese. There was a
> complete blank. The only thing to be done was to devise some plan for
> getting back to the country, to find out how the resistance movement was
> going and to further it if that was possible. The only way to get back to
> Malaya at that time was by submarine and the only submarines that were
> available were Dutch ones. So I found myself with five stalwart Chinese
> preparing to land on the Malayan coast. The Dutch submarine dropped
> us about five miles from the shore and we went off in canoes. We had one
> slight alarm on the way when we were surrounded by motor boats and I
> thought 'My God, the Jap patrol boats,' but then the penny dropped: of
> course they were the local fishing boats going out. And as we neared the
> shore after an hour or so, the lovely spicy warm smell of the Malayan coast
> and the swishing of the jungle trees almost overwhelmed one and we
> didn't think any more of being two thousand miles from our friends, we felt
> we were just coming home again where we had lived for many years. We
> went ashore and we hauled the boats up into the jungle above, to hide
> them, and then we went and had a bathe. We were extraordinarily sticky
> after ten days in a submarine.
>
> We Europeans couldn't leave the jungle, we couldn't be seen outside. So
> we were totally dependent on our own Chinese. They made contact with
> the local Communists. The deal was that the Communists would obey
> allied instructions in fighting the Japanese and on the British side we
> should supply arms, medicines and personnel for training and liaison.

The Malays, following their spiritual and secular rulers, the Sultans, were not inclined to join any organisation dominated by Chinese. By and large they kept clear of the Communist Party. So John Davis spent the war hidden and protected by Malayan-Chinese Communists, one of whom, a young commissar named Chin Peng, became particularly friendly with him. A strong mutual respect combined with a careful avoidance of talk about politics brought the British officer and the young Chinese to a relationship of trust.

The Second World War exhausted the British in all parts of the Empire. In Malaya they were defeated and humiliated, and when, in August 1945, American atom bombs caused Japan to surrender, the country was left without an administration. Many British officials were in Changi jail on Singapore island and other jails or camps where the Japanese had kept them since 1942; others were in India or dead. No British or allied forces reached Malaya – except the half dozen liaison officers like John Davis – until two weeks after the Japanese surrender.

The local Communists, sweeping aside their British advisers, tried to take advantage of this gap. On learning of the surrender they strode into many Malayan villages as the conquering heroes. But they had not prepared for such a sudden end to the war, did not have a plan ready to govern the whole of Malaya and soon found themselves displaced by the returning British, who not only had such a plan but also enjoyed good relations with the traditional Malay rulers.

The British were not as firm in repressing their erstwhile allies as some would have wished. A few Malayan Communists were invited to London to take part in the parade before King George VI to celebrate victory over Japan; some were decorated; all who had fought as guerillas (and who handed in their weapons) received a campaign medal and 250 Malayan dollars (about £45 at that time) – a poor return, they thought, for three years in the jungle. As Guy Madoc, Deputy Director of security services in Malaya in 1945–8, put it:

> We all had a rather silly attitude about the Malayan Communist Party. We knew that it had fought on our side during the war, or had been prepared to fight. We knew that it had most loyally looked after people like John Davis, and other liaison officers. And it seemed it just would not be public school to treat that lot as the enemy.

Some of the British weapons supplied to Communists were not returned, and the Communists had captured many Japanese weapons that were also not handed over. British and Malay police found some, hidden in dumps in the jungle, but there were more. It was a time of violence and revenge. Chinese Communist guerillas slaughtered many Malays and some Chinese traders who they thought had collaborated with the Japanese. Some Malays brandishing their *kris* ran 'amok' in reprisal. Order was not restored for many months.

The Communists did not immediately use against the British either the

*Chin Peng, the Communist guerilla leader, in Singapore to receive the thanks of the British Empire from Admiral Lord Louis Mountbatten.*

weapons or the training in guerilla warfare that the British had helped them acquire. They changed their manifesto, however. During the war the MCP's nine-point programme began with objective '1: To drive the Japanese fascists out of Malaya.' Immediately the war ended the words 'Japanese fascists' were replaced by 'British'. The Communists' purposes were plain: the British had to be removed because they took an undue share of wealth and power, lived in ostentatious luxury and treated other races as their inferiors; the Muslim sultans had to be removed because they were reactionary, autocratic landlord-rulers, and the get-rich-quick Chinese millionaires had to be removed because they exploited the masses.

The Communists began their effort to drive out the British by taking over trade unions and organising demonstrations and strikes. The new Labour Government in London wanted to encourage trade union activity in Malaya. They also wanted to treat the Malayan Communist Party as a wartime ally deserved. So the party, which had been illegal before the war, was now free to organise meetings, publish pamphlets, win converts. The MCP apparently believed for a while that they could topple the Government by such methods as disrupting tin mines and rubber plantations and demanding public demonstrations on the anniversary of the fall of Singapore. Gerald Da Cruz, a member of the MCP at the time, recalled that Chin Peng and the party leadership were determined to bring about economic chaos:

> Instead of calling for individual strikes as we'd been doing before, we were going to call for nationwide strikes by occupation. All the rubber workers would be pulled out, Malaya's major industry. Then all the tin workers would be pulled while the first strike was unsettled. So you would have the two major industries crippled. Then we would call all the transport workers out, then we would call all the dock workers out and the country would be, after a few months, in a state of total economic chaos. And, mind you, through the Pan Malayan Federation of Trade Unions, eighty per cent of the workers were under the direct control of the Communist Party of Malaya.

These activities were nuisance enough to convince the Government that the MCP must be banned and failure enough to persuade the new Secretary-General of the party, Chin Peng, that a resort to guerilla warfare from jungle bases was the only way to drive the British out. The Government's decision to ban the MCP and the MCP's decision to go underground and to use all-out violence were reached independently in mid-1948.

The British had not been blind to the need to win over the Chinese, including the Communists. When they returned to Malaya at the end of the war they had set about trying to create a new Malayan citizenship that would give a fair deal to the Chinese residents, not least the ex-guerilas. In London during the war a Cabinet committee under the chairmanship of the Deputy Prime Minister, Clement Attlee, had overseen the preparation of new constitutional proposals for Malaya. Instead of an untidy disarray of three tiny colonies (the Straits Settlements) directly ruled from London and nine small states (federated and unfederated) formally ruled by traditional Malay sultans but under British 'protection', Attlee's committee proposed a unified state to be called the Malayan Union with Singapore administratively separated from it and governed from London as a strategic colony and military base. And instead of the old Malay states' citizenship, open only to Malays, Attlee's committee proposed citizenship open to all, including the immigrant Chinese. Equality under the law was a principle in which the British believed; equal citizenship for the Chinese was a right that had been earned; and it seemed useful to tie the wealthy Chinese merchant families closely to the administration. When Attlee became Prime Minister, he sent the head of the Colonial Office's wartime planning unit for Malaya, Sir Edward Gent, to be governor of the new Malayan Union and to introduce equal citizenship for all.

The scheme failed. The Malay sultans would have none of it. They boycotted Sir Edward Gent's installation, boycotted the Malayan Union, demanded the return of their traditional status and flatly rejected equal citizenship for the Chinese. Opposition to the Malayan Union became the first cause to arouse the Malays, mostly kampong (village) dwellers with a slow, settled lifestyle, to political action. The fertile industrious Chinese, already more than a third of the population of Malaya and commercially and intellectually dominant, had long been the Malays' greatest fear. Their principal protectors against the Chinese had been the sultans. Now suddenly the British were introducing changes which at once offered full citizenship to the Chinese and removed the formal sovereignty of the sultans. The Malays felt threatened.

The Malay response amazed the British. This normally sleepy and acquiescent people, who had allowed their states to be taken over and run as virtual British colonies without a fight, who had come out to cheer when the British returned as colonial rulers at the end of the war, now showed an iron political will. They came to meetings in their thousands; they held together to press a single policy line; and they gave overwhelming support to a new body created to respond to the threat, the United Malays National Organisation. UMNO grew from nothing into a powerful political party not only because of the support it enjoyed from the Malay sultans and the vast bulk of the Malay population, but also because it had the other requisite for success: organisation. This was provided by Malay Government servants. Throughout the Malay states, the small Malay middle class was heavily dependent on government jobs, which were in effect reserved for Malays. Now almost all the Malay civil servants devoted their organisational skills to building up UMNO and opposing the policy that had arrived from London. Led by Dato Onn bin Ja'afar, the adopted son of the Sultan of Johore, UMNO mobilised almost the entire Malay population. They did not demand independence, or that the British must go. Dato Onn considered the Malays to be backward and in need of help from a sympathetic British administration to protect their interests: too sudden independence would mean the Malays being dominated both economically and politically by the Chinese. An UMNO resolution mourned 'the loss of faith and confidence of probably the only race in the world today who would voluntarily remain loyal to the British Empire'. UMNO's opposition to the British was restricted to the Malayan Union proposals, and against these the Organisation and the Malay rulers used every instrument of resistance available to them, including, as their ultimate deterrent, some aged ex-Advisers, Residents and Governors, retired to Britain's home counties, who insisted on seeing the Colonial Secretary in Whitehall and wrote angry letters to *The Times*. Under this bombardment, the British Government capitulated. The Malayan Union – and with it equal citizenship for the Chinese – was abandoned.

Instead a Malayan Federation was created, with the sultans' sovereignty and limited powers restored, citizenship reserved principally for Malays, and British colonial-type rule evidently to continue for a long time. The objectives of the new federal constitution, as approved by UMNO, the sultans and the British, included the following: 'That the new arrangements should, on a long view, offer the means and prospects of development in the direction of ultimate self-government.' No hurry in these words, and no pressure.

Equal citizenship rights would not have won over the Communists to support the colonial government; but, although most Chinese in Malaya were apathetic about political rights, citizenship was attractive to some of them and its withdrawal made them more responsive than they would otherwise have been to the Communist argument that nothing could ever be gained from the British except by force. They had been robbed of their promised reward.

In February 1948, the month in which the Federation of Malaya came into being and six months after India's independence, two conferences of Asian Communist parties were held in Calcutta. Some European Communists attended and strongly encouraged their Asian colleagues openly to revolt. Such verbal encouragement, unsupported by either money or arms, was not decisive, but violent outbreaks nevertheless followed in India, Burma, Indonesia and Malaya. In June 1948, the British Commissioner-General in south-east Asia, Malcolm MacDonald, the senior British official in Malaya and Singapore from 1946 to 1955, spoke on Radio Malaya of Communist agitators making a desperate attempt to impose the rule of gun and knife. Soon after, three leading Chinese anti-Communists were shot in daylight in

*Malcolm MacDonald, front row centre – in bow tie, with a group of businessmen in Kuala Lumpur.*

Johore and three European planters were killed on rubber estates in Perak. The British Government declared a State of Emergency. This lasted twelve years and was really a war, but since the insurance policies of the many businesses in Singapore and Malaya contained clauses suspending them in time of war, the Government throughout denied that a war was in progress. It was always 'the Emergency'.

The MCP's technique, from early 1948, was to hide its few thousand fighters in the jungle and, by quick sorties, to kill rubber planters, tin miners, policemen – any isolated lackeys of capitalism. If they could keep this up for long enough, it would become impossible for the British to find new recruits for these jobs, so they would withdraw.

To understand what followed, it is necessary to know a little about the Malayan jungle. Malaya is in one of the world's three areas of tropical rain forest (the other two are the Amazon basin in Brazil and the Congo basin in West Africa). Rain is heavy throughout the year; the heat is constant and equatorial; plants grow everywhere and fast. But the richness of the growth does not lead to an abundance of nuts and fruits. The trees grow tall and crowded, leaving a dark, wet atmosphere below in which a lost human being soon dies – of hunger, disease or the bites of tropical insects, his blood sucked by leeches, his skin reduced to a blue-white pastiness by the steaming half-light. Although the British – with the manual labour of the Chinese and Indians – had cleared parts of the jungle to plant rubber trees, four-fifths of Malaya remained primeval jungle, dangerous to man. So when the MCP decided to take their guns and withdraw to the jungle they needed friends outside, to supply them with food, clothes, ammunition and information. Although it was frightening to be a rubber-plantation or tin-mine manager, isolated and liable to be murdered in one's bed or shot while patrolling one's estate, it was no less frightening to be a guerilla, hungry and prone to disease in the hot jungle gloom. The guerillas' supply and information systems were vital. Whoever controlled these systems would win the war.

The guerillas began with the advantage. During the 1939–45 war, the extreme Japanese brutality to the Chinese had caused many Chinese labourers to flee the towns and villages and settle in the jungle fringes, where they had cleared patches to grow vegetables, keep pigs and eke out a subsistence. These small communities of 'squatters' beyond the convenient reach of the Japanese were also out of sight of the returned British administration. They were perfect targets for jungle guerillas' demands for help – as indeed they had been during the war. So long as the squatter villages survived unsupervised by the British, individual guerillas could withdraw into them for brief periods of relief from the jungle; food could be bought or, more usually, extorted; information could be obtained – some of the squatters were now working, once again, on rubber plantations and under pressure would reveal the managers' movements. Security was enforced by terror: squatters believed to have given information to the British were flayed alive and left tied to a jungle tree to be slowly devoured by the insects, or sometimes tied between two trees whose recoil slowly stretched them apart.

The early advantage of the Communist terrorists (CTs as the British called them) was reinforced by the post-war weariness of the British. The police were demoralised. The British officer put in charge of the Malayan police in 1948 reported that, even after the Emergency had been declared, central and subordinate police headquarters regularly closed down overnight from 6.30 pm to 8 am and between midday Saturday and 8 am Monday. And when they were open to receive news of a CT attack, the police stations had no radios with which to call for reinforcements. One was overrun by CTs; several others were closed down. By early 1950 the guerillas were murdering more than a hundred civilians a month and the police seemed powerless to prevent them.

Some managers of rubber estates, feeling exposed and unwilling to risk their lives, quit; one, amid considerable publicity, was given a police escort to Singapore airport and retired to Australia. Estates with Chinese managers were a particular problem because the police were less vigorous at providing protection to Chinese-run than to British-run plantations, and some Chinese planters, observing the rising tide of Communism in their homeland as well as in Malaya, put their money on the favourite. Many Chinese-run rubber plantations, and a few British-run, paid the CTs regularly to keep away.

*An armed planter with his bullet-shielded car.*

The main problem for the British was that they had little intelligence about the CTs – where they were, where they might strike next, who was helping them. So the army's attempts to capture or kill terrorists were usually unsuccessful. Indeed at first the army's ideas on how to combat jungle terrorists came largely from an official handbook published in 1906, based on the campaign against the Boer guerillas in South Africa. The soldiers attempted large 'sweeps' through the jungle, which merely obliged the CTs to withdraw into neighbouring parts until the sweep was over. Europeans in Malaya became increasingly worried. Some, whose view was taken up by an English-language newspaper, the *Malay Mail*, demanded public executions and an end to civil rights: catching the enemy – or the suspected enemy – at any price.

*A principal reason for the end of empires: in a free society it is all but impossible for governments to keep massacres secret. Recent research in Batang Kali puts the number killed at twenty-four.*

This mixture of impotence and impatience led to some vicious conduct by the British forces, who routinely beat up Chinese squatters when they refused, or possibly were unable, to give information about CTs. The worst known case was the murder of twenty-four Chinese villagers by Scots Guards at Batang Kali in Selangor in December 1948. After this massacre of innocent civilians, the military and civil bureaucracies conspired to conceal the facts, claiming first that the twenty-four killed were guerillas (an improbable tale when the army was failing to find any guerillas at all), then that they were men who had been detained and were trying to escape. These fabrications were believed in Britain, but among the Malayan Chinese the massacre became well known: twenty-four men whose deaths cried aloud for

# The People

No. 4598     Sunday, February 1, 1970     8d.

## British guilt revealed

## HORROR IN A NAMELESS VILLAGE

ON DECEMBER 12, 1948, at a nameless village in a clearing deep in the Malayan jungle, a patrol of the 2nd Battalion, The Scots Guards, shot and killed 25 suspected terrorists they had held prisoner overnight.

Officially the villagers, Chinese plantation workers, died while ⸺o escape. But for 21 years the memory of the massacre has ⸺ of the men who took part and today the truth can be told.

shoulder as he did so. I think he must have known he was going to get shot.

"When he had gone about ⸺wards, Douglas dropped to ⸺e, aimed his rifle and ⸺outh in the back. He ⸺ to me or go to ⸺e youth was dead. youth on the ⸺ and his ⸺ ⸺ hu

### Why we are publishing this report

WE PUBLISH this report without any satisfaction, but in the certain knowledge that it is our duty to do so.

It arose because of a "Voice of the People" article in our issue of November 30, attacking Mr. George Brown.

Commenting on the Pinkville massacre in Vietnam, he had said: "I suspect there are an awful lot of spectres in our cupboard, too."

We called upon Mr. Brown to produce the evidence, or withdraw the slur. And we gave

that in either of the two world wars or since any such crime as Pinkville has been committed by British soldiers.

"If any such evidence were produced, we and other newspapers would search out the truth relentlessly."

After reading this Mr. William Cootes came forward and told us his story. We have, as promised, searched out the truth relentlessly.

It is not the story of another Pinkville. Women and children were not killed in cold blood. All of them in the village were spared. But what happened is appalling enough in all conscience.

that this unhappy story would be best left untold so many years after the event. But a newspaper has a simple duty to its readers which is best summed up in the Biblical phrase "Know ye the truth."

The truth, in this case, illustrates—as at Pinkville and elsewhere—the corrupting and fearful effect of war on otherwise decent men, and what can happen when the highest standards of discipline are allowed to fall.

That is the lesson, and it can never be taught too often.

There is nothing unusual about the men who took part

in the crime. One ⸺ another they told us, in most moving terms, how it preyed on their minds since, and how relieved are to get it off their truth.

It is falsely said that truth never hurt anyone. At least in this case it prevent such an act ever committed again by soldiers, with all the d⸺ it did not only to the ⸺ but to the soldiers them⸺

Robert Edw⸺

E⸺

justice, which the British denied and which, many argued, only the Communists could bring. (The facts did not come out in Britain until an investigation by *The People* newspaper led to questions in the House of Commons, twenty-two years later.)

In October 1951, when Attlee's Labour Government was defeated in the general election, the outgoing Colonial Secretary, James Griffiths, said of Malaya: 'It has become a military problem to which we have not been able to find the answer.' The new Prime Minister, Winston Churchill, promptly sent his Colonial Secretary, Oliver Lyttelton, to inspect the country. It was a bad moment. At the beginning of the British election campaign the Communists had shot dead the British High Commissioner, Sir Henry Gurney, in his official Rolls Royce as he was travelling to a resort in the hills. And 1951 was the year the terrorists killed the largest number of security forces (504) and even more civilians (533). Following the Communists' victory in China in 1949, their Malayan allies were widely thought to be unstoppable. Churchill and Lyttelton responded by appointing as the new High Commissioner not another Colonial Service official but General Sir Gerald Templer, a former Director of Military Government in Western Germany.

Templer was a tense, nervous man with a crisp manner and a high-pitched voice, who seemed to have buzzing engines within, driving him into constant physical, mental and social activity. He barked orders and jabbed people in the stomach with his cane. He insisted on seeing everything for himself, travelling to parts of Malaya no Governor had ever visited before. Stories about him abound. When he arrived at Government House and the entire staff stood in line to meet him, he inspected them, briskly saying a few words to some, and then announced that he was going to inspect the staff quarters. An official quietly told him that Governors did not normally inspect the staff quarters, especially without warning. 'Well this one does,' said Templer. He found that many of the staff lived in shacks in a kind of shanty town behind Government House. He ordered that the lot be bulldozed within a fortnight and replaced with modern sanitary dwellings. A second story concerns his attempts to make the administration more vigorous. He ordered no golf on weekdays. His reputation caused his order to be obeyed without question near his headquarters. But a District Officer in a remote up-country post could not believe that it was meant to apply to him. He played, word got back, and within days he found himself on an airliner back to Britain.

Templer's first concern was the war. A mere five thousand guerillas were tying down a huge force of British and Commonwealth troops, a quarter of a million at the peak of the emergency, the largest group being Malay Special Constables. The MCP guerillas, for a time outnumbered fifty-to-one, were constantly replaced, at the rate of about 1,600 a year, making up for those killed, captured or persuaded to surrender. For the British soldier, it was unpleasant to be eight thousand miles from home, carrying a heavy pack and weapons through the stifling jungle, seeking the elusive but dangerous CTs.

One national serviceman (i.e. a conscript), Roy Armitage of the Manchester regiment, described his experience:

> On long jungle patrols it was atrocious. Apart from all the insects, animals and such like, you were fighting the CTs. It was not often that contacts were made, but when they were the action lasted only for a few minutes (before the guerilla was killed or captured, usually killed). You lived very rough, slept in hammocks. Washing facilities were non-existent, unless you crossed a river or stream. When we came out, after three or four weeks, the drivers who used to pick us up insisted that we smelt absolutely vile, from undergrowth and non-washing and jungle sores.

In capturing terrorists, propaganda was almost as important as soldiering, as Hugh Carleton Greene, Head of Emergency Information Services, Malaya, 1950–1, explained:

> My main task was to increase surrenders in order to get more information, more killings and thereby more surrenders. Over an area of many thousands of square miles we dropped about two million leaflets offering the CTs safe conduct and assuring them that they would be given treatment for their diseases and so on, if they came out. We knew that they were interested in money and many of the people who came in got rewards and set up as small capitalists and are probably quite wealthy people in Malaya today. In one case in the state of Selangor, the second in command

*Templer strode rapidly through villages, his British civil servants often struggling to keep up.*

of one of the Communist units came in carrying a sten gun in one hand and his commanding officer's head in the other. He got quite a lot of money for that.

Guy Madoc, by now promoted Director of Security Services, commented:

It was quite extraordinary to all of us, European officers and Asians alike, how completely these prisoners lacked loyalty. The moment they came out of the jungle, we would say, 'Right, we're going to give you a good dish of food and you're then going to tell us exactly what you know: how many camp sites and paths you know. Then you're going back in with us to attack them.' And they were quite happy to do it.

Many were hungry and ill and desperate to escape from the jungle.

Templer's arrival is widely held to mark the turning point in the Malayan Emergency. By appointing a general and giving him virtually dictatorial powers, Churchill's Government showed that they meant business and Templer left no one in any doubt that he was taking all the decisions that mattered. For example, two months after he arrived, the main water pipeline into the town of Tanjong Malim (population 20,000) was cut by CTs. Of the twelve-man repair party, eleven were killed or wounded, again by CTs.

*Templer addresses the citizens of Tanjong Malim.*

None of the townspeople admitted to knowing anything about those responsible; indeed most of them were probably both angered by the cutting-off of their water and shocked by the murders. Templer came to Tanjong Malim, had the elders assembled and said, 'It does not amuse me to punish innocent people, but many of you are not innocent. You have information which you are too cowardly to give. Have some guts and shoulder the responsibility of citizenship.' When they still gave no information, Templer imposed a twenty-two-hour curfew. For only two hours each day were they allowed out. He further cut the town's already tight rice ration. He then distributed questionnaires for all households to complete, promising that only he would open them and that afterwards he would destroy them; nobody would know who had given information about the CTs. The curfew lasted thirteen days; not much information was received; the few arrests that followed did not lead to any charges for membership of the murder gang. But Templer had shown who was boss; his many admirers from Malaya in those days point out that Tanjong Malim had a peaceful record for the rest of the war; and the whole of Malaya had been given a warning. Complaints were raised in the House of Commons in London, but Templer could dismiss them contemptuously because he was backed by the Government with its secure majority after the recent election.

Templer's military strategy was largely that of his predecessors. (The Cabinet ruled, soon after he arrived, that his forces must stop decapitating enemy dead to help identify them: hands must be taken instead.) The CTs' attacks on rubber planters had already, by the time of Templer's arrival in 1952, become less effective. The rubber companies and the Government provided armed guards, the plantation-managers' houses were fortified, police visits and telephone links were organised, and helicopters were used to

*Tanjong Malim under curfew. The only thing that moves is a police truck.*

*In 1952 helicopters were brought into use in the jungle war, to drop troops behind the Communists.*

guide the specially trained jungle platoons. Luckily for the British, the Malayan Emergency began within a month of the end of British rule in Palestine. Consequently many ex-Palestine policemen were available to be shipped in. They had deficiencies – they were accused of being too rough – but they had recent experience of being fired on by both Arab and Jewish terrorists, which meant that their reflexes were conditioned for anti-terrorist action. It was partly thanks to their arrival that rubber and tin exports were maintained in spite of the murder of many who worked on the plantations and mines and of the constant strain on those who survived.

The principal technique in fighting the war was 'resettlement'. The vital need of the CTs, isolated in the jungle, for supplies and information from the squatters on the jungle fringes provided a challenge for the British military planners. This was met by what came to be known as the Briggs plan, after Sir Harold Briggs, the Director of Operations before Templer. Squatters were all to be moved into 'new villages' where they could be supervised by the police and thus prevented from helping the CTs. It was an ambitious policy that would eventually require shifting half a million people, most of whom, understandably, objected. Before Templer came resettlement had begun, but he brought extra money and drive. A community of squatters would be surrounded in their huts at dawn, when they were all asleep, forced into lorries and settled in a new village encircled by barbed wire with searchlights round the periphery to prevent movement at night. Before the 'new villagers' were let out in the mornings to go to work or to their paddi-fields, soldiers or police searched them for rice, clothes, weapons or messages. Many complained both that the new villages lacked essential facilities and that they were no more than concentration camps. The description of a national serviceman, William Rees, conveys something of their early disorganisation:

> Some of the villagers were so frightened of the Communists that they were paying them and passing things through the barbed wire. In one village the wire was actually cut and rolled back sufficiently to allow a three ton vehicle to drive through. Yet the villagers insisted they hadn't heard a sound. So my company commander briefed me to take the platoon down and harass them, as if to say, 'You can't serve two masters. You're going to get it one way or the other.' This was to unnerve those people so that they were more worried about us than they were about CTs.

Slowly Templer revealed a velvet fist inside his iron glove. Indeed those who had feared the danger of authoritarian government if a military man were put in charge of Malaya – and Malcolm MacDonald, Britain's Commissioner-General in south-east Asia, was one of them – were relieved when Templer's most famous remark in Malaya proved to be: 'The answer lies not in pouring more troops into the jungle, but in the hearts and minds of the people'. He is remembered above all for his 'Hearts and Minds campaign'. Following policies laid down by MacDonald, he pressed for the concentration-camp character of the new villages to be minimised. He sought to make sure that they had facilities such as running water, medical centres and schools (largely financed by lotteries which, with Government encouragement, the Chinese ran themselves). He made sure the Chinese could acquire title to the land they occupied, thus giving them a permanent stake in the villages. Above all, he involved the Chinese ex-squatters in the government of the villages, so that, by the time he left in 1954, two hundred village councils, most of them popularly elected, were imposing limited local taxes and spending the revenue on road-making and other works.

By the time of Templer's arrival, the police, thanks to a rapid seven-fold expansion of the force to 41,000 regulars plus 100,000 voluntary auxiliaries,

most of them extra Malay constables, had greatly restricted terrorist activity. But that was not enough, as Templer recognised. Most of the police had no experience of normal policing – of service to the community, showing sympathy to law-abiding citizens, helping with everyday problems. So Templer's new police commissioner, Arthur Young, had as his principal task making the Malayan police less of a force and more of a service. By 1952, following the start of the Korean war, rubber and tin prices had boomed and Templer was able to inject the money thus made available not only into maintaining the force of the Government's measures, but also into significantly increasing services to the community generally. Once enough of the Chinese in a new village came over to the Government's side against the CTs, not only could the severe restrictions on them be lifted but they could be brought into the Home Guard and themselves armed. This last stage had always been envisaged as the final part of resettlement, but until Templer came it was mostly theoretical. The decision that the Chinese inhabitants of a new village had abandoned their allegiance to the CTs (or were safe from their threats) and were now ready, first, for a share in their own government and, second, to bear arms, was always a risky one, but taking the risk was the only way finally to win the war.

The way to convince the Malayan Chinese that Communist propaganda was untrue was to do what the Communists said the British never would do: place both the powers of local government and guns in villagers' hands. And the same thing happened on the larger scale. To defeat the Communists,

*A public-address van brings advice to resettled Chinese in a 'new village' in Selangor, 1951.*

Britain was now to give Malaya independence (though the British army stayed on afterwards to make sure nothing went wrong). Where normally the decision to grant independence to a colony was taken by the British Cabinet, in this case it crept up on the Government in London as a result of the tactics in warfare adopted by the men on the spot.

Such a topsy-turvy sequence of events arose partly from the absence, until late in the Emergency, of any powerful Malay demand for independence. While colonial governments were swept from India and Burma, Ceylon and Indonesia, the jungles of Malaya remained politically backward. Thus, although the British Cabinet acknowledged as early as 1944 that British rule could be re-established in Malaya only if the country was launched on the road to independence, the absence of pressure from the Malays between 1945 and 1948 meant that this intention did not have to be implemented in a hurry. Then, when the Malayan Chinese Communists in 1948 turned on the pressure, ostensibly to win independence for Malaya, a quarter of a million Malays in the police and the army supported the British against them, and many died in the fighting. The war drove the Malays into siding with the British, first, because of their long-standing fear of the Chinese and, second, because they were Muslims and therefore opposed to the godlessness of Communism.

A guerilla war cannot be won without widespread popular co-operation. In order to cut off the CTs from their own community, the Government had encouraged the setting up of the Malayan Chinese Association, a body of rich Chinese to provide anti-Communist leadership and to raise money for social services (its initials, MCA, were widely held to stand for Money Collecting Association). These efforts to encourage political organisation and social welfare among the Chinese led to resentment among the Malays, who in turn had to be given political and social benefits that were at least as good. So in the end the war brought political advance to Chinese and Malays alike.

This was the opposite of the policy that came from the top. Oliver Lyttelton, when he visited Malaya as Colonial Secretary in 1951, made it plain that 'the restoration of law and order in Malaya has first priority and political reforms must come after that'. Similarly the Cabinet's instruction to Templer on taking up office in 1952, while stating that 'Malaya should in due course become a self-governing nation', went on: 'The British Government will not lay aside their responsibility in Malaya until they are satisfied that the Communist terrorism has been defeated.'

Political reform came before terrorism had been defeated because it was a necessary step towards achieving that very defeat. As we shall see, the Malayans (i.e. Malays, Chinese, Indians and others resident in Malaya) found themselves whistled through the stages of constitutional advance, first represented (by people of their own races nominated by the High Commissioner) on the federation's War Council (1950), then voting in local elections (1952), then voting for more than half the seats in the Legislative Council in a federal election (1955), and finally, with the legislative still only half elected, becoming independent (1957).

The 1948 Federal Constitution, which the Malays had demanded to replace the Malayan Union, contained no provision for democracy. The High Commissioner was nominally the King's representative to the sultans, to assuage their hurt pride and to calm their followers, but in fact he was a Governor with full authority over a largely centralised state. His Executive Council was chosen entirely by him and only he had the power to submit questions to it. The members of the Legislative Council likewise were chosen by the High Commissioner. The slight hint of democracy in the preamble to the Federal Agreement, promising elections and eventual self-government, carried no date and was not acted on quickly. Instead the High Commissioner in 1951 introduced the 'Member system'. This replaced some of the officials, who had hitherto headed all government departments, by Members of the Legislative Council. Three Malays were able to get their first experience of top-level policy-making, the most senior of them, Dato Onn bin Ja'afar, being made Member for Home Affairs. They were not ministers, they were not elected, but, in the midst of the Emergency, when some of them had complained at their exclusion from the Federal War Council, they became part of a system which helped forestall any possible dissension in the Malay–British alliance.

The Member system was a success. British officials retained the portfolios of economic affairs, defence, Chinese affairs, industrial and social relations and railways and ports; so the new, appointed Members had none of the most sensitive departments. But they co-operated loyally with the Government and took responsible decisions. That was success from the British point of view. And when the Members, their appetites whetted, asked for more authority, it was granted in the form of powers roughly ministerial. That was success from the Malay point of view.

The next step, voting in local elections, came before demands for it were pressed by either the Malay or the Chinese settled communities, partly because the British needed maximum local co-operation in the conduct of the war, partly because, with all Malaya's neighbours by now independent, the British felt the need to push forward the country's education in democracy.

The larger step of nationwide elections for seats in the Legislative Council was handled in typically British fashion by choosing a large committee of Malayans to advise. This produced a Legislative Council of 99 members of whom 52 were to be elected – a sure prescription, UMNO leaders thought, for the elected seats to be divided between parties, leaving power with the officials. But when the first federal elections were held in 1955, a totally unexpected result made independence possible far faster than anyone had expected.

In the words of Sir John Martin, a Colonial Office official centrally involved in the negotiations, the leaders of the Malays had independence given to them 'on a silver platter'. It had to be so, because they did not have a Gandhi or Nehru, a Nkrumah or Kenyatta to lead them in pressing the British to go. In the End of Empire story, Malaya is an oddity. The two principal Malay leaders in the years preceding independence, Dato Onn bin Ja'afar and Tunku Abdul Rahman, enjoyed some political triumphs, but these more often reflected the strong Malay racial jealousy towards immigrants, especially the Chinese, than any real pressure to get rid of the British.

Dato Onn bin Ja'afar, the Mentri Besar (Chief Minister) to the Sultan of Johore until 1950, was the first and more impressive Malay leader. Onn's great victory was to force the abandonment in 1948 of the Malayan Union with its equal-rights-for-Chinese constitution and its reduction of the traditional powers of the Sultans. His party, the United Malays National Organisation, was both the first Malayan political party and the focus of the common allegiance of almost all Malay civil servants, whether working for the British Government or for the nine Sultans. Thus UMNO had the makings of much more than a political party: it was potentially like the Communist party in Russia or the Broederbond-Nationalist party alliance in South Africa, a state within the state. But Onn soon decided that UMNO's primary role as an association for the protection of Malay communal interests was not sufficient: for the needs of the future of Malaya, the party had to be multi-racial.

In the thinking that led towards this decision, though not in the decision itself, Onn was greatly influenced by Britain's Commissioner-General in south-east Asia, Malcolm MacDonald, who reappears at several key points in the End of Empire story, always bringing the principal nationalist leaders and the British Government closer together, always trusted by both, always discreet or silent in public. His job placed him above the Governors of Singapore and British North Borneo and above the High Commissioner in Malaya. MacDonald was not merely the son of Britain's first Labour Prime Minister, Ramsay MacDonald, but his confidant. He was an MP and close to the centre of affairs when his father formed a National Government in 1931, destroying the Labour Party as a political force for a decade, and he later served as both Dominions and Colonial Secretary. He had lived through the ruin of a political party and the decline of a great political career when saving the national economy had seemed to his father and himself more important than saving their party. He is widely remembered in Malaya for his voice, which was exactly like Charlie Chaplin's, and for his easy-going personal lifestyle, well represented by a famous photograph of him with two bare-breasted Dyak women. When newspapers published this picture, the dismay of most colonial officials was outshone by MacDonald's glee.

MacDonald respected Onn as the man who had rapidly built UMNO into a national party with sufficient power to cause the British totally to reverse policy on the post-war system of government for Malaya. He was grateful to

Onn for not using UMNO to bring out the Malays in anti-British demonstrations and violence comparable to the anti-Dutch violence that brother Malays were taking part in across the Straits in Sumatra. And he considered Onn a political leader of such force and independence that he was unlikely ever to be regarded as a tool of the British: his leadership of the Malay defence campaign, creating a Malay national movement, had been a political *tour de force*.

MacDonald's principal concern was to help the Malays and Chinese (and the Indians and other races in Malaya) to learn to work together in government, so that the country could be handed over to an administration that would not be immediately destroyed by racial violence. He was therefore anxious to have Onn take a course similar to that which he believed his father had taken in Britain in 1931: to shift from being the leader of a party and an interest within the state into being the unifying force for the state as a whole. Ramsay MacDonald had failed. His son had now to help Onn to succeed.

The instrument through which he made the attempt was called the Communities Liaison Committee (CLC), which MacDonald invited leaders of the various communities to attend in private to sort out matters that could split the country. Over possible electoral arrangements, over jobs in government, over education, over control of the economy, the interests of the different racial groups clashed. MacDonald used the CLC not merely to teach the leaders of the communities the art of compromise, but also to draft proposals for government: whatever was acceptable to all the communities' representatives on the CLC was likely to work. Onn threw himself enthusiastically into the business of the committee. His standing among the Malays was so strong that he could lead them to make substantial concessions when doing deals with the other races. Also, as a result of a CLC proposal, he became chairman of a Government-funded development authority to help Malays increase their share of the country's commerce.

Before long, influenced by these experiences, Onn decided to broaden UMNO into a party to which not only Malays but also Chinese and Indians could belong. He consulted MacDonald, expecting his support. Instead MacDonald warned him that the Malays would not welcome non-Malays into their party, that the proposed multi-racial party was an attempt to go 'too far too fast'. Onn set aside the Commissioner-General's advice and pressed forward with his campaign. But the majority of UMNO members rejected his non-racial approach and insisted on the slogan 'Malaya for the Malays'. So Onn resigned and – in a daring political gamble – set up a new multi-racial party. That was the end of Onn as a popular political leader. He enjoyed continuing support from the British, notably from Malcolm MacDonald; and his party was consequently heavily represented on Government-nominated bodies, like the Legislative Council; but the Malays cared more than anything else for protection from other races, and Onn's pleas for inter-communal tolerance and co-operation seemed to most of them merely a threat to expose them to unfair competition from the Chinese and Indian immigrants.

UMNO had been Onn's creation and when he left no leading Malay could be found to replace him. The party seemed likely to disintegrate in confusion. Eventually an improbable and apparently second-rate choice, Tunku (Prince) Abdul Rahman, was invited to take over the leadership. He was a long-established playboy who, although younger brother of the Sultan of Kedah, had occupied only a junior position in the Kedah administration. At Cambridge he had earned the lowest number of marks possible for a pass degree; at the Inner Temple he took twenty-five years to qualify as a barrister, partly because he preferred horse-racing, dog-racing and dancing to the law. His principal strength was his membership of a ruling family. Though Kedah was the most northerly of the Malay sultanates and the Tunku himself was half Thai, a prince was, in the eyes of the Malays, a man to follow.

At first the Tunku did little to rebuild UMNO. He was an uninspiring speaker and a poor administrator. 'Malaya for the Malays' was the party slogan and the Tunku accepted it. Most British officials did not take him seriously. A playboy prince leading a party of racial exclusiveness was hardly a serious candidate for the post they wanted filled: Malaya's leader to independence. The British continued to back Onn. The racial divisiveness of UMNO after Onn's defeat was a serious worry for senior administrators, who had spent a significant part of their working lives suppressing inter-communal violence (usually taking the form of Malay *kris* sharpened for use against Chinese).

The Tunku, however, surprised the British. Like Onn, he came to realise that Malaya must be a multi-racial state. The many British administrators who came to Malaya from Palestine brought with them the warning that people who refuse to come to terms with recent immigrants may lose their land. When a local alliance was agreed between the Selangor branch of UMNO and the Malayan Chinese Association to fight one of Malaya's first municipal elections, in Kuala Lumpur in 1952, the Tunku backed it. This was not a multi-racial party like Onn's but a temporary trans-communal arrangement that most political observers did not expect to do well. But the Tunku had judged things right: the Malays trusted him – as they had long trusted the Sultans – to protect their interests; and because it was clear that UMNO remained a separate party, able to campaign on its own again if Malay concerns failed to receive first priority, the vast majority of Malays voted for the Alliance, as did sufficient Chinese to secure clear majorities in nine of the twelve Kuala Lumpur municipal constituencies.

This success led Templer, with MacDonald's backing, to co-opt the Tunku onto his Executive Council. The new Member often failed to read the papers for meetings and consequently either had nothing to say or spoke irrelevantly, when Templer promptly reproved him. But the Tunku travelled constantly round Malaya, kept in touch with Malay opinion and so was able to perform the main task of a politician: voicing the feelings of those he represented. He also built on the unexpected success of the Alliance in the Kuala Lumpur election, encouraging UMNO–MCA alliances in local elections in the towns of Johore Bahru, Muar, Batu Pahat and Malacca, and later in the states of Johore and Trengganu. Each time the Alliance won a majority of the seats, soundly beating Dato Onn's multi-racial party. These victories increased the Tunku's standing and he moderately asked whether the time had not come for elections to the Legislative Council; after all, by now Kwame Nkrumah was Leader of Government Business in the Gold Coast, which had had elected Africans in its Legislative Council since 1925. Templer's reply was to ask him to submit two names for 'Members' of the administration. The education of the Alliance for political responsibility was under way.

With the war in the jungle by now going increasingly well for the Government, the Tunku felt the need to keep pressing for elections to the Legislative Council. He discussed with his fellow Alliance leaders whether, like Gandhi and Nehru, they should back their demands with boycotts and disruptive demonstrations, so that the British would have to put them in prison. When in 1954, after long consultation, the British proposed elections but with a large proportions of seats in the Legislative Council still to be nominated by the High Commissioner, the Tunku thought here at last was the issue on which he could prove his anti-colonial credentials. He threatened (and even gently launched) a boycott of public office by all UMNO and Alliance members, demanding that a sufficiently large majority of the Legislative Council members be elected to ensure power for the largest party without having to seek the support of 'officials'. The Colonial Office was flummoxed: it was standard procedure and thought to be rather clever to begin progress in central legislatures by compelling the party most successful at the polls to seek the support of nominated members, thus restraining excesses inspired by the hustings; then, when the political parties had learned to take charge of the administration, they could progress to straightforward majority rule. Oliver Lyttelton, the Colonial Secretary, was not prepared to rush things. The Tunku addressed some meetings and blustered for a while but, over whisky, Templer's successor as High Commissioner, Sir Donald MacGillivray talked him out of his boycott and thus deprived him – in spite of much heart-searching – of his chance to go to prison.

In the first federal election, held in July 1955, the Tunku showed his qualities not only as a tireless campaigner but also as a loyal ally. He had agreed with Tan Chen Lock, the leader of the MCA, that the Alliance would put up a candidate for each of the 52 seats: 35 Malays, 15 Chinese and two Indians. In proportion to the electorate, this was generous of the Tunku: of the 1,280,865 voters, 1,077,562 or 84 per cent were Malays, many of them little inclined to vote for a Chinese candidate. So the Tunku raced round the country, urging Malays to vote for the Chinese who were standing on the

Alliance ticket. He faced Malay xenophobia almost everywhere and he stood up publicly to oppose it. He was an honest, likeable, slow-spoken man who earned people's trust. His improbable Alliance of three communal parties won 51 of the 52 elective seats.

This result led to the Tunku's being made Chief Minister and to the Alliance's forming the first representative government of Malaya – subject, of course, to the High Commissioner's supervision. The election also placed the Tunku in a new light for the British. Where once he had been the irresponsible leader of a Malay racial party, he emerged now as the one leader who could carry Malay voters into an alliance with the other two main racial groups, so probably containing inter-communal violence. If he could do that, he was the man to lead Malaya to independence. He was thus in an extraordinarily strong position when, shortly after the election, the Communists asked for peace talks.

By now the resettlement of the squatters in 500 'new villages' had greatly increased the difficulties the CTs faced in obtaining food and information. The British army had learned how to deal with jungle guerillas, primarily by winning the confidence of the population and thus securing the intelligence that enabled the huge Government forces to surround and capture the tiny guerilla bands. And the creation of the Alliance Government, to which the British soon announced that they would hand independence, robbed the Communists of one of their principal claims – that only they could remove the British. Chin Peng, the Communist leader, decided his party must get onto the new Malayan political stage before either the British and their new Alliance allies defeated him militarily, or the Alliance, by leading Malaya to independence, acquired overwhelming authority. The Tunku agreed to a meeting, hoping to secure a Communist surrender and thus the end of the war, and John Davis was brought in as 'accompanying officer' to give some personal reassurance to his former comrade, for whose capture alive the then enormous reward of £30,000 had been offered. Davis describes this remarkable episode:

> It was about Christmas 1955 that I found myself up at dawn on top of a tin mine at Baling in Kedah and we waited. We were surrounded with troops as a precaution. In half an hour, a couple of red-shirted figures with their guns appeared. It was rather a thrill to see them again, particularly as I hadn't got to shoot them, as we would have had to do if they'd come our way for the last several years. And behind them emerged Chin Peng, moving very slowly. He came up to me and we greeted each other in Cantonese and shook hands and strolled up the path to the waiting vehicles. It was rather terrifying when we got back to the entrance because these talks had rather hit world publicity and large crowds of people had turned up, and there were journalists and cameras clicking. Chin Peng was very changed from when I'd last known him. He'd become very much bulkier and heavier. And it was quite obvious after a short time that that

was not mere fat. It was oedema from beriberi, which I think was somewhat to his credit. Many rumours had gone around about how he was just living it up in Siam in complete comfort. This obviously was not true. He, a true leader, was still sticking by his men.

*John Davis (in front, half hidden by a soldier) leads Chin Peng and his guerillas to the Baling talks, December 1955.*

A newsreel commentary of the time is less cool:

> And then the Communists escorted by Mr John Davis, the famous Force 136 guerilla leader and former colleague of Chin Peng during the Japanese occupation. All necks crane for a glimpse of the number one terrorist. There he is, that's him, Chin Peng, the man responsible for a brutal seven-year campaign of murder and terrorism against the ordinary people of Malaya.

Chin Peng came to the talks with a weak hand. He offered to disband his forces if the Communists could take part in the normal political process in Malaya. Tunku Abdul Rahman turned him down, insisting on unconditional surrender and the disbanding of the MCP. His memory of how the Malayan Communist Party had used the normal political process in 1945–8 persuaded him that they were not to be trusted now. 'I was glad to meet him,' the Tunku said, 'because it became quite clear he is Communist, I am anti-Communist. And the two of us can never work together. On that basis we ended our talks.'

John Davis describes what followed:

> It was then that Chin Peng and I got down to a jolly good talk. We got a considerable amount of our old companionship coming back. He said, 'I

know that the Tunku said there was to be no talk of terms, it was only to be surrender; I admit I know that. But you see, when people come out to talk, you always give a little bit, take a little bit, you always do it that way. And I assumed completely that he would. I can't understand why he didn't give way a little bit.' And of course Chin Peng had fooled himself from the very beginning. He was aiming, although completely beaten in the emergency, to start gaining on the political scene straight away, by some good concession. Next morning, just after dawn, we took him down to the jungle edge, which was lined at the front by British troops, and I said 'Look, I'll go with you into the jungle for any distance you like as a *bona fide* that nobody's going to shoot you in the back.' And so off we went into the jungle and walked I suppose two or three hundred yards with him and his guerillas – rather nice, rather like the old days with him – until he stopped and said, 'Well, thank you very much, that's enough, we'll go on now. And I'll send a couple of men to see you safe back.' And I was able then to say to him: 'You don't think that I need to be escorted in our own jungle do you?' And he laughed and said, 'No, not really, I don't think so.' And we shook hands, quite friendly. I turned back, wandered back to the camp and that was the last I've ever seen of him.

The Tunku and David Marshall, the Chief Minister of Singapore who was also at the talks, thought that John Davis's accompanying Chin Peng was essential to save his life. Both recalled that, once the talks were over, the British military commanders planned to shoot Chin Peng as he was walking back into the jungle and were convinced that but for John Davis's presence they would have done so. Naturally the British deny this. Chin Peng soon resumed his guerilla war and his men continued into the mid-1980s, though with diminishing frequency, to kill Malayans in remote jungle areas.

By rejecting Chin Peng's plea, the Tunku showed himself to be a man the British could trust to keep up the pressure on the Communists, even after independence. Though his civil servants found him not very diligent at reading the briefs they put before him, and despite his tendency to make mistakes when announcing policy, obliging officials to scurry about correcting what he had said, he was sound on the essentials: first anti-Communism, second inter-communal co-operation and third, the importance of the free enterprise system (which meant he was likely to protect the interests of British and Malayan companies that invested in the country).

In return for his service as the best available man to take over Malaya – and, with British help, to complete the biggest victory yet achieved over a Communist guerilla insurgency – the Tunku demanded and obtained one parting gift: the preservation of Malay privileges. The British had long favoured a fully equal citizenship for all permanent residents in Malaya. They had tried to introduce it in 1946 with the Malayan Union but were defeated by Dato Onn, UMNO and their nationwide demonstrations and boycotts. So the 1948 constitution and its subsequent amendments maintained protected status for the Malays and disabilities for non-Malays. With independence in prospect, the British prejudice in favour of equal rights for all again reared its threatening head. But this time the Colonial Office, not wanting to get into another dispute with the leading Malays over this sensitive issue, caused an independent constitutional advisory commission to be set up under Lord Reid, widely regarded as the leading House of Lords judge of his generation, with judges and constitutional experts from Britain, Australia, India and Pakistan. They went to Malaya to take evidence, heard the UMNO case for protected status for the Malays, booked themselves into a fine hotel in Rome, where they could write their report immune from the pressure of any interested party, and came out in favour of full equality under the law.

The Malays were horrified. Given the rapid Chinese birth rate, the Reid report threatened them with the prospect of being outvoted and dominated once again. The Tunku had no choice but to demand that the British Government, in drafting the independence constitution, reject Lord Reid's non-discriminatory proposals and substitute protection for the Malays. Malay was to become the sole national language and Islam the state religion. The Tunku won on all points, largely because he persuaded his Alliance partners, the Malayan Chinese Association and the Indian National Congress, that they must support him, even though these changes adversely affected their communities. They did so because they were the smaller partners in the Alliance (neither of them very effective at getting its racial group to the polling booths) and they knew that the Tunku, like Onn before him, could lose his position in UMNO if he did not ensure the preservation of Malay privileges. From first to last in the history of the end of British rule in Malaya, the Malays, the largest community, were more concerned to maintain their protected status than to expel the British.

Malaya's progress to independence, by way of the defeat of a major Communist guerilla insurrection, helped remove the belief, then widespread, that Communist movements in primary economies were irresistible. Alan Lennox-Boyd concluded: 'When I was Secretary of State for the Colonies, I realised that the eyes of the world were on us in Malaya – particularly the eyes of Asia and Africa – and had we not defeated the Communists, then the Communist central powers would have done their utmost to start up similar problems in Africa and elsewhere.'

The Communist defeat in Malaya might have been avoided if either Stalin or Mao Tse-Tung had been determined to help, but no evidence has been produced to suggest that any material aid came from the great Communist powers to rescue Chin Peng. When his guerillas surrendered or were captured, their weapons and clothes were generally British- or Japanese-made, captured from police posts and ambushes or bought in Thailand. None came from Russia or China. The great Communist powers decided to let Chin Peng go under in accordance with their long-standing principle of backing winners rather than fellow Communists. And Chin Peng, while

*Tunku Abdul Rahman
at Malaya's
independence celebration,
31 August 1957.*

certainly not a clear loser from the beginning, proved to have insurmountable forces against him. The most important of these were the Malays, who formed the vast bulk of the rural population. Their hostility to the Chinese and their loyalty to Islam, their sultans and the British meant that the MCP had negligible success in recruiting Malays and that most of the settled countryside was hostile to them. The second force was the wealthy citizenry, particularly the rich Chinese. Unlike Vietnam, Malaya was a highly prosperous country with a substantial community of business and professional people opposed to Communism. The final force was the British, not so much for their innovative military tactics (though both the 'new villages' and the use of helicopters in anti-guerilla warfare were pioneered in Malaya) as for their political flexibility. The Dutch in Indonesia and the French in Indo-China fought unsuccessfully in the years after 1945 to retain colonial power. Given the enormous profitability of Malaya, the Communists thought the British would fight to retain colonial power there too. But the British had stated in 1944 that self-government was their ultimate objective for Malaya. While the system of government embodied in the Malayan

Federation agreement was basically old-fashioned colonial rule, with future steps towards both democracy and self-government promised, but nothing firmly specified and no timetable, it was the Emergency that unexpectedly led to speedy independence. The old rule, 'No political concessions until law and order are restored', crisply expressed by Colonial Secretary Oliver Lyttelton in 1951, proved not to be British policy after all. On the contrary, political concessions came first and in 1957 Tunku Abdul Rahman and an UMNO-led Alliance Government presided over Independence Day celebrations – very much as usual – to cries of *Merdeka*, freedom. In the later stages, the Tunku had pressed the British to speed up the process. Instead of going through the Colonial Office's full constitutional obstacle course, Malaya sped to independence with only a partially elected legislature. Instead of independence having to wait until the Communist insurgency was finally defeated, independence came when British and Malayan troops still had a further three years of mopping-up operations to complete. Then, in 1960, the Emergency was declared to be over. This did not mean that Chin Peng was captured or finally gave up, merely that most of his colleagues had been killed or captured and that the small band of Communists he was left with had been driven from most of Malaya and could now operate only from the jungles in the far north, or sometimes from across the border in Thailand. From these remote hiding places they maintained their revolt, occasionally killing a few Malayans; but henceforth their only impact on the Malayan state was that the Communist Party remained illegal there.

After the Malayan defeat, Communists did not again offer an effective military threat anywhere in the British Empire. Although Communism was making great advances worldwide at precisely the time the Empire was crumbling, although the destruction of imperialism was one of the major objectives of Communism, although the red menace was constantly described by newspapers and politicians as an immediate threat to this colony or that, the imperial demise proceeded under its own momentum, almost entirely unaffected, except in Malaya, by its noisiest proclaimed enemy.

## After Independence

In the twenty years after independence, Malaya stayed on the course on which the British had launched it: a free enterprise community in which economic growth proceeded rapidly. The world's fastest growing economies in these years were all in south-east Asia – Japan, Taiwan, Hong Kong, South Korea and Singapore (which continued after Malaya's independence to be directly ruled from Britain as a colony and military base). Malaya followed close behind these wonder economies, her prosperity protected by stable governments democratically elected, and with most of the western freedoms (apart from the freedom to join the Communist Party).

The country continued to be ruled by multi-racial Alliance governments, led first by Tunku Abdul Rahman, then by others who had served with him in the early years of UMNO, including a son of Dato Onn bin Ja'afar. The Finance Minister was always a prominent businessman drawn from UMNO's partner in the Alliance, the Malayan Chinese Association. Generally racial harmony was preserved, despite vicious Malay–Chinese riots in 1969.

The state was enlarged and renamed Malaysia in 1963, when Singapore and the former British North Borneo colonies of Sabah and Sarawak became independent and were added to it. The racial arithmetic of this change was that the one and half million Chinese of Singapore, had they alone been added to Malaya, would have produced a Chinese majority. Since that would have been unacceptable to the Malays, the people of the two North Borneo territories were incorporated also, to preserve the non-Chinese majority.

Singapore had fought its own battles against Communism, not by means of guns, as in Malaya, but by political back-knifing. The crowded and prosperous island city exhibited the ugly side as well as the splendours of capitalism. When free elections were held, Communist candidates did well. A socialist lawyer, Lee Kuan Yew, determined to reach the top in Singapore politics, entered a political alliance with the Communists which, once he had won power, he abandoned. He is said to have ridden the tiger and survived to tell the tale. Had he not imprisoned his former Communist allies, Lee argued, they would have seized power, dumped him, and never allowed another election to be held in Singapore.

This effective handling of Communists impressed the Tunku, who welcomed Lee into Malaysia as an ally. But the relationship between the two men deteriorated. The Tunku had scraped a pass degree at Cambridge, Lee gained a double first there; the Tunku had struggled to become a barrister, Lee won all the prizes; the Tunku was straightforward, steady and slow, Lee subtle, surprising and fast. Within a year of Singapore's joining Malaysia, Lee had begun to extend the influence of his political organisation, the

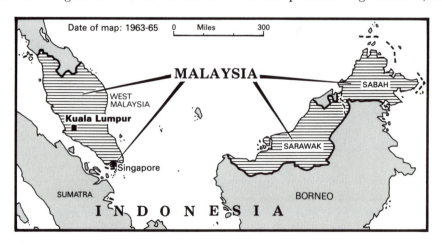

*The enlarged, racially balanced state created on 16 September 1963.*

People's Action Party, into mainland Malaya. With such a dynamic leader, the PAP seemed likely soon to be challenging the conservative Alliance's position as the permanent Government in Kuala Lumpur. So after less than two years the Tunku had Singapore thrown out of the federation. Lee Kuan Yew was heart-broken and amazed. He could see no reason why the democratic process of Malaysia should not be used by a political party eager for power. Once again, the Malays had sensed a Chinese takeover and forestalled it.

Singapore went its own way as a small independent state, leaving Malaysia without its greatest city. Sabah and Sarawak remained part of Malaysia, which now faced a military 'confrontation', the 'crush Malaysia' campaign, launched in the form of another guerilla war by President Achmed Sukarno of Indonesia. Against this challenge, as against the declining challenge of Chin Peng's forces, the Tunku enjoyed British military backing. Like Chin Peng, Sukarno claimed that the Tunku's government was a lackey of British imperialism; he added that Malaysia was a scheme by the British to prevent the unification of the Malay peoples in a single state, a greater Indonesia. Sukarno was not exactly a Communist, more a nationalist with Marxist leanings, and his motives in launching his 'confrontation' against Malaysia were complex; but the trenchant anti-Communism of the Tunku and Lee Kuan Yew and their willingness to enter defence agreements with Britain and to retain a major British naval base at Singapore were certainly among his reasons for assaulting Malaysia. He was offended by the Tunku's efforts to create an association of anti-Communist south-east Asian states (a challenge to Sukarno's non-alignment) and by his semi-feudal family background.

On this last point Sukarno was misguided. Although the Tunku was the son of a Sultan and became leader of the UMNO largely because of his princely standing, he caused UMNO to become the dominant voice in the independence of Malaya by mastering the skills of a democratic politician. By the time of independence he was a major influence in limiting the power of the Sultans, including that of his own nephew. Malaya became at independence a constitutional monarchy with – a unique institution – the office of Yang Di-pertuan Agung (King) circulating among the Sultans every five years. This formally put the Sultanate into the position it had really occupied under the British, that of constitutional monarchy. In trimming the status of the Sultans, evicting Singapore, holding the racial balance in the government and securing British help to keep out both the MCP and the Indonesians, the Tunku showed consistently good judgment – above all of what the vast majority of Muslim Malays wanted or were prepared to tolerate.

Thus he survived as the dominant leader in both the approach to independence and in Malaya's adaptation into an enlarged Malaysia. He headed the Government from the first Malayan federal election in 1955 until he retired in 1970. No one could have survived in office for so long without political skills of the highest order, above all the patience and sympathy to keep closely in touch with Malay feelings and, almost as important, the tact and flexibility to manage coalition partners, especially the Chinese, whom he knew to be much cleverer than himself. No one could confuse an issue more verbosely than the Tunku: soft spoken and unemotional, he could keep talking until persistent questioners were lost. Few politicians shared his ability, when asked a difficult or embarrassing question, to appear genuinely not to understand. He did not like being compared unfavourably to Lee Kuan Yew, but, that apart, he did not mind Chinese and western intellectuals dismissing him as dim. He knew he could outlast them and that he could maintain something they all respected: a tolerant, multi-racial government.

Perhaps his oddest weakness was his belief that, to prove that he had been a true nationalist leader, he should have fought ferociously against the British Empire and been sent to prison, a belief associated with his great admiration for Jawaharlal Nehru, who had visited Malaya in 1934 and 1946, each time making inspiring speeches and meeting the Prince. In his book *Looking Back* the Tunku exaggerates his own militancy and explains his failure to go to prison as due to Templer's subtlety: he 'called me to his office and declared, "Why should I make a martyr of you?"'

In reality the transfer of power from the British to the Tunku and his government went more smoothly than any other colonial handover in the Third World. He secured the interests of the Malays without fighting the British, and he preserved the institutions – impartially administered law, free elections, a thriving business economy – which the British were most concerned to pass on to whoever succeeded them. With his princely ways, his instinct for compromise and his robust modesty, he was one of the most acceptable to the British of all the leaders who assumed power from them. Perhaps it was the fact that many of them looked down on him intellectually – he always consulted the racing calendar before agreeing to an official engagement – that made them so fond of him.

# CHAPTER 4

# Iran

Iran was never formally part of the British Empire. Colonial Office staff never set foot there. But agents of the British government of India were present in strength and detachments of the Indian army effectively protected British interests in southern Iran not merely during the First and Second World Wars but also for long periods of peace. During the first quarter of the twentieth century and the decade after 1942, British soldiers and diplomats decided who should rule the country. Indeed Iran proved by contrast one of the advantages of direct imperial rule: a Governor with his plumes and his executive council enabled both colonisers and colonised to define their relationship and to know where power lay. The people of Iran, nominally independent but actually for much of the period from 1907 to 1951 a British client state, were never sure. As Abol Hassan Bani Sadr, briefly president after the fall of the Iranian monarchy in 1979, recalled:

> A great number of Iranians blamed the British all the time. If it rained it was because the British wanted it; if that character was Prime Minister, then the English must have put him there. In towns across Iran, if something happened, even a crime, it was thought the intrigues of the British were always behind it.

In 1921 General Sir Edmund Ironside, commander of the British troops in north Persia, decided the country was in need of a military dictatorship. He encouraged Reza Khan, an officer he had put in charge of the Persian Cossack regiment, to move on Tehran, the capital, and carry out a coup d'état. Reza Khan soon had himself made Shah (King). He did not reward his sponsors but drew Germans into Iran and removed Britons from positions of power wherever he could. So in 1941, soon after the start of their war against Germany, the British deposed him and, having canvassed a range of alternatives, placed on the throne his pliable young son, Mohammed Reza Shah, who survived as monarch until the Ayatollah Khomeini's coup d'état in 1979.

Reza Shah forbade the use of the name Persia by which foreigners had known the country since ancient times: it was a name based on the language, Farsi, and on the southern province, Fars, where British influence was particularly strong. Reza Shah insisted that the country be called only Iran. After his death both names were again acceptable.

Britain's eventual departure from Iran is one of the saddest events in the End of Empire story. A passionate constitutionalist, Dr Mohammed Mussadeq, became Iran's Prime Minister in 1951. He was exactly the kind of man colonial Governors in the directly ruled parts of the Empire were seeking out and encouraging: well-connected, incorruptible and dedicated to the principles of liberal democracy. What was more, he had the one quality above all others that made the British in the colonies recognise a political leader of substance: he dominated the nationalist movement and could generate mass support. But the British were determined to remove him because Iran was in one vital respect peculiar. Although all colonies were acquired for British profit – either to get wealth locally or to protect routes to wealth – the needs of the colonised people commonly occupied most of the attention of British colonial officers. In Iran in 1951, such preoccupations were at best secondary. The Anglo-Iranian oil company was so big – the largest single British overseas investment – and its income so important to a British Government battered by economic crises that the political judgments of businessmen settled policy instead of the experience of normally more liberal-minded politicians and administrators. In Iran in 1951–3 Britain conformed to Lenin's model of imperialist power – exactly the opposite of its behaviour in India, Burma, Ceylon, the Gold Coast, Nigeria, Sudan and a dozen other places. Iran was the exception that proved the rule.

## The Sands Run Out, 539 BC–1948 AD

According to the Bible (Daniel, Chapter V) Belshazzar King of Babylon was carousing in his palace with his nobles and courtesans when the fingers of an unseen hand wrote on the palace wall 'MENE, MENE, TEKEL, UPHARSIN' roughly translated, 'Your time is up, your empire will fall to the Persians.' Soon after, the Persian King Darius and his army slew Belshazzar and conquered Mesopotamia. As usual with Bible stories, archaeological evidence confirms the important facts, as does the evidence of Greek and Roman historians. In the age of classical Greece, the tiny states of Athens and Sparta trembled at the arrival of the Persians, whose capital, Persepolis, was larger, more splendid and better administered than any city in Europe. The Persian Empire was the eastern limit that Greek and Roman armies were repeatedly unable to pass, save when Alexander the Great broke through and reached India. Persia has been for thousands of years the barrier between east and west. Huge, mountainous and sparsely populated, it preserved much of its ancient character. Outsiders rarely penetrated. More often the Persians descended to conquer their neighbours.

When the British acquired their empire in India, Persia became important to them. But not for itself. Its significance lay in its northern neighbour, Russia. In the 'great game' between the British Empire and the Russian, Persia was at the centre of the chessboard. The nineteenth century saw

Russia expanding southwards, its rulers determined to capture a warm water port. Had they succeeded, the Russians could have challenged British naval domination of the sea route to India and the Far East. So to stop Russian access to the Mediterranean, Britain and other European powers propped up the regime of the Ottoman Turks; and to prevent access to the Persian Gulf, a British lake since the end of the eighteenth century, Britain propped up the shahs of Persia.

As the nineteenth century advanced they needed more and more propping. They developed a powerful taste for court luxuries and European voyages but were unable to raise enough taxes to pay for them. The easiest way to pay both for pleasures and for the strong army they needed was by selling to foreign companies the sole right to do business in their land. In 1862 the British government of India obtained the concession to build and operate the land telegraph line across Persia and in 1889 an English company was empowered to establish the Imperial Bank of Persia, with the sole right to issue and control the country's currency. In 1901 a British syndicate, headed by William Knox d'Arcy, received the sole concession to find, produce and refine petrol in Persia (outside the northern provinces where all rights went to the Russians).

The Persian court, like a deer feeding two tigers, attempted to preserve its independence by doling out concessions to Britain and Russia even-handedly. When British plans for a railway became known in the 1870s and 1880s, Russia insisted on their cancellation, with the result that Persia had no railways until after the First World War. When the Shah was bankrupted at the turn of the twentieth century, Russia nipped in ahead of Britain to give a loan in return for control of the Persian customs and the right to their future revenue. As this competition gathered momentum Britain and Russia felt it was dragging them towards war. To avoid it they signed a Convention in 1907. The Persian Government was informed in the following terms:

> Desiring to avoid any cause of conflict between their respective interests in certain regions of Persia, in the neighbourhood of the Russian frontier on the one hand and of the frontier of Baluchistan and Afghanistan on the other, the Governments of Great Britain and Russia have signed a friendly Arrangement on the subject . . . Each of the two States binds itself to seek no concession of any kind whatsoever in the neighbourhood of the frontier of the other . . . The sole object of the Arrangement is the avoidance of any cause of misunderstanding on the ground of Persian affairs between the Contracting Parties. The Shah's Government will be convinced that the Agreement concluded between Russia and Great Britain cannot fail to promote the prosperity, security and ulterior development of Persia in the most efficacious manner.

Thus did the tigers divide up the deer.

The 1907 Convention, together with the failure of the Shah to call a Majlis (parliament), provoked a revolution. For five years Persia was at war with itself: monarchists and conservatives backed by Czarist Russia against liberal democrats and radicals supported by Great Britain.

On the side of the democrats was a young lawyer called Mohammed Mussadeq. Tabriz, Persia's second largest city, was the scene of a liberal insurrection and suffered a six-month siege in which not only was an American schoolteacher killed leading a bayonet charge but the correspondent of the *Times* was obliged to fight at the barricades. Victory finally went to the liberals, in alliance with the British-backed tribes of the south. Persia became a constitutional monarchy and a Majlis was assembled. Within twelve months Russia and Britain had whittled these hard-won rights to nothing. The monarch returned to being as absolute as he was inefficient and the Majlis degenerated into a marketplace for bribery. For the young Mohammed Mussadeq it was a bitter lesson.

Russian troops entered the northern provinces. British garrisons were established at Shiraz and Isfahan. The Persian Governors of the southern provinces soon came to be generally regarded as merely British agents. Before the 1913 elections for the Majlis, the Russian and British envoys in Tehran jointly urged the Persian Cabinet to take care, according to British Foreign Office records, 'to insure the return of more suitable members than on the two previous occasions'. What the Russians and British meant was that liberal nationalists of the kind who had only a few years earlier caused the Shah to create a Majlis and who had been openly critical of the granting of concessions to foreign powers should not be elected. The presence of such people in the Majlis caused deplorable instability. Landowners who wanted Russian or British help understood that they must instruct their tenants and labourers to vote for traditionalists. Those Persians who had derived the idea of a liberal constitution from the many British in Persia were disappointed and baffled.

In 1904 Baron 'Jackie' Fisher became First Sea Lord at the Admiralty in London. He saw that the ships of the future would be fired by oil. This would place the British navy at a disadvantage because, while Britain mined the best steam coal in the world, the British Empire was not well endowed with oil, so he was anxious to find a source that would flow reliably to Britain in time of war.

William Knox d'Arcy, the man who had been granted the oil concession, was by now in need of money. An English solicitor who had made a fortune by investing in a gold mine in Australia, he lived lavishly, maintaining the only private stand at Epsom apart from the Royal Box and paying Caruso and Melba to sing for his guests at dinner. His efforts to find oil in Persia were a drain on his capital. Among British oil-men he is reverently described as the father of the Middle East oil industry, but he never set eyes on Persia. He just bought the concession and provided the money while his team of Canadian and Polish drillers, an American engineer (the Rockefeller finds in the United States were d'Arcy's inspiration), an Indian doctor and a labour force of tribesmen who had never before handled any sort of machinery

*William Knox d'Arcy,
solicitor and legend in
the oil industry.*

struggled in the desert heat. Their first two wells gave off 'the true oil gas smell' and an explosion, then a flow of oil. D'Arcy, on receiving the news, began to celebrate. After a few weeks, the flow stopped.

Some investors directed his way by the Admiralty enabled d'Arcy to set his team to work again. In all they spent seven years dragging their equipment through a mountainous area devoid of roads where the summer temperature is over 100° in the shade. In the spring the harsh land blossomed with jonquil, sweet-scented nightstock, tulips, narcissi and anemones. Then the sun turned the earth brown and nothing grew. The drillers counted not the years they worked in Persia, but the summers.

By 1908, d'Arcy had lost £250,000 and his Admiralty-introduced backers more than £100,000. Enough was enough; a cable was sent to the men at Masjid-i-Sulaiman, 'the Mosque of Solomon', a ruin in the desert where they were 1,100 feet down yet another apparently dry well. The engineers should cease drilling, dismiss the staff and come home. Fisher had won authority from the Cabinet to start converting his ships to oil, which now seemed not available; d'Arcy had lost a large part of his gold fortune. But the drillers had given seven years of their lives. For two weeks after the order to stop they continued to drill. In May 1908 they struck oil. One of the cables bearing the good news read – for want of a company code – 'see Psalm 104 verse 15', which reads, according to the translation in the Book of Common Prayer, 'That he may bring food out of the earth . . . and oil to make him a cheerful countenance'.

By 1912 investors in Britain had paid enough for shares in a new venture, the Anglo-Persian Oil Company, to enable it to take over the d'Arcy concession and build a refinery at Abadan. In July 1914, six days before the start of the First World War, Parliament authorised the British Government to purchase a controlling interest in Anglo-Persian, an untypical decision, motivated by concern about the German navy rather than any desire to go into business. Indian troops were by now permanently stationed at Bushire, where the British chief political agent in the Persian Gulf was based. From there they could control the province of Fars, just south-east of Persia's main oil area. As soon as the war started, additional troops were sent from India, to make sure that the Turks, who had sided with the Germans, did not interfere with Britain's oil supplies: their province of Mesopotamia was worryingly near. British officers raised the South Persia Rifles, the only regular armed force in its area during the war.

*Laying Anglo–Persian's first pipeline.*

In 1917 the Russian Revolution led to the withdrawal of all Russian troops and the renunciation of all privileges previously possessed in Persia by the government of the Tsar. For an imperialist group within the British Cabinet led by George Nathaniel Curzon a great moment of opportunity had come.

Britain could take over Persia, Mesopotamia and Palestine, thus acquiring a continuous land mass from the Mediterranean to India.

Curzon had travelled in Persia as a young man. In 1903, as Viceroy of India, he had paid a state visit to the Persian Gulf, impressing its sultans by the ships of the Royal Navy that accompanied him and the dignity of his own bearing and entourage.

> We opened these seas to the ships of all nations [he told them] and enabled their flags to fly in peace. We have not destroyed your independence but have preserved it. We are not now going to throw away this century of worthy and triumphant enterprise; we shall not wipe out the most unselfish page in history. The peace of these waters must still be maintained; your independence will continue to be upheld; and the influence of the British Government must remain supreme.

Curzon was referring to the conversion of the Gulf into a secure area for British traders and of its rulers into princely subordinates in the Indian manner. Curzon's viceregal party had dropped anchor off Persia itself, but problems of etiquette had prevented his landing at Bushire: he refused to play second fiddle to the representative of the Shah. However, he did land at Bandar Abbas and Lingah, where he and the Persian Governor of the Gulf ports exchanged flowery compliments while the issue of precedence was skilfully avoided.

By the end of the 1914–18 war Curzon was Foreign Secretary in a Cabinet in which Alfred Milner, as Colonial Secretary, and Winston Churchill, as Minister of War, shared his imperial ideas. For a while Britain used Persia as a base from which to help the White Russians conduct their war against the new Communist Government. In August 1919 Britain signed a treaty with Persia under which, in return for a loan, Persia would accept British advisers to reorganise the army and the national finances, the country becoming, in effect, a British protectorate. 'A great triumph', Curzon wrote, 'and I have done it alone.' He was of course concerned mainly with Britain's interests but his desire to help Persia was also genuine: the state was in chaos and needed to assert central control, to collect revenue efficiently, to learn to work its parliamentary constitution; all these things would help ensure its effectiveness in keeping out the Russians. Neighbouring Mesopotamia, captured from Turkey, was at this time being run by British officials, mostly shipped from India. The imperialist group in the Cabinet thought a splendid new fruit had dropped into Britain's hands.

The army of revolutionary Russia soon proved, however, like that of revolutionary France just over a century earlier, more than a match for the forces of imperialism. The operation that Churchill had called 'reaching out for Persia' overreached itself. A British naval flotilla had been set up on the Caspian Sea and a British army headquarters at Kasvin in north Persia. To deal with an unexpectedly vigorous Russia these required expensive reinforcement. But the Liberal Prime Minister, David Lloyd George, a solicitor from Wales, enjoyed dominating Curzon, his haughty Foreign Secretary, and wanted to build homes for heroes (the demobilised British soldiers, who now all had the vote) and to use the army to suppress disorder in Ireland. So the scheme for Persia was dropped. When both the naval presence on the Caspian and the army were withdrawn, the Majlis in Tehran, which had delayed ratifying Curzon's treaty, rejected it. The formal acknowledgement of Britain's suzerainty over Persia had been refused, though the fleet in the Gulf, British India to the east and British Iraq to the west, as well as the oil company, the South Persia Rifles and all the concessions of the previous hundred years, left Persia under British protection in fact if not in name.

At the time of the rejection of the treaty with Britain, Persia was in a bad way. Ahmed Shah, the young king, was immature and indecisive, and the members of the Majlis, mostly local landowners, had no desire to see a strong central authority diminish their autonomy. With the sources of control thus out of action, political circles in Iran assumed that the British would organise a coup to put a strong man into office. In 1921 they did so. But the colonel who, armed and encouraged by General Ironside, marched his Persian Cossack regiment into Tehran to seize power, first as Prime

*General Sir Edmund Ironside, later Chief of the Imperial General Staff, the man who in 1921 armed and encouraged Reza Khan to seize power.*

Minister, then, with the approval of a frightened Majlis, as Shah, proved to be no British puppet.

He had the Majlis proclaim him Reza Shah Pahlavi, and soon gave voice to the Anglophobia which the British occupation of their country had aroused among the Persians. The British, seeing their own strong man turn against them, decided they had little choice but to give him their blessing. The local warlords and feudal landholders whom he imprisoned or killed had little support. He quickly showed that he knew how to reassert central control, which both the British and most Iranians wanted.

Reza Shah set out to follow the lead of Kemal Atatürk in nearby Turkey. Having seized a deteriorating empire by force, he proposed to drive it into the twentieth century. He treated the ineffective Majlis as Roman emperors had treated the senate – a servile group of yes-men to whom he formally deferred merely to establish that his actions were constitutional. The western-educated upper class, mostly professionals from land-owning families, included many who cared about the maintenance of parliamentary forms. When the docile Majlis invited Reza Shah to assume the throne, only four of them had the courage to oppose him. One was Dr Mohammed Mussadeq, the radical young lawyer of 1907 who had since for some years been Governor of Fars province where he had worked well with the British. He held the curious belief that the provisions of the constitution concerning democracy were meant to be taken seriously. Under the constitution, he argued, the Shah was supposed to reign but not rule; if Reza Shah attempted to reign while continuing as a minister to rule, 'this would be contrary to the fundamental law'. Mussadeq had been an ally of Reza before he became Shah, helping to introduce his early reforms. Soon, however, Reza Shah decided that Mussadeq's attachment to his principles made him dangerous, so he placed him under house arrest.

Reza Shah was determined to restore the greatness of Iran. One of the obstacles, as he saw it, was the strong hold of Islam. The ancient Persian religion of Zoroastrianism had been replaced by Islam when Arabs conquered the country as part of the great invasions that followed the death of Muhammad. The *ulema*, the Shi-ite Muslim clergy, gradually acquired a grip on the Persian people. The first widespread upsurge of Persian nationalism had been led by the *ulema* in 1890 when a small group of Englishmen (who included a cousin of Lord Salisbury, the Prime Minister) bought from the then Shah the concession to sell tobacco throughout the country. Orthodox Muslims believed that merely by passing through the hands of Christians the tobacco would become impure. They therefore organised a boycott of smoking and became involved for the first time in nationwide opposition to the sale of concessions to infidels.

The success of the tobacco boycott led the *ulema* to pursue further their opposition to foreign concessions and the introduction of foreign ways. As a Cossack officer, Reza Shah had learned that western equipment was essential for military victory. To him boycotts for religious reasons were an impediment to the progress of the country. In 1924 the American Consul-General, wandering past a religious ceremony at a holy fountain, took out his camera; the worshippers, spurred on by the *mullah* (priest), beat him to death to cries of 'evil eye'. Reza Shah was determined that such outbursts must cease.

The *ulema* also held that secular rulers had no legitimacy. All real authority came from Allah and the only real law was the Koran. They wanted the *sharia*, the Koranic code, restored as the basic law of Persia. Reza Shah was determined to weaken *sharia* courts and introduced a codified system of secular law. Following the lead of Kemal Atatürk, he put an end to many of the *ulema*'s privileges and forbade women to wear the veil; he even made it obligatory for adult males to wear western dress, in particular the 'international hat', the European, brimmed felt hat, which made it difficult to conform to the Muslim rule of prayer which requires the faithful to touch the ground with their foreheads.

To modernise and industrialise Reza Shah needed help. An American was brought in to set up the central bank which displaced the British-owned Imperial Bank; Belgians reformed the customs; French the law and public health; Swedes the army; Italians the navy and, above all, Germans built up state industries and directed Persian trade away from the old imperialists. Reza Shah did all he could to reduce Persia's subservience to the two powers that in 1907 had carved up the country. He was determined to make Persia as independent as possible, given that the reality of Russian and British power could not be removed and that much foreign skill was needed for his plans.

The biggest British affront to Reza Shah was the Anglo-Persian Oil Company. He claimed that when he passed Abadan on his yacht he looked the other way (into Iraq) rather than see the gleaming expanse of the refinery. He referred to the British as *Junubis*, southerners, because they controlled the one region of which he could not become master. The remoteness of the oil fields and refinery from Tehran had encouraged the oilmen to feel that they were not part of Iranian society; until Reza Shah ended the privilege, they were not subject to Iranian law; they had negotiated with a local sheikh rather than in Tehran for the rights to build the refinery and their main pipeline; they hid from the Shah the low price at which they sold oil to the British navy; finally, when the world slump caused oil revenues to collapse in 1931, their royalty payment to his government collapsed also, at a time when he was building a railway and badly needed the money. He responded by informing the company that its concession was cancelled. This was celebrated throughout Iran as a great national triumph, with holidays, illuminations and fireworks. In the south, however, Reza Shah's soldiers kept the excited crowds away from the oil installations so that pumping and exporting could go on.

Reza Shah was a pragmatist. He did not want to throw the oil company out of Persia but to make his authority plain and increase his government's revenue. Having given the company and the British a shock, he promptly

offered to negotiate a new concession. The price agreed under a sixty-year contract – Iran was to receive twenty per cent of the dividend on ordinary shares and four shillings for each ton sold – was not ungenerous by the standards of the time. Once this deal was done, in 1933, Reza Shah visited Abadan, eager to see Iranians learning the skills that might eventually enable them to run the refinery themselves. The company, renamed Anglo-Iranian, increased its exploration and well-drilling and soon the refinery became the largest in the world.

By 1939, when war started in Europe, Reza Shah had deteriorated into an increasingly brutal and unpopular despot. He declared Iran neutral, but the British mistrusted the large number of German businessmen and techni-cians he had attracted and his increasing sympathy for Hitler and Mussolini. When Hitler's armies attacked Russia in 1941, it became vital for Britain to get war supplies to its new ally, the Soviet army. The northern route, past German-held Norway, was both dangerous and liable to freeze. A southern route, along the new railway Reza Shah had built from the Persian Gulf to the Caspian Sea, offered the ideal alternative. A quick invasion was arranged, using the Shah's failure to expel the German businessmen as the excuse. The oil fields and refinery were secured. Knowing he could not win, the Shah ordered his army to offer no resistance.

The Prime Minister Reza Shah had appointed to negotiate with the

*Reza Shah, centre, visits the refinery at Abadan.*

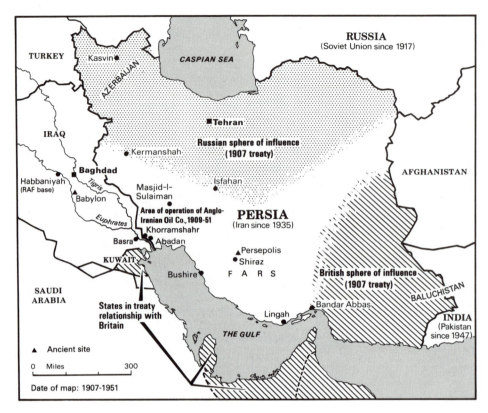

RUSSIA
(Soviet Union since 1917)

TURKEY

Kasvin

CASPIAN SEA

AZERBAIJAN

IRAQ

Kermanshah

■Tehran

Russian sphere of influence
(1907 treaty)

AFGHANISTAN

Baghdad

Habbaniyah
(RAF base)

Babylon

Tigris

Masjid-I-
Sulaiman

Isfahan

Area of operation of Anglo-
Iranian Oil Co.,1909-51

Khorramshahr

PERSIA
(Iran since 1935)

Basra

Abadan

Persepolis

KUWAIT

Euphrates

Shiraz

British sphere of influence
(1907 treaty)

SAUDI
ARABIA

Bushire

F A R S

BALUCHISTAN

States in treaty
relationship with
Britain

Bandar Abbas

Lingah

INDIA
(Pakistan
since 1947)

THE GULF

▲  Ancient site

0    Miles       300

Date of map: 1907-1951

invaders, Ali Foroughi, an independent-minded lawyer, soon entered discussions with the British about removing him. Names were canvassed in London for a successor, candidates discreetly examined. According to the diaries of a principal court adviser, the British gave Foroughi the choice of becoming president of an Iranian republic or remaining Prime Minister under a constitutional monarchy and he chose the latter. The BBC's Iranian service began transmitting from London talks on the proper methods of constitutional government and on Reza Shah's misdeeds and cruelty. Iranians clustered round their radios. In the normally subservient Majlis deputies acquired new courage. Reza Shah boarded a British ship at Bandar Abbas and three years later died, in British custody, in South Africa.

For the rest of the war Iran was under Anglo-Russian control, which was sufficiently strong for the first meeting of the big three allied leaders, Roosevelt, Churchill and Stalin, to be held in Tehran, Stalin's choice because of its proximity to Moscow. The huge British legation compound, its gardens surrounded by a brigade of Sikh soldiers, and the even larger Russian compound, surrounded by Soviet soldiers, became briefly in November 1943 the centre of the world. Reza Shah's young son, promoted to the throne by the British, tried to persuade the three leaders to pay some attention to his country, but their minds were elsewhere. So long as Iran remained docile, however, the British and Russians allowed the Majlis and the young Shah to run its internal affairs.

In fact the war brought Iran a welcome spell of liberalism. A small group of politicians, of whom the most prominent was Dr Mohammed Mussadeq, enjoyed the unexpected freedom to speak out against the Russians and the British alike. In 1944 Mussadeq carried a bill through the Majlis making it illegal for any minister or official to discuss oil concessions with any foreign government or oil company. Although some in the west thought him merely a xenophobic aristocrat, within the Majlis, where the principal battles for power increasingly took place, he acquired a small but devoted following of professors, engineers, lawyers and civil servants, most of whom had been to university in either Paris or Berlin. To them he was the man who had chosen detention under Reza Shah rather than abandon his principled belief in democracy; he was by contrast with most members of the Majlis, incorruptible; his patriotism was beyond suspicion. The British House of Commons always contains a few such upper-class radicals, usually a nuisance to the government, often to their own party leaders. Of them it is seldom said, 'He is a sensible man who knows where to draw the line.'

After the war ended in 1945, Britain's Indian troops were soon withdrawn, but Russian troops stayed. The Russians had some basis for their claim that the Persian province of Azerbaijan, where they were firmly dug in, was culturally and linguistically one with the Russian province of the same name; but while they wanted to use the base they had established there to secure control of the rest of Persia they did not want to start another war. So they applied pressure to secure Tudeh (Communist) party members in the Cabinet in Tehran. A similar technique was successful in capturing several East European states without starting a new war. In Iran it failed, partly because Britain promptly sent troops to Basra (Britain's last overseas use of its Indian army) and encouraged southern tribes to rebel and demand the dismissal of the Tudeh ministers, and partly because the Prime Minister, Qavam Saltaneh, used Britain's interference as an excuse to resist the Russian/Azerbaijan demands and to drop his Tudeh colleagues. Qavam's method was to flirt with the Russians, offering the carrot of his full co-operation and then to hit them with such sticks as the nationalism of the Majlis, the revolt in the south and the threatened intervention by the Americans. Finally the Russians had to choose between using force to conquer Persia and giving up; and, with growing opportunities in Eastern Europe to keep the red army busy, they withdrew their troops in 1946.

Nevertheless the Russian pressure had worried the young Shah as well as the American and British Governments. Whereas Reza Shah had rejected the help of foreign governments, his son now felt he needed it. He asked for American arms and got them, and he signed an agreement with the Anglo-Iranian Oil Company which preserved its concession and increased his government's income. He seemed to many patriotic Iranians, particularly Dr Mussaddeq, to be leading his country back into subservience to the West.

The British relationship with Iran was curious. In 1920 the country had escaped the protectorate status Curzon had planned and had asserted under Reza Shah a national will to pay allegiance to no foreign power. Yet Reza

Shah had been taken away in 1941 by the British and Mohammed Reza Shah, his son, had been placed on the throne by them and had spent his first four years as Shah co-operating loyally with the British and later the Americans in the use of his country as the supply route to Russia. The Persian Gulf, Iran's only outlet to the open seas, remained in effect a British lake, dominated by the Royal Navy and surrounded by small states whose rulers relied on the advice of British Residents. On top of all this, Iran's principal source of foreign revenue and the main source of government income, the Anglo-Iranian Oil Company, was half owned by the British Government and was Britain's largest single overseas investment. Everyone in Tehran knew that, following the withdrawal of the Russians in 1946, Iran had three power centres: the Shah's court, the Majlis and the British. The British legation was in the centre of Tehran, indeed much of Tehran had grown around it, and its power was generally thought to be supreme.

Members of the Majlis liked to keep up contacts in the British legation. Partly this was due to a genuine respect for British ideas, as Dr Mussadeq explained in a speech to the Majlis in June 1950:

> I would like to take this opportunity to reveal the advice I gave the young Shah in August 1941 when I was freed from political confinement. I advised him to follow the example of the British monarchy. The King of England is highly respected because he stands outside politics and avoids the dirty business of appointing and dismissing ministers, deputies and governors.

After the experience of Reza Shah, the Persian ruling class, mostly powerful landowners, wanted, like the British in the seventeenth century, to prevent the restoration of an absolute monarchy. A coarser reason for their close relations with the British legation was succinctly expressed by Sir George Middleton, chargé d'affaires in 1951–2: 'Deputies expected to be bribed.'

## The Man in Pyjamas, 1948–1953

Mohammed Reza Shah was regarded as weak and malleable, not only by the British, the Russians and the great Persian landowners who took advantage of these deficiencies for their several purposes, but also by his forceful twin sister, Princess Ashraf, who throughout his reign did her best to strengthen his will and make him behave more like their father. It followed that once the Russians had been removed, the young Shah became the perfect candidate for a paternal relationship in which Britain's prime purpose was, as always, the 'great game': to contain the Russians by helping a friendly regime in Tehran stay in command. The British paid the Shah's government what they thought a fair price for Iranian oil and, in order to save him from trouble with his nationalists, avoided flaunting their influence. While the United States considered that, in the worldwide task of containing Communism, the Persian front was Britain's responsibility.

The weak link in these arrangements was the unusual position of the
Anglo-Iranian Oil Company, which through its board in London, controlled
the largest part of Iran's national revenue. In 1948, as in 1931, a cut in the
company's payments started trouble. Britain's Labour Government, facing
a financial crisis, required all British companies to limit their dividend
payments. This automatically reduced the income of Iran, and neither the
British Government nor the company realised how seriously it was to anger
Iranian nationalists.

Anthony Eden, who was Under-Secretary at the Foreign Office in 1933
when Reza Shah told the company its concession was cancelled, had studied
Persian at Oxford, had often visited Persia and was there in 1948. On his
return to London he told the Chancellor of the Exchequer, Sir Stafford
Cripps, that the feelings of Persians were understandable: the British
Government was increasing its tax revenue from the company while the
dividend, on which the Persian Government's revenue was based, was being
kept down. Cripps, though well known for his sympathy with the nationalist
movement in India, showed none for Persia. He replied that dividend
limitation was a general treasury policy to which no exceptions could be
made.

The company, based in London and Abadan, far from the tense political atmosphere of Tehran, made offers it thought generous but always too late to forestall the next round of demands. In 1949 an agreement was signed to replace that of 1933. It contained important concessions in response to Iran's claims. But public feeling against the company had grown so fierce that the Prime Minister who negotiated the agreement was afraid to put it to the vote in the Majlis for ratification. By now any deal would be denounced as a sell-out to the British imperialists and the man responsible could expect rough handling from crowds in Tehran.

The oil industry had become the central issue in Iranian politics thanks to a simple analysis by Dr Mussadeq. So long as a foreign company had an oil concession, Iran's sovereignty would be in doubt, its domestic politics influenced by outside forces. Any Iranian who negotiated an oil concession was therefore selling the country's independence. All the frustrations of a weak state that had suffered occupation and a change of Shah at foreign hands became focused on the Anglo-Iranian Oil Company. Dr Mussadeq's earlier political career had been governed by his belief in liberal constitutional procedures. Now that he spoke against foreign oil interests he evoked a new, more powerful response. Both in the Majlis and in public meetings in Tehran the company's stranglehold on Iran's nationhood proved a challenge that brought Iranians to their feet.

*Abadan 1951, then the largest oil refinery in the world.*

The Shah wanted British help in equipping his army and a steady flow of revenue from Anglo-Iranian to finance his government. He and senior

diplomats in the British embassy considered that Mussadeq's whipping-up of an oil hysteria would soon exhaust itself. So in June 1950 the Shah appointed a strong man, General Razmara, as his Prime Minister to secure Majlis ratification for the oil agreement and calm the country down. A paradoxical situation developed: the company was advancing money to the Iranian Government to help it out of its troubles, but the Government, afraid of being called a paid tool of the British, insisted that the payments be kept secret. Dr Mussadeq continued to denounce the company for withholding money and no one was allowed to say publicly that it was not doing so.

General Razmara tried to persuade the company to make concessions on points the Majlis had recently demanded – to sell oil at cost within Iran and give the Iranian Government the right to vet the books and know where the oil went – but the company always refused to budge until too late. Razmara therefore submitted the oil agreement to the Majlis without these amendments. By now deputies and public meetings in Tehran addressed by Dr Mussadeq were calling for nationalisation – the recovery by Iran of assets which, they said, should never have been granted to a foreign company. Razmara argued that nationalisation was not practical politics – that both the operation of the refinery and the sale of the oil worldwide were totally dependent on the British – but public passion was roused and in March 1951 Razmara was assassinated by a Muslim fanatic. His death led to much rejoicing in Tehran, where he was described as a traitor and a British agent.

The Shah was reluctant to appoint Dr Mussadeq Prime Minister in Razmara's place, but found he had no choice. While Mussadeq remained in opposition, he and the forces backing him made government impossible. Mussadeq was deputy for a part of Tehran and noisy crowds of his supporters mobbed the Majlis, decisively influencing the votes within. A doctor of medicine who was also a deputy, Hassan Alavi, described one incident to a British official in Iran, C. M. Woodhouse. While Mussadeq was making an impassioned speech he suddenly collapsed on the floor of the Majlis, apparently unconscious; Alavi rushed forward, crying, 'Let me through! I'm a doctor.' He took Mussadeq's pulse, in dread that the great national leader had been taken from them; then Mussadeq slowly opened one eye and winked at him. He took to sleeping on an iron bedstead in the Majlis building (to avoid assassination, he claimed). He normally wore what to western newspapermen looked like pyjamas and, like Churchill, transacted much government business from his bed. He became the favourite character of cartoonists throughout the world. In the end, perhaps he was more actor than politician. No man ever wept more copiously in public. His frequent fainting was caused by an ailment, but it often struck at the climax of a speech or when he needed sympathy.

Support for Mussadeq came from all sides. Members of the traditional landowning élite were prepared to back him because he was a man of property, came from a family with long experience in government service and could be trusted to resist any tendency of the Shah to become tyrannical

*Iranians greet the raising of their flag over the main office at the Abadan refinery.*

like his father; nationalists and the mob backed him because he offered a clear, simple solution to a problem others made complicated; the *ulema* backed him because they too wanted to remove foreign concession-holders and restrain the powers of the Shah; his standing-out twenty-five years earlier against the enthronement of Reza Shah and his years in detention proved he was brave and honourable. His eloquence and integrity between them had brought him the support of all the powerful groups in the state. Even the Shah became his reluctant ally. When the British ambassador pointed out that Mussadeq had no party organisation, merely a loose coalition of existing groups, and could therefore easily be ditched, the Shah explained that Mussadeq's popularity in Tehran was so great that to oppose him now would be to set his own throne at risk: better to leave him in power while the fury of the mob worked itself out.

Immediately the Shah made him Prime Minister in May 1951 Mussadeq sent the Governor of the province of Khuzestan to the Anglo-Iranian Oil Company's head office at Khorramshahr. Accompanied by a crowd of about a thousand the Governor sacrificed a sheep and announced that the oil was now nationalised. The Iranian staff were thrilled, believing that discrimination against them would cease and that the industry would at last be in

Iranian hands. A new supervisory board began to issue orders. Sir Eric Drake, then the company's General Manager in Iran, recalled:

> There was no question of violent resistance, but it was extraordinary how pieces of plant would go wrong. The Iranians soon realised that we weren't being very helpful really. We weren't handing over files or accounts which they asked for. I said I had no authority to hand them the British company's accounts, unless I was told from London.

In effect the company responded to nationalisation by going on strike. By July 1951 all oil exports had ceased. By September most non-Persian staff had left and Mussadeq gave a week's notice to the few who remained.

The instrument by which the company throttled production was the tanker business: Mussadeq insisted that tanker-masters must sign receipts stating that the oil they had loaded belonged to Iran; the company caused all major-buyers to order their tanker-captains not to sign. In the words of Sir Hartley Shawcross, a Labour Cabinet minister and later a lawyer representing Anglo-Iranian, 'Whoever bought Iranian oil bought a lawsuit with it'. So the storage tanks at Abadan filled up, the refinery and the oil wells had to be closed. Mussadeq had done as he promised; the result was exactly as his predecessors, the Shah and the British had predicted.

The nationalisation of Iranian oil confronted the Labour Government in London with several dilemmas. They had themselves nationalised more industries than any previous government in British history, including the entire coal-mining industry, which, like Iranian oil, was then the country's main source of energy. In these circumstances they could hardly deny Iran's right to nationalise. The company, on the other hand, argued that the 1933 agreement was binding under international law and that the Government must stand up firmly for British rights. Besides the Government owned half of Anglo-Iranian and the loss of its concession would be a major blow to the British economy. Britain at the time still owned more overseas assets than any other country. To acquiesce in an illegal nationalisation would be to invite the seizure of more British assets by other hysterical nationalists.

Sir Eric Drake was summoned back to London and invited to Number 10 Downing Street:

> The entire Cabinet [he remembered] and the three chiefs of staff in uniform were all seated round a table. The Prime Minister bade me take a seat on his right between him and Mr Morrison, the Foreign Secretary. I pleaded that we should not allow the biggest foreign asset of Britain to go without doing something about it. I didn't say what was to be done. I had in my own mind that at least we should make a struggle for it. I thought the nationalisation was a completely unilateral act and I said that if we didn't do anything about this within five years we should lose the Suez Canal, which proved to be right, almost to the day.

The Cabinet were divided. Herbert Morrison, and the Minister of

Defence, Emanuel Shinwell, favoured a prompt use of force to seize back the oil installations. They persuaded the Cabinet to seek United States support for such measures, sent the destroyer HMS *Mauritius* to evacuate British personnel or start any necessary bombardment, sent a paratroop brigade to Cyprus, reinforced British air-bases in Iraq and instructed the company to conduct negotiations with the Iranian Government on compensation and other matters, the main purpose of which was to play for time.

Mussadeq was deflected neither by the Labour Government's huffing and puffing nor by the total loss of his country's foreign income. He demanded 75 per cent of the oil revenue and offered the company 25 per cent as compensation. When Britain complained to the UN Security Council that Iran was acting illegally by breaching a freely-made agreement, he flew to New York to put his country's case, dazzling the General Assembly by his performance and winning sympathy and admiration for his style. The Security Council, however, declined to hear Iran's arguments until they had been heard by the International Court, so he went to The Hague to supervise the presentation of Iran's case there and, when the judges eventually decided they had no competence in the matter, presented their finding as a triumph.

While he was in the United States Mussadeq tried to persuade President Truman to give Iran aid to prevent collapse during the conflict with Britain. He failed, but he charmed and delighted. Dean Acheson describes him as 'small and frail with not a shred of hair on his billiard-ball head; a thin face protruded into a long beak of a nose flanked by two bright shoe-button eyes. His whole manner and appearance was birdlike, marked by quick, nervous movements as he seemed to jump about on a perch.' When visiting the President, he sat in a chair with his legs tucked under him like a child. Suddenly he dropped his normal mood of gay animation and turned pathetic, saying, 'Mr President, I am speaking for a very poor country – just sand, a few camels, a few sheep . . .' When Acheson interrupted to say that, with its oil, Persia was as rich as Texas, Mussadeq laughed with delight: his gambit had failed but no one was more amused than he.

The Americans were sympathetic. He was a constitutionalist and an anti-Communist whose determination to end Iran's imperial relationship with Britain matched America's anti-colonial instincts. The British suspected also that the desire of American oil companies to get their hands on Iranian oil had something to do with Washington's hospitable behaviour towards Britain's antagonist. In 1939 Middle East oil amounted to less than six per cent of the world's total; even Britain then imported only twenty-two per cent from the Middle East, compared with fifty-seven per cent from the Americas. But during and after the war the assessment of Middle East reserves rose to more than half the world's total. A US company developed production in Saudi Arabia, another took a half share in Kuwait. American companies repeatedly offered better terms to governments in the Middle East than did the previously dominant British.

To Truman and Acheson, Morrison's threat to send ships and soldiers to enforce a commercial contract that the British company had been unable to negotiate was a hundred years out of date. The Americans thought price was largely the issue and sent one of their cleverest negotiators, Averell Harriman, to Tehran; they feared that a British invasion in the south would lead to a Russian intervention in Azerbaijan in the north. Harriman would avert the danger by a political and financial compromise.

The task proved impossible. Mussadeq insisted on total Iranian control; the British insisted that Anglo-Iranian must run the oil operation. Harriman, however, achieved something: he persuaded the two governments to open high-level talks. But the British Government was functioning as little more than the agent of the oil company and would not concede what Mussadeq considered essential for Iran's self-respect. The negotiator sent from London, a Cabinet minister, Richard Stokes, wrote to Prime Minister Attlee that he was impressed with the Iranian case: he thought the company was being unreasonable. Harriman thought the same. But the British Government was too pressed financially to act with generosity and too much jostled by jingoism – in press and parliament – to act rationally. A British possession had been stolen by a seventy-year-old trouble-maker in pyjamas;

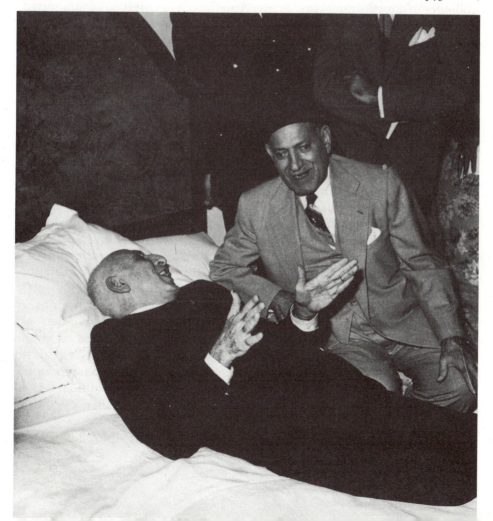

*Dr Mussadeq working in bed. Here he is seen with Nahas Pasha, Prime Minister of Egypt.*

it must be recovered. Only after the American Government had made clear its strong opposition to the use of force did Attlee take charge of Iranian policy in the Cabinet and overrule his Foreign Secretary's determination to settle the matter by gunboats and grapeshot.

Soon afterwards the October 1951 election brought Winston Churchill and the Conservatives to power. Churchill complained that the Americans were still giving financial aid to Iran and criticised his predecessors in office 'who had scuttled and run from Abadan when a splutter of musketry would have ended the matter'. The US Secretary of State, Dean Acheson, argued that on the contrary the British should settle with Mussadeq: threats of force and continued strangulation of Iran's oil exports might bring about the fall of this popular liberal in which case extreme instability in Iran was likely to open the way to a renewal of Russian influence. Acheson did not find Mussadeq easy to deal with: 'It was like walking in a maze and every so often finding oneself at the beginning again. On price particularly he pretended to be very vague and stupid.' But a man who in his own country was adored by vast public meetings in the capital, was supported by a majority of the main power groups, was firmly anti-Communist and was as passionate an upholder of constitutional law as any American was surely to be supported. Acheson continued to urge British ministers to do a deal with Mussadeq, rather than find themselves faced with someone worse.

Anthony Eden, the new British Foreign Secretary, thought this threat unreal:

> I did not accept the argument that the only alternative to Mussadeq was Communist rule. I thought that if Mussadeq fell, his place might well be taken by a more reasonable government with which it would be possible to conclude a satisfactory agreement.

His confidence was based on information he did not reveal to the Americans. Soon after Mussadeq came to power, C. M. Woodhouse, a senior officer of MI6, the British equivalent of the US Central Intelligency Agency, arrived in Tehran; so did Robin Zaehner, later Professor of Eastern Religions at Oxford, who had worked in Tehran during the war, building up Iranian contacts. Woodhouse, Zaehner and a team in the British embassy had a clear instruction from the Labour Foreign Secretary, Herbert Morrison, later confirmed by Eden: to organise Mussadeq's fall.

Eden, an old Persia hand, knew that the chance of British embassy officials installing a Prime Minister more satisfactory than Mussadeq was high. It was only ten years since Eden had himself been consulted about the choice of the Shah. Before long the mob support for Mussadeq would subside; deputies in the Majlis would resume their friendly contacts in the embassy; the Shah would summon up courage and Iran would be returned to the sensible management of someone who understood the British point of view.

Meanwhile, to keep the Americans happy, Eden and Churchill allowed further talks to be held. After the failures of Harriman and Stokes, the third mission to Mussadeq was conducted by the World Bank, which proposed a neat compromise: oil production should resume and it would receive all payments for overseas sales and hold the money as trustees until the terms of a settlement were agreed. Had Mussadeq accepted this proposal, as he almost did, his hand would have been much strengthened: the stranglehold that the British were applying would have been removed and his chance of obtaining a prompt American loan improved. But he had told the people of Iran that anything less than total control would be a sell-out of their sovereignty. Fearing the accusation that he too had given in, he insisted that the agreement should say that the Bank would be acting 'on behalf of the Iranian Government'. Since the entire basis of the scheme, unenthusiastically accepted by the British Government, was that the Bank was to act impartially, as a trustee, this proviso scuppered the arrangement. The American Government regarded the doctor's rejection as unreasonable, turned down his request for financial aid and swung from its previously neutral role in the dispute towards supporting the British.

Mussadeq's failure to secure the American loan lost him an important section of his supporters in the Majlis and made him increasingly dependent on the Tehran crowd. In September 1951 the British chargé d'affaires, George Middleton, had written that Mussadeq, 'being unable to deliver a speech in the Majlis, was obliged to make it in the street to a crowd of passers-by, whom he described as the real Majlis'. The image of John Bull being kicked into the Persian Gulf continued to inspire a thrill of pleasure in the town and Mussadeq used it to override the question being asked by many of his parliamentary colleagues: how did he propose to extricate them from the mess he had led them into? A veteran politician, Jamal Emami, said in the Majlis:

> Is our premier a statesman or a mob leader? What type of premier says, 'I will speak to the people' every time he is faced with a political question? I never imagined that an old man of seventy would turn into a rabble rouser. A man who constantly surrounds the Majlis with thugs is nothing less than a public menace.

The changing public mood in Iran encouraged the British to think their opportunity had come. Many British officials were honestly convinced that to remove Mussadeq was not only in Britain's interests but in Iran's, since he had unleashed forces he could not control. Sir Peter Ramsbotham, a Foreign Office official who accompanied the Stokes mission, later described him as:

> . . . incapable of bringing any form of stability or prosperity to Persia. He could not govern, and the sooner that he left power, the better for Persia. Not for us, for Persia.

Sir Donald Logan, who served in the British embassy in Tehran from 1947 to 1951 and then in the Foreign Office, recalled:

Our policy was to get rid of Mussadeq as soon as possible. We didn't think he would do any good to Iran. The two years he was there was too long for our thinking. He did nothing for Iran.

Even Sir Sam Falle, a junior official in the Tehran embassy whose job was to keep in touch with the younger political elements in Iran, concluded that 'Mussadeq was leading the country to hell on a wheelbarrow'.

Julian Amery, a backbench Conservative MP with connections – his father, Leopold, had been Secretary of State for India and his father-in-law, Harold Macmillan, was in the Cabinet and a longstanding ally of Churchill – recalled:

> The question was whether we could overturn the Mussadeq government. I had a long association with Iran because of my father. Iranians who were opposed to Mussadeq kept getting in touch with me. One of these was their greatest elder statesman, Qavam Saltaneh. He got in touch with me several times and said that he was prepared to do something about it if only the British Government would give him their blessing. He came and talked to me about it in my house in Eaton Square. But the Labour Government and even the Churchill Government were a bit slow at first.

Sir George Middleton approved of Qavam as Britain's candidate for the Prime Ministership:

> He was a very wily politician and an operator and far more likely than anyone else to manipulate the various parties in the Majlis. He was a professional and I won't say devious but an elastic politician: the man to get a majority together.

In July 1952 luck came Britain's way. Mussadeq insisted on his right to appoint the War Minister. The Shah refused and Mussadeq resigned. So the Shah appointed Qavam Prime Minister, and royalist and pro-British deputies in the Majlis voted for him. He had successfully double-crossed the Russians in 1946 and was thought able to win public support. His diplomatic and parliamentary skills were, however, of little use. Mass demonstrations in Tehran demanding the return of Mussadeq led to twenty-nine deaths. Some army units called in to crush the rioters contained pro-Mussadeq troops, who refused to fire and had to be hastily sent back to barracks. Qavam, finding himself powerless, resigned and the Shah quickly capitulated. Sir Donald Logan commented:

> The popular reaction to the resignation of Mussadeq in Tehran was such that Qavam couldn't continue. This was a real setback. I think at the same time the military takeover in Egypt was taking place. It was a bad week.

Mussadeq returned to office, ordered the Shah's powerful twin sister, Princess Ashraf, to leave the country, cut the royal budget, appointed himself War Minister and compelled the Majlis to concede him greater powers than anyone in Iran had enjoyed since Reza Shah. He continued to appeal over the heads of elected deputies to the students and political dissidents of Tehran as the embodiment of that same 'general will' that Rousseau identified in 1760 and that in the 1790s Robespierre saw himself representing in Paris.

Sir George Middleton concluded in a cable to the Foreign Office:

> Mussadeq's megalomania is now verging on mental instability . . . It looks as though the only thing to stop Persia falling into Communist hands is a *coup d'état*.

British arrangements for such an extreme had been carefully prepared. Some of the details have come to light, including an arrangement for bribing members of the Majlis and paying crowd leaders to bring mobs onto the streets to counter the apparently spontaneous demonstrations of Mussadeq supporters. Such matters were largely handled for the British by three brothers, Seyfollah, Qodratollah and Assadollah Rashidian, one of whom was a close friend and ally of the Shah, another a merchant and cinema-owner. The Rashidians had helped Robin Zaehner win Majlis support for Britain during the war; they helped Zaehner, Woodhouse and their colleagues now. The brothers were regular visitors to London, where they kept a family suite at the Grosvenor House hotel, overlooking Hyde Park. They sent their children to school in England. Faced as they thought with a choice between an Iran dominated by either the capitalist west or Russian communism, they opted for the west. Buying votes in the Majlis was no more unusual than buying votes in the English parliament in the eighteenth century. The Rashidians invested their own money in the cause. The suitcases of English money that they received – well over £1.5 million according to the MI6 man responsible for delivering them to Zaehner – represented simply a bonus for the cause.

The Rashidians, with an increasing number of anti-Mussadeq allies among the bazaar merchants, were widely known to be British agents. One of the complaints the Prime Minister's supporters made against him was that, given such knowledge, he failed to take vigorous action against them; but Mussadeq believed in democracy; he thought that so long as he had the support of the people he would be safe; he had no desire to organise either a political party or a pre-emptive coup.

His British enemies had no such scruples. C. M. Woodhouse in his autobiography describes how, late in July 1952, he went to the British airforce base at Habbaniyah in Iraq to pick up arms, which he flew to Iran and had buried. Their purpose was to strengthen the local tribesmen who had on previous occasions helped the British apply pressure on the Government in Tehran.

In October 1952 Mussadeq broke off diplomatic relations with Britain. Until the day before, he maintained smiling personal terms with Middleton, the British chargé d'affaires.

We'd be sitting together at his bedside for hours [Middleton remembered] and getting very heated. Suddenly he rings a little bell and in comes a servant with a great plate of sweetmeats. And he said, 'Now we'll have the cameramen in.' And I said, 'Look, we're in the middle of a discussion, Prime Minister. Is this the moment really for sweetmeats and photographs?' He said, 'Yes, because sweetmeats will do you good, sugar is very good for you. And it is an instinctive reaction for all human beings, when a camera comes in they smile. We've got fifty cameramen, you'll have to do fifty smiles, then I'll kick them out and we shall resume and you'll be in a much better frame of mind.' Of course he'd got something there. He really was a highly civilised person.

Mussadeq claimed when he expelled the British embassy staff that they had been spying. He did not know the half of it. The financiers of the Rashidians and the secret arms importers were all on the embassy payroll and therefore compelled to leave. To the Prime Minister's dismay, the British Council left too, depriving Iranians of English teachers whose work he warmly approved. But the English engineering firm Alexander Gibb and partners stayed; they were installing the first piped water supply to Tehran and Mussadeq's supporters at the poorer end of town wanted the clean water.

Britain's network of plotters had now to be helped from a distance. The Rashidian brothers were provided with a radio transmitter to maintain contact with MI6 and Woodhouse put his opposite number in the US Central Intelligence Agency in touch with other useful allies in Iran. Woodhouse then flew to London and with Robin Zaehner met Anthony Eden at the Foreign Office. Zaehner was understandably downhearted and

*Allies in a dangerous venture: left to right, Seyfollah, Qodratollah and Assadollah Rashidian, photographed in Paris and . . .*

the officials present were relieved at what they took to be the end of underhand procedures, but Eden authorised Woodhouse to renew his efforts by setting up a joint operation with the CIA. Woodhouse and some Foreign Office officials went immediately to Washington.

At this point, November 1952, Dwight D. Eisenhower won the presidential election, opening for the CIA the prospect of a leadership more enthusiastic for vigorous action than President Harry Truman's had been. Woodhouse stressed to his CIA opposite numbers the growing risk of a Tudeh (Communist) party coup which, he argued, Mussadeq would be unable to resist. He therefore took to Washington plans for a pre-emptive coup, based on Britain's longstanding links with tribal leaders in the south and the well-financed organisation of the Rashidian brothers in Tehran, which, Woodhouse writes, included 'senior officers of the army and police, deputies and senators, *mullahs*, merchants, newspaper editors and elder statesmen, as well as mob leaders'. These forces were to arrest Mussadeq and his ministers, capture key towns and install a prime minister acceptable to both Britain and the United States. Sir Sam Falle, who was part of the Foreign Office team that flew to Washington, recalled:

We went there to persuade the Americans that we weren't going to get anywhere with Mussadeq and that his remaining in power was very dangerous to both our interests; also to tell them a little bit about the means we had at our disposal for changing the government. We felt that, after we had been talking for some time, they accepted that Mussadeq remaining in power would eventually lead to a Communist takeover.

Richard Cottam, a leading United States expert on Iran who worked at the University of Tehran in 1951–2 and was advising the State Department on policy towards Iran when the British visitors arrived, commented:

> It was my feeling then – it remains my feeling – that the British understood the extent of paranoia in the United States concerning Communism. These were the days of Senator Joseph McCarthy's Un-American Activities Committee, and the British consciously played on that fear in order to help persuade us to involve ourselves in the coup.

Woodhouse had a list of fifteen candidates approved by the Foreign Office for the post of Prime Minister of Iran. The Americans whittled it down until both sides agreed on the most likely man for the job: General Fazlollah Zahedi, whom Middleton, Woodhouse, Sam Falle and other embassy officials had secretly contacted before leaving Tehran and who was known to be favoured by the Shah. He was not top of the British list: he had been arrested as pro-German in 1941 and held in detention in Palestine until 1945; but the plotters agreed he showed no anti-British feelings. As with Nehru and Patel in India, who had both spent much longer in British custody, the experience proved no bar to British support.

While Woodhouse and Sam Falle were in Washington, Kermit Roosevelt, the head of CIA operations in the Middle East and grandson of the interventionist US President Theodore Roosevelt, happened to be passing through London on his way home from Tehran. Woodhouse's colleagues intercepted him and put the British proposal to him. He had been thinking along similar lines and had received offers of backing from influential Iranians. Since no British official could now enter Iran, Roosevelt had become the obvious man to take charge of the coup.

The Anglo-American meeting of minds in the closing weeks of 1952 did not lead to immediate action. Eisenhower's administration took time getting into the saddle and it was not until July of the following year that the firm decision to proceed was finally taken. Secretary of State John Foster Dulles presided over a meeting at which the go-ahead was given in Washington. Prime Minister Winston Churchill had a number of conversations with Woodhouse and gave the authority for the coup to proceed from London. The date was set for mid-August 1953.

In Iran Mussadeq was being carried along on the torrent. He caused the Majlis to give him emergency powers to legislate by decree and passed laws for land reform and a major redistribution of wealth; he dismissed many civil servants and army officers. The senate objected to some of these measures, so Mussadeq caused the lower house, the Majlis, to close it down. Then the opposition plucked up the courage to resist and Mussadeq's men withdrew, leaving the Majlis without a quorum and therefore unable to function. He held a referendum and won a victory of Soviet proportions, sealing his apparently total dominance. But he was no longer pursuing the policies to which he had devoted his life: defender of the constitution against the Shah, he was now allied with street mobs to overthrow the constitution; opponent of foreign influence, he was now backed by the Tudeh and their Soviet sponsors; his former allies began actively turning against him.

One group who had supported him but now turned were the *ulema*, the Islamic leaders. He was proposing, along lines laid down by the Tudeh party, to nationalise businesses and enfranchise women: both anti-Islamic moves. One pious deputy found that Mussadeq's doctoral dissertation, written thirty-five years earlier in Switzerland, contained strong secular views. Another said that Mussadeq had been made Governor of the province of Fars in 1920 because of his British connections, and, though the deputy cannot have known it, a report from the British envoy in Tehran to Lord Curzon in 1920 had indeed described Mussadeq as 'honest, intelligent, well-educated, capable and very friendly to us'. Now Mussadeq drove the *ulema*, the constitutionalists, the Shah and much of the army and the civil service as well as the British and the Americans into a temporary alliance. The Tudeh won him to their side in face of all these dangers because they were the party of intelligent young Iranians who wanted to get rid of western dominance, religious obscurantism and the purchasable politicians whom Mussadeq had always despised. They expressed their rational, enlightened views in well-written newspapers and journals and in a theatre in Tehran that became famous for the high quality of its performances. The Prime Minister drifted closer to them; he was convinced that these culturally admirable manifestations were not a Soviet front, and he naively ignored the risk that they would unite all Russia's enemies against him.

The coup d'état is a curious form of political activity requiring above all the active co-operation of the ruler who is to be removed. For the coup to succeed he must expose his chest to the dagger, which he does by antagonising those who are normally, in the interest of stability and continuing reward, disposed to back whoever is in power. By August 1953, Mussadeq had bared his chest.

The Anglo-American plan came into operation principally because the Shah refused to act. The son of Reza Shah totally lacked his father's ruthlessness. He had constantly opposed Mussadeq and lost nearly every battle. Now, as the Tudeh party grew openly more assertive and Mussadeq flirted with republicanism, he was convinced that Mussadeq was a disaster for Iran and a danger to the monarchy; but Mohammed Reza Shah still would not strike first. His allies, however, were more decisive and in July 1953 Kermit Roosevelt entered Iran to take charge of the operation.

The plotters required the Shah merely to sign two *firmans* (decrees), one dismissing Mussadeq as Prime Minister and the other appointing General Zahedi. But he was nervous. He did not believe the coup could succeed; he did not believe that both the British and American Governments were really backing him; he suspected that, whoever was running the coup, he was likely to be its victim.

Two officers, a Briton from MI6 and an American from the CIA, visited Princess Ashraf in Paris and gave her evidence of the commitment of their governments, persuading her to fly to Tehran to boost her brother's confidence. Mussadeq insisted that the Shah order her to leave. A second emissary bringing information and reassurance, Brigadier-General Norman Schwarzkopf, an American who had served for six years as head of the Shah's gendarmerie, also aroused Mussadeq's distrust – and still the Shah remained indecisive. Kermit Roosevelt himself had to meet the Shah, which had not been part of the plan. The Rashidian brothers arranged a succession of secret meetings in cars at night during which Roosevelt almost talked the Shah round – but still not quite. As final proof that the American and British Governments really supported the plan, two code phrases were inserted in broadcasts, a speech by President Eisenhower and a Persian-language broadcast by the BBC. These finally convinced the Shah that he should sign the two decrees, but he insisted on quitting Tehran before the coup for one of his houses by the Caspian Sea and made arrangements to leave the country should anything go wrong. In his haste, he left Tehran before the decrees were given to him to sign and Roosevelt had to arrange for them to be flown after him to the Caspian.

The delay and dithering gave Mussadeq warning. When a colonel of the royal guard brought the decree dismissing him from office, Mussadeq had army units loyal to him arrest the message-bearer. The next morning Tudeh party supporters came onto the street shouting anti-royalist slogans and smashing statues of the Shah and his father. According to Richard Cottam, who was by this time working for the CIA, the Rashidian brothers

> . . . saw the opportunity and sent the people we had under our control into the streets to act as if they were Tudeh. They were more than just provocateurs, they were shock troops, who acted as if they were Tudeh people throwing rocks at mosques and priests.

The purpose was to frighten the majority of Iranians into believing that a victory for Mussadeq would be a victory for the Tudeh, the Soviet Union and irreligion. Pro-Mussadeq elements took control of the army and General Zahedi had to be concealed in a house in the American embassy compound. For two or three days Mussadeq seemed to be winning again. The Shah fled to Rome.

This time the forces against Mussadeq were too strong. The Rashidian brothers proved to have built a reliable organisation and Roosevelt to be an able commander. When Mussadeq's supporters took charge of the streets, Roosevelt hid in a temporary radio station, his only means of communicating, via the British relay in Cyprus, to the United States. From there he had thousands of copies of the Shah's decrees dismissing Mussadeq as Prime Minister and appointing Zahedi printed and distributed, and sent a messenger to the military commander in Kermanshah, causing him to advance his tanks on Tehran.

In such conditions of turmoil, power swings erratically. Roosevelt, sitting in his radio station, had the greater weight on his side: more of the army was pro-Shah than pro-Mussadeq; so was the moneyed class of Tehran; and the apparent dominance of the Tudeh in the pro-Mussadeq street demonstrations helped inspire rival and larger pro-Shah demonstrations. For two years the people of Tehran had been Mussadeq's followers. Now the Rashidians and other allies of the Shah made a gigantic effort to buy rival crowd leaders. Richard Cottam states:

> That mob that came into north Tehran and was decisive in the overthrow was a mercenary mob. It had no ideology. That mob was paid for by American dollars and the amount of money that was used has to have been very large.

From the bazaar, the trading centre of Tehran, a demonstration was led by a famous weight-lifting team, calling 'Long live the Shah' and marching towards Mussadeq's house. Well-known Iranian jugglers and tumblers helped draw the crowd; so did the bazaar barkers. The Tehran mob that finally turned against Mussadeq was brought onto the streets by every entertainment that money could buy, but they kept going, joining in the pro-Shah and anti-Mussadeq choruses, because their patience with Mussadeq was at last exhausted.

> There were lots of people in the street [Homa Katouzian, an Iranian university teacher remembers] standing on the pavement and wondering what was happening – lots of talk and conversation and debate as well as speculation. I saw a few lorryloads, people standing in lorries looking like ruffians and thugs carrying clubs and sticks and shouting slogans against Mussadeq and occasionally in favour of the Shah. That was what was happening in the morning. We didn't take it very seriously. We knew that something was wrong but we thought perhaps that things would turn the other way. But in the afternoon it became clear that things were much more serious and the news came that Mussadeq's house had been surrounded.

For two years the loss of the oil-revenue had failed to turn the mob against him. Most of the oil money had been accustomed to find its way into the Swiss bank accounts of the rich, providing them with foreign holidays, Cadillacs, jewellery and, of course, Royal Iranian caviar; a society where the majority had never enjoyed wealth was at first little affected when the source of wealth was cut off. But gradually the effect seeped through. The price of basic foods rose sharply; Mussadeq's promised reforms failed to materialise; his developing alliance with the Tudeh ran against the people's deep-seated religious feelings; his repeated assertion that simple nationalism was the key to success became less convincing; and when he came into open conflict with

*Chosen by Anglo–American agreement, General Fazlollah Zahedi sits in the Tehran Officers' Club a few hours after the coup that made him Prime Minister and restored the Shah to the throne.*

the Shah, Mussadeq's core of followers was reduced to students, radicals and the Tudeh.

The conservative element in both the moneyed classes and the mob had been waiting for its moment, and the coup devised by Woodhouse and directed by Roosevelt released their pent-up feelings. The crowd came to Mussadeq's house, forcing him to flee over a back wall. He had risen by inspiring the crowd. Now that a crowd, differently inspired, demanded his removal, he acquiesced. He did not attempt to resist by force. General Zahedi emerged discreetly from the basement in which he had been hiding to be acclaimed in the streets and the officers' club. He chose his Cabinet and invited the Shah to return from Rome.

This was the last time a plan drawn up in London determined who should be both head of state and Prime Minister of a major country in the Middle East. Kermit Roosevelt was discreetly flown out of Iran the day after he had seen the Shah restored to power. He flew immediately to London to report to his MI6 colleagues and to describe his exploits to Britain's great imperialist, Winston Churchill, at 10 Downing Street. For two hours Churchill, sitting up in bed, listened to the story of the coup he had authorised. The details of the triumph, known in Britain to only a tiny inner circle of Conservative politicians, helped to encourage their belief in the whiff-of-grapeshot theory of foreign policy.

The Iranian experience implanted two ideas that were to shape the even more decisive imperial clash over Egypt in 1956. To Gamal Abdel Nasser it

The gate of the Shah's town palace on 23 August 1953, four days after the coup.

brought the idea of nationalising a foreign asset; for Anthony Eden it was confirmation that Britain still had the power to overthrow inconvenient rulers in countries traditionally protected by Britain's imperial crinoline.

## After the British

The restoration of the Shah marked the end of British overlordship in Iran. Dean Acheson, the American Secretary of State until January 1953, had repeatedly insisted to sceptical colleagues that Britain should remain the alliance's lead partner in the Middle East, including Iran. From August 1953 the Shah's Government moved into the American sphere of influence.

The British company and its principal shareholder, the British Government, did not suffer as much as might have been expected. Their share in the ownership of Iran's oil output and of the refinery were reduced from one hundred to forty per cent, a further forty per cent in the new consortium being bought by five American oil companies, the remainder by Royal Dutch Shell (fourteen percent) and Compagnie Française des Petroles (six per cent). This arrangement ensured that Anglo-Iranian was compensated for the partial loss of its investment. The international oil companies felt a collective glow of pride: they had stood together and demonstrated that a national government could not isolate one of them. On the contrary, their cartel had made up for the enormous loss of Iranian oil to the market by increasing the output of the Arab oil-producing countries, which, while professing to support Iran, allowed their incomes to be increased at Iran's expense. Consequently the terms offered by the consortium to Prime Minister Zahedi in 1954 were little better than those offered by the company to Prime Minister Razmara before he was murdered in 1951.

Dr Mussadeq was tried for treason in an open military court. This provided him with a perfect platform for addressing the people of Iran. He explained the nature of the coup against him, described the Shah's new regime as illegal, wept, laughed, shouted, went on hunger strike and fainted. Running a government and compromising with the realities of world power were not his strongest points. Inspiring his fellow Iranians with constitutional nationalism was. By the time he was sentenced to three years' solitary confinement, he had restored himself to the standing among Iranians that only a man who is somewhat unworldly can attain.

The Shah, who had previously been regarded as intelligent but weak, appeared to have learned from his experience. He took charge of his government and won the confidence and approval of his new principal ally, the United States. He determined to use his enormous oil revenue to turn Iran into a modern industrial country, to maintain the most powerful armed forces in the Middle East and to overcome the hold of medieval Islamic ideas on his people. For many years he appeared to be succeeding. But he faced the fundamental dilemma of the Middle East: Islam, formerly a great world force, had declined into an age of darkness. Most Muslims were resentful at the intrusion into their lives of western science and irreligion.

The Shah, like his father, frightened the Iranian people with changes they did not understand. He decided that to allow them freedom to oppose him would destroy his family's attempt to follow the path of Kemal Atatürk in neighbouring Turkey. Unfortunately for the Shah, his investment in industry built up a class of urban workers whose expectations of a rising standard of living proved beyond Iran's economic capacity. Thus his newest class of supporters became his enemies, turning either to the *ulema* or to the Communists. He exiled leading members of both groups, but the protests continued. He extended the activities of his secret police, the SAVAK, until its reputation for torturing and killing his political opponents became a major embarrassment to his western allies.

The Shah remained a frequent visitor to Washington and London, the proud leader of a westernising élite who hoped to revive the greatness of

*Dr Mussadeq at his
trial, eloquent . . .
fainting . . . weeping.*

ancient Iran. In 1971 he held a spectacular celebration at Persepolis of the
2,500th anniversary of the Persian monarchy, the great kingdom that had
held sway over Greece and Ethiopia as well as Babylon. But when he was
challenged, he proved once again to lack his father's ruthlessness. Although
the vocal and well-educated opposition raised outcries against him in the
west for being a torturer, and although, like his father, he became increasingly repressive with age, his regime was less harsh than those of many of his
neighbours and, in 1977–8 as in 1951–3, he hesitated to strike decisively
against his internal enemies.

In 1979, the Shah's regime was again threatened and again he left his
country, but this time for good. The Persian monarchy was swept away by
an Islamic revival led by the Ayatollah Khomeini: the religious impulse that
Reza Shah, Mussadeq and Mohammed Reza Shah had in turn been
determined to defeat, finally buried them all. Islamic courts, the veiling of
women, the stoning of adulterers and the chopping-off of the hands of thieves
were all reintroduced. When British and Russian and American power were
finally driven out, Iran turned back to Allah.

By plotting the overthrow of Mussadeq and the restoration of an autocratic Shah, Britain helped unleash forces that by the mid-1980s appeared to
be driving the country some hundreds of years back. The judgement of such
tough Americans as Harry Truman and Dean Acheson, that Mussadeq, for
all his many drawbacks, was a leader who could have assisted the west and
controlled events in Iran, was probably right. The meanness of the Anglo-
Iranian Oil Company and the British Government – arising from Britain's
sheer economic weakness and its embassy's outrage at being faced with an
Iranian Prime Minister it could not influence – caused a grave mis-
judgment, so far as both the Iranians and the British were concerned.

# CHAPTER 5

# Egypt

The start of British rule in Egypt in 1882 and its closedown in 1956 were remarkably similar. In each case a spasm of assertiveness, of which at least half the Government in London disapproved, led British ministers to tell lies in order to justify military aggression. On both occasions the British were dragged into their bullying posture by the French. On both occasions the British failed to understand Egyptian nationalist leaders, Colonel Ahmed Bey Arabi in 1882 and Colonel Gamal Abdel Nasser in 1956. In each case British action was directed by an obsessional desire to topple the nationalist leader and was preceded by an ultimatum of breathtaking outrageousness – in 1882 that the Egyptians dismantle defensive guns at Alexandria or face bombardment, in 1956 that they withdraw ten miles from the Suez Canal or face invasion. The difference between the two cases was that 1882 was a complete success, 1956 the culminating humiliation that hastened the British Empire to its end.

Throughout its period of military occupation, Britain underestimated the strength of Egyptian nationalism. In 1882 the mistake was understandable. Egypt had been ruled by non-Egyptians for so long – three thousand years – that the notion of Egyptian nationalism seemed to make little sense: all the top people in Cairo were non-Egyptians, mostly Turks, French, Lebanese, Circassians and Greeks. The ruling family was Albanian. Persons of quality did not speak the language of the people, Arabic, except to servants. Cairo and Alexandria were not so much part of Egypt as of a separate cosmopolitan world: they creamed off the wealth of the Nile valley and of the international markets that gave the two cities their importance. These markets have enriched non-Egyptians throughout recorded history because of their position astride the land link from central Asia to Africa and the sea link from Asia and east Africa to Europe.

## From the Pharaohs to Farouk, 1198 BC–1945 AD

Since the twelfth century BC and the Pharaoh Rameses III, Egypt has been in decline. The Persians ruled here. So did Alexander the Great, whose successors, the Ptolemies, made Alexandria, with its library and museum, the leading Greek city. The Romans treated Egypt principally as a source of grain and under their rule most Egyptians were converted to Christianity. Under the Byzantine rule that followed, the Christian patriarchate of Alexandria played a major role in shaping Church doctrine. Then, in 640 AD, following the death of the prophet Muhammad, Arab power surged forth from the desert and a succession of Islamic rulers, from Damascus, Baghdad and Istanbul, came to govern Egypt; most Egyptians were duly converted to Islam.

Britain became interested because of Napoleon Bonaparte's statement, 'To ruin England we must make ourselves masters of Egypt.' Control of Egypt, he believed, would enable French troops to travel quickly to India, outdistancing the British ships that sailed round the south of Africa, so that France could challenge Britain's hold on its greatest overseas possession. From the victory of Horatio Lord Nelson at the battle of the Nile in 1798, Britain's first concern in Egypt was to keep out the French. Palmerston explained:

> We do not want Egypt, any more than a rational man with an estate in the north of England and a residence in the south would wish to possess the inns on the road. All he could want would be that the inns should be always accessible and furnish him, when he came, with mutton-chops and post-horses.

One of the most remarkable sustained efforts of British foreign policy was the resistance to the construction of the Suez Canal. Napoleon wanted it dug for the passage of French ships and successive French Governments courted the rulers of Egypt to win the contract. Britain, particularly Palmerston, pursued every possible alternative. British ships were fastest in the voyage round Africa to the Far East, so strong British interests opposed the development of any shorter route. If one was to be developed, the British preferred a railway from Cairo to Suez, which, given Britain's dominance of early railway construction, would inevitably have been British. Better still was a route that avoided Egypt and its French connections altogether. To this end the British Government financed an attempt to open the Euphrates from the point near Alexandretta where it comes within fifty miles of the Mediterranean through to the Persian Gulf, territory entirely controlled by Britain's allies the Ottoman Turks. In 1834 the parts to make two complete river steamers were sent in crates from Birkenhead, assembled on the Euphrates and dispatched down the river to prove that the route could become commercially navigable. The experiment failed: one of the steamers was caught in a sandstorm and capsized.

That was not the limit of British ingenuity in opposing the scheme to build a canal at Suez. Robert Stephenson, the great engineer and railway builder, was commissioned to study the feasibility of the canal and reported that the difference in height between the Red Sea and the Mediterranean made it impossible. His findings scared off investors for a while. And when French determination revived, Britain used diplomatic pressure. Egypt was ruled by a Khedive or viceroy appointed in Istanbul and nominally subordinate to the Ottoman Sultan, whose authority was needed for a major project with international repercussions. British ambassadors to Istanbul repeatedly persuaded the Sultan to refuse permission. Disraeli described the canal scheme as 'a most futile attempt and totally impossible to be carried out'. When, in 1869, the canal was finally opened, Britain sent the Prince and Princess of Wales to a ceremony that marked the defeat of sixty years' steadfast opposition to the inevitable.

The opening of the Suez Canal was a triumph for the current Khedive, Ismail, for whom it was the largest of a series of projects. He built irrigation canals, railways, telegraph lines, bridges, harbours, lighthouses, sugar mills; he reclaimed more than a million acres from the desert; he also built himself palaces and entertained lavishly. The Khedive financed most of these activities by borrowing against future tax income, but the interest on his debts became larger than the income from his taxes. To bridge the gap he decided in 1875 to sell the forty-four per cent he owned in the Suez Canal Company. The purchaser was Britain. The Prime Minister, Benjamin Disraeli, now converted to enthusiasm for the Canal, told Queen Victoria:

> You have it, Madam . . . Four millions sterling! . . . There was only one firm that could do it – Rothschilds. They behaved admirably; advanced the money at a low rate; and the entire interest of the Khedive is now yours, Madam.

However, the sale of the Suez shares did not solve the Khedive Ismail's problem, and the British and French Governments, normally inclined to turn a blind eye to the distress of citizens whose foreign bonds collapsed, decided in Egypt to intervene. They leapfrogged each other in their eagerness to help the Khedive reschedule his debts and sent expert advisers to increase his revenue. Soon an Englishman was appointed Egypt's Minister of Finance and a Frenchman Minister of Public Works. For two parties merely bent, as Palmerston had put it, on using the roadway, the British and French showed surprising enthusiasm to manage the inn. The trouble was, as Ferdinand de Lesseps, the Frenchman who built the canal, was told in 1885 when he was made a member of the Académie Française:

> You have created . . . a serious embarrassment . . . In case of a maritime war, everyone will be striving to occupy it. You have marked out a great battlefield for the future.

In 1881 a group of Egyptians, led by an army colonel, Ahmed Bey Arabi, demanded the promotion of Egyptians in the army and government and the setting up of a parliament and a constitution. This demand that Egyptians should run their own affairs was something new, but the British Government, now Liberal and headed by Gladstone, favoured constitutional progress, opposed imperialism and was content to accept that Arabi's

*Ferdinand de Lesseps, the visionary who, with the help of the French Government, raised the money to build the Suez canal.*

movement, which enjoyed the reluctant acquiescence of the Khedive as well as wide popular support, must be allowed its way. The French, however, were mistrustful partners with the British in Egypt and, having recently secured Tunis from the Ottomans (in a deal that allowed Britain to acquire Cyprus), were afraid that Arabi's demand for the removal of foreign overlordship might spread throughout north Africa. The French Prime Minister, Léon Gambetta, therefore drafted a joint note to be sent to Egypt and by sheer force of personality he bullied the British Foreign Secretary, Lord Granville, into signing:

> The two Governments being closely associated in the resolve to guard by their united efforts against all cause of complication, internal or external, which might menace the order of things established in Egypt, do not doubt that the assurance publicly given of their formal intentions in this respect will tend to avert the dangers to which the Government and Khedive might be exposed and which would certainly find England and France united to oppose them.

This aggressive bluster, sent on 2 January 1882, matches ill with a letter Gladstone wrote two days later:

> 'Egypt for the Egyptians' is the sentiment to which I would wish to give scope: and could it prevail it would I think be the best, the only good solution of the 'Egyptian question'.

Unfortunately Gladstone's letter was private, the joint note was public. Gladstone was giving most of his attention to Ireland at this time and, as was common in the nineteenth century, left his Foreign Secretary a free hand.

The note created a sensation in Cairo. It arrived just before the meeting of the Egyptian Chamber of Notables which was to advise on Colonel Arabi's new constitution. One item which the leaders of the chamber had been prepared to accept was continued European control of the budget, but the note created such an angry reaction that the moderates were outvoted and Arabi found himself the leader of a movement more assertive than he had planned. The hostility aroused led the British and French Governments to send warships to Alexandria as a precautionary measure, although the British consul had warned that to do so would put the European residents there in danger. Riots broke out and several hundred were killed or injured, including at least fifty Europeans. Although it has since been accepted that Arabi and the military did not start these riots, the accusation was widely put about at the time, particularly by those Turks, Syrians, Albanians, Circassians and others who had good reason to be opposed to the constitutional movement. Arabi had by now been appointed Minister of War by the Khedive and was doing his best to restore order, but the Khedive and the British became convinced that to end the riots and the danger of revolution he must be removed and his movement crushed.

To this end Sir Beauchamp Seymour, the admiral in charge of the British fleet in Alexandria, issued a remarkable ultimatum: he required that the forts in Alexandria harbour be surrendered to him for dismantling or else he would bombard them. The French had nothing to do with this threat; Gambetta's Government had fallen and his successors, not wanting to make war on Arabi and a revolutionary movement which, if successful, might turn to France for support, withdrew their ships. The Egyptian Government politely explained that 'the requirements of the British admiral are contrary to the laws of public international right'. So the admiral commenced a bombardment that continued for ten and a half hours and destroyed the forts. The population fled Alexandria, which was left in flames.

Jingoism now seized both the Egyptians and the British. A Liberal-Imperialist group among Gladstone's ministers persuaded him to ask the House of Commons for £2.3 million to pay for an expeditionary force which quickly defeated Arabi's army and established British occupation of Egypt – a British army on Egyptian soil, the most powerful force in the country. The stated reason for the invasion was to support the Khedive in putting down a rebellion; but when the British arranged to try Arabi (the Khedive wanted to hang him without trial) the evidence to support the charge of rebellion could not be mustered. So the British persuaded him to plead guilty in return for a promise that his death sentence would be commuted to exile in Ceylon, where he lived for eighteen years in some style.

Victory in Egypt did not please Gladstone. Asked whether the Government contemplated an indefinite occupation, he replied 'Of all things in the world, this is a thing which we are not going to do'. The British hoped to reform Egyptian law and government largely along the lines Arabi Pasha had demanded and then leave. Formally, Egypt was to remain part of the Ottoman Empire with internal independence. This was in deference to the sensibilities of the Egyptians (after the Indian Mutiny wise Britons were chary of taking on the management of more orientals), of the Ottoman Sultan (who was thought the best agent to secure Britain's interests throughout the Middle East) and above all of the French. To pacify France, British governments repeated endlessly that the army of occupation in Egypt would shortly be withdrawn. At the same time British control tightened under what Alfred Milner, later Colonial Secretary, called 'the veiled protectorate': maintaining friendly charge of a buffer state by loans, advice and the occasional gunboat, was cheaper and less trouble than annexation. The man who ruled Egypt went under the modest title of British Agent and Consul-General.

From 1883 to 1907 the occupant of this post was Sir Evelyn Baring, nicknamed 'over-Baring' because, whatever formal gestures he made to the Khedive and the parliament, everybody in Egypt knew that Baring was the boss. And, however sincere British protestations that they were in Egypt only temporarily, Baring could not find Egyptians whom he considered able to run the place. He complained of 'the utter incapacity of the ruling class' and later wrote that 'the Englishman' (himself) was convinced his mission was to save Egyptian society, but,

> . . . How was he to accomplish his mission? Was he, in his energetic, brisk, northern fashion, to show the Egyptians what they had to do and then to leave them to carry out the work by themselves? This is what he thought to do, but alas! he was soon to find that to fulminate against abuses which were the growth of centuries was like firing a cannon-ball into a mountain of mud . . . If he were to do any good he must not only show what was to be done but he must stay where he was and do it himself.

To judge from his years of work in Egypt, reducing the burden of taxation on the *fellahin* (the small, peasant farmers), struggling to reduce the rate of interest on Egypt's debts, reorganising and improving the administration, westernising the legal system, restoring year-round irrigation to large parts of the country, his sentiment was sincere. But Egyptians were increasingly offended by his schoolmasterly tone and by the growing number of young men he imported to run the Civil Service – the 'annual British invasion of new recruits' who, like their Turkish, Greek and Persian predecessors, were not required to learn Arabic. To the nationalist-constitutional movement of Colonel Arabi and to critics in London the occupation appeared far from temporary. But Baring – who also never learned Arabic – had the power and the skill to get his way. His British subordinates found him almost as autocratic and unapproachable as did the Egyptians.

No sooner had Gladstone's Government gone to war for Egypt, which it

*Sir Evelyn Baring, 'over-Baring', who patiently reorganised the public finances and government of Egypt.*

said it did not want, than it was faced with a demand to go to war for the Sudan, which it wanted even less. The vast area of the Sudan had been conquered by Egypt early in the nineteenth century. During the 1880s a revolt arose there against Egyptian rule. The Government of Egypt tried to put it down, but failed. Baring had scarcely arrived in Cairo when the Sudanese swept towards him, led by a Muslim fanatic known as the Mahdi (or messiah) whose followers were determined to restore the purity of unadulterated Islam and whose victories over Egyptian armies were a far more serious threat to the stability of Egypt than Arabi's constitutional movement had been.

Gladstone wanted nothing to do with the war, but luck was against him. Living in London was a retired imperial character, General Charles Gordon, a muscular Christian whose activities in many parts of the world, including China, had been wholeheartedly dedicated to the service of God. His most recent office had been the Governor-Generalship of the Sudan, to which he had been appointed by the Khedive because of his competence and honesty. While there he devoted himself to the God-given task of suppressing the Arabian slave trade.

Gordon was a popular figure in England, and anti-slavers, Christians and imperialists all clamoured for him to be sent back to the Sudan. Gladstone eventually gave in, but instructed Gordon merely to secure an orderly withdrawal. The reluctance of the great Liberal Prime Minister to be an imperialist was now proved. When the Mahdi besieged Gordon in Khartoum, Gladstone was so slow to send a relief force that Gordon was killed, along with most of his men, and the Sudan was lost. The best the British could do was to keep Mahdist troops out of Egypt.

After Gladstone's Government had fallen, Lord Salisbury and the Conservatives raised the money to avenge Gordon's death and conquer the Sudan, a task that was sealed by the Sirdar (Commander-in-Chief) of the Egyptian army, Sir Herbert Kitchener, at the battle of Omdurman in September 1898. (During this battle a young subaltern, Winston Churchill, joined in a rash charge into a gully full of Dervishes and, unlike many of his fellow Lancers, came out alive on the other side.)

Thus the British came to rule both Egypt and the Sudan, while refusing publicly to admit ruling either. In Egypt the Khedive continued to enjoy all the ornaments and pageants of his office; in the Sudan the Governor-General, nominally appointed by the Khedive, was always a Briton, as was most of the administration. The fiction was maintained that the Sudan was a 'condominium', half Egyptian-ruled, half British, but few were deceived. The British habit of recruiting sportsmen from Oxford and Cambridge to run its administrative service led to the Sudan's becoming known as the land in which blacks were ruled by blues.

In 1906, towards the end of Baring's time as Consul-General, an incident occurred which reinforced Egyptian detestation of British rule. A group of Britons went pigeon-shooting at Denshawai, a small village in the Nile delta. The locals, who had raised the pigeons, protested, a scuffle broke out and two men died, one British, one Egyptian. Had the matter ended there, Denshawai would be forgotten, but the British, including Baring, saw the incident as an example of the xenophobic fanaticism that threatened their safety. English newspapers demanded exemplary punishments, a tribunal was set up, dominated by an English judge who knew little Arabic, and drastic sentences were imposed. At the scene of the incident, with the villagers compelled to be present, four men were hanged and nine flogged, each receiving fifty lashes. Such punishments had been normal under Britain's predecessors in Egypt – the introduction of lenient European penal methods to the Egyptian courts had been followed by a crime wave under Baring – but now Britain's own professed standards helped to generate a wave of revulsion amongst Egyptians.

Nevertheless the spread of Egyptian nationalism did not stop the British from increasing their control. In 1904 Britain had signed the *Entente Cordiale*, which gave France a free hand in Morocco and Britain the same in Egypt. What was more, France conceded Britain the right to waive international supervision of passage through the Suez Canal. Napoleon's dream, built by a Frenchman, was at last openly in British hands.

Eldon Gorst, who succeeded Baring in 1907, wrote:

Throughout the British Empire there is no place in which the occupant enjoys greater freedom of action than that of British agent and Consul-General in Egypt. The Consul-General is the *de facto* ruler of the country, without being hampered by a parliament or by a network of councils like the Viceroy of India.

Gorst's successor, Lord Kitchener, the victor of Omdurman, proved the point; of the Khedive's few remaining powers, Kitchener took away his authority to preside over the Cabinet and to confer titles without the approval of the British Agent.

In 1914, the process was completed. Turkey, still nominally the sovereign power in Egypt, declared for Germany in the war. Britain had to choose between annexing Egypt as a colony or declaring a protectorate. Kitchener happened to be in England at the time, where he was made Minister of War; his deputy in Cairo was against direct administration, which a colony would have required, so a protectorate was declared with a new princeling, called the Sultan, chosen by the British from Egypt's Albanian ruling family and with ministers more than ever under the thumbs of their British advisers. Some academic dispute followed as to whether Egypt was or was not part of the British Empire. Baring, now ennobled as Lord Cromer, thought it was:

> After hanging in the balance for thirty-three years, the political destiny of Egypt has at last been definitely settled. The country has been incorporated in the British Empire. No other solution was possible.

A Turkish army with an able German adviser promptly set out to seize the Suez Canal. They hoped to stir up a rising of Egyptian troops and civilians against the British occupiers, since the replacement of the Muslim Sultan at Istanbul by the Christian King in London as their overlord was bound to dismay Egypt's Muslims, especially the many influential Turks who served as ministers and officials and the many distinguished Turkish women who lived in the harems of the aristocracy. British efforts to raise forces by conscription were resisted by the new Egyptian ministers, who said they could not carry such a measure and retain public support. The British were sufficiently worried to ban all political meetings, impose total censorship on Egyptian newspapers and ship in a new army. For two years they could not remove the Turkish threat from the Canal, nor could the Turks induce the rising that they hoped would open Cairo to them. German aircraft bombed Port Said and even, once, Cairo itself.

Then the numbers of British, Australian and New Zealand troops in Egypt were increased, Cairo's famous brothels received a huge, new spate of business and, with the help of some twenty thousand Egyptian auxiliaries and their donkeys and camels, requisitioned without Egyptian Government approval, the campaign against the Turks was launched. The operation involved building roads, railways, barracks and pipelines in the Canal zone so that it became a huge military base. From there British offensives pushed the Turks northwards, first out of Palestine, then out of Syria.

The collapse of the Ottoman Empire at the end of the war left Britain, long its prop, as principal inheritor. Yet the only substantial place in the area where the British were established and from which they could run this great new empire was Cairo. A. J. Balfour, the Foreign Secretary, told the House of Commons: 'British supremacy exists in Egypt, British supremacy is going to be maintained. Let no one in Egypt or out of Egypt make any mistake on the cardinal principle.'

Some Egyptian nationalists led by a lawyer and former minister Zaghlul Pasha ('pasha' was a title equivalent in the Ottoman empire to 'Lord' in the British) asked to be allowed to attend talks about the post-war settlement, first in London then at the peace conference in Paris. They wanted to send a delegation (in Arabic *Wafd*). The first reaction of the British Government was high-handed and insulting. Unlike the Arabians, whom the Egyptians with reason considered less politically advanced than themselves, unlike the Cypriots and the Armenians, the people of Egypt were to have no say in their own future. Zaghlul, a great speech-maker and campaigner, given so strong a cause, organised committees and petitions nationwide. He was striking the same nationalist chord as Colonel Arabi almost forty years earlier and, like Arabi, he quickly had the Egyptian nation marching to his tune. The movement that sprouted up at Zaghlul's summons called itself the Wafd; soon it absorbed all other political parties: every politically conscious Egyptian was a nationalist, so they nearly all joined.

The British responded by deporting Zaghlul to Malta. He became a national hero. Students paraded through Cairo chanting his name, overturning trams, breaking windows. The riots worsened and, to the surprise of the British, fresh ones erupted in the countryside. When the police shot rioters, their funerals became great political processions addressed by nationalist speakers. Within days Britons were being killed, eight on a train from Luxor to Cairo, their mutilated bodies displayed to frenzied crowds at every station.

Britain had enough troops in Egypt to reassert control and David Lloyd George, the Prime Minister, sent General Sir Edmund Allenby, the conqueror of Jerusalem, to Cairo to take charge. Allenby, a thinking soldier with some knowledge of nationalist feeling in the Middle East, knew that force could subdue Egypt's nationalism but not destroy it. He assembled notables in Cairo and told them that when he had brought the disturbances to an end he would redress legitimate grievances. He went on: 'It is you who can lead the people of Egypt. It is your duty to work with me in the interest of your country.' Within a week he advised the Government to release Zaghlul. Thus Allenby reversed the policy that had evolved steadily through the efforts of Cromer and Kitchener and that had become the clear purpose of Balfour and the Cabinet in London. Officials in Cairo and Whitehall were shocked but the Cabinet could not reject the first recommendation of the war hero it had just appointed. Zaghlul was released and travelled directly to the peace conference in Paris.

Lord Milner, the Colonial Secretary, led a mission to Egypt to sort out the mess. He was a leading imperialist and his instructions required him to find a solution 'under the protectorate'. Prominent Egyptians refused for this reason to talk to him. When a member of his mission visited a law court, the Egyptian lawyers walked out. Milner reluctantly concluded that to impose

imperial rule on so sullen a population was impossible: 'It appears to be frequently assumed that Egypt is a part of the British Empire. This is not and never has been the case.' A mere five years after Cromer's assertion Zaghlul and the Wafd had forced Milner to withdraw it.

In London the Cabinet faced a problem: Allenby, newly awarded a peerage and a £50,000 grant by a grateful nation, and Milner, a senior Cabinet minister, both reported not only that Egypt could not be part of the Empire, it could not even be run as a protectorate: the Egyptians' demand to run their own affairs was so strong it must be met. However, Australia, Canada, New Zealand and South Africa had by their support in the war decisively helped Britain to victory; their leaders had a claim to be heard when, at the post-war Imperial Conference, they insisted that the Suez Canal route must be kept secure. Moreover, Cabinet ministers like Balfour and Churchill recognised a unique opportunity. The Bolshevik revolution had temporarily obliterated the foreign ambitions of Russia, which would otherwise have demanded a substantial share of the Ottoman Empire and a say in its carving-up; France, exhausted by the war and relieved to be given Syria, which the British had conquered, was in no position to object;

*In the embassy garden, which swept down to the Nile, Lord Allenby kept a pet stork.*

Germany and Turkey were defeated; now was the moment to enlarge the Empire, not to give in to the whims of a rabble-rouser like Zaghlul. While the Cabinet had been unable to reject Allenby's advice to release Zaghlul, Milner's conversion – he thought it necessary to recognise Egypt as a nation – was too much. His report was not accepted. He resigned and Churchill succeeded him as Colonial Secretary in 1922.

The Cabinet's new policy was to reintroduce Baring's system of ruling with an Egyptian puppet government. Allenby knew that such a policy would never be acceptable to Zaghlul and therefore had him once more deported, this time to the Seychelles. Strikes and boycotts continued until the British agreed to give Egypt nominal independence, but limited by a treaty allowing Britain to keep vast forces there and to be responsible for defence and all dealings with foreign nationals.

Even with Zaghlul deported, Egyptian public opinion rejected this as a sham. Since no Egyptian Government was prepared to sign a treaty embodying such provisions, Britain simply declared them to be so: 'The British protectorate over Egypt is terminated and Egypt is declared to be an independent sovereign state.' The scion of Egypt's Albanian royal family whom the British had recently named Sultan Fuad became, by British decision, King Fuad. He had been brought up in Italy and liked to talk

Italian. With Allenby and his successors he spoke – or rather, as the result of a gunshot wound to his throat caused by the husband of a lady friend, barked – in French.

Fuad wanted to turn the clock back even farther: he claimed all the powers of an absolute monarch. Allenby overruled him and, with widespread support from Egyptians, imposed in 1923 a liberal constitution with a parliament elected by all adult males. For this Fuad never forgave him. For the next twenty-five years the government of Egypt resembled a three-legged stool: leg one, the King, trying to take power away from both the main political party, the Wafd, and the British, but needing either popular support in Egypt or British backing to get his way; leg two, Zaghlul's party, the Wafd, winning nearly all elections but frequently rendered ineffective by being opposed to both the King and the British; and leg three, the British, trying to win their political battles by persuading the King or the Wafd, or sometimes other politicians, to support them, but repeatedly having to rely on force.

Zaghlul, soon released from his second deportation, had established good relations with Ramsay MacDonald and when Labour came to power in 1924 visited him in London. But even though the Labour Party was publicly committed to complete independence for Egypt, Zaghlul got nothing. MacDonald insisted on retaining all the restraints on Egyptian sovereignty imposed in the declaration of 1922. In the disappointment and anger that swept Cairo, a group of extreme Egyptian nationalists murdered the Sirdar of the Egyptian army (who was also, inconveniently, Governor-General of the Sudan), Sir Lee Stack. The sequel to this event revealed the reality of power. Zaghlul went to the British residency to express his regret and Allenby, accompanied by a fully equipped cavalry regiment, publicly admonished the Council of Ministers and reasserted British primacy in the Sudan by reducing the modest number of Egyptian officers and army units there almost to zero.

This pattern recurred several times. When King Fuad, with popular backing, tried to declare himself King of the Sudan, Allenby threatened to depose him. When Zaghlul, carried away by an election victory in 1926, was bent on measures London regarded as anti-British, a battleship of the Royal Navy arrived in Alexandria and the Wafdists, remembering 1882, persuaded Zaghlul to stand down in favour of a more pliant prime minister. When in 1927 the Wafdists attempted to secure Egyptian control of the army, another warship had to visit Alexandria before they would agree to a British Commander-in-Chief and second-in-command and a British majority among the officers.

For fourteen years – from 1922 to 1936 – no Egyptian Government would sign a treaty with Britain. The British were in Egypt by force and could not obtain formal Egyptian consent. But by 1936 the Wafd had softened. Zaghlul had died, and the young British Foreign Secretary, Anthony Eden, skilfully used the Italian aggression in nearby Ethiopia to make Egyptians feel that Britain's presence and willingness to defend Egypt were after all of some use. Eden wanted the legal right for British troops to be in Egypt in the event of war. The new Wafd leader, Nahas Pasha, wanted the same, though he did not like to say this in public.

So a treaty was signed. Every such action diminishes somewhat the sovereignty of the states that sign it. The 1936 Anglo-Egyptian treaty went farther, making it plain that Egypt was not sovereign at all, but a princely state on the Indian pattern. Every political party in Egypt, thirteen in all, was persuaded to send a representative to London to sign, to prevent their campaigning against the treaty. Most of the parties, however, were unimportant. The one that mattered was the Wafd, which, like the Congress in India had established itself as the national movement for independence.

The Wafd did win some concessions: the treaty would be renewed or reviewed in twenty years, i.e. in 1956; if British troops were then no longer needed in Egypt they would go; meanwhile, as Egypt's ability to defend itself grew, British forces would withdraw from Cairo and Alexandria into the Canal zone and Sinai; the Inspector-General of the army would be an Egyptian; the number of Europeans in the Egyptian police would be reduced; foreigners in Egypt would henceforth be subject to Egyptian law.

Each side interpreted the treaty in its own way: to the British it meant permanency; to the Egyptians it meant twenty years. Since the Wafd was a popular party that had to win elections, the treaty was presented as a triumph for Egyptian nationalism. The British High Commissioner, Sir Miles Lampson, was re-titled Ambassador and ceased to drive through Cairo in his Rolls-Royce with two police-cars before and behind and a fleet of motorcycle outriders. He reduced his procession to one police-car and two outriders.

From the Egyptian point of view the best that could be said was that, while the earlier Wafd demand for immediate, unfettered independence had led nowhere, the 1936 treaty opened some prospect of removing the British slowly by stages. Anthony Eden, the British Foreign Secretary, and all the other signatories appeared on an Egyptian postage stamp to commemorate the treaty. Nahas, the Wafd leader, was applauded in the streets.

The circumstance that had made Britain anxious to have the treaty soon arose. Article eight placed all Egypt's facilities at Britain's disposal in the event of war. In 1939, therefore, with the start of the Second World War, Egypt fell again under formal British control. All the arguments about colony or protectorate or treaty became irrelevant. Cairo was soon the military hub of the British Empire. While Lampson was master of the embassy, conferring with the King and his ministers, pulling the strings that kept the puppet theatre of government performing to a British script, the British Middle East Command was installed in the Garden City, close to the embassy, directing campaigns not only in north Africa but in Greece, Crete, Somaliland, Ethiopia, Syria, Iraq, Persia and Yugoslavia. Anthony Eden, now Minister of War, repeatedly visited Cairo to oversee the work of the generals and the busy assembly of staff officers. Nearby at Alexandria was the Royal Navy's Mediterranean headquarters. Oliver Lyttelton, a full Cabinet minister and a close colleague of Churchill, was installed in Cairo to keep the Prime Minister constantly in touch. So important to Britain's strategy was Egypt considered that in September 1940, only three months after Dunkirk, when German armies were massing for the invasion of Britain, Churchill ordered reinforcements including aircraft to be sent from the British Isles to help hold Egypt and the Suez Canal. Singapore could be sacrificed; Egypt could not.

Cairo was a bright, bustling city, providing Australian, British, Indian, Kenyan, New Zealand and South African troops with every service an army requires. The officers and gentlemen who commanded this vast enterprise enjoyed in Cairo the wines, the caviar, the grouse, the gaming rooms, the racecourses and the polo fields – as well as the company of journalists, politicians and entertainers stopping over at this imperial crossroads – that made war tolerable.

It came naturally to the British to treat with dignity traditional Islamic rulers like the emirs of northern Nigeria, the princes of Arabia and the sultans of Malaya. In Egypt, by contrast, the thousands of years of acquiescence in foreign rule, the readiness to bow the head, the unreasonable refusal of the nationalist leadership, as the British saw it, to face the realities of power, the predisposition of the King and the political leaders to intrigue and double-deal, led many British to show contempt. To them Egypt was not an ally in the war – Egypt did not declare war until February 1945, when it was certain which side would win – but a subordinate. To most Egyptians Britain was an unwelcome and arrogant occupying power: indifference to the outcome of a war between Europeans was to them a natural and reasonable attitude.

Early in 1942, Sir Miles Lampson faced a problem. The war had begun well for Britain in North Africa. Late in 1940 Germany's ally, Italy, ruler of Libya since 1912 and recently conqueror of Ethiopia, attempted to invade Egypt and was swept out by British troops under General Wavell. The 22-year-old King Farouk, however, like his father Fuad whom he had succeeded in 1936, was fond of Italians; when Lampson urged him to dismiss his Italian court officials, Farouk had them made Egyptian citizens (and compulsorily circumcised). The King was particularly friendly with the palace barber, an Italian who, the British believed, procured him girls. In spite of the 1936 treaty, Egypt's loyalty to the allied cause was suspect.

In 1941, as General Erwin Rommel's Afrika Korps began its assault on the British in an attempt to recover the Italian losses, Farouk decided to appoint as Prime Minister a man called Ali Maher who, while not openly pro-German – that would have been foolishly provocative – made it plain he would do nothing to discipline the pro-German element in Cairo, where cries of 'Long Live Rommel' were heard on the streets and elements in the army, including the Chief of Staff, wanted actively to side with the Axis powers. At the start of what promised to be a difficult campaign, Lampson repeatedly asked Farouk to appoint a wholeheartedly pro-British government. A suitable Prime Minister was available in Nahas Pasha, the principal Egyptian politician behind the decision to sign the 1936 treaty and leader of the Wafd.

The King refused. He did not want to commit himself to the British when it seemed that a German army might soon arrive in his capital. In London Churchill complained it was intolerable that Cairo should contain 'a nest of Hun spies, that the canal zone should be infested by enemy agents'. How was Lampson to persuade King Farouk to abandon his own plans and appoint Nahas Pasha Prime Minister?

Lampson consulted the minister of state, Lyttelton, and with the approval of Anthony Eden and in the face of some misgivings from the generals, they decided on 4 February 1942 to send the King an ultimatum: appoint Nahas Prime Minister by 6 pm or accept the consequences. At 6.15 the King delivered his reply. The ultimatum was an infringement of the Anglo-Egyptian treaty and of the rights of Egypt: the King could not assent to it. Lampson sent a message to say that he would be calling on the King at 9 pm. By the time he did so, British tanks and armoured vehicles had surrounded the Abdin palace. The King prudently ordered his royal guard not to resist and Lampson went in accompanied by General R. G. W. Stone, the officer commanding British troops in Egypt, and a squad of officers, all fully armed. Lampson read the King a statement which ended:

> Your Majesty has refused to entrust the government to the leader of the political party which, by commanding the general support of the country, is alone in a position to ensure the continued execution of the treaty . . . Such recklessness and irresponsibility . . . make it clear that Your Majesty is no longer fit to occupy the Throne.

He then handed Farouk a document to sign. Drafted by Walter Monckton, the man who had handled the abdication of King Edward VIII in London and was now serving in Cairo as Lyttelton's deputy, it read:

> We, King Farouk of Egypt, mindful as ever of the interests of our country, hereby renounce and abandon for ourselves and the heirs of our body the throne of the kingdom of Egypt and all sovereign rights, privileges and powers in and over the said kingdom and the subjects thereof and we release our said subjects from their allegiance to our person.

Farouk appeared to be about to sign when his chief palace adviser spoke to him quietly in Arabic, after which, Lampson wrote, 'Farouk, who was by the time completely cowed, looked up and asked almost pathetically if I would not give him one more chance.' The King then promised to invite Nahas to form the government. Lampson and his party left. Later that evening the chief palace adviser telephoned the embassy to say that the King had summoned Nahas, but Britain's nominee could not get into the palace

*Sir Miles Lampson, British ambassador, arriving with Lady Lampson for the opening of the Egyptian Parliament, November 1939.*

because British troops were blocking all approaches. Less than an hour later Nahas became Egypt's Prime Minister.

Thus Lampson solved his immediate problem, but the events that day at the Abdin palace, like the public hangings and floggings at Denshawai, were to help make the next confrontation between British imperialism and Egyptian nationalism even more ugly. A young Egyptian officer fresh from serving in the Sudan, Lieutenant Gamal Abdel Nasser, wrote to a friend of the events of 4 February 1942:

> What is to be done now that this has happened and we accepted it with surrender and servility? . . . I believe that colonialism, if it felt that some Egyptians intended to sacrifice their lives and face force with force, would retreat like a prostitute.

Lampson and Lyttelton were convinced that they had done their job well: the danger of a vacillating or disloyal government in Cairo was removed and Nahas not only interned suspected pro-Germans, including Ali Maher, but remained staunchly pro-British through the worst days of the war, as Malaya, Singapore and Burma fell to the Japanese, all mainland Europe was overrun by the Germans and Rommel came to within sixty miles of

Alexandria. If such gains could be bought only by browbeating the King and arousing anti-British feeling in the Egyptian army, the price seemed, in the midst of war, none too high.

## Anthony Eden and Gamal Abdel Nasser, 1945–1956

The Labour Government that came to power in Britain at the war's end in 1945 gave Egypt new hope. The British insisted that France give independence to Syria and the Lebanon, and the new British Foreign Secretary, Ernest Bevin, planned to evacuate British troops from Egypt to Cyrenaica, the north-eastern part of Libya, where the British were on good terms with the dominant tribe, the Senussi, and hoped to be granted a UN trusteeship. If this scheme failed – as it did – Bevin was prepared to move the British troops to Palestine, Cyprus, Aden, Malta, Transjordan, anywhere that would keep them on hand in the Middle East but get them out of Egypt. In May 1946 he told the House of Commons that the Government was offering to withdraw all British forces from Egypt before discussing with the Egyptian Government future defence arrangements for the area. Churchill attacked the policy and the two men were for some time, in the words of Pierson Dixon, Bevin's private secretary, 'on their feet on either side of the mace shaking their fists at one another'.

The parliamentary rough-house did not deflect Bevin, but foot-dragging by the military for a while did; he asked Attlee to press the Chiefs of Staff to speed the evacuation of Cairo and Alexandria, adding, 'It needs a warlike operation to get them to move.' Slowly Bevin and Attlee overcame the demand of their defence advisers that the army keep a maintenance staff in the canal zone with a right to move back if trouble threatened and secured Cabinet approval for a complete withdrawal as the prelude to a genuinely voluntary Anglo-Egyptian treaty. The Cabinet had eventually to overrule the Chiefs of Staff, who were convinced that the mass of workshops, dormitories, railways and warehouses centred on Ismailia and surrounded by a training area the size of Wales were essential for Britain's defence. Sergeant-Major James Hilden recalled:

> There was fifteen miles of jeeps in crates at Ismailia. The Egyptians thieved everything. It used to be said that if there was anything you couldn't get at the base, you could get it at the village nearby. At Tel-el-Kebir there was a mountain of brass shell-cases. We guarded it, we surrounded it, but we couldn't keep them out. We even used landmines. One Egyptian had his legs blown off. Six months later we caught the same one – on crutches – climbing over the shell mountain.

Bevin's firmness enabled him, in October 1946, to reach agreement with the then Prime Minister of Egypt, Sidki Pasha, that Britain would have its troops out of the main towns by March 1947 and out of the canal zone by

September 1949. In return Egypt agreed to consult with Britain on Middle East security. The agreement looked as though it would bring Britain's troubled involvement in Egypt to an end. The Egyptian nationalists had obtained all they wanted with the single exception of the Sudan. Bevin insisted and Sidki agreed that the Sudanese must be consulted about the future of their country. This was to prove the undoing of the deal.

The British administration in the Sudan had developed unique qualities. With few British traders or missionaries and no settlers to challenge it, recruited not by the Colonial Office but by the Foreign Office (because of the formal condominium with Egypt), it ran like a school prefects' room: bossy, inconsistent and ruthlessly protective of its charges. Its members were determined to teach the Sudanese to run their own country and not to let them be taken over by Egypt. They had promised the people of the Sudan the chance to decide their own future – whether to be fully independent or to join Egypt – and that promise could only be reversed by the Foreign Secretary at the price of dishonour and, they warned, violent resistance by Sudanese nationalists. Remembering how the Mahdi had killed General Gordon and driven out both Egyptian and British forces – Kitchener's reconquest being achieved only after the Mahdi's death – policy-makers in London noted that the leader of the main party demanding independence was the Mahdi's posthumous son, Sir Abdel Rahman el Mahdi, who had been carefully looked after by the British and had amassed a fortune growing cotton in the British-created Gezira irrigation area, but who still had the power to rouse his followers with the inspiration of Islam and the memory of his father.

The Foreign Office had failed to provide Bevin with Eden's 1936 reinforcement of a full flush of Egyptian politicians brought to London to sign. Equally damaging was Bevin's timing: he made his offer to withdraw British forces before obtaining his *quid pro quo*. When Sidki Pasha returned to Cairo, he found that the enormous concessions he had gained were not enough. The Wafd, in opposition, demanded in addition that the British withdraw from the Sudan and recognise Farouk as its King. Since Sidki could not meet this demand, the Egyptian parliament refused to ratify the agreement. Sidki resigned and Anglo-Egyptian relations reverted to their usual state of mutual exasperation. The British carried out their promise to withdraw their troops from Egypt's towns by 1947, but most of them did not leave the country; they were transferred to the canal zone. There, instead of the ten thousand stipulated in the 1936 treaty, Britain retained almost eighty thousand men. Egyptian nationalists felt that Britain, as usual, had completely disregarded them.

This feeling was made worse by the events of 1947–9 in Palestine. The Mufti of Jerusalem (see p. 120 and p. 136) was living in Cairo and helped to persuade Egyptians that the handing of Palestine to the Jews was an act of British perfidy. Although Britain did not support the partition of Palestine nor openly back the Jews in 1947–8, Egyptians were familiar with British deception and took the Mufti's word. He was particularly influential in an organisation, the Muslim Brotherhood, whose growth had been a problem to Farouk for many years. Its members wanted Egypt to be an austere Islamic state, whereas Farouk's taste was for gambling, extravagance and things European. The partition of Palestine boosted the popularity of the Brotherhood to new heights. It demanded that Egypt lead a holy war, a *jihad*, to save fellow-Muslims from being robbed of their land. The headquarters of the Arab League was in Cairo, and Egypt, of all League members the largest and most advanced, was urged to give a lead. Farouk's Government reluctantly entered the war in the hope that victory in Palestine might strengthen their hand in dealing with both the British and the malcontents at home. The war, however, did Farouk no good. The Egyptian armies failed. The Government gave them too little time to prepare, their equipment was antique, their training irrelevant and their senior officers – all appointed by Farouk – were incompetent. The defeats suffered at the hands of the unexpectedly effective Israelis made Egyptian officers angry both with the regime that governed them and with the British who had for so long prevented them from serving effectively in the defence of their country. No doubt the British had been right to suspect during the 1939–45 war that to put modern arms into the hands of some Egyptian units would be as good as handing them to the Germans. The result was that Egyptian soldiers blamed Britain for keeping them ill-equipped and ill-trained.

The growing demand for Britain to get out of Egypt found vigorous

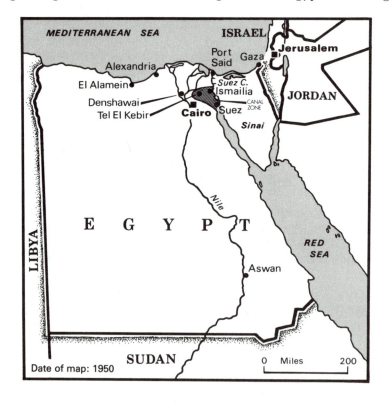

expression when the Wafd came back to power after an election in 1950. The movement Zaghlul had founded in 1922 retained popularity mainly by being more stridently anti-British than any other party – all the more so after its co-operation with the British in 1942–5. Having failed to persuade the British to reduce the number of troops in the canal zone to the 10,000 specified in the 1936 treaty, the Wafd Prime Minister, Nahas Pasha, and his interior Minister, Serag-ud-Din, cut off fresh food supplies to the zone and moved the 40,000 Egyptians on whose labour the zone depended *en masse* to Cairo. Many of the workers were led to think they would find jobs in the Egyptian public service in return for giving up their income from the British; some gave up their jobs as a patriotic sacrifice; some were intimidated. These moves made life unpleasant for the British troops but did not cause their withdrawal. On the contrary, the position of the Labour Government had hardened. Egypt's failure to ratify the Sidki–Bevin agreement strengthened the hand of those in the British establishment who demanded that Egypt agree to a new Middle East defence arrangement *before* Britain relinquish the Suez base. A proposal to this end was worked out with the United States, France and Turkey by which Britain would return the base to Egypt, which would immediately place it under a joint Middle East command in Cairo that would include Egyptian officers. The American ambassador in Cairo

*The man who nearly brought Britain painlessly out of Egypt – Ernest Bevin visits the Sphinx.*

*King Farouk greets the British ambassador, May 1950. Second from right is Nahas Pasha.*

pointed out that the only way to secure Egyptian agreement was to hand over the Sudan to Egypt. Since the British remained unwilling to do this, their efforts to arouse Egyptian interest in the four-nation proposal made no progress.

The Egyptian Government, badly needing to retain popular support, took an unexpected initiative. In October 1951 the parliament in Cairo unilaterally abrogated the 1936 treaty and declared Farouk King of the Sudan. This coup was transacted just as a general election in Britain brought the Conservatives back to power and the new Foreign Secretary, Anthony Eden, disdainfully treated this 'purported abrogation' as impudence: the Egyptians had not the power to cause King Farouk to set foot in the Sudan and the 1936 treaty contained no provision for unilateral abandonment. Nahas knew as well as Eden – since they had been the principal signatories – that the treaty was to expire in five years' time and that Britain and Egypt must, under its terms, agree on what should follow. The treaty was binding in international law. Eden considered that Nahas was merely playing to the Egyptian gallery for reasons of internal politics.

Certainly Nahas was under pressure. With his Wafd colleagues and even his wife publicly accused of corruption, the King widely unpopular and the army crawling with discontent, he needed the one brilliant success for which his movement had been founded – the complete restoration of Egyptian independence – to save his Government from collapse. For Egyptians another treaty, another defence arrangement, would seem to be 1922 or 1936 all over again. This time the British departure must be real. Nahas' reply to Eden took the form of a guerilla war against the British base. Serag-ud-Din had the Egyptian army train volunteers to shoot off-duty British soldiers and blow up buildings. Before long the British command had to declare the main towns in the canal zone – Port Said, Suez and Ismailia – out of bounds. A British soldier, Corporal Alex Ingram, remembered:

> The sporadic activities of the Egyptian guerillas effectively tied us up: they almost made us prisoners within our own camp. The boredom was terrible. One of our sergeants said that, apart from the fact that the food was a little better and that we got it regularly, the situation was not dissimilar from what he had experienced as a prisoner of war in Germany.

The zone's supply of fresh water from the Nile could not be cut off, but the British water filtration plant was put out of action, spreading fear of dysentery among the troops. The guards on the filtration plant had been shot and the action launched, the British believed, by a group of *fedayeen* (commandos) hiding in the mud huts of the village of Kafr Abdou. The British therefore turned their tanks' guns on the village and demolished it. This may have been a military necessity but it was a serious political

*Art students in Cairo in 1951 express their feelings about Britain.*

mistake. The Egyptian Government and press denounced the action as an atrocity, since the British were attacking Egyptians' homes and villages. Volunteers came forward to join the 'liberation battalions' attacking the zone and reinforced the auxiliary police, under the sympathetic eye of Serag-ud-Din.

In January 1952, with the Suez base under virtual siege, the Egyptian irregulars launched their biggest assault – on the garrison at Tel-el-Kebir, the principal depot for materials and munitions in the Middle East. The British responded by occupying the town from which the assault had been launched, Ismailia. British troops surrounded the auxiliary police head-quarters with overwhelming superiority of arms. The commander of the two hundred or so police officers inside, Captain Mustafa Ibrahim Rifaat, was awkwardly placed: two days earlier a group of auxiliary police had sur-rendered to the British and Serag-ud-Din, the Interior Minister, had said on Cairo Radio that henceforth all policemen, regular or auxiliary, would be expected to 'fight to the last bullet'; if they failed to do so they would be brought before a military tribunal.

> I met Brigadier Exham [Rifaat recalled] at the gate of the police station and he gave me his warning, that we were to leave our arms, go out raising our hands and there is a train at the station to take us to Cairo. I told him, 'If you stay a hundred years we shall resist. This is our land and we shall die on our land.' I went inside and I distributed the ammunition and everyone took his position. At about eight o'clock in the morning the switchboard man said, 'The Minister of the Interior wants to speak to the officer in charge.' I gave Mr Serag-ud-Din a true picture of what had happened and he asked me, 'What are you going to do?' I said, 'We are ready to take our position. We are going to fight. If the British enter this place they will find only dead bodies.' He said, 'All right; God will be with you.'

Brigadier Exham, according to his wife, described what followed as 'a distasteful task, like shooting sitting duck – a disaster'. Some fifty were killed in the police post and a hundred wounded before Rifaat eventually sur-rendered. He had subjected himself and his men to a three-hour massacre, on the instruction of the minister. Militarily the resistance was pointless, but politically and psychologically Serag-ud-Din knew what he was doing: he was stirring up the Cairo mob, angered by the earlier razing of Kafr Abdou, to a state of frenzy.

The next day, 26 January 1952, 'Black Saturday', the frenzy was unleashed. The British embassy advised Britons to keep off the streets and stay at home: the massacre of Ismailia was about to be avenged. Students marched to a huge meeting at the university to demand arms with which to remove the British from their land. Auxiliary policemen went on strike in protest at the fate of their colleagues and joined the march, as did soldiers and sailors. A demonstration assembled outside the Cabinet offices, where a

Wafd leader addressed them, promising that the Government was with them in their determination to kick out the British. So far the crowd were angry, potentially dangerous, but not violent. At midday, however, a new element became active in the centre of Cairo: an organised group of fire-raisers.

The first building put to flame was a 'cabaret'. The police stood by watching. Then began a routine: the Rivoli and Metro cinemas were set alight by the same group of men, who, according to many witnesses, arrived by jeep equipped with cans and bottles of petrol and crowbars to break open doors. Their next target was the Turf Club, where members of the British colony were relaxing. Here, once the fire was started, the mob, avenging the previous day's massacre, stopped club members from fleeing, striking them down with iron bars and leaving them to the flames. Nine people – including the Canadian trade commissioner – were burned to death in this way.

The fire-raisers had a list of targets: the tea shop Groppi's, the Cecil bar, the Ritz café, the St James's, the Parisian – haunts of the Europeans and those who aped them. Jewish stores were set aflame: Cicurel, Robert Hughes, Adès. The fire-raisers leading the mob would use their tools to prise the shutters or break open the doors of the premises on their list, then some of them would rush in to pile up the furniture or goods for sale and soak them with petrol. They would then leave, throwing in lighted rags or using tapers on long sticks to start the blaze. The operation was organised, disciplined and fast. At first there was no looting.

British, French and American firms all had their premises burned. Shepheard's, where Gordon waited in 1883 while Cook's arranged his travel to Khartoum to face the Mahdi, was probably the most famous of all the British Empire's hotels: founded for travellers on their way to and from India, it became, thanks to imperial stability, the place in which millionaire Englishmen and Americans and half the royalty of Europe enjoyed Cairo's winter season: the antiquities, the opera (just across the gardens from the hotel) and the wonderful dry heat. At about 2.30 the fire-raisers arrived, swept aside the staff and guests, made a bonfire of the furniture and carpets in the centre of the elegant hall and fled. From Shepheard's the guests were allowed to escape, although one jumped to her death.

The brisk work of the fire-raisers, often observed by the police but not impeded, soon had much of the centre of Cairo ablaze. General Neguib (of whom more later) summarised the damage:

> Before the army was permitted to re-establish order, seventeen foreigners (including nine Britons and one Canadian) and fifty-odd Egyptians had been killed. A British club, a Jewish school, an office of the Moslem Brotherhood, four hotels, four night-clubs, seven department stores, seventeen cafés and restaurants, eighteen cinemas and seventy other commercial establishments, including banks, automobile show-rooms and airline ticket offices had been destroyed.

Firemen arrived to fight the fires, but the crowds repeatedly slashed their hoses. By mid-afternoon, the fire-raisers had worked through their list and the crowd turned to looting. Had there been a breeze, all Cairo would have been aflame.

At lunchtime on Black Saturday, King Farouk gave a banquet for six hundred, including almost every senior officer in the Egyptian army. Just as Cairo was starting to burn, they sat down to eat their eight-course lunch in the Abdin palace, to celebrate the birth ten days earlier of the King's first son. Later Serag-ud-Din wrote an article in the Wafd newspaper *El Misr* in which he described his efforts from 1.30 onwards to get General Haydar, the Commander-in-Chief, to send troops to stop the rioting. But Haydar was at the palace and could not be brought to the telephone. General Neguib described how Haydar and the King held 'frequent whispered conferences with various couriers [which] indicated that they were aware of what was happening' but though both 'seemed preoccupied throughout the banquet . . . neither so much as mentioned the riots.' Having failed to get Haydar on the phone, the Interior Minister drove to the palace, where, at 2.45 pm, Haydar came to an ante-room to tell him the King was going to order the army into action and that they would be in the city by 3.30. But, according to Serag-ud-Din, the first army unit did not arrive until 5 pm. Since his telephone calls, his visit to the palace and the arrival of the first troops were verifiable events, Serag-ud-Din's account has some credibility. Whoever organised the fire-raisers – the facts have not been publicly established – the King either knew what was afoot and chose to let it proceed or else he was criminally negligent.

Black Saturday happened because the imperial relationship with Britain had made the Egyptian monarchy and government irresponsible: they had become Britain's eunuchs. When Serag-ud-Din ordered the police post to commit suicide, when Farouk delayed calling the army to Cairo, they acted like men who did not care about the outcome of their orders. The decades of uncertainty about Egypt's status, the repeated attempts to secure independence repeatedly rejected or side-stepped by Britain had reduced the Egyptian regime to a state in tinsel.

Britain had enough troops in the canal zone on Black Saturday to put down the Cairo demonstrations. Eden, after seeking American backing and being told he would not get any, decided the soldiers should not intervene. Anthony Nutting, then Parliamentary Under-Secretary at the Foreign Office recalled:

> I remember the meeting very well. Eden was acting Prime Minister because Winston was on a slow boat coming from the United States, and Eden sent for Field-Marshal Sir William Slim, the Chief of Staff, to discuss what should be the British reaction. Slim said, 'You can move the troops in if you want. Anybody can get into Egypt. But how do you ever get out? Last time we sent an expeditionary force into Egypt, we didn't get out for a very long time. In fact we are still there.' Eden decided that the troops

*One of the British camps in the Suez Canal Zone.*

should not be moved and that Farouk must be left to deal with the situation.

Within six months the King and the Wafd were both finished. The 'free officers', a group in the Egyptian army who had been plotting for several years, expelled Farouk and took over the government. The operation was all but bloodless because the leader of the free officers, Colonel Gamal Abdel Nasser, overruled those of his colleagues who pressed for the King to be executed. Nasser was to prove a ruler of Napoleonic impact, revolutionising his own country and winning followers throughout the Middle East. Like Napoleon, he will be the subject of hundreds of biographies. In the story of the End of Empire his significance is peculiar. Unlike Gandhi, who was determined to achieve independence for India but took no action intended to undermine imperial rule elsewhere, Nasser believed he could lead an Arab resurgence that would put an end to the rule of the imperialists and their stooges in all the countries of the region. This brought him into conflict with

Anthony Eden, Britain's Foreign Secretary and later Prime Minister. The final years of Britain's imperial relationship with Egypt are best understood as the tragedy of Anthony Eden and his obsession with Nasser.

Eden's relationship with the new military regime in Egypt began well. To his surprise, the nominal head of the regime from 1952 to 1954, General Mohammed Neguib, was eager to sort out the biggest single stumbling-block in Anglo-Egyptian relations, the Sudan. Neguib himself was half Sudanese and as anxious as any Egyptian for the 'unity of the Nile valley', as Egyptian control of the Sudan was tactfully called. He recognised, however, that the British promise of self-determination for the Sudan could not be set aside and believed he could persuade the Sudanese to exercise this option in favour of unity with Egypt rather than independence. An Anglo-Egyptian agreement on the Sudan was therefore reached. Britain would go within three years; during this transitional period the Egyptian Government and some others would advise the British Governor-General while elections and other parliamentary processes enabled the Sudanese to settle their own future. In return Neguib dropped the insistence of Farouk's governments that Egypt's title to the Sudan be recognised immediately.

This agreement shows Anthony Eden at his best – and taking the first steps on the road to his tragedy. Eden was as much a diplomat as a politician. He often removed himself from broad issues of principle to give his full attention to mastering the complex details of a negotiation. He used immense skill in bringing irreconcilable parties together. Over the Sudan, the transitional period that preserved the possibility of both union with Egypt and full independence was the kind of diplomatic mechanism at which he excelled. The achievement was all the more considerable in the light of the sustained American pressure to give in to Egypt's demand in order to get talks started on the canal base and wider issues of Middle East defence.

Eden's greatest difficulty, having had the arrangement accepted by all parties in Egypt and the Sudan, was with his own Prime Minister. Churchill did not want to give the Sudan to Egypt, nor did he wish to give it independence. Sir John Colville, Churchill's private secretary, said later that the Prime Minister 'positively desired the talks on the Sudan to fail'. Eden threatened to resign if his policy was not accepted and won over both the Cabinet and the Conservative backbench foreign affairs committees by reportedly brilliant speeches. The Anglo-Egyptian agreement was signed in February 1953. Churchill, the veteran of Omdurman, sulked. In January 1952, in a speech to a joint session of Congress in Washington, he had gone so far as to say that he favoured a token US force joining the British in the canal zone. This confirmed the US Government's belief that the British still held an outdated, imperialist view of Egypt, and America's consequent non-cooperation increased Eden's difficulties.

Churchill's activities in the House of Commons caused Eden problems that were ultimately to prove even more serious. Eden's Private Secretary, Sir Evelyn Shuckburgh, said of those days:

Eden was, from the time I came to know him in 1951, constantly preoccupied with the problem of how to get this country into a tenable position, because we were stretched all over the world in places which we had no possibility of continuing to dominate. It was a question of persuading not only his own party but the nation. He was not helped and he was really rather frightened by the opposite view in the party, rather under the umbrella of the great war leader. Churchill realised the crucial importance of the Suez canal zone, the strong point for the navy, the air force and the army, linking the Commonwealth as a defence unit. He was therefore very much against the proposed withdrawal. On the other hand he was eighty, Eden his crown prince was for it, and the Americans were for it, so he was in a difficult position.

Julian Amery, a member of the Conservative backbench 'Suez Group':

... made a speech in the House of Commons attacking Anthony Eden, who I saw was going right over to withdrawing from the Canal zone. It was quite a bitter little speech. At about half past ten the next morning, the telephone rang and a voice said, 'This is the Prime Minister's secretary.' I thought I was going to get a reprimand. He said, 'The Prime Minister asked me to congratulate you on your speech. He thinks you got all the right points.' Then, a month or two later I happened to be at a talk and Mr Churchill asked me how I was getting on about Egypt. I told him what I felt about it and he said, 'You keep it up. You're on the right lines.' Considering that I was attacking his Foreign Secretary, this was not at all discouraging.

Sir Evelyn Shuckburgh noted in his diary:

*20 January 1953*: Prime Minister passionately interested in the Egyptian situation . . . Questions down in Parliament about this . . . and he wanted to see the drafts of what A.E. [Eden] would say. The latter much upset: 'If he has so little confidence in me, I had better go.' . . . *30 January 1953*: The Private Secretaries at No. 10 all attacked A.E. and the Foreign Office for their policy on Egypt . . . they thought it ridiculous that we should not be able to cope with the Egyptian army with the eighty thousand men we have in the zone. The Chiefs of Staff, they said (obviously quoting the Prime Minister), always say that the force available in any emergency is insufficient. You have to prove the contrary. If we go out of the Sudan and Egypt it will be another stage in the policy of scuttle which began in India and ended at Abadan. It will lead to the abandonment of our African colonies . . . Sir John Colville [Churchill's principal Private Secretary] tells me that the PM is very bellicose against A.E. 'If he resigns I will accept it and take the Foreign Office myself.'

In June 1953 Churchill, temporarily in charge of the Foreign Office while Eden was ill, persuaded a conference of Commonwealth prime ministers that together they could play a great new role in preserving world peace –

and it all depended on keeping the base at Suez. He even induced the Prime Ministers of India and Pakistan to call at Cairo on their way home to make his case to the Egyptians.

In these circumstances, Eden required courage and skill to continue his preparations for a retreat. He and Churchill had separate conversations about Egypt with Dwight D. Eisenhower, who had become US President in January 1953. The agreed policy that emerged was the kind of complicated, interdependent package at which Eden was adept: a phased withdrawal of British troops; the canal base to be maintained ready for use in the event of war; Egypt to join a Middle East defence organisation and to receive military and economic aid. For months the negotiations proceeded, with Eden stressing to his unhappy colleagues in London that British interests were preserved by Egypt's being required to agree to the maintenance of the base and a British return in the event of war. Arguments with Egypt centred on who was to maintain the base (British servicemen, British civilians or Egyptians) and which countries had to be involved in a war to permit reoccupation of the base. Ali Sabri, one of the free officers who now had the title Minister of Presidential Affairs, recalled:

> Whenever we came to a disagreement in the negotiations, the guerillas would start their activity against the British base – to put pressure and to give the impression to the British commander that it could not become a safe base for military action. So it was going on and off all the time according to the course of the negotiations – sabotage of communication lines and within the camps and killings of British soldiers.

Gradually Eden and the chiefs of staff persuaded Churchill that moving the base facilities to Jordan, Cyprus or other parts of the Middle East would strengthen Britain's position. In July 1954 the agreement was concluded.

> The agreement with Nasser, which I negotiated myself, [Anthony Nutting said] was a compromise. Nasser wanted the British garrison to be withdrawn. He wanted no British troops on Egyptian soil, which was understandable, because their presence offended against his concept of national dignity. At the same time he was prepared to concede that we needed some form of military assistance, which the canal zone was equipped to provide. We needed somewhere our tanks, armoured cars, guns and so on could be looked after in an ordnance depot. So the essence of the compromise was that the Egyptian army would move in, that we would share the Suez canal base with the Egyptians, but only the Egyptians should be in uniform and the British ordnance people should be in civilian clothes. I think Anthony Eden shared my hope that we would enter into a period of good relations with Egypt. After I'd signed the agreement he sent me a telegram saying, 'Don't come home immediately. You've had your head in details of negotiations with Nasser. Go off and find out what makes the man tick. Talk to him and find out how he sees the

future.' And I came back and reported that I thought he was a great patriot, determined to remain neutral as between the power blocks, but anxious to have good relations with Britain and open this new chapter on a friendly note. And Anthony Eden seemed to share this hope at that time.

Britain conceded more than Egypt did. The withdrawal of the British troops – due to be completed by June 1956 – began, but Egypt did not agree to participate in a Middle East defence system. Eden needed Egyptian co-operation in such a system, partly because Egypt had the most advanced economy of any Arab country, partly to retain the maximum possible British say over the canal zone, but mainly to keep his Prime Minister and backbenchers quiet. Nasser, however, who had by now displaced Neguib as leader of the Egyptian regime, would not join any pact. He feared showing any weakness towards the British, particularly as the canal agreement did not provide for the total, immediate break with Britain that was popularly expected and had therefore brought him some criticism at home. So Eden turned to Iraq and Turkey, which together in February 1955 formed what became known as the Baghdad Pact. Eden saw this as the basis for the defence arrangement he required to keep the peace in Westminster – a pact that several Middle Eastern states would join and that Britain would dominate. He tried to persuade Egypt to take part and visited Cairo for this purpose. In keeping with Eden's status as one of the world's great statesmen of the previous twenty years, Nasser came to the British embassy rather than grant him an audience in the presidential palace. It was to be their only meeting. Mahummad Heikal, a journalist and friend of Nasser, recalled:

Before dinner Mr Eden was talking about his being an expert on Egyptian affairs. President Nasser did not utter a word at that point. It was Eden talking about his experience in Arab affairs, about his role in the signing of the treaty of 1936, about the picture which he still had in his country home with all the Egyptian negotiating team and him sitting among them. He even greeted President Nasser when he entered in Arabic. Nasser was astonished. I think that was a mistake.

Field Marshal Lord Harding, then Chief of the Imperial General Staff, said:

The object of the meeting was to try and persuade Nasser that it was in his interest to become an active member of the Baghdad Pact. We got down to business after dinner and Anthony Eden started off by a few remarks about the political situation and then I was put on to explain our strategic thinking about developing the Baghdad pact, that is to say, Turkey, Iraq, Iran and Pakistan would provide the front-line defence and we and the Americans would provide the major logistics and air support. And for that Egypt was vital, because it had a double entry through the Mediterranean and through the Red Sea, it had air fields, it had an industrial capability; it was absolutely suited in every way as the main support area. After I had finished, Anthony asked Nasser if he would like to comment and Nasser

*Eden is said not to have liked Nasser's holding his hand for the photographers. The two men only met once, in the British embassy, Cairo, in February 1955.*

said, 'Well, I agree, I agree completely.' What flummoxed me was that Anthony then went on for the best part of an hour to try to convince Nasser of what I would have thought was the logical conclusion, that they should join the Baghdad Pact. But Nasser said the time was wrong. I think that meeting was the beginning of Eden's complete mistrust of Nasser.

Ralph Murray, a member of the Foreign Office team at the dinner, remembered:

Eden tried rather insensitively to lecture Nasser on what his defence arrangements should be. It produced a rather bad effect upon Nasser, who didn't like being lectured. Eden seemed to think that he could make common cause with Nasser in defence arrangements concerned with the possibility of Soviet eruptions from the north. But it was perfectly plain that Nasser was not interested in that kind of thing.

Nasser's own comment on the meeting (in an interview with the *Sunday Times* in June 1962) was that Eden behaved as though 'he was talking to a junior official who could not be expected to understand international politics'. Nasser was strengthened in his belief that Britain wanted to use the pact to dominate the Middle East and he became more determined than ever not only that Egypt should stay out but that other Arab states should be dissuaded from joining.

During the next months Pakistan and Iran joined the pact, but its principal sponsor, the Iraqi Prime Minister Nuri-es-Said, had little success with his fellow Arabs. Nasser had told him that the Arabs should have a pact of their own, with no outside powers involved, except in supplying arms. Nuri replied, 'Zero plus zero plus zero equals zero', meaning that, since the power of each Arab state was zero, a major western member was needed to give the alliance substance. He wanted fellow Arab states to join primarily to make the pact palatable to young radicals and for this reason asked the British to persuade Jordan to become a member.

Nuri was a good friend of Britain, the kind of Arab nationalist Eden understood and liked. During the 1914–18 war, he had been a young officer in the Ottoman army and he was one of the small group of Arab soldiers who sided with the British against the Turks. He became a close associate of the Emir Feisal and found that the British kept their word, both in making Feisal King of Iraq and in helping him develop his new country. Governments came and went in Iraq, but Nuri was always near the centre, frequently Prime Minister, reliably if brutally keeping the country in order and ensuring that the British stayed in touch with developments there. Iraqi oil was extracted mainly by the British; an RAF base had been maintained at Habbaniyah since 1920; Nuri's generation of Arab nationalists saw no reason to allow either themselves or their British allies to be driven from the area by crowds of idealistic but simple-minded young students and junior officers. By 1955 Nuri was seventy, a regular and welcome visitor to London. Nasser, then aged 37, thought that, like King Farouk and his ministers, Nuri was due for retirement.

Nasser had begun to use a remarkable new instrument of persuasion throughout the Middle East – the radio. Each of the Arab countries run by a Nuri-like regime – Libya, Lebanon, Jordan and Iraq – contained young people of an Arab nationalist turn of mind. Cairo Radio helped make Nasser their hero, the man who was finally throwing the British imperialists out of Egypt and would lead the Arab world to real independence. As Mahmoud Riad, Nasser's Foreign Minister, said:

> The transistor radio was more important than guns. Nasser sent tens of thousands of radios to the Yemen. I saw illiterate tribesmen ask for 'the radio with Nasser's voice', and they would only buy it if the set was turned to the appropriate station. It would be impossible to overestimate the impact of the radio, the Voice-of-the-Arabs, in the liberation struggle.

Nasser considered a resurgent Egypt to be the natural leader of the Arab world. To help secure that leadership he had Cairo Radio direct a constant flow of bitter abuse at 'reactionary regimes', especially those of Nuri-es-Said in Iraq and King Hussein in Jordan. The Voice of the Arabs, founded by General Neguib in 1953, became a convenient outlet for those Cairo writers whose radical energies now needed to be turned away from the home front. Cairo Radio was Nasser's instrument. Precisely for that reason he could not turn it off without risk.

When Nuri-es-Said asked Britain to persuade Jordan to join the Baghdad pact, Nasser felt challenged. To him this was the reactionary alliance that he must oppose if he was to hold his position in Egypt, let alone in the Arab world. He used his key weapon, the radio, to remind students and young officers in Jordan that the pact was the tool of the imperialists and that therefore King Hussein must not join. When Britain sent an emissary to Jordan to work out with the King details of the additional British military aid he would receive on joining the pact, public feeling had become inflamed against any British-backed deal. Riots in Amman were quelled only when the King changed prime ministers in order to announce that he would, after all, not join the pact.

Anthony Eden, who had by now succeeded Winston Churchill as Prime Minister, was becoming obsessed by Nasser, yet no final breach had occurred. Many British officials understood Nasser's difficulties. With British troops still not completely gone from the canal zone, nationalist feelings remained touchy and dangerous. Nasser continued to buy arms from Britain and America and showed a preference for dealing with the western powers, so long as they did not attempt to dominate the Middle East. But during 1955 his ideas broadened. The western powers were balancing the supply of arms to Israel and its Arab enemies, preventing Nasser from obtaining all the weapons he needed both to keep his senior officers happy – a key problem for one who had come to power by a military coup – and to defend Egypt against Israel. In February 1955 a major Israeli raid into Gaza convinced Nasser that new and additional arms for his forces were essential. In April he left Egypt for his first trip outside the Middle East, to attend an Afro-Asian conference at Bandung in Indonesia. The conference was dominated by the idea of neutrality and non-alignment. Nehru, the Prime Minister of India, encouraged Nasser to obtain all he could from both the west and the Communists. President Tito of Yugoslavia explained how he had maintained his country as a Communist state independent of Russia and the rest of the Soviet bloc. Communist China's Prime Minister, Chou En-lai, advised him to buy arms from Russia.

Later in 1955 Nasser acted. He bought a large quantity of arms from Soviet Russia, via Czechoslovakia. For the British this was almost like an invasion of their own territory. They had fought a war in the Crimea and devoted a century of diplomacy to keeping the Russians out of the Mediterranean, and Russia had scarcely shown its head in the area since 1917. Now, at Nasser's request, Russia had reappeared. Western domination – of the oil, of the sea routes, of defence arrangements – seemed to be threatened. Eden's response was that the errant Egyptians must be won back. Nasser was eager to build a great dam for irrigation and hydro-electricity at Aswan, where the British had built a dam in 1902, one of the prouder legacies of British rule. Nasser's arms deal with Czechoslovakia and Russia convinced Eden that the new dam must be western-financed; the Russians must not be allowed to extend their influence.

The Aswan high dam was to be one of the largest engineering projects in the world. It would revolutionise Egypt's economy, bringing vast areas of desert into cultivation and preventing the disastrous Nile floods. Some knowledgeable observers dismissed it as Nasser's twentieth-century pyramid, but when Eden learned that the Russians were seriously thinking about paying for it he sent urgent telegrams seeking the help of President Eisenhower. Eden wanted to organise a consortium of Britain, the United States and the World Bank to provide the foreign exchange that would be required. Putting together such a deal takes time: the US Congress must be persuaded to vote the money, the World Bank's studies must show that the spending is justified. Such obstacles apart, Eden believed by early in 1956 that, in the competition to be generous to Egypt, the west was winning.

An incident then occurred that tipped Eden's growing concern about Nasser into a form of obsessive madness. This honourable diplomat-politician had at last become Prime Minister and led his party to a comfortable election victory in which the Conservatives' slogan 'Working for Peace' was recognised by voters as a fair tribute to him. He had bravely worked for agreements – on the Sudan, on withdrawal from the canal zone and on financing the Aswan dam – which a large section of his own party thought feeble. What now shifted him into a state of mind totally out of character with his entire previous career was the sudden dismissal in March 1956 by the young King of Jordan, Hussein, of the English officer who commanded his army, Sir John Glubb.

Hussein's motives were clear. Glubb had been in charge since 1939, thirteen years before Hussein came to the throne, and was therefore less easy to command than the young King required. Jordanian officers, inspired by the spirit of Arab nationalism as well as ambition, wanted an Arab in the top job. It was all perfectly understandable. Eden's own Foreign Secretary, Selwyn Lloyd, understood it. He later wrote:

> When the King was in London in the autumn of 1955 I had spoken to him about Glubb. We knew that Glubb was nearly sixty. We suspected that he irritated the King. It was obvious that the time for his retirement could not be long delayed.

Anthony Nutting, now Minister of State, understood it. On the night of Glubb's dismissal, Nutting was in temporary charge in the Foreign Office. He recalled:

> Eden's reaction to Glubb's dismissal was violent. He blamed Nasser and

he decided that the world just wasn't big enough to hold both of them. One had to go. He declared that night a personal war on Abdel Nasser. I spent most of that night with him, first in the Cabinet room and then, when he retired to bed, I sat with him and we went on arguing until five o'clock in the morning. He simply would not accept that the dismissal of Glubb was not Nasser's doing. He called me nothing but a Foreign Office clerk and said I didn't understand anything about politics and the implications of this dismissal for Britain and her Prime Minister. At one point he said, 'You won't accept any arguments against Nasser, you are in love with Nasser.' He was becoming irrational.

I decided that I must try and get the Prime Minister to think on positive lines. So, with the help of Foreign Office advisers, I drew up a set of proposals, the effect of which was that we would attempt to consolidate our position in those countries where we had still considerable influence, namely Iraq, the Gulf states and Jordan, and that we would try to quarantine the Nasser influence. . . Some days later I was horrified to get a telephone call over an open line to the Savoy Hotel in which Anthony Eden said, 'What is all this poppycock you have sent me about isolating and quarantining Nasser? Can't you understand that I want Nasser murdered.' He actually used that word.

In his book *No End of a Lesson*, Nutting, for reasons of discretion, toned down the word to 'destroyed'. His 1984 recollection in a recorded interview for *End of Empire* was that the word Eden used was, however, 'murdered'.

Eden's first official reaction to Glubb's dismissal was to instruct Selwyn Lloyd to tell the Cabinet that Britain might have to withdraw its offer of help for the Aswan dam. Lloyd told the British Ambassador in Washington that the west should not give Nasser the money for the dam 'unless he genuinely changed his attitude towards western interests in the Middle East'. Lloyd wrote later: 'We agreed to let the Aswan dam project "wither on the vine".' US Secretary of State John Foster Dulles was becoming disillusioned with non-aligned countries that drifted towards the Soviets. He agreed with Eden that Nasser must be taught a lesson. Backing away from this vast scheme proved, however, almost as slow as had assembling support for it. Not until July did Dulles inform the Egyptian Government that the US offer of help was withdrawn. William Clark, Eden's Press Secretary, recalled:

This came through, as messages tended to, on the Reuters tape before it came through on the Foreign Office tape. I took it up, always glad to get credit for the press, to the Prime Minister in his bedroom. His comment was, 'Oh good, oh good for Foster. I didn't really think he had it in him.' Then there was a pause and, 'I wish he hadn't done it quite so abruptly.'

In London Eden quickly followed Dulles's lead. Nasser had had enough warning to see this blow coming and, though deeply disappointed, he had a reply ready.

Nasser's speech at Alexandria on 16 July 1956 was a turning point both for

*The view from the platform: the crowd in Alexandria listening to Nasser speak, 16 July 1956.*

him and for the British Empire. He had until now appeared the least charismatic of the free officers, a quiet, determined staff officer, fanatically secretive as one who had for years built up a movement of conspirators had to be. He was also shy and awkward. It was well known in Egypt that the Russians had said that the dam was too large a project for them to finance. After raising popular hopes so high, Nasser had doubly misplayed his hand. A failure on such a scale, it was widely thought, would topple him. His speech was awaited with interest, since he plainly must offer some explanation. He had been locked away with his closest advisers for several days. The speech, to mark the fourth anniversary of the exile of King Farouk, was a much-heralded event. Some 50,000 people assembled in the main square of Alexandria to hear him. Although Nasser was not a great speaker, this promised to be an intriguing occasion.

The young colonel who had for two years been President began in an unexpected style, using *baladi* language, the Egyptian equivalent of the cockney of a music-hall comedian, to tell the vast crowd the funny story of his adventures with the American diplomats and the President of the World Bank, Eugene Black. He told it like a French farce, with people following each other in and out of rooms, confused and accident-prone. The audience, to its surprise, was convulsed with laughter.

Then he spoke a sentence in an oddly different tone: 'Mr Black suddenly reminded me of Ferdinand de Lesseps.' The crowd did not know it, but those words were a signal. The speech was being broadcast on radio throughout Egypt and the words 'Ferdinand de Lesseps' were Nasser's coded instruction to units of the Egyptian army and police to move into the Cairo offices of the Compagnie Universelle du Canal Maritime de Suez which had run the canal from the start and of which the British Government, thanks to Disraeli, owned forty-four per cent. Nasser went on. He said that the benefits that de Lesseps's imperialistic company had stolen from the people of Egypt when they were dying of hunger were about to be recovered. The audience began to clap. Nasser had achieved an extraordinary state of control – over the crowd and over events throughout Egypt. The managing director of the company, M. Ménessier, was at dinner with the Governor of Ismailia, where Nasser knew that the radio was on. It was just one month since the last British troops had left the canal zone. The Government press, Nasser announced, was at that very moment printing a new law nationalising the company and outlining arrangements for compensating its stockholders. As he was speaking, armed units were taking over the company's premises at Port Said, Ismailia, Suez and Port Tewfik. The crowd at Alexandria roared with approval. Nasser was seized by a fit of laughter at his own daring. 'The canal will pay for the dam . . . This, oh citizens, is a battle against imperialism and against Israel, the vanguard of imperialism . . . Arab nationalism has been set on fire from the Atlantic Ocean to the Persian Gulf . . .' Before he finished speaking the entire canal was in Egyptian hands. 'Today, in the name of the people, I am taking over the company. Tonight our Egyptian canal will be run by Egyptians. *Egyptians*!' He laughed with delight as he said it. The crowd erupted in applause and he left the rostrum.

This was a feat of showmanship and planning. The soldier who in 1942 had written, 'I believe that colonialism, if it felt that some Egyptians intended to sacrifice their lives and face force with force, would retreat like a prostitute,' had matched his words with action.

While Nasser spoke, Anthony Eden was holding a dinner at 10 Downing Street for the King of Iraq and his Prime Minister, Nuri-es-Said. A secretary brought a telegram giving the news of the nationalisation to Eden, who read it out. Nuri was outraged. Not only did Nasser's seizure of the canal endanger the oil exports of Iraq and other Arab countries, but more triumphs for the radical Egyptian ruler threatened further to weaken conservative regimes such as his own. He was confident he had the young Nasserites in Iraq under control, but other Arab regimes were, he thought, less secure. William Clark recalled:

I got into Number 10 at the end of the dinner. The guests were just walking out, it was court dress, and the Prime Minister was escorting the King. Nuri was just behind him and could be heard saying quite clearly, 'Prime Minister, hit him hard, hit him soon, and hit him by yourself.'

Immediately after the dinner Eden called a meeting of his senior Cabinet colleagues and the chiefs of the army, navy and air force. The ministers agreed a statement that Eden would make in the House of Commons the next morning and he asked the Chiefs of Staff for a quick assessment of what military action was open to Britain. Their main advice was that, now the troops had left the canal zone, British tanks could not longer rumble straight onto Egyptian roads. To assemble a force capable of invading Egypt with the necessary heavy guns and tanks, which could be transported only by sea, would take weeks. The Prime Minister ordered preparations to begin immediately.

One of the strangest effects of imperialism now appeared. Sensible men in both England and France became convinced by reports put about by the Suez Canal Company claiming that the Egyptians could not manage the canal, which would quickly silt up and become useless, and that the departures of the mostly French and British pilots would make it impossible for ships to pass through. The London *Times* wrote: 'An international waterway of this kind cannot be worked by a nation of as low technical and managerial skill as the Egyptians.' That such nonsense was commonly accepted suggests that Britons and Frenchmen were desperately seeking a justification for the continuing exercise of their imperial instincts. Eden cabled to Eisenhower:

> My colleagues and I are convinced that we must be ready, in the last resort, to use force to bring Nasser to his senses. For our part we are

*The offices of the Suez Canal Company on the bank of the canal at Port Said.*

prepared to do so. I have this morning instructed our Chiefs of Staff to prepare a military plan accordingly.

This indication of an *ultimate* willingness to use force was misleading. Eden and his few closest colleagues had already decided on it. Eisenhower promptly sent to London as his personal emissary Robert Murphy, one of his political advisers when he was allied Commander-in-Chief in the Mediterranean during the 1939–45 war. The other had been Harold Macmillan, who was now Eden's Chancellor of the Exchequer. Macmillan had Murphy to dinner four days after Nasser's nationalisation speech and explained that the Suez crisis was a test that could be met only by the use of force or 'Britain would become another Netherlands'; that the French too were prepared to take part in a military operation; that military moves might start in a month and 'would not take much', a division or two at the most; that it would all be over in ten days with the Suez Canal returned to international control; that the British Government had set aside £5 million for the venture; that 'Nasser had to be chased out of Egypt'.

By the time Eisenhower received these reports he had confirmation in a private message from Eden, saying that he had decided the only way to break Nasser was to resort to force without delay and without any attempt at negotiation. Eisenhower responded by sending an even more senior emissary to London, John Foster Dulles, his Secretary of State who was himself a lawyer and who brought with him the legal adviser to the State Department. Eisenhower, while agreeing that Nasser must be reined in, was determined to prevent military intervention, and the two lawyers arrived armed with a series of delaying tactics. The Americans did not argue with Britain and France but set about prolonging negotiations until the heat of the Anglo-French reaction died down. Dulles told Eden that they must 'mobilise world opinion' and should convene a large conference of the main maritime nations with interests to protect. He also recommended that the nationalisation should be referred to the International Court. The more it appeared to Dulles that Eden and his colleagues were bent on war, the more he urged legal procedures.

The principal danger spot in the world at this time was in the mind of Anthony Eden, itself shaped by the experience of the past twenty-five years. In 1940 the leader of the Conservative Party, Neville Chamberlain, had fallen from power because he had appeased the dictators Hitler and Mussolini. Eden had then been against Chamberlain; he had himself resigned as Foreign Secretary in 1938 over his Prime Minister's weakness towards Mussolini. When Chamberlain was succeeded by Churchill in 1940, Eden re-entered the government and soon became the Prime Minister's number two. Churchill had then quickly grasped the reality that Britain could be no more than a junior partner to the United States in the war, but he had deliberately exaggerated the grandeur and importance of the Empire's role. Without Churchill's proud vision, the supreme effort of will that kept

Britain fighting in 1940–1, when all seemed lost and the United States had not yet entered the war, would have been impossible. Such moments of hyperbole have to be paid for. A large part of the Conservative Party believed the things Churchill had said at that time about the continuing greatness of the Empire. Many in Britain saw the turning point of the war as Montgomery's victory at El Alamein in 1942, when a German army was prevented from capturing Egypt and the recovery of Europe began, from North Africa over the Mediterranean and up through southern Italy. The Middle East had long been under British control. British and Empire troops had fought and died to defend the region. It made no sense a mere decade after the war, when oil discoveries were revealing it as one of the richest regions in the world, to give it up.

As Foreign Secretary from 1951 to 1955 Eden had struggled to achieve compromise between such feelings in his party and Egypt's insistent nationalism. His success had won him the firm enmity of the 'Suez group' of back-bench Conservative MPs who had long regarded Nasser as nothing more than a dictator. As Prime Minister, and particularly as the events of 1956 piled upon him, Eden became unable to bear their charge of 'appeasement'. William Clark remembered:

> Eden stopped even the limited amount of sitting in the smoking room of the House of Commons that he had done until that time. He found himself very uneasy. Back-benchers would try to talk to him, as they can in the smoking room, as equals. Some were now saying, 'I told you so, you should never have given way to Nasser and removed our troops. You certainly ought to send them back.'

For Eden the dismissal of Glubb, Cairo Radio's attacks on Britain and all Britain's friends in the Middle East, the purchase of Soviet arms and finally the nationalisation of the canal proved that Nasser was both a dictator and an implacable enemy of Britain. Worse, they seemed to prove that Churchill and his friends had been right. The grumblers within the party who had accused Eden of appeasement and weakness in the Middle East would now be silenced: nationalisation had provided the occasion for him to behave with Churchillian firmness. Recent experience in Persia confirmed him in his new strength of purpose. When Mussadeq nationalised Britain's oil assets, the dithering and negotiations of the Labour Government had achieved nothing. It was the Conservatives' ruthless determination to topple Britain's enemy that had won the day. So while Dulles's scheme for an international conference of maritime nations was allowed to occupy world attention, the British and French Chiefs of Staff got on with their preparations to invade. Eden was determined that a way must be found 'to make Nasser disgorge' (a phrase coined by Dulles). Eden states in his memoirs, 'I did not wish to lose momentum or to allow discussion to drag on from conference to conference.'

His problem was that he could not find grounds for the use of force. With the French he tried to provoke Nasser by asking all British and French shipping companies to continue to pay their dues to the old Canal Company's accounts in London and Paris (fifty-five per cent of canal payments were British, ten per cent French). This could be justified as an interim measure pending an agreed settlement; but Anthony Nutting, then the Minister of State at the Foreign Office, has written that it was done in 'the hope that Nasser would now overstep the mark and prevent the passage of a British ship'. Eden states in his memoirs: 'The French and ourselves intended that as little money as possible from ships passing through the canal should find its way into Egyptian hands.' Egypt's sterling balances in London were frozen. British army, navy and air force units were moved to the eastern Mediterranean. Twenty thousand army reservists in Britain were called up. Nasser made no response. His organisation kept the canal operating as efficiently as before. British ships continued to pass through it.

The conclusion of Dulles's meeting of maritime states went some way towards providing the *casus belli* Eden sought. The purpose of the meeting was to remove control of the canal from Egypt and place it in the hands of an international consortium of nations, of which Egypt would be a member. To Nasser this seemed merely an attempt by the imperialist powers to reoccupy the part of Egypt the British had just left. He therefore refused to be represented and, when the conference sent him its proposals, he promptly rejected them. Sir Robert Menzies, the Prime Minister of Australia, who went to Egypt to explain the consortium idea to Nasser, warned him that to turn it down might well invite the use of force by Britain and France. Nasser felt able to ignore the warning. That very day, President Eisenhower told a press conference that the United States was 'committed to a peaceful settlement of the dispute, *nothing else*'. This was said for American domestic reasons: a presidential election was three months away and Eisenhower did not wish to be described as the war candidate. The effect was to diminish to zero the already slim chance that Nasser would acquiesce.

Since eighteen countries, including the United States and neutral Sweden, had agreed that the canal as an international waterway should be internationally administered, Nasser's rejection of this proposal strengthened the Anglo-French case for the use of force. Dulles's fertile brain was equal to this challenge. His first idea for a conference had occupied most of August. He now came up with an ingenious scheme that was to keep governments busy during September. He engineered the formation of a Suez Canal Users' Association (SCUA). (Originally it was named CASU, the Co-operative Association of Suez canal Users, but this turned out to be a dirty word in Portuguese.)

Again the lumbering processes of international co-operation forced the British and French to hold their hand. SCUA was empowered to accept the canal dues of all its members. Had Dulles backed the Anglo-French proposal that shipowners of all member states be *obliged* to pay their canal dues to SCUA, Nasser would have faced a counter-coup at least as effective as the international companies' refusal in 1951–2 to buy Iranian oil, possibly more so. Harold Macmillan, a member of Eden's small Suez advisory group within the Cabinet, wrote in his diary on 10 September:

> If SCUA's members, including the US, were really to sail their ships (with pilots) through the canal, disregarding Nasser, it would either cause Nasser to 'lose face' altogether or get the western countries into an 'incident' which would justify forceful action. But does Dulles really mean business?

Two days later in the House of Commons Eden echoed Macmillan's sentiments:

> If the Egyptian Government should seek to interfere with the operations of the association or refuse to extend to it the essential minimum co-operation, then . . . Her Majesty's Government and others concerned will be free to take such further steps as seem to be required, either through the United Nations or by other means for the assertion of their rights.

Selwyn Lloyd, Eden's Foreign Secretary, confirmed that the inner Cabinet were by now committed to war. In his book *Suez 1956*, he wrote:

> It was unlikely that effective international control of the canal would be achieved without the use of force. SCUA would be a step towards that.

Dulles had hoodwinked Eden again. He intended SCUA not to provide an occasion for war but as a means to avoid it and gain time. The memoirs of Eden, Lloyd and Macmillan become increasingly bitter about Dulles at this period because he so completely outmanoeuvred them. When Dulles replied to a press question about SCUA, 'There is talk about teeth being pulled out of the plan, but I know of no teeth,' Eden was enraged. He decided that the use of force when it came would have to be without the Americans' knowledge.

When the issue was belatedly brought before the United Nations (it had been delayed mainly to help Dulles, who did not want discussion of the parallel issue of the Panama Canal to be stimulated, especially before the presidential election), Eden's war plans received a further setback. Egypt, it turned out, was willing to compromise. Dr Mahmoud Fawzi, Nasser's Foreign Minister, agreed to work out a co-operative arrangement between Egypt and the canal's users. Pressure had been applied on Nasser both by India's Prime Minister, Jawaharlal Nehru, anxious to avoid war between his Commonwealth partner Britain and his non-aligned partner Egypt; and by Arab states concerned at the damage a war would do them. Likewise Selwyn Lloyd had been pressed by the Americans to withdraw in practice the Franco-British demand for 'international management'. Fawzi and Selwyn Lloyd held private talks under the chairmanship of the United Nations' Secretary-General, Dag Hammarskjöld. Lloyd had spelled out six 'principles' to govern a settlement: 1. open transit through the canal without discrimination, 2. respect for Egyptian sovereignty, 3. canal operations to be insulated from the politics of any one country, 4. dues to be agreed between users and owners, 5. a proportion of canal dues to go for development in Egypt, 6. issues between Egypt and the old Canal Company to be settled by arbitration.

On 12 October, at a meeting with Hammarskjöld and the French Foreign Minister, Christian Pineau, Fawzi agreed to all six principles, as Hammarskjöld announced to the next session of the Security Council. How to implement the principles remained to be worked out, particularly principle 3 on insulating canal operations from politics in Egypt; but Egypt had made major concessions by agreeing to organised co-operation with the canal users and by allowing them a say in the allocation of canal revenues for maintenance and development. The prospect for a peaceful settlement appeared encouraging.

Eden, however, did not trust Nasser to honour a negotiated settlement, parts of which might be unpopular in Egypt, and he continued in his efforts to find a *casus belli*. He dismissed Fawzi's concessions as 'paper contracts' designed to entangle Pineau and Selwyn Lloyd, and instructed his Foreign Secretary to emphasise the extent to which Fawzi's acceptance of the six principles fell short of the earlier requirements of the maritime powers. At the next meeting of the Security Council, France and Britain pressed a resolution that had been drafted before Fawzi's meeting with Lloyd and Pineau and that they knew was unacceptable to the Egyptians. Hammarskjöld continued to pursue the agreement the three foreign ministers had reached, but events now moved too fast for those who wanted a settlement.

*In Paris to discuss their joint policy on Suez: left to right, Pineau, Eden, Mollet, Lloyd.*

On Sunday, 14 October 1956, while Selwyn Lloyd was still at the UN, two French visitors came to the Prime Minister's country house, Chequers. One was Albert Gazier, acting Foreign Minister during Pineau's absence at the UN; the other was the air force general Maurice Challe. They described to Eden and Nutting, who attended in Selwyn Lloyd's absence as the senior available Foreign Office minister, a scheme for Israel to attack Egypt and capture most of Sinai, at which point Britain and France would order both parties to withdraw ten miles either side of the Suez canal. The Anglo-French force already under arms would then occupy the canal and the ports at either end, Port Said and Suez, on the pretext of separating the combatants. Thus not only would the canal be restored to Anglo-French management but the terminal ports would be for the first time under direct control. Nutting reports that Eden could scarcely conceal his excitement at the scheme, which at last offered a justification for using force. Eden told Nutting he was to discuss the scheme only with two senior officials and forbade him to mention it to the Foreign Office's legal adviser. Nutting, who had signed the agreement on the withdrawal of British troops from the canal zone, was particularly distressed that one of its clauses, binding Britain to come to Egypt's aid in the event of aggression, was to be so flagrantly breached. As he explained to Eden's inner circle of Cabinet ministers the next day, Britain would be attacking the victim of aggression instead of the aggressor.

Selwyn Lloyd was summoned back from the UN and Nutting described the French scheme to him. The Foreign Secretary thought the idea of Britain's inviting Israel to attack Egypt a poor one, he subsequently wrote, but he was quickly talked round by the Prime Minister, who took him to Paris for further talks. Until this point Selwyn Lloyd had believed that the threat of force would be enough to make Nasser 'disgorge'. He thought that the combination of international pressure, the denial of the canal dues to Egypt and the mobilisation had produced the concessions Fawzi had made at the UN. What now converted him to Eden's view, he later wrote, was the weakening of the American position. Dulles, who had first talked of making Nasser disgorge, was now proposing to have ninety per cent of canal dues paid to Egypt. That would remove the main pressure on Nasser and be tantamount to capitulation. With the presidential election less than a month away, the one thing that could destroy Eisenhower's chances was entanglement in an escalating overseas conflict.

Eden persuaded Lloyd that the six principles to which Fawzi had agreed were no more binding on Egypt than the paper signed by Hitler that Neville Chamberlain had brought back from Munich in 1938 – the embodiment of appeasement. Nasser was trying to undermine all the governments in the Middle East that were friendly to Britain; he had to be removed, and no better reason for intervention than the seizure of the canal was ever likely to occur. Selwyn Lloyd was unhappy and confused but he allowed himself to be hustled along; after all, Eden was the most complete master of foreign policy in the Conservative Party and could be the most skilful conciliator. What was more, Harold Macmillan, another close associate of Churchill and Selwyn Lloyd's immediate predecessor at the Foreign Office, was as determined as Eden that this moment of opportunity must be seized. Macmillan reported, on the basis of his many personal connections in Washington, that although the American Government might make peace noises, in the end Eisenhower would firmly back his old ally. A visit to Eisenhower in the White House in September had reinforced Macmillan's confidence. The Foreign Secretary, newly promoted to the Cabinet, would have had to be remarkably self-confident to resist. He was not. The doubts of Nutting and the two Foreign Office officials whom he had been allowed to consult were set aside.

France had its own reasons for wanting Nasser toppled. In Algeria French troops were fighting a bigger war to retain power over a colonised territory than the British ever undertook for such a purpose. The French believed that Nasser, with his vision of a united Arab nation, was not merely helping to inspire the Algerians against France, he was also giving them vital help. In 1882 Gambetta had thought a success for Arab nationalism in Egypt would weaken France throughout the Maghreb, and Guy Mollet, the French Socialist Prime Minister, thought so now. In scheming to slay the Nasser dragon the French were way ahead of Eden. They had been supplying aircraft, tanks and other military goods to Israel and had acquired a clear understanding of Israel's needs in the proposed joint action. The one need that France could not meet was the capacity quickly to hit Egypt's airports. The Israelis had explained that the new aircraft delivered by the Soviet Union to Egypt could fly in from the sea and bomb Israel's cities before Israeli fighters could leave the ground to intercept them. Israel needed those Egyptian aircraft destroyed before it launched the invasion of Sinai. Only Britain, with its air bases at Aden and Cyprus, could carry out the necessary pre-emptive bombing raids on Egypt's military airfields. Eden therefore had the power to decide whether the Franco-Israeli plan for an attack on Egypt should proceed. He did not hesitate.

When he returned to London, however, Eden did not dare tell his Cabinet colleagues of the collusion he was involved in; he restricted the knowledge to a small group of like-minded ministers and an even smaller number of Foreign Office officials. Instead he persuaded the British Cabinet to agree to something innocuous: that Britain would intervene to protect the canal *after* it had been threatened by an Israeli attack, which Eden told them he thought likely. Britain's ambassador in Egypt, Sir Humphrey Trevelyan, was one of those who knew nothing about the real plan. Britain's ambassador in Israel was told by Prime Minister Ben Gurion, 'I think you will find your government knows more about this than you do.'

Eden sent Selwyn Lloyd back to Paris, this time to meet not only the French but also the Israelis. He travelled incognito in a military aircraft and was taken to a villa at Sèvres near Paris. Moshe Dayan, then Israel's Chief of

Staff, wrote of this meeting: 'Lloyd's manner could not have been more antagonistic. His whole demeanour expressed distaste – for the place, the company and the topic.' David Ben Gurion, Israel's Prime Minister, wrote that Selwyn Lloyd treated him like a subordinate. The Foreign Secretary took part in the conspiracy with the enthusiasm of a judge in a brothel. He kept explaining that an Israeli–French–British agreement to attack Egypt was impossible, that British subjects and property throughout the Middle East could not be set at risk. Britain could only indicate what she would do if Israeli action threatened the canal. Ben Gurion's requirement that British aircraft bomb Egyptian airfields at the start of the Israeli attack was, Lloyd explained, impossible. When he returned to London he gave Nutting the welcome news that it did not now look as though the French plan could work.

It was necessary for Pineau to visit London two days later to satisfy the Israelis that Eden's approach was warmer than Lloyd's and that the dominant voice in the British Cabinet remained the Prime Minister's. Still, however, Eden could not deliver Cabinet approval for a pre-emptive bombing raid on Egypt: once the Israelis had attacked he would have an excuse to launch the bombings, but not before. Pineau persuaded the Israelis that this was the best they could hope for, and Eden and the French ministers drew up the ultimatum they would present to Israel and Egypt immediately after the Sinai invasion. The time limit in the ultimatum would be only twelve hours; then the British would destroy Egypt's air force. The Israelis' response was that, though the delay exposed them to great risk, they would go ahead nevertheless.

On 29 October 1956, ostensibly to destroy *fedayeen* bases from which terrorist attacks had been launched, Israeli forces invaded Sinai, moving quickly towards the Suez Canal. Eden now bounced his Cabinet into the policy he had agreed with France and Israel. One minister complained of being rushed. Eden replied that those who had been in the War Cabinet would understand. Iain Macleod, the Minister of Labour, said, 'We didn't know we were at war.' Eden faced down the doubters and got his way, and Britain and France duly issued their ultimatum. At the time it was delivered, Israeli troops were between 75 and 125 miles short of the places from which they were ordered to withdraw; in effect the ultimatum required Egypt to withdraw west of the canal and Israel to move forward on the east. Egypt could only reject such an ultimatum.

Once Eden had decided to attack Egypt in collusion with France and Israel he began systematically to conceal information from the United States. The British ambassador to Washington was conveniently brought home to a new post on 11 October and no replacement was sent until 8 November. Eisenhower and Dulles knew nothing of Israel's invasion of Egypt nor of the Anglo-French follow-up until they read reports on news agency tapes. Dulles quickly became convinced that the Israeli attack had been arranged in collusion with France and Britain. A year earlier Eisenhower had timed his announcement of a summit conference with Russia to help Eden in his election. He was furious at being double-crossed a week before his own election. He immediately had a resolution placed before the United Nations Security Council calling on Israel to stop its aggression. The Security Council majority, including the Soviet Union and Australia, supported the resolution. Britain and France used their veto, placing themselves in a minority of two, because they needed Israel to press home its attack in order to justify their intervention.

As soon as the ultimatum to Egypt expired, the British launched the bombing raids Eden had promised. They continued for five days. During that time ships carrying men and armour were steaming the 900 miles from the British naval base at Malta to bring the main force that was to capture the canal and the towns at either end. The voyage took six days because the landing craft that were needed to put tanks and armoured vehicles ashore could not sail faster than five knots and because the nearest British military centre at Cyprus had no harbour from which an invasion force could be launched.

Eden's position was now odd. He announced to the House of Commons that British and French troops were intervening to separate the belligerents and secure the canal, but no damage to the canal had occurred and no British or French troops arrived. To the world's surprise, however, British aircraft bombed nine Egyptian airfields, some near Cairo and in no way connected with the canal. When asked to explain this in the House of Commons, Eden had no answer. When the accusation of collusion with France and Israel was levelled at him, he again had no answer. When asked if Britain was at war with Egypt, he answered no, but that the two countries were in a state of 'armed conflict'.

The Anglo-French veto prevented the Security Council from passing any resolution concerning the Suez fighting, so the matter was transferred to the General Assembly, where the veto did not apply. Here the United States took the lead in moving that 'all parties now involved in hostilities agree to an immediate cease-fire'. This was carried by sixty-four votes to five. Only Australia and New Zealand supported Britain, France and Israel.

Then the very thing happened that the still unconsummated Anglo-French intervention had been advertised as being aimed to prevent. Egypt sank forty-seven ships filled with concrete in the canal. The main passage through which Europe received its oil was blocked and plainly would remain so for some months. Tankers from the Persian Gulf required so much more time to reach Britain via the Cape than via the canal that extra oil would have to be bought from the Americas – particularly Venezuela – to keep Britain's industry functioning. Such oil could be paid for only in dollars, of which the run on the pound sterling provoked by Suez had left Britain desperately short. A US loan was essential.

Almost as bad from Eden's point of view, both Israel and Egypt agreed to the UN demand for a cease-fire, destroying his excuse that the invasion was necessary to separate the combatants. Nevertheless, when the ships carrying the Anglo-French force reached Egypt on 5 November the soldiers proceeded with their task, 'separating' Egyptian and Israeli troops who were already separate, 'stopping' a war that had already stopped. At the United Nations, to avoid being pilloried as an aggressor, Britain announced its agreement to a Canadian proposal to set up a UN Emergency Force (UNEF) to take over from the Anglo-French armies the policing of the canal. Britain and France now amended the purpose of their intervention: it was not, as previously, to restore the canal to international control but to facilitate the arrival of UNEF. The necessary resolutions were carried unanimously at the UN, but all representatives made it clear that neither British nor French troops would be acceptable as members of UNEF. At Port Said, in the face of Egyptian resistance, the Anglo-French force caused heavy civilian casualties and great damage to the city. Part of the force began making its way southwards down the canal towards Ismailia.

At this point Harold Macmillan, Eden's strongest ally in support of the invasion, abruptly deserted him. As Chancellor of the Exchequer Macmillan was responsible for Britain's gold and dollar reserves, which had been falling for some weeks and were now collapsing disastrously. Holders of sterling

*British tanks in Port Said, 8 November 1956.*

throughout the world understandably lost confidence and sold. Companies due shortly to make international payments and individuals anxious to protect the value of their savings dumped sterling to buy more reliable currencies. Macmillan believed that the selling was stimulated by the United States Treasury and Federal Reserve Bank, which he thought off-loaded far more sterling than was necessary to protect the value of their own holdings. To keep up the value of sterling, the Bank of England had to buy every pound that was offered. By 6 November the attempt to do so was dangerously depleting Britain's gold and dollar reserves. Macmillan had asked for short-term loans from the United States and the International Monetary Fund to tide Britain over its difficulty. To his surprise both were made conditional on a cease-fire in Egypt. Macmillan told his Cabinet colleagues that they had no choice. The money had run out. The invasion must stop. Thus he obtained his reputation over Suez for being first in and first out. The British troops, barely a third of the way along the canal, were told, a mere day after they had landed, that it was all over.

For most people most of the time, politics are a subordinate interest. Only once in a generation does a political issue dominate the minds of the public for a sustained period. For the British, Suez was such an issue. When Nasser nationalised the canal, the British response was almost unanimous. The Labour leader, Hugh Gaitskell, like Eden, thought Nasser another Hitler who must not be allowed to get away with a criminal act. But as Eden's will to war became increasingly manifest, the nation divided. Eden and the Suez group saw their critics as appeasers; Gaitskell, most of the Labour and Liberal parties and some Conservatives, came to see Eden and his claque as devious bullies. Most of Eden's critics disliked Nasser's seizure of the canal, not least because grabbing it by armed force at night seemed the act of a thief, and they favoured economic and other sanctions. But they were firmly opposed to the use of force, especially in defiance of the United States and the United Nations. All over the country meetings and rallies were held to protest against Britain's aggression. Counter-meetings were held to support the Government. Three ministers resigned – Lord Monckton, the Minister of Defence, who was in the Cabinet, Sir Edward Boyle, Economic Secretary at the Treasury, and Nutting. After Eden had spoken on the radio on 3 November explaining his action to the nation, Gaitskell claimed the right of reply the next night. Eden's staff tried to silence the Labour leader, arguing that the BBC had no right to divide the nation in the midst of an armed conflict; but the BBC rejected the Prime Minister's demand. Consequently the British officers approaching Port Said – other ranks were not allowed to listen – heard Gaitskell argue that the mission they were engaged on should be abandoned and that the Prime Minister should resign. The BBC's world service reported in its news bulletins the many voices raised against the Government's policy. Probably the only official British institution that emerged from the Suez crisis with its reputation enhanced was the BBC.

In every purpose that the Suez invasion was intended to achieve it was a failure. It brought British power in Egypt to an end. The Soviet Union, on the day Macmillan persuaded his colleagues to stop the advance on financial grounds, announced that they would intervene with nuclear weapons unless the invaders stopped. This threat did not influence the British Government's decision – Russia had no base at that time from which it could intervene in Egypt and was not thought likely to bomb Britain – but the propaganda effect was exactly as planned: it helped deflect world attention from the simultaneous Russian invasion of Hungary. Most Egyptians thought the Russian intervention had been decisive; their Islamic predisposition to mistrust Communists was consequently weakened and within a year Egypt became the base for a growth of Russian influence in the Middle East. Soviet bloc countries replaced the west as the main buyer of Egyptian cotton. Soviet-style nationalisation of western banks and businesses was adopted as Egyptian Government policy. Nasser, instead of being toppled, became more popular and powerful, not only in Egypt but throughout the Middle East. The Anglo-French invasion enabled him to escape popular condemnation for having been defeated by the Israelis. The leaflets the British dropped on Cairo urging Egyptians to rise against him only increased his standing. His propaganda and pressure against Britain's allies were redoubled.

The effect of Suez spread widely, particularly in Africa. Within three years Britain's policy of gradually bringing on colonised peoples to self-government and ultimately to independence was replaced by one of rapid scuttle. Nationalist movements that might have advanced at the pace of India or the Gold Coast, mastering the skills of modern government over a decade or more, now had to insist that Britain's departure be immediate. Radio Cairo helped carry the message to East Africa with its regular broadcasts in Swahili, but the message of Suez did not need Nasser's own propagandists to put it across. Just as Clive had proved at Arcot in 1751 that the rulers of Indian states would not stand up to a determined Englishman, so Nasser proved at Suez in 1956 that the British could not stand up to a determined nationalist.

Two months after the débâcle Anthony Eden, sick and ruined, resigned. On 20 December 1956, he told the House of Commons, 'There was not foreknowledge that Israel would attack Egypt' – an outright lie. Harold Macmillan, who succeeded him, continued to speak like an imperialist, but promptly set in train a major reduction of Britain's defence commitments and soon dismantled what remained of the Empire. Much the same happened in Paris. The Suez invasion not only failed to ease France's Algerian problem but made it worse. Within two years the politicians of the Fourth Republic resigned their powers to General Charles de Gaulle, who, like Macmillan, spoke with nostalgic grandeur while actually reducing France's imperial role. The Suez operation wrote *finis* not only to the British Empire but to all the empires of western Europe.

# CHAPTER 6

# Aden

In the late 1950s Aden – a bay on the edge of a desert – was the busiest harbour in the world except for New York. Most ships on the way from Europe to India, Australia, the Persian Gulf, the Far East and South and East Africa stopped there for fuel and supplies after passing through the Suez canal. The harbour was huge, deep and sheltered, the bunkering service fast and competitive. For passengers and crew the duty-free shops were irresistible. Aden was a free port, bustling with Indian and Arab traders.

The British were happy to run so profitable a colony, but profit was not why they were there. The prime purpose was strategic. The British acquired Aden in response to French ambitions in Egypt, inspired initially by Napoleon. In attempting to establish themselves astride the shortest route to India the French in the 1830s energetically supported the ruler of Egypt, Mehemet Ali, in his efforts to conquer Yemen. Thus France seemed to be on the way to acquiring allies on both sides of the Red Sea. From the Governor's residence in Bombay, nothing on earth appeared more threatening.

Throughout Britain's period of rule from 1839 to 1967, Aden was not run for the benefit of its citizens or even of Britons. It was a military facility from which guns could be sent against Egypt. Units sent to its intense heat and isolation regarded it as a 'punishment station'. When decades went by, however, with no threat arising from Egypt, British defence planners forgot why they possessed Aden. Lord Rawlinson, Indian Commander-in-Chief, wrote in 1920: 'As long as we command the Indian Ocean, Aden is in no danger, and if we do not, I cannot see that it is of any use to us.'

## The Busiest Port, 1276–1956

In 1276 Marco Polo wrote that the great wealth of the Sultan of Aden arose 'from the imposts he lays on merchandise that comes from India and on the returning cargo; this being the most considerable mart in all that quarter for the exchange of commodities and the place to which all trading vessels resort'. Aden, with 80,000 people and 360 mosques, was then known to Egyptian and Arab traders as the gateway to China.

Like Singapura (see p. 151), however, another of the world's great natural

harbours, Aden's splendour disappeared. Once Vasco de Gama had opened the sea route round southern Africa to the East Indies, the Portuguese and then the Dutch, British and French sent their goods on the long sea voyage to the Far East precisely to avoid the taxes of the Sultan of Aden and his like. Aden tried to make up for lost trade by raising its charges. So Egyptian- and Persian-controlled ports took a growing share of the trade between the Muslim world and the Indies. In 1538 the Ottoman Turks seized Aden. Their taste for coffee grown in the Yemen led them to prefer Mocha on the Red Sea as the main harbour for ships trading south of Egypt. They let Aden decline. By the beginning of the nineteenth century this once-great city was reduced to fewer than a thousand inhabitants.

In 1838 the Governor of Bombay, Sir Robert Grant, wrote of his concern at 'the gradual approach of France to India by way of Egypt simultaneously with that of Russia by way of Persia'. He thought it necessary to seize 'places of strength' in the Red Sea–Persian Gulf area for India's defence. The little-used port of Aden seemed ideal for his purpose. What was more, the strong opposition of public opinion in London to imperial acquisitions could in the case of Aden be overcome. In 1829 an experimental run from Suez to Bombay had been made by the *Hugh Lindsay*, a ship with a coal-fired engine. Coal had been deposited at Aden (by sailing boat) to enable it to refuel. The

*A view from within Aden Bay, looking east over the docks.*

success of this enterprise led to the development of a regular service. The British public could be persuaded of the need for a coaling station, to speed the mails and the transit of goods. So in January 1839, negotiation to secure its peaceful cession having failed, Commander Stanford Beresford Haines of the Indian Navy led a small squadron of ships and 700 British and Indian troops in an assault. The ships' guns pounded the local Sultan's meagre defences. Aden thus became the first colonial acquisition of Queen Victoria's reign.

No sooner had Britain conquered the territory than its reason for doing so evaporated. France's ally, Mehemet Ali of Egypt, withdrew from Arabia, and the Governments in London and Bombay, with danger removed, entirely lost interest in their proposed military base. Haines, a naval officer, found himself left in charge of a coaling station, while his superiors could not decide whether to keep or abandon it. Haines ran Aden as a private fiefdom and when he retired after fifteen years the Government in London prosecuted him for fraud and embezzlement and had him consigned to a debtor's prison in Bombay, from which he was released only a few days before his death in 1860.

Nevertheless the place prospered. Mail-steamers were soon regularly calling for coal en route from Egypt to India and Australia, and when the Suez canal was opened in 1869 Aden's trade enjoyed a substantial extra boost. As the ships refuelled, the passengers went ashore to do their shopping and to explore this strange volcanic outcrop with no hint of green vegetation but only rocks in intriguing shades of amber. Soon Indian traders from Bombay and Arabs mostly from the neighbouring state of Yemen were making fortunes.

Aden was isolated from its hinterland. No roads led through the desert – only camel tracks. Although evidence survives that in ancient times cities existed in South Arabia, indicating that food must have grown nearby, when the British arrived Aden looked only to the sea. Incense-growing in inland valleys to the east of Aden, in the area known as the Hadramaut, had once been a major item in international trade but now had almost entirely ceased. South Arabia had reverted to sand, its coast utterly barren. Not a single stream flowed all year or reached the sea. Few irrigation works survived. The thin and wiry inhabitants of the interior kept sheep near occasional waterholes.

Haines adopted the policy of buying the goodwill of these locals. Learning of fat traders and rich pickings in Aden, they were inclined to raid and rob. Rather than send soldiers far into the scorched interior to punish the raiders, Haines paid their leaders annual allowances to stay away and keep the peace. Between 1839 and 1954 Britain signed ninety protectorate treaties with local sheikhs, sultans, amirs, sharifs and naibs, each one being at the time the top man in his village or area of desert. The treaties provided that the local worthy would sign no treaty and enter no arrangement with any outside power but Britain, and that in return Britain would protect and pay him. Thus, behind Aden colony, an isolated town which was thought strategically as well as commercially important, Britain acquired sway over the Aden protectorates, a scattering of negligible pirate states, separated by sand and rock.

The outside power against whom these provisions were principally directed was the Imam of Yemen, hardly a power at all by the nineteenth century but a subordinate ruler within the Ottoman Empire. Yemen was once a state of some substance. The Romans had called it 'Arabia Felix', the only corner of cheerfulness amidst the sandy wastes of Arabia. Here the mountains force the monsoon winds upwards to cool and so to drop their final rains. Consequently Yemen has always been the most fertile area – almost the only fertile area – in the peninsula, its steep and rocky surface notched with terraces planted with maize, peaches, bananas, melons, figs and, once Turkish taste came to dominate the Middle East, coffee. However, after some two hundred years of virtual monopoly, the Yemen's coffee exports were undercut by the product of Dutch, French and British colonies. Nevertheless the Imam in his mountains was the greatest ruler within a thousand miles of Aden and maintained a historical claim to its ownership. The desert tribesmen inland from Aden showed no disposition to assist the Imam in attacking the British – he belonged to a different sect of Islam – but, given the undisputed ability of the Royal Navy to keep out any danger from the sea, Yemen was the direction from which the British in Aden felt most vulnerable.

In the 1920s the Imam tried to assert his claim, seizing some desert waterholes and apparently bent on marching across the sands to attack Aden itself. The Ottoman Empire had collapsed, releasing him from its overlordship, so perhaps the British would collapse also. The Imam was a man of the hills to whom the sea was unknown – he never visited his state's two miserable harbours in the hot, desert fringe of the Red Sea – and he therefore could not appreciate the basis of British power. Even less had he imagined the power of Royal Air Force bombers, the new and economical device by which the British kept the peace in inaccessible areas. When his troops took over some desert villages that the British considered under their protection, small aircraft based at Aden bombed the villages and the Imam's men. When this failed to persuade the Imam to give in gracefully, the RAF bombed sites in the Yemen, including the town of Taiz. Thus some kind of understanding with the Imam was reached. He accepted that the British required him to keep out. The 1934 Treaty of Sana, in which, according to the English version, the Imam agreed to keep out, is held to mark the last enlargement of the British Empire.

The British themselves were never quite sure about their policy towards Aden and even less about the protectorates. In 1921 the Prime Minister Lloyd George gave a parliamentary answer which indicated that neither he nor his staff knew which Government department was responsible for the place. This was understandable. Acquired by the Government of India and

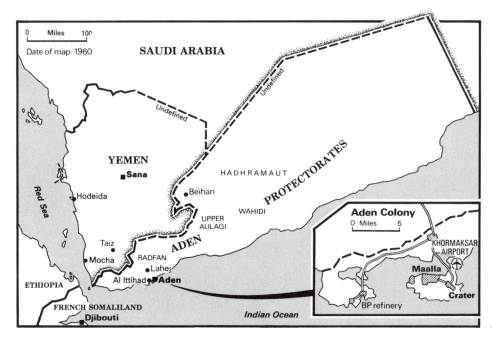

ruled from Bombay, Aden became an obvious candidate for transfer to the Colonial Office after the 1914–18 war when a Middle East department was set up there to administer the spoils of the Ottoman Empire. However Indians were acquiring a voice in their own Government by this time and considered the Colonial Office racially prejudiced. It was, they held, discriminating in favour of whites and Africans and against Indian labourers and traders in Kenya; such practices must not be introduced into Aden. The Bombay legislature argued that Aden was a military outpost of the Indian empire and that the principal traders there were Indian, so Indian interests came first. The Colonial Office maintained that it was part of the Arab world. From 1920 to 1937 the dispute remained unresolved and all decisions concerning Aden passed from out-trays in Whitehall to in-trays in Bombay and back again. Then the 1935 Government of India Act settled the matter. With India about to become internally self-governing and plainly due before long to make further constitutional progress, the British Government announced that it was unwilling to share control of this imperial base with an independent Indian administration. In 1937, therefore, Aden was formally transferred to the Colonial Office.

In the 1939–45 war, as in 1914–18, Britain controlled Egypt and therefore made only limited use of its military facilities at Aden. It was after the war that the colony suddenly expanded into one of the world's busiest harbours, mainly on account of the sharp rise in the number of oil tankers travelling from the Persian Gulf to Europe. In 1954 British Petroleum, thrown out of Iran, opened a huge new refinery at Aden to serve the growing traffic. This was the biggest investment ever made in Aden and, at a time when the British were being forced to leave Egypt and faced growing nationalist pressure throughout the Middle East, it was some consolation to them to know that the port and town of Aden were sovereign territory, British for ever, as well as prosperous and stable.

The only pressure on the British came from within Aden town itself. The port and the refinery were by now employing thousands of people. Business was booming. Some traders set up a polite nationalist organisation, the Aden Association, asking for a measure of self-government, with a view ultimately to independence. To calm and reassure those who wondered where such things might lead, the British Government in May 1956 sent Lord Lloyd, Under-Secretary of State for the Colonies, to address the Aden Legislative Council. He told the eighteen members (four elected by Aden's wealthier citizens, the rest appointed by the Governor):

> Many of you have a perfectly legitimate desire to take a greater part in the affairs of Government and there is no reason why this desire should not be realised. But I should like you to understand that for the foreseeable future it would not be reasonable or sensible, or indeed in the interests of the Colony's inhabitants, for them to aspire to any aim beyond that of a considerable degree of internal self-government ... Her Majesty's Government wish to make it clear that the importance of Aden, both strategically and economically, within the Commonwealth is such that they cannot foresee the possibility of any fundamental relaxation of their responsibilities for the Colony. I feel confident that this assurance will be welcome to you and to the vast majority of the inhabitants of the Colony.

The moderate nationalists, disposed to be pro-British, were surprised to be rebuffed.

## To the Helicopters, 1956–1967

Lord Lloyd's statement closely resembled that of another Colonial Office minister, Henry Hopkinson, on the subject of Cyprus two years earlier (see page 321). Both were made for the same reason. With Britain forced to remove its troops from the huge base in the Suez canal zone, the Government thought it must hold on to substitutes that would be both safe and permanent. Ministers did not want to move men and equipment to Aden only to be faced with a nationalist demand to move them out again.

Coming a mere six months before the Suez invasion, the announcement was unfortunately timed. Nasser was soon to become the inspiration of Arabs everywhere. David Holden, of the London *Sunday Times*, reported:

> When I was in Aden at the end of 1956, I could see, in room after dark room, in shop after cramped shop, the familiar face of President Nasser gleaming from the walls, all teeth and self-confident bonhomie; and from somewhere in every street came a harsh and crudely amplified Arabic voice [which] even a novice could identify as the 'Voice of the Arabs' on Cairo Radio attacking British imperialism.

Cairo Radio described any Arabs who co-operated with Britain as 'traitors to Arabism' conspiring with the colonialists in 'a union of slaves'. After Suez, Arabs everywhere clamoured to listen. In the tiny, stone villages of the protectorates where no political meeting had ever been allowed, traders on camels brought transistor radios and tribesmen began to hear the new ideas: that the day had come to kick out both the British and all reactionary rulers. Some Arabs, however, who had a legitimate claim on Britain's attention, begged the imperial overlords to stay. The sheikhs, sultans and amirs who lived near the border with Yemen were anxious to avoid coming under Yemeni control. Each of their 'states' was by treaty a British protectorate and they were grateful to the Royal Air Force for saving them from Yemeni attacks in the 1930s. The British had since pressed them to form a federal government, which they had refused to do. They disagreed too much among themselves – often in decades-old blood feuds – for federation to seem possible. The Suez fiasco exposed them to outside pressures. It encouraged both the Imam of Yemen and Arab nationalists in Aden to attack Britain and its friends. A group of sheikhs, feeling threatened, turned to Britain and asked for the scheme for a federal government to be implemented.

After the humiliation of Suez, this was a request to which Conservative ministers were eager to respond. In the wave of anger that swept the Arab world, Britain was evicted from the former RAF airfields in Jordan and Iraq. Even Cyprus was now under threat from Grivas and EOKA. The retention of Aden as a staging post to enable troops and supplies to be flown to the Far East in time of war and as a base from which forces could be rapidly deployed to Jordan, Iraq and the Gulf, where Britain still had treaty commitments, therefore seemed vital.

The former British proposal which the South Arabian sultans now took up was for a federation in a treaty relationship with Britain, which would provide money, advice and administrators. A federation would be better able to resist attacks from the Yemen than individual sultans were, and, being an Arab state on the way to independence, it would be less vulnerable than a British colony to pan-Arabic invective. A federation, once established, might even win Aden into membership and thus smother the influence there of the Nasserites.

When the Imam of Yemen and the Sultan of the most fertile of the would-be federal states, Lahej, announced that they too had joined the majority of Arab peoples in the Nasser camp, the remaining sultans, afraid of both Nasserite radicalism and Yemeni attack, pressed with growing urgency for a federation to be created. In 1958 the régime of Prime Minister Nuri es Said in Iraq, Britain's most loyal ally in the Middle East, fell to a coup by young officers. The bodies of Nuri and the young King were dragged through the streets. This evidence from the far side of the Arabian desert of the post-Suez mood of Arab mobs towards traditionalist rulers strengthened the feeling of the sultans that they needed increased protection.

So, in February 1959 the Federation of Arab Amirates of the South eventually came into existence; villages that had never before received any British aid – except a little cash and a few rifles for the amir – were suddenly given help to develop a school, a medical clinic or a road. Modernising the protectorates was not easy. 'Road-making was one of the first things we tried to do (remembered Sir Kennedy Trevaskis, adviser and British agent to the western Aden protectorates). The moment we started building a road, the tribes who had got their money from hiring out camels immediately closed the road by shooting up all the lorries that went up it.' Of the sixteen larger protectorates within reach of Yemen, twelve soon joined the Federation, although the eastern 'states' in and around the Hadramaut felt no fear of the Yemen, hoped vainly that they were about to strike oil, and kept out.

The setting-up of the Federation did not prevent eruptions of Nasserite feeling in its tiny member-states, and many subjects of those sultans who had joined the Federation followed the instruction of Cairo Radio that they should oppose the scheme by all possible means. Every male tribesman in the protectorates carried a gun. To go out without one was unthinkable. Shooting each other was their national sport. They had formerly used their guns in skirmishes with the sultans' guards and continued to shoot at the guards in their new uniforms as the federal army. Usually the federal forces reacted quickly and decisively. When villagers remained unsubdued, British bombers would be sent in to deliver the *coup de grâce*. It was all, to the British, 'military tiddlywinks'. They held that RAF bombing was a humane and efficient way of maintaining control: first, leaflets were dropped, warning tribesmen to leave the village; then any buildings thought to belong to the ringleaders would be bombed to teach their owners a lesson. Often villagers would gather on a nearby hill to watch the aircraft in action. After such a display of overwhelming military superiority a proud and rebellious Arab could give in to the sultans and their federal partners, the British, without dishonour.

In Aden colony itself a similar, though less violent, pattern of conflict developed between, on the one side, the British and their merchant allies and, on the other, Arab immigrant workers organised after 1956 in the Aden Trades Union Congress (ATUC). British confidence in Aden's stability was boosted by the creation of the Federation to protect its hinterland, and in 1960 Aden was made the headquarters of the British Middle East Command. This role, added to the great expansion in trade since the opening of the BP refinery in 1954, drew thousands of work-seekers into Aden, mostly Yemenis and Federation tribesmen, who were new to the modern wage economy. The ATUC campaigned for Arab unity and the need to remove imperialism, so the new arrivals – already enthused with such ideas by Cairo Radio – joined up. The ATUC version of Arab unity began with an independent, socialist state to be made up of Aden, the protectorates and the Yemen, whose brutal and dictatorial Imam would first be removed.

While these ideas were spreading, Aden was changing character. Previously the British had ruled but kept out of sight. The traders were mostly Indians and Pakistanis, the workforce mostly Arab and Somali. But in the 1950s, after the opening of the refinery, the military base added to the few hundred RAF men already present an influx of 8,000 British soldiers, sailors and airmen, many of whom also brought their wives. The new Federal Government also increased the British presence. Previously the sultans had enjoyed the benefit of an occasional visit by a British adviser. Now a new federal administrative capital was built just beyond the boundary of Aden, and named Al Ittihad (Arabic for 'the Federation'). Here an influx of British officials arrived to administer all the new aid schemes. Cairo Radio was spreading the conviction that the imperialists must go and the British were publicly declaring that the Federation was merely a scheme to enable the independent rulers in the protectorates to exercise a full and modern independence in an enlarged state. But the number of Britons in newly-built, air-conditioned dwellings in Aden – soldiers, civil servants, refinery technicians, agricultural advisers, irrigation engineers, doctors, teachers – mushroomed.

They were greatly outnumbered, however, by the building labourers, vegetable sellers, cleaners, carriers and runners who flocked into Aden to serve them. Many, particularly those who worked in the refinery, the base and the port, were recruited into the Aden TUC. The largest group of its supporters were Yemenis, of whom some 50,000 were by now earning quick money in Aden before returning to the green hills of 'Arabia Felix'. Indeed the Yemenis formed the largest group in Aden's total population of 138,000, as measured by a census in 1955. Given the general British commitment to the introduction of elections and the progressive extension of the franchise, this group seemed destined to destroy the British plan to absorb Aden into the Federation of the conservative – indeed autocratic and mostly reactionary – sultans. This problem was dealt with by a neat electoral device. When the first elections were held in 1955 for four members of the Aden Legislative Council, the franchise was restricted to those born in Aden and to British subjects long resident there – Indians, Pakistanis and Englishmen as well as some Arabs. The Yemenis and the Arabs from the protectorates, though together they formed a majority, were only 'temporary residents' and so were excluded. The ATUC, since most of its members were disfranchised, instructed those few with the vote to boycott the election. Sir Kennedy Trevaskis defended the arrangement, though with reservations:

> A great majority of the Yemenis were transitory labourers. They came and worked for a year, got enough money to get married and went back to the Yemen. And possibly a couple of years later they would be back again. It wouldn't have been right to have given those the vote. Some of course came and settled. It would have been fair to have given the vote to householders. Then at least you would have known that they had a stake in Aden. But that wasn't done.

Most of those who had the vote, the long-term residents and British subjects,

wanted the British to stay. They found the administration competent and honest and, above all, reliable at keeping the peace. One of them, Antonin Besse (by origin a Frenchman), made enough money in Aden to give more than £1 million to the University of Oxford to found a new college, St Antony's. Such people on the Legislative Council gave the Governor sensible and informed advice. They were also helpful in other matters. When the Governor expressed dismay at the donation to Oxford, already adequately endowed with colleges, M. Besse immediately made further donations to set up institutes for technical and women's education in Aden.

The Imam of Yemen launched armed attacks on the Federation. The ATUC launched strikes and demonstrations in Aden. In the face of such blows, the British Government saw only one way of keeping its Aden base: by reinforcing its links with the businessmen in the Aden Legislative Council and with the pro-British rulers in the Federation. If they would agree to make Aden part of the Federation, secure political defences might be constructed. Britain's Prime Minister, Harold Macmillan, noted in his diary in May 1961: 'The real problem is how to use the influence and power of the Sultans to help us keep the Colony and its essential defence facilities . . . We agreed to merge the Colony with the Federation of Rulers and give as much power as we can to the Sultans who are on our side.' So the British cajoled and bullied the merchant Adenis and the federal sultans into a shotgun marriage. The imminent event that the ceremony was to forestall was the advent in Aden of an Arab majority in the Legislative Council. By gerrymandering – changing the date of an election so as to avoid the damaging impact of a franchise revision – the British clung on to a narrow majority in the council. Arab businessmen in Aden were worried at being required to vote in the council chamber for a measure against which thousands of less wealthy Arabs were demonstrating in the streets outside. British ministers and officials forced the passage of a major constitutional reorganisation, with only the lukewarm support of an unrepresentative legislature, in the face of strong popular opposition and by one vote. Nevertheless, in September 1962 they pulled it off. The Aden Legislative Council voted for the colony to join the Federation.

The next day the scene abruptly changed. The Imam of Yemen was overthrown by a revolutionary republican coup backed by Egypt. The opponents of the Federation in Aden had previously been obliged to dissemble. They had said they wanted Aden and the protectorates unified with the Yemen, even though they knew that the Yemen, under its medieval Imam, was not a country with which modern Aden could become involved. The revolution, however, brought Yemen a Government in sympathy with Nasser and his modernising, pan-Arabic ideas. So the ATUC Nasserites and their immigrant Yemeni supporters, within days of the vote that secured Aden's absorption into the Federation, acquired a powerful nearby backer. Sir Charles Johnston, the Governor of Aden, subsequently wrote: 'If the Yemeni revolution had come one day earlier or the Legislative Council vote one day later . . . the agreement would never have obtained the support of a majority of local members.'

The leader of the Aden TUC, Abdullah al Asnag, greeted the Yemen coup in a speech on 28 September 1962: 'We declare in the names of the citizens of the Occupied South, that we shall fight . . . to strengthen and stabilise the popular revolution in the north . . . This occupied part belongs to the sons of the natural Yemen . . . not to a handful of satellites. . . . Be sure the day of liquidation is at hand.' He was soon flying to the Yemeni capital, Sana, where four of his colleagues became ministers in the new republican Government.

So the political foundations of Britain's principal military base in the Middle East were further undermined. Things soon became even worse. Had the new Egyptian-backed régime in the Yemen secured itself in authority throughout the country, the British and the new Federal Government – since Aden's accession renamed the Federation of South Arabia – would have had to come to terms with it. Indeed officials in the Foreign Office, who had almost to a man opposed the Suez invasion, were now eager to recognise the new régime in the Yemen. They argued that Britain's only hope of retaining influence in the Middle East lay in winning the consent of the main Arab political leaders. Nasser had been prepared until 1956 to allow British military technicians to stay in the Suez canal zone, provided

*A demonstration in Crater with Nasser, as always, held high.*

they were not in uniform, and his new policy of playing off East against West might have led him to welcome some form of continued British presence in Aden. It would not be a wholly British base inside a sovereign British colony, but that position had in effect already been abandoned by the agreement to advance the new South Arabian Federal state towards independence.

The Foreign Office argued that a reduced British presence in Aden secured with the consent of the Pan-Arabists and Nasserites would be more stable than a large base held with the consent only of the federal rulers and Aden's business leaders. The possibility of improved relations with Nasser was clearly indicated by a change in the tone of Cairo Radio, whose anti-British invective was abruptly restrained. The prospect of peaceful co-existence between British Aden and Republican Yemen was, in the words of Sir Kennedy Trevaskis, 'dangled alluringly before American and British eyes'. The first step towards such a policy was the recognition of the new régime in the Yemen. This should have been easy, given Britain's rule that the Government which is in effective control of most of a country must be recognised.

In 1962–3 in the Yemen, however, it was not altogether clear who was in effective control. The republicans held the towns and a large part of the countryside, but – the old Imam having died – his son was leading a royalist resistance strongly backed by Saudi Arabia. Since the Saudis were, thanks to their oil, the richest state in the peninsula, the side they supported could not be considered certain losers. Furthermore Britain was eager to resume diplomatic relations with Saudi Arabia, broken off at Suez. And the Ministry of Defence and Colonial Office argued that it was sound policy to withhold recognition. A hasty deal with the republicans and the Nasserites would mean abandoning the sultans and the Adeni leaders who had just voted to join with Britain. To the chagrin of the Foreign Office, after its ministers in London had for four months argued in favour of recognition, the new Yemen Government settled the issue by evicting the British mission. Macmillan noted in his diary in February 1963:

> The Colonial Secretary is triumphant – so is the Minister of Defence. I think it's the best thing 'in the short term', for (had we recognised the new Yemeni regime) we would have lost the confidence of all our friends in the new Aden Federation. In the long run it may bring us trouble. But Arab politics change with startling rapidity and one can never be sure.

In this way Britain's desire to stand by its friends led it to take the side of the royalist resistance in the Yemen. The United States Government took the opposite view. In spite of Macmillan's efforts to persuade him, President Kennedy recognised the new republican régime in Sana. The State Department, like the Foreign Office, had warned against supporting a reactionary royalist régime that was opposed by the modern pan-Arabist movement. Since the republican Government in Sana was rapidly reinforced by the arrival of an Egyptian army of 20,000 men, the joint view of Anglo-American diplomats was that delay in recognition would merely encourage a hopeless royalist resistance and oblige the Egyptians to stay in Sana to support their ally. Macmillan, faced with conflict between his ministers, was finally responsible for the British decision and revealed the spirit that had made him the Government's leading hawk over Suez. He wanted to see Nasser given a bloody nose and he received reports – notably from a Conservative MP, Colonel Neil McLean, who paid an extensive visit to eastern and northern Yemen under royalist protection – that the tribesmen and the royalists would not be easy to defeat. Mercenaries trained in the British army went to fight for the young Imam. Arms reached him via one of the federal sultans.

Britain's policy for Aden had now entered a whirlpool, in which it was to be drawn disastrously ever downwards. Pan-Arabism threatened it on all sides, capable of bringing crowds onto the streets to burn a British embassy anywhere in the Middle East. President Nasser had become a more implacable enemy than ever, his initial help for the Yemen republican coup now growing, in the face of the British backing of the royalist resistance. The Egyptian army in Yemen soon numbered 70,000. The majority of the 150,000 population in Aden were supporters of a movement that took the side of Nasser, Egypt and the Yemen republic. And the half-million tribesmen in the protectorates, while their views had never been tested, were mostly armed and probably volatile. Against such forces, Britain's frail craft was the Federation, a vessel whose two halves fitted ill together and whose officers were never on the bridge. The sultans from the protectorates were not really suited to be ministers in a modern government. They shared out ministries amongst themselves, and the ruler of every newly recruited 'state' became a minister in the federal Cabinet, even though he was barely literate and blatantly incompetent. The dominating figure among the sultans, the Sherif of Baihan, a minister in the Federal Government, refused for two years to visit the federal capital. The chairmanship of the ministers rotated monthly, ensuring lack of leadership or continuity. The sultans were tribal leaders, constantly suspicious of their neighbours and their subjects, good men with a gun or a goat. The Aden members of the Federal Government were no better. First and foremost they were businessmen, liable to flit off to Djibouti, Mombasa or Bombay, more concerned with their own profits than with the subtleties of statecraft. Insofar as the Federal Government continued to stay afloat, it depended entirely on its British crew of dutiful civil servants, most of them hard-working, many unhappy at being posted to Aden, none really abreast of the fast-changing and variously financed pressures of Arab politics.

The appointment in 1963 of Sir Kennedy Trevaskis as High Commissioner (as the Governor was henceforward to be known) was against Colonial Office practice. Usually a new Governor was brought from another colony, to avoid any charge of favouritism towards groups with whom he had previously worked. Trevaskis was the man who had patiently nursed the sultans into the Federation. They and it were his babies. Most governors by the early 1960s had concluded that the rulers of the small. primitive states in treaty relationship with Britain were unequal to the task of running a modern government. The successful inheritors of British power had all been men who could win popular mass support. In appointing Trevaskis the Conservative Colonial Secretary, Duncan Sandys, took a gamble. As Trevaskis himself later wrote: 'It was clearly questionable whether my long and intimate association with the federal ministers, as their adviser, might not prove a liability when it came to ironing out the continuing differences between them and their Adeni colleagues.' The Conservative Government, in effect, was wholeheartedly backing the federal sultans. A Cabinet that was led by Harold Macmillan, who had three years earlier made his 'winds of change' speech acknowledging the irresistible force of nationalism in Africa, and that included Iain Macleod, who as Colonial Secretary had backed African nationalists against both traditional rulers and white settlers, was in Aden taking the huge gamble of putting its money and its reputation on the traditionalists. The rationale behind this policy was that Britain's defence needs were paramount, that the Adenis were making so much money from the British presence that they would calm down, and that Nasser's Arab nationalist movement was a flash-in-the-pan: if the British and the federal rulers kept their heads down, they would pull through.

Their difficulty is illustrated by a visit Trevaskis paid to New York in the

*The Governor, Sir Kennedy Trevaskis, and Conservative Colonial Secretary, Duncan Sandys.*

spring of 1963. In the United Nations, the Federation was depicted as an imperialist plot. The Egyptian Government sent leaders of the Aden TUC and its new offshoot, the People's Socialist Party, to New York to describe the iniquities of this engine of British anti-democratic oppression. In the 'Committee of 24', set up by the General Assembly to harry the imperial powers out of their colonies, Britain found that Egypt, in the aftermath of Suez, could call the tune. Third World countries and Soviet satellites would launch strings of allegations against the oppressor régime. The British delegate to the committee would try to obtain the facts to answer the charges, but votes regularly ended with unanimous condemnation of the colonial power.

Trevaskis took the brightest of the federal sultans, the finance minister Muhammad Farid, to New York to appear before the committee. Farid was the ruler of the federal state of Upper Aulaqi, had been educated at Oxford and had served in the British protectorate administration. He told Trevaskis that he backed the British because they would give genuine help to the area and then, eventually, depart; Egypt and Yemen, on the other hand, were seeking control over South Arabia; they were expansionist powers and once let in would be determined to stay. Farid described the Federation to the committee and explained that the south Arabians did not want to be ruled by Yemen which had repeatedly attacked them. The committee, however, paid no attention to his words. They regarded him as a stooge of the British. When the committee visited Cairo in May 1963 its request to visit Aden to hear further evidence was rejected by the British Government.

Trevaskis responded to his disappointing experience at the UN and to the need to forestall a popular uprising which would enjoy both Egyptian and Yemeni support by persuading the Government that it must grant the Federation independence as fast as possible. In December 1963 he prepared to leave for London for the first stage of a constitutional conference which would open the way to an independent federation ruled by the sultans and the richer traders of Aden. It was no doubt a forlorn mission, but in any case it was forestalled. When the Governor was saying goodbye to colleagues at Aden airport before boarding his plane, a grenade was thrown at him. It killed one of his assistants and an Indian lady by-stander and wounded fifty-one others. Nevertheless ministers in London decided to let Trevaskis proceed with his efforts to bring Aden and the Federation jointly to independence under the rule of the sultans and the Adeni businessmen. The target date for independence was set as 1968.

Such was the legacy of the Conservative Government. In October 1964 Labour was elected to power in Britain, determined to reverse its predecessor's policies. The new Colonial Secretary, Anthony Greenwood, had some knowledge of Aden and the Federation acquired from sources independent of the Government, especially from Abdullah al Asnag, the leader of the Aden TUC and of the Yemeni nationalist movement in the colony. Asnag's father was for many years an inspector in the Aden

Government's health service, a member of a family long settled in Crater (the main Arab residential area inside an extinct volcano). Asnag himself ran the booking office of Aden Airways with effortless efficiency. While as leader of the ATUC he was organising protests and campaigns against the British and those he considered their puppets, successive Governors and lesser officials relied utterly on his services in fixing their air passages in and out of the colony. They were impressed by his skill in making the ATUC the single nationalist voice of a heterogeneous population. The Labour Party and the Fabian Society in London came to know Asnag as a reasonable man and found his arguments convincing. The Conservative Government, he explained, had backed the wrong horse. It was totally against the British colonial tradition to fix a constitutional arrangement with an unrepresentative minority. What Britain had to do was to come to terms with the majority, whom he represented, as proved by his ability repeatedly to bring them out on strike. Anthony Greenwood accepted Asnag's arguments and within two months of taking office summoned Sir Kennedy Trevaskis to London to dismiss him. Greenwood determined that Asnag and his Adeni colleagues, who were popular nationalist leaders, competent administrators and on good terms with Nasser and his pan-Arabist movement, should as quickly as possible be given power and independence.

Greenwood, however, was not a strong minister. He was overruled. The President of the United States, Lyndon Johnson, fighting an unpopular war in Vietnam, was anxious for all possible help from Britain in the role of world policeman. While it was impossible for a Labour Prime Minister to send troops to Vietnam, as Johnson would have liked, the maintenance of Britain's overseas bases could relieve America of military burdens elsewhere. In return, Johnson was prepared to help the Wilson Government in its overriding policy objective, avoiding a devaluation of the pound sterling. Therefore retention of the Aden base, which Labour had previously opposed, now became essential.

Having reversed its policy on the base, Labour also reversed on the Federation. Ditching the sultans accorded with Labour Party principles, but the promise to protect them had been made extremely recently and repeated in the independence talks held only weeks before Labour came to power. Was Britain's word to be shown as worthless? Furthermore, since the isolated incident of the airport grenade, Aden had been generally peaceful. Cairo Radio and Sana Radio daily promised bloodshed and revolution, and the Aden TUC, the most sophisticated and militant trade union organisation in the Arab world, was constantly holding strikes in support of political demands, but the base and the refinery were continuing to function satisfactorily. Al Asnag made threatening speeches, visiting Moscow, Peking and, much more frequently, Cairo, but Labour ministers judged that he was a man of peace with whom a deal could be struck.

The Labour Government therefore pursued a scheme that might bring it the best of all worlds: a unitary state of South Arabia in which the bulk of power would lie less with the sultans than with the elected majority in Aden. The more able of the sultans would be brought into the new government, while the less able would be treated as respectfully and honourably as possible. Anthony Greenwood flew to Aden to put together this arrangement. He talked the sultans into giving up a substantial portion of their powers and the Aden TUC and Al Asnag into agreeing to the retention of the British base. After some months a new chief minister was appointed in Aden, Abdul Makawee, a member of Al Asnag's party who came from a wealthy trading family and was trusted by some of the traditional Aden élite. If Al Asnag could deliver Nasser's support for the scheme and the sultans were prepared to place their trust in a Makawee-led Aden Government as the major force in the new unitary state, it appeared that a solution might be at hand.

It was not to be. In the federal sultanate of Radfan in 1964, a new force had appeared on the South Arabian scene. Many Yemenis had gone home from Aden to fight for the republican cause. Some tribesmen from the federation had joined them. Since 1962 they had become war-hardened and had been formed into a new organisation. They were called the National Liberation Front.

The NLF was founded in the Yemen in late June 1963. The republican Government that came to power in Sana the previous year was faced with Britain's refusal to recognise it and the prospect of active help to its royalist opponents from both the sultans and the British in the South Arabian Federation. It therefore sponsored the setting-up of the NLF to oppose the British and the Federation, its members drawn from those who had hurried to Yemen to welcome the new régime: tribal leaders, army officers who had been serving as mercenaries in Saudi Arabia and the Gulf, workers from Aden, young men from the federal states who had gone to Aden to study and had been inspired by Arab nationalism. The Yemen republican Government employed an adviser on South Yemen affairs, Qahtan Asshabi, who came from the federal state of Lahej, had been educated in Aden and was well-connected with Arab civil servants and journalists there. Kennedy Trevaskis remembered him as 'an agricultural officer with mischief in his eye and a sly grin on his face'. When Asshabi set up the NLF, radical Aden newspapers reported the fact, but the news made no impact on the British administration because organisations dedicated to the overthrow of imperialism were ten a penny in the Arab world. Most had eloquent titles and explicitly subversive objectives, and achieved nothing. This one performed unexpectedly effectively in Radfan in 1963–4, tying down federal and British troops (including two thousand who had to be specially flown from England) for nine months before withdrawing. It then held its first Congress at Taiz in June 1965. The charter that was there approved included many paragraphs about 'reactionary imperialist plots' and 'the Revolution of 26 September', and contained one key declaration of purpose: the NLF would organise 'a popular revolutionary army'.

With hindsight it is clear that the circumstances were perfect for such a venture. Neither the federal sultans nor the Government in Aden enjoyed the legitimacy of popular support; both were heavily dependent on the British, whose continued presence was doubtful; both Cairo Radio and Sana Radio had broadcast years of political education about the need to wipe out the imperialists and their stooges; the young men of the sultanates were accustomed to carrying guns and were good shots; and the civil war in the Yemen provided plenty of opportunities for training and the acquisition of modern arms and equipment. Furthermore the NLF had teachers and advisers from Egypt and from among the Palestinians who since 1948 had been fighting the Israelis. Mahmoud Riad, then Foreign Minister of Egypt, recalled: 'We helped in two ways, by sending arms directly to groups who were asking for them and by establishing a centre for training in Taiz. Many young men from southern Yemen used to come for training and arms.' The NLF rapidly proved to possess the most important attribute of a guerilla movement: the ability to surprise. The British simply did not know what had hit them. In the words of Lt.-Colonel Julian Paget of the Coldstream Guards, posted to Aden in 1965, 'A major problem which was to recur throughout the campaign was the lack of any specific, reliable intelligence about the enemy – where they were, what their organisation was, what their aims or objectives might be, or indeed, who they were.' The British did not realise that they were up against a new type of enemy with a new kind of strategy. Hitherto dissident tribesmen fighting their sultans had been fairly easy to deal with. Their whereabouts, even their names, were usually known. Similarly agitation in Aden had been manageable. The Governor could always phone Al Asnag at home early in the morning or later in the airline office to obtain a fair idea of what was going on. The NLF, organised in tiny cells whose members knew nothing except the task they had been given, presented a challenge of a different order. Saleh Musleh Qassem, an NLF leader, explained:

> The internal party cells were made up of three to five members and there were periodic secret meetings, mostly at night. That was the time when the armed commandos would tour the villages and meet with each of the organisation's secret cells separately. During such meetings they would clarify the latest developments, gather information, assign tasks and distribute pamphlets, as well as gather contributions for the National Front Political Organisation. These were the most important activities undertaken by the party's secret cells in the villages. No cell knew of the others except in extraordinary circumstances related to security. A member joining any of the secret cells of the Organisation had to go through a probationary period of six months at the most before being accepted as a full member.

Major-General James Lunt was the commander of the South Arabian Federation army:

In every battalion we had four, five or six British officers and many British warrant officers and NCOs [he reminisced]. They called the shots. And of course the Arabs in the army saw this. If I had been a young Arab I would have been a nationalist just like them. The appeal is to run your own country. When these Arabs were sent on courses and met Arabs from Syria or Jordan or Iraq they were regarded as imperialist stooges.

It was not long before cells of the NLF included serving members of the federal army. Saleh Musleh Qassem recalled:

Members of the police and the army – mostly NCOs and junior officers – were transporting a fair quantity of arms for us. This was especially true of the out of bounds areas or those where only the military and the police could move freely. They were the ones who were carrying out this task, as well as hiding the weapons. Most of them were the sons of poor workers and peasants and as such had a genuine stake in the revolution.

Greenwood had only just concluded his first talks with Al Asnag and the federal sultans about creating a unitary state when, in December 1964, grenade attacks against British servicemen began in Aden. Rapidly the NLF proved that they could kill whomever they wished without getting caught. When in February 1965 Greenwood announced that Britain would hold a constitutional conference in London to work out the details of the proposed unitary state, the NLF threatened to kill anyone who attended. Participants threw up obstacles and the conference was cancelled. Later in the year, with Adenis in the Government frightened to take any action against the NLF after the Speaker of the Legislative Assembly and the superintendent of police had been murdered, Greenwood was reluctantly obliged to suspend the constitution of the town and impose direct rule by the High Commissioner.

The NLF's success on the streets led to further recruitment. Success also encouraged the leaders to develop an ideology dedicated not only to expelling the British and all imperialists but also to destroying the traditional merchant and ruling classes; some spoke of creating a proletarian state. Much of this became clear at its June 1965 congress in Taiz, which enabled British officials for the first time clearly to identify the NLF and therefore to ban it. Becoming an illegal organisation did not, however, reduce its activity. Nor did the ban help the British to learn more about it.

The arrival of the NLF in Aden drove Al Asnag to attempt his own violence, to avoid being overtaken on the final stretch in the race for power. He set up a military organisation with Egyptian backing and headquarters in Cairo. Egypt's reason for giving its support to a second guerilla movement was that the NLF was proving impossible to control. President Nasser did not want a Marxist-Leninist movement, which the NLF appeared to be, to dominate south Arabia. He hoped to win the NLF into the new movement which, through the political skill of Al Asnag, moderate friends of Egypt would dominate. Mahmoud Riad recalled: 'Sometimes there were clashes between Asnag's party and the NLF and the sultans. We wanted only the independence of the country and to avoid civil war. Nasser thought that there must be some kind of coalition.' However, this attempt to bring the NLF under Egyptian control worked only briefly. Nasser, unable to win the war in the Yemen, signed an agreement with Saudi Arabia's King Feisal which obliged him to withdraw the 70,000 Egyptians backing the republican Government in return for Feisal's withdrawing his aid to the royalists. The NLF proved able to look after themselves without Egyptian help. They raised money by armed visits to Aden businessmen, billeted their men on a largely willing – but also terrified – population, and arranged their own arms and training. Al Asnag's guerillas – known as FLOSY, the Front for the Liberation of Occupied South Yemen – were not so independent. The NLF soon decided that FLOSY was a tool of the Egyptian bourgeoisie and began to use grenades and guns against them. For the British, Aden and south Arabia were becoming ungovernable. They rarely caught the killers and arsonists and never brought any of them to trial.

When they did catch people thought to be NLF supporters, the British interrogated them harshly. The International Red Cross were refused permission to interview detainees and the Welsh lawyer, Roderic Bowen Q.C., who conducted an independent inquiry for the British Government, found little to complain of, but NLF men made frequent allegations of torture. A subsequent British commission of inquiry (into ill-treatment of detainees in Northern Ireland) reported in 1971 that 'disorientation' techniques had been developed by British army interrogation units in Palestine, Malaya, Kenya and Cyprus, as well as Aden. Suspects were compelled to stand leaning towards a wall, their weight borne on outstretched fingers and their heads hooded. Being kept in such a position for long periods, deprived of sleep and with continuous high-pitched noise directed at them, the suspects' willpower and sense of identity were weakened. Such procedures were against the law in Aden, but no NLF man had lawyers raise the point, since they were looking for more traditional beatings and torture, which were not used systematically. None of these methods enabled the British to catch NLF cells. On the contrary, the few British intelligence officers who were fluent in Arabic and beginning to acquire an idea of the way the NLF worked were promptly assassinated.

In the light of Britain's promise to grant independence to the Federation, many were puzzled by the worsening violence. Cairo Radio, in January 1966, gave an explanation:

Some may ask, why fight for independence when the British will grant it freely in 1968? Comrades, true independence is not given but taken. For this reason, my brothers in the south, there is no way but war and armed struggle. The people must wage armed revolution against the enemy, in which they must pay the highest price in life and blood.

What this really meant was that the battle for the succession was on. Whichever group could win popular support by actions against the British could then turn its force against the local competition. By creating a system of government in which both the workers of Aden and the gun-carrying tribesmen of the protectorates were unrepresented, the Conservative Government had in effect challenged both to do their worst. It was the misfortune of the Labour Government that it inherited this primed grenade.

In February 1966, as part of a review of Britain's excessive defence commitments overseas, the Government announced that it would quit not only the government of the colony but also possession of its military base at Aden by the end of 1968; Britain could no longer afford to police the Persian Gulf or the route to India, even to please President Johnson. The effect of the announcement was to make it clear that Britain now had no further interest in Aden, except to hand over to a stable successor. However, neither of the two favoured candidates – the sultans who were, jointly with Britain, running the Federal Government, and Al Asnag's fundamentally accommodating party – was able to negotiate for the succession because the NLF were raising hell in both the villages of the sultans and the centre of Aden. Real power was slipping into the hands of a group of gunmen who included disciplined Marxist murderers, primitive tribal pursuers of the blood feud, teenage tearaways and dedicated nationalists.

The 1966 announcement of the closure of the base shocked and angered the Conservative Party, particularly Duncan Sandys who as Colonial Secretary had promised the sultans of the Federation that Britain would stand by them. It shocked the sultans even more. Immediately before publishing its defence review, the Labour Government sent a junior minister, Lord Beswick, to break the news to them. Mahommad Farid, the Oxford-educated Sultan of Upper Aulaqi who had gone with Trevaskis to the UN, recalled:

We had been assured by Lord Lloyd, who was a British Conservative minister, and by Duncan Sandys, who was the Commonwealth and Colonial Secretary, and also by Mr Healey, who was the Labour Defence Minister, by Mr Greenwood, who was the Colonial Secretary, and by George Brown and by Lord Beswick, who was Minister of State, by every one of them, that the British Government would carry out its obligations to the Federation. They promised to lead us into independence and ensure that we had defence arrangements as long as we needed them. And we needed them only for a limited period. Then at twenty-four hours' notice the High Commissioner told us that Lord Beswick, who had the responsibility for South Arabia, wanted to meet the Council of Ministers. We had no idea what it was all about. He came in the morning to our Cabinet meeting and told us that the British Government had decided unilaterally to get out of Aden and to liquidate the base, whether there was a broadly-based Government in the Federation or not. And there was a tremendous shock amongst the ministers. We sensed that the British Government had no interest any more in the Federation and in seeing it go to proper independence. One of my colleagues described that sort of behaviour as dishonourable and a betrayal on the part of the British Government, which we all felt it was. We had a very stormy meeting.

From that moment on, the war for the spoils was uncontainable. Britain tried to encourage prominent Adenis to join the Federal Government, which still seemed the only formal body to which it was possible to transfer power, but nobody with popular backing would agree. The Federal Government devoted its energies to trying to persuade Britain to enter a defence treaty at independence. That way it would have some prospect of surviving. But the Labour Government was now determined on a total military withdrawal.

So officials continued to run the Federal Government in co-operation with federal ministers, while in practice opening the way for the enemies of the Federation to take over. To Conservatives in London and federal ministers in Al Ittihad, this policy made no sense. To ministers in London it made perfect sense: the prime objective of policy was to avoid getting involved in a war, more particularly to avoid being accused by Labour Party members of killing socialists and the representatives of the Aden majority in order to bolster the power of feudal sultans.

Al Asnag was caught in a similar but opposite trap. Since the Labour Government was plainly determined to go and to give representative Adenis as much control as they could over the successor Government, his ideal would have been to negotiate his way peacefully into power. But the successes of the NLF made this impossible for several reasons. The only way to maintain popular support in a world where the British were seen as the allies of Zionism and the co-conspirators of 1956 against the great Nasser was to appear at least as militant as the NLF. In earlier times Al Asnag had sometimes made anti-British speeches which he explained to friendly colonial officials were not to be taken too seriously: they were merely necessary rhetoric. But now, to demonstrate that he was as anti-British as the NLF, his guerilla movement had to prove itself more heroic and effective than theirs.

President Nasser did everything he could to help. He provided training camps, arms and equipment for FLOSY and, when the NLF refused to subordinate themselves to a movement led by Al Asnag, Nasser compelled Qahtan Asshabi to stay in Cairo. Asshabi had started the NLF as a paid official of the republican Government of Yemen and now found himself paid instead by the Government of Egypt to stop running the NLF. Al Asnag, by contrast, was now paid by Egypt to run a more co-operative guerilla movement. In 1965, seeing that the British lacked either the will or the ability to hand him power, he had left Aden and based himself in Taiz, travelling regularly to Cairo.

Following the March 1966 announcement of Britain's withdrawal from

*The reluctant guerilla. Abdullah Al Asnag, centre, at his headquarters in Taiz, Yemen, in 1967.*

the Aden base by 1968, Nasser reversed his decision to quit the Yemen. He thus reneged on his agreement with King Feisal because it was now plain that the rich plum of Aden was about to fall from the tree and it would have been sheer imprudence for an Egyptian President with an ambition to head a united Arab nation not to have his army on hand at the moment it dropped. Denis Healey, who was Labour's Minister of Defence from 1964 to 1970, recalled: 'Nasser once told me he saw himself as performing Lord Lugard's role in the Yemen.' He intended to take control in both north Yemen (Arabia Felix) and south Yemen (Aden and the protectorates).

Nasser found it as difficult as the British did to control events in the states of Arabia. Putting Qahtan Asshabi and other NLF leaders under virtual house-arrest in Cairo and putting Egypt's resources behind Asnag's military organisation merely led NLF supporters to brand Asnag as an agent of Egyptian imperialism. Cairo Radio's call for Arab unity against the imperialists encountered an unexpected new development which, in Aden and the Federation, appeared to be stronger even than pan-Arabic nationalism.

New NLF leaders emerged who demanded total independence for South Arabia – from Britain, from the Yemen and from Egypt. The NLF leaders who made this demand proved able to win support within their cells and to maintain their organisation's military momentum. Many of them happened also to be the strongest believers within the Front in the creation of a

*Sir Richard Turnbull,*
*High Commissioner,*
*inspects federal troops at*
*Al Ittihad, the capital.*

Marxist–Leninist state, a policy which had the advantage in a complex political situation of being uncompromising and clear.

Egypt was now as keen to destroy the NLF as Britain was and a curious alliance developed. It had been the policy of the Labour Government in London ever since it came to power in 1964 to restore diplomatic relations with Egypt, which had been broken off in 1956, restored in 1961, then broken off over Rhodesia in 1965. Foreign Office officials were as keen as ministers to come to terms with the reality that Nasser's Egypt was the key state in Middle East diplomacy. The residues of Conservative policy in the region had been slowly cleared away – including the commitment to keep a 'permanent' base in Aden and to back the federal sultans – and in August 1966 Britain acquired a new Foreign Secretary, George Brown. He was a man of enormous charisma with clear ideas both on policy and on the role of personality in shaping it. He was determined to reopen relations with Egypt and, more particularly, with President Nasser. Apart from all its other advantages for Britain in the Middle East, an understanding with Nasser looked like being the only way to secure a peaceful transition of power in Aden, since Nasser controlled FLOSY and had the leaders of the NLF in Cairo under his control.

When Anthony Greenwood had dismissed Sir Kennedy Trevaskis in 1964, he appointed as High Commissioner in Aden Sir Richard Turnbull, whose colonial service record included a brilliant success in bringing

Tanganyika peacefully to independence, defusing conflict with the often explosive nationalist leader Julius Nyerere. Turnbull handled the impossible Aden situation with like skill. He managed to keep the Federal Government in control but he restrained its inclination to act so brutally against the nationalists as to render impossible the more broadly-based Government which Britain hoped to assemble. All informed parties praised Turnbull's performance. But George Brown, who had taken over responsibility for Aden, decided to dismiss him.

Brown had had a brilliant idea. To secure a British–Egyptian deal over Aden that would put a stop to terrorism and enable Britain to hand power in a civilised way to a locally popular and generally well-regarded successor régime, someone must be appointed High Commissioner who was both respected and trusted by Nasser. In the British colonial service nobody fitted the bill. But the recently retired British ambassador to Moscow, Sir Humphrey Trevelyan, was not only one of the most able men in the public service, he had earlier in his career occupied a peculiar position: he had been ambassador to Egypt in the run-up to the Suez invasion, and on the day of the Anglo-French ultimatum to Egypt to withdraw ten miles west of the Suez canal he told Nasser that he had known nothing of it until it was delivered. Nasser knew him well and believed him. Their relationship was good enough for the President to invite the former ambassador to visit Egypt as his personal guest. If, as the British Government believed, Egypt was the main cause of the troubles now afflicting Aden and the Federation, then the appointment of Trevelyan was a stroke of genius.

His first step was to open the door to the gunmen. He and British ministers doubted whether the Federal Government was capable of carrying the country through to independence. Yet Britain did not have the power to remove it. In former times Britain had been able to dismiss sultans, but now, with NLF and FLOSY gunmen active everywhere and Britain's departure imminent, the word of Westminster counted for little. The protectorates were always legally independent, not British territory at all; Britain had merely persuaded the sultans that it should help them to run *their* Federation. Until Nasser's allies came forward responsibly to take the share that the federal rulers had been persuaded to offer in their government, Trevelyan, like Turnbull, was stuck with the federal Cabinet of erratically attending sultans under its revolving chairmanship. He therefore announced, immediately on arriving, that he 'started from the position' of supporting the Federation. No clearer indication could be given of willingness to hand power to the gunmen.

A Foreign Office official who was fluent in Arabic, Sir Sam Falle, was part of a British team sent to open talks and he succeeded in getting himself taken to a house in an area of Aden controlled by the NLF where two representatives of the organisation came to meet him.

One was a little guy with a club foot, packing two guns who looked as if

*The last High Commissioner, Sir Humphrey Trevelyan, left, with ministers of the Federation.*

he'd come straight out of a horror movie [Sir Sam recalled] and the other was a smooth, American-educated graduate. I think I was the first western representative to have a friendly conversation – rather than an interrogation in prison – with the NLF. I explained that the British Government wanted to negotiate independence and to involve all parties concerned so that the government that emerged would be acceptable to the people of Aden. I said that the NLF were a very important party to this and that if we could start talking with them we would of course consider releasing their detainees and taking the ban off their party, so that we could discuss things in a reasonable and relaxed atmospere. But there was just one minor condition that we'd like to make. If it were possible we would be very grateful if they would stop killing us. And the two representatives roared with laughter. And one of them said, 'Very sorry, Abu Sami, this is quite impossible.' Being young, naïve and foolish I said, 'But why? We come with peace and we want to talk to you. It would be rational if you'd stop killing us.' He said, 'No, you must understand, FLOSY constantly accuse us of being the running dogs of the imperialists. If we at this moment were seen to be talking to you this would simply give credence to their story. And so, Abu Sami, we are very sorry, but we have got to drive you out of Aden. And we have to be seen to drive you out. When we have reached that stage then we can negotiate.'

Falle's invitation was not accepted. Al Asnag was now trapped in the role of guerilla leader by the repeated successes of his rivals, the NLF. He and Nasser and the British were alike ignorant of who was running the NLF, if, indeed, anybody was. With its leaders out of action in Egypt, its cells were now independent teams of young toughs, a genuine popular movement with no time for conferences to decide on policy. The one idea that clearly united them all was that any form of compromise with the British would be the act of a traitor. Both in Aden and in the sultanates they were shooting people and letting off bombs apparently at will. Thanks to a mixture of fear and popular support, they were fed, housed and safe from informers.

Trevelyan, unable to talk to FLOSY or the NLF, tried the only alternative – to increase the effectiveness of the Federal Government, the only body in sight capable of providing the structure for the successor state. He tried to make the sultans abandon their revolving chairmanship and invite some Adenis of political standing to join them. He had no success. Instead the main support of the Federal Government – its army and armed police – went out of control in what became known as the army mutinies.

These began with the issue of who was to be commander-in-chief after independence. The federal sultans chose a man whose competence was in doubt, but whose tribal loyalty as an Aulaqi gave them confidence. Other senior officers protested and division quickly spread through the ranks. A group of cadets burnt down an army camp, and a group of armed police, told that the British were about to attack them to restore order, shot at two passing Land-Rovers carrying British soldiers, and killed nine men. Other armed police fired on passing British vehicles until the total of British soldiers killed in this way reached twenty-two.

The worst of these incidents occurred in Crater, the most densely occupied area of Aden where most of the middle-class Arabs and Indians lived. Suddenly, on 20 June 1967, it had become a no-go area for British troops. Worse, the mutiny created fear between the British and their only allies. Some British officers demanded a show of authority and the punishment of those who had killed British soldiers. Tribesmen in the federal army, familiar with the blood-feud, expected reprisals and were ready to resist. The action demanded by understandably angry British troops could quickly have led to total chaos. One British officer, at least, agreed with his men. Lieutenant-Colonel Colin Mitchell of the Argyll and Sutherland Highlanders became known as 'Mad Mitch' because of the way he complained about 'prowling journalists . . . and squeamish politicians' who prevented him from 'sorting out the Arabs'. He put the word about in Crater 'that we were wild Bedouin tribesmen from the Scottish Highlands who could get very rough if provoked'. The General Officer Commanding British troops in Aden, Major-General Philip Tower, said later of Mitchell:

It would have been very easy to 'sort the Arabs out', if we had so desired. But that was not what we were trying to do. Our object was to get out with

*Lieutenant Colonel Colin Mitchell has a cameraman aboard his Land Rover as he drives through Crater.*

minimum casualties and with as much equipment as possible and leave a government behind. Colonel Mitchell for reasons of his own wished to cut a dash with the Argylls in Crater. There were six other battalions in Aden all of whom were doing an equally good job. So I stopped Colonel Mitchell and made him do what everybody else was doing: keep the place as quiet as possible.

The British were fighting only the NLF and FLOSY. To be fighting half the federal army as well would have been too much. Further, the Indian middle class were moving out of Crater as fast as they could get flights to India and Pakistan, and some of the Arab middle class too were beginning to move out, somewhat reducing the British sense of obligation to maintain policing there. So the case for taking no action against the mutineers was strong. However, the Federal Government was the only successor in sight, so restoring discipline in the federal army and armed police was essential. And Crater had to be brought back under British control for another reason that constantly preoccupied Sir Humphrey Trevelyan. It looked increasingly likely that the final British departure would be a hurried rush to the airport, with neither FLOSY nor the NLF nor the Federal Government in control of the territory; and, as Trevelyan repeatedly noted, 'The Khormaksar airport was in mortar range of Crater. We had to keep control of Crater to protect the evacuation.'

For Trevelyan's immediate purpose of recovering control in Crater, it was fortunate that the NLF gangs, in the absence of Asshabi and their other leaders, failed to seize the opportunity to set up a rebel administration there. Consequently, after some days' delay to allow passions to cool – senior officers feared that British soldiers might go on the rampage to avenge their dead comrades – a skilful, bloodless operation by night, led by Mitchell, brought the British army into total charge of Crater. But the mutiny had delivered a fatal blow to the Federation. Always politically weak, it was now no longer in command of its own forces. To restore some measure of discipline, the sultans had to depend on the very officers who had protested at being passed over for the post of commander-in-chief. From this point on the federal army, while not quite as difficult for the British to deal with as FLOSY and the NLF, was a third major armed force whose actions could not be relied on.

The NLF had been gaining ground steadily over FLOSY, but had been unable to obtain dominance because Egypt's substantial backing kept FLOSY going. The possibility that George Brown's understanding with Nasser might lead to a broad-based successor government had remained open. Then in June 1967, the month of the mutiny, that slim hope was ended. In a war with Israel, Egypt was humiliatingly defeated and Nasser had promptly to summon home his troops from Yemen. The urgent crisis in Egypt left him no freedom to pursue ambitions in South Arabia. The money and logistical support on which FLOSY had relied were promptly withdrawn.

Two coincidental events, the mutiny and the Arab–Israel war, had thus raised the NLF from the favourite to win the murderous race for the succession into the unchallenged winner, cantering down the home straight. Asshabi was released from Cairo and took charge of the Front. As the British speeded up their evacuation plans and, by the end of June, withdrew all their forces into Aden, Asshabi's men placed their guns between the shoulders of the federal sultans and, one by one, took charge of their states. Most of the sultans went into exile in Saudi Arabia. The federal army, though shaken by the mutiny, still survived, but the Federal Government it was supposed to serve was vanishing. Some sultans went to Geneva to make their case to a United Nations committee that was looking into the issue. When they had given their evidence the rulers were shocked to be told that the British could not guarantee their safety if they returned to Aden. One, the ruler of Wahidi state, returned nevertheless and persuaded an RAF officer and helicopter pilot to fly him on to his home. When they landed, the two British were killed and the ruler was sent into exile.

On 5 September 1967 Sir Humphrey Trevelyan announced that the Federal Government was no longer functioning and invited 'the nationalist forces as representatives of the people' to talks about forming 'an effective Government'. Asshabi, newly released, said he would be pleased to come to talks if the NLF was recognised as the sole voice of the people. When this

condition was rejected, he agreed to attend a meeting in Cairo at which the Egyptians tried once more to persuade the NLF and FLOSY to work together. But by now it was too late. The NLF were winning and had no need to compromise. Asshabi did not himself know who half his supporters were but while detained by the Egyptians he had become a hero – the founder of the movement. He judged that his men were radicals who would take it amiss if they heard of his engaging in talks with the imperialist British. So Trevelyan and his team were in the extraordinary position of being anxious to leave within a few weeks but having nobody to whom they could hand the keys of the offices. The NLF and FLOSY continued fighting, murdering each other's men, in the battle for the succession. However, the NLF reduced their attacks on property, realising it might soon be theirs.

The evacuation went steadily ahead, troops now withdrawing within Aden to limited and defensible areas. Internal security was progressively handed over to the federal army, now called the South Arabian army, and FLOSY and the NLF each tried to hold the allegiance of officers and men. Too few British troops were now left in Aden to maintain control and the British had to go, whether or not the NLF came forward to learn about the mechanisms by which their country was governed. Lord Shackleton, the Government spokesman in the House of Lords, put the matter clearly:

We consider we are not in a position to help South Arabia any more by our

*A shot came from the crowd and they all wait to be searched, April 1967.*

presence. We still hope that there will be a government there, but if there is no government to hand over to, we can't hand over to a government.

Trevelyan could not contact Asshabi or any NLF leader. He could only pass messages to them through army officers sympathetic to the NLF. He urged them to come to a meeting in Geneva at which the British would arrange the handover. The NLF delayed and did not finally come to Geneva until 22 November 1967, eight days before the final British departure. By then the British had left their Middle East Military Headquarters, moving their command to Khormaksar airfield, and Sir Humphrey Trevelyan had left Government House on Steamer Point empty, bringing in decorators to smarten it up for the new owners, whoever they might be.

The NLF, however, continued to shoot British soldiers and European civilians, to keep up their nationalist image. While the number of these murders declined with the shortage of targets in the last few weeks of British rule, the killings by the NLF and FLOSY of each other's members rose to a new intensity. The British figures for guerilla actions in Aden town alone show the growing struggle for the succession: 36 in 1964, 286 in 1965, 510 in 1966, 2,900 in January to October 1967; in this period 57 British military were killed and 651 wounded. British figures for local people, again in Aden town only, were 290 killed and 922 wounded. The protectorates remained to the end places where men could kill each other without entering British statistics.

Colonel Dai Morgan of the Royal Marines had been in Aden twice before, in 1946 and 1960, and was posted back two months before the final withdrawal.

Everything was being run down [he recalled]. The whole picture was very sad. The blocks of flats at Maalla had their window shutters fluttering in the breeze, glass was broken, doors were open, the air conditioners had disappeared. The cruise liners weren't calling there because the canal had been closed. So commercial activity in Aden town itself had run down. And the NLF and FLOSY were battling it out. We'd see for example from our observation positions uniformed men and non-uniformed going to the back doors of houses and there would be two or three shots and they would run out again. When we investigated of course we'd find a body there. This was a situation in which we had been told we shouldn't interfere at all. It was particular to the last days of Aden.

The Egyptian withdrawal from the Yemen took place, ironically, at the same time as the British withdrawal from Aden. FLOSY, therefore, was not yet deprived of its arms supply and in the final weeks before the British departure tried to make one last gigantic effort to come out on top. Its Egyptian weapons were excellent, it had plenty of ammunition. The NLF had secured the sheikhdoms, but Aden was Al Asnag's base and in parts of it FLOSY gunmen had never yet been defeated. As the battle raged between

the two groups, the South Arabian army, which was ordered to be neutral, found occasion to side with the NLF, using its tanks and heavy guns to destroy FLOSY's last resistance. The NLF then set about arresting, imprisoning and murdering those it considered its enemies, both prominent FLOSY supporters and allies of the British. In Government offices, army barracks and hospitals, the few remaining British stood helplessly by as their colleagues were dragged away by NLF gunmen.

The meeting in Geneva with the British Government team, led by Lord Shackleton, that Asshabi eventually agreed to attend was not an easy affair. Asshabi had discovered that the state he was about to take over was impoverished. One of the main sources of jobs and money, the British base, had just been closed down. The port, recently so busy, had been all but put out of business by the closing of the Suez canal as a result of the Arab–Israel war. And the sultans had none of the stores of gold some NLF members expected. Britain offered £12 million – a lot less than Asshabi wanted. He had to make do.

The last day in Aden was unlike any other. The British assembled a great fleet to take them away and make sure nothing went wrong at the last minute. (One of the ships, HMS *Fearless*, was to be posted from Aden to accommodate the second Wilson–Smith meeting on Rhodesia: see p. 503.) The last British civilians to depart assembled at Khormaksar airport,

*Eleven hours before the British departure and the proclamation of independence, a British minister, Lord Shackleton, left, is at last able to sign a deal with the NLF leader, Qahtan Asshabi.*

surrounded by troops. Dai Morgan, the Marines' colonel, recalled:

> At a quarter to two the helicopters returned from HMS *Albion* and they lifted the final 330 men from about ten positions around the airfield perimeter. And as soon as the men were lifted off I got into my own helicopter and went round the final positions to make sure that everything had been picked up safely and there was nobody left behind. As I was tearing out across the Aden bay to go back to HMS *Albion*, I had a feeling of sadness that I was the last man and we were leaving Aden after a British presence had been there for over 128 years.

Saleh Musleh Qassem of the NLF saw it differently: 'At that moment I had the feeling that Captain Haines has been defeated and that he had been thrown out of our country in the same manner that he had forced his way into it. He had used force to come in and it was with force that he had been turned out.'

Qahtan Asshabi returned from Geneva to the kind of welcome independence leaders expect: multi-coloured lights, NLF flags, taxis and lorries honking N-L-F, a national holiday and crowds from across the desert come to celebrate their freedom. Asshabi was the only successor of the British Empire to escape altogether that course in the British constitution which Governors were prone to teach. He had, however, had a little experience of the British system of government, as an assistant in the Aden protectorates' agricultural service and then as Director of Agriculture to the Sultan of Lahej. Richard Crossman recorded in his diary on Friday 27 October 1967:

> At the Overseas Policy and Defence Committee of the Cabinet, George Brown started a discussion on Aden by apologising for having to tell us that we'll be out by November instead of January. The rest of the committee couldn't be more pleased. Really we've been miraculously lucky in Aden – cancelling all our obligations and getting out.

## After Independence

The NLF took Aden and the Protectorates further to the left than most citizens can have expected. The new state was before long named the People's Democratic Republic of Yemen and soon proved itself a whole-heartedly Marxist, Soviet satellite. Ships of the Russian Navy became regular visitors to Aden harbour, Bulgarian and East German advisers helped develop new industries. The journalists who, until 1967, had been freely reporting on the failures of the British in Aden were now firmly kept out. By 1984 the concept of editorial freedom had become totally baffling, if not unintelligible, even to sophisticated Government officials. Not only was the PDRY unique in the aftermath of the British Empire in turning to Soviet Marxism, it was also unique in the Middle East. The departure of the British from Aden was certainly the worst shambles in the End of Empire, the successor régime the most completely opposed to all Britain had stood for.

# CHAPTER 7

# Cyprus

For thousands of years powerful rulers have considered Cyprus strategically important. That is why the island was ruled by Egypt until the time of Cleopatra and by Rome under the governorship of Cicero; it is why the Duke of Venice sent Othello to prevent the Turks from seizing control and why the Turks persisted and eventually succeeded. Set in the Eastern Mediterranean, by the great trading crossroads of the world, little Cyprus, its population around half a million both in ancient times and today, has repeatedly been seen as a vital fortress. Ironically Cyprus has always proved a strategic disappointment, more ornamental than effective.

Cyprus is a mere forty miles from Turkey but five hundred from mainland Greece and although since ancient times a large majority of the population have been Greek-speaking and felt themselves to be Greek, Cyprus has never been ruled from Greece. As far back as Homeric times Greeks sailed to Asia Minor and conquered cities like Troy. They dominated the Byzantine Empire and retained a privileged status in the empire of the Ottoman Turks. Three hundred years later in 1830, the Greeks managed to break free from the Sultan's rule and set up a small, independent Greece. The inspiration to Ottoman Greeks of this event was like that to the world's Jews of the creation of the state of Israel. Some Greeks from Cyprus went to see the first President of Greece, Count Capo d'Istria, to ask him to annexe the island. He lacked power to do so, but the gesture was significant.

## A Greek Dream, 1878–1954

The British crown acquired Cyprus twice: in 1191 Richard I captured the island while leading the Third Crusade to recover Jerusalem from the Islamic leader Saladin (however, Richard found Cyprus of no use and soon sold it); and in 1878 Benjamin Disraeli pulled off a remarkable diplomatic *coup*. In pursuit of what had by then become the traditional British policy of preventing the Ottoman Turkish Empire from being gobbled up by Russia, Disraeli proudly told Queen Victoria that he had obtained a *place d'armes* from which Britain's interests could be secured: Cyprus was, he said, 'the key to Asia'. The Ottoman Turks had just suffered damaging defeats by

Russia and lost substantial territories. Disraeli persuaded them that their surest protection against further Russian aggression would be to entrust Cyprus to Britain. He had sent seven thousand Indian troops to Malta to encourage the Sultan to see his point of view and immediately afterwards moved four hundred to Cyprus, to be at hand in any crisis. He hoped to ensure that the Ottoman Empire, while paying its own way and fighting most of its own battles, would find the presence of British troops near its heart a beneficial influence: through a lease on a part of the Sultan's territory, the British would shape the policy, insofar as it concerned them, of a great but declining ruler.

As usual Cyprus was strategically upstaged because immediately afterwards Britain took control of Egypt, with far better military bases than Cyprus could offer from which to dominate the Middle East. And thirty years later the Ottoman Sultan made the mistake of siding with the Germans in the 1914–18 war. Consequently what remained of his empire was carved up between the victorious British and French and a number of nationalist movements. The policy of indirect control that Disraeli had favoured was replaced by the policy of grabbing the remains.

From the start of British rule the most powerful political and economic force in Cyprus, the Greek Orthodox Church, was demanding 'enosis', union with Greece. The Bishop of Kition, reading an address of welcome to the first British High Commissioner and Commander-in-Chief in July 1878, said he hoped Britain would help Cyprus to be united with mother Greece. King George I, crowned in Athens in 1863, had taken the title 'King of the Hellenes' rather than 'King of Greece', to stress his standing with Greeks everywhere and the determination of his governments to absorb them all into the Greek state. Bit by bit they succeeded. The Ionian Islands, British since the Napoleonic wars, were ceded to Greece. Thessaly was taken from the Ottomans as, after some years of struggle, was Crete. The excitement these successes stirred in Greece itself and among Greeks overseas drove Greek governments to push forward and seize more by a direct war against the Ottomans in 1912–13 which nearly doubled the territory and population of the Greek state.

The Pan-Hellenic movement of Greek Orthodox Christians determined to resume control of the eastern Mediterranean had been supported by some notable Englishmen. Lord Byron died at Missolonghi in 1829 fighting for the Greeks in their war of independence. Admiral Sir Edward Codrington in 1827, when the British were supposed to be allies of the Turks, sank the Turkish–Egyptian fleet at Navarino Bay. This action played a crucial part in securing independence for the Greeks and the British Government later apologised to the Sultan for their 'error'. Greek nationalists recognised the British as important allies. Gladstone publicly urged the union of Cyprus with Greece, though he did not carry through this policy when he became Prime Minister. Winston Churchill visited Cyprus in 1907 as Under-Secretary for the Colonies and was ever after quoted as saying it was:

. . . only natural that the Cypriot people, who are of Greek descent, should regard their incorporation with what may be called their motherland as an ideal to be earnestly, devoutly and fervently cherished. Such a feeling is an example of the patriotic devotion which so nobly characterises the Greek nation.

Lloyd George in 1919 when Prime Minister said, 'It is my intention to give the island of Cyprus to Greece', but his Conservative coalition partners and the chiefs of staff quickly made him withdraw. To many Greeks, Cyprus in British hands was merely on its way home. Indeed until 1922, when a Turkish army under Kemal Atatürk put a stop to it, Greater Greece seemed to be an idea whose time had come. Philhellenes from Oxford and Cambridge who had studied Plato, Aristotle, Homer, Herodotus and Aeschylus; Christians who were appalled that the lands in which much of Christian theology had evolved should for a thousand years have been ruled by Muslims; humanitarians shocked at the massacres by which the Ottomans put down European nationalist movements; others who simply admired Greek sculpture and architecture: all joined in supporting the Greeks in their ambitions.

British rule of Cyprus began promisingly. A constitution was introduced in 1882 with a Legislative Council of eighteen of whom six were officials and twelve elected members (nine Greeks, three Turks, proportionate to the population). But the Greek members kept demanding enosis and opposing efficient administration, so an alliance of the six officials and the three Turks reinforced by the casting vote of the British High Commissioner regularly outvoted them to transact government business. The British frequently pointed out to the Greek Cypriot leaders that enosis was impossible because Cyprus was on a kind of lease; if the British left, the island reverted automatically to the administration of the Ottoman Empire, whose sovereignty was unimpaired.

This argument collapsed in 1914 when, after Turkey sided with the Germans, Britain formally annexed Cyprus. Greek Cypriot delight at this removal of the principal stated obstacle to enosis was increased in 1915, when the island was offered to Greece in return for Greek support in the war. King George V's secretary had written to the Prime Minister, H. H. Asquith:

> The King desires me to express the earnest hope that the Government will decide to . . . offer Cyprus to Greece on condition of her joining the allies . . . Financially Cyprus is I suppose a loss to this country [Britain was paying an annual grant to keep the island solvent]. Strategically His Majesty understands that it has proved a failure.

The offer was made but King Constantine of Greece rejected it. He thought German victory likely and wanted to avoid taking sides.

To the Greek Cypriot leaders, the position was clear. The objection concerning Turkish sovereignty was removed by British annexation; the willingness of Britain to cede sovereignty was proved by the 1915 offer. Cyprus could now expect to take its proper place as part of the Greater Greece that should be one of the successor states to the Ottoman Empire.

Until 1925 this hope remained open. Then the British Government declared that Cyprus was a colony and that the issue was closed. This was pure imperialism. The strategic reasons advanced were as unconvincing as in the days of Richard I. Economically Cyprus was insignificant. Britain's assertion of a duty to protect the Turkish minority was a mere excuse. In the past the Turks in Cyprus had generally been tolerant rulers of the Greeks and now, in spite of massacres on the mainland, Greeks in Cyprus behaved well towards the Turks. The reason enosis was rejected was a spasm of Middle Eastern imperialism which seized colonial secretaries like Alfred Milner and Winston Churchill. The steps towards self-government in India that followed Edwin Montagu's statement in 1917 offended them; they wanted Britain's imperial role to expand and the obvious area was now the Middle East, where the collapse of Ottoman power had left vast territories in British hands. But in several of these, notably Egypt and Iraq, and in the nearby state of Persia, Britain faced local revolts. This was not a moment, therefore, to hand over a safe and largely docile island that might serve as a base from which to reassert control. The objective of a greater Greece had to take second place. Even the Labour Governments of Ramsay MacDonald, after years of Labour support for enosis, now turned it down flat. Eleftherios Venizelos, the man who won enosis for his native island of Crete and then went on to be Prime Minister of Greece, did not press the matter: if Britain wanted to hold on to Cyprus, Greece would be foolish to risk antagonising the most powerful state in the eastern Mediterranean by resisting. The Greek Cypriots found themselves facing no longer the Ottoman but the British Empire, unenthusiastically backed by the Government of Greece, as the principal obstacle to enosis.

This brought a change of style. Instead of putting their case to a government they thought might listen, those Greek Cypriots who wanted enosis became more hostile. Some made passionate speeches calling for civil disobedience, boycotts of British goods and non-payment of taxes. Some resigned from the Legislative Council and on 21 October 1931 led a march. This ended in a demonstration outside Government House, which was a prefabricated structure built entirely of wood and intended for military use in Ceylon but diverted to Cyprus in 1878. The High Commissioners and Governors who lived in it complained of its inadequacies. So it was not an architectural disaster that it caught fire and was destroyed. But symbolically it was a serious matter and rioting spread round the island. Six Cypriots were killed and more than thirty wounded. The British Government reacted harshly: they suspended the constitution, banned political parties, removed all elected representatives from the Legislative Council and introduced the Governor's absolute rule. They made it a criminal offence to question British sovereignty, to raise the Greek flag or even to ring church bells. Whereas the guiding principle of British colonial administration as a whole was to maintain the consent of the governed and to get them to help run the show themselves, the constant demand of the Greek Cypriot leaders for enosis had finally snapped British patience.

Sir Richmond Palmer, Governor of Cyprus in 1933–9, justified the new policy by saying that a liberal regime requires loyalty; if a significant part of the population repudiate allegiance to the state, democratic government is impossible; the cry for enosis was not sincere, but merely a stick with which to beat the Government; the rural two-thirds of the population were indifferent to such political trouble-making and were certainly not anti-British. He thus implied that the 1882 constitution was far too liberal for enosis-minded Cypriots; certainly many British administrators were pleased to be rid of it. And the firm measures seemed to work. Economic development was advanced. Promises of eventual self-government were made. The British were confirmed in their view that the demand for enosis was primarily operatic. The island's garrison of a hundred British troops, briefly reinforced from Egypt, did not have to act against the population. From 1931 to 1939 all appeared quiet.

The Second World War, like the First, went on all round Cyprus without the island's being militarily involved, thus confirming again its strategic insignificance. But enosis was given a boost. Britain and Greece were allies, more than 14,000 Cypriots volunteered to serve in the British army, and, after the defeat of the Italian attack on Greece in 1940, Cyprus was bedecked with Greek flags brought out of drawers and cupboards after nine years. When Britain's Foreign Secretary Anthony Eden visited the island in 1941 crowds cheered him. The Greek Prime Minister, speaking from London in November 1941, mentioned Cyprus as among the daughters of Greece that would be reunited with the motherland after victory. The Atlantic Charter, in which Franklin Roosevelt and Winston Churchill set out their war aims, promised self-determination to dependent territories, which to Greek Cypriots meant enosis. Churchill, briefly visiting Cyprus in 1943, used ambiguous but encouraging words.

The political life of Cyprus revived in other ways during the war. The British Government had promised to restore democratic institutions, beginning with local government elections. These were held in 1943 and the Communist party AKEL (its initials in Greek) won control of two of the five main towns, Famagusta and Limassol. Trade unions were now developing fast. Previously Cypriot politics had been dominated by bishops, lawyers and professional men, a small élite inspired by the idea of a Greek national revival. AKEL and the unions were more concerned with conditions of life and work in Cyprus: a problem for the British administration, but a change from the demand for enosis.

At the end of the war Britain's new Labour Government announced that it would call a consultative assembly in Cyprus to discuss constitutional reforms, lifted the ban on all exiled Cypriots, released trade unionists convicted of sedition and published a ten-year economic development plan for the island. This was as liberal a package as a British Government could be expected to offer, except that it excluded self-determination and, therefore, the possibility of enosis. For that reason the ethnarchy (the Greek Cypriot religious and political leadership), needing to emphasise its nationalist passion to defeat the challenge of the left, turned it down. The new Governor, Lord Winster, did his best to get round this obstacle. He put his proposals before the AKEL-trade unionist representatives and the Turkish Cypriots. But the Archbishop had ordered Greeks to boycott the consultative assembly, and the AKEL-trade union group soon joined him in demanding enosis or nothing. This was a little odd as the Athens Government, having recently defeated Communists in a bloody civil war, would have given AKEL short shrift had enosis come. AKEL judged that the Greek Cypriot voters wanted more than anything else to be Greeks.

As in 1915–25, the British Government seriously considered granting enosis. Many officials recommended it. But the Foreign Office feared Greece would face another civil war, which the Communists might win; to hand to Greece an island that was supposed to be strategically important might therefore amount to handing it to Russia; this could not be risked.

Further, with British troops removed from Palestine in 1948 and with the British base at Suez under such constant attack from Egyptian irregulars that it was almost useless, Britain faced the prospect of having no conveniently located base in the Middle East from which to protect its by now vast oil interests – one of Britain's main sources of income in the post-war years. Cyprus was therefore, as ever, held to be vital by strategic planners. The British Government repeated the formula that had for years upset leading Greek Cypriots when they petitioned London. British sovereignty over the island was not to be questioned. The only topic that could be discussed was internal constitutional progress.

The British proposal of 1948 included an advance on the constitution that had ruled Cyprus from 1882 till 1931: the Greeks would have an overall majority in the legislature; no longer could an alliance of Turks and government officials win every vote. British ministers and officials explained that such a majority could not easily be overruled by the Governor; it could form the basis for further constitutional advance. But because enosis was ruled out the Greek Cypriot leaders would have none of it. So Cyprus entered its final phase under British rule with still no representative Cypriots in its government. The Governor invited a few Cypriots onto his advisory council, but they had no formal role and no popular support. The Governor was a reluctant autocrat. This state of affairs was awkward, but not yet disastrous. Cyprus remained on the surface a quiet, beautiful island, betraying no sign that it was ready to explode before the world like a bomb.

## 'Never', 1954–1960

Archbishop Makarios III of Cyprus liked to tell stories to describe his political methods. He was born in the Cypriot village of Pano Panaghia where one of the main activities was breeding donkeys. Traders would come over the mountain passes to buy them. A trader having made his offer, the villager would reject it and let him walk off. Only as he was disappearing over the pass, proving his unwillingness to pay more, would the villager call him back and accept. Makarios left the village and was ordained as a priest of the Greek Orthodox Church in the monastery of Kykko. The Abbot congratulated him, for he was a brilliant student, and said that now, like all Greek orthodox priests, he must grow a beard. Makarios refused. The Abbot gave him the night to think it over: unless he consented by morning, he must leave. He spent the night planning his tactics. He would let the taxi take him away and drive to the monastery gate. If the Abbot let him get that far, he would return and give in. Next morning, the abbot invited him to change his mind, but he persisted. A taxi was duly called and, with his little cardboard suitcase, Makarios got into it to return to his village and a lay future. The taxi set off. But before it had even left the inner courtyard, the Abbot called it back. Makarios had demonstrated whose will was dominant. Only much later, and by his own choice, did he grow a beard.

Makarios first came to British attention when, as Bishop of Kition, he played a leading part in organising the 'plebiscite' of January 1950. Every Greek Orthodox priest in Cyprus was ordered to end Sunday morning service at nine, peal the church bells and collect signatures under the alternative headings, 'We demand union with Greece' and 'We oppose the union of Cyprus with Greece'. The result was 96 per cent in favour of enosis; the figures were circulated to the delegations at the United Nations in New York. Later in 1950 the 37-year-old organiser became Archbishop Makarios III. He knew his way round. The World Council of Churches had sent him

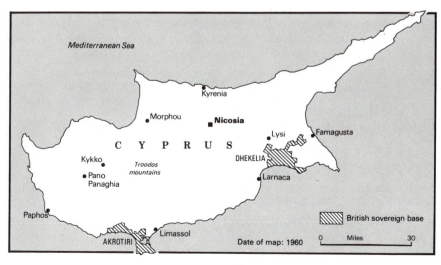

*Beardless in Boston. The young Makarios, a student-priest at Boston University School of Theology in 1946, shortly before his election as Bishop of Kition.*

to study in Boston for two years and he understood that a report of a 'plebiscite' sent to UN members and to rich Greeks living in the United States would bring the cause of enosis important backers. His position as archbishop gave him standing in Athens, where he worked hard to attract the support of both journalists and politicians. For centuries the Archbishop had been recognised as the ethnarch or political leader of the Greek Cypriots, by both the Ottoman authorities and the British. The ethnarchy had been demanding enosis since 1820. Makarios III brought new skills and drive to the leadership. He also involved the ethnarchy in new methods.

In July 1952 Makarios became chairman of a revolutionary committee that met in Athens and recruited as its military organiser Colonel George Grivas, a Cypriot by birth who had served in the Greek army since 1915. Grivas seemed a strange colleague for a Christian archbishop. After the 1939–45 war the Greek army had terminated his service because, although he was a brave and skilful officer, he had a reputation for harshness and cruelty and a fanatical commitment to the extreme right in politics that embarrassed even his royalist colleagues. During the war, after the defeat of the Greek army, Grivas formed a group of officers in Athens called *X* (the

Greek letter *Chi*), whose purpose was not to resist the occupying Germans but to prepare for the return of the Greek monarchy at the end of the war by eliminating Communists. For this task, the Germans provided $X$ with weapons. The leading British officer in Greece in the final stages of the war, C. M. Woodhouse, himself a distinguished Greek scholar and historian and later a Conservative MP, described $X$ as 'reactionary thugs' with 'the sinister significance of a Ku-Klux-Klan'. The $X$ gangs ruthlessly killed civilians, aroused widespread fear and were soon after the war proscribed by the Greek Government. Grivas tried to form $X$ into a political party to join the royalist coalition fighting the post-war Greek elections, but the royalists refused to have him. They thought his reputation for extremism and violence would be an electoral liability. Both the Greek army and the right-wing royalist parties had rejected him.

Makarios believed Grivas to be the best man available to lead and discipline the secret army that would apply pressure on the British. He meant to hire a ferocious guard dog, but his recruit turned out to be more like a man-eating tiger. Grivas accepted that Makarios was the political leader of the Greek Cypriots and of the enosis movement, but he mistrusted and despised all politicians and was therefore not a wholly reliable subordinate. He thought that the cause of Greek greatness could be won in Cyprus only by a military campaign that would inspire popular support in Greece, gain the attention of the world and thus make the British withdraw; he was convinced that he alone had the skill, knowledge and power of leadership for the task. Makarios did not believe in the will of the Greek Cypriots to fight and if necessary die: in the past they had shown no such will; 'Not fifty men will be found to follow you,' he told Grivas, and ordered him not to come to Cyprus to start military preparations until so instructed. But Grivas went ahead, obtained a visa from the British embassy in Athens and openly arrived in October 1952 for a five-month preparatory visit. So deeply did Grivas mistrust Makarios that he made detailed notes of all their meetings and hid them, so that, should Makarios betray him, the evidence would eventually be found and Grivas's role vindicated. Thanks to this practice the story of their secret movement can be told, albeit from a squint-eyed view, with some confidence.

Since the time of Eleftherios Venizelos, Prime Minister between 1910 and 1930, Greek political leaders, while personally sympathetic to the Greek Cypriot desire for enosis, had avoided any action that might anger the British. But the idea of uniting overseas Greeks with the motherland continued to excite Greek voters. So Cyprus posed a dilemma for Greek governments: to please their principal ally and avoid trouble with the voters, ministers in Athens kept the issue quiet. This Makarios and Grivas were determined they should no longer be able to do.

Makarios's technique was to make speeches in Greece that aroused Greek public feeling so that politicians both in office and out would have to support him. He thought it would be useful to organise some sabotage on the island, so that he could claim Cypriots were blowing up British installations as the only way to express their resentment at the oppression and injustice of British rule. Grivas insisted from the start that a little sabotage would not be enough: successful sabotage required a secret organisation able to hide people suspected by the British, to carry out operations with precision and discipline, to punish Cypriots disloyal to the cause. Makarios, while uneasy about Grivas's schemes, provided the money from Orthodox Church funds to pay for the arms, explosives and equipment the colonel said were needed. Grivas's contacts with army officers and arms dealers enabled him to buy the material discreetly. Nevertheless Greek ministers and officials soon heard of his preparations.

To stop Makarios's campaign from sweeping Greece, with disastrous electoral consequences for a Government held to be handling the issue unpatriotically, and in an effort to restrain Grivas's activities – which could lead Britain to hold Greece responsible for action against British persons and property – the Government in Athens decided that it must itself support enosis. It did not, however, show sufficient vigour to dissuade Makarios and Grivas from their joint activities. On the contrary, Greek ministers did all they could to prevent Makarios's going to the United Nations, on the grounds that his presence would prejudice their own attempt to raise the issue there. They also tried to discourage the inevitable anti-British fervour of the enosis movement, on the grounds that progress would best be made by bilateral Greek–British talks. It was not the speeches of Makarios, though they had made Cyprus a national obsession in Greece, nor the threats of Grivas, though he was known to be dangerous, obsessive and skilful, that drove the Greek Government into active support. That was achieved by Anthony Eden and some of his colleagues in the British Government.

Eden was British Foreign Secretary when, in September 1953, he visited Greece to convalesce after an operation on his gall bladder. The visit was private and medicinal, but the Greek Prime Minister, General Alexandros Papagos, pressed for a meeting. Towards the end of their informal talks, Papagos raised the Cyprus question, asking Britain's intentions and indicating that, whatever happened, Britain could keep the military bases she needed on the island. Eden replied with an outburst of anger: there was no Cyprus question now, there never would be and he would not discuss it: why did not Greece claim New York, which contained more Greeks than Cyprus? This explosion, strange in an experienced diplomat and doubtless partly attributable to his health, upset Papagos, who immediately afterwards said in an outraged voice, 'He told me *never!*' When, later, Eden invited him to come to London, Papagos asked the British Government to place Cyprus on the agenda for their talks. Eden refused and Papagos did not go. This time Eden's gall bladder could not be blamed: he simply did not like the Greeks, preferring Britain's traditional and tough allies, the Turks.

Now followed an event which stands high in the mythology of Cyprus and of the end of the British Empire – a second and far more devastating 'never'.

Henry Hopkinson was the Minister of State at the Colonial Office in London and on 28 July 1954 he announced in the House of Commons that a new constitution for Cyprus would be introduced. A junior minister making a business statement about a tiny island might seem small beer. But all the passions and errors of the years since 1878 exploded in the Commons that afternoon. Hopkinson, an old Etonian and former diplomat, had served in Greece and after the war joined the Conservative Central Office, where he briefed Churchill and Eden. He was a member of that class of Englishman who are plainly born to rule. Yet one word was to destroy his ministerial career.

Hopkinson was unlucky. Oliver Lyttelton, the Colonial Secretary, knew there might be trouble over the Cyprus announcement and that therefore he ought to make the Commons statement himself. But he was resigning from office that day to return to business and did not want bitterness to mar his farewell. So he asked Hopkinson to speak for him. Immediately before Hopkinson rose to speak, Anthony Eden had announced that Britain was to withdraw its troops from their huge base in the Suez Canal zone. Prime Minister Churchill had agreed to this decision only reluctantly after the chiefs of staff had explained to him the damaging effects of the long campaign of sniping and sabotage by Egyptians against the base. That they were capitulating to illegal methods could not, of course, be announced but was known to all. It hit many Conservative MPs as a terrible blow, an abasement of their own pride as well as Britain's. Some sixty of them warned that they would vote against the Government on this issue, at the end of the debate the next day. If their revolt was not contained it could bring down Churchill. Cyprus was to be the new Middle East military headquarters, so the Cabinet gave Hopkinson one instruction: in answering questions after his statement, he must make it clear that from Cyprus there would be no withdrawal. The 'Suez group' of Conservative MPs must not be further upset.

Even so the word 'never' was a tactical mistake. It slipped out inadvertently and Hopkinson immediately tried to gloss it over. Lyttelton later that day denied that the word had even been used. But it was the same word Eden had used to Papagos.

Hopkinson successfully avoided provoking the Suez group, but ran into trouble from the left. In announcing new constitutional arrangements for Cyprus he promised the islanders less elective representation than under the Winster terms of 1948. Then they had been offered an elected majority; now they were to be given an assembly with a majority of officials and nominated members. But, said Hopkinson, it was a first stage. Predictably he was asked about the final stage: was it to be dominion status and the ultimate right of self-determination? The Hansard report of Hopkinson's answer reads:

It has always been understood and agreed that there are certain territories in the Commonwealth which, owing to their particular circumstances, can never expect to be fully independent. (Hon Members: 'Oh!') I think the right Hon. Gentlemen will agree that there are some territories which cannot expect to be that. I am not going as far as that this afternoon, but I have said that the question of the abrogation of British sovereignty cannot arise – that British sovereignty will remain.

Within minutes a group of Labour MPs had raised the roof. Aneurin Bevan, Tom Driberg, Richard Crossman and others demanded and got an immediate emergency debate. This was 1954: India, Pakistan, Burma, Ceylon and Palestine were independent; the Sudan and the Gold Coast were close to it; the principle that Britain's purpose in running the Empire was to advance subject peoples to self-rule had been published by the Labour Government in a white paper in 1948 and accepted, though without enthusiasm, by their post-1951 Conservative successors. Many Labour MPs believed that Hopkinson's words revealed that the Conservatives were about to back away from this consensus.

Hopkinson had merely repeated in public what Eden had already said privately to Papagos. In fact the 1945–51 Labour Government had adopted a similar policy towards Cyprus, but had not been hard-pressed on the issue and so had been able to avoid stating it crudely. Hopkinson's 'never' rang round all Britain's colonies: it enraged anti-imperialists everywhere. Some slighting remarks about Greece by Lyttelton as he tried to back Hopkinson in the subsequent debate turned the Cyprus situation into a crisis. The Greek Government had kept trying to settle the issue by talking to Britain, had kept trying to restrain Makarios and Grivas. But 28 July 1954 was the last straw: the British were not only being unreasonable in refusing to talk, they were being publicly insulting as well. Three weeks later Prime Minister Papagos was forced to ask that Cyprus's right to self-determination be put on the agenda at the United Nations. The Government in Athens had at last publicly taken up the cause.

Thus 1954 saw Cyprus change from a British colonial problem, difficult but not necessarily insoluble, to an international issue which the Colonial Office could no longer handle alone. The Governor appointed in 1953, Sir Robert Armitage, had come to Cyprus from the Gold Coast, where he had been Finance Minister in the Cabinet alongside Dr Kwame Nkrumah. His task in Cyprus was to find a way to make constitutional progress. Archbishop Makarios and the leading Greek Cypriot politicians boycotted his informal constitutional talks, on the familiar ground that they wanted enosis or nothing. Nevertheless Armitage believed progress could be made. He consulted as many Cypriots as he could, lawyers, businessmen and others, and concluded that a large part of the Greek population was indifferent to enosis and would soon come round to supporting a Government in which they saw some Greek Cypriot ministers exercising power. So Armitage's proposed constitution emphasised the prospect of office for nominated Cypriots. And, to help these moderates win support, Armitage urged his ministers in London to repeat plainly that enosis was ruled out. Thus he hoped that Makarios and his allies would be seen by sensible Cypriots to be pursuing a hopeless line. Makarios himself feared that this tactic might succeed: after four thousand years governed by others, occupying an island too small to hope to overrule a succession of great empires, the Cypriots had grown docile. When Makarios said that not fifty men would follow Grivas in his guerilla campaign, he was in effect admitting that Armitage might win the day, as he might well have done had not Eden and Hopkinson turned the Greek Government from its discreet acquiescence in the British policy to open opposition.

Armitage of course did not know of Makarios's involvement in smuggling arms to Cyprus; he did not know about Grivas; nor did he know that Greek Government officers, who had formerly restrained and threatened Grivas, began after the end of 1954 to offer him some help. Grivas reports that Makarios now told him the Greek Prime Minister was 'in full agreement with our activities'. Caiques of arms sailed from Greece to Cyprus (one was intercepted by the British); Grivas set up his first secret headquarters, in a smart suburb of Nicosia, the capital; the stage was set for violence.

Grivas proved to be a brilliant commander for the guerilla movement, now named EOKA (the Greek initials of the words National Organisation of Cypriot Fighters). He was a fanatical, dominating man with a high-pitched voice and piercing eyes: when he gave an order, he required it to be obeyed to the letter. His instructions were always in writing, so no misunderstanding could arise. If things went wrong, he held a post-mortem. Given the easy-going ways of the Cypriots, who had not previously formed a fighting army (in the Second World War Cypriot volunteers had served only as military auxiliaries – muleteers, pioneers, launderers, etc.), Grivas imposed iron discipline: all recruits had to be church-going Orthodox Christians, who would swear the EOKA oath under the supervision of a priest and would take it seriously; anyone revealing information about EOKA to the Government was to be shot. For hours Grivas himself sat cleaning and oiling the first weapons to arrive from Greece. He had given up everything. He had left his wife in Greece. He was to live sparsely, changing his dwelling whenever necessary. When the British were at hand, he was to march across mountains or hide under floorboards to avoid them. They had no idea that such a determined and skilful military leader was preparing war on them.

The principal preoccupations of the British who were then running Cyprus were quite different. The Greek Government's espousal of enosis had led to a British diplomatic success. The United Nations had voted in 1954 not to consider the Cyprus question. This decision was followed by noisy street protests in Greece and Cyprus, and the problem troubling the British in Cyprus was how to stop seditious demonstrations, in order to reassure the moderates that they could safely come forward and play a part in Britain's new constitutional arrangements. One difficulty was the organisation of Greek education in Cyprus. From the beginning of British rule, the Greek ministry of education in Athens had provided textbooks and teachers for

Cypriot schools and dominated the curriculum. This was allowed not because the British rulers were high-principled liberals but to avoid expense and bother: if the Greeks were prepared to run the schools, good luck to them. The result was that the Greek schools in Cyprus taught pan-Hellenic nationalism and enosis, making the schoolchildren ready recruits for demonstrations and for slogan-painting in support of Makarios. Both schools and children were difficult targets for repressive action.

The same was true of Makarios himself. His main role was as political leader of the movement demanding enosis. He was frequently away from the island campaigning internationally, and when he was at home the authorities always found their work harder: they did not yet realise that he was stirring up even more trouble for them when he was abroad. To call for a change of sovereignty in Cyprus was sedition, as the law stood, and the Attorney-General, a Greek Cypriot, announced that breaches of this law would be prosecuted. In a typical Makarios move, the following Sunday, before a huge crowd, the Archbishop repeated his demand for 'Enosis and nothing but enosis,' adding, 'No fire on earth can extinguish the flame.' The Government had not the courage to prosecute him. He was the Archbishop, the ethnarch, the supreme leader of the Greek Cypriots; to arrest him might stir up riots. The Government found itself in a similar situation with the Greek Cypriot newspapers. These were regularly blazoning the cause of enosis, equally in defiance of the sedition law. The Governor, Armitage, wanted to prosecute but he was brought before Churchill in Downing Street who told him he could have as many soldiers as he needed to put down trouble, but he must not interfere with the freedom of the press.

In the face of all these obstacles the Governor's constitutional talks were failing to make headway when, just after midnight on 1 April 1955, EOKA presented its visiting card. This took the form of several bombs placed in towns on the island. Not all the bombs exploded. Of the sixteen that did, one damaged the Cyprus broadcasting station. Makarios's policy of striking at property not persons was followed, except that one of the EOKA men accidentally killed himself. Grivas issued what he called his 'first revolutionary proclamation':

> We have taken up the struggle to throw off the English yoke . . . the warriors of Marathon, the warriors of Salamis . . . are looking to us . . . International diplomacy is unjust . . . The Cypriot soul is brave . . . We have RIGHT on our side and that is why we WILL WIN. . . . Greeks, wherever you may be, hear our call: FORWARD ALL TOGETHER FOR THE FREEDOM OF OUR CYPRUS.

The announcement was signed, 'EOKA, The Leader, Dighenis'. According to Grivas, Dighenis was a legendary Cypriot guardian of the empire of Alexander the Great, and therefore an appropriate *nom de guerre*, although scholars agree that he was wrong about the original Dighenis, who was not a Cypriot.

During the next three months EOKA's best reported action was to place a bomb under the seat of the Governor, Sir Robert Armitage, at an Empire Day film show (it did not explode until after he had left). More significant were the organisation's attacks on police stations which killed a sergeant and a bystander and launched one of Grivas's most effective strategies, the systematic intimidation of the police until they could no longer be relied on.

Anthony Eden, who succeeded Churchill as Prime Minister in April 1955, a few days after the first EOKA bombings, responded by inviting the Greek and Turkish Foreign Ministers to a conference in London. This was partly a clever piece of United Nations tactics. Britain had won the vote against the Greek proposal in 1954, but the British minister who attended the debate, Anthony Nutting, thought Britain's only argument – that Cyprus was British sovereign territory and the UN did not interfere in its members' internal affairs – was thin. Some show of a positive effort to solve the problem would be needed, he argued, to persuade the UN to keep out again when Greece next raised the issue. Further, Eden was convinced that the Turks would never let the Greeks have Cyprus, but thought the Turkish Government was acting with undue restraint in not saying so publicly. He wanted the Turks to 'speak out' against the Greeks and in support of Britain's continued control of the island. In these purposes Eden's London conference of August 1955 was successful: Britain was able to tell the UN that it had made an effort to consult all interested parties, and Turkish opposition to enosis was made public. Indeed it was declared with greater vigour than Eden could have hoped for, with huge anti-Greek riots in Izmir and Istanbul, where a rich Greek minority was at risk, launched with at least the connivance if not the active sponsorship of the Turkish Government (this was one of the charges subsequently levelled against the Turkish Prime Minister Adnan Menderes before he was hanged in 1961 by the military regime that replaced him).

The effect in Cyprus was less satisfactory. No Cypriot representative was invited to the London conference. That was upsetting to Makarios. The invitation to the Turks to have a voice in the island's affairs outraged him. He preached a sermon urging Cypriots to continue the fight for self-determination 'unto death'. Rauf Denktash, a Turkish Cypriot who was a lawyer working in the Cyprus Attorney-General's department, said later about the summer of 1955:

> On 1 April everyone looked upon EOKA as the movement of a misguided few under the guidance of the Church. And even the Greek police – they were very good, the CID men in the police force, excellent people – looked upon it as just a criminal activity by misguided youth whom they were very effective in catching. But the terrorism against informers and the police was such that within six months the people who had been saying 'This is the criminal activity of a misguided few', began to say 'We are EOKA too'.

As the bulk of the Greek Cypriots fell in behind EOKA, Britain's control over the island fell apart. Bombs went off inside British bases wounding scores of servicemen. Greek Cypriot customs men helped EOKA slip arms into the island. Greek Cypriot policemen leaked anti-terrorist plans to EOKA. Sixteen top EOKA suspects held in the supposedly impregnable Kyrenia castle escaped. To get the island back under control, Eden appointed as Governor Britain's top soldier, Field Marshal Sir John Harding, Chief of the Imperial General Staff.

Harding was Commander-in-Chief south-east Asia during the Malayan Emergency and oversaw Templer's planning; then as CIGS he visited Kenya in 1952 when the Mau Mau rebellion broke out and he was consulted about the possible appointment of a military Governor. He was the most senior of the military advisers who said if, after the loss of Palestine and the Suez Canal base, Britain was to fulfil its treaty commitments to Iraq, Jordan and Turkey, full sovereignty over Cyprus was required. He did not say Cyprus was a satisfactory base, merely that it was the best facility available in the area, should Britain be called on to fly in men and equipment to help her allies.

For Greece and the Greek Cypriots, therefore, he was a worrying choice: not merely a soldier renowned for his brains, organisational skills and toughness but also one of the architects of the policy that required Cyprus to remain British. His appointment flattered Grivas but was greeted with dismay by the Greek press, which presented him as a butcher about to commit crimes against the patriots of Cyprus. Makarios, who had refused to consider meeting Armitage, let it be known that he would be willing to talk to Harding, on the grounds, of course, that it is better to get to know a dangerous enemy than to turn your back on him and that talking to him might delay the impact of his inevitable assault on EOKA.

The meeting took place the day after Harding's arrival, and the talks that followed over the next five months, the Harding–Makarios talks, were the saddest missed opportunity in the Cyprus conflict. Harding, aware of the Archbishop's enormous influence among the Greek Cypriots, wanted to get him to denounce EOKA's use of violence. That seemed the quickest and easiest way to restore law and order. Makarios indicated his price and Harding reported it to London: no progress would be made with Makarios so long as Hopkinson's 'never' remained British policy. This was the kind of challenge to which the first-class minds of Whitehall respond with vigour. Within a few weeks they had produced a verbal solution, the 'double negative'. Harding said later, 'You can't talk to troops like that', but he hopefully carried the formula back from London. 'It is not,' the document stated, '[the British Government's] position that the principle of self-determination can never be applicable to Cyprus. It is their position that it is not now a practicable proposition.'

Nikos Kranidiotis, the Archbishop's political secretary, was host to Harding's meeting with Makarios on the Governor's return:

He came from London with new instructions and we met in my house in Nicosia [for secrecy] on 21 November 1955. Marshal Harding came first, ten minutes earlier, maybe for security reasons, and Makarios came a few minutes later. And immediately Marshal Harding took out from his pocket a paper. He gave it to Makarios and said, 'I have very good news for you.' Makarios read his paper and when he finished Harding asked him, 'What is your answer, Your Beatitude?' And the Archbishop said, 'Your Excellency, I cannot accept this,' and he passed the paper to me. I read it and I was really surprised because it was the first time the British Government conceded the right of self-determination to the people of Cyprus. Harding was really upset and he left immediately without waiting even to eat the sweets and coffee which we offer in Cyprus on such occasions. When Marshal Harding had left, the Archbishop said to me, 'Well, we have that in our pocket. We must now try to make it better.'

Like the donkey-seller in the mountain village, Makarios broke off negotiations, in the hope of pushing the price a little higher.

When the new Greek Prime Minister, Constantine Karamanlis, saw the double negative, he recognised it as a significant shift in the British position and sent an emissary to Cyprus to persuade Makarios to resume the talks. The Archbishop agreed. He tried to get the Governor to offer a British guarantee that the period of partial self-government proposed would be followed by self-determination. Harding could only say that the will of the majority in an elected assembly would be hard for the British Government to ignore. Makarios appeared convinced, but asked for time to consult the ethnarchy council. With only one exception, they agreed to a settlement. It was all but concluded.

Makarios, however, felt he must consult Grivas and, for the only time in the emergency, arranged to meet him, high in the mountains at Kykko monastery. Lambros Kafkallides, Grivas's bodyguard, was not present at the talks but remembers that the next day Grivas called his men around him and said, 'We should prepare ourselves to go down because an agreement is on the way between Harding and Makarios.' They packed their suitcases and 'were joking and took photographs'.

Makarios had Grivas's agreement to cease campaigning and accept the British offer on two conditions: a complete amnesty for EOKA fighters and control of the police to be taken from British into Cypriot hands before independence. He had also requested cast-iron guarantees that Britain would carry through the agreement, which the Archbishop interpreted by asking for a guarantee of a Greek Cypriot majority in the assembly. He wrote to Harding that, if these three conditions could be met, he would help frame a constitution for what he called 'interim self-government'.

Makarios said later that he thought the talks were making good progress and that if Harding had not been impatient they could have reached agreement. Harding, however, found Makarios slippery to deal with:

*Grivas (third from right) allowed no photographs of EOKA. This was the one exception, because he thought Harding and Makarios had reached an agreement that would before long lead to enosis.*

whatever the British Government conceded, the Archbishop immediately raised a new demand – constantly upping the price. And, crucially for Harding, Makarios agreed to denounce violence only after all his conditions were met. During the five months of the talks Harding came increasingly to suspect that Makarios was involved with EOKA, whose violence increased whenever the talks broke down. But to the British the idea that an Archbishop could be the leader of a group who undertook killings and bombings was unthinkable. The Governor, in a final attempt to get the matter settled, asked the Colonial Secretary, Alan Lennox-Boyd, to come to the island. Even the Prime Minister, Anthony Eden, offered to come to talk to the Archbishop, but after his tactlessness with Papagos this was not thought a good idea. So the Colonial Secretary came, and read the Archbishop a statement spelling out the latest responses Harding had been authorised to make: the constitution would be 'in accordance with normal, liberal constitutional doctrine', which can only have meant a majority voice for the Greek Cypriots who formed 80 per cent of the island's population; the Government was prepared to pass control of the police into Greek Cypriot hands before independence when violence had subsided, which required as a

*The final session of the talks. Left to right: Harding, Kranidiotis, Makarios, Lennox-Boyd.*

first step that the Archbishop publicly call for it to do so; an amnesty would be granted to all prisoners, except those found guilty by a court of violence against persons or of carrying arms. The British thought they had moved as far as they could to meet Makarios on all three points. But the Archbishop, as usual, demanded more. He later claimed that he was surprised Lennox-Boyd took him at his word and terminated their talks after a mere two hours and ten minutes.

The breakdown of the negotiations was a disaster for the Cypriots and British alike. A large part of the blame must attach to Makarios, who failed to accept a compromise when to do so would have brought his people great benefits and the prospect of self-determination within a few years. Later the Turkish Foreign Ministry official who dealt with Cyprus at this time, Orhan Eralp, said of the final British terms:

Had Makarios accepted them I think we would have been in a very difficult position, because although they ruled out immediate enosis they left the door open, 'Let's see what will happen in ten years' time' and that sort of thing. Anyway Makarios, much to our content, refused them.

The British, of course, were partly to blame also. The patient Harding sat through seven long sessions with Makarios over five months, became increasingly unhappy with the Archbishop's Levantine method of bargaining and ended up suspecting his good faith. Nevertheless he achieved wonders: he dragged both Makarios and the British Government farther towards each other than either would have thought possible. Lennox-Boyd, who actually terminated the talks after he had taken part in them for only two hours, was along with Eden one of the hawks in the Conservative Cabinet, anxious to sustain Britain's imperial role in the Middle East, angry at Britain's being forced out of Egypt, looking for a chance to show old-fashioned imperial muscle. For all that, a careful review of the Harding–Makarios talks shows the British willing to compromise again and again, while Makarios, as the talks proceeded, became harder. Almost certainly he wanted a compromise, underestimated his own ability to lead the Greek Cypriots to accept one, feared that, in the light of the votes won by AKEL, the Cypriot Communist Party, in the municipal elections and of the Greek Government's policy towards Communists, an elected assembly might not vote for enosis, overestimated the patience and the room for manoeuvre of the British and thus dragged his own people to disaster.

The next step towards disaster came a few days later. The British arrested Makarios and sent him to detention in the most remote place they could think of, a tiny group of islands in the Indian Ocean where aircraft never called and tramp steamers only once or twice a month, the Seychelles. Within the narrow terms of British thinking, this made sense: clearing Makarios out of the way facilitated a vigorous campaign to destroy EOKA; when that task was completed, political negotiations with more reasonable Cypriots could resume. But detaining a religious leader without trial is widely regarded as the act of a totalitarian government: the Archbishop of Canterbury said in the House of Lords that the action made Christians everywhere feel shocked and uneasy. The Greek Government, which had been discreetly steering Makarios towards compromise, condemned the deportation as an uncivilised act of violence; riots in Athens protesting against his detention increased the pressure on Greek ministers fully to back EOKA.

The United States Government pointedly announced that it favoured the continuation of negotiations in Cyprus. And in Britain Labour Party leaders who had played down the Cyprus issue during the Harding–Makarios talks were roused by the deportation to outraged opposition. This was to weaken the Government's hand in Cyprus greatly as the next general election approached.

The scene was now cleared for a clash of arms: Makarios's removal left Grivas in total charge of EOKA, and Harding, no longer restrained by the need to negotiate, determined on his elimination, having only recently learned who Dighenis was. Harding and Grivas both knew that the British were bound to win a war against EOKA. Greece was too far away and

British control of the sea too effective for the rebels to have a secure base for retreat and reinforcement. But Grivas had used his long period of preparation well for winning something less than a war, but equally decisive. From the Greek schools and the church youth movement, long disciplined by the Archbishop to support enosis, his few close collaborators chose the young people they thought reliable and God-fearing, and organised them in Cyprus's five main towns into forty-seven sabotage and killer gangs, each of about six members. And in the mountains, Grivas had set up seven similar small guerilla gangs. The total size of EOKA grew until by March 1956 when the Archbishop was deported, in face of some 36,000 British troops on the island, Grivas claimed authority over 273 men armed with one hundred guns, backed by 750 villagers armed with shotguns. Only a few were paid full-timers; the majority served EOKA in the evenings or days off work, when they would steal explosive from Cyprus's copper mines, place bombs and, in the case of the killer gangs, shoot an opponent in the street and run. Grivas and Makarios expected these activities to lead to a British attempt to restore law and order by repression, which they hoped would stir up increased anti-British feelings amongst the Greek population.

Harding turned the entire government machine into an instrument of security. The forestry officer, the tax clerk, the agricultural adviser were no longer interested only in forestry, taxes or agriculture; their main job now was to look out for anything unusual in the places they visited and report. The police, largely composed of Greek Cypriots, many of whom had been passing information to EOKA, were totally reorganised, with Turks recruited for a newly created riot control force, and army units enlisted for police work. A State of Emergency was declared, introducing the death penalty (previously in force only for murder) for using weapons against people, life imprisonment for illegally possessing guns or bombs, deportation, collective punishment, censorship and whipping. Extra judges were appointed, mainly from England and Ireland, to conduct a special court dealing with offences against public order. It functioned like a normal English court, but took pressure off the Cypriot judges who had become increasingly subject to threats when they passed unpopular sentences.

The first impact of Harding's measures was ugly. Soldiers whose colleagues had been shot or blown up searched Cypriot houses. Many Greek families who had no contact with EOKA found the soldiers rough. When searching for weapons or explosives the soldiers would empty sacks of grain onto the floor or tip a load of fruit and vegetables off a van. Sometimes they found what they were looking for. When Makarios's palace was searched, they found evidence that arms had been stored there and money raised for EOKA. But in the months after the deportation Grivas made the running. His men penetrated the security of Nicosia airport and persuaded a Greek Cypriot policeman to place a bomb in an aircraft and destroy it (fortunately without loss of life). A Greek Cypriot household servant even placed a time bomb under Harding's bed, but it failed to go off and merely led to the

*British soldiers conduct a spot-check in Nicosia.*

dismissal of the Greek Cypriot staff from Government House. EOKA gunmen accomplished many successful shootings in streets and cafés, enlarging their range of victims from soldiers, policemen and Greek Cypriot 'traitors' to British civilians.

The intensive searches soon had Grivas and his men on the run. The once safe houses in the towns where Grivas stayed had to be abandoned and he took to the hills, living with his tiny guerilla groups. The searchers moved after him. Grivas recounts in his memoirs how he and a group of six guerillas were hunted down in the mountains of the Paphos forest in June 1956, trudging over rocks that were too hot to touch, seeking water in streams that had dried up, at one point being fired on by a patrol from only a dozen yards, so that Grivas left his diary, spectacles, binoculars and other belongings as he fled. He reports that after this incident he and his band hid stock still among the trees and that one of the British soldiers posted to guard the area stood within touching distance of the tree behind which he, the 59-year-old EOKA commander, was hiding.

Though the British failed to catch Grivas, they captured other EOKA men and supporters, from many of whom they obtained information about the whereabouts and plans of their colleagues. A large number of these men claimed – and still continue to claim – that the British routinely tortured them. This allegation was trumpeted to the world by EOKA and its Greek allies. It was an allegation that a man who had squealed to the British might be expected to make. The British denied that they had used torture or brutality and pointed to two cases of officers in Cyprus who were charged and found guilty of assaulting a prisoner as evidence of British correctness. The truth, of course, lay somewhere between the two. 'Rough handling', which Harding admitted occurred after suspected killers had been captured, was inevitable. Harsh interrogation of those thought to have information that could lead to the capture of killers was also inevitable. EOKA killed 'traitors'; a police questioner could make the counter-threat of a trial that might lead to hanging if no information was given. That was as far as the questioner was supposed to go, and some of them sometimes went farther. But as deliberate policy the British did not respond to EOKA brutality by counter-brutality. When a bomb exploded among a group of British service-men off-duty after a game of football, when the wife of a British soldier was shot dead, British troops went on ferocious retaliatory rampages, injuring many innocent bystanders. In the privacy of the interrogation room, some intelligence officers gave vent to their feelings. Many former EOKA mem-

*'Disperse or we shoot', in English, Greek and Turkish on a British army lorry.*

bers described ill-treatment. One was Nicos Koshies, who missed going to university because he joined EOKA instead and later became publisher of a Cypriot newspaper.

> They took me to the Special Branch [he recalled] and they started beating me. They took off all my clothes; they tied my hands and my feet. Then they asked somebody to come in, a Cypriot. He was always either drunk or taking drugs. He was really mad with me, crying at one time, laughing at another: he was unbalanced. He was taking a stick to put up my bottom, he was putting cloths in water and then putting them on my face so I could not breathe, he threw me down and danced on my stomach when he was wearing boots. After twelve days my body was really bad. I could not recognise myself.

James Callaghan, then Labour's colonial spokesman, described another case. He told the House of Commons:

> On 29 June 1957 an inquest was held into the death of Nicos Georghiou at Limassol. Dr Clearkin was the Government pathologist. He is an Englishman, and said in evidence that bruises in the head were sufficiently severe to have caused the injuries to the brain, perhaps by bumping the head against a hard object. The coroner returned a verdict that the cause of death was intercranial haemorrhage occasioned by some unknown external agency of which there is no direct evidence.

Callaghan asked why, in the light of this case and others, the Government would not agree to an impartial inquiry to establish the facts. Harding's answer was that the morale of troops and police would be damaged by such an inquiry.

Nevertheless right through the emergency the British courts worked to normal standards of evidence. EOKA men conceded that once their cases came to court they received just hearings; they were able to make their allegations of torture in open court. And though these allegations were usually dismissed, the EOKA gunman Nicos Sampson, who subsequently boasted of the way he led killer gangs on the streets, was acquitted of the murder of a British police officer because the rough way he was treated on arrest made the judge doubt whether his confession was freely given. In short, facing the provocation and horrifying violence of EOKA, the British behaved, as Gandhi had predicted, better than any other imperial power would have been likely to.

Harding's first campaign in 1955–6 was successful. Grivas on the run had difficulty controlling EOKA with his detailed written instructions. Seventeen leading guerillas were captured and the mountain gangs never fully recovered. They had brought the exciting notion of guerillas in the hills to the Cyprus conflict – more attractive than the urban killing that was EOKA's main activity – and their disruption was a blow. Grivas himself survived, thanks largely to the rich and numerous monasteries: the Greek

Orthodox monks were a constant source of money, food and protection. In August 1956 he called a truce, to give himself time to repair his organisation. He had by now settled in his permanent headquarters, a house in Limassol known only to two girl couriers. He slept in a specially constructed cell beneath the kitchen sink, where he wrote his orders and proclamations on tiny scraps of paper, tightly folded.

The deportation of Makarios in March 1956 marked the start of a campaign to secure British interests not just in Cyprus but throughout the Middle East. Only days before, the English general, Sir John Glubb, widely known as Glubb Pasha, had been sacked from his post as commander of the Arab Legion, the army of the King of Jordan. The Prime Minister, Anthony Eden, and other British Conservatives felt that the dismissal of Glubb, who was to many Arabs and Englishmen the symbol of the British presence in the Middle East, was a slight to British prestige that had to be reversed. Deporting Makarios and launching an all-out campaign against EOKA demonstrated in a small way the imperial will that the Suez group demanded. But the Prime Minister's main attempt to prove that he was not a weakling in Middle Eastern affairs was his decision in the autumn of 1956 to attack Egypt (see chapter 5, p. 265). This had numerous effects on Cyprus, direct and indirect. The most immediate was that Harding became short of men. Paratroopers were withdrawn from Cyprus to take part in the Suez invasion, others were put on stand-by to be flown to Egypt or loaded supplies and helped the British and French airforces in the Akrotiri base prepare for bombing raids. Consequently Harding lost the initiative that he had earlier won. After the launching of the Suez campaign on 31 October 1956, EOKA had their best three weeks of the entire four-year emergency, causing thirty-three deaths, a strike rate of well over one a day.

The effect of the Suez affair on Cyprus was also decisive in the long term. American refusal to back the invasion almost bankrupted Britain. The Prime Minister, Eden, resigned. The Government had to cut its spending, particularly on defence. The emphasis shifted from conventional forces to nuclear weapons, which were much cheaper; the number in the services was to be reduced from almost 700,000 to 375,000. This meant a change in the role of Cyprus. Never again would it be a launching point for a major land force; its task now would be to provide secure airfields for strategic bombers. That no longer required the whole of Cyprus to be sovereign British territory: the airfields and their environs would be enough. And for this reduced role, it was disproportionate to have some 30,000 British troops tied down pursuing three hundred EOKA men. The new Prime Minister, Harold Macmillan, who in 1954–5 was a staunch upholder of the policy that all Cyprus must remain for ever British, in 1957 abandoned it.

Macmillan hoped this change of policy would stop the killing, but the Greek Government that had earlier wanted a quiet compromise with Britain now refused even to come to talks; brother Greeks were being killed and tortured by butcher Harding; the peace-loving Archbishop had been deported; Athens radio was broadcasting constant support for EOKA; the Greek public were too excited by regular reports of British atrocities in Cyprus for any but a brave and secure Greek Government to dare to come out publicly in favour of a settlement.

In an effort to find someone to deal with, the British released Archbishop Makarios from the Seychelles in April 1957 and let him return to Athens, though not to Cyprus itself. The release aroused anger and violent public demonstrations in Turkey. Harold Macmillan wrote about the problem:

> It really is one of the most baffling . . . which I can ever remember . . . like one of those children's puzzles where the effort to get three or more balls into their right position is continually frustrated; two would fall into place but then the third would immediately escape. To whatever Turkey might agree Greece would object. To whatever Greece might demand Turkey would be obstructive. What Makarios might be inclined to accept, EOKA under General Grivas would refuse.

The release of Makarios was one of Macmillan's first major decisions as Prime Minister. It marked Britain's withdrawal from a tough policy in the Middle East and provoked the resignation from the Cabinet of the Conservative grandee Lord Salisbury, who had recently been one of Macmillan's key backers for the Prime Ministership. The release was, however, what Harding, the Governor, wanted. He had had an amazing piece of luck. In a field near the village of Lysi the army had found some large, screw-topped glass jars which contained diaries in Greek. The handwriting matched that of the visa application George Grivas had made for his visit to Cyprus in 1952. The British Government quickly published extracts and used the full version as their best source of information about EOKA's organisation, learning definitely that Makarios was the Commander-in-Chief. The Greek Government and some British newspapers and politicians dismissed the diaries as forgeries made for British propaganda, but Grivas himself, in his memoirs eight years later, confirmed their authenticity. The diaries showed that Makarios had had the authority to order Grivas when to start military action and when to stop. With Harding's pre-Suez grip on the island restored by the spring of 1957, with Grivas's gangs so weakened that he offered a truce, and with Britain ready to quit the island, now seemed the moment for Makarios to order an end to the violence.

This view was pressed upon him in the Greek Foreign Ministry. Although his return to Athens was a triumph and he was greeted by the Greek Prime Minister, Constantine Karamanlis, his private briefing from Greece's consul-general to Cyprus, Evangelos Vlachos, was blunt: 'I insisted to Makarios that the action of Grivas and EOKA should reach an end.' Vlachos argued that there was no further point in fighting the British. The problem was now the government of Turkey, which, having remained quiescent while Britain was committed to stay in Cyprus, was becoming anxious and aggressive now Britain was keen to go. To the Turks, Greece was a state bent on expansion at Turkey's expense. So they made it plain they would not have Cyprus, a mere forty miles from their coast, in Greek hands. Vlachos warned Makarios that, with Turkish Cypriots in the auxiliary police helping Britain fight EOKA, the Turkish and Greek Cypriot communities might soon start slaughtering each other. Already Turkey was beginning to arm a Turkish Cypriot defence organisation, VOLKAN, much as Greece had armed EOKA: if violence between the two communities erupted, Turkey, being both nearer to Cyprus and much stronger militarily than Greece, would be the more powerfully placed to intervene. Vlachos reports that Makarios said he agreed absolutely and wrote a letter to Grivas which Vlachos carried to Cyprus in the diplomatic bag. The letter, however, did not order Grivas to cease fighting; it asked his opinion. Grivas replied by flatly rejecting the idea of a permanent cease-fire. He remained in Cyprus. Makarios backed down. Later Vlachos, the Consul-General and message-carrier, commented:

> I can't say Grivas was controlling him, but Makarios was afraid to come to a clash with him. This is my impression. Makarios was a very clever man, but I don't think that he had the power, the bravery I would say, to confront public opinion.

Makarios, having agreed with Grivas in refusing to face the reality of Turkish power, clutched at a straw proffered by the British Labour Party. After the Suez fiasco, Labour was expected to win the next general election and a group of Labour left-wingers gave their support to Makarios. Barbara Castle, speaking for Labour's national executive at the Party conference in October 1957, said Labour would try to complete the process of giving self-determination to the people of Cyprus during its next term in office. In view of the increasingly strong line being taken by Turkey, this implied a readiness by Labour to impose self-determination, meaning enosis, even at the risk of war with Turkey. It was not realistic, but thanks to Barbara Castle's speech and some effective work among left-wing Labour MPs by Makarios's many emissaries in England, it seemed to give justification to Grivas for keeping up the struggle and to Makarios for refusing to talk to the Conservative Government.

Harold Macmillan showed his mastery of British politics in the way he handled this dilemma. As the new Governor to succeed Harding he appointed Sir Hugh Foot, a man close to the Labour Party. Foot's brother, Michael, was a prominent Labour politician and a close ally of left-wingers like Barbara Castle. Foot himself was a career colonial officer, duty bound to obey government orders but famous within the service for the enthusiasm and effectiveness with which he had carried out Labour Government policies in the late 1940s. He was then Chief Secretary in Nigeria, where he was the driving force behind a major innovation – the preparation of a new constitution by getting Nigerians to sound out fellow Nigerians. The idea was that the system of government should not be imposed by Britain but that the colonised people should be made responsible for their own fate. This was the policy of the then Labour Colonial Secretary, Arthur Creech Jones, and of the Labour Party think-tank on such issues, the Fabian Colonial Bureau. Added to Foot's family links, it gave him a standing with the Labour Party that no other colonial civil servant enjoyed.

While Foot's appointment helped win Labour MPs to the Government's policies in Cyprus, it had an opposite effect in Turkey. The government there had liked Harding's effectiveness against EOKA, but Foot's reputation for liberalism and for a principled belief in self-determination appeared to them akin to support for enosis: why, they asked, appoint such a man unless to change policy? Foot arrived in the island in December 1957 and soon began to reinforce the Turks' fears. Invited by Macmillan to propose his own solution, he announced that he had an open mind and toured the island bravely on horseback. He released detainees and lifted restrictions. The Greek Government and Archbishop Makarios were impressed and persuaded Grivas to maintain a truce. Turkish Cypriots became convinced that their protectors had abandoned them.

The Turkish Government responded by insisting on the partition of Cyprus, an option that had been put to them some months earlier by the British, and the establishment there of a Turkish military base. Turkish Cypriots in Nicosia launched violent demonstrations, burning Greek shops and houses and in one incident killing eight Greeks. Such actions enraged the Greek Cypriot community and Grivas. So the arrival in the island of the peaceable, well-intentioned Sir Hugh Foot was soon followed by Greek and Turkish Cypriots' engaging in virtual civil war. In effect the partitioning of the island was starting as terror drove both Greek and Turkish families out of areas where they were in an isolated minority.

Nor did this mean that EOKA held off their anti-British activities. After the blows to the organisation struck by Harding, the truce for negotiation had given Grivas, once again, time to rebuild. He was isolated by now, seeing nobody but the owners of the house in the cellar of which he was living, dangerously at risk of his girl couriers' giving him away. He continued methodically writing his orders to his deputies, receiving their reports, issuing public pronouncements over the signature Dighenis and, remarkably, maintaining his authority. His instructions to the people of Cyprus were increasingly those of a puritan zealot, more monkish than Makarios. When Grivas ordered his EOKA gangs to stop tradesmen on the island from selling British goods, appeals to Makarios came not only from the traders. The only sanitary towels then available in Cyprus came from Britain. Grivas's leaflets included tirades against gambling and against those who opened coffee shops during church services on Sundays. Makarios by comparison seemed catholic, indulgent and forgiving.

By now it had become generally accepted that 'Dighenis, the Leader' was indeed George Grivas. Many Cypriots, particularly left-wingers, had at first dismissed this allegation as British propaganda to blacken EOKA: a sadistic fascist known as the leader of *X*, the war-time bully-boy allies of the Germans, surely could not be the inspiration of their battle for freedom and justice? While such doubts shook some supporters of enosis, they did not appear to affect Archbishop Makarios or the Greek Orthodox Church. Grivas now turned EOKA's energies against AKEL and trade unionists, murdering some left wingers with particular brutality. Grivas was a religious man; Makarios and Grivas were alike passionate anti-Communists; for both it was essential to secure Church- rather than AKEL-rule, once the British were forced to leave. But Grivas was now going too far in his anti-Communist crusade even for the Archbishop. Greek Cypriots from the island went to Athens to appeal to Makarios to stop Greeks murdering Greeks.

By 1958 Turkish and Greek Cypriots were using violence against both the British and each other; the Athens and Ankara Governments, pressed by fanatical demonstrations, were giving secret support to the organisers of violence on both sides; and the British Governor was trying to promote a constitutional plan to which none of the parties principally involved would listen. Cyprus moved up from being a Colonial and Foreign Office matter to become a principal preoccupation of three Prime Ministers, Harold Macmillan in England, Constantine Karamanlis in Greece and Adnan

*Ataturk Square, Nicosia, January 1958. Turkish flags fly from the buildings and an overturned police car burns in the background.*

Menderes in Turkey. Macmillan himself visited the island and worked on
what became known as the Macmillan plan: a scheme under which Greek
and Turkish Cypriots would each have a representative assembly and would
each have places in the Government, while the Governor, who would be
British, would have resident advisers appointed by Greece and Turkey.
Macmillan succeeded in selling this proposal to Menderes. He then flew to
Athens, where Karamanlis demanded changes, and then to Ankara, where
Menderes pronounced the changes unacceptable. In short the plan gave
major gains to the Turks: the concession of a separate assembly was for them
a step towards partition; the proposal to have a Turkish – as well as a Greek –
representative on the island to advise the Governor gave Turkey a standing
that was the Greeks' worst horror.

The Macmillan plan had one extra ingredient, a tactical trick that was to
prove its most important element: the Prime Minister informed the Greeks
that it would be implemented in two months' time – with a Turkish
representative taking up residence in the island to advise the Governor
whether the Greeks agreed or not. The Turks prudently named their consul
in Nicosia to the post, thus avoiding the risk of Greek demonstrations against
the representative's arrival. Macmillan hoped he had forced the Greeks and
Makarios to see the realities of power. Turkey was the strongest state in the
area, Britain was determined to go; if the Greek Government did not force
Makarios into accepting a settlement, then Greece would have to fight
Turkey for possession of the island, a war the Greeks were certain to lose.
After years in which Makarios's refusal to face reality had prevented Greece
from coming to terms, the timing device in the Macmillan plan brought the
Cyprus conflict to a head. Evangelos Vlachos, the Greek Consul in Cyprus,
said later:

> One of the best Cypriots that I knew, Mr Paschalides, came into my office
> and he crossed his hands on his breast and said in Greek, 'Tetelesti', which
> means, 'It is finished'. These are the last words which our Lord murmured
> on the cross – that is, 'Everything has come to an end.'

Makarios still did not give up. He turned to his last allies in Britain, the
Labour Party. He invited Barbara Castle to come to Athens to find out
whether Labour still stood by its promise to grant union with Greece.
Barbara Castle brought bad news. The Prime Minister's choice of Governor
was having its effect. Sir Hugh Foot was bringing the Labour Party round.
Unless Makarios offered some compromise, they too would back the
Macmillan plan.

Makarios reacted with uncharacteristic impulsiveness. He told Mrs
Castle that in the circumstances he was prepared to give up enosis. If Cyprus
could have its status guaranteed so that neither Greece nor Turkey could
control it, he would accept independence. He consulted neither his ethnarchy council nor Grivas. His last hope for union with Greece having
evaporated, he authorised Mrs Castle to announce his change of mind to the

world. This procedure appalled the sophisticated diplomats in the Greek Foreign Ministry who had been working for some years to back him. Why had Makarios thrown everything away?

> We were completely astonished [Evangelos Averoff, then Foreign Minister, recalled] because this was something that, treated diplomatically, could lead to many things. If we could have secretly approached the Turks and the British and told them, 'Let's try to convince Makarios,' we could have found terms which would have been very favourable.

The ethnarchy council, the mayors, AKEL and the trade unions in Cyprus promptly agreed to Makarios's abandonment of enosis. His authority as ethnarch remained supreme. The only objector was Grivas, angry at not being consulted and outraged that the purpose of their struggle was to be abandoned. Not for the first time or the last, Makarios wobbled on finding himself out of step with Grivas. He gave an interview to the *New York Times* in which he said that independence did not rule out enosis, which could follow later. But this half-withdrawal did not remove the impact of his change of mind. He had opened a path.

As the Cyprus situation had worsened from 1954 onwards, the Greek Government had placed it on the agenda of the United Nations, each year gaining a few extra votes but otherwise achieving little. Now an event at the UN was to lead to the resolution of the conflict. Every November since 1954 Greece had tried to get a motion calling for self-determination for the Cypriot people, in accordance with principles laid down in various fundamental UN documents, passed by the appropriate committee and then the General Assembly. With like regularity the British replied that the motion should not be put – or if put that it should not be passed – on the grounds that it would increase conflict, the avoidance of which was an equally if not more fundamental purpose of the UN. Skilful British tickling of UN votes had regularly prevented the motion for self-determination from obtaining the two-thirds majority it required. It must be said for the effectiveness of the UN that each year, as the time for the Greek resolution approached, the Government in Cyprus did its best to avoid committing atrocities, introducing illiberal laws or in any other way giving the Greek delegation and their regular supporters (including the Russians and members of the eastern block) any new arguments to prove that the Cypriot people were oppressed. Similarly each year Makarios and the Greek Government pressed Grivas to declare a truce or at least to restrict EOKA's violence to military targets while the speeches for the debate were being prepared. Thus the effect of the UN on the Cyprus conflict had been to impose an annual rhythm, like that of primitive warfare regularly interrupted for the harvest. But during the annual UN Cyprus manoeuvres in November/December 1958, a meeting occurred in a lobby that was to be decisive. The two who met were Evangelos Averoff and Fatim Zorlu, the Foreign Ministers of Greece and Turkey.

In the political committee they had been locked in conflict, daily rebutting each other's every point in hour-long speeches based on fast and brilliant research done by their embassies throughout the world. Averoff argued Makarios's case for independence with guarantees: no links with either Greece or Turkey. The Greek Government were desperately using this plea in the UN in a last attempt to prevent the implementation of the Macmillan plan and the inclusion of Turkey in the government of the island. Zorlu argued that Cyprus contained two national communities and that Averoff's demand for independence was just a Greek ruse to achieve annexation. The implications of partition in international law were displayed in terms of the latest pronouncements of the leading authorities; likewise the circumstances in which an oppressed people might use force to secure fundamental rights; and much besides. The one consistent feature of the debates was that whatever Averoff said Zorlu contradicted and vice-versa.

Britain, Turkey and their allies had always managed to prevent a resolution satisfactory to Greece and EOKA from being passed and they succeeded again this year. Evangelos Averoff remembered his terrible disappointment at that time:

> We went with some members of the delegation to the end of a corridor to smoke. We were frantic of course, desperate: how do you go back to your country beaten in an international forum? Then I saw Zorlu coming towards me. I told my people, 'There he is coming, I am afraid I'll slap him in the face. I'm so nervous I don't think that I will be able to keep my nerve.' So he came smiling, and he told me, 'I came to congratulate you.'

Zorlu smoothed the Greek Foreign Minister's ruffled feathers and suggested that the two of them should meet privately. The Greek Government was by now desperate to get off the Cyprus hook. It was embarrassing for so staunchly anti-Communist a regime to be dependent each year on Communist votes at the United Nations and to be regarded by their British, American and Turkish allies as a wrecking force in the NATO alliance. It was debilitating for both Greece and Turkey to have to devote a large part of their Foreign Office manpower to one small issue. Both countries needed a way out.

Two days later, in the deserted UN cafeteria in New York, Averoff and Zorlu sat down to settle the Cyprus issue, which Britain had by now proved unable to do. Zorlu again took the initiative, spelling out the kind of independence for Cyprus that would be acceptable to Turkey: a federal structure, with small areas set aside for sovereign British and Turkish bases. Averoff was far from certain that continued discussion along these lines was worthwhile, but Zorlu insisted that he consult the Greek Government and the Archbishop and that they meet again. Zorlu's only condition was that secrecy must be preserved; above all, he said melodramatically, the British must not be informed.

The talks were bound to be difficult and complicated and before long the

British had to be informed. Two Greek Cypriots had been condemned to death for murder. They had killed another Greek Cypriot while he was asleep. The law provided that an appeal for clemency in such cases went to the Governor. Sir Hugh Foot wanted to find an excuse for a reprieve, because this was the first such appeal he had had to decide and he did not want his influence with the Greek Cypriots destroyed in the demonstrations and retaliatory killings that were bound to follow an execution. Also he did not relish his predecessor's nickname, 'Harding the Hangman'. But the evidence in the case was clear, the murder particularly brutal. He signed the death warrants. Averoff and Zorlu were meeting in Paris at the time and realised that Averoff's position would be impossible if it became known that he was negotiating behind EOKA's back while the British were hanging EOKA heroes. The two Foreign Ministers told their British counterpart, Selwyn Lloyd, that a deal was in progress but that negotiations would be called off if he did not prevent the hangings. After some delay the Colonial Secretary, Alan Lennox-Boyd, managed to telephone Sir Hugh Foot, informing him of the negotiations and telling him that the Cabinet would back him whatever he decided: as the Queen's representative in Cyprus, the decision was his. Foot, unaware of the precise time fixed for the hangings, immediately phoned the director of prisons and later reported the following conversation:

Governor, 'I'm coming down to see you.'
Director, 'Could you give me half an hour?'
Governor, 'What do you mean by that?'
Director, 'It will all be over in half an hour.'
Governor (shouting), 'No, you don't understand, I'm coming down to stop it.'

A few days later, just before Christmas 1958, the Greek Government asked Grivas to call off all EOKA violence. Averoff and Zorlu were making progress, but they still did not tell the British Government the details. They merely asked for and obtained a statement that Britain was prepared to give up sovereignty over Cyprus as a whole provided it could keep sovereignty over its military bases there. The Greek–Turkish negotiations continued throughout January 1959, including a further four-day Averoff–Zorlu meeting in Paris, conducted in back rooms at an international conference. In February the two Prime Ministers, Menderes and Karamanlis, with their Foreign Ministers and advisers, assembled in the Dolder Hotel on the outskirts of the Swiss lakeside city of Zürich to draw up a settlement. The Greek Government had conferred with Makarios beforehand and Averoff, a precise man, thought he had Makarios's approval for the positions he was to take; but no Cypriots were present at the Zürich meeting, where two months of informal sounding out, adjustment of positions and formulation of draft clauses were to be translated into firm agreements between governments.

The main clash that dominated the Zürich proceedings was Turkey's

demand for a base in Cyprus and Greece's refusal to allow it. Menderes and Zorlu had the Greeks on the run: enosis was dead and partition of the island was the likely consequence of the British Government's continuing to implement the Macmillan plan, so the Turks ruthlessly pressed their demand for a base. The solution finally agreed, after many reports that the talks were about to break down, was that Greece and Turkey would sign a treaty with Cyprus guaranteeing her independence and providing for a headquarters garrison there of Greek, Turkish and Cypriot soldiers. The Turks thus secured a military presence on the island of six hundred and fifty men. The remainder of the Zürich agreement provided for a President elected by the Greek Cypriots, a Vice-President elected by the Turkish Cypriots, each with substantial veto powers over government action, and all subordinate parts of the Government intertwined and mutually restraining, as precise and delicate as a Swiss watch. Proudly Averoff and Zorlu brought the documents their Prime Ministers had initialled to London.

The British were delighted and agreed that a short formal conference should be held in London at which all parties, including leaders of the Greek and Turkish Cypriots, would sign their acceptance. Karamanlis, now in Athens, reported this proposal to Makarios and accepted it only when the Archbishop said he agreed. Thus the clear purpose of the London meeting, apart from dealing with a few supplementary British concerns, was to sign the agreement. Karamanlis had reason to be confident that Makarios accepted this, not only because he had explicitly put it to him but also because, immediately on his return to Athens, the Greek Prime Minister had given the Archbishop a full and detailed account of the Zürich terms, after which Makarios had issued a press release filled with nothing but warm enthusiasm:

> The agreement lays the foundations for an immediate final settlement, whereby Cyprus is to become an independent sovereign state . . . a new era of freedom and prosperity . . . I have congratulated Prime Minister Karamanlis . . .

The Greek Government were surprised, therefore, to learn that Makarios was proposing to bring to London thirty-five Greek Cypriots of various shades of opinion and walks of life. Averoff, as soon as he heard of it, begged Makarios to change his mind, because to ask such a group to pass a quick verdict on a package of previously agreed compromise measures was to ask for trouble. Makarios was the acknowledged leader; whatever he recommended the Greek Cypriots would accept. Makarios insisted. His motives were mixed: he could use the thirty-five to justify delay and thus get a better price, but he could also tie an influential group of Cypriots to him in the awkward task of selling the eventual deal to his more extreme supporters. Greece had to acquiesce.

As soon as he arrived in London, Makarios held a meeting with the thirty-five, many of whom he had not met since his deportation three years earlier. As one of the party, Glavkos Clerides, said later:

> Two things became obvious, the one, that it was not a question of enosis, and the other that it was a question of a constitution which gave far too many rights to the minority community, as we saw it. Therefore there was a lot of opposition to Makarios signing that agreement.

When Averoff was told that Makarios was refusing to sign unless changes were made to the agreement, he telephoned Karamanlis in Athens. The Greek Prime Minister flew immediately to London and summoned Makarios and others to a meeting in the Greek Embassy. According to Averoff, Karamanlis said, 'How can you possibly have objections now, when you agreed in Athens to accept the proposal and that there should be no further discussion here of any issues that had been settled in Zürich? You knew what those issues were and you gave your assent.' Makarios replied, 'You are right, but I have to do what my conscience tells me and I cannot take on any further responsibilities.' Karaminlis then pointed out that a renewal of bloodshed for no possible gain was the probable consequence and concluded, to all present, 'If Makarios wants to carry on the struggle he will have to look elsewhere for support.' He then left and flew back to Athens.

Makarios and Averoff held a meeting with Makarios's Cypriot group. Averoff addressed them, arguing for the settlement, Makarios said nothing and, according to Averoff, everyone who spoke, and they nearly all did, supported the signing of the agreements. Yet each had a specific objection.

Most said they wanted the Greek–Turkish ratio in the public services to be changed from 70–30 to 80–20, to match the proportions in the population. Some argued against the provision for separate Greek and Turkish municipal authorities (not knowing that this had been Makarios's idea, because he did not think the Greeks wanted to subsidise the poor Turkish areas). One argued against the clause requiring separate Greek and Turkish majorities in the house of representatives for votes on tax legislation, on the ground that this would enable the minority to block the budget. But none of them said the agreements should not be signed; on the contrary, many insisted that they must be signed, in spite of all their flaws, to rescue Cyprus from stalemate and horror.

That afternoon the British called a full session of the conference. Selwyn Lloyd, the British Foreign Secretary, was in the chair. Their purpose, he said, was to ratify a compromise settlement to a complex and painful problem. Now he was told the Archbishop objected. Could he persuade him to change his mind?

The Archbishop asked for 'modifications on certain points', nearly all of them, Averoff remembers, the very points that the Turks had required as preconditions of their acceptance. The delegates listened with astonishment and displeasure and, on the Greek side, despair and humiliation. Averoff himself spoke, saying that the word of the Greek Government was to be trusted: in negotiating for the Greek Cypriots, 'in every case we kept Makarios informed and we never moved onto the next step without first obtaining his consent'.

*The London conference, February 1959. At the table, right to left: Sir Hugh Foot, Selwyn Lloyd, Alan Lennox-Boyd, with Archbishop Makarios at the far table, centre.*

After an adjournment, unwillingly granted by Selwyn Lloyd who thought all was lost, Zorlu made a passionate speech about the reluctance of many Turks to make concessions, how well he understood and sympathised with the Archbishop's similar stance, and how in the next phase the Turkish Cypriots would co-operate with the Archbishop, who, although they had crossed swords with him, they respected for his many outstanding qualities. The Greek Foreign Minister delivered more in the same vein. Selwyn Lloyd was due in Moscow the next day and saw no point in extending the conference further. Makarios, pressed for an answer, said, 'If it is now, it is no.' He wanted one more night to reflect and pray. Lloyd had to agree.

Makarios shared his thoughts that night with nobody. He smoked constantly in his bedroom in Claridge's hotel. To understand his dilemma it is necessary to recognise that he was not an Archbishop in the modern English sense. He was more like a medieval cardinal who used the Church as the ladder to political power. He had acquired the senior archbishopric in the Greek Orthodox Church. He admired Eleftherios Venizelos, the Cretan who skilfully secured enosis for his island and went on to become Prime Minister of Greece and the dominant figure in Greek politics from 1910 till 1930. Makarios too had shown the ability to master Greek politics. During his many long periods in Athens he had used the pulpit successfully to rekindle the passion for a greater Greece that he considered the only force able to civilise the eastern Mediterranean in the face of Muslim backwardness. He had led Cyprus into war for the cause; he had suffered exile for it. To give up now would not only end his chance of becoming leader of a greater Greek state, it would mean abandoning a great ideal.

On the other hand, Makarios knew that his determination not to waver had twice cost the people of Cyprus dear. When he pressed Governor Harding and Colonial Secretary Lennox-Boyd farther than they would go he had lost an offer that would have kept open the door to enosis and that was never to be renewed. When he returned from exile and failed to order Grivas off the island, the intercommunal killing of which he had been warned drew Turkey actively into the island's affairs. Both times the Greek Government had urged him to settle. Both times he had chosen the policy favoured by Grivas. Both times he had been wrong.

This time he had not consulted Grivas. The thirty-five did not include any representative of the colonel. Even though the Greek Prime Minister's brutal statement had intimidated the thirty-five into accepting that he must sign, Makarios knew that Karamanlis was bluffing. The Grivas–Makarios axis could still work: if he, the Archbishop, went back to Athens and appealed to the Greek people, they would vote for enosis and a greater Greece. Karamanlis would fall. The Greek nation and EOKA could keep up the struggle. But – and this was the factor he had been amazingly slow to recognise – if they did this they would lose. Karamanlis and Averoff were not the cowards he and Grivas had thought, they were Greek patriots who recognised that Turkish feeling was now so strong that a further attempt by Greece and

*Grivas returns to Athens, March 1959, wearing his battle kit, to be greeted by vast, enthusiastic crowds.*

EOKA to secure Cyprus would inevitably mean war with Turkey and defeat for Greece. Only on the last night of the London conference did Makarios fully recognise that this was the clinching argument. Early the next morning he told the Greek representative in London that he would sign.

That effectively marked the end of British rule in Cyprus. It took eighteen months to tidy up the unsettled issues: an amnesty was agreed for EOKA and their leader, George Grivas, who returned to Greece a national hero and was awarded a general's rank and pay for the rest of his life; a negotiation about the exact size of the sovereign areas for the two British bases compelled a British minister, Julian Amery, to bargain at Makarios's speed and therefore stay on the island for five months; a request for illegal arms to be handed to the Government, on the promise that there would be no prosecutions, left many guns in the hands of those who still thought they needed them; an election in December 1959 made Makarios President of Cyprus and Dr Fazil Kutchuk, leader of the Turkish Cypriots, Vice-President. Finally, with a constitution that made it illegal to campaign for either enosis or partition, Cyprus became an independent republic in August 1960.

So eager were the British to put an end to the horrors of Cyprus that they left the island with an independence constitution of doubtful validity. Its main purpose was not to secure good government in Cyprus but to avoid war between Greece and Turkey. To this end the sovereignty of Cyprus was restricted: it could not form part of a political or economic union with any other state and the forty-eight basic articles of the constitution could never be changed. The three guaranteeing powers, Britain, Greece and Turkey, were given the right to intervene, together if possible, otherwise individually, to restore the constitutional arrangements should they be upset. The UN Charter requires every member state to have full and equal sovereignty. Cyprus was given a Supreme Constitutional Court whose President could be neither Cypriot nor Greek, neither Turkish nor British. The first President, Professor Forsthoff, a German, concluded in 1963: 'I consider it wrong to regard Cyprus under the present agreement and constitution as an independent state.' By then the British, to their relief, and amid an unexpected show of friendliness on all sides, had got away.

## After Independence

If Cyprus was a violent place in the five years before independence it was much more so in the fifteen years after. Within three years the British were summoned back, not as rulers but as a military 'green line' to try to keep the warring Greek and Turkish Cypriots apart.

As a result of the pre-independence amnesty, many EOKA men were free to roam the island, discontented and armed. Makarios failed to use his authority as independence leader immediately to subdue them and insist on obedience to the constitution. On the contrary, he appointed EOKA men to key positions in the Government, notably Polykarpos Georkatzis, whom he made Interior Minister with authority over the police.

Makarios needed to use the post-independence honeymoon period to unite the whole of the new nation, both because the minority partner had been given disproportionate powers under the constitution and could be induced not to use them only by persuasion, and because Turkey, which now had its own armed men on the island, had shown it could act decisively in Cypriot affairs. The first requirement was for Makarios to secure the personal trust of Dr Fazil Kutchuk, the Turkish Cypriot Vice-President. But the Archbishop and his Greek-Cypriot ministers were tactless with Kutchuk. They allowed him to feel belittled and mocked: he was not consulted about the making of policy and issues were settled by the Greeks in private before they came to Cabinet. In December 1961, only just over a year after independence, the Turkish Cypriots used their ultimate constitutional weapon of refusal to vote for the budget, depriving the Government of the legal power to collect customs duties and income tax.

*Dr Kutchuk, the Turkish Cypriot Vice-President, with the Archbishop-President.*

Cyprus soon reverted back to the violent days of 1958. In December 1963 Makarios and his Cabinet sanctioned a major campaign of violence by Greeks against Turks in Nicosia. Georkatzis, who ran his ministry as if he were still in EOKA, disarmed the Turkish police shortly before the attacks, many of them led by his Greek Cypriot police, others by ex-EOKA groups built up by Georkatzis with the authority of Makarios. Scores of Turks, including women and children, were killed, houses were sacked, seven hundred hostages were taken. A Turkish intervention to protect their people was forestalled only by the setting-up of the British 'green line' in Nicosia and Larnaca. This soon proved ineffective at protecting the Turkish Cypriots: the Greek Cypriot authorities would not allow their police, largely ex-EOKA men, to be impeded in their continuing attacks. The 'green line' was taken over by the United Nations, but it still could not protect the Turks. The Turkish Cypriot leaders withdrew from a Government that was effectively at war with them and Grivas came back to the island to lead further attacks on Turkish villages. UN mediators and international conferences put their minds to the problem without success.

The first instalment of civil war in 1963–4 completed the virtual partition of Cyprus. The Turkish Cypriots retreated into enclaves where they took over complete military and administrative control. Cyprus Government troops, police and officials were not admitted, nor, usually, were Greek Cypriots. In these enclaves the 25,000 refugees from the Greek-held areas tried to make a new life. The Turkish area of Nicosia contained the Ministry of Justice, with all legal records such as wills, birth and marriage certificates and the land registry. The Turks refused to allow these documents to be moved. Turks in government service were nearly all now jobless (Turkish judges were among the few who continued at their posts); many could not get to their farms or workplaces; of a Turkish population of 116,000, fifty-six thousand were living off relief supplies from Turkey.

The island remained thus divided, with the Greeks trying to blockade the Turkish areas amid sporadic outbursts of violence, from 1964 till 1967, when a bloodless *coup d'état* overthrew the elected government in Greece and elevated three colonels to power. The previous Greek Government, in agreement with Makarios, had sent thousands of soldiers to Cyprus. The arrival in power in Greece of a right-wing junta encouraged Grivas to overstretch himself. He launched an attack on a Turkish enclave which provoked a muster of Turkish troopships and quickly led the UN Secretary-General, U Thant, to report that 'Greece and Turkey are now on the brink of war'. Following UN intervention, the Turks held back their invasion, on condition that the 10,000 or so illegal Greek troops were removed from the island. This episode at last taught Makarios that he must stop provoking the

*Nicos Sampson (centre with revolver) holding up a Turkish flag captured after a gun-fight, December 1963.*

Turks. But he learned the lesson too late. In the early days of independence he might have had the authority to discipline EOKA. Now he no longer had. Grivas created a new organisation, EOKA B, backed by the Greek colonels, whose target was no longer the British Government or the Turks but Makarios himself. They saw the Archbishop as a conciliator and therefore the main obstacle to enosis; they were as blind to the danger of provoking Turkey as Makarios had previously been. So in July 1974 they had him overthrown, in a *coup* executed by Greek officers. In his place as President of Cyprus they placed Nikos Sampson, the former EOKA street killer whom the British courts had released because of the rough way he was arrested. Makarios escaped to the safety of the British sovereign base at Akrotiri, from where he was flown to London.

The Greek breach of the 1960 Treaty of Guarantee was flagrant and the Turkish Prime Minister flew to London to seek British military help in restoring the Cyprus republic as defined in the Zürich and London agreements. The Labour Government of Harold Wilson refused to send troops: the obligation to do so was clear, but the consequences of such action were not. Britain had two areas of the island under her sovereignty, with troops based there, but rather than risk being accused of reviving imperialist practices in an operation that promised Britain no advantage, the Government preferred to let Greece and Turkey fight it out in Cyprus once again.

So Turkey invaded Cyprus. The Greek and Greek Cypriot troops there resisted fiercely but unsuccessfully. An immediate and unexpected effect was the fall of the Greek military dictatorship and the return of democracy to Greece. At first the Turks seemed to be restoring the Cyprus Republic, as defined in 1960. For this they had substantial international support. But after negotiations in Geneva failed they went farther, securing the whole of northern Cyprus under their control and turning 180,000 Greek Cypriots, nearly a third of the total population, into refugees. Turkey seized much more of Cyprus than was necessary merely to protect the Turkish enclaves, continuing to pour in Turkish troops and civilians until the Cyprus problem was, so far as Turkey was concerned, settled. Only a counter-invasion by Greece could now drive out the substantial Turkish military presence. The Cyprus Republic, to which Makarios was soon restored as President, was restricted to the southern half of the island, some sixty per cent of the whole. By July 1974 Turkey, which had moved out in 1878, was back.

The British period in Cyprus is a story of errors from beginning to end. The island performed none of the tasks for which Disraeli acquired it, was of no major service to any British interest and provided one of the nastier episodes in the end of the British Empire as Greek delusions of imperial grandeur came into conflict with British delusions of an imperial revival in the Middle East. Many Cypriots died and many more were made homeless because of the fevered visions and implacable stubbornness of Anthony Eden and Archbishop Makarios.

# CHAPTER 8

# Gold Coast

In the fifteenth and sixteenth centuries the Gold Coast exported a tenth of the world's supply of gold. In the seventeenth and eighteenth centuries the country remained one of the three or four largest sources of a major element in world trade but gold sales were overtaken as the principal export by slaves. By the late nineteenth century the West African slave trade had been suppressed and – by the methods of extraction then available – the gold was almost exhausted. The principal export became cocoa, of which the Gold Coast was soon the world's leading source.

The area was so hot, damp and disease-ridden that it became known as the white man's grave. Only a few Europeans penetrated inland from the surf-beaten, harbourless coast. That successive world trading opportunities were seized was mainly the work of a number of well-organised small nations or tribes, of whom the most powerful were the Ashanti. They had extracted gold and kept slaves for many years before the Europeans arrived.

This small territory thus played a role in international trade for more than four hundred years, unlike most of black Africa. So it was not surprising that in the mid twentieth century it took the lead in obtaining independence from European empires. For a few years after 1957 it became the world's leading exporter of pan-African revolution.

## The Slave Trade and After, 1475–1947

The first Europeans to reach the Gold Coast were the Portuguese in 1475, who named their landing-place Mina, the mine (now Elmina). They built warehouses on islands off the West African coast, where they later developed sugar plantations. These were worked by African slaves bought from the local traders and provided the idea of exporting slaves to work the Spanish silver mines in Mexico and Peru and the first sugar plantations of Spanish America and Brazil. Gradually the Portuguese built up their trade until the African gold panners and traders, fifty miles or more inland, who had formerly sent their gold dust north in exchange for goods brought by Muslim traders from across the Sahara, now sent the bulk of it south to the coast. And the more powerful of the Gold Coast states, formerly purchasers of slaves from other parts of West Africa, turned their energy to capturing and selling them.

The northern Europeans gradually moved in. First the Dutch in 1642 drove the Portuguese from the trading posts they had developed in the previous 160 years. Later the English and French tried to drive out the Dutch. They wanted the gold because it enabled them to buy goods and defend themselves throughout the world; and they wanted the slave trade both because it was profitable and because slaves were the key to the successful development of their new sugar plantations in the West Indies.

Sugar tickled the palate of the northern Europeans. Never before had they known a taste that so pleased them. The history of the Gold Coast from the sixteenth to the nineteenth century was to be dominated by the trans-Atlantic slave trade. Europe's insatiable sweet tooth had a bitter consequence.

The Venetians and Genoese had long been shipping Christian slaves – especially young boys – eastward over the Mediterranean to the Arab world. The slave trade from West Africa grew into a much bigger business and intense competition developed between European merchants to control what were really prisons for the storage of slaves. State monopolies were granted by Britain, France, Denmark, Sweden and Brandenburg to companies which by the start of the eighteenth century had built twenty-five huge forts of stone or brick on the 250 miles of the Gold Coast. These forts were attacked, captured, sold, exchanged and abandoned in bewildering succession. African merchants became principal suppliers of slaves for the new world, willingly selling to any customer. The European forts – mostly tourist rest-houses today – were never sovereign: the land on which they were built was rented from the coastal states, the African sellers of slaves and the European buyers dealing as equals.

The demand for slaves grew sharply. Between 1700 and 1786 the island of Jamaica alone imported 610,000. The calculations of historians suggest that more than six million African slaves reached all parts of America during the eighteenth century. This works out at an average of roughly twelve hundred a week. They did not all come from the Gold Coast, nor were they all carried in British ships, but the Gold Coast was one of the largest sources (along with what are now Nigeria, Liberia and Ivory Coast), and the British were by the end of the century the principal carriers. In the 1780s, the British were transporting some 26,000 slaves a year, their nearest rivals, the French, fewer than half as many. In 1770, 192 British ships regularly plied the trade.

The slave ships made a notorious 'triple passage'. They sailed for West Africa from Liverpool or Bristol with a cargo of cloth, firearms, knives, cutlasses, metal bars, gin and stone (as ballast and for reinforcing the forts). On reaching the Gold Coast, these goods were unloaded for sale and the crews set about chaining down the human cargo for the notorious 'middle passage'. During this voyage from Africa to the Americas roughly two in every ten aboard died, slaves and crew alike. The stench of a slave ship could be smelt miles down wind. After the slaves were sold and the ships scrubbed down came the most pleasant, the homeward leg, from the Caribbean with sugar, or occasionally from Virginia with tobacco. The elegance of Bristol and Bath, the sumptuous town hall of Liverpool, the fortune that saw William Ewart Gladstone through Oxford and into Parliament, were all founded on the triple passage.

The Ashanti, the dominant military power just inland from the Gold Coast, evolved a routine of body-snatching from neighbouring peoples. African slave-owners increased their holdings in order to speculate in slaves. The practice of 'panyarring' developed – seizing not merely one's debtor but any fellow-townsman of one's debtor and selling him or her to a slave merchant. Passing strangers were kidnapped and sold.

In most ages and places slavery had been the common fate of criminals, prisoners of war and debtors. The trade to America was different in kind and

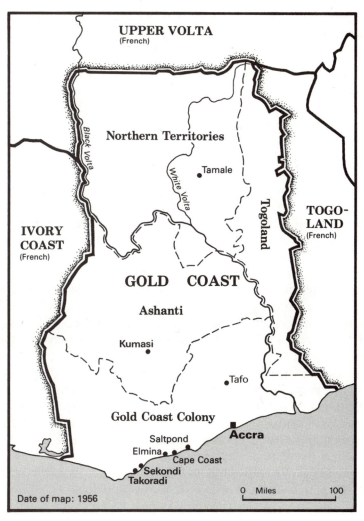

the country that was making the most profit from it now turned against it. William Wilberforce was an English evangelical Christian from Hull who devoted his political life to the suppression of the slave trade. The group who surrounded him, known as the 'Saints of Clapham', were well-connected, conservative moralists. Wilberforce himself was a close friend of William Pitt the younger, Prime Minister from 1783 till 1806, who spoke in support of the campaign in the House of Commons. The Saints obtained information, notably from former officers on slave ships, produced pamphlets, held meetings, mostly at evangelical churches, and petitioned Parliament. They were the first of the modern pressure groups.

Against them were ranged powerful interests and strong arguments. James Boswell wrote in 1777:

> To abolish a status which in all ages God has sanctioned and man has continued would not only be robbery to an innumerable class of our fellow-subjects but it would be an extreme cruelty to the African savages, a portion of whom it saves from massacre or intolerable bondage in their own country.

Plantation-owners from the West Indies were well represented in Parliament. Many had bought seats along with their great English country houses, on retiring with a fortune from the rigours of sugar-growing. They were straightforward, self-interested protectionists. But India and other countries were producing sugar more cheaply than the West Indies and it was difficult to justify tariffs to protect high-priced sugar in an age of laissez-faire (Adam Smith's *Wealth of Nations* had been published in 1776), especially when the processes of trade and production were so abhorrent. In the face of pressure from the East India Company it was impossible.

Nevertheless the struggle lasted more than thirty years, in Parliament, the press and the English and Scottish courts. In 1807 Parliament passed an Act that made it illegal for British subjects to engage in the slave trade. A similar Act had been passed four years earlier by Denmark and over the next decade the United States, Sweden and the Netherlands all followed. Britain quickly took the lead in enforcing the measure by sending a naval patrol to West African waters to catch slave ships. The penalties for British subjects convicted of slave-trading rose in severity until in 1824 they became liable to be hanged.

British traders conceded victory to the evangelists and rapidly quit the business. The gap was filled by French, Spanish, Portuguese, Brazilians and others. So the Foreign Office applied strong pressure on all these countries to allow British ships to arrest their slavers and British courts to punish them. They nearly all passed the necessary laws, but the trade remained profitable and so, when the British navy stopped their ships, captains would often produce papers which showed them to be owned in a country that permitted the trade. Captains who had no such papers would dispose of the evidence on sighting the naval patrol by throwing their slaves into the sea.

Until the 1870s a squadron of the Royal Navy was regularly stationed in West Africa – the commitment of forces reached a peak in the 1840s with twenty warships and a thousand men – for the purpose of catching slave-ships. Between 1825 and 1865 more than twelve hundred were captured and an average of one hundred slaves released alive from each. The navy took the slave-ships to Freetown in Sierra Leone, the headquarters of the anti-slavery patrol and the seat of the slave-trade courts. Here thousands of freed slaves were to remain, creating a colony determinedly British in character, the model for Liberia, the republic settled by freed American slaves, and Libreville by former French slaves.

The country most active in resisting the British patrols – ignoring its own law of 1809 abolishing the trade – was the United States. It was determined not to suffer interference in commerce by its former imperial ruler. The fastest slave clippers, always able to escape the British patrols, came from Baltimore or New York.

Britain's 1807 Act abolishing the trade did not change the relationship between existing slaves and their owners. So it was followed by an Act in 1834 making all slaves throughout the British Empire free. The slow, expensive task of arresting slave-ships went on. Lord Melbourne, Prime Minister when Queen Victoria came to the throne in 1837, thought the operation pointless: 'Religion, morality, law, eloquence, cruisers,' he wrote, 'will all be ineffectual when opposed to a profit of a cent per cent and more.' In 1839 Viscount Palmerston, his Foreign Secretary, proposed to punish the Portuguese for breaking their promise to put down the trade. He wanted to seize their Indian colony of Goa. Melbourne would not allow it. Such enthusiasm wearied him. The Ashanti and other slave-sellers continued for decades to find ways round the British, selling to captains willing to brave the blockade. Slavery was not abolished in the United States until 1862, in Cuba until 1886 and in Brazil until 1888. For many years it looked as though Melbourne would prove right. However free trade and the invention of machines that did the plantation work more cheaply than slaves eventually completed the task Wilberforce had begun.

The determined Christians who drove Parliament to make the slave trade illegal – and who also pressed for prison reform, improved factory conditions and the end of child labour in Britain – saw a great opportunity for doing good among the coloured peoples. Indeed they had to undo harm. While the abolition of the slave trade was good for those who might otherwise have become slaves and for the conscience of Europe, its effect on the economy of the Gold Coast was disastrous: the principal source of foreign earnings was blocked.

Slave-trading was a labour-intensive business and its abolition deprived tens of thousands of their livelihood. The quantity of gold that could be obtained by primitive panning techniques was now declining. The followers of Wilberforce recognised a duty to help the Africans find new sources of income; for the West African traders it was an urgent need. The evangelists also began setting up missions to convert the natives to Christianity. Whereas most British in the Gold Coast were primarily interested in profit, by the middle of the nineteenth century a second group had arrived with another purpose – humanitarianism.

It was not easy. The Ashanti were warlike and determined to continue selling slaves. Rice, maize, indigo and timber, the alternatives the British pressed the Gold Coasters to produce, were not so profitable. Coffee and cotton were total failures. Only palm oil sold well. The British Government gave grants to help pay for local defence and administration until the new products began to prosper, but for decades derived no benefit and were minded to withdraw. The missionaries brought results only slowly and not primarily in the form of profits.

The British traders in the Gold Coast forts asked the Government in London to provide defence and proper administration. The response was an economical device: in 1830 one man was appointed a President of the Joint Council of the British Forts. His name was Captain George Maclean. His task was to maintain the forts and defend the traders. He proved, however, to be a great judge and spent most of his time adjudicating. Bulwer Lytton, the novelist, described him as 'a dry, reserved, hard-headed Scotchman, of indefatigable activity – not of much perceptible talent'. Since London was indifferent, Maclean's seventeen years of shrewd and parsimonious administration shaped Britain's role in the area. Disputing chiefs and traders came to him from all parts of the Gold Coast for his patient and honest arbitration, even though he had no power to enforce his judgments. With the decline of the business in slaves and gold, the traders of the rival European nations departed. Through Maclean's influence an informal British protectorate developed over the states near the coast.

In 1852 Maclean's successor called an assembly of chiefs and elders and persuaded them to place themselves under the formal protection of Queen Victoria and vote a poll-tax of one shilling a head to be collected by officers appointed by the British Governor, to pay for education, law courts, roads and medical aid. The money was not collected, but the arrangement shows the readiness of southern chiefs in intermittent need of military help against the Ashanti to place their trust in the British. This was an important step towards Britain's decision, in 1874, to declare the coastal area a colony.

It almost did not happen. The need to guard the sea route to India and to provide fresh vegetables for ships on the long passage to the east required Britain to maintain facilities in West Africa, but the Gambia and Sierra Leone were better located than the Gold Coast for this purpose and the case for withdrawing altogether was strong. However, the lure of a monopoly over even the modest trade remaining after the abolition of slavery persuaded the Government in London to take the key step: send an army to stop the Ashanti from attacking British-protected chieftaincies, which were mostly of a group called the Fanti. A young British general, Sir Garnet Wolseley, with a force of 2,500 British soldiers and many African auxiliaries, soon overcame the Ashanti army. He burnt down their capital, Kumasi, and imposed a humiliating treaty. Ashanti, however, remained independent until the turn of the century, when it made a final attempt to assert its power, was again put down by force and this time annexed.

The British Empire transformed the fortunes of two colonies with trees transplanted from Latin America. One was the rubber tree in Malaya, the other the cocoa tree in the Gold Coast. Although the first cocoa seed was almost certainly brought in by an African from a Portuguese plantation on one of the offshore islands, it was missionaries and government botanists, in their continuing pursuit of a product to replace the vanished profits of slaves and gold, who were mainly responsible for supplying farmers with cocoa seeds. Chocolate was selling throughout the world. Cocoa proved admirably suited to the small farms which Gold Coasters in the southern half of the country hacked out of the forests. By the 1930s the Gold Coast was the world's largest producer.

Railways were built in the surge of commercial confidence that followed the declaration of the colony and made it possible for mining machinery to be imported to extract gold from deep mines and thus revive it as an export; manganese and bauxite were mined and also some diamonds; mahogany trees were exported, changing the appearance of British dining-room tables and sideboards; but above all it was cocoa that made the Gold Coast the richest territory in West Africa. The gold and slave trades had developed a sophisticated, moneyed class of city dwellers. The cocoa trade paid for an élite to be educated to standards unique in Africa, brought wealth to hundreds of thousands of farmers, and enabled the Gold Coast to become Britain's model colony.

In the 1880s, France, Germany and Belgium, seeing British traders monopolising the most profitable coasts of Africa, did their best to catch up by defining their own areas of control. But these were generally less well endowed and less densely populated than the British areas: most of French West Africa was desert. So the scramble for Africa obliged the British to define the borders of the Gold Coast and to assert that they were thoroughly administering the areas within. The British instinct – to stick to the coast, work up a profitable trade and intervene in native affairs as little as possible – was overridden by agreements reached at conferences in Europe defining which countries controlled which regions. Were the British to fail to demonstrate control of the interior, their rivals were keen to move in. To prevent this in the Gold Coast the British conquered an area beyond Ashanti which became known as the Northern Territories. The name Gold Coast, which had been appropriate for the two hundred and fifty miles of harbour-less coastline with forts every ten miles, was now applied to areas with no gold, no coast and no great interest for their new British rulers.

The scramble made the British think about their colonial system. Most African states, particularly in the area now administered by the Governor of the Gold Coast, had well-established systems of tribal authority, under which chiefs had to obtain the consent of village headmen and the headmen the consent of the villagers themselves before decisions affecting them all were taken. The British had intervened to stop the slave trade, outlaw human sacrifice and secure safe passage for traders. Otherwise they let the tribes run their own affairs, corrected by the occasional destruction of a rebellious capital by naval guns or a punitive military expedition. Hilaire Belloc accurately summarised the late nineteenth- and early twentieth-century British method of colonial administration:

> Whatever happens we have got
> The Maxim gun and they have not.

This rough and ready procedure was now marginally humanised and dignified by a theory. Sir Frederick Lugard, formerly a captain in the Indian army, later the Colonial Office official largely responsible for conquering northern Nigeria to forestall the French, became acknowledged as the leading expert on colonial administration by making a virtue of necessity. Having neither the funds nor the trained administrators to run his conquests in an orderly, European manner, he called the alternative 'the system of indirect rule'. British administrators greeted Lugard's theory with the delight of Molière's Monsieur Jourdain on being told he had for forty years been speaking prose. Lugard went on to become a Lord.

In the Gold Coast his system worked reasonably well. When Britain annexed the territory in 1874, many of the coastal élite of Africans from chiefly families were angered: they had learned from George Maclean how to manage European-style courts and considered the imposition of British sovereignty unnecessary. They found, however, that the British needed them to run offices, medical centres and schools and they had begun to congregate, like the Congress in India, in the British colonial administration. Then British officials began to arrive to take the senior posts to which these Africans aspired. What was seen in London as clearly a step forward, to many sophisticated Gold Coast Africans was a step back. As the administration grew larger, the proportion of Africans in senior posts fell from a fifth of the total in 1883 to a twentieth in 1926. Consequently men who had hoped to serve the Government began to turn their energy to opposing it.

When a bill was introduced to take unused or common land into public ownership, the organisation that successfully resisted it developed into the Aborigines' Rights Protection Society, the first western-type political organisation in tropical Africa. It was an alliance between lawyers and businessmen on the one hand and their cousins the coastal chiefs on the other, seeking elected African representatives on the Legislative Council. The Gold Coast Legco had since 1850 advised the Governor on local opinion to assist him in making laws and since 1861 had normally included a full-blooded African. By 1901 its membership was four officials, four nominated non-officials, two of them African, and the Governor and Chief Justice. It

*Sir Frederick Lugard, conqueror of Uganda and northern Nigeria and author of* The Dual Mandate *(1922), the bible of colonial administrators in Africa.*

was through securing an elected African majority that the Gold Coast élite hoped to take control of their country.

In 1919 Sir Gordon Guggisberg was appointed Governor. Like George Maclean, he was a soldier who found the Gold Coast chiefs likeable and trustworthy. A former army engineer in the Gold Coast Survey, Guggisberg at the end of the 1914–18 war was an unemployed brigadier-general. He secured the governorship with a clear statement to the Colonial Office's selection committee that he was determined to bring about major changes. The sales of cocoa were by now generating sufficient revenue to enable him to do most of what he had planned and to carry the African élite with him. He brought about the construction of Takoradi harbour, the first deep water port, allowing merchant ships to dispense with the former practice of anchoring off the coast and conveying goods over the surf in small boats; he planned and launched Achimota College, the first degree-level institution in black Africa (it entered its brightest pupils for London University external degrees); he built a modern hospital at Korle Bu, completed the Accra–Kumasi railway line and more than three thousand miles of motor roads. He worked according to the principles of Lugard, under whom he had served in

Nigeria: he himself decided what needed doing and enlisted the support of the chiefs.

Nearly thirty years after independence, Guggisberg's statue still stood in the centre of Accra, his vigour in seeking improvement still respected. But he drove the new class of lawyers and doctors, the urban intelligentsia, into a state of simmering discontent. While he gave each of the three principal towns of the coast, Accra, Cape Coast and Sekondi, a member on the Legislative Council elected by ratepayers, he made sure they were thoroughly outnumbered by representatives of the chiefs, the white traders and the Government.

Yet inevitably the Lugard–Guggisberg system, including measures to stimulate both trade and education, enlarged the class of urban Africans wanting control of their own affairs. Meanwhile Guggisberg was concerned to protect the majority, the rural, tribal Africans, from the quick-talking traders, lawyers and journalists of Accra. Thus in the 1920s and 1930s, Gold Coast governments were progressive in practical policy but conservative in the distribution of power. After Guggisberg retired in 1928 some young nationalists began to demand complete and immediate autonomy. The Gold Coast newspaper the *African Morning Post* carried such stirring calls to the youth of Africa to assert themselves that its Nigerian editor Nnamdi Azikiwe

*Sir Gordon Guggisberg (left) with colleagues from Ceylon, Barbados and the Colonial Office, in Downing Street, 1927.*

(later first President of his country) was fined and imprisoned in 1936 for sedition. The sentences were soon quashed by the Court of Appeal and he later wrote an affectionate portrait of the Governor who had him prosecuted. The threat that the young radicals of the Gold Coast would come into violent conflict with both the chiefs and the British was never quite realised. In the 1930s the paternalism of Lugard and Guggisberg still worked.

Towards the end of the decade British policy in Africa was critically reviewed by a retired Indian Civil Servant, Lord Hailey. He was Governor of the Punjab for four years and then of the United Provinces, the highest post in the service, for six. A committee of Empire governments and scholarly trusts then employed him on a fresh task: to survey the entire continent of Africa and advise whether it was satisfactorily governed. His *African Survey* was published in 1938 and, with all the discretion of a great mandarin, demanded the down-grading of Lugard's system of indirect rule. Hailey described the African native authorities as no more than 'executive powers for the purpose of local government' and rejected them as a basis for political evolution. 'Africans,' he argued 'must before long be given a material addition to their very limited representation in the legislative councils.' He wanted Africans appointed to the colonial administrative service and said the best place to begin would be the Gold Coast.

Hailey's arguments impressed many, including Malcolm MacDonald, appointed Colonial Secretary in 1938, who began the slow process of persuading all the governors, attorneys-general, finance officers and district commissioners in the sixteen British-run territories in Africa that the old order would have to change. The start of the 1939–45 world war impeded MacDonald's preaching of Hailey's gospel, but in 1941 a new Governor, Sir Alan Burns, was appointed to the Gold Coast and he promptly acted on some of Hailey's recommendations, appointing Africans to the administrative service and to his Executive Council.

As soon as the war was over Burns brought a new constitution into effect. Of the thirty-one members of the Gold Coast legislature, twenty-two were now to be Africans, five directly elected by ratepayers in the coastal towns, thirteen nominated by chiefs in provincial councils, four nominated by the Governor. This looked like a first step towards the Hailey line and it was at first welcomed by the leading Gold Coast politicians.

For Dr J. B. Danquah it seemed that his moment had come. A member of a chiefly family, he had studied at London University, acquired a PhD, written a highly regarded book, *Akan Laws and Customs*, and qualified as a barrister at the Inner Temple. He had organised the Gold Coast Youth Conference, the most radical body of educated Africans in the early 1940s, demanding immediate steps towards dominion status. It was he who had the idea of dropping the colonial name Gold Coast and calling the territory Ghana, after the earliest known Negro empire. With colleagues from the youth conference he had submitted evidence in 1940 which was sufficiently impressive for Lord Hailey to arrange to meet him.

*Sir Alan Burns arriving to take the salute at the victory march-past in Accra, May 1945.*

The good relations between the 'intellectuals' of the coastal towns and the traditional chiefs were cemented by Danquah and some others like him. He understood and belonged to both camps, as he showed when his half-brother, Nana Sir Ofori Atta, a paramount chief, moderniser, member of the Gold Coast Legislative Council since 1915 and one of the first Africans to be knighted, died in 1943. The tribal practice of the Ashanti required a human sacrifice as part of the obsequies of a great chief. A village chief was ritually killed. Burns insisted on a thorough investigation and eight men were charged with the murder. Danquah organised their defence with great ingenuity (mostly through political pressure on London and obfuscation) until eventually only three of the eight were hanged.

Although he was a chiefs' nominee to the new Legislative Council in 1946, Danquah learned the lesson of Lord Hailey. During the war African soldiers recruited in the Gold Coast had been flown to East Africa to defend the British territories there against the threat of an Italian attack and two West African divisions fought alongside British and Indian forces against the Japanese in Burma. These men returned to the Gold Coast with the expectations of victors. In a total Gold Coast population at the start of the war of fewer than four million, more than 65,000 experienced military service of some kind – a significant proportion of the young males, particularly in the towns where many of them looked for work on their return.

Britain's war-time deputy Prime Minister, Clement Attlee, had told the West African Students Union in London that the undertaking in the Atlantic Charter about self-determination applied to all races, black, brown and white. Attlee was now Britain's Prime Minister and some students from London returned to tell their fellow Gold Coasters that they were not being given what they were promised. On the contrary, immediately after the war economic conditions in the Gold Coast deteriorated. Prices rose, demobilised servicemen could not find jobs, transport and machinery to revive the export industries were unobtainable. In an effort to harness the upsurge of discontent in the country Danquah and a group of colleagues

*Dr Joseph Danquah. The British hoped he would be the first African to head the Government of the Gold Coast. He died in irons, imprisoned by President Nkrumah, in 1965.*

turned against the new constitution and in 1947 set up a new party, the United Gold Coast Convention (UGCC). They looked around for a vigorous, young organiser to be their paid secretary and were told of a student in London who had all the qualifications. His name was Kwame Nkrumah. Danquah – a cantankerous lawyer – wrote to invite him to take the job and arranged for him to be sent the money for his fare.

## 'Seek Ye First the Political Kingdom', 1948–1957

On Saturday, 28 February 1948 a riot in Accra sparked a change in the course of African history. Ex-servicemen, angry that they had not been paid their war bonus, wanted to complain to the Governor. The police persuaded their leaders to march to the secretariat office instead to hand in a petition. The timing and route were agreed. The marchers assembled at the Legion ex-servicemen's club, where, in the way of old comrades, they had a few drinks. When the march started the leaders soon lost control and the straggle of over two thousand supporters abandoned the agreed route and set out for Christianborg Castle, the once Danish slaving fort that was now the Governor's residence. The small police force that rushed to the Christianborg crossroads to try to stop them, two white officers and a dozen African constables, met with threats and stone-throwing.

*Slave fort turned Governor's residence. Built by the Portuguese and captured in 1657 by the Danes, who named it Christianborg Castle, it was bought by the British in 1850.*

When we got to the crossroads [one of the marchers, Mike Adjivon,

remembered] we were held up. We were then marching in a column, and all we saw was a resistance. The British Superintendent of Police, Mr Imray, would not allow us to further our advance to the castle.

The Superintendent, Colin Imray, had ordered the marchers to halt. He recalled:

My own men behind me I think were probably stunned by the general sequence of events. The crowd started to move forward again. They came very close, perhaps twenty to twenty-five yards. I gave the order to fire, and nothing happened at all. We were obviously going to get overrun at any moment. I retreated back onto the firing party and tore a rifle out of the hands of one of the men, and I myself fired at the man in front, who was urging the crowd forward with a sort of wooden bugle which he was blowing. And I killed him. I think I fired a total of another five shots. And the crowd turned around and made off.

The man with the bugle was killed instantly; another died in hospital; four were wounded. The demonstrators rushed into the trading quarter of Accra.

One of their complaints was that the European firms which during the war had received licences to import goods and which therefore dominated trade were exploiting world shortages to make grossly excessive profits. A boycott of such firms had recently become effective and before the ex-servicemen reached the trading quarter, Accra youths had started action. The offices and shops of the United Africa Company (part of the Anglo-Dutch Unilever organisation and the biggest trading company in West Africa) were set on fire. Other European and Lebanese firms were burned and looted. Next morning the rioters battered down the gates of the prison at Usher Fort. James Moxon, then a District Commissioner in Accra, remembers:

We brought out the fire brigade but there was little we could do. We did save a few buildings from burning but some of the citizens were actually slashing the hoses with cutlasses. So we had to arm the fire brigade.

On the Monday riots were breaking out in other towns, including Kumasi, the capital of Ashanti. By the time this whirlwind was exhausted, twenty-nine people had been killed, 237 injured and the trading district of Accra was in ruins.

When the violence began in Accra, Dr Danquah and his organisation's new secretary, Kwame Nkrumah, were some seventy miles away in the small coastal town of Saltpond. On learning of the shooting and clashes they drove to Accra and held a meeting with UGCC colleagues to plan how to take advantage of the day's events. Danquah, a great drafter of protests, wrote a telegram of nearly a thousand words to the Colonial Secretary in London, offering the services of the UGCC working committee to take over an interim government and ending, 'God Save the King and *Floreat* United Gold Coast'. Nkrumah sent shorter versions to the United Nations and newspapers in London, New York and Moscow.

The Government in Accra were completely surprised by the riots. Sir Alan Burns had retired in August 1947, applauded throughout the Gold Coast for the liberal constitution he had just introduced. Indeed Burns's last gubernatorial memorandum to his staff – sent to every British official in the Gold Coast – embodies the best that British colonial administration under the post-war Labour Government aspired to:

> The fundamental policy of this Government is to educate the people of the Gold Coast, both individually and collectively, so that they may be able to stand on their own feet without support, to manage their own affairs without supervision, and to determine their own future for themselves . . . Our principal duty is to use such superior training or qualifications as we may possess to help and educate our African colleagues to take an ever-increasing share of public responsibility . . . I am aware that there are some 'die-hards' who consider that we are moving too fast in giving greater political power to the Colonial peoples and in the Africanisation of the Service. If there are any such 'die-hards' in the Public Service of the Gold Coast I suggest to them that they should consider seriously whether they can conscientiously continue to serve a Government with whose policy they are in fundamental disagreement. For this policy is clear and there is no prospect of it being changed except in the direction of still faster progress.

The happy, model colony seemed in no need of an urgent replacement, so the new Governor, Sir Gerald Creasy, a Colonial Office desk man since 1920 with no previous field experience, did not arrive until January 1948, five months after Burns's departure. Creasy was still learning his way when the riots erupted. His advisers, convinced that, under Burns's leadership, they had achieved a daring and welcome leap forward in African administration, were baffled.

Burns and the senior colleagues he had left behind had not liked Danquah, partly because of his stratagems to save the perpetrators of human sacrifice from the gallows, partly because of his two-faced attitude to the new constitution. Communists had seized power in Czechoslovakia a few days before the Gold Coast riots and Creasy's senior officials soon convinced him that Danquah and his new party must have planned the riots, that they had 'links with the Communist organisation overseas', that part of the riots followed 'a pattern familiar . . . when the Communists are seeking to seize power', that 'their ends were revolutionary' and that there was a danger of terrorism and assassination (quotations from the Governor's report on the riots). The Governor had Danquah, Nkrumah and the four other leading members of the UGCC removed to the Northern Territories. No evidence was produced to enable charges to be brought against them and the police who arrested them showed some doubt about the propriety of the action. William Ofori-Atta, one of the six, commented:

We were not expecting to be arrested, but we were. We weren't very angry because the police came and said, 'We don't really know whether you are the cause of it, but your presence here does not seem to conduce to peace, so we will take you away.'

Detention turned the group for the first time into national heroes. Seized by panic, Creasy asked for more troops, declared a State of Emergency and prepared for a struggle.

In London the reactions of two decision-makers were different. One was Arthur Creech Jones, the Colonial Secretary, who had long believed in bringing colonised peoples as fast as possible to independence. He was a former official in Ernest Bevin's Transport and General Workers' Union and had in the 1930s been the MP who kept most in touch with Africa, regularly asking awkwardly well-informed Parliamentary questions at a time when nobody else was interested. He helped prod the Labour Party forward from its simple view that Britain should not have any colonies towards a range of policies designed to help the tribes of Africa to acquire the skills and institutions needed to run modern national states. Once he became Colonial Secretary, Creech Jones was looking for a chance to carry his policies into effect.

His even more daring ally was the young, left-wing head of the Africa division of the Colonial Office, Andrew Cohen, a Cambridge classicist who became Britain's most effective anti-colonialist. He was physically huge, like an elephant, always bursting into rooms, his hands full of stuffed briefcases and his keys or the rim of his Homburg clenched between his teeth. Unlike Creech Jones, Cohen came from a wealthy and well-connected background. The modest, quiet minister, who was hopeless in the House of Commons but clear on the principles he was determined to pursue, and the superior, self-confident civil servant, who was equally dominant in committees and at dinner parties, made an odd but highly effective couple.

Creech Jones and Cohen were frustrated because change was not easily initiated from their offices in Great Smith Street. Each colony was self-governing, subject to only a tenuous oversight from London. So long as a colony ran calmly, raising enough revenue to pay its bills and causing no awkward questions to be asked in Parliament, the Colonial Office could do little to intervene. Creech Jones and Cohen had tried their best, issuing circulars and holding conferences. Their argument for change was simple. Post-war Britain was desperately hard-up and needed the colonies to raise their profits by modernisation and investment. This meant getting some Africans to do the growing, packing, manufacturing, transporting and clerking that were required and others to co-operate in assigning land, planning roads and clearing administrative blockages. All this called for Africans to run the local government and public services in an innovative, energetic spirit. The urban, educated African could help; Lugard's friends, the traditional chiefs, could not. A new system of government would

*Sir Andrew Cohen moved in 1951 from the Colonial Office to be Governor of Uganda. Here he addresses the Great Lukiko, the parliament of Buganda, at Kampala.*

therefore have to be introduced throughout the African empire. It involved nation-building hand in hand with educated Africans.

When Creech Jones and Cohen advanced these ideas to a Cambridge conference of colonial governors they faced revolt. Lord Milverton, Governor of Nigeria, and Sir Philip Mitchell of Kenya objected that the introduction of democracy would undermine imperial authority: loyal Africans would be driven into the arms of extreme and irresponsible nationalists. Cohen's reply, his favourite slogan in this campaign, was, 'Self-government is better than good colonial government'. The governors were not impressed. Cohen, who had a hand in all policy developments in Colonial Africa, had helped draft Sir Alan Burns's memorandum quoted on page 368. Because of the comparatively advanced social and educational state of Gold Coast Africans, Burns was able to back the Smith Street radicals. But Milverton and Mitchell and several other governors objected that Africanisation, like democratisation, would corrupt colonial government from top to bottom. Creech Jones and Cohen, convinced that responsible Africans given power now would remain friends of Britain but that delay would lead to aggressive demands from leaders with no sympathy for the Empire, bided their time. By the end of 1947 five governors of colonies in Africa were due to retire. Their successors would have the right attitudes.

The shooting of demonstrators by the police in Accra followed by riots that killed twenty-nine presented Creech Jones and Cohen with their opportunity. Such an episode called for a judicial enquiry and the choice of the man to preside over it could be decisive. A traditional, conservative judge would present the detailed facts and do all he could to avoid overt political judgments. Creech Jones and Cohen, in consultation with the Lord Chancellor's office, chose someone of another type. Aiken Watson was a recorder (a junior judge) who had stood as a Labour candidate in the 1935 general election and was a supporter of the Fabian Society, of whose Colonial Research Bureau Creech Jones had been Chairman and Cohen an influential friend (as a civil servant he was not allowed to join even a gradualist political organisation). Colonial leaders when in London visited the Bureau's office near Parliament to meet Labour MPs and sympathisers.

Watson was sent with two fellow commissioners (one of whom was also on the committee of the Fabian Colonial Research Bureau) to tour the Gold Coast and question witnesses. When he came back to London he did not, as is usual in a judicial inquiry, retire to the seclusion of his chambers or a quiet library. Extraordinarily for a lawyer drafting a report which might criticise Colonial Office staff, he wrote it in the Colonial Office. Here he had been briefed by Andrew Cohen before departing and was further briefed now. The report has Cohen's fingerprints all over it.

Cohen had secured Watson wide terms of reference – 'to report on the . . . disturbances . . . and their underlying causes: and to make recommendations on any matter arising' – and encouraged him to interpret them liberally. Instead of submitting their report to the Governor, who had nominally appointed them, Watson and his colleagues wrote the Governor a note: 'The nature of our recommendations, involving as they do proposals to amend the constitution, appear to us as more appropriate for address to the Secretary of State for the Colonies. Accordingly . . . we have adopted this course.' Creasy had not known how to handle the riots. He was equally at sea with a report which plainly had authority much greater than his own.

The Watson report reads less like an inquiry into a few days of rioting than a total survey of the Gold Coast Government, economy and society: 'The ordinary type of report . . . might well be useless . . . a broad outline of remedies appeared to be called for.' The breadth is breathtaking. The Burns constitution, though less than two years old and widely welcomed, was damned as:

> . . . outmoded at birth. The concession of an African elected majority in the legislature, in the absence of any real political power, provided no outlet for a people eagerly emerging into political consciousness . . . The constitution and government must be so reshaped as to give every African of ability an opportunity to help govern the country . . . In all appointments or promotions in the public services the first question to be asked is: 'Is there an African capable of filling the appointment?'

Watson and his colleagues state, 'We do not propose to draft a constitution', but then spell out in considerable detail how the new constitution they consider essential should provide for local authorities, regional councils, town councils, the Gold Coast Assembly, the Executive Council and the role of the Governor. They want the Government as far as possible to be like that in the United Kingdom: ministers should be salaried, full-time politicians, chosen by the Governor but collectively responsible to the assembly; instead of being all officials, as at that time, the majority of ministers should be elected; each should head a department whose civil servants, through the Permanent Secretary, would be responsible to him.

Many colonial officials in the Gold Coast and some civil servants in the Colonial Office in London thought the Watson report a gross over-reaction. They considered that the riots had been about the ex-servicemen's war bonus and high prices and that an economic response by the Government would have been enough to calm the place down; although the Gold Coast Africans were the most advanced in the continent, fewer than ten per cent of them were literate and the slow educational process of working the Burns constitution was what they needed; to reward troublemakers would only encourage more of them; rapid constitutional advance of the kind recommended by Watson and by Cohen's conferences and memoranda would put power into the hands of Africans before they were ready for it, with disastrous consequences for both the British Empire and the colonised peoples.

Cohen not only thought the opposite, he considered it vital to take rapid and irreversible steps in the Gold Coast and Nigeria in case the return of a Conservative government in Britain should stop political advance. Remembering how during the war Churchill had undermined the position of Congress as government-in-waiting in India, causing the transfer of power in 1947 to be rushed, destructive of Indian unity and murderous, he was determined to prevent such mistakes in Africa. Creech Jones did not go quite so far. He said he was startled by the radicalism of the Watson report and felt bound, honourable minister that he was, to defend Sir Gerald Creasy publicly. However, 1947–8 was a busy time for Creech Jones. He was overwhelmed by the problems of Palestine, for which he had to answer in the United Nations, the House of Commons and the Cabinet. The supervision of the Watson commission and the implementation of its recommendations were therefore largely handled by Cohen. The Labour Cabinet approved of Cohen's views so Creech Jones did not need to refer his decisions to ministerial colleagues, though he kept Attlee informed. Both the Minister and the Government were content to take their lead from a strong-minded civil servant.

Cohen used the Watson report to stand the Gold Coast Government on its head. Whereas Governor Creasy had in March detained the six main UGCC leaders without trial or the right to appeal to a judge – 'the assumption of such a power was excessive to the occasion and we unhesitatingly condemn it', wrote Watson – a few months later five of the six were invited to sit on an all-African Committee to propose constitutional reforms, chaired by a fifty-five-year-old African judge. By the time the committee published its proposals, largely following the Watson blueprint, Cohen had discreetly removed Sir Gerald Creasy from the scene (having him appointed to the less arduous post of Governor of Malta) and not only brought in a new Governor, Sir Charles Arden-Clarke, but also promoted a new Deputy Governor, Reginald Saloway, who had served through the final stages of independence in India.

The shared purpose of Creech Jones and Cohen was to strengthen the hand of Danquah and the moderate leaders of the UGCC by giving them a full share in government before it was too late. Already in Malaya a Communist insurgency had compelled the British Government to send thousands of troops who were bogged down in the tropical jungle. In the Gold Coast the danger of the nationalist movement's becoming dominated by Communists could be forestalled, they believed, by rapidly anointing Danquah and his colleagues with the oil of constitutional authority. Creech Jones told Arden-Clarke before he left London, 'The Gold Coast is on the edge of revolution. We are in danger of losing it.' The Governor's first job was to introduce the new constitution that would bind the Gold Coast again to the Empire. The young secretary of the UGCC, Kwame Nkrumah, possessed a Communist Party membership card. With his enthusiasm for Marxist ideas and his dangerous skill as a mass orator, he could, they believed, be excluded from the political scene.

Dr Danquah and the other UGCC leaders were already uneasy about Nkrumah's personal ambition and left-wing beliefs. He had been recommended to them as a vigorous young organiser, but as soon as he arrived it was plain that he was something more. His background, as the son of a poor fisherman in a coastal village, gave no clue to his political effectiveness. His years working his way through universities in the United States, where he was influenced by the movement for Negro rights and the ideas of equality and freedom, equally do not explain his phenomenal powers. He was a brilliant political leader whose abilities exactly matched the needs of the time. He had not concealed from the UGCC leaders that he considered them reactionaries, with whom he would co-operate only temporarily. While they had readily accepted seats on the constitutional commission from which Nkrumah was excluded, he proved the more astute politician. The thirty Africans on the commission were tied down in meetings redrafting subclauses, moving closer to those in authority. Nkrumah toured the country building up the local UGCC youth societies. In June 1949, he announced the launching of a new party, the Convention People's Party (CPP), with himself as leader. Nkrumah, the most effective mass recruiter for Dr Danquah's UGCC, now took most of the recruits with him.

When Nkrumah formed local branches he kept in touch with them, listened to their anxieties, encouraged them to keep minutes and organise themselves efficiently. He took account of their views in forming his own policies. He did not lightly leave the position of secretary of the UGCC but waited, continuing to work with people whose moderation irked him, until he was sure that most of his UGCC recruits would follow him. The recruits were of a new political class.

The idea of education as the principal means to advancement had taken hold of parents and children throughout the Gold Coast, but few could go to the excellent secondary schools on the coast that had helped educate Nkrumah and Danquah. So they did the next best thing. By 1948, according to an official report, half the children of infant–junior school age in Ashanti and the coastal area were in schools, many of them newly set up, unregistered, unsupervised, their teachers untrained. These semi-educated elementary school leavers were scarcely employable; they worked if they were lucky as market-stall assistants, messengers, mates to motor-mechanics or carpenters. The language they wanted to hear and, with difficulty, read was English. The local party leaders who could hold their support were primary school teachers, clerks, stall-holders, one-lorry transport contractors. Nkrumah was the first political leader in black Africa who successfully cultivated this new territory.

Thus by 1949 a remarkable change occurred. Dr Danquah and his colleagues secured most of what they had been asking for in the way of constitutional advance and felt obliged publicly to defend some of the compromises to which they had agreed, but their political base had been taken from under them. Nkrumah had two close colleagues with whom he shared all decisions, Komla Gbedema, a self-made businessman, and Kojo Botsio, an Oxford graduate. In the CPP they were the triumvirate and they chose as their slogan the phrase best calculated to separate them from the UGCC, 'Self-government NOW'. The proposed new constitution, by contrast, promised self-government fairly soon. The CPP leaders judged that intransigent rejection of whatever had been agreed between the imperialist British and the African élite was the way to keep their followers' enthusiasm. Nkrumah had read about Gandhi, always refusing to take office, always voicing the instincts of his followers. Gandhi was the model for this phase of his career.

The new Governor, Arden-Clarke, presented to the Gold Coast the constitutional proposals which had the support of all responsible political leaders. Illegal opposition to them would, he warned, be severely dealt with. Nkrumah and his CPP produced a Gandhian response: the proposals were 'bogus and fraudulent' and must be resisted by civil disobedience with, as a last resort, 'strikes, boycotts and non-cooperation based on the principles of absolute non-violence'. Nkrumah added that he might call his supporters to take 'Positive Action'.

This ill-defined threat led Reginald Saloway, the Deputy Governor, to persuade Arden-Clarke that Indian experience must be brought to bear on the Government's side too. Remembering the Gandhi–Irwin talks (see Chapter 1, p. 45), Saloway overcame the predominant official view that the CPP were a rabble and that to talk to them would undermine the authority of the chiefs. He sent for Nkrumah and said afterwards that he had convinced him that the election to be held when the new constitution took effect would be fairly run and that the CPP should put up candidates. Sir George Sinclair, head of the Gold Coast Government's intelligence committee, was present at the meeting because Nkrumah was regarded as a menace to public order:

> Saloway was quite superb. 'Positive Action' had dominated Nkrumah's *Accra Evening News*, his newspaper, for weeks and weeks. Saloway said that, from his short knowledge of the Gold Coast, the claim that they would run this as a non-violent campaign was an illusion. It would lead to violence and to bloodshed, which were unnecessary. The constitutional commission had promised general elections within six months, and Reg Saloway said, 'If your claim to represent the vast mass of people in this country is substantial then put it to the test in six months, instead of putting the country to violence now. That is a clear choice that you have. But if you choose to launch "Positive Action" now, I tell you it will end in violence and any bloodshed will be on your head.'

Then, at Nkrumah's request, Saloway put his case to other members of the CPP executive committee; but, Saloway wrote later, 'Dr Danquah taunted Nkrumah with having sold himself to the Colonial Secretary and thus infuriated the rank and file of the CPP, who forced Nkrumah to retract.' With the public aroused and the new railway and lorry workers' unions declaring a general strike, Nkrumah and his colleagues had little choice if they were to retain the political initiative.

On Sunday, 8 January 1950, Nkrumah announced that Positive Action was to start from midnight, taking the form of a general strike and a boycott of British goods. As in India, the leader's instruction on non-violence was not completely obeyed: rioting and disorder broke out. Sir Robert Armitage, Financial Secretary in the Governor's Executive Council, recalled:

> They were creating a great deal of trouble, turning people against the chiefs and against government officials. You could do nothing except stop it. And stop it we did. I attended a meeting with Arden-Clarke and Branigan, the Attorney General, and we decided that there had to be a declaration of a State of Emergency. All the ringleaders were immediately arrested. Almost overnight about a hundred people were taken into custody. There were no deaths except for two policemen and the whole affair fizzled out in a matter of a few days.

This time Nkrumah was tried and found guilty of fostering an illegal strike and of sedition, for which he was sentenced to three years in prison. The Governor insisted that the law had impartially taken its course and that anyone could have attended the court to hear the evidence of Nkrumah's guilt. Most Africans, however, were convinced that the sentences were political, that Nkrumah and his CPP colleagues had been cast into prison because they alone challenged British imperial control. The effect was again to raise the popularity of the imprisoned men. Arden-Clarke, in a letter to his family, wrote, 'I have been preoccupied with our local Hitler and his *Putsch*.'

The British Government now acted in a way which was regarded by some as brave, by others as foolhardy. Although widely urged to be cautious, to use Positive Action, the riots and the imprisonments as justification for delay, Cohen, the elephantine force, pressed firmly ahead. The recommendations of the constitutional commission were, with some modifications, accepted: the Government announced that an African-dominated Assembly was to be elected and from the largest group within it African ministers were to be appointed. Arden-Clarke said he did not think the first election would produce a single party able to maintain a majority in the House or elect a government leader, but Dr Danquah and his UGCC colleagues, having helped shape the constitution, believed they would now inherit power. With Nkrumah and his friends in prison, Danquah said, 'the wolf had been driven away'. The authority of the wolf over his party was, however, undiminished. Nkrumah acted on Saloway's promise that the election would be fairly conducted and sent his party colleagues streams of messages, mostly written on prison lavatory paper, about how the campaign should be managed.

Much now turned on the coincidence that as Nkrumah entered prison one of his two closest colleagues, Komla Gbedema, was coming out. Imprisoned for an earlier offence, Gbedema had been unable to take part in the Positive Action campaign or to be sentenced with Nkrumah and the other leaders for causing the riots. He now proved to have a genius for propaganda and party organisation.

> I realised that somebody had to keep Nkrumah's image before the people [he recalled] and I felt that was my duty. I had a life-size photograph made of him which I carried as part of my paraphernalia, going round the country. Raising it I let the people see, here's the man who is in jail, we must go on fighting. His body is in jail, but his spirit must go marching on.

Gbedema also invented the title Prison Graduate.

> When I came out of jail [he explained] my father and a friend were the only two people who met me at the prison gates. I didn't like that. So I thought other people who were then in jail should come out as heroes. And I organised the prison graduate idea.

Those who had been to prison for the cause were honoured by the CPP with the prison graduate insignia, a white hat and a Northern-Territories-style smock. Gbedema went on:

> The first few had maybe a hundred people to meet them. But after the first two or three the supporters came out in thousands. And we paraded the streets. The Government didn't like the idea so they thought they should stop us. But the nationalist tide was moving so high, they didn't want to do it by force. They thought they could let the prisoner go some time before he was due to come out. I remember the first instance, we went to his house,

he had been let out at about four o'clock in the morning. We went and brought him back to the prison gate and performed our ceremonies there.

Government officials began preparing for the first general election on an adult franchise ever held in black Africa – marking out constituency boundaries, preparing lists of eligible voters, arranging where polling stations would be. The sudden grant of the parliamentary franchise to an illiterate, tribal African population, utterly remote from the political experience of western nations, was without precedent. In rural areas the preparations were viewed with suspicion as evidence of the Government's predatory intentions. The antagonism of local people was repeatedly calmed by the CPP. One junior registration officer reported: 'At eight villages I had a nil registration. When I go they turn me out. They say they will not register until they have CPP registration forms.'

In this tedious part of the democratic process the UGCC leaders showed little interest. This was a worry to the Government. Although the constitution was designed to bring the UGCC alliance of 'intellectuals' and educated chiefs to power, the urban constituencies, where direct one-man-one-vote elections would be held, required energetic canvassing. In the rural areas of Ashanti and the Northern Territories indirect elections were to be held in which local worthies, chosen by peasants who knew them well, would not so easily be swayed by facile southerners. Even here, however, Gbedema, following Nkrumah's energetic lead, proved more effective than Danquah and the UGCC élite at visiting, listening to and winning over the emerging rural organisations, particularly associations of cocoa farmers, trade unions and the powerful 'market mammies'.

Joe Appiah, an Ashanti friend of Nkrumah from his student days in London and a prominent CPP member, said of Gbedema and his organising teams:

> When they went out to the villages they sat down together with the verandah boys [who slept on the verandahs of the rich because they had no homes of their own], drank palm wine in street bars, stood on street corners with them and generally were prepared to throw their lot in with them. Now this Danquah and the others were not prepared to do. Nor would it have been honest if they had attempted to, because it just didn't suit them. It wasn't in their character.

Well before the election was held the Government began to fear that the CPP might win.

The extent of the victory, was, however, a surprise. Kwame Nkrumah, though in prison, was able to stand in Accra, on account of an oversight in the drafting of the election law. He received 20,780 votes. The UGCC committee member who less than four years earlier had suggested inviting him home to become the UGCC's secretary, Ako Adjei, a barrister, stood against him and received only 1,451 votes. In the indirect elections in the tribal areas the CPP won a scattering of the thirty-seven seats. Of the thirty-eight seats filled by popular ballot, Nkrumah's party won thirty-four. Komla Gbedema said of 8 February 1951:

> I remember that night very clearly, even after thirty years. In the old polo ground there were crowds, thousands of people, waiting anxiously for the results. Soon after midnight, the final results were known. The CPP had won by a large majority and Mr Saloway, who was the chief secretary, called me and said, 'Mr Gbedema, you must tell your people.' So quite unprepared I stood up and I said: 'Now at long last the people of this country have spoken the language which the imperialists understand: the language of the ballot box. We have won this election.' And the roar which came from the thousands still rings in my ears.

Sir Charles Arden-Clarke now faced a dilemma. Not only had the wrong horse won; the CPP was demanding that Nkrumah, properly convicted by a court and with two years of his sentence still to run, should be released from prison. 'The decision,' Sir Charles later wrote, 'however unpalatable, was in fact inevitable. To have refused would have undoubtedly led to a head-on collision and would have received little or no support from the UK press or Parliament.' Gbedema had a difficult time restraining victorious CPP supporters from marching to the prison and releasing Nkrumah by force. His success in doing so provides the theme for the next phase of Gold Coast history. Arden-Clarke ordered the release and invited Nkrumah to Christianborg Castle. The two men who had till now been enemies met for the first time. Nkrumah wrote five years later:

> He came towards me with his hand outstretched . . . As we both sat down I sensed that he must be feeling as alert and suspicious of me as I was of him . . . I did my best to make it clear to him that I would be prepared at all times to play my cards face upwards on the table because it was only by frankness that mutual trust and confidence could be established . . . He was, I thought, a man with a strong sense of justice and fair play, with whom I could easily be friends . . .

Arden-Clarke later wrote in *The Times*:

> The meeting was redolent with mutual suspicion and mistrust. We were like two dogs meeting for the first time, sniffing at each other with hackles half raised trying to decide whether to bite or wag our tails.

The Governor offered the man he had a few months earlier called 'our local Hitler' the post of leader of Government business. Nkrumah readily agreed to take office, under a constitution – stipulating that three British officials should serve as ministers – which during the election campaign he had described as 'bogus and fraudulent'.

Arden-Clarke and Nkrumah were quickly to form a close alliance. Many of the Governor's staff, particularly those remote from Accra, later com-

plained that he became in effect a member of the CPP. His biographer, David Rooney, writes that, in addition to being Governor, he was 'joint political leader and party manager'. The two men spent much time alone together, both determined to prevent the caution of British administrators or the eagerness of CPP supporters from destroying peaceful progress to complete self-government.

A severe test of their alliance was presented by a disease that had been killing cocoa trees since 1943. Trees affected by swollen shoot go on producing cocoa pods for two or three years, infecting neighbouring trees, before dying. A cocoa research institute was established at Tafo, just north of Accra, in 1944, but the scientists there could find no antidote. Their only advice was to cut down and burn all infected trees. Remaining trees then nearly all had a chance of surviving. Most farmers, however, refused to cut down trees which were still bearing pods. The Government's agriculture department tried to persuade them to do so; it obtained court orders requiring them; it hired gangs of labourers to chop down trees without their owners' consent. By the end of 1947, of 400 million trees in the Gold Coast, two and a half million had been destroyed, an estimated forty-five million more were infected, and the disease, spreading to some fifteen million new trees each year, threatened the country's biggest source of foreign revenue. To a farmer whose trees in spite of visible infection were still bearing pods, however, the arrival of a government gang with axes was alarming and

*Making a bang together. Sir Charles Arden-Clarke, Governor, and Dr Kwame Nkrumah, leader of Government business in the Legislative Council, jointly set off the first blast to launch a harbour development.*

tyrannical. Chiefs who normally backed the Government said publicly that there must be a plot to grow cocoa in Europe and destroy the Gold Coast's production.

Fear of 'cutting-out', as it was called, fed the riots of 1948 and became an issue in the 1951 election. A few weeks after they came to power, the new ministers explained in the Executive Council that they must stop it or the farmers would never again trust them. Arden-Clarke confronted them head on: the scientific evidence showed that compulsory cutting-out had to continue.

Nkrumah had violently attacked cutting-out and he led the majority of ministers in voting to suspend compulsion pending an official inquiry. They thought Arden-Clarke would use his veto. He did not. Three months after the election the Government stopped compulsory cutting-out. Arden-Clarke later wrote: 'Had I decided that it should continue despite the Cabinet decision, I would have had to ask for a division of troops, because there was a recent popularly elected Government out to please the farmer voter.' Although the official inquiry predictably confirmed that cutting-out was essential, Nkrumah would not give way on compulsion, though he asked local branches of the CPP to help persuade the farmers. The disease resumed its advance.

Eighteen months later, in October 1952, Nkrumah's Cabinet reintroduced compulsory cutting-out. Nkrumah announced the new policy in a broadcast: 'If there was ever a test of our fitness to control our own affairs,' he said, 'this is it.' The interval had enabled those farmers' leaders who were open-minded to appreciate the Government's case.

Over swollen shoot disease – as over almost everything else – Nkrumah and Arden-Clarke were lucky. The world cocoa price was soaring. The CPP was able to take responsibility for compulsory cutting-out because the Government had the money to pay both substantial compensation for the trees cut and grants for planting new ones, as well as for new schools, harbour developments, roads and concrete open sewers in hundreds of villages. When fellow ministers asked for money for their pet projects, the Finance Minister, Robert Armitage, was usually able to say yes. In the British Empire only Malaya was as rich.

The Gold Coast tradition of 'dash' – bringing a gift to a chief when asking a favour – encouraged ministers to get their own hands on a proportion of this money. George Levak, a civil servant in the Chief Minister's office, recalled: 'We didn't meet corruption face to face in the office but it did become reflected in the kind of people who were passing through all ministers' offices. There were a number of carpet-bagging businessmen, who made one feel uncomfortable.' Another civil servant, Sam Macdonald-Smith, said:

One case came to us in the Ministry of Communications and Works. An American chap produced some fantastic housing scheme which only cost three and a half million, something of the sort, and we examined it and were able to shoot it down. This made us very unpopular because it cut the ministers off from the 10 per cent or whatever it was that they were going to get on this contract. After one or two occasions like that, they kept these things very quiet and didn't put them to us to be examined and considered. They signed on the dotted line and then told us what was going to happen and that it was for us to put the thing into effect.

One minister resigned when it became known that he had accepted a £2,000 bribe from a contractor. Other ministers built themselves large houses in Accra – disdaining to live in the officially provided bungalows, even though the extravagant standard of their construction had caused an outcry in the press – and the relationship with a German company of Krobo Edusei, chief whip of the governing party and a founder-member of the CPP central committee, was described by an independent commission of inquiry as 'below any acceptable standard for men in the public service'. Nkrumah readily agreed to Edusei's removal from his government job as Ministerial Secretary to the Minister of Justice, Sir Patrick Branigan, who later recalled:

> When Nkrumah first asked me to take on Krobo as my junior minister in 1951 – the idea was that the junior minister should share all the work and see all the papers – I was taken aback. I explained that my office had such sensitive files on people, police recommendations and so on, that Krobo, though a great asset to the party in rallying support in Ashanti, was hardly the man. Nkrumah said, 'You needn't show him any files. Just give him an office and a telephone and make him happy.' Krobo spent his time in the office conducting party business.

Nkrumah and his principal colleagues, particularly Gbedema and Kojo Botsio, showed themselves as able as British politicians to take charge of the administration. They were also leading a nationalist movement and if they did not keep up the momentum of the advance towards independence, the CPP could lose support. The party's first slogan, 'Self-government NOW' was quickly overtaken. Nkrumah's next and most original slogan was, 'Seek ye first the political kingdom': this meant complete independence, again putting the CPP at the front of the demand for constitutional progress. The party pressed for the removal of the three British civil service members of the Cabinet (responsible for finance, justice and foreign affairs and defence) and for the rapid promotion of Africans in government jobs. It was a task, Reginald Saloway commented, 'like laying down a track in front of an oncoming express'. Arden-Clarke depended on Nkrumah to keep their Government clear of political trouble from rioters like those of 1948 and so was forced to move towards independence at Nkrumah's pace.

In 1951 Winston Churchill was re-elected Prime Minister of a Conservative Government in Britain. His Colonial Secretary, Oliver Lyttelton, agreed with him that the Gold Coast was moving too quickly out of British control and that the brake should be applied. But Creech Jones and Cohen had made delay impossible, and Cohen himself was now taking an even more direct hand in pushing Africa quickly towards independence, having become Governor of Uganda (where the Africans were less sophisticated but their political demands equally strong). He was therefore out of the Colonial Office when Lyttelton arrived.

The new Minister went to the Gold Coast to look for himself. He later wrote that he saw there, by a roadside, 'two black boys, whose combined ages could not have been twenty and who were completely naked, holding up a large blackboard. On it in impeccable copperplate was written in chalk, "Away with the three ex-officios".' Lyttelton accepted that

> . . . a successful leader in Africa had to deliver to the people large and visible constitutional gains or he would be swept aside. [But he added:] On the other hand the wiser leaders – and there were not many – realised that to fulfil a true and not a meretricious mission, the standard of life and education of their peoples must be raised. For this the help of the British and other white men was necessary, with capital, powers of organisation, skilled direction, skilled supervision and skilled workmen. If they went too far or too fast with freedom and constitutional advances, the sources of this capital and these skills would dry up.

Cohen's successor as head of the Africa division in the Colonial Office, Sir William Gorrell Barnes, agreed with his new minister.

> There would have been great advantage in slowing it a bit [he said] first of all for the benefit of the people in the Gold Coast themselves, because of the state of readiness they were in, and secondly from the point of view of the repercussions which were bound to follow elsewhere, first on the west coast and then in the rest of Africa.

Nkrumah, however, had already raised with the Governor the need to amend the year-old constitution and pressed on Lyttelton the demand for rapid further steps towards full self-government. Lyttelton did not want to listen, but Arden-Clarke persuaded him he had no choice and a year later brought detailed proposals to London. While there Arden-Clarke wrote to his mother:

> A powerful body of opinion in the highest quarters here think that I am going too far and too fast but as no one has been able to put forward an alternative policy that has the remotest prospect of working I am being allowed to have my way. Nevertheless there are those who will weep no tears if the Gold Coast comes a cropper and delude themselves with the idea that failure or breakdown in the Gold Coast will provide them with an excuse to slow down the rate of political advance in Africa. They forget that you cannot slow down a flood – the best you can hope to do is to keep the torrent within its proper channel.

Arden-Clarke had tried to dissuade members of the Gold Coast assembly from insisting on a new constitution by telling them it would require an election, in which they might lose their seats. Nevertheless by mid-1954 they had pressed the demand successfully. Lyttelton, reluctantly convinced he had no choice, persuaded the Cabinet in London that the Gold Coast should have an all-African government responsible to a legislative assembly elected by universal adult suffrage. Conservative ministers who did not like the idea consoled themselves with the thought that this was only West Africa, a steamy, unhealthy place where no whites had settled permanently and no strategic interest was affected. The Government announced in London that the new constitution, providing full internal self-government (the Governor remaining responsible only for foreign affairs and defence), was the last step before complete independence.

The election that followed, in June 1954, did not prove the simple step forward Nkrumah and Arden-Clarke had hoped. The CPP's substantial victory made a number of groups throughout the Gold Coast realise that they were about to be handed over from rule by the British to rule by Kwame Nkrumah and his 'verandah boys'. The Cabinet now contained no white men and its installation marked the beginning of a huge effort by chiefs, traditionalists, 'intelligentsia' and a number of regional groups to wrest power from Nkrumah and the CPP or to persuade the British not to leave as

*The first all-African cabinet in any colony. Seated, centre, is Nkrumah, with, as always, Kojo Botsio on his right and Komla Gbedema on his left. Standing far right is Krobo Edusei.*

they had promised. In this struggle Arden-Clarke threw his full weight behind Nkrumah and his party, while many British officials in the Northern Territories and Ashanti fought equally hard to protect their own charges. Instead of completing a smooth transition to independence, the model colony became a battleground.

The spearhead of the resistance was Ashanti, the central forest region. The Ashanti peoples had dominated the whole of the Gold Coast before the British took control. They had been the main gold merchants; they had captured slaves from other tribes for sale to the Europeans and they kept the slave trade going when the British tried to stop it; they had fought longest and hardest against British rule. Then, once they had succumbed, they rapidly became the most successful cocoa farmers. Kumasi, their capital, was a bustling market town, with a third of its inhabitants, more than in any other town of the Gold Coast, in business on their own account. Like trading peoples in Europe – the Venetians, the Flemish, the British – the Ashanti had developed a stable, flexible system of government, under which their principal ruler, the Ashantehene, consulted all subordinate rulers in a formal assembly before taking decisions. The sacred Golden Stool of the Ashanti was the symbol of their state much like the crown and sceptre in Britain. Their senatorial process of debate and consultation was so deep-rooted that, although the British abolished it when they conquered Ashanti, it persisted and revived. Thus Ashanti remained a coherent state under British rule, its Ashanteman council conservative in the manner of the Doge and his council in Venice. The prospect of all power being taken to Accra and the CPP did not appeal to them. Even the Ashantehene, who normally stood above the clash of politics, was persuaded to give his backing to the new opposition body which some of his close advisers helped form, the National Liberation Movement.

The old 'intelligentsia' joined the NLM because most of them were now out of the assembly – Dr Danquah lost his seat to the CPP in 1954 – and they resented the sight of people they thought less educated and able than themselves monopolising positions of power. The cocoa farmers joined the NLM because, while the world price for cocoa rose dizzily, the price paid to them was kept fixed by the new Finance Minister, Komla Gbedema, through the Cocoa Purchasing Company, the only organisation to which they were allowed to sell. The NLM enjoyed the energetic support of General Sir Edward Spears, former Conservative MP, a frequent writer in the London *Daily Telegraph* and board member of one of the biggest British mining companies, Ashanti Goldfields. He caused every example of corruption, inefficiency and Marxist hyperbole by Gold Coast ministers – and there were many – to be vividly presented to the public, in both Britain and the Gold Coast, where his company ran the *Ashanti Times*.

In October 1954 the national propaganda secretary of the NLM, E. Y. Baffoe, was stabbed to death in Kumasi by the regional propaganda secretary of the CPP, K. A. Twumasi Ankrah. The murder unleashed gang warfare in Ashanti between the NLM's Action Groupers and the CPP's Action Troopers. The leader of the Action Groupers, Alex Osei, said, in tones still vibrant with menace thirty years after the event:

> After Baffoe's death we decided that if they have started killing, then we shall also wake up and kill. We started vigorously with anybody. We were fighting here and there and we could do the same as they did. We swore that if anybody dares to commit a crime on any of our members, we shall revenge. And then it became a hectic game. Instead of the normal campaigning for each party, it became a threatening affair.

CPP leaders in Ashanti were attacked. Thirteen people were killed in Kumasi. CPP members of the assembly, elected only months before, were now afraid to return to Ashanti. Many CPP supporters, particularly in Ashanti, went over to the NLM.

Krobo Edusei, the CPP boss in Ashanti, became the key figure. He was a member of a chiefly family and if, like Joe Appiah and many other Ashantis, he now deserted the CPP and sided with the majority of Ashanti chiefs, the chance of Nkrumah and the CPP leading a united Gold Coast to independence looked slight. Edusei stood firm. He controlled almost all CPP patronage in Ashanti. He kept his own paramount chief loyal to the CPP, it was alleged, partly by providing government money for a piped water supply. He faced Alex Osei's gangs with his own circle of followers who were no less violent.

In mid-1955 the death of an assembly member led to a by-election in a CPP seat in Ashanti. The NLM candidate, himself a defector from the CPP, won decisively. The NLM asserted that the people had shown they no longer wanted Nkrumah's party. They called for a new nation-wide election and demanded that the negotiations for independence between the CPP government and the Colonial Office should cease.

Part of the CPP's response was to develop a personality cult. An extract from the CPP paper, the *Evening News* of 19 June 1954, is typical: 'Kwame Nkrumah, Man of Destiny, Star of Africa, Hope of Millions of down-trodden Blacks, Deliverer of Ghana, Iron Boy, Great Leader of Street Boys, personable and handsome boy from Nzima, Kwame Nkrumah has given his answer to all the twaddle and tripe and the dirty scribblers . . .' But the answer was not enough. NLM support spread throughout Ashanti with strong allies in the Northern Territories and Transvolta, the section of German Togoland that had been mandated to the Gold Coast in 1919. NLM petitions to the Governor, the Colonial Office and the Queen combined with NLM power on the ground to make it difficult for the British Government to keep its promise that the CPP would proceed to independence on the basis of the 1954 elections. The Government could not get witnesses to court to secure convictions against NLM gangs; to use force to suppress the NLM would seem to confirm the assertion of General Spears that the Government was an unpopular one-party dictatorship. Unexpectedly, on the point of inheriting sovereignty, Nkrumah and the CPP faced the prospect of having it taken from them.

Arden-Clarke was now less powerful than formerly, but as Governor he still carried weight, both in the country and the Colonial Office. He continued decisively to back Nkrumah and the CPP, partly because they had won a general election and still had a huge majority in the assembly so that he was constitutionally bound to support them, partly because the Government in London was committed to proceed to independence, and partly because Nkrumah and members of his Cabinet, particularly Nkrumah himself and Gbedema, the Finance Minister, were plainly mastering the complex skills of governing. Arden-Clarke thought as Governor he should be seen to stand publicly above the dispute between the NLM and CPP, but he did not succeed. The principal demand of the NLM was for a federal constitution, giving the regions enough autonomy to resist dictatorship from Accra. Arden-Clarke made a speech in which he said, 'There is too much talk of "federalism" and "regionalism". As a practical administrator . . . I am suspicious of "isms".' By declaring publicly what his officials in Ashanti and the Northern Territories already knew, he nailed his colours to the CPP mast.

The NLM taunted Nkrumah with being afraid to visit Ashanti. Arden-Clarke was not afraid and in March 1955 drove to Kumasi in his new, official Rolls-Royce. Among the leaflets greeting him was one purporting to advertise the post of propaganda secretary for the CPP, with a Rolls-Royce and accommodation at the castle among its perks. Victor Owusu, a lawyer and former CPP man in Ashanti, commented:

> The Ashantis had come to the conclusion that he was Nkrumah's mouthpiece and that anything he came to say he had previously discussed with Nkrumah. Therefore they decided, if Nkrumah could not visit Kumasi his surrogate shall not come.

The Governor did come. He visited the palace of the Ashantehene, who was determined that proper courtesy should be shown to the Queen's representative. However the crowds booed the Governor's arrival and, as he was leaving, in his own words:

> . . . the police had difficulty clearing the way for the car, the screaming and booing rose to a frenzy, then some people at the back of the crowd started throwing gravel and mud and stones. The Rolls received a few dents, lost a few chips of paint . . .

A bomb was placed in Nkrumah's house in Accra, but failed to kill him.

The ferocity of the anti-Government movement persuaded Nkrumah of the need for compromise, but the NLM leaders were suspicious of the invitations he sent them, believing they could get satisfaction only from London. Eventually the Colonial Secretary, Alan Lennox-Boyd, became convinced that the CPP could not be given independence as things stood.

*Nkrumah, after victory in the 1956 election had confirmed that he would be the first African to lead his country from colonial rule to independence.*

The NLM must have a chance to demonstrate the extent of their support in another general election. The CPP resisted, fearing they might lose, but Lennox-Boyd told them they had no choice.

The Gold Coast's third election in five years was therefore held in July 1956. Joe Appiah, a former close CPP colleague of Nkrumah who now stood for the NLM, said:

> I told the voters of the corruption. I told them of the burgeoning tyranny that we could foresee ahead. I told them why we had struggled for independence. I told them we did not want to sack the British Raj in order to substitute a Black Raj.

Nkrumah, Gbedema, Botsio and Edusei remained, however, the masters at winning votes. The CPP used the power of office and its skill in making local alliances to secure overall victory. Independence under the leadership of Kwame Nkrumah was now certain.

Even at the last moment, however, all did not go smoothly. The NLM continued to foment violence. The opposition had won majorities in both Ashanti and the Northern Territories and said they would resist the handing over of these regions to an untramelled CPP government. So Alan Lennox-Boyd decided to visit the Gold Coast to talk to the chiefs and the rest of the opposition, assess for himself how bad things were and see if he could help. Arden-Clarke opposed Lennox-Boyd's visit and much was made of the fact that when the Colonial Secretary went to Ashanti and the north, Arden-Clarke did not go with him. The reason was that the Governor was thoroughly distrusted, by his own civil servants in the north as well as by the dominant politicians there. It was an unusual – probably unique – humiliation for a Governor to be unable to accompany the Colonial Secretary on an important mission of persuasion to parts of his colony.

Lennox-Boyd's Private Secretary, Sir John Moreton, said of their visit to Kumasi:

> We were greeted by a crowd of, I don't know, ten thousand Ashanti, chanting and waving banners, some of them dressed in brown, the colour of mourning, the banners saying things like, 'British don't go' and 'We don't want independence'. This was five weeks before the declared date for independence, and there was a great deal of noise and shouting and display.

Sam MacDonald-Smith, the official responsible for organising the visit to Tamale, the capital of the Northern Territories, remembered:

> We called a meeting of the major chiefs and the NPP leaders [northern allies of the NLM] and they wanted to put their case to Lennox-Boyd that the north was still a protectorate, deriving from the treaties of Queen Victoria's time, and that some arrangement should be made whereby Britain could go on protecting them from exploitation by the south. He listened sympathetically and tried to get them to make a public statement to the effect that they were not ready for independence, didn't want it and could it please be postponed. But he couldn't get them to. He pointed out that they were cutting the ground from under his feet because unless they come out with a firm statement to this effect he couldn't go back to Parliament and say that the north just wouldn't have this rapid independence.

Lennox-Boyd told Nkrumah and his colleagues that they must agree to some additional provisions in the constitution to provide a measure of regional autonomy. The CPP leaders acquiesced, but without sincerity. Komla Gbedema commented: 'If we accepted any ideas about regionalism, it was just a sop to get independence given to us. But we never really intended to divide the country up.' Nkrumah expressed himself even more strongly to his British Private Secretary, John Codrington, who said later:

> Just before full independence, when I was working directly with Nkrumah for a period, he was proposing to do something or other which wasn't in accordance with the constitution. When I told him, very directly and positively, that this was unconstitutional, he said, 'Mr Codrington, I can drive a coach and horses through this constitution and after independence I certainly will.' And sure enough he did too.

Arden-Clarke's judgement about the CPP had proved right. Although it had not won a majority in either Ashanti or the Northern Territories, it had come a good second in both, with more than forty per cent of the votes. These successes combined with an overwhelming victory in the south to justify its claim that it was the only party able to unite the whole country. Thus Arden-Clarke, who had started out as a traditionally minded Governor, and Lennox-Boyd, who would greatly have preferred to see independence delayed, together carried out the policy of Andrew Cohen. They gave independence to the modern, popular party over the protests of the traditional chiefs whom British rule had formerly encouraged.

The advance to independence of the Gold Coast held the attention of the world. The 1948 riots helped white supremacists in South Africa to terrify voters with the prospect of rampant black power, and the South African election soon afterwards brought the Nationalist Party of Dr Daniel Malan to power, obsessed through the next forty years by, first, Nkrumah, then Patrice Lumumba of the Congo, followed by a succession of black rulers supposed to be rapists, terrorists and Communists. (The word 'rapists' here is not hyperbole: members of Dr Malan's party were morbidly interested in the alleged sexual illnesses and oddities of black political leaders.) The world's press came to see Africa as a battlefield over which two ideologies must fight: Dr Malan's theory of *apartheid* and the African nationalism, thought to be tinged with Communism, of Kwame Nkrumah.

To black people throughout Africa, Nkrumah's advance was an inspiration. Dr Hasting Kamuzu Banda, later to lead Nyasaland to independence as Malawi, and Robert Mugabe, later to lead Southern Rhodesia to independence as Zimbabwe, both settled in Accra during Nkrumah's years in power, to learn from the master. The message of the Gold Coast led many Africans in the French, Portuguese and Belgian colonies for the first time to think that speedy independence was possible. The administrators of these colonies, on the other hand, assumed that the perfidious British were merely up to another trick, that real power in the Gold Coast would remain in British hands, Nkrumah's 'independent' government a disguise to win local popularity. The Russians, dutiful followers of Lenin's theory of imperialism, were equally unable to acknowledge that the British were really handing over power. Lenin had argued that as the capitalist economies declined, they had to exploit colonies where high profits could be made. The Gold Coast's cocoa exports were a major source of dollars for the sterling area, enabling Britain to import American goods, therefore the transfer of power in Accra, the Russians maintained, could not be real. For all these reasons, the independence celebrations in the Gold Coast, which became Ghana on 6 March 1957, captured world attention. Where India's independence ten years earlier was the culmination of a process, Ghana's was the result of an unexpected lurch forward that was to lead the entire continent of Africa even more rapidly to independence.

## Ghana after Independence

Ghana was the biggest disappointment of all the British ex-colonies, partly because it was launched in such high hope. With a full treasury, a highly profitable principal export crop and substantial new investment under way, with a government that in six years in office had learned to administer responsibly while maintaining popular support, with a competent civil service, largely African but stiffened by a British contingent of enthusiasts for African advance, with an able and independent judiciary, Ghana was expected to succeed. Above all Ghana had a national leader who seemed too good to be true.

Kwame Nkrumah impressed almost everyone who met him. He was calm, relaxed, quiet-spoken and sweet-mannered. His extreme personal considerateness was combined, in his early years, with indifference to his own comforts. Even Oliver Lyttelton, when he visited the Gold Coast as Colonial Secretary, regarding Nkrumah as little more than a rabble-rouser, was won over by his charm and intellectual speed:

> I said to him, 'There are two great tragedies in human life . . . One is when you want something with all your heart and cannot get it.' 'Oh yes', Nkrumah replied, opening wide his expressive eyes, 'the other is when you have got it.'

Those who thought Nkrumah primarily a Communist were wrong. He was primarily a pan-Africanist. During his ten years in the United States from 1935 working his way through three university degrees and his three years in London intended for the study of English law but mostly devoted to West African and pan-African politics, his vision was always of the removal of white domination from the whole continent. But he repeatedly found the British enemy less evil and oppressive than he expected. He wrote of his stay in London, 'There was nothing to stop you getting on your feet and denouncing the whole of the British Empire.' His favourite newspaper then was the Communist *Daily Worker* which he read among the businessmen on the Underground:

> I used to unfold my *Daily Worker* as ostentatiously as I could and then watch as pairs of eyes were suddenly focused on me. But the gaze of these bowler-hatted gentlemen was not in any way hostile and the atmosphere was always one of mild amusement.

Nkrumah found many British willing to help him in his pan-African and anti-imperialist objectives. In England in 1945 he helped organise a pan-African conference in Manchester to which many participants came, thanks to the Colonial Office, which had paid for their travel to a conference a week earlier on trade unionism. In London, when he took charge of the West African National Secretariat, the tiny office he borrowed in Gray's Inn Road from a Gold Coast barrister was soon crowded with middle-class English

girls, willing to type for hours on end in the evenings for no payment. Nkrumah later wrote about one whom he took to the cinema. An Englishman insulted her for being with a black man; she slapped his face and told him to mind his own business.

When he returned to Africa and Arden-Clarke proved ready to perform a similar role on a larger scale, Nkrumah's natural courtesy as well as his political instinct led him to accept in the appropriate manner: by learning the skills of government in the way Arden-Clarke required and saying nothing of his enthusiasm for Marxism and pan-Africanism. In this Nkrumah did not set out to deceive Arden-Clarke. Like all outstandingly charming people, he was something of a chameleon. In the company of the Governor he became himself gubernatorial: he showed a ready understanding of the Governor's problems and did his best to cause the CPP to respond appropriately. Nkrumah was similarly affected by the Queen, whom he was thrilled to visit after independence at Balmoral and to welcome on a state visit to Ghana in 1959. The impeccable courtesy and friendliness with which she treated him evoked a full and equal response. British businessmen with interests in Ghana found him, in spite of his public professions of Marxism and his dislike of neo-colonialism, straightforward and co-operative.

Once independence was achieved, Nkrumah allowed his first and main enthusiasm to come to the fore. In his own words, 'there would be no

*The Queen rarely has foreign visitors to Balmoral. Dr Nkrumah, Prime Minister of Ghana, was invited there in August 1959. Left to right: Prince Charles, the Queen, Nkrumah, Princess Anne, Prince Philip.*

meaning to the national independence of Ghana unless it was linked with the total liberation of the African continent'. He saw Ghana's independence as the first step towards the creation of a united government of the whole of Africa. Nkrumah's diplomatic and political skills were so great that he almost certainly could have woven the quarrelling groups within Ghana into a successful, prosperous and even a democratic state. But he placed these objectives second to his plans for the continent. He tried to use this small west African state for a purpose that was beyond his or its power.

Soon after Ghana became independent so did the French colony of Guinea, but in a quite different way. France's President, Charles de Gaulle, wanted to create a 'French Community', a federation of all French colonies presided over by France. He toured the colonies explaining that they must vote for membership of the Community in a referendum or become independent 'with all the consequences'. The colonies all fell into line except Guinea, where the sparkling left-wing oratory and chiefly background of the political leader, Sekou Touré, led to a 'no' vote. De Gaulle promptly ordered the withdrawal of all French funds and government personnel from Guinea, leaving it independent but vulnerable and distressed. Nkrumah approached Sekou Touré and agreed with him that their two states should become one to form the United States of Africa, which other states were invited to join. Ghana gave Guinea a substantial loan, which was never repaid. For Nkrumah this was the first step on the road to pan-African unity.

In late 1958 Nkrumah assembled in Accra an All-African People's Conference, attended by delegates from twenty-eight countries (including Northern Rhodesia and Nyasaland: see p. 476), making use of the grand State House, with its Italian marble, silks, brocades and crystal chandeliers, which had been built for independence day. His purpose was to help advance them all to independence and then into close political union. In 1959 an All-African Trade Union Federation was created during a conference in Accra to help mobilise trade-union members throughout Africa in support of first their own nationalist movements and then Pan-Africanism.

When the Congo was suddenly given independence by Belgium in 1960, Nkrumah welcomed its Prime Minister, Patrice Lumumba, into the union of African states. He had entertained Lumumba in Accra and now backed him firmly when regional secessionists threatened the new state. He sent forces from both the Ghanaian army and police to help restore order – and they were widely praised for their discipline and competence. He made great but unsuccessful efforts to create an African joint command to resolve the worsening Congo crisis.

In 1960 the French Soudain became independent as Mali and was soon welcomed by Nkrumah and Sekou Touré into their United States of Africa. However Nkrumah's efforts to persuade the Republic of Upper Volta to join, which would have given the embryonic pan-African state a continuous land surface from two coastal strips far into the Sahara, were unsuccessful. He kept trying, nevertheless, and was a moving force behind the Casablanca

KWAME NKRUMAH
FOUNDER OF THE NATION

*The President on his podium.*

group of African states, with its radical-socialist approach to change throughout the continent. This eventually came together with the more conservative Monrovia group of states in 1963 to form the Organisation of African Unity, of which Nkrumah is generally acknowledged as one of the architects. By then his United States of Africa had collapsed, his African high command proposal had been repeatedly rejected and Ghana itself was falling into severe difficulties.

What went wrong in Ghana was simple: Nkrumah insisted on spending huge sums of money on spectacular projects which would confirm Ghana's position as the leader of independent Africa: an extravagant airport terminal building, an airline, modern steel production facilities, an atomic reactor, a navy, a great stadium and many modern factories which remained empty because the money and men to operate them were not available. Nkrumah believed that colonialism had held Africa in the subordinate role of primary producer. To bring Ghana and then Africa into the twentieth century, industry had to replace agriculture as the main source of wealth. He thought

*Komla Gbedema, Nkrumah's closest and most able ally in the years leading to independence.*

the economists and bankers who told him that this objective had to be approached slowly were either neo-colonialists or lacking in courage. He ignored their advice and accepted the help of eastern European governments in setting up complex industrial plants. Such projects – in addition to the vast sums that went into the pockets of CPP politicians – meant that the cocoa farmers and others far from Accra, whose production provided all the Government's revenue, grew increasingly discontented.

Nkrumah, pursuing his greatest ambitions outside the country and, facing growing frustration and opposition within, tried to keep Ghana orderly by repression. First he scrapped the provisions in the independence constitution designed to increase regional powers. Then he introduced measures authorising the restriction of individuals without trial. Not only members of the opposition but fellow members of his own party were detained. Komla Gbedema, who in 1951 when Nkrumah was in prison had carried his life-size portrait round the country, in 1961 spoke out against a measure creating a Special Criminal Division of the High Court from which there would be no appeal. He told the National Assembly:

When we pass this Bill . . . the low flickering flames of freedom will be for ever extinguished. We may be pulled out of bed to face the firing squad

after a summary trial and conviction . . . Today we may think that all is well, it is not my turn, it is my brother's turn, but your turn will come sooner than later.

Gbedema then promptly left the country.

In 1963, after a trial in which some former government ministers were acquitted on charges of treason, Nkrumah dismissed the Chief Justice, Sir Arku Korsah. In 1965 Dr J. B. Danquah, the man who brought Nkrumah back to the Gold Coast in 1947, died in prison after three years without trial, kept by Nkrumah's officials in leg-irons. Nkrumah attacked Ghana's new university for teaching students ideas critical of government. He set up the Kwame Nkrumah Ideological Institute, where ministers, party officials, civil servants and assembly members attended seminars on 'Nkrumaism'. Nkrumah himself defined this new political philosophy in a talk at the institute in February 1962:

When you talk of Nkrumaism you mean the name or term given to the consistent ideological policies followed and taught by Nkrumah . . . Nkrumaism, in order to be Nkrumaistic, must be related to scientific socialism [and] . . . must:
  a) be all-pervading

*In March 1966, a week after Nkrumah had been ousted by a National Liberation Council, the Accra crowd showed their feelings.*

b) provide both the aims and principles and the intellectual tools by which these aims are achieved and

c) offer the ordinary man and woman hope.

Nkrumah became more of a Marxist as the economy of Ghana declined. He created state companies and institutions whose incompetence and corruption merely increased the difficulties arising from the fall in the world cocoa price. In the end he became a megalomaniac dictator out of touch with the real world, surrounded by a corrupt and harsh security force. Many able Ghanaians moved overseas to work for international organisations. Nkrumah's great expenditures overtook the income from cocoa – declining but still enormous – and the country fell into debt. In Accra vegetables could not be had, the hospitals could not obtain drugs.

In February 1966, while on a visit to China, Nkrumah was deposed by a military coup. In nine years he had turned the model colony into an economic and political disaster area, which, under a succession of military and civilian rulers, it has remained.

# CHAPTER 9

# Kenya

Kenya was a colony the British Government never wanted and from which – except briefly in the 1939–45 war – it derived no benefit. For its first thirty years under British rule, Kenya did not even have a name, being called merely the East African Protectorate. The upper class Englishmen who bought land there cheaply and in vast estates were notable mainly for the urgency and style with which they established hunts, the ebullience of their extra-marital sexual relations, which caused the colony to become known as 'Happy Valley', and their constant demands on successive British Governments. They asked for subsidies to help them buy and develop their farms, for legal power over the natives, for exclusive rights in law to all the best land and to grow the most profitable crops and then, when the Governments' reluctant acquiescence in demand after demand led some of the Africans to rise in revolt, the Kenya settlers required that armies be sent from Britain to protect them.

Kenya had no minerals or marketable established skills. All it had, in its vast, overheated, infertile area, was a small zone, plumb on the Equator, which was high enough to be cool and to attract rain. Here the early settlers, by dint of many a massacre, subjugated the natives. The young Winston Churchill in 1908, when Under-Secretary for the Colonies, wrote of one punitive expedition, 'It looks like butchery, and if the House of Commons gets hold of it all our plans in the East African Protectorate will be under a cloud. Surely it cannot be necessary to go on killing these defenceless people on such an enormous scale.' From start to finish the Colonial Office tried to restrain the excesses of the settlers, but with little success.

So in the end, the Africans rose in a revolt which the panic and anger of the settlers made famous. They called it Mau Mau and put about the idea that it was the most brutal, bloodthirsty, murderous rising of black men against white in the history of mankind. Never can a Minister have reacted with greater horror than Colonial Secretary Oliver Lyttelton when he wrote about Mau Mau. In Britain it was widely believed that Mau Mau fighters had slaughtered white people in their thousands. But it was not so. The actual number of white civilians killed was thirty-two. The plain truth about Kenya is that it was a country of myths, the only country where the events that led to the end of the British Empire were described, in the writings of

Minister, Governor and Official commission, as due to the Devil, witchcraft, spells and the taking over by alien forces of the personality of subject peoples. In short the British in Kenya, while they had some real and severe difficulties to deal with, were so totally unable to understand them that they reverted to a primitiveness almost as extreme as that they believed they faced.

## A Settlers' Dream: the Last White Dominion, 1890–1948

The British acquired Kenya by accident. They regarded it as merely a passageway to Uganda. Established in Egypt in 1882, they felt vulnerable so long as enemies – the Germans and French – were in a position to raise a great army inland and sail down the Nile to attack them from the south. So British strategic planners wanted control of the headwaters of the Nile in Uganda. Treaties were signed with the local rulers there, above all the Kabaka of Buganda, king of a sophisticated people with whom profitable trade could be developed.

The quickest way to get British troops to Uganda, should the need arise, was by rail. The railway had totally revolutionised warfare, enabling a naval power like Britain for the first time to defend territories far inland. So Britain built a 600-mile-long railway, starting at the old Arab slaving port of Mombasa and running towards the centre of the continent, through land that was semi-desert in places and only sparsely populated even where it appeared fertile. The logic seems convoluted: protection of the route to India required Britain to control the Suez Canal; British passage through the canal in time of war could be secured only by controlling Egypt; the defence of Egypt required British power over the headwaters of the Nile; and the quickest way to get an army to Uganda was by train. Thus reasoned Lord Rosebery, Britain's Liberal-imperialist Foreign Secretary in 1892–94. His Prime Minister, Gladstone, was opposed to imperial adventures, but Rosebery used campaigns by missionaries and the Anti-Slavery Society to win his case for sending a mission and declaring Uganda a British protectorate in 1894. Construction of the railway began at once.

Military hardware always costs more than estimates allow for. The Uganda railway was no exception. The local Africans knew nothing of engineering work so Indians from the Punjab were imported for the enormous task of construction, which was not completed until 1901. By then the Government's main concern was how to pay for the Foreign Office's extravagant military device. Trade with the Kabaka's people, the Baganda, could be useful. Ivory was a profitable product, but not in quantities large enough to pay for a railway. The only solution, as railway-builders everywhere discovered, was to encourage settlement along the line, in the area now known as Kenya. Industrious trading people had to be attracted. A report to Parliament in 1901 favoured the large-scale settlement of Indians, making East Africa 'the America of the Hindu'. The Foreign Office con-

sidered immigration from Finland. Joseph Chamberlain, the Colonial Secretary, travelled up the Uganda railway in 1902 and decided that the fertile lands along the way would make an ideal area of settlement for the Jews who were then fleeing from persecution in Russia and Poland. He put the idea to Theodore Herzl, the founder of the Zionist movement, who raised it at the sixth Zionist congress meeting at Vienna in 1903.

*Engineers and construction workers on the Uganda Railway. They laid down about three-quarters of a mile a day.*

Chamberlain's proposal became known as the 'Uganda offer' because the area he chose was in territory still considered part of Uganda. But the Jews wanted to go to Palestine and the Finns to stay in Finland, so the recruiting officers turned to more usual sources of imperial migrants – Britain, Australia, New Zealand, Canada and, especially, South Africa. What was needed to attract settlers from these countries was a large acreage of productive land available both cheap and freehold.

However, it was not clear that the British Government had the right to sell land freehold. East Africa was a protectorate and Britain's rights in the area derived from treaties with local tribes. The Government's lawyers faced a dilemma. To stick to the letter of the treaties would mean no freehold land to sell, no settlers and therefore no end to the Treasury subsidy. So they found a typical lawyer's solution. Land which was 'vacant' could be held not to belong to any tribe. Therefore it could be disposed of as the Government wished.

In the 1890s drought and locusts had brought famine and, with smallpox, had killed off a large part of the African population. Therefore much land appeared to be vacant, even though neighbouring families and tribes remembered it as their own. From 1901 onwards Britain introduced a vigorous policy of offering such land cheaply to settlers. The resentment this might cause among the Africans was not seen as a problem. One large tribe of settled agriculturalists, the Kikuyu, were particularly badly affected. Frederick Lugard, a young soldier from India who in 1890 led the first British armed caravan to Uganda, making treaties as he went, and who later came to be regarded as the greatest authority on how Africans should be governed, wrote of the Kikuyu:

> I lived among them for close on a month and I was more favourably impressed by them than by any tribe I had as yet met in Africa. We became the greatest of friends and I had no hesitation in trusting myself alone among them, even at considerable distances from camp . . . I found them honest and straightforward, I had little trouble of any sort among them.

The Kikuyu had vacated a substantial amount of land, temporarily as they thought, owing to the recent natural disasters. And this land, on the plateau near the railway sidings that were to grow into the city of Nairobi, was especially fertile and therefore attractive to Europeans.

The promotion of the new country – still known as the East African Protectorate – was skilfully handled. Soon, enough upper-class English had bought estates for the Nairobi hotel where they gathered to become known as the 'House of Lords'. This small, élite group, led by the third Baron Delamere, tried to keep the best of the former Kikuyu land for themselves. They did not want either Jews or Indians admitted and soon persuaded the Colonial Office that, like Australians and New Zealanders, they must be granted a Legislative Council to protect their interests. The settlers asserted that this new dominion was rightly theirs. The British commissioner for the East African Protectorate in 1901–4, Sir Charles Eliot, agreed. In 1905 he wrote:

> The interior of the Protectorate is a White Man's country. This being so, I think it is mere hypocrisy not to admit that white interests must be paramount and that the main object of our policy and legislation should be to found a white colony.

This view was strongly advanced in London in the real House of Lords. The Colonial Secretary, Lord Elgin, retorted in 1907 that such assertions were baseless, as the two thousand whites were outnumbered by an estimated four million Africans. The Under-Secretary, Winston Churchill, visited Nairobi where he told the Colonists' Association: 'Never before has a Legislative Council been granted where the number of settlers is so few.' But the settlers got their way. A Legislative Council was set up and land grants in what soon became known as the White Highlands – areas vacated by the Masai,

Kalenjin and Kamba tribes, as well as the Kikuyu – were restricted to whites.

Officials in the Colonial Office and in the Colonial Government tried to resist settler pressure. When in March 1907 the President of the Colonists' Association, an Englishman named E. S. Grogan, publicly flogged three Kikuyu servants in front of the Nairobi Court House, his nomination to the Legislative Council was withdrawn. The Colonial Office maintained that the East African Protectorate was an African country and would one day be returned to its black inhabitants – when they had been taught how to run it. Delamere and his fellow lords were determined this would not happen and showed skill in winning over the Governors whom the Colonial Office appointed.

Sir Percy Girouard, Governor from 1909 to 1912, backed the view of Sir Charles Eliot and the settlers. The Colonial Office forced him to resign. Still London could not impose its will. Sir Edward Northey, Governor from 1919, wrote: 'European interests must be paramount throughout the Protectorate.' Like dozens of officials compelled to choose between occasional instructions from London and constant pressure from settlers, he sided with the whites among whom he lived. In 1922 Northey too was recalled to London and dismissed. When important decisions were in the offing, Lord Delamere, in particular, knew how to lay on lavish hospitality. In 1920, in order to help raise money for economic development, the name and status of the territory astride the Uganda railway were changed from the East African Protectorate to Kenya Colony, after the highest mountain there, Mount Kenya. Becoming a colony meant formal annexation by Britain, abrogating all former treaties with tribes and giving the Crown clear legal authority to dispose of land as it wished. Natives became, in the words of a subsequent High Court judgement, 'tenants at will of the Crown on the land actually occupied'. It was a change the settlers had long been demanding.

The Colonial Office succeeded in preventing total white settler domination mainly because of the presence of Indians. The insistence of the European settlers on securing advantages relative to the Indians, both in representation on the Legislative Council and in the allocation of land, led to trouble. The Indians in Kenya asked for help from the National Congress in India, which was already being nuisance enough to the authorities. The Congress pointed out that, in return for Indian sacrifices in the 1914–18 war, the imperial Government had formally promised equal citizenship for Indians throughout the Empire. What Congress told the Viceroy, the Secretary of State for India soon told the Cabinet. So in 1923 the Colonial Office issued a white paper: 'Primarily Kenya is an African territory . . . the interests of the African natives must be paramount.' These fine words at first led to no more for the Africans than the appointment of a white missionary to the Legislative Council to represent them. Some Indians joined the council too. The apparently unstoppable progress of a few thousand white settlers towards dominion status had met its first obstacle.

In the face of heavy settler resistance the Government set about developing native councils and encouraging peasant agriculture. Africans in Uganda had been successfully growing cotton and this plant was introduced into the neighbouring Nyanza area of Kenya, over settler protests that it would deprive them of their labour supply. The settlers fought back. The principal tribe in the region of Nairobi had developed a political presence through its Kikuyu Central Association. In 1925 it petitioned the Governor for permission for Africans to grow coffee (the most successful crop on the European estates) as well as, among other things, for the publication of the laws in the Kikuyu language and for direct African representation on the Legislative Council. All three requests were turned down.

The white settlers' conviction that they could go on winning such battles was reinforced during the years 1924–29 when a sympathetic Colonial Secretary, Leopold Amery, sat in the Cabinet in London. Amery had been a member of Milner's 'Kindergarten', the group of young intellectuals who joined Alfred Milner in South Africa when he was High Commissioner there at the start of the century and began the manoeuvres which led the warring Dutch- and English-speaking communities into forming the Union of South Africa. Milner and Amery believed their policy had secured a vital extension of British influence by this voluntary association of European settlers. They considered such arrangements to be the model for British imperial interests in the future. To Amery and to some of the aristocratic landowners in Kenya, South Africa pointed the way forward. Since white settler control was being impeded by Indians in Kenya and by do-gooders in London, the Amery-settler alliance propounded a grand idea: the federation of the British East African territories, Kenya, Uganda and Tanganyika (the area to the south acquired from Germany in the 1914–18 war), perhaps also with Northern Rhodesia. This would make possible both major economic development and improved standards of common services, such as transport, disease-control and African training for modern agriculture. So ambitious a project could be undertaken only with the active help of the local people who possessed the appropriate skills, i.e. the white settlers. To bring it to fruition they would have to be given control of Kenya.

In 1927 Amery set up a commission of inquiry under the chairmanship of Sir Edward Hilton Young to look into the federation idea. But Hilton Young took evidence from Africans, Indians and missionaries, as well as settlers, and his report, published in 1929, was a blow alike to the settlers and to Amery. It did not recommend federation, but stated that the Kenya Legislative Council must retain a majority of British officials, appointed from London, until the natives could take a share in government 'equivalent to that of the immigrant communities'.

These reverses for the settlers' hopes of entrenched white domination were driven home with additional force when Labour came to power in Britain in 1929 and Lord Passfield (Sidney Webb) became Colonial Secretary. He withdrew funds from the settlers' pet projects, insisted that rules previously laid down from London to protect native land were enforced, and forbade the Governor to restrict the meetings and money-raising activities of the Kikuyu Central Association. In a white paper he stated that the British objective was 'in Kenya as elsewhere ... a ministry representing an electorate in which every section of the population finds an effective and adequate voice', something impossible while 'less than one per cent of the population' was enfranchised.

The leaders of the settlers spent most of the 1930s locked in combat with London Governments, Conservative as much as Labour, sometimes boycotting the Governor's Legislative Council, often flying to London to try to put their case to the Colonial Secretary over the Governor's head. They frequently got their way. When in 1937 some disputed land was returned to a Kikuyu chief called Koinange, he asked for permission to continue to use it for growing coffee, as its European occupant had done. The District Commissioner ordered him to grub out the bushes. The settlers pressed for a law to guarantee that in the highlands land grants would be made only to whites. After repeated refusal, the request was granted in 1939 in an Order in Council which outraged Indians as well as Africans. The Government of India joined the protest, pointing out that the Order discriminated in favour of foreigners and even ex-enemies over British subjects.

It discriminated above all against the Kikuyu, who maintained that the highlands had been theirs and never voluntarily relinquished. The Kikuyu Central Association therefore did all it could to oppose the Government. Many Kikuyu chiefs had been disposed to use the law to recover their land, as Koinange had successfully done, but the Order in Council reinforced the bitterness of those who held that the settlers always got their way and that the Government's professions of even-handedness were not to be believed. The KCA therefore expanded into areas outside the highlands, building up the first widespread African movement opposed to the Government. In Mombasa, Kenya's principal port, a section of the workforce were Kikuyu and in 1939 the KCA encouraged the Indian-led trade union there in a widespread strike – forcing the Government to hold an inquiry into working and housing conditions (which were found to be scandalous and commonly in breach of the law). In 1940, after the outbreak of the Second World War, the Government proscribed the KCA and its associated organisations as subversive, and interned their leaders. The KCA had sent one of them, Jomo Kenyatta, to London as their representative. He was therefore not available to be interned. But growing Kikuyu pressure and the war had their effect. The arrival in Kenya of 75,000 soldiers and the Government's need to supply armies in the Middle East brought prosperity to white and black farmers alike. The Government set up boards to make sure production targets were met, and had to appoint Africans to them since it was seeking African cooperation. In 1944 the first African was appointed to the Legislative Council – Eliud Mathu, son of a Kikuyu medicine man and educated at Balliol College, Oxford. By 1948 the number of Africans on the Legislative

Council was raised to four – chosen by the Governor from lists submitted by local native councils – along with six elected Indians, eleven elected Europeans and eighteen officials.

The Africans observed that on many issues the officials and the Europeans would form an alliance to get their way. They knew that the Governor since 1944, Sir Philip Mitchell, owned an orange farm in South Africa and believed quite wrongly that he was a white settler at heart (in fact he had been appointed largely because of his known contempt for white settlers). They knew that Government officials and leading settlers visited each others' homes and shared a profound sympathy of view.

Paradoxically the settlers too felt defeated. Their desire that Kenya be recognised as a white man's country had been overruled first by the admission of Indians to the Legislative Council, later by the arrival of Africans there. The Colonial Office had repeatedly asserted that it would keep power in its own hands until the other races were fully able to share it with the Europeans. And Mitchell not only despised them, he also took his orders from London where the Colonial Secretary from 1946 to 1950, Arthur Creech Jones, watched them with mistrust. In the 1930s Creech Jones had frequently asked parliamentary questions critical of Kenya's labour laws. From 1937 Jomo Kenyatta had been regularly supplying Creech Jones with information about Kenya, and Creech Jones had sent Kenyatta copies of letters he received from the Colonial Office, so that he could keep his KCA friends in Kenya informed. In 1946 Creech Jones had visited Kenya, where he discussed a scheme for equal numbers of representatives for Africans, Indians and Europeans in an East African federal assembly. To the 9,000 white voters the scheme was horrifying: a threat to all they had devoted their lives to building.

Post-war Kenya was consequently a political battleground. White settlers, African farmers and Indian traders, encouraged by the war-time boom and the share it had enabled them to acquire in running the country, were all demanding more. The slump that follows every war intensified their competition for Government favours. As usual, whatever the Colonial Secretary in London might say, the settlers got most of what they wanted from the Kenya Government. They even wheedled their way around Mitchell. The 97,000 Kenyan Africans who had become soldiers and fought for Britain came home to none of the fruits of victory. Seventy thousand of them were reckoned to be literate, 600 of them had been trained as teachers, 15,000 as drivers. The majority wanted jobs in Nairobi or Mombasa, where work was scarce. Their experience, serving alongside British soldiers, whom thay had seen for the first time as no more than their equals, made them a dangerous, volatile group.

*A picture designed to mislead. It appears as the frontispiece of* Facing Mount Kenya, *captioned 'The Author'. Jomo Kenyatta was settled in London in 1938 and habitually wore western clothes. He borrowed the tribal gear for the pose.*

## Mau Mau and its Consequences, 1948–1963

In 1938 Jomo Kenyatta's book, *Facing Mount Kenya*, had been published in London. It purports to be an anthropological study of the Kikuyu. Perhaps the most remarkable chapter is a warm defence of the Kikuyu practice of female circumcision. According to Kenyatta the tribal matrons who performed this operation worked 'with the dexterity of a Harley Street surgeon . . . With a stroke she cuts off the tip of the clitoris . . . the girl hardly feels any pain.' The attacks on this practice by missionaries were 'misinformed': 'The overwhelming majority of [the Kikuyu] believe that it is the secret aim of those who attack this centuries-old custom to disintegrate their social order and thereby hasten their Europeanisation.' The book contains an enthusiastic introduction by the great anthropologist, Professor Bronislav Malinowski, who describes it as 'one of the first really competent and instructive contributions by a scholar of pure African parentage . . . a pioneering achievement of outstanding merit'.

In reality the book is something else: namely, propaganda. Kenyatta responded to the Europeans' constant assertions of superiority with a counter-assertion of Kikuyu superiority. Living in London, penniless but refusing to return to Kenya where he would be treated as an inferior, he wrote a book consisting of a series of celebratory descriptions of primitive customs, mixed with a trumpeting, traditionalist political view:

In the old order of the African society, with all the evils that are supposed to be connected with it, a man was a man, and as such he had the rights of a man and liberty to exercise his will and thought in a direction which suited his purposes as well as those of his fellow-men; but today an African, no matter what his station in life, is like a horse which moves only in the direction that the rider pulls the rein . . . The African can only advance to a 'higher level' if he is free to express himself, to organise economically, politically and socially, and to take part in the government of his own country.

Jomo Kenyatta, the author of this manifesto, was to become the most misunderstood and misrepresented of all the nationalist leaders in British Africa. To him and the Kikuyu the British were *thieves* in a way they were not for Gandhi, Nkrumah, Makarios or even Nasser. The Kenya settlers were an immediate and dangerous threat, the protection of the Colonial Office was verbal and distant. So Kenyatta was no more than voicing the feelings of his people when he told the Manchester Fabian Society in 1938: 'I not only say there is British fascism in the colonies but can give you examples and facts for you to judge whether the Jews in Germany are treated worse than we are.' Colonial Office staff built up files of press cuttings from British local newspapers on Kenyatta's speeches. They judged him subversive in intention – he had been to Moscow for training in 1932 – but harmless.

In September 1946 Kenyatta returned to Kenya. In 1929, when he had left, he was the paid organiser of the Kikuyu Central Association, chugging around the countryside on a motor-bike. His powers as a speaker had led the KCA to send him to London – though Fenner Brockway, an English pacifist and anti-imperialist, later recalled that Kenyatta's English was so poor in the early 1930s that when he spoke, audiences melted away. On his return seventeen years later, crowds came out to greet him at Mombasa, along the railway and at Nairobi. He was given charge of the main Kikuyu school and teacher-training college, Githunguri, an English-language institution through which the tribe showed their determination to control their own future. He received a large salary, based on collections from Kikuyu farmers and traders, and within a year he was elected President of KAU, the Kenya African Union, Kenya's first moderate, inter-tribal nationalist organisation. While strengthening his position as leader of the Kikuyu, Kenyatta tried to make KAU represent an all-Kenya nationalism. His task was not difficult. African population in Kenya had increased enormously in the 1930s and 1940s. Pressure on the areas allotted to the Africans was therefore intense. Yet the settler lobby stopped the Government from extending these areas, insisting instead on the further recruitment of white immigrants. Africans could not understand why, if there was plenty of room on the richest land for more settlers, no room could be found for them. The argument which persuaded Mitchell and the Labour Government was that with growing African unemployment, a dangerous situation would arise unless jobs were

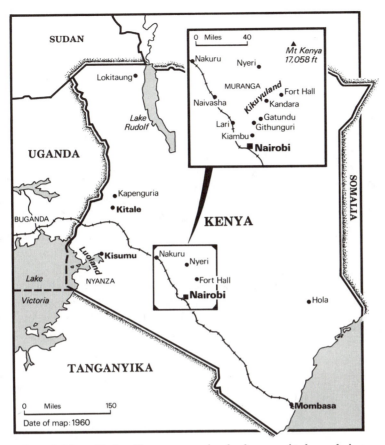

Date of map: 1960

generated quickly. Only Europeans had the capital and international contacts to make profits fast. Therefore, once again, the settlers had to have their way. African reaction was such that Kenyatta did not have to strain himself to organise a movement. The Africans of Kenya were looking for a leader with the skills and contacts to beat the settlers at their own game. The Kikuyu and some others flocked to Kenyatta's meetings.

The speeches he made as he toured Kenya had a consistent pattern. The Africans, he said, must gain independence by peaceful means. They must then protect the other races living in Kenya. To win freedom they must abandon the laziness, theft and crime that were so prevalent among them (on this theme he spoke far more severely than any European official would have dared and was quoted approvingly in settler newspapers). He asked to see the Governor, Sir Philip Mitchell, and hinted that he would like to be nominated to the Legislative Council. Mitchell replied that he should start by standing for the Local Native Council in his area. This was a mistake. It both insulted Kenyatta and was at variance with current British policy. The slow education of Africans for government, enforced by restricting them to native authorities, had been criticised by Lord Hailey in his African Survey in 1938. Arthur Creech Jones and Andrew Cohen at the Colonial Office spent the post-war years trying to persuade governors that African national-ists who were ready must be offered participation at the national level. So it was no surprise that Kenyatta did not take up Mitchell's suggestion. Nevertheless the Governor had him appointed to the African Land Utilization and Settlement Board, whose meetings he attended regularly for two years.

Kenyatta's position was that of a saddened elder. He demanded independence, but he could not see how to obtain it in the face of the alliance of Colonial Government and settlers. He built up KAU, winning African members with spicy speeches, full of the homely saws of the Kikuyu, but he thought the struggle ahead would be a long one.

Some younger Kikuyu believed they could achieve more rapid results by mobilising the tribe in a secret movement to kill white settlers and take over the country. Kenyatta knew they would be defeated after much bloodshed. He tried to discourage them. But they were not under his authority. To help keep their organisation secret, they insisted that it be nameless, but others soon called it Mau Mau (a term with many alleged origins and no known meaning). Bildad Kaggia, a Kikuyu who during the 1939–45 war had served in the British army in the Middle East and in England, where he helped run a reception camp for African prisoners of war repatriated from Germany, recalled:

When I returned from the war I thought about joining KAU, but it was led by Eliud Mathu and others who were collaborating with the colonial authorities. So I joined the East African Trade Union Congress which was quite progressive at that time. In 1946, when Kenyatta came back, I thought he would change KAU, so in 1947 I joined it. But KAU went on following the old tradition of submitting memoranda and petitions to the colonial Government. Some of us, particularly those who had been in the army, decided that these petitions were doing nothing. For instance, during that period we kept asking for increased African representation in the Legislative Assembly but the Government would always reply that we were not fit to represent our own people. We found in the trade union that we were managing to represent our workers, but in politics things were not moving fast enough. So we joined the KAU and in a very short time we succeeded in taking over the Nairobi branch, thanks to our strength as trade union leaders.

Mau Mau started in a small way in 1946–47. Then in 1949–50 the Nairobi branch formed their own group, training them with arms. This group had grown very fast. By 1951 we had trained people, we had managed to get guns, we were thinking that the time must come soon to fight. Then in 1952 KAU sent a delegation to London and its leader addressed a meeting at Nyeri on their return, explaining how the Colonial Secretary would not see them. This experience helped us in the Mau Mau group to convince others that these delegations would do nothing. After that, almost everyone was convinced that armed struggle was the only solution and most of the members of the Nairobi branch joined Mau Mau.

The Kikuyu were themselves divided by the shortage of land. The chiefs who remained on the land and most of their followers wanted the British to concede constitutional advance, but did not want this to be achieved in a way which would cause power to pass into the hands of the young, landless Kikuyu whom they called the wild boys of Nairobi. The chiefs, who were effectively the landowners in Kikuyu society, had been directly responsible for forcing these young men and their families out of Kikuyuland and were wealthy enough to pay most of the costs of KAU and the teacher-training college, Githunguri. The Kikuyu were among the few African people in the whole continent to live on well-watered, fertile land, served by road and railway and close to the capital city. Both the chiefs and their people in the Kikuyu reserve and the many Kikuyu squatters in the designated white areas had, by African standards, a high income from the sale of their produce. The chiefs were government-appointed agricultural entrepreneurs who were adapting the Kikuyu way of life to meet the needs of modern business. The wild boys of Nairobi, on the other hand, were reverting to traditional tribal practices. In the booming capital city, a short ride from their family lands, they saw big houses, cars, hotels and shops full of luxuries. But none of this was for them. They had lost their land and found little reward in being ill-paid wage-labourers. But they remembered something of Kikuyu tradition. They used an adaptation of the Kikuyu manhood initiation oath as a way to secure loyalty to their secret political army. One reason for the enormous success Mau Mau was to enjoy among the Kikuyu was that its appeal to the tribal spirit was genuine and convincing. Fred Kubai was another early member of the Nairobi Mau Mau, later described in a Government report as 'the recognised leader of the Kikuyu thugs in Nairobi'. He recalled:

> Kenyatta was very important to us. People in all tribes knew him and respected him. We found it very difficult to convince old people they should support us. We wanted Kenyatta to join us so that he could get the old people on our side. He was a very good orator and people used to pay 100 shillings for him to talk at their meetings to cover his costs. Soon Nairobi branch meetings became very successful and we were able to collect large contributions. So Kenyatta started to come to our meetings.

Kenyatta, anxious to build up support among the five million Africans throughout Kenya, was at first nonplussed by the division among the million Kikuyu. He tried to avoid taking sides and, until 1952, managed to do so. He skilfully chose his words so as to offend neither chiefs nor Nairobi wild boys. But as Mau Mau built up, its violence increasingly frightened and offended the non-Kikuyu and the businessmen-chiefs.

> Organisation in Nairobi was very difficult at first [Bildad Kaggia recalled] because of the police. So after the ex-army people we started to recruit criminals. Most of our people, except for those who had been in the army,

were afraid to touch guns. Criminals were prepared to do so. We also recruited taxi drivers and we used them to take us anywhere at any time in Nairobi.

Fred Kubai added:

We had a team of thieves. We organised them. We asked them to steal guns. They stole money as well from the Asians. Most of the Asians don't keep their money in the bank. The ex-servicemen trained young people in shooting. This was 1949–50. Kenyatta was not saying much at this time, so we didn't bother to inform him what we were doing. At most of the meetings of the Kenya Africa Union he would be there with the elders, but we acted as if we didn't know each other.

Mau Mau soon found recruits in the countryside. Most white farms had, in the 1930s, been too big for their owners. So they allowed African squatters to occupy sections, partly in return for labour, partly for rents, which the squatters earned by selling their produce in Nairobi. After 1945, white settlers and Government set about evicting these squatters, to make room for more white immigrants and secure the character of the highlands. The evicted Africans, mostly Kikuyu, tried to return to the native reserves, but they were unwelcome and the chiefs barred them. They therefore became ready allies of the Nairobi wild boys. So did a few dissident chiefs, like Koinange, the man who had been forced to grub out the coffee plants on his land, who was a close associate of Kenyatta.

The early violence of Mau Mau was of the press-gang variety, directed against those of their fellow-Africans who refused to swear the initiation oath and were thought likely to report the organisers to the police. Bodies of members of the tribe were found in rivers tied with wire. Kikuyu policemen disappeared and were later found dismembered. When Mau Mau recruitment teams forced Kikuyu still living on the reserve to take the oath, their action was like forcing churchgoing Catholics to perform the rituals of the holy sacrament – symbolically eating the flesh and drinking the blood of Christ – as part of an oath to support a band of political killers.

During August 1952 Kenyatta's attempts to avoid backing either side became impossible and he found himself backing both. Waruhiu Itote, known as 'General China', records in his book *'Mau Mau' General*, published in 1967, that on 16 August 1952 he and eight younger men came to seek Kenyatta's guidance. The secret central committee had ordered them to set up a guerilla base in the forest. What should they do? Itote, who had served with the British in the Burma campaign, was well qualified. He claims that Kenyatta told him:

You learnt many things in the army, my son, and now you can lead our people. If you had died in Burma, no one would have remembered you, for you were fighting for the British. But should you die tomorrow in our struggle, you will die for your own people and your name will live in our hearts.

Six days later, at Kiambu on 24 August 1952, Kenyatta addressed a crowd of some 30,000, including journalists: 'This meeting is of the Kikuyu elders and leaders who have decided to see what the disease in Kikuyuland is and how this disease can be cured. We are being harmed by a thing called Mau Mau. Who wants to curse Mau Mau?' Thousands of hands shot up. Kenyatta went on: 'Mau Mau has spoiled the country. Let Mau Mau perish for ever. All people should search for Mau Mau and kill it.'

Government officials thought Kenyatta's speech a major blow against Mau Mau. Fred Kubai and his colleagues in Nairobi thought so too:

Kenyatta made a very strong denunciation of Mau Mau. At the Kiambu meeting he cursed Mau Mau with a powerful Kikuyu curse. He said that the Mau Mau should be banished to the roots of the 'Mikongoe' tree. This is a mythical tree but it meant that the Mau Mau should be thrown into a very big hole from which it could never be recovered – into the abyss. Meetings were arranged for Kenyatta to speak at Nyeri and in Muranga district. We felt that if he continued with this kind of denunciation, people would become confused. Some of them might not follow what we wanted to do. So we decided to call him in. We said, 'We are Mau Mau and what you have said at this Kiambu meeting must not be said again.' This was the central committee, about fourteen of us, on 24 or 25 August 1952. We called Kenyatta into an office and we told him that we didn't want him to go to another meeting. If Kenyatta had continued to denounce Mau Mau, we would have denounced him. He would have lost his life. It was too dangerous and he knew it. He was a bit shaken by the way we looked at him. He was not happy. We weren't the old men he was used to dealing with. We were young and we were serious. So he didn't go to either of those two prepared meetings. He refused to address them.

Achieng Oneko, a member of Kenya's second largest tribe, the Luo, was secretary of KAU and present at the office when his colleagues summoned Kenyatta.

He did not argue with them [Oneko remembered]. He tried to change his words to convince those people that he was not against them. But he had to survive also. Kenyatta used very convincing language. He said he was like a tongue between the molars and the lower teeth. So he stood between Mau Mau and the then Government.

Assassinations of chiefs and headmen reinforced the warning.

As recently as February 1952 – six months earlier – a report to the Governor, Sir Philip Mitchell, by his Director of Intelligence had concluded that the oath-taking campaign was a legitimate activity, 'to rouse political consciousness, unite the African people in their objectives, in particular the acquisition by the Kikuyu of more and better land, and to raise money'. Only the last item might be held to be criminal. Settlers, angry, tough and many of them afraid, pressed Sir Philip to clamp down firmly, declare a state of emergency and nip the Mau Mau menace in the bud. Large numbers of colonial officials supported these recommendations, but Mitchell did not respect the judgement of the settlers or of officials he thought too much under their sway. He relied on efforts to persuade Kenyatta to denounce violence and showed himself not to be the settlers' tool that many Africans supposed. Hysterical movements among the Kikuyu, he considered, were nothing new. He responded with the same coolness Hailey had shown in India when, on the day of an expected riot, he went off fishing and left his deputy in charge.

In February 1952 Mitchell greeted Princess Elizabeth and her husband, Prince Philip, when they arrived in Kenya to spend part of a long holiday watching wild animals from the Treetops Hotel, Nyeri. While in Kenya they learned that King George VI had died and that the Princess had therefore become Queen Elizabeth II. Whatever the risk, Mitchell's judgement had proved correct and the royal visit went off safely. In June 1952, four months later, he left Kenya, still insisting that all was well there, and wrote to his nominated successor: 'There really is a genuine feeling of desire to cooperate and be friendly.' Much of the letter was devoted to advice on how to behave towards divorced people among the colony's white community: 'It is of somewhat unusual complexity as we have the amateur champion out here who has, I think, been divorced by five if not six husbands.'

Settler venom was heaped on Mitchell for not acting forcefully against Mau Mau. After three governorships – Uganda, Fiji and Kenya – he was expected to receive a peerage on his retirement, but he did not get it. During his last months Mau Mau had spread threateningly in Kikuyuland, but Mitchell told the Colonial Office nothing about it. In the three months following his retirement twenty-four headmen and thirty-six potential witnesses in Mau Mau cases, all Kikuyu, were murdered. The police could obtain no evidence to bring the killers to court. It was not until late September that his successor, Sir Evelyn Baring (son of 'over-Baring', the first British ruler of Egypt), arrived. A thoughtful man who normally made decisions slowly after considering all the evidence, he flew into Kenya amidst intense security precautions and demands for immediate action.

> Five days after I arrived I started a tour which I shall never forget [he later told the great scholar of Africa, Margery Perham, in a taped interview]. The first place I visited was a town called Kandara, near the original home of the Kikuyu people, and I rode through the main street to have a meeting in the school. The people stood in shops and houses. I've never seen such faces. They were scowling, they looked unhappy, they were intensely suspicious. It was an expression I saw a great deal during the early years of Mau Mau. My first meeting was entirely African, civil servants, the local chief and headmen, some teachers. They all said there

had been a complete breakdown of law and order, a murder every night, and unless you proceed against the people who are doing this our position is impossible. The same thing was repeated to me in other places. At Nyeri a group of European Christians said the same and I said, 'Who do you mean?' 'Kenyatta', they all said. 'If you don't get Kenyatta and those around him and shut them up somehow we are in a terrible, hopeless position.'

*Across the grave of Chief Waruhiu: extreme left with microphone, Sir Evelyn Baring; in centre foreground of picture on right, Jomo Kenyatta.*

While he was on his tour, one of the most senior Kikuyu chiefs, Waruhiu, was murdered. Baring went to the funeral and faced Kenyatta across the grave. According to his aide and biographer, Charles Douglas-Home, Baring 'was conscious of some of what he felt was the demoniac force of Kenyatta's personality. But they did not speak. The two men had to wait nearly twenty more years before they actually met.'

On 9 October 1952, twelve days after arriving in Kenya, Baring cabled the Colonial Secretary in London, Oliver Lyttelton:

I have regretfully come to the conclusion . . . [that] most of the KAU leaders, including Kenyatta, are the planners of Mau Mau . . . Jomo Kenyatta, when he chooses, has induced most Kikuyu to obey him. He practically stopped the drinking of European beer by Africans in Nairobi. Yet his denunciation of Mau Mau crimes is ineffective and has often, I'm told by Kikuyu, been accompanied by sayings and gestures making clear he did not mean what he said . . . Kikuyu chiefs, African administrative officers, Kikuyu teachers, missionaries of three denominations, all said KAU (particularly Jomo Kenyatta) were backing Mau Mau and JK allowed his name to be inserted blasphemously in hymns and prayers . . . I conclude that we must remove Jomo Kenyatta and several of his henchmen during the next few weeks. If we do not, the chiefs, headmen, Government servants and missionaries who still support us will cease their support and may be killed [and] trouble will spread to other tribes . . . who provide men for the Kenya police.

Within five days the Cabinet in London informed Baring that his proposal for a state of emergency was approved. It was expected to be a brief matter. The ringleaders would be arrested, violent protests would erupt, then the leaderless movement would shrivel within a few weeks, and peace would be restored. The arrests were carried out with no trouble, but failed to kill the movement. Young new leaders quickly took over and launched a wave of killings of African elders. Reports arrived of widespread oath-taking ceremonies and of horribly mutilated African corpses. Mau Mau was tightening its hold on its own people. When white farmers found their cattle hamstrung – the tendons in their legs cut so they could not walk and would therefore starve to death – their outrage increased. The declaration of a state of emergency seemed merely to have stimulated an increase in violence.

Baring faced a further problem. Having arrested Kenyatta and the other alleged Mau Mau leaders, what was he going to do with them? If he held them without trial they would become martyrs. Kenyatta in particular would be proclaimed worldwide as the innocent victim of British imperialism. MPs at Westminster required evidence of his guilt and an open trial, so that the world, and especially the Africans of Kenya, could judge the facts. A ton and a half of books and papers, taken from Kenyatta's house on the night of his arrest, provided no clues. The decision to hold a trial in these circumstances was a risky one, but Baring felt he had no choice.

If the British were given the chance to have their Empire judged by one achievement alone, they would surely choose the law. The high standards of the courts, their openness and fairness, were praised on all sides. No Briton would deliberately have tarnished that achievement by a defective trial of a major political leader. No Governor had more reason than Baring to maintain the standard. He knew how the brutal mismanagement of British justice at Denshawai (see page 234) undermined the twenty years of painstakingly constructive effort by his father in Egypt. The panic and anger of the white community there had broken the thin veneer of civilised conduct of which the law is the highest expression. The panic and anger of the white settlers now drove the younger Baring to do the same in Kenya. He wrote to Lyttelton of his doubts:

> If witnesses will repeat in open court what they have said on affidavit to magistrates, convictions should be obtained. Every possible effort has been made to offer them rewards and to protect them, but no one can tell what will happen when they are confronted in court by Kenyatta's formidable personality. If they speak they will disclose a degree of close connection between the Kenya African Union and Mau Mau greater than has ever been mentioned before in public.

The words 'every possible effort has been made to offer them rewards' can mean nothing other than that the Governor wanted the Colonial Secretary to know witnesses were bribed. Nor was this the least of the peculiarities. The Government chose to hold the trial at Kapenguria, an agricultural station near the edge of the desert that covers the northern half of Kenya. Here were no telephones, no railways, no hotels and no safe water. The advantage of the location lay in the ease with which Mau Mau men or Kenyatta supporters could be kept out. The drawbacks included difficulty of access for the press and even for the lawyers and others who had to be present. The place was so little known that the officials who drew up the warrant for the Governor to sign, formally appointing the magistrate to try the case, attributed Kapenguria to the wrong province. What was worse, something smelt wrong about the appointment. Ransley Thacker QC was a civil-service lawyer, once attorney-general of Fiji, later a judge in Kenya and for twelve years on the Supreme Court there. He had retired to practise in Nairobi where he was regarded by the settlers as one of themselves. The sentiment 'Thacker will convict, he's a sound chap', spoken in the white bars of Nairobi, was overheard by many Africans. If one of the purposes of the trial was to convince Kenyan Africans and their supporters throughout the world of Kenyatta's guilt, the choice as judge of one who was no longer on the bench but a member of the community of accusers and who chose to live for much of the trial in the Europeans' club in nearby Kitale was at best self-defeating. However well and fairly Thacker conducted the case, Africans would have grounds to cavil if he produced a verdict of guilty.

Worse still, it later emerged, Thacker and Baring had unexplained dealings. An *ex gratia* payment of £20,000 was made to Thacker – more than ten times the annual salary he had recently been earning as a judge – drawn from a Government emergency fund at Baring's instruction. Thacker had let it be known that if he found Kenyatta guilty his life in Kenya would be forfeit and he would therefore need to be helped to move. It was, however, no business of the Governor to have dealings concerning such a matter with a temporary magistrate. Baring's biographer, Douglas-Home, concludes: 'He desperately wanted a conviction and a quick one at that.'

Thacker, the presiding magistrate, also performed the role of the jury. He placed great faith in one prosecution witness, Rawson Macharia, who swore that Kenyatta had tried to administer a Mau Mau oath to him. Five years later, while Kenyatta was still in prison and the British were still ruling Kenya, Macharia swore in court that his evidence at the trial had been false. He then produced papers in court showing that the Colonial Government had undertaken in writing to pay for him to be flown out of Kenya to study at an English university, there to be kept with his family and given a Government post on his return. British officials confirmed in court that once he had completed his evidence at Kapenguria, these promises were kept. Thacker, in summing up the Kenyatta trial, said : 'Although my finding means that I disbelieve ten witnesses for the defence and believe one for the

*Kenyatta and his five fellow accused are taken handcuffed from the court at Kapenguria to return to jail.*

prosecution, I have no hesitation in doing so. Rawson Macharia gave his evidence well.'

The evidence against Kenyatta covered three allegations: that he had administered the Mau Mau oath, that when he denounced Mau Mau he was insincere and really supported it, and that he had allowed his name to be blasphemously used in place of Jesus Christ's in Mau Mau hymns (JK substituting conveniently for JC). Evidence on these themes was supposed to prove the charge that Kenyatta was guilty of 'managing an unlawful society'. Since the strongly contested evidence about administering oaths concerned a period before Mau Mau was made illegal, the totality of the evidence can be seen, more than thirty years afterwards, as offering no proof of the charge of 'managing an unlawful society'. When the prosecution had completed the presentation of its case, D. N. Pritt, QC, the defending counsel, said as much: 'It is the most childishly weak case made against any man in any important trial in the history of the British Empire.' He put it to Thacker that there was no case to answer. Thacker felt obliged to adjourn for a weekend to ponder the arguments.

The weekend of Saturday 24 January 1953 proved a bad time for judicious pondering. Since the arrest of Kenyatta and his fellow defendants, Mau Mau had begun to kill Europeans. A lone settler was killed and disembowelled in

October, an elderly farmer in November, two partners on a farm in January 1953. Then, on 24 January, a family named Ruck, mother, father and a six-year-old boy, were all hacked to death with *pangas* (heavy-bladed agricultural implements). Mrs Ruck, a doctor who ran a clinic for Africans, was expecting a second child. She and her farmer husband were found outside the farmhouse, their son Michael upstairs in his bedroom. The murder of the Ruck family galvanised the settlers. An explosion of rage shook the colony; demands for action reflected a desire to get after the murderers and tear them to pieces. It would not have been an easy weekend for a judge properly isolated from settler feeling to decide that Kenyatta and his colleagues had no case to answer. Thacker spent the weekend among the settlers and was fully aware of the intensity of their conviction that they must all do their duty in cracking down on the murderers.

Thacker went back to Kapenguria and ruled that the prosecution had established a case. The Nairobi whites stormed Government House, demanding to see Baring. They were determined once again to tell London's appointee how to run *their* colony. Baring declined to see the crowd, fearing to set a precedent, but spoke to two representatives in his study. They passed on his message that new, vigorous policies were being prepared and the crowd should disperse. Instead the settlers pressed forward. Baring's *askaris* (African guards) had the unpleasant task of keeping them at bay. Outraged at being pushed back, the settlers called the *askaris* 'dirty niggers', stubbed out cigarettes on their bare arms and tried to storm the front door. One settler leader, Michael Blundell, wrote later:

> A little woman dressed in brown who was the respected owner of an excellent shop in Nairobi was crying out in a series of unprintable words . . . A musician and scientist with a quiet, scholarly, intellectual face was crouched down, twitching all over and swirling with a cascade of remarkable and blistering words, while an occasional fleck of foam came from his mouth . . .

Blundell eventually persuaded them all to go home.

The schoolroom at Kapenguria where the trial was being held became a popular outing for whites. They sat at the scratched school desks during the sessions and picnicked on the grass at lunchtime, along with the lawyers. Nobody lived nearby except the Suk tribe, naked save for ostrich feathers in their hair and some beads or bracelets. Sometimes, embarrassed at being watched by strangers, the Suk would cover their faces with their hands. Alongside Kenyatta those tried included Fred Kubai and Bildad Kaggia – both of whom subsequently admitted they were Mau Mau organisers – Achieng Oneko, the Luo secretary of KAU, who has always denied it, was released on appeal and re-arrested, and two other Kikuyu. But all attention centred on Kenyatta. He was the man the settlers wanted removed. After Thacker had ruled that there was a case to answer, Kenyatta was the first defence witness. During his ten days in the witness box he was cross-examined at length by Anthony Somerhough, counsel for the Crown, a large, round-faced, balding man.

Q:   The Crown case is that at no time have you denounced Mau Mau at all with any intention to be effective.

A:   That is not true. I have denounced Mau Mau in the best way possible . . .

Q:   And that in general the most that you did, the Crown say, is to deny the connection of Mau Mau with KAU which of course you had to do as Mau Mau was a proscribed society.

A:   That is not true. I have denounced Mau Mau in the most strong terms I could use.

Q:   And that when, on occasions such as Kiambu, you were forced . . . to say something more definite . . . you used such terms and with such double meaning and in such forms that –

A:   That is a lie.

Q:   Let me finish my sentence – that your hearers were not deluded or deceived for one moment as to your true views.

A:   If you are doubtful I ask you to call this 40 to 50,000 people to come here and tell you if they did not understand what I said. And at Kiambu I was not forced. I was one of the organisers of the meeting. Therefore I could not have been forced to say what I said.

Q:   You will agree, will you not, that your so-called denunciation had very little effect at all?

A:   That is a lie.

Q:   You think it has?

A:   It has, yes.

Q:   You think Mau Mau is much better since you started denouncing it?

A:   You people have audacity to ask me silly questions. I have done my best and if all other people had done as I have done, Mau Mau would not be as it is now. You made it what it is, not Kenyatta.

Q:   What, 'you Europeans', 'the Crown', or who made it what it is?

A:   The Government is not handling Mau Mau in the proper way and you blame it on me.

Q:   It is the Government's fault that Mau Mau exists and goes on?

A:   Well I say yes.

Q:   I will take that answer. Thank you.

Kenyatta could not, of course, describe the response of the actual managers of Mau Mau to his Kiambu speech without giving evidence against his fellow defendants (of whose Mau Mau activities the prosecution knew surprisingly little). He did, however, point out that the Government had recorded his speech: 'So do not beat about the bush. Bring the record and you can hear what I did say.' Pritt arranged, with the help of the Kenya Government's Director of Information, for the recordings to be brought to Kapenguria. Thacker then ruled – in accordance with English court practice at the time – that such mechanical devices were not admissible as evidence.

In late March 1953, as the trial was drawing to a close, two more Mau Mau attacks frightened the settlers and the Government. The police station at Naivasha was overrun and guns and ammunition from its armoury were taken away in a lorry. If the police station could not protect itself, what hope was there for the surrounding population? That same night an even more traumatic event occurred: the Lari massacre. A British-appointed Kikuyu chief and his family and followers had moved out of land designated as 'white' in return for a substantial area in Lari. The long dispute between the displaced Lari cultivators and the chief led them to join Mau Mau. During the night of 24 March they bound the circular huts of the intruders with cable so that the doors could not be opened, poured petrol onto the thatch and set all the huts alight. Many of the men in the community were away, serving in the Kikuyu guard that was being established for anti-Mau Mau service; most of the ninety or so who died were women and children. Those who managed to escape from the burning huts were attacked with *pangas*. Such a vast attack on 'loyal' Kikuyu and so complete a success against a police station reinforced the lesson of the Rucks' murder. A white settler in Kenya at this time knew his duty. So it was no surprise when, two weeks later, Thacker found all the defendants guilty and gave them the maximum sentence of seven years' hard labour. It was more of a surprise that the Judicial Committee of the Privy Council refused leave to appeal. Pritt later wrote:

> In the forty years in which I practised before the Privy Council, during which time I presented hundreds of petitions for special leave, I never had another which was as strong as this one of Kenyatta and his colleagues, and when I came to present it I did not believe that any consideration of any kind could prevent my obtaining leave. But I was wrong; after listening to my arguments for a day and half, the Privy Council rejected it without giving any reasons.

Pritt's view was, for an Englishman at the time, unusual. He had been a Member of Parliament from 1935 to 1950, at first a Labour Party member, then an independent when his views became too left-wing for the Labour Party. His conduct of Kenyatta's case came to be regarded as not merely anti-settler but anti-British. A more typically British view was expressed by Oliver Lyttelton, Secretary of State for the Colonies, who was generally acknowledged as an unusually able businessman and politician and one of the most senior members of the Cabinet. He wrote in his memoirs, published in 1962:

> The Kikuyu . . . came under the influence of Kenyatta, a daemonic figure with extreme left-wing views. The driving force of the Mau Mau movement was, nakedly, power and the expulsion of the white man: its methods of gaining adherents were the methods of African witchcraft. The Mau

*Oliver Lyttelton, the Colonial Secretary, meets senior Kikuyu chief Njiri at Fort Hall. By November 1952 when this picture was taken, the other senior Kikuyu chiefs had been killed by Mau Mau.*

Mau oath is the most bestial, filthy and nauseating incantation which perverted minds can ever have brewed. I am not unduly squeamish, but when I first read it I was so revolted that it got between me and my appetite. It shocked even lawyers who had [acted] in cases of ritual murder in Africa . . . I can recall no instance when I have felt the forces of evil to be so near and so strong. As I wrote memoranda or instructions, I would suddenly see a shadow fall across the page – the horned shadow of the Devil himself.

Lyttelton is here describing his feelings as he sat in his large, comfortable office in Great Smith Street, with civil servants and secretaries in the private office next door and the House of Commons three minutes away. If in these circumstances he saw 'the horned shadow of the Devil himself' fall across the page he was working at, how much worse was the sense of horror, disgust and fear felt by many whites in Kenya? Even Father Trevor Huddleston, a missionary who became famous for supporting African anti-colonialists, wrote in December 1952: 'Mau Mau is a movement which in its origins and development is wholly evil. It is the worst enemy of African progress in Kenya.' What caused such intense feelings in the minds of sane Britons? What was it that had turned the process of the law into the tool of the settlers' will to imprison Kenyatta? Graham Greene was sent to Kenya by the *Sunday Times* and wrote that from the gallery of the House of Commons,

> . . . you cannot see the group of burnt huts, the charred corpse of a woman, the body robbed of its entrails, the child cut in two halves across the waist, the officer found still living by the roadside with his lower jaw sliced off, a hand and a foot severed . . .

Violence, however, was only part of the reason for the extreme British reaction. If Mau Mau consisted simply of the killers and thugs associated with certain nationalist movements – Kenya's equivalent of the Irgun Zvai Leumi or EOKA – Lyttelton would not have responded as he did. Something about Mau Mau's oaths and activities created feelings beyond even the normal hatred, fear and misrepresentation inspired by an enemy in war. The British came to believe that Mau Mau was black African witchcraft and savagery in all their ancient fearsomeness. And Kenyatta, with his piercing eyes, dominating personality and the messianic enthusiasm for Kikuyu tribal practices revealed in his book, was seen as the ultimate witch or wizard – the Devil himself.

The Kenya Government employed a psychiatrist, Dr J. C. Carothers, to write a report entitled *The Psychology of Mau Mau*, published in 1954. To help explain what was happening in Kenya he turned to late medieval Europe:

> At the midnight assemblies, homage was paid to the Devil by rituals that reversed and mocked the Catholic rituals, recitals were made of the evils recently committed, obscene songs and dances followed, a meal was taken which sometimes included human blood and urine and the flesh of infants who had been exhumed or murdered, and the meetings ended in a sexual orgy. Incredible though it seems, there is little doubt that behaviour of this type did occur, and not uncommonly, in Europe until the end of the sixteenth century, if not later . . . If one substitutes pagan culture and Christianity for the Catholic faith, and Jomo Kenyatta for the Devil, the two are often virtually identical. Jomo Kenyatta is very certain to have made some study of European witchcraft; he had the opportunity and it is easy to imagine more than one incentive . . .

The British Government published another report, *The Origins and Growth of Mau Mau*, by F. D. Corfield, former Governor of the provinces of Upper Nile and Khartoum in the Sudan, in 1960 when it wanted to justify continuing to keep Kenyatta in prison. Corfield used the statements of informers to official interrogators to support the settler view that Mau Mau was the embodiment of evil. He stated that by late 1953 Mau Mau soldiers were commonly taking an oath,

(a) to burn European crops and to kill European-owned cattle
(b) to steal firearms
(c) if ordered to kill, to kill, no matter who is to be the victim, even one's father or brother
(d) when killing, to cut off heads, extract the eyeballs and drink the liquid from them
(e) particularly to kill Europeans.

Corfield continues:

As the terms of the Mau Mau oath became increasingly more violent and bloodthirsty . . . the ritual increased in bestiality . . . forcing the initiate to reach the necessary pitch of blood lust and degradation to make it possible for him to pronounce the ghastly words . . . Public intercourse with sheep and adolescent girls were a common feature of most of these ceremonies . . . Young women were kept with the gangs for this purpose. Concoctions of the foulest ingredients were eaten and drunk . . . For one of the more notorious, known as the 'Kaberichia cocktail', semen produced in public was mixed in bowls with menstrual and sheep's blood and drunk while repeating the oath . . . These orgiastic ceremonies took place in deep forest clearings by the flickering light of bonfires . . . If any refused to take the oath they were subjected to violence. If they still refused, they were killed in the presence of others attending the ceremony.

After further detail of Mau Mau oaths and practices – including a Mau Mau 'general's' description of their ceremonial cannibalism – Corfield writes:

There is only one reasonable conclusion to be drawn from the above, and that is that the general pattern of this evolution must have been planned by a man knowing the psychology of his peoples . . . All this indicates that Jomo Kenyatta arrived back from England in 1946 with the outlines of a plan to enslave the Kikuyu and subjugate them to his will.

Like the judgement of the courts in 1953–54 that Kenyatta was the manager of Mau Mau, this conclusion – laid before Parliament in London as Command Paper no. 1030 in May 1960, seven years after Kenyatta had been locked away – went far beyond the evidence adduced. It also failed to challenge the evidence which, coming from ex-Mau Mau anxious to please their British captors, was by its nature suspect and, even if true, was not shown to be typical. The British authorities, from the Secretary of State in 1954 to the Government Commissioner in 1960, really did think they were in the presence of the Devil.

What some see as the Devil others see in more prosaic terms. The Kikuyu were agriculturalists who, before the British came, had been subjected to some fearsome experiences. They were regularly attacked by the warlike

Masai, the seasonally nomadic people of the nearby plains. And they were occasionally victims of raids by Arab slave traders. To these experiences, which taught the Kikuyu that survival was achieved by moving to the forest and keeping quiet, was added proximity to the settlers. In consequence the Kikuyu became generally cleverer than other tribes, clannish and mistrustful, quicker to see opportunities for money-making. They were called the Jews of East Africa. In the white highlands Kikuyu squatters grew cash crops and most settlers had Kikuyu servants. In Nairobi the Kikuyu were, second to the Indians, the most enterprising traders.

Kenyatta began his career in the service of Nairobi municipality, reading water-meters. While many African tribes were cut off from European ideas and ready to take their lead from the District Commissioner, all Kikuyu in the reserves had friends and relatives in Nairobi or had been there themselves. This, added to their grievance over land, made the Kikuyu the most serious challenge the settlers faced.

The action that unleashed the blood lusts and brutalities of the British–Mau Mau confrontation was the declaration of a state of emergency. By arresting Kenyatta and the younger leaders who had some political judgement, the Government left Mau Mau totally in the hands of its stormtroopers. They happened to include numerous wild youngsters, of the kind every army attracts, but whom Bildad Kaggia, Fred Kubai and their colleagues might have been able to control. This second echelon of Mau Mau leaders took all the techniques developed before the state of emergency and used them with extra crudity and viciousness. The oaths, which had been little more than the necessary guarantee of the organisation's secrecy, became, as the Mau Mau gangs retreated into the forest and found themselves isolated and prone to fear, increasingly like the sexual and sadistic fantasies of demented adolescents. The killing of selected targets became the mindless and uncontrolled mutilation of hundreds.

All these changes happened after Jomo Kenyatta was imprisoned, when he was clearly not responsible for them. Why, then, did so many apparently rational European officials see Kenyatta as the principal devil? The experience of Sir Walter Coutts, who came to be widely regarded in later years as one of the chief enemies of Kenyatta in the British administration, helps explain. In 1947, after Kenyatta returned from England, Coutts was a young District Commissioner in Kenya's Fort Hall district. Kenyatta applied for permission to hold meetings and many DCs turned him down. They thought he was a Communist, an agitator and out to talk their natives into parting with their money for his benefit. Some were influenced by settler gossip about the white wife he had left behind in England. They were made uncomfortable by his contacts in the Labour Party and the House of Commons. Coutts stood out against such prejudice. He invited Kenyatta up to Fort Hall, toured the district with him and gave him permission to hold meetings. Coutts explained to Kenyatta the policies he was trying to implement, in particular the difficult soil conservation process of terracing,

*The harshest and most effective force fighting Mau Mau was the African resistance movement, some of whose members are here seen arresting two suspects in Nyeri district in December 1952*

which required heavy labour, mostly done by unenthusiastic African women. Coutts says that Kenyatta accepted his explanation of the wonders achieved by terracing and was persuaded that, given the population increase, the measure was essential to raise output from the land. Coutts recalled, 'he would stand up in public with me and talk about the virtues of soil conservation'. Coutts was dismayed, therefore, when Kenyatta chaired a large KAU meeting at Fort Hall which resolved that terracing should cease. Worse, 'young men in natty suits would drive up from Nairobi in smart cars after every Kenyatta meeting' to organise a boycott of terracing. Coutts believed that Kenyatta, to win easy popularity, deliberately wrecked measures that he knew were for the benefit of the Kikuyu in the area. He recalled: 'Within three months of Kenyatta coming up to the district, the whole soil conservation scheme fell to bits.' Worst of all, Kenyatta had double-crossed a young official who had taken a risk in inviting him into his area. Coutts concluded: 'This man was not straight in any way whatsoever. I felt that Kenyatta was evil.'

Such a conversion of a liberal-minded young DC helps to explain how older officials and settlers felt. Kenyatta threatened everything they had devoted their lives to building up. Only he could dominate vast Kikuyu audiences with his appeals to their tribal memory. He plainly enjoyed using the knowledge of Kikuyu practices that he had displayed in *Facing Mount Kenya*. If a single intelligence lay behind Mau Mau then, the British and many Kikuyu concluded, it must be Kenyatta. Mr Justice Thacker had spoken for most Europeans in Kenya at the end of the trial at Kapenguria:

> You, Jomo Kenyatta, stand convicted of managing Mau Mau . . . You have protested that your object has always been to pursue constitutional methods on the way to self-government for the African people . . . I do not believe you . . . It is my belief that soon after your stay in Europe when you came back to this Colony, you commenced to organise this Mau Mau society, the object of which was to drive out from Kenya all Europeans, and in doing so to kill them if necessary. I am satisfied that the master mind behind this plan was yours . . . You have taken the fullest advantage of the power and influence which you have over your people and also of the primitive instincts which you know lie deep down in their characters . . . You have persuaded them in secret to murder, to burn, to commit evil atrocities.

Thacker then recommended that at the conclusion of his seven-year sentence Kenyatta should be restricted. The power to restrict lay only with the Governor and in September 1954 Sir Evelyn Baring announced that as soon as Kenyatta had completed his sentence a restriction order would take effect requiring him to live 'in a remote place'. The order, Baring said, 'will remain in force indefinitely'. The Government did its best to erase the memory of Kenyatta. His college at Githunguri was destroyed, his home at Gatundu was pulled down, his farm was given over to an agricultural college. A prison was specially built for him and his fellow Mau Mau 'managers' at Lokitaung, in the northern desert. The guards spoke no Kikuyu. So far as they could, short of murder, the British obliterated him.

Beside the problem of a British settler community and a large part of the British Government hysterically over-reacting to Mau Mau, the practical problem of dealing with it was comparatively easy. Mau Mau affected only one tribe and a limited area of Kenya. In both Malaya and Cyprus a senior British soldier was brought out as Governor to turn the entire resources of the country against the terrorist challenge. In Kenya this was not necessary. The Governor, Sir Evelyn Baring, a notably unmilitary figure who was repeatedly ill and could therefore easily have been relieved, stayed in charge throughout. The number of European civilians killed by Mau Mau was thirty-two – each case horrifying but the total fewer than the number of Europeans killed in traffic accidents in Nairobi in 1952–6, when Mau Mau

*Part of one of the camps in which suspected Mau Mau were held.*

was active. The number of African civilians killed by Mau Mau was officially recorded as 1,819. The settlers made sure the story of their suffering reached the British newspapers and Parliament, but most of the whites, though frightened, were not prevented from continuing with their business. Mau Mau caused an emotional shock to the British and created panic among many of them, but the danger was more psychological than military.

The military problem was handled quickly and fairly efficiently. The Mau Mau, driven into the forest by the declaration of the state of emergency, had to be cut off from their sources of food and support both in the Kikuyu reserve and in Nairobi. So, as in Malaya, the scattered rural population was forced to move into 'new villages', surrounded by troops and barbed wire, where the Mau Mau could not get at them. And in Nairobi a mass arrest of young Kikuyu – any who could not satisfy the police and army as to their reason for being where they were – led to 17,000 being interned in April 1954. This drastic measure shattered the Mau Mau hierarchy and cells in Nairobi, in addition to removing many innocent people from their homes. Militarily the campaign was far shorter and easier than those in either Malaya or Cyprus.

It was conducted, however, in a pathological atmosphere. Settlers formed their own auxiliary forces to help the security effort. John Wainwright, a young settler in 1952–53, recalled:

> We set up two private armies, mounted cavalry. For us it was a bit like being cowboys – *Boy's Own* stuff. Our idea was to help isolated farmers. What we did was we went from farm to farm and we spent a night on each so that the farmer and his wife could have a night's sleep. We didn't always stay near farmhouses. We simply rode until we were too tired to ride any more and then we fell off our horses and slept. So the terrorists never had any idea where we were or where we were going to be next. Our biggest success was in the Nanyuki area. An old Kikuyu told us that a gang was hidden up in some rocks and we left our horses and went up there and sure enough we found three people asleep and one of them was the gang leader who we'd been looking for, Brigadier Kago, and we shot them and put Kago in the back of an open truck down to Nanyuki so that the local people could see that he had been killed. Then we took him to the police station.

Settlers also joined auxiliary police and army units. To many of them every Kikuyu was a Mau Mau. Sir George Erskine, the General appointed in June 1953 to command the Kenyan security forces during the emergency, had within a week of his arrival become appalled at the 'indiscriminate shooting' in which he found British and Kenyan army units indulging, including scoreboards and £5 rewards for 'kills'. He tried to put a stop to such conduct and warned his subordinates that he would not protect them or their men against murder charges. Consequently settlers complained that he failed to pursue his task with proper vigour and formed a general dislike of him. Erskine reciprocated their hostility, writing to his wife: 'Kenya is a sunny place for shady people . . . I hate the guts of them all. They are all middle-class sluts.'

Labour MPs at Westminster maintained a regular assault on abuses in the colony, helped by young national service officers with political ambitions who sent them reports. John Whyatt, the Attorney-General in Kenya, genuinely wanted to prosecute all breaches of the law. A parliamentary delegation came to Kenya from London in February 1954 and found that 'brutality and malpractices by the police have occurred on a scale which constitutes a threat to public confidence in the forces of law and order'. It went on to report that, since the start of the emergency, Whyatt had launched 130 prosecutions for police brutality, obtaining 73 convictions. The sentence, however, was usually only a small fine. When Brian Howard, a young settler in the Kenya Police Reserve, was found guilty of burning suspects' ear-drums with cigarettes and sentenced to a fine of £100 and three months' hard labour, the Young Settler Defence Fund and others competed to pay his fine and protested so angrily at the 'savagery' of his sentence that he was allowed to spend his three months in a hotel.

Between Whyatt's determination to enforce the law and the settlers' zeal to kill Mau Mau, Baring was trapped. The income of the country and Baring's plans for its future depended on the settlers. He could not ignore their strongly-held views. He rejected their demands for summary justice, wider death sentences, movement controls, forfeiture of Mau Mau land and representation in an inner Cabinet. However, if they considered that the Government was failing them, they could take the law into their own hands even more than Wainwright and others had already done. His solution was generally to allow Whyatt to take action against settler and army excesses, but to back local administrators when they argued that they must protect 'loyal' Kikuyu, whose excesses against Mau Mau suspects were often worse. One Kikuyu woman described 'loyal' Kikuyu holding down Mau Mau suspects and castrating them with a pair of pliers. When they reported suspects 'shot while trying to escape' the circumstances frequently belied the excuse. Baring feared that to prosecute and punish the 'loyal' Kikuyu for pursuing Mau Mau with vigour would confuse and discourage them. So he stopped Whyatt from prosecuting. Each decision like this was distasteful to him, but to propitiate the white settlers in Kenya and many in the Conservative Party in London who were convinced that Mau Mau was the army of the Devil, he overruled both Whyatt and his own instinct.

He had his eyes on the future when the Mau Mau madness would be over, and he took advantage of the state of emergency to push through economic and social reforms with a firmness that would not otherwise have been possible. The strength of Mau Mau was broken by mid-1954. Baring wanted to grant an amnesty as soon as possible to persuade the remaining Mau Mau in the forest to surrender (also to enable him to grant an amnesty to lawbreakers on the Government side, who Whyatt continued to demand must be prosecuted). The settlers bitterly opposed an amnesty for the Mau Mau, which they variously described as 'grasping hands stained with blood', 'parleying with murderers' and 'the Governor taking the Mau Mau oath'. Lyttelton backed Baring in overruling them and in carrying into effect the first of Baring's major steps towards reconstruction: a new constitution. Where hitherto the Government had been mainly in the hands of officials, from 1954 representatives of all races were brought in as Ministers. At first officials remained in the majority, but three local Europeans, two Asians and one African were given ministerial posts. Lyttelton wrote later: 'I tried hard to get the other races to accept one more African in the Ministry, but to have insisted would have been to break down the agreement which I had secured.' The appointment of one African minister was a breakthrough, achieved only by Lyttelton's browbeating of the settlers.

The obvious candidate for this job was Eliud Mathu, the ex-Balliol man who had been on the Legislative Council since 1944, proving himself a sound government man. But the settlers would not accept a Kikuyu, suspecting even Mathu of having Mau Mau links. So a little known Luo became Kenya's first black minister. The same fear of the Devil-tribe affected the first election in which Africans were enabled to vote, in 1957. Rules of great complexity, designed to keep out extremist candidates and to give additional votes to the highly qualified, included the provision that no Kikuyu could vote unless he had a 'loyalty certificate'. Few did.

Eighty thousand Kikuyu – almost a third of the tribe's adult males – had been removed to detention camps, where the Government was trying to 'rehabilitate' them. A large proportion of the tribe had been forced to take one or other of the Mau Mau oaths and, following Dr Carothers' report, the administration considered that these people had been made psychiatrically ill and needed to be cured. The therapy ranged from vigorous, compulsory outdoor activities of a generally boy-scout type to lectures by Christian missionaries and the exorcising efforts of men who came to be known as HM Witch-Doctors. Plainly the Government had to return the Kikuyu to normal life as soon as possible, if only to relieve the pressure on the makeshift camps, where disease was rife. So dangerous were the hardcore Mau Mau judged to be that the latrines in the camps – holes the inmates were ordered to dig – were provided with no stone footholds, in case inmates used the stones as weapons. Officials had promised both the settlers and the 'loyal' Kikuyu that the hardcore would not be allowed to return. The first task in the camps, therefore, was to separate them from those who could be saved. Like the non-person Kenyatta, the hardcore were effectively under a life sentence.

*An anti-Mau Mau oath being administered by a 'loyal' witch doctor to Kikuyu women.*

Baring, meanwhile, was devoting his energies to land reform. The key to politics in Kenya, as in most African countries, was land, above all the rich land of the Kikuyu. The emergency made possible a revolution in Kikuyu land-holding. This was the decisive change in Kenya's politics and economics that was to shape the future of the country. It was Baring's main enthusiasm and was in his view always more important – though less urgent – than the emergency itself.

The Kikuyu system of land ownership was to cultivate strips, rather like the medieval English open-field system. Baring saw that to increase African income the strips must be consolidated into farms that could be more efficiently managed, rather like the English enclosure movement. But where enclosure took England four centuries, Baring forced it through in Kenya in five years, depriving many Kikuyu farmers of their strips so that their more efficient neighbours could obtain consolidated farms. And to prevent this process from rendering the deprived strip-cultivators landless and discontented, Baring secured the funds to buy substitute farmland. The essence of the policy was the active encouragement of the Africans to grow cash crops – coffee, tea, pyrethrum, pineapples – for overseas sale. The settlers had always opposed attempts to help the Africans compete with them in these markets. Baring used the emergency to overcome settler objections, obtain the vast sums of money needed and, in effect, to carry through in a decade a complete agrarian revolution. He argued convincingly that Kenya needed both the revenue and the political stability that would result from strengthening the prosperous, black, peasant class.

Baring, until his appointment to Kenya, had not been a member of the Colonial Service. He had started in the Indian Civil Service and had then joined the family bank, Barings, in the City of London, of which he was offered the chairmanship. He turned this down and joined the Foreign Office instead, and he had gone on to hold the mainly diplomatic posts of Governor of settler-ruled Rhodesia and High Commissioner to South Africa. One of his great skills was at international financial management, and he used the emergency to extract large sums of money from the British Treasury for land schemes, which he was truthfully able to describe as essential to rehabilitate the Kikuyu. As the 'loyal' Kikuyu began to run their new, consolidated farms, their need for finance grew – for plants, fertiliser, farm equipment. Baring again used his financial credit and know-how, this time with the World Bank, to set up loan schemes for the farmers. Inevitably he soon had to extend the policy to other tribes.

Oliver Lyttelton told the settlers bluntly that Britain would not pay for an army to protect them against a revival of Mau Mau. The only protection available to them was African consent, and that meant starting to share power at once. The main settler leader, Michael Blundell, understood and tried to win over his fellow-whites. The Mau Mau revolt converted just enough of them from their commitment to white supremacy to enable Baring and the new Colonial Secretary appointed in 1954, Alan Lennox-Boyd, in co-operation with Blundell, to edge their way towards a system of partnership in government, the power-sharing between Africans, Asians and Europeans that the Colonial Office had been urging since 1923.

What the British needed to carry through this policy was an African leader capable of both maintaining popular support in the tribes and inspiring confidence among the settlers. In 1957 the ideal man arrived in the Legislative Assembly. He was Tom Mboya, one of the first eight elected African members of the Legislative Assembly (Mathu and previous members had been appointed). His constituency was Nairobi, where he had built up widespread support as a trade union leader. Although a Luo by origin, his trade union activity and his extraordinary mastery of European culture, legislative processes and politics had made him the first non-tribal political leader of Kenya Africans. Only 27 when he joined the Legislative Council, Mboya had already won himself friends and admirers in the British Labour Party and in the trade union movement in the United States. His level of accomplishment as writer, speaker and political operator quickly made him the most powerful force in Kenyan politics.

Mboya arrived in the Legislative Council to demand that the number of African members there should be raised from eight to twenty-three, so that African representatives would equal the number of Europeans and Asians put together. He soon got a substantial increase. The independence of the Gold Coast as Ghana in March 1957 marked a change in African politics. The inspiration to nationalist leaders afforded by Nkrumah's assuming supreme power stimulated others to demand the same. If multi-racialism was to be preserved in Kenya, Mboya's demands had to be partly met. The Colonial Secretary, Lennox-Boyd, and the Governor, Baring, did their best to drag the reluctant settlers along with them in their attempts to satisfy Mboya. Neither of them approved of his impatience. Baring was particularly dismayed when Mboya opposed the extension of land consolidation to Luo areas. Here was a repeat of the occasions when Kenyatta shocked Sir Walter Coutts over terracing and when Nkrumah opposed the cutting-out of infected cocoa trees (see p. 379). African politicians, like any others, would support popular prejudice against wise policy if that was the best way to win votes. But, though they disapproved of his constantly escalating demands, Lennox-Boyd and Baring needed Mboya as an ally. He was able to inspire vast crowds of Africans, to manage and direct his fellow African members of the assembly and to handle the complexities of Government affairs with easy mastery. While he reinforced his popular support by calling for ever more power for the Africans and pouring scorn on Uncle Toms who accepted ministerial office in a white-dominated Government, the Europeans in the assembly who spoke to him privately – as only a few did – recognised him as a rational man whom they could deal with. A new leader was emerging who plainly, like Kwame Nkrumah in Ghana who advised him on political tactics, was determined to be top man.

In the course of so rapid a political rise, Mboya could not help offending the senior politician of his own tribe, Oginga Odinga. An older man, Odinga was in general agreement with most of Mboya's policies but discomforted by Mboya's skill, particularly at self-advertisement. In parliamentary and party committees Mboya repeatedly made sure Odinga had the senior position, as chairman, while himself controlling decisions, usually as sec-retary. With most of the Kikuyu disenfranchised, these two Luo became the dominant figures in African politics in Kenya. In June 1958, with his position relative to Mboya slipping, Odinga took the dangerous step of breaching a taboo.

In the Kenya Legislative Council the name of Jomo Kenyatta had been unmentioned and unmentionable for the best part of five years. He was the Devil and he had been exorcised. Some of his fellow prisoners at Lokitaung had managed to have complaints published in the *Observer* newspaper in London about their conditions of detention. They accused the Kenya Government of trying to starve them to death. The Chief Secretary in Kenya replied to the charges:

> Lengthy and careful inquiries have been carried out and no evidence of any irregularities has come to light . . . These were men who inspired superstition and fear among the masses of the Kikuyu . . . to obtain the greatest possible security it has been necessary to keep them in a very remote spot . . .

Odinga rose in the Legislative Council and said:

> These people, before they were arrested, were the political leaders of the Africans in the country, and the Africans respected them as their political leaders, and even at this moment in the hearts of the Africans, they are still the political leaders . . .

Odinga was howled down. African members of the Legislative Council, hoping soon to have power in their hands, white settler members horrified at this praise of the Devil, Government officials fearful for public order, all rose to speak, expostulate, shout and heckle. The Speaker, as soon as he could make himself heard, adjourned the assembly.

Odinga had tried, after Kenyatta's return to Kenya in 1946, to help him win support for KAU among the Luo. He had been deeply impressed by Kenyatta's oratory and political skill. They had shared many campaigns. Odinga was not to be silenced now. He was pressed to apologise for his outburst and, when the assembly session was resumed next day, he said:

> Just as when Archbishop Makarios was arrested by the British Govern-ment, he was taken to the Seychelles . . . [and] nearly every day there was a report of his health, of his activities, in the press, the same thing should be done for Mr Kenyatta . . .

Now he had actually spoken the taboo name. The cries of rage were redoubled. Members shouted 'Mau Mau' and demanded that Odinga be hounded out of public life. He recalled :

Other African members said I must apologise. I had gone too far. They wanted to expel me from the African Elected Members Association [a body that partly compensated for the Government ban on nationwide political parties]. Then I challenged my colleagues to hold meetings in Kisumu, Nairobi and Mombasa and let the people denounce me for saying that Kenyatta is the leader. If the people denounced me, then I would agree to withdraw. If they didn't, then my colleagues should apologise to me. In Kisumu the Provincial Commissioner called together all the chiefs in Luoland. For two days they tried to persuade me not to support Kenyatta, not ever to mention him, and to go back to the Legislative Council to apologise to His Excellency the Governor for having spoken Kenyatta's name. The Chiefs all said: 'We know Kenyatta and the Kikuyu – they are all killers. These Kikuyu, they steal anything. We do not want any trouble here.' So I told them: 'You should call a big public meeting here in Kisumu. At that meeting you, the chiefs, will be able to speak, and so will I. And then if the people decide that I should drop Kenyatta's name, I will do so. If they decide that I should go on with Kenyatta, then you also should come along with it. Then the Africans met in Nairobi, Kisumu and Mombasa and passed a vote of confidence in me. My colleagues changed their tune after that, because the pressure was coming from the people.

Tom Mboya was deeply embarrassed by Odinga's tactic. The last thing the rising star wanted was the return of the old leader. He said nothing for some weeks, but eventually saw that Odinga had judged the African mood correctly. Kapenguria had given Kenyatta the crown of martyrdom among the Kikuyu, the largest tribe, and Odinga had persuaded the Luo, the second largest tribe, to recognise that their interests were best served by a close alliance with the Kikuyu. Mboya had no choice but to follow Odinga's lead.

All the African political leaders in the Legislative Council except Odinga were happy to have Kenyatta kept out of the way. The several smaller tribes, who together represented as large a population as the Kikuyu and Luo combined, had no desire to see either Kenyatta or the Kikuyu restored to dominance in the politics of the country. The 'loyal' Kikuyu too, increasingly prosperous thanks to land consolidation, preferred Kenyatta and the Mau Mau leaders forgotten. The release of Kenyatta was now back on the political agenda, but the effective majority were against it.

The dominating issue in African politics was a conflict between those who wished to take office under the 'power-sharing' constitutional arrangements which Baring and the Colonial Office devised to ensure a safe future for the whites and the Indians, and those like Mboya and Odinga who insisted that unfettered power must be placed in the hands of the majority. Mboya's friends in London and America were disappointed by his refusal to take up the ministerial office that his early success in the Legislative Council had made available to him. He judged, however, that African voters would soon have to be given power proportional to their numbers and that the political leaders who entered deals with the settlers would then be swept aside. So Mboya and Odinga campaigned together for full democracy, full independence and the release of Kenyatta – Mboya because he calculated that these were the causes that would be victorious and Odinga because he passionately believed in them. The Government, in pursuit of its objective of independence by 1975 or thereabouts was obliged to recruit African ministers who, though often able men, were not from the top rank.

In March 1959 an incident occurred in a remote camp for hardcore Mau Mau detainees which compelled the British Prime Minister, Harold Macmillan, to give his mind to Kenya. The Hola massacre, as it came to be known, changed the direction of British policy in a way the arguments of Mboya, for all their undisputed quality, had no hope of doing. Government forces, in the course of defeating Mau Mau, had killed some 10,000 Kikuyu. In addition more than 1,000 had been hanged. Many of the 80,000 taken to rehabilitation camps responded willingly to a régime designed to turn them into loyal, hard-working citizens. Others refused to confess to swearing oaths or to crimes committed while in Mau Mau and adopted a negative attitude to the manual work they were ordered to do. Those who confessed and co-operated soon found themselves in a pipeline that led back to freedom and their families, though under the surveillance of a local official to whom they had to report. Those who did not became increasingly a problem for the administration. The Government's theory, following Dr Carothers, was that the Mau Mau oath and the vile deeds they had done in the forests had turned the detainees into amoral creatures, cut off from Christianity, normal Kikuyu tribal life and the will to work. Rehabilitating them for citizenship, like dealing with a negative child, involved threats, promises and the use of 'compelling force' (though not, the rules stated, 'overwhelming force').

By 1959 some 77,000 detainees had been released. The Government decided that the residue of some 1,100 would be concentrated in one camp at Hola, a remote spot near a small river, where the detainees could work on an irrigation scheme that should eventually enable those of them who could not be trusted to return home to grow their own food. Those detainees who had refused to work were to be compelled. Once they had cleared the hurdle of their resistance to work, officials argued, their rehabilitation could begin: making them work was for their own good. To this end, force was permitted. Warders were instructed to 'manhandle the detainees to the place of work and force them to carry out their tasks'. On the first day this procedure was applied to 88 detainees. Eleven of them died and some twenty others were severely injured – the result of beating with sticks by African warders.

News of the murders seeped out slowly. The Governor, who was responsible for the policy of forcing the detainees to work, sent three senior officials to Hola to find out what had happened. On the basis of their hastily gathered information, he issued a statement implying that the deaths were the result

of drinking contaminated water. But the truth could not be suppressed. A coroner had to report on the cause of death and his descriptions of the injuries suffered by the eleven men who died – a fractured skull, brain lacerations, fractured jaw, broken limbs – led to a worldwide outcry.

In the same month as the Hola massacre, more than fifty Africans were killed by police and troops in Nyasaland (see p. 480). When the reports on both events came before Parliament, Harold Macmillan found himself responsible for defending actions that were horrifying and of no benefit to Britain. By now, mid-1959, France had announced that it would give independence to all its colonies in Africa and Belgium had been shaken by anti-white riots in the Congo. Talks were under way about progress towards independence for Tanganyika and Uganda. If Britain hung on to Kenya to protect its white settlers, it risked being left behind there – the final anachronism.

After the British general election in October 1959 Macmillan appointed a new Colonial Secretary, Iain Macleod, who later wrote:

> It has been said that after I became Colonial Secretary, there was a deliberate speeding-up of the movement towards independence. I agree. There was. In my view any other policy would have led to terrible bloodshed in Africa. This is the heart of the argument.

Macleod had been principally interested in British domestic policy until Hola, but the killing of eleven detained men who had not even been tried for

*Hola. Left is the open camp, where detainees lived with their wives and children and worked four-acre irrigated plots. Right is the closed camp for the 'hard core'.*

a crime outraged him. He decided that Britain must quickly grant independence and must not be held up by the requirements of a white settler community. Macleod's younger brother, Rhoddy, was a farmer in Kenya who in 1953, soon after the declaration of the state of emergency, became an inspector in the intelligence branch of the Kenya police force. The knowledge that the new Colonial Secretary had such a brother was reassuring to most Kenya settlers, but the younger Macleod was not a typical settler. He was one of the whites who went to Kapenguria to hear parts of the trial of Jomo Kenyatta and was not convinced that the prosecution's case was conclusive. He headed one of the interrogation teams appointed to divide interned Kikuyu into innocent farm labourers and Mau Mau, and was surprised at the large numbers who were held for three or four years before their innocence could be established. He went into the forests to talk Mau Mau members into surrendering, shook hands with them, satisfied them of his good faith and brought them out to be rehabilitated. He was, with Michael Blundell, one of the founders of the New Kenya Party, dedicated to a multi-racial Kenya.

Iain Macleod followed a policy of which his brother approved. He brought all forty elected members of Kenya's Legislative Council to London for a conference whose purpose was to advance Kenya rapidly towards independence by creating an African-led multi-racial Government. He was able to do this thanks mainly to his brother's political associate, Michael Blundell, who recognised that the only way to secure inter-racial partnership was promptly to concede a substantial share of power to the Africans. Most of the settlers disagreed. The hard-liners were amply represented at the London conference, but a surprising change had occurred among those the settlers had elected to Legco. They had been converted by the force of Blundell's arguments and the evident quality and adaptability of Mboya as a political leader. Thus although the view of the majority of settlers was unchanged, among their representatives, Blundell's view was predominant.

The Africans began the conference with an unexpected demand, advanced by Oginga Odinga: that Kenyatta be released and brought to London. Knowing the pandemonium it would provoke from the hard-line settler leaders, Macleod refused even to discuss this idea. The Africans then came up with a second demand: that an old and trusted friend of Kenyatta, Peter Mbiyu Koinange, son of the chief who had been made to grub out his coffee plants, be admitted. Peter Koinange had been expelled from Kenya at the start of the emergency and subsequently worked for a while in London as a milkman. When Macleod turned down the demand for him to attend, the Africans walked out. The hard-line settler group warned: 'If Koinange is in, we are out.' Macleod solved this problem by a neat dodge. A blank card was issued on which the Africans could write Koinange's name. This did not admit the bearer to the conference room, but it did let him into the conference building, Lancaster House. Sir Hilton Poynton, Permanent

Secretary to the Colonial Office, celebrated this diplomatic triumph with a quatrain:

'Mau Mau milkman, have you any pass?'
'Yes sir, yes sir, but only second-class.
Good for the cloakroom and good for the loo,
But not for the Music Room among the chosen few.'

Macleod built an alliance between the Blundell group of whites and the Africans, with a constitution that provided for an African majority of one among elected members of the legislature – 33 seats out of the 65 which were to be elected on a common roll, of which 20 were reserved for the Europeans and Asians – and four elected African ministers against three European. Mboya and Odinga had long said they would not accept such a deal, preserving as it did a disproportionate share of power for the whites. But the principle of an African majority had been conceded and the hard-line white delegates were so apoplectic in their rage with Macleod and Blundell for contriving such a deal that even the radical Africans at the conference accepted it. When Blundell arrived at Nairobi airport, a settler threw thirty pieces of silver at his feet and many Europeans ostentatiously refused to speak to him. The hard-line European party called the agreement the 'cynical abandonment of the Europeans in Kenya' and 'a victory for Mau Mau'. A year later Blundell wrote to Macleod:

Although our agreement at Lancaster House practically killed me politically, nevertheless we were right. I have now spoken to more than 20,000 Africans at public meetings and hundreds privately, and I have been left with an impression of great friendliness – all the jealous racial questions have gone . . . the alternative to Lancaster House was an explosion. The result of it is a real chance of success here.

A Government was quickly set up with an African majority among its Ministers, though neither Mboya nor Odinga would join it. A national political party of Africans – the Kenya African National Union – was created, with Kenyatta as President. When the Governor, Sir Patrick Renison, said that he would not allow KANU to function with Kenyatta as President, an acting President, James Gichuru, was appointed to keep the seat warm until Kenyatta's release. Odinga was the man behind this arrangement, still preserving the Luo alliance with the Kikuyu and manoeuvring with skill to keep Tom Mboya from becoming too powerful. The competing ambitions of the two leaders made it convenient to hold the nationalist movement together by keeping the top post open for the leader who was absent. Minority tribes were reinforced in their fear that a Kikuyu-Luo alliance under Kenyatta's leadership would override their interests.

At this point, in the first half of 1960, the Belgians were preparing to leave the Congo. A total breakdown of order was rapidly to follow, with whites fleeing by car and train, and a savage civil war engulfing the entire country.

*Sir Patrick Renison, Governor of Kenya, left, and Iain Macleod, Colonial Secretary, at Nairobi airport, March 1960.*

Whites throughout Africa were terrified. Many decided that they too must leave. In Kenya house and share prices slumped. Capital began to flow rapidly out of the country.

To restore European confidence and hand over to majority rule a country that was still economically prosperous, Macleod authorised Renison to make a statement confirming that the Government would not release Kenyatta. At a press conference in May 1960, immediately after he had returned from seeing Macleod in London, Sir Patrick said:

> Jomo Kenyatta was the recognised leader of the non-cooperation move-ment which organised Mau Mau. With its foul oathing and violent aims, Mau Mau had been declared an unlawful society. He was convicted of managing that unlawful society . . . He appealed to the Supreme Court and the Privy Council . . . [and] his guilt was established and confirmed. Here was the African leader to darkness and death. He was sentenced by due process of law . . . The readiness [of Africans] for self-government will be measured by the readiness of their leaders to acknowledge those facts and their ability to carry their followers with them.

Renison's use of the words 'Leader to darkness and death' has been the subject of much criticism and speculation. Macleod had strongly advised him to delete these words from his statement, because sooner or later they would probably have to do business with Kenyatta. The Governor threatened to resign. His closest advisers, including the former D.C. from Fort Hall, Walter Coutts, who was now deputy Governor, told him the words were true; the Corfield report which set out to prove that the settler view of Mau Mau was right and Kenyatta was the Devil, had just come into the Governor's hands and was about to be published; many settlers were determined to disrupt the peaceful transfer of power into the hands of moderate Africans. Further, officials reported that Kenyatta was old and growing feeble in detention. He would soon die and the demands for his release would be forgotten. Macleod concluded that Kenya was in so dangerous a state it would be imprudent to provoke Renison's resignation.

The positive case for letting Renison go ahead was that the words could ease Macleod's difficulties with the Conservative Party in Westminster. His Kenya policy was moving too fast for many backbenchers and a tough line on Kenyatta could reassure them. More important still was the need to stop the settlers from taking their money, skills and families out of Kenya. It was, after all, only a matter of a few words. If it stilled settler panic it might save Kenya's economy.

And so it did. In the election held in February 1961 on the basis of the new constitution, the main African political leaders, Mboya, Odinga and their colleagues in KANU, campaigned on the claim that they would not accept office unless Kenyatta was released, and they won the majority of the votes. But the Governor was able to form a ministry of minority tribal leaders, European settlers and officials. It bought enough settler confidence to secure the transition. Within weeks the Government decided to build Kenyatta a house near the one that it had destroyed in 1953 and began preparations for his release. With some of their own number in responsible positions in the Government, the settlers could accept a policy which, coming from the Governor alone or from an all-African Government, would have revived European panic. In their role as ministers, white settlers accepted that an insistent demand from KANU, the largest single party in the legislature, could not long be resisted without provoking disorder. In the election KANU posters had carried Kenyatta's picture and KANU speakers had referred to him as the national leader. So the Government decided that politicians and journalists must be allowed to visit him. Their reports gradually spread the word that he was not the ogre the settlers had thought. He remained puzzling and arrogant. Asked what were his feelings about the Governor, he said he bore no grudge, Sir Patrick had been poorly advised, and added that he, Kenyatta, would borrow the words of Jesus: 'Father forgive them for they know not what they do'.

Slowly, by stages, he was released. In October 1961 he became President of KANU. A seat was found for him in the Legislative Council and in April 1962 he was appointed Minister of State for Constitutional Affairs and Economic Planning in a coalition Government. KANU had made him its figurehead, but it was by no means clear at first that he was effective either as party leader or minister. He was a far less skilled performer in the Legislative Council than Mboya. Only in huge open-air meetings, where his tribal

*Kenyatta greets crowds at Nairobi airport on his release from detention, August 1961.*

intimacies and his old-fashioned oratory excited crowds, was he at his best. Many such meetings were arranged for him.

With the British rulers soon to depart, competition for the succession broke out between tribes, parties and individuals. The only man with the skill and standing to hold himself above such conflicts was Kenyatta. He again employed all the evasiveness he had shown in the early days of Mau Mau. He could thrill an audience, making them cheer and howl with delight, leaving all parties convinced he was on their side. Yet the tape-recording or shorthand note revealed no commitment to any but the most bland generalities:

> I do not feel bitter towards anyone at all because I know my cause and my activities were just. I regard everybody as my friends. You know the commandment, 'Love thy Neighbour'? Well, the world is my neighbour.

Kenyatta had the power to make such sentences sound at the same time threatening and mystical. He began to make the multi-racial, multi-party coalition Government of which he was a junior member seem an irrelevancy. After nine years he was a more fully qualified prison graduate than any colonial nationalist leader since Nehru. He had returned to take up where he left off – uniting the people around him. It was only a matter of time before he became formally leader of the nation. The mechanisms – another constitutional conference in London, a general election in 1963 – became almost like the stages in a procession. Enthronement was the inevitable culmination. Carrying his huge fly-whisk as though it were the sceptre of a king, Kenyatta re-established himself as the monarch of the Kenya Africans.

But what of the whites? How were they to be persuaded to keep their skills and capital in Kenya as it slowly came under the control of a man they had recently described as the Devil, wholly responsible for the oath-taking and the vile and primitive murders perpetrated by Mau Mau, the leader to darkness and death? Someone had to make the white settlers understand that their security in Kenya depended on coming to terms with the Kikuyu and Luo, the largest and most powerful tribes. That meant accepting Kenyatta. The final stages of the British transfer of power to the Africans therefore needed a Governor of outstanding political deftness. The man chosen, Malcolm MacDonald, had shown such qualities in Malaya (see page 178) and subsequently as Britain's High Commissioner to India. Before leaving London he consulted the Government's experts about the part-mythical monster he was to deal with. The clear impression they gave him of Kenyatta was:

> That I would meet in him a wicked old man who was fortunately past his prime, quickly declining in physical and mental powers, and whose influence was being progressively subordinated to that of younger and abler political colleagues. He might still have a certain temporary importance because his name was something to conjure with among the African masses – but this too, I was informed, would linger but briefly, since he was rapidly boozing himself to death . . . The authorities in London not only suspected Kenyatta of increasing feebleness but also the Kikuyu as a whole of innate viciousness.

MacDonald found this fabulous personality and his tribe not quite as described. First, when drink was offered, Kenyatta restricted himself to Coca-Cola. Second, although some of his younger colleagues, particularly Tom Mboya and James Gichuru, exerted more influence than Kenyatta in settling important issues, his mastery of events was slowly reviving after his long detention. As he travelled around the country, renewing his contacts, learning the needs of different areas, weighing the willpower and support of local leaders, he revealed that in the art of striking a political balance, judging what measures would be most widely acceptable, he was unsurpassed. Both Mboya and Gichuru separately said to MacDonald: 'We didn't know the old man had it in him.'

As for the Kikuyu and KANU, the party which they were now free to dominate, MacDonald recorded:

> When I arrived in Nairobi I discovered that the British Colonial officials (with the consent of Whitehall) were doing everything they discreetly could in marginal constituencies to ensure that KANU candidates would

be defeated, so that [the party of the minority tribes] would . . . gain a . . .
majority in the new legislature.

MacDonald changed this policy, which seemed certain to fail. KANU duly
won the election in May 1963. Kenyatta became Prime Minister and allotted
a large number of Government jobs to the most capable tribe in the country,
the Kikuyu.

However, he also understood the need to bind the nation together. He
preached the unity of all tribes, as he had done since he returned to Kenya in
1946, and in August 1963, a few weeks after firmly establishing himself as
Prime Minister, he delivered a decisive address to a meeting of some 300
white farmers at Nakuru, in what had until a few months earlier been called
the 'White Highlands'. This was Lord Delamere's country and many of
those who came to hear him felt betrayed. They had accepted that open
white rule in Kenya was not possible, but until recently the British
Government had assured them that, even though black faces might have to
occupy the more prominent positions in the Government of Kenya, the
constitution would preserve a substantial white voice in all decisions that
mattered. Now not only were they faced with a black Prime Minister, but of
all conceivable blacks the worst. Every settler was contemplating selling his
farm, restrained in large measure by the low state of the land market.
Kenyatta had made statements intended to reassure them, but this was the
first time he had come to address a meeting exclusively of white farmers.
Their mood was glum. He said:

> There is no society of angels, whether it is white, brown or black. We are
> all human beings, and as such we are bound to make mistakes. If I have
> done a wrong to you, it is for you to forgive me; and if you have done
> something wrong to me, it is for me to forgive you. The Africans cannot say
> the Europeans have done all the wrong; and the Europeans cannot say the
> Africans have done all the wrong . . . You have something to forget, just as
> I have.

He went on to speak of his imprisonment:

> This has been worrying many of you; but let me tell you Jomo Kenyatta
> has no intention of retaliating or looking backwards. We are going to
> forget the past and look forward to the future. I have suffered imprison-
> ment and detention; but that is gone and I am not going to remember it.
> . . . Many of you are as Kenyan as myself . . . Let us join hands and work
> for the benefit of Kenya, not for the benefit of one particular community.

The white farmers found themselves not merely convinced but also liking the
man. They laughed at his anecdotes and frequently interrupted him with
cheers. When he sat down they stood to give him a long ovation.

The next evening, at a party Malcolm MacDonald gave in Government
House, Kenyatta's speech, extensively reported in all Kenya's newspapers,
was the main topic of conversation. MacDonald noted:

Some of his own lieutenants in the new Cabinet, as well as others, expressed disagreement with part of his remarks, asserting that he had gone too far in assuring the European settlers that their earlier, often viciously racialist hostility to African majority rule would now be forgiven. But Kenyatta vigorously defended his theme.

Kenyatta's reason was not simply magnanimity. Kenya had become a prosperous country. Its whites ran their farms efficiently and were big consumers. Many foreign firms had come to Kenya to produce the goods the farmers wanted and to sell, from their bases in Nairobi and Mombasa, to neighbouring markets, particularly Uganda and Tanganyika. The entire structure of economic prosperity depended on the white farmers. If they went before Africans acquired the know-how to earn as much, the foreign investment would go and Kenya would come to independence crippled. So it was partly to secure the confidence of the white farmers that Kenyatta gave Cabinet office to Bruce Mackenzie, a white farmer himself. For the same reason Kenyatta appointed settler leaders who had been the enemies of African rule to such posts as Speaker of the House of Representatives and Chairman of the National Museum.

It was surely out of pure magnanimity, however, that following independence (in December 1963) and after he had become President, Kenyatta appointed an English judge of the East African Court of Appeal to be Kenya's acting Chief Justice. The appointment was only temporary, but

*At the conference in London to agree Kenya's independence constitution, left to right, Oginga Odinga, Minister of Home Affairs, Jomo Kenyatta, Prime Minister, and Tom Mboya, Minister of Justice.*

*Independence Day. The Mayor of Nairobi confers the freedom of the city on the Duke of Edinburgh, the Queen's representative, on his right, and Jomo Kenyatta, the Prime Minister, on his left. On Kenyatta's left is Malcolm MacDonald, the Governor.*

this man was the judge who, twelve years earlier, had dismissed Kenyatta's appeal – after leave to appeal to the Privy Council in London had been turned down – and had thus sent him to his nine years' exile in the desert. MacDonald, by then Britain's High Commissioner in Nairobi, asked Kenyatta if it was the same man. The President replied: 'Yes . . . He's a good lawyer and he'll be a good acting Chief Justice.'

## After Independence

Kenyatta became not merely the father figure of the Africans but the most trusted by the whites of all the leaders in independent Africa. Within two years the near-unanimous view of the white settlers that he was the Devil was replaced by the equally widespread view that good old Jomo was the best protector European farmers and businessmen could possibly have. The seventeen years he had lived in Britain and the fact that he had an English wife had previously been held against him. But when his English wife flew to Nairobi to join him and his two surviving Kenyan wives at the independence celebrations, everything changed. It was as though he had become every white settler's brother-in-law. They saw him as an ugly caterpillar miraculously changed into a butterfly.

Kenyatta was above all an African nationalist, but he was also a pragmatic politician and a master of compromise. So, while he outlawed any form of white racialism, he kept whites who were useful in positions that many Africans would themselves have liked to occupy. He was criticised for going too slowly both in Africanising the public services and in distributing land to Africans. Loans from the British Government, arranged before independence, financed the buying-out of white farmers, but Kenyatta was reluctant to use compulsion. He overruled not only those of his colleagues who favoured seizing and distributing the land but also some who pressed him to force the whites to sell quickly. He thought it more important to maintain the standards of the Highlands in both agriculture and lifestyle than to satisfy land-hunger. But he kept the pace up fast enough to re-establish the market in land, to prevent squatters on abandoned farms from resurrecting the ghosts of Mau Mau, to draw the sting from Kikuyu land-hunger and to stamp Government control on black re-colonisation.

Post-independence Kenya was a thriving business economy, with Kikuyu increasingly replacing whites, but otherwise little changed. Soon, however, resentments arose at the power enjoyed by the Kikuyu and at their corruption, which Kenyatta certainly tolerated and to which he was widely accused of being party. Poorer Kikuyu, including many former Mau Mau fighters, resented their exclusion from the fruits of independence. Oginga Odinga became the political leader of a movement for a socialist redistribu-tion of the country's assets and in 1966 resigned the vice-presidency. Mboya, backed by Kenyatta, stood firmly for maintaining the economic system of the west. Kenyatta at first directed the resentments – and consequent riots – at those members of the Asian community, a minority, who had opted at independence to retain their British passports, on the understanding that they would thereby secure the right of entry to Britain. Some 20,000 were rendered homeless.

The squeezing of the Asians and the opportunities created by taking over their businesses and property relieved the social and political pressure only temporarily. Kenyatta accumulated land and his family grew wealthy. The Kikuyu, sensing themselves challenged, resumed their secret oath-taking ceremonies, encouraged by Kenyatta himself. In July 1969 Tom Mboya, Minister for Economic Planning and Development, by general agreement the most brilliant member of the Government of Kenya and rumoured to be Kenyatta's chosen successor, but by tribe a Luo, was shot dead in the centre of Nairobi. A Kikuyu was hanged for the murder, but Luo resentment against Kenyatta and the Kikuyu grew. Kenyatta became convinced that Oginga Odinga was plotting to overthrow him and placed him and other Luo leaders in detention for a year. Kenyatta's dream of creating a truly united country appeared to be collapsing, but he stayed in command, leading Kenya in the 1970s through a period of political stability and rapid economic growth.

After Kenyatta's death in 1978, the Presidency was taken over by a leader of one of Kenya's smaller tribes, Daniel Arap Moi. The power of the Kikuyu was somewhat reduced, but the general air of Kenya remained that of a modernising, free-enterprise state, successfully overcoming both its lack of minerals or significant natural resources and the general backwardness of its people. In this Kenya followed, in the first twenty years after independence, the path the British hoped for. The problems caused by tribalism and corruption were serious and worrying, but nothing compared to the disasters that after independence struck Ghana, Nigeria and Uganda. By the standards of ex-British colonies in Africa, Kenya was the big success.

# CHAPTER 10

# Rhodesia

This is the story of a colony that Britain never governed. Troops under the command of the British Government came threateningly close to its borders, but they entered only in ceremony or in the pay of a company that had a royal charter to govern on Britain's behalf. And that company used the British troops for its own purposes. The usual determination of London to spend no money on imperial adventures led in Rhodesia to a disastrous absence of control. Britain had responsibility without power.

Britain's title was restricted in this curious way because of one man, Cecil John Rhodes. His achievement was both creative and destructive. It dwarfs that of any other British imperialist, including Robert Clive. Alone of the imperial creators, Rhodes took the government in London by the nose, blindfolded it and led it where he wished, leaving generations of British ministers in a tangle until the very last moment of the End of Empire story.

On the day Britain gave up sovereignty in April 1980 the police in Southern Rhodesia still bore on their epaulettes the letters BSAP, standing for British South Africa Police, the force belonging to Rhodes's company to which in 1889 he had persuaded the British Government to grant the power to make laws and treaties and to govern Rhodesia. His purpose, as will become clear, was to strengthen British – and his own – rule in Rhodesia's big, rich, troublesome southern neighbour, the assortment of Dutch- and English-speakers which in 1910 were to form the Union of South Africa.

The anomalous British colony on South Africa's frontier was known as Southern Rhodesia. Two adjacent colonies, Northern Rhodesia and Nyasaland, form part of the story, but they escaped the control of Rhodes's company and came under the protection of the Colonial Office. Even Southern Rhodesia was eventually to escape the destiny Rhodes had planned for it. He wanted to absorb the land and its black inhabitants into an enlarged South Africa.

## Offspring of South Africa, 1652–1947

South Africa presented a peculiar problem for the British Empire. The British took over many colonies from the Dutch, who had themselves taken over from the Portuguese. But in South Africa the British took over more than the colony. Since 1652 Holland, as part of its control of the eastern trade, maintained a base at the Cape of Good Hope. Dutch farmers (Boers) had established themselves in the countryside behind, mainly to supply vegetables to the ships sailing to and from the East Indies. In 1815 the Cape was transferred from the Dutch to the British Empire and the Boers chose to stay. Many of their families had lived there for more than a hundred years and they saw themselves as the indigenous population.

Britain's purpose in acquiring Cape Colony was to have a base that, in the event of war, would enable her to keep the route to India secure. As it became clear that the predominant local population, the Boers, were inflexibly opposed both to modern ideas and to British rule and that in a war they might well side with Britain's enemies, settlers from Britain were sent out as a counter-balance. Thousands of Boers responded by trekking out of Cape Colony, escaping the British flag and the British tax-collector, to set up 'independent republics' of their own – puny, penniless little areas of settlement whose citizens' prime characteristics were extreme hardiness, great skill with the gun and bitter dislike of the British. What the British Empire wanted behind its naval base at the Cape was peace and co-operation. The disaffection of the Boers denied them both. So Britain tried to persuade the Boers to join a union in which the small inland republics to which they had retreated would co-operate with the larger and more prosperous British provinces of Cape Colony (where diamonds were discovered in 1869) and Natal.

Britain was trying to create such a federation when South Africa was hit by as big a shock as ever struck a British colony. In 1886 gold was discovered at Witwatersrand in the Transvaal. It soon became clear that Rand gold could make the Boers even richer than Kimberley diamonds were making the British in Cape Colony. The ore was of unusually low gold content and its location was exceptionally deep, but throughout an area 170 miles by 100 the mines seemed bottomless.

Among those who came to get a hand on the gold was an Oxford graduate in his early thirties, Cecil John Rhodes. He was the son of a wealthy English clergyman in Hertfordshire and he had been sent to South Africa at the age of seventeen in the hope that the hot dry climate would improve his poor health. He stayed several years, first farming, then diamond mining. He supervised 'kaffirs' (local blacks) as they dug and sieved, then sorted the earth himself to pick out the stones: 'I found a $17\frac{5}{8}$ carat on Saturday,' he wrote to his family, 'and I hope to get £100 for it . . . I find on average thirty carats a week.' Soon he was a millionaire, and skilful further investment in Rand gold helped to make him a multi-millionaire before he was thirty. He had no further need to devote a moment to securing an income: he spent the rest of his life pursuing a political dream.

At Oxford Rhodes was inspired by the inaugural lecture of the art critic John Ruskin:

There is a destiny now possible to us, the highest ever set before a nation
. . . We are still undegenerate in race; a race mingled of the best northern
blood . . . Will our youths of England make your country again a royal
throne of kings, a sceptered isle, for all the world a source of light, a centre
of peace? . . . This is what England must either do or perish: she must
found colonies as fast and as far as she is able, formed of her most energetic
and worthiest men; seizing every piece of fruitful waste ground she can set
her foot on, and there teaching her colonists that their first aim is to
advance the power of England by land and sea: and that, though they live
on a distant plot of land, they are no more to consider themselves therefore
disfranchised from their native land than the sailors of her fleets do,
because they float on distant seas.

Rhodes returned to South Africa, determined to pursue Ruskin's aim by
ensuring that a continuous band of British territory ran from south to north
the length of the continent – from the Cape to Cairo. But he had to win the
support of the Boers, who would otherwise cause trouble. By the 1880s the
Boer–British competition was taking many forms, including the acquisition
of inland tracts of territory. In 1885 the British acquired the vast semi-desert
of Bechuanaland. The Boers seemed bent on acquiring the area immediately
to the north, then known as Zambesia. A Boer occupation of this area
threatened to block Rhodes's dream.

Zambesia was dominated by a warlike, Zulu-related tribe, the Matabele,
who had fled north ahead of the Boer trekkers. The African peoples of this
area were in their Iron Age. Portuguese missionaries and traders had come
and gone two hundred years earlier, bringing the wheel and the ability to
write, but the Africans had retained neither. Such people were easily
defeated by well-organised groups of Europeans with guns. Since the
Matabele held sway over high plateau country where the climate is tolerable
for white men, one of the European groups was certain to take their land.

Rhodes was no scholar, but he liked to read Gibbon's *Decline and Fall of the
Roman Empire* which, with Ruskin, helped shape the grand trans-continental
ideas which he voiced with unusual eloquence. He talked Sir Hercules
Robinson, British Governor at the Cape, into having a treaty signed between
Britain and Lobengula, King of the Matabele. The British promised peace,
Lobengula promised to make no concessions to any outsiders without the
prior approval of Britain.

The year was 1888, a curious moment in African history. By now several
powerful European countries had decided that the time had come to take a
share of Africa. Europeans had not yet succeeded in penetrating far inland
because the continent consists to a large extent of a high central plateau off
which most of the rivers, which might have been expected to provide the
routes to the interior, tumble in successions of great cataracts that make
navigation impossible. The lowlands between the sea and the plateau were
mostly infested with tsetse fly – fatal to horses, mules and cattle. It followed

that, while the European explorer in a small boat that could be carried on foot past the cataracts might clamber to the centre of the continent, armies and larger expeditions requiring pack animals or substantial river craft were excluded. In general, therefore, Europeans had been restricted to coastal points of contact, where they traded with African merchants and provided services for ships *en route* to the far more profitable East Indies. Inner Africa was a mystery, to be circumnavigated. South Africa provided the exception to this general pattern because, far south of the equator, its lowlands were less hot and free of both cataracts and tsetse fly.

The 'scramble for Africa' that began in the 1880s may be ascribed to the desire by several European governments to write their names across the huge blank areas on their maps. Naturally the British, Germans, French and Belgians expected the territories thus acquired to be profitable, but the scramble was not managed in the previous manner of the British and Dutch Empires; this was not a case of traders finding profits, establishing themselves and then demanding guardianship from the government at home. The scramble was a matter of planting flags and then hoping trade would follow. The dictum 'trade follows the flag' was a late-nineteenth-century slogan for governments that hoped to justify a spree of land acquisition in the last great available area of the world.

The strange process whereby ministers and civil servants in Europe pored over maps of Africa and marked out their respective claims produced an even stranger process in the kraals (villages) and huts of hundreds of African chiefs. Europeans literally scrambled, their objective being to secure a piece of paper. They wanted a concession or treaty from the local chief – or failing him someone who could convincingly pass for the local chief. In return for cash, guns or the promise of protection against rival tribes, chiefs were persuaded to mark their crosses or thumb-prints, and these, in the hands of foreign ministry staff in Europe, helped establish a national claim. At the appropriate conference, lines on the map would be adjusted to take account of 'reality on the ground' as proved by such documents.

A trader, adventurer or scoundrel could thus obtain both the backing of his own government and the acquiescence of other European governments in claims whose validity was at best doubtful. Once signed and sealed by foreign ministers in Europe, such claims had the backing of international law. Except where major national interests were involved, European governments observed them.

Cecil John Rhodes was the most effective of all the adventurers who took part in the scramble. He did not himself walk hundreds of miles to the kraals of chiefs; nor did he crouch in the hot sun politely listening to the chiefs' speeches day after day, or ply chiefs with drink night after night in an effort to persuade them to sign. Instead he sent agents or bought concessions at high prices from rivals.

Many concession-seekers had friends and highly-placed contacts in their capital cities. None had such powerful connections or so much money as

Rhodes. Lord Salisbury, the Prime Minister in London, dismissed Rhodes's Cape-to-Cairo idea as fanciful nonsense, but he approved of Rhodes's securing claims in central Africa to keep out both the Boers and the Portuguese.

Rhodes acquired the country that later became known as Southern Rhodesia by trickery. He sent a trusted colleague, Charles Dunnell Rudd, accompanied by a young Fellow in Law from All Souls College, Oxford, to the kraal of the Matabele king, Lobengula. Boers and other British groups had already approached Lobengula, but Rhodes's team outbid them, offering £100 a month, a thousand rifles, ammunition and – a typical piece of Rhodes panache to clinch the deal – an armed steamboat on the Zambezi river. What Lobengula promised in return has remained the subject of argument. He put his mark and his elephant seal on a paper drawn up by Rochfort Maguire, the All Souls man, granting 'complete and exclusive charge over all metals and minerals situated in my Kingdom', but a missionary who interpreted during the negotiations, signed the document as a witness and was trusted by Lobengula, the Rev. C. D. Helm, wrote to the London Missionary Society that Rhodes's men 'promised they would not bring more than ten white men to work in his country and that they would abide by the laws of his country and be as his people'. What is clear is that Lobengula granted only a mining concession, while Rhodes, as his negotiators well knew, was planning a full-scale European settlement.

Once Rhodes had obtained Lobengula's seal he bought another and incompatible concession which the Matabele King had sold to a rival European. Thus equipped he could set about winning his next requirement, the backing of the Government in London. Squaring opponents was Rhodes's greatest skill. Some pointed out that granting a monopoly to a rich Cape mining group would be an outrageous breach of Britain's principle of free trade; ministers feared that Rhodes's colonists would provoke from the natives a violent response which the British Government would be required expensively to overcome; missionaries and imperial paternalists sincerely feared for the Africans. Each group had to be won round and for each Rhodes dispensed the right tranquilliser – appointing respected men, including two dukes and an earl, to the board of his proposed company, and making large contributions to the party funds of both the Liberals and the Irish Nationalists (who still had eighty votes at Westminster). Rhodes devoted a year to cosseting Government, Parliament and Privy Council through all their necessary processes and finally, in October 1889, Queen Victoria signed the charter of the British South Africa Company. Like the former East India Company, it was given powers not merely to trade but also to govern, raise its own police force, fly its own flag, construct roads, railways and harbours, establish banks and allocate land to settlers.

Rhodes's company was granted such extensive powers because the British Government was concerned about the Cape. The Suez Canal had by now been opened, but defence planners feared it could be rendered useless in war

by France – Britain's most likely enemy – blocking access through the Mediterranean. Therefore the defence of India depended on secure facilities at the Cape. For Lord Salisbury, granting Rhodes's company its concession was a way to secure imperial defence on the cheap: any increase in Boer or anti-British activity in the Cape's hinterland was dangerous; giving Rhodes his way promised to strengthen the British in the Cape and renew their attachment to the mother country. Salisbury distrusted empire-building by private enterprise – government action and treaties were more his style – but he needed Rhodes and did not want awkward questions asked. His Government therefore failed to discover that the company to which it had granted its charter did not own Lobengula's concession (this was owned by Rhodes and a small group of associates, who sold to the company for a high price) or that the concession did not allow for most of the activities the chartered company was explicitly created to perform.

Promising 'the gold of fifty Rands', Rhodes promptly launched British South Africa Company shares onto the market. Speculators snapped them up. Rhodes had completed the construction of an imperial venture in which he deceived almost everyone he dealt with, above all Lobengula and the purchasers of the shares. They thought his purpose was to mine gold and secure profits. His real plan was to settle a new colony for Britain.

*The Queen's envoys, two officers of the Royal Horse Guards, bearing a letter from London to tell Lobengula that the Royal Charter had been granted and he could trust the company.*

Rhodes himself returned to South Africa to oversee the recruitment of the 'pioneers'. His advertisements promised them daily pay, three thousand acres of farmland each and fifteen gold claims. Two thousand applied. The two hundred chosen were unmarried young men who included farmers, artisans, miners, doctors, lawyers, engineers, builders, bakers, sailors, soldiers, men of good family and no employment, three parsons and a Jesuit. Their advance into Zambesia was guarded by five hundred armed and mounted police, their route cleared by three hundred native porters. At Rhodes's request the British Bechuanaland police conducted manoeuvres close to Lobengula's territory, suggesting that if the chief sent his *impis* (warriors) against the pioneers his capital at Bulawayo would be attacked. Lobengula, knowing that he was outgunned, restrained his men. Thus Rhodes obtained some British Government cover for his pioneers while making certain that in the territory they entered the Company alone was in charge.

He had planned to accompany the pioneers but was prevented by a political crisis in Cape Colony, as a result of which he became its Prime Minister. The Cape remained both his and Britain's central concern.

The pioneer column, after a five-week trek through the steamy low country, reached the steep climb to the central African plateau, where they named their first stopping place Fort Victoria. On 13 September 1890 they raised the British flag at their 'capital', calling it, in honour of the Prime Minister in London, Fort Salisbury.

Rhodes, meanwhile, was continuing the scramble. He bought concessions farther afield in what was later to become Northern Rhodesia, he tried to buy concessions in Nyasaland, he drew up plans for the Cape-to-Cairo railway line. To avoid the obvious route north, through the Boer republic of the Transvaal, Rhodes sent the line of rail looping instead to Rhodesia by way of Bechuanaland. That he planned the railway not through the rich Rand goldfields, with their vast and growing business, but by the circuitous route through Britain's new semi-desert colony is proof that Rhodes's purpose was more strategy than profit. Neither passengers nor goods required the Bechuanaland line, but it was the ideal way to send rapid military reinforcements through territory that was securely British. Building the railway at the Company's expense was one of the conditions on which the British Government had granted the charter.

The pioneers soon faced disappointment. They had trekked to Zambesia for gold but few found any, and once they had paid a half share in their finds to the chartered Company, as the terms of their concessions required, the profits were only moderate. They had been given land to farm, but most of them did not relish the tough job of clearing and tilling isolated tracts. Many sold their concessions and returned to South Africa. Those who stayed and the immigrants who replaced them lived for some years in primitive hardship. It soon became clear that the main resource available to them in Zambesia was native labour.

In most colonies by the start of the twentieth century, the British administration did what it could to protect the natives from brutal exploitation. British governments had, from Burke's time, developed some principles in the matter, and missionaries and other Christian watchdogs were prone to cause embarrassing questions to be raised in Westminster. In Zambesia, however, the Colonial Office had no representative. Rhodes was the king of the area, which soon came to be known as Rhodesia in simple recognition that it was his. The British Government's ability to influence him was slight. He was Prime Minister of the Cape, whose European population Britain was anxious to keep friendly. To instruct them how to treat the natives was certain to offend. The idea of sending an imperial Resident to Rhodesia was seriously considered in London, but Lord Ripon, the Colonial Secretary at the time and himself a convinced Liberal (see India Chapter 1, pp. 28–30), was persuaded that to do so would cause dangerous problems at the Cape. So Britain averted its gaze.

To Rhodes it did not matter that Lobengula had granted him the right to mine only if the number of miners was limited; or that he had assured the British Government that the Company would adhere to agreements reached with native chiefs. Like a Mafia boss, Rhodes was loyal to those who were totally loyal to him, but not averse to the use of illegal violence by his subordinates, so long as he could deny any knowledge of it. In London, Oxford and Cape Town, when he was dealing with powerful people, his charm was magical. Few recognised that he was a shark. Away from the eyes of men in formal suits, suddenly there would be blood in the water.

With such a man at the apex of power in Rhodesia, settlers and company officials knew they could use natives in any way that suited them. At first this meant that the Shona peoples, the natives of the concession area, were made to work for the settlers for negligible wages. But Lobengula's Matabele continued to treat the Shona as 'their dogs'. The Matabele lived by war, preyed on the Shona and, when they went on a punitive expedition, disembowelled women, roasted children alive, reduced kraals to ashes, assegaied (speared) the men, then cut off their genitals. Lobengula was wise enough to forbid his *impis* to do such things to white men. But when a Shona chief failed to pay his dues, the full violence was directed against his tribe. This had two consequences the settlers did not like: they found their workers dead, often gruesomely treated; and the rumour of *impis* arriving repeatedly led the entire Shona labour force to flee to the hills.

Rhodes and his chief assistant in Rhodesia, Dr Leander Starr Jameson, concluded that the situation had to be resolved: the Shona could not serve both the white settlers and the Matabele; the invasions had to be stopped. Lobengula, recognising the power of the Europeans, tried to negotiate. He sent a peace mission whose members were murdered by company troopers. The British Government also pressed for a peaceful settlement, so Rhodes made himself unavailable to receive messages while Jameson assembled and dispatched the force which was to wipe out the Matabele kingdom.

For the most part this was an easy war for the Europeans. Lobengula had received the rifles and ammunition promised in return for his concession, but his men had not yet learned to use them properly (the gunboat to sail on the Zambezi was never delivered). The Matabele capital at Bulawayo was quickly overrun and some white traders were found there alive, having been protected by Lobengula. The Matabele armies were destroyed. One of the Company's officers, Benjamin Wilson, wrote:

> I was sorry for King Lobengula but for the people of his nation I have not the slightest sympathy. They have felt for the first time what they have been making the surrounding tribes feel for fifty years.

During the final stage of this short war, a British patrol of thirty-six men were sent to capture the fleeing Lobengula, found themselves surrounded by Matabele *impis* and were annihilated to the last man. Known as the Shangani patrol they became the national heroes of white Rhodesia. Imaginative paintings of their brave final moments were displayed in every school, home and public building.

The soldiers who defeated the Matabele, like the original pioneers, were rewarded mainly with grants of land, along with most of the Matabele cattle, as the victors' loot. For Rhodes and Jameson it was essential to increase the number of white settlers, and generous land grants combined with many tempting – if small – discoveries of gold continued to attract both British and Boers from South Africa. In addition, Rhodes now made huge land-grants in Matabeleland to relatives of the well-connected who might win him political support in London. Most of these remained absentee landlords. The Matabele were made squatters on their own land. Rhodesia, Rhodes explained, was white man's country.

Land needed labour, so the Company appointed a 'native commissioner' in every district to compel the local headmen to supply able-bodied young men. All were obliged to work for a number of months each year at a fixed rate of pay. This forced labour system was later described by Sir Richard Martin, eventually appointed as Britain's first Resident Commissioner in Rhodesia, as 'synonymous with slavery'. One of the first of the Company's native commissioners, M. E. Weale, wrote that his hardest task was to prevent the Shona from fleeing at the sight of a white man. In addition to seizing them for labour, white men were, he wrote, given to 'assaulting and raping any native woman they found in the veld alone'.

In October 1895 Jameson withdrew all but forty of the Company's police from Rhodesia. He and Rhodes needed these servants of the chartered company to launch what became known as the Jameson raid, an attempt by these two war-lords to seize the Transvaal – and in particular the Rand – from the Boers. The raid was a disaster in itself and had unhappy effects in Rhodesia, where both Matabele and Shona took the opportunity to rise, killing hundreds of Europeans on outlying farms, forcing survivors to scurry to Bulawayo, Salisbury and some other small towns, there to cling together for defence.

The rebellions came at a bad time for Rhodes. Public outrage at his involvement in the Jameson raid led to his having to resign both the Prime Ministership of the Cape and his formal position in the chartered company. When he arrived in Rhodesia, however, he soon proved to have as much authority as ever. He went out to meet Matabele warriors to sign a peace which most settlers did not want and he offered concessions by the Company which he had no formal right to make. Even at his moment of humiliation, he remained a colossus with mythical standing among the whites of Rhodesia – and even among some of the blacks.

The Jameson raid almost ruined his plans for Rhodesia. A parliamentary inquiry was set up in London to investigate the background to both the raid and the Company's rule; it became known as 'the lying-in-state at Westminster'. Fortunately for Rhodes the committee exhausted themselves on the raid and never got round to the administration of Rhodesia. Had they done so, demands for the Company's charter to be revoked would have become irresistible. On the raid alone Rhodes had to use all his ingenuity

*The parliamentary committee's task was to investigate his guilt but Rhodes (centre) soon charmed and dominated them. On the right, with monocle, is Joseph Chamberlain. (Print from* Vanity Fair.*)*

to prevent evidence of his direct involvement from damning him publicly: he arranged lucrative posts in Rhodesia and South Africa for potential witnesses, making it impossible for them to appear.

The clamour for the removal of the charter was deflected by the Colonial Secretary, Joseph Chamberlain. He had had prior knowledge of the Jameson raid and believed that if he let Rhodes down over the charter, information in Rhodes's possession would end his political career in Westminster as surely as Rhodes's had been ended in Cape Town. Thus Rhodes's ideal for Rhodesia survived – it remained a British colony but with no Colonial Office presence. His colonial scheme did not, however, emerge unscathed. Nyasaland was kept out of his grasp. His many enemies in the Colonial Office, among missionaries and in the Liberal Party got the better of him, and here direct Colonial Office control was introduced.

Rhodes died in 1902 at the age of forty-eight. Twenty-one years later his dream for Southern Rhodesia almost reached fulfilment. He had been determined that the white settlers should be given the vote and that, as a self-governing colony, they would join the federation of South Africa, thus increasing British predominance there. Instead in 1923 the majority, 8,774, voted for 'Responsible Government', against 5,989 for union with South Africa. The occasion for the vote was the exhaustion of the chartered company, which had paid for the government, built the railway and kept trying to attract settlers, whom it saw as the only way to make the country profitable. But the Company came increasingly to be disliked by the settlers. The compensation it received from the British Government for the loss of its privileges enabled it in 1923 to make its first dividend payment since Rhodes's charismatic flotation thirty-four years before.

Northern Rhodesia, where few whites had settled, was now transferred from Company rule to the Colonial Office. Southern Rhodesia became nominally a British colony but was in practice a self-governing dominion like Australia or Canada. The Colonial Office tried to establish the right to oversee law-making there, particularly in matters affecting the Africans, and formally Parliament in London had the authority to overrule the legislative assembly in Salisbury. But it never exercised this right, and the Colonial Office soon transferred responsibility for the territory to the Dominions Office, which from 1926 dealt also with Australia, Canada, Eire, New Zealand and South Africa. The only respect in which the government of Southern Rhodesia's 19,000 registered voters was less than autonomous was in dealing with the 850,000 Africans. The Native Affairs Department was subject to oversight by the British High Commissioner (who was also Governor-General of South Africa and lived in Cape Town). The arrangement was designed to prevent any increase in discrimination against Africans, but Rhodes had fixed the odds so strongly in favour of the settlers that increases in discrimination were hardly necessary.

Southern Rhodesia was in practice as much a colony of South Africa as of Britain. In British colonies the entire government service was manned from

London; in Southern Rhodesia the service was locally recruited, responsive entirely to local interests and more in the tradition of Rhodes than of Lord Salisbury. The final authority in most colonies was the Governor, answerable to London. The final authority in Southern Rhodesia from 1923 onwards was the electorate, which, thanks to property and literacy qualifications, consisted of all Europeans who were British subjects aged over twenty-one and a handful of Indian shopkeepers and prosperous African farmers. A large proportion of the electorate were of South African origin and all had South African connections. Many were Boers. The law in Southern Rhodesia, drawn from South Africa, was Roman-Dutch.

Rhodes's dream of finding great mineral wealth in Rhodesia was eventually fulfilled. In the 1930s major copper reserves began to be mined. They were, however, not in Southern Rhodesia, where Rhodes's big settler community might share the benefits, but in Northern Rhodesia, now firmly under the control of the Colonial Office. Rhodes's British South Africa Company at last began to pay regular and substantial dividends, thanks to

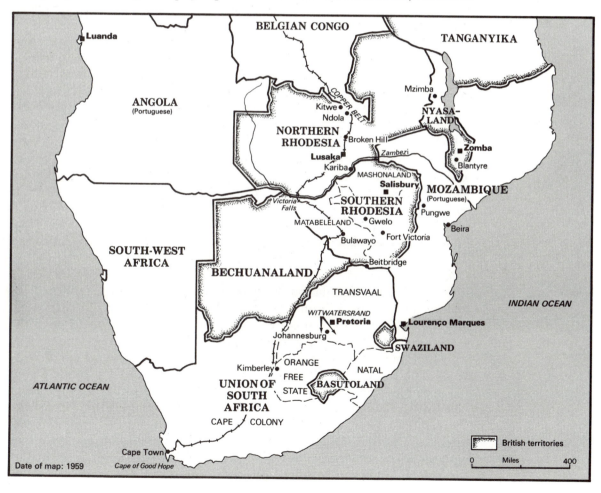

the Northern Rhodesian mining concession which it retained, but the whites
in the south suffered a frustrating experience: they saw train-loads of copper
steaming across their territory *en route* for the sea. The Southern Rhodesian
whites were not poor. They mined a little gold and copper as well as
tungsten, chrome, zinc, antimony, asbestos and coal. Thanks to plentiful
native labour, their farms did well, particularly selling tobacco to Britain.
They enjoyed an even higher standard of living than whites in South Africa.
But they could not see why the realisation of their dream of a great mine
should bring them no benefit.

Consequently from the 1930s on a growing theme in Southern Rhodesian
politics became the need for 'amalgamation'. Rhodes had secured both
Northern and Southern Rhodesia for Britain and he had wanted them
amalgamated. The settlers believed that the narrow policy of the Colonial
Office, obsessed, as they saw it, with protecting the interests of the blacks in
the northern territory, must now be set aside to make way for the founder's
ideal of a unified Rhodesia under the elective rule of white men.

To the British Government it did not seem so simple. Britain felt obliged
to undo the damage done by Rhodes's and Jameson's abuse of the authority
of the 'great white Queen' when they had made promises in her name and
then disregarded them. Promises made to Northern Rhodesian tribes,
particularly to the King of Barotseland who had freely accepted British
protection, must be guaranteed by the British Government itself and not left
to the whim of Southern Rhodesian voters. Equally important, copper was
becoming, with the development of electrical equipment, radio and motor
vehicles, a vital strategic raw material. Northern Rhodesia was one of only
half a dozen places in the world where it was mined on a huge scale. It was
too important a resource to be entrusted to a government of settlers. Control
was much easier to enforce under direct Colonial Office rule. For these
reasons Northern Rhodesia and Southern Rhodesia remained separate with
contrasted forms of government. Colonial Office men appointed from
London ran the north, local settlers strongly influenced by South Africa ran
the south.

The contrast between the territories increased. Southern Rhodesia's
substantial white population insisted on laws that clearly established the
inferior status of the Africans. The Land Apportionment Act of 1930 made it
illegal for Africans to own or rent property in any of the towns or in the
greater part of the country: this meant that those enterprising Africans who
were profiting from European economic development were kept out of white
areas. The Industrial Conciliation Act of 1934 introduced a formal colour
bar in employment by excluding 'natives' from the definition of 'employees'.
The British Government, in failing to prevent the passage of these measures,
showed that it considered its publicly proclaimed duty to protect native
interests in Southern Rhodesia less important than preserving good relations
with the white settler electorate. Similar measures were never permitted by
the Colonial Office in Northern Rhodesia – or any other colony.

Consequently when, in 1939, a Royal Commission reported on the possibility of closer association between the territories, it found the main obstacle to be Southern Rhodesia's 'native' policies. The Commission stated that Africans in the north were opposed to being put under the power of the white settlers in the south. The demand which the Southern Rhodesian whites had been pressing for more than a decade was set aside.

The spirit of Cecil Rhodes could not, however, be quashed among white Rhodesians. After the 1939–45 war they pressed again for amalgamation. Many of them and rather more Rhodesian Africans – some 16,000 – had fought for Britain in the war. The whites had shown considerable ability in running their country, making it stable, efficient and prosperous. Their treatment of black Africans was closer to the South African pattern than British imperial policy could approve, but they did not go as far as South Africa. Some qualified blacks still had the vote (of which almost all South African blacks were deprived). Had the Southern Rhodesians in 1945 demanded full dominion status, they could probably have had it.

## All Things to All Men: the Federation, 1947–1963

In 1947 King George VI and Queen Elizabeth and their two daughters, the Princesses Elizabeth and Margaret, visited South Africa. Their tour was part of Britain's effort to thank the South African Prime Minister, Jan Christiaan Smuts, for bringing his country to Britain's aid in the 1939–45 World War. They came to celebrate both victory over Germany and Japan and the hope, shared by Smuts and the new Labour Government in Britain, that South Africa and the British people would continue to support each other against the illiberal forces that had threatened them.

Within a year, in the South African general election of May 1948, Smuts fell to illiberal forces closer to home. His vanquisher, Dr Daniel Malan, was the leader of the Boers or, as they now preferred to be called, Afrikaners. True to his people's traditions he had supported Britain's enemies in the 1939–45 war. In the South African Parliament in September 1939 Malan's Nationalist Party had come within thirteen votes of causing this British dominion to stand neutral between Britain and Germany. Malan himself was pro-Nazi. Smuts had narrowly held South Africa to the British alliance only by employing every kind of political skill. Victory in 1948 brought Malan and his party their chance for revenge.

Malan was a republican, determined to cut South Africa's links with the British Crown. He was also the inventor and arch-priest of *apartheid*, which, Malan explained, meant 'separate development', a way to provide 'separate but equal' rights to all races. Afrikaner voters welcomed *apartheid* for what it really was: a mechanism to secure white supremacy for ever.

To the Government in London the Afrikaner Nationalists with their policy of *apartheid* were a challenge. In April 1948 Labour ministers declared unequivocally the final purpose of the British Empire: to bring colonised peoples to independence on the basis of majority rule. Clement Attlee and his Colonial Secretary Arthur Creech Jones were determined to pursue this objective as quickly as the subject peoples could be trained to take charge of their own affairs. South Africa had enjoyed complete independence since 1910. Britain had neither the power nor the legal obligation to control the Union's internal policy. But South Africa's adoption of *apartheid* threatened several nearby British-ruled territories – Bechuanaland (now Botswana), Basutoland (now Lesotho) and Swaziland were all in Dr Malan's sights. The most awkward threat, however, as seen by British ministers and officials, was to Southern Rhodesia. How could Britain prevent this most wayward of its colonies from slipping towards Dr Malan?

South African and particularly Afrikaner migrants were settling in Southern Rhodesia in growing numbers. If the 1923 referendum were repeated, the white majority might well now vote to join South Africa. If the Southern Rhodesian Government demanded independence – as India, Ceylon and Burma had recently done – it would be difficult for Britain to refuse, and Southern Rhodesia's drift towards South Africa would follow via an alternative route. The Labour Government felt responsible for advancing the 1.6 million Southern Rhodesian Africans towards democratic independence but, thanks to the deals done with Rhodes in the late nineteenth century and with the settler electorate in 1923, faced the prospect of impotently watching as they were taken farther into *apartheid*-style subordination.

Britain's answer to this problem was above all the work of one man, Andrew Cohen, the head of the Africa department of the Colonial Office in London. From the South African election of 1948 he took three years to evolve his solution and bring both the Labour Government and the Rhodesians to accept it. He identified the common interests of apparently irreconcilable groups and brought them to an arrangement to which all had at first been opposed.

The process had begun for Cohen in 1944 when he was in charge of the Colonial Office department in London that dealt with Northern Rhodesia. The leader of the 'unofficials' on the Northern Rhodesian Legco, Stewart Gore-Brown, met Cohen and impressed him as a most untypical settler. Gore-Brown agreed with Cohen and the Colonial Office that the first duty of the Empire was trusteeship – to advance the interest of the colonised peoples – and that the Southern Rhodesian proposal for amalgamation of the territories was merely a takeover bid for the copper revenue which, if granted, would be followed by attempts to remove Colonial Office protection from the Northern Rhodesian Africans. But he saw two advantages in closer association between the territories: economic co-operation could bring obvious benefits; these could be used to induce Southern Rhodesia to alter its political-racial direction.

Cohen built on these ideas. His superior in 1948, the Colonial Secretary

Arthur Creech Jones, wanted nothing to do with closer links between the Rhodesias. A Central African Council existed for consultation between the governments of the two Rhodesias and Nyasaland, and Creech Jones was convinced that any closer link would merely give more power to Southern Rhodesia's whites to hold back Northern Rhodesia's blacks. Cohen disagreed. He thought copper could be the bait to win the Southern Rhodesians into a federation in which their policies towards blacks could be gradually modified away from the South African pattern.

From 1948 to 1950 Cohen made little headway. Creech Jones visited the territories, found that the Africans in the north were strongly opposed to closer relations with the south and supported them. However in the 1950 election in Britain Creech Jones lost his seat. Labour was returned to power with a reduced majority and the new Colonial Secretary was James Griffiths, an ex-miner with no experience of colonial policy-making. Cohen soon persuaded him that the federal idea should be explored further. The decisive event, held primarily because Cohen talked Griffiths into it, was a meeting in London of officials from the Commonwealth Relations Office, the Colonial Office and the Governments of Northern Rhodesia, Southern Rhodesia and Nyasaland.

Cohen had persuaded Labour ministers that now was a moment for vision. Not only could a Central African Federation save the blacks of Southern Rhodesia from creeping *apartheid*; it could also form a buffer of moderation between the dogmatic, short-sighted nationalisms of the Afrikaners in South Africa and the blacks in territories to the north. Here in the centre of Africa, British common sense and skill at compromise would create a middle way – racial partnership – with white and black sharing power for their common benefit.

Many in the Labour Party thought Southern Rhodesia very nearly as bad as South Africa. Colonial Secretary Griffiths, Commonwealth Secretary Patrick Gordon-Walker and Prime Minister Attlee needed courage to advance a scheme to sup with the devil – as many in their party considered it. Only Cohen's patent sincerity in pursuit of African advancement (see Gold Coast, Chapter 8, pp. 369–73) and his unique combination of visionary inspiration and administrative skill caused them to allow the exploratory meetings of civil servants to be held. Cohen hoped that once he had the officials of all the governments assembled he could give his plan irresistible momentum. The able white Rhodesian civil servants persuaded him of their *bona fides*.

The extent to which the next step in the history of Rhodesia was Cohen's personal achievement was recalled by Sir Arthur Benson, who was present at the officials' conference in March 1951 as Secretary of the Central African Council:

Cohen was ill for a while and unable to take part and problems started, particularly from the Southern Rhodesian delegation, who were insisting that all financial and economic powers be taken from the territories and given to the federal government: they were still hankering after amalgamation. It looked as though Cohen's whole scheme would collapse. So I went up to his house in Hampstead and he got straight up from his sick-bed and came and calmed the Southern Rhodesians down. It took him a week. He also talked all the other delegations into making adjustments in their positions. He was the one man with the authority and self-confidence to change the terms of what was being agreed because he knew exactly where he was going. When he returned to the conference, even though he was still ill, he got it back on course.

Cohen achieved at that conference the balanced structure that the governments were two years later to carry into effect, creating a new superstate – the Federation of Rhodesia and Nyasaland. A federal legislature and cabinet would take over defence, economic policy, currency, customs, European schools, all higher education, foreign trade and transport. Northern Rhodesia, Southern Rhodesia and Nyasaland would each retain their own constitutions and control over law and order, African affairs, agriculture, forestry, health, labour, mines and relations with the British Government.

Each party to the agreement saw it as delivering something different. The tiny élite of Southern Rhodesian white ministers and civil servants wanted the great mining wealth that Rhodes had promised and an enlarged state over which to exercise their considerable skill at governing. Cohen wanted that small élite, whose views seemed comparatively liberal, strengthened in relation to its white electorate, whose views were self-protective and reactionary. The British Treasury wanted to stop paying an annual subsidy to Nyasaland. The Government of Nyasaland, ruling more Africans than either Northern or Southern Rhodesia, many of them obliged to go to the Rhodesias to get work, wanted money for development. The Northern Rhodesian and Nyasaland whites wanted to rid themselves of Colonial Office rule and join a club which would make them feel less of an isolated minority and seemed to guarantee them a place in central Africa for ever. The Northern Rhodesian Government, the least enthusiastic party, wanted to make sure it retained all powers to protect its African subjects.

The agreement among officials was to prove decisive but the scheme they put forward had to be agreed by the politicians of all four countries (the two Rhodesias, Nyasaland and Britain). Opposition came from Africans in the two northern territories. Harry Nkumbula of Northern Rhodesia and Hastings Banda of Nyasaland, two prominent African nationalists then living in London, published a paper in 1949 in which they declared:

> Under the government provided for us by the United Kingdom the relationship between us and the authorities is one of ward and warden or trust and trustee. The cardinal principle in administration is guidance or guardianship. But under the government provided by Southern Rhodesia [i.e. the proposed Government of the Federation], the relationship

between us and the authorities will be one of slaves and masters, and the cardinal principle in administration will be domination.

Sophisticated Southern Rhodesian blacks, on the other hand, saw hope in the Federation: they believed it could be the mechanism they needed to rescue them from the legacy of Rhodes.

Soon after the officials' recommendations had been published the 1951 election in Britain brought the Conservatives to power. They pressed on with the plans for Federation but the Labour Party turned against its own scheme, while Cohen went off to govern Uganda. The new Colonial Secretary, Oliver Lyttelton, had jointly with Sir Miles Lampson planned the browbeating of King Farouk in Cairo in 1942 (see Chapter 5, p. 242). He saw the federation as economically advantageous for all and thought it his duty to improve the lot of the Africans, even if they were so foolish as to oppose his methods. He did not accept that the handful of African leaders from the two northern territories whose opposition was vocal truly reflected the views of the mass of Africans, who were illiterate, dispersed and uninterested. The African languages did not contain a word for Federation, Lyttelton declared – so how could they meaningfully oppose it?

Lyttelton's energetic support for Federation was reinforced at a conference he held in May 1952. Joshua Nkomo, the leading African spokesman, one of the two blacks brought to London as a member of the Southern Rhodesian delegation, moderately explained that his suspicions about Federation had been allayed and that he would try to persuade Africans to see its advantages. However, the failure of the Southern Rhodesian Government until this time to invite any Africans to the many official meetings to plan for Federation had fuelled African suspicions.

To Lyttelton, African opposition was no obstacle. Nor could the scheme be impeded by the governments of Northern Rhodesia or Nyasaland, which had to do what the Colonial Office told them. The only problem, as he saw it, was the electorate of Southern Rhodesia. As in the referendum of 1923, they faced a decision affecting their constitutional future and – since they controlled their own police and army – had to be offered the final say.

Consequently the Prime Minister of Southern Rhodesia, Sir Godfrey Huggins, was granted some concessions. The British Government toned down provisions for African representation in the Federal legislature and for the composition of an African Affairs Board (with the power to refer proposed Federal laws to London if it held them to be discriminatory). Lyttelton was determined that the Southern Rhodesian voters should neither opt to join South Africa nor demand independence as a separate state: Federation was a great British venture which they must be persuaded to support.

Huggins went back to Southern Rhodesia and said, 'The United Kingdom are trusting the Europeans of Central Africa sufficiently to hand over six million primitive Africans to a Parliament dominated by local Europeans

. . . It is a great testimonial to us.' He described the African Affairs Board as 'a frightful waste of money and manpower' and 'a little piece of Gilbert and Sullivan'. He begged his hearers not to worry about remarks made in Britain concerning the primacy of Africans' interests. The British, he explained, 'suffer from a kind of unctuous rectitude and apparent hypocrisy which is disliked by foreigners and their overseas kinsmen'. The idea of 'partnership', he explained, included the partnership of the rider and his horse. Lyttelton did not contradict him.

The Southern Rhodesian whites were persuaded. They voted for Federation and Lyttelton pushed the measure through the British Parliament. The huge new central African state – almost as big as Canada – came formally into existence on 1 August 1953. But the words of Huggins and the absence of Colonial Office contradiction were not noticed by the Southern Rhodesian voters alone. The feelings of blacks in all three territories were strengthened against the new state into which they had been shovelled; Colonial Service officers in Northern Rhodesia and Nyasaland were shocked at the open contempt shown for their ideal of trusteeship for the African; and the Labour Party in Britain stopped being embarrassed about opposing a measure it had itself originated. The Party now regarded with wholehearted loathing what it saw as Conservative collusion with the imperialism of the white settlers.

Some Southern Rhodesian Africans also turned against the scheme. Although Joshua Nkomo had been convinced by the honourable intentions of the ministers and officials he met in London, once back in Southern Rhodesia and faced with Huggins's public statements he reverted to opposing Federation. He now warned that his people would return to savagery in their struggle to resist it.

The defect at the core of the Federal scheme had been spotted by one of the keenest minds applied to the issue, the Chief Justice of Southern Rhodesia, Sir Robert Tredgold. He considered 'native policy' the key problem for the Federation and did not see how the three territories could be left to handle it separately. He drew an analogy with slavery in the United States:

> It took one of the bitterest civil wars in history to prove what should have been obvious from the beginning, that a problem the concern of the whole union could not be settled one way in some states and another in other states. This, to my mind, is the fatal defect in the [Federation scheme]. They seek to avoid an issue which is unavoidable. They endeavour to postpone a decision which can only be made vastly more difficult by delay.

Nevertheless the Federation began well for Southern Rhodesia. Its stagnating economy was seized by a boom. Copper was heavily in demand, leading to high prices, plentiful jobs and new investment. The creation of the Federation attracted businessmen with its prospect of a large single market and, it was thought, long-term political stability. Great plans were afoot for the biggest hydro-electric scheme in Africa to be built at Kariba, on the

Zambezi river frontier between Northern and Southern Rhodesia, to provide the power both for refining copper and for expanding industry throughout the Federation. Such developments matched Lyttelton's hopes.

The hopes of Attlee, Gordon-Walker and Cohen also received some encouragement. During the early years of the Federation some of the discriminatory laws which the British Parliament had allowed white Rhodesia to introduce were amended. Changes in the Land Apportionment Act, for example, allowed restaurants, hotels and clubs to become multi-racial – though few did – and African professional men to rent offices, though not dwellings, in European areas; the setting-up of a new university college was announced, to be multi-racial from the start and therefore exempted from the Act. Dining cars on the railways were declared open to all races. The first meeting of the Federal Assembly was held in the Southern Rhodesian legislative building in Salisbury. The few African MPs were asked not to use the toilets for fear of offending their hosts. In a state now dedicated to racial partnership the request was a tactless error from which the whites of Salisbury learned that they must not discriminate openly, at any rate not against black MPs.

The mood of hope is conveyed by Nathan Shamuyarira, a young black journalist who came to work in Salisbury in 1953:

> Before Federation there had never been any idea of such a thing as equality; so that, although the equality likely after Federation was heavily qualified even in theory, nobody paid any notice to the qualifications: they were ready to grab anything. The preamble to the federal constitution, a non-racial federal civil service, a common federal voters' roll, six Africans in the Federal Parliament: these were all wonderful novelties, and it did not enter into the heads of many Southern Rhodesian Africans that their two African MPs were there only on white votes.

The hopeful signs for a better deal for the African in Southern Rhodesia centred mainly on one man, Garfield Todd. In 1953 Sir Godfrey Huggins, who had been Prime Minister of Southern Rhodesia for twenty years, was elevated to the Prime Ministership of the Federation and most of his leading colleagues joined him in the Federal Cabinet. Running Southern Rhodesia seemed, by comparison, county council work. So Todd, who had never held any government office under Huggins, was suddenly catapulted from the backbenches to the Prime Ministership.

Todd, unlike other Southern Rhodesian politicians, had expressed mildly liberal views on race relations. For example, in June 1952 when supporting Federation in the Rhodesian parliament, he said:

> If we federate these three countries we are committing central Africa to a liberal policy, to a policy of racial co-operation, which we are not so fully committed to under our present state government.

He was exactly the man supporters of partnership needed to take the helm in

*Garfield Todd's four years as Prime Minister of Southern Rhodesia prove that the Federation's ideal of partnership had some powerfully placed and honest supporters.*

Southern Rhodesia at this moment. By origin he was a New Zealander, by style a relaxed and self-confident mission school headmaster. He had become a rancher, with at one time a 90,000-acre farm, and Huggins, who was always looking for men of talent, had invited him to join his United Party. Todd was a spellbinding orator with a broad world view. Huggins liked talking to him and approved of his remark, 'We're taking the African people by the scruff of the neck and saying, "Come with us into the twentieth century". But they'll be glad they came.'

Todd began the slow process of liberalisation which was the price Southern Rhodesia's whites were being asked to pay for Federation. He chipped here and there at racial discrimination, moving Southern Rhodesia away from the South African model without significantly undermining any of the privileges of the Europeans. The electorate were uneasy about Todd's committed Christianity and his belief that all men – *all!* – are created equal, but the white professional and governmental élite were doing well out of Federation and did not expect to lose by any of the concessions to Africans that were in prospect. Todd was able to persuade even some white artisans and factory workers – who were normally paid ten times the black rate for the same job – that his measures were the way to secure Rhodesia and the Federation the world's approval. Now that Salisbury was the Federal capital as well as the capital of Southern Rhodesia, all the Western European governments and the USA, Canada, Turkey and India opened legations there. Foreign businessmen were arriving. Salisbury airport was becoming busy. Skyscraper offices and new hotels were built. In such hopeful times Todd was able to introduce a scheme to provide five years' schooling for every African, paid for by a rise in African taxes. The whites even put up with Todd's announcement in November 1956 that in future the Government would address African males as 'Mr'. Such Prime Ministerial whims would not stop any settler from hailing an African – even an eighty-year-old – as 'Boy!'

Todd was far and away the most talented minister in the Southern Rhodesian Government and he showed considerable skill in bringing forward reforms by stealth, but he was leading in a direction that all whites, except those with technical qualifications, knew must end with their being displaced by Africans. That he survived as Prime Minister from September 1953 until February 1958 is a measure of his political skill and his superiority in brains, style and charm to any alternative candidate. It is also a measure of the mood of liberal optimism that Federation brought to Rhodesians, white and black. In the words of Nathan Shamuyarira, who during this period rose to become editor-in-chief of the white-owned African Newspapers Ltd as well as Salisbury correspondent of the *Guardian*: 'The whole country sailed on this little sea of hope for five years.'

Todd's Cabinet colleagues eventually became convinced he would lose them the next election. They did not object to his policy of making some concessions, so long as the number of Africans admitted to the electorate was low. And Todd himself was inclined to move slowly. But his way of speaking aroused African expectations and enthusiasm. His colleagues objected to his being regarded by many Africans as 'a sort of saviour'. They objected to his having conversations with Joshua Nkomo in an attempt to win the co-operation of the African National Congress (even though Todd was tough and threatening with Africans he regarded as 'troublemakers').

Two issues brought about Todd's downfall. The first was sexual. A law of 1903 had made intercourse outside marriage between a black man and a white woman a punishable offence. In April 1957 a demand was raised for relations outside marriage between white men and black women also to be an offence. Todd thought the proposal idiotic: it would require the police to spy on activities that were widespread. He said not only that the new law was foolish but also that the old one should be repealed – a view which caused some whites to see him as a defender of black rapists. When the proposed new law was raised in Parliament, Todd voted in the minority against it; the other four members of his Cabinet voted in favour. He showed a Gladstonian indifference to the fact that his actions would outrage many voters.

The second issue that led to Todd's overthrow was the franchise. Todd believed in extending the vote to educated Africans. He explained at a public meeting:

Southern Rhodesia finds itself the custodian of Rhodes's liberal dictum of equal rights for civilised men regardless of colour. If legislation further to implement that policy, when introduced to our House, were so changed as to keep off the rolls our six thousand Africans who have had ten years' education and who work as teachers, agricultural demonstrators, medical orderlies and so on, we would be so betraying the spirit of Rhodes that I would not continue to lead my party. However, I am confident that our legislators will meet the challenge.

Todd's success in nudging the Southern Rhodesian electorate into accepting liberal policies towards Africans had convinced him that a kick was needed to get them over this next step. He appeared to be right. Cabinet and legislature accepted his amendment to the franchise. It was not yet respectable to be openly illiberal. The current cliché had it that full equality should be granted the Africans *when they were ready*. Whatever Todd and the professional élite meant by these words, to most white Rhodesians they meant 'not in my lifetime', and some said they believed the Africans would never be ready. Over the franchise Todd proved what they had long suspected: that he was not really one of them. He might own a big farm but deep down he was still a missionary with dangerous egalitarian beliefs. Soon after the franchise vote, Todd's four Cabinet colleagues announced that they would not serve with him and his party rejected him as leader. Nathan Shamuyarira wrote later of those times:

Hope for peaceful co-operation and swift progress towards racial equality was over . . . An African composed a song which became a best-selling record:

> Todd wasichya
> Hamba Kahle mudale . . .
> Todd has left us
> Go well, old man . . .

While Todd remained Prime Minister of Southern Rhodesia it was possible to believe that the logical chasm in the Federation – the contrasted racial policies of Southern Rhodesia's Government and of the Colonial Office in the two northern territories – might be bridged. Todd honestly wanted to bring educated, politically conscious Africans into the governing élite. He made contact with African nationalist leaders. He courageously led his party from the front. But he fell into the logical chasm. The white Rhodesian voters wanted the Federation, but they did not want the partnership between white and black which alone could preserve it.

The Federal Government never had a Todd to lead it. Sir Godfrey Huggins, the first Federal Prime Minister, was near the end of a long career in politics which he combined with general medical practice. He had a shrewd doctor's understanding of the fears of the majority of whites. He knew they would never voluntarily share power with the blacks. For him it was useful to have Todd as Southern Rhodesian Prime Minister, to provide evidence for Britain and the world that a sincere white leader was pursuing the policy of partnership and that he enjoyed widespread black approval. Huggins hoped to persuade the British Government to grant the Federation complete independence before he retired, so that the further evolution of partnership would be for the predominantly white electorate and his successors to control.

Before agreeing, the British Government insisted that further steps towards partnership must be taken. Therefore the next stage in the history of Rhodesia and the Federation turned on the issue that finally brought down Todd: who should be entitled to vote. Ultimately this was a simple matter. More blacks had to be enfranchised. In practice it turned out so complicated that people who were jointly involved in preparing electoral arrangements have ever since disagreed about their impact. Four legislatures were elected – for the two Rhodesias, Nyasaland and the Federation – and each had separate and complicated rules which were the subject of public argument and revision in 1957–61. Sophisticated Africans were not so naive as to press for one-man-one-vote in the Federation. With the whites outnumbered 12–1 in Southern Rhodesia, 30–1 in Northern Rhodesia and 330–1 in Nyasaland, elections on that basis would have led to prompt white emigration on a scale that would have been economically disastrous. So the Federal objective was to raise the number of black voters fast enough to win African consent and international approval, while keeping power firmly in the hands of the minority.

The problem was the word 'qualified'. Given economic development and the spread of education, the rise in the number of 'qualified' blacks was quickly going to lead to a black-majority electorate. To make sure that the candidates elected were not black nationalists, whites and blacks were placed on separate electoral rolls and their votes were weighted. The objective was to ensure that, in order to be elected, a white MP had to win a significant proportion of the black vote in his constituency and a black MP a significant proportion of the white. This mechanism, it was hoped, would exclude racial extremists of either colour from the legislature. A core of moderate multi-racialists in and around government would ensure that partnership became a reality.

In the first Federal election in 1953 this system worked. Joshua Nkomo, the leading African nationalist of Southern Rhodesia, had stood for the African seat of Matabeleland and, thanks to the overwhelming impact of the whites' cross-voting, had been defeated. An African whom the whites found more 'moderate' was elected. Those who believed partnership could be made to work saw Nkomo's defeat as harsh but necessary. He and his supporters must learn that the only route to power was by way of compromise. Such mechanisms for averting a black-white clash were eventually rejected both by the whites of Southern Rhodesia and by the blacks of Northern Rhodesia and Nyasaland. The blacks' disillusionment with Federation became complete when the Federal Franchise came up for review in 1957. The Federal Assembly proposed that its own membership should be enlarged from thirty-five to fifty-nine, including six extra African MPs; so far so good. But hitherto African MPs for Northern Rhodesia and Nyasaland had been elected by Africans. The new proposal was for four of the six to be elected by a cross-voting arrangement like that which had led to the defeat of Joshua Nkomo, i.e. by a predominantly white electorate.

The African Affairs Board, the official committee to protect African rights, about which Huggins had been so scathing, now had its moment. It considered the proposed measure, judged it discriminatory and referred it to Westminster, thus using its ultimate weapon. It advised, in effect, that by making four out of six of the extra Africans in the assembly dependent on European votes, the Federation would be effectively reducing African representation as a proportion of the total. Against this the Federal Government argued that twelve Africans in an Assembly of 59 was a higher proportion than six in an Assembly of 35; therefore the change meant an increase for Africans. The British Government accepted the Federal argument and set aside the view of the Board.

Lord Home, who was Commonwealth Secretary at the time, later explained the Government's thinking:

> As far as the franchise was concerned we had to try to keep the Federal Government on our side. There was always a danger that they could break away and claim dominion status. When we came to making concessions on the franchise they were on the whole ones we thought were reasonable. The Federal Government did let more Africans in on the act; not enough in our view, but they made progress; and so we did make some concessions.

Sir Arthur Benson, then Governor of Northern Rhodesia, recalled:

> When I got the telegram saying that the British Government was going to allow the bill on the Federal franchise to go through – 'Despatch follows explaining reasons' – my reaction was one of absolute profound shock. I was shattered by it. It seemed to me that that was probably the end of the Federation.

In five years this was the first time the African Affairs Board had referred a Federal law to London. To the Africans, the Board's role as their protector was shown to be hollow. This episode and Todd's dismissal confirmed the suspicions of Africans in the two northern territories: only by all-out opposition to the Federation could they hope to save themselves from *apartheid* Rhodesian-style. African leaders, who for some years had shown moderation in the hope that partnership would work, now turned militant. Most whites saw them as increasingly crazed and vicious.

The most bitter invective of Southern Rhodesian whites came to be reserved for a small Edinburgh-trained doctor – the black response to Sir

Godfrey Huggins – Hastings Banda. It was he who had written the paper in London in 1949 arguing for colonial rule rather than Federation. He had not changed his mind and he was now to strike Federation its fatal blow. Its internal contradictions suggested that it was bound to collapse. Banda made sure of it.

Banda, a Nyasa village boy, had been taught by Scottish missionaries, long the predominant Europeans in Nyasaland following David Livingstone's work there in the 1850s. The mission teachers encouraged the young Banda to seek further education in South Africa, and in 1919, at the age of sixteen, he walked to Johannesburg, a distance of more than a thousand miles. His trek was not unique. The British rulers had imposed on all Nyasaland Africans a hut tax, which had to be paid in cash. Since Rhodes had been denied Nyasaland, his railway did not run there, so it was almost impossible for the natives to earn cash locally. However, with their Scottish mission training, they were among the best educated natives in central Africa and were welcomed as employees throughout Rhodesia. Obtaining a 'Nyasa-boy' was the settler's wife's best step towards a well-managed home. To find the cash for their families' hut tax, many Nyasa men also went to work in the mines of South Africa. Banda worked as a clerk in a gold-mine there while continuing his education. An American missionary then encouraged him to study in the United States, where he gained a degree in history and political science at the University of Chicago and qualified as a doctor of medicine in Tennessee. His qualification did not permit him to practise in the British Empire, so he came to Britain to obtain a medical diploma at Edinburgh. He became an elder of the Church of Scotland and settled down to general practice, first in Liverpool, then near Newcastle, later in Kilburn in north-west London.

Banda was away from Nyasaland for more than forty years, from 1915 to 1958. He wanted to return when he qualified, but decided not to when he was told that the Government of Nyasaland would not pay him as much as they paid a British doctor. He took an interest in politics, joining the Fabian Colonial Bureau, publicly opposing the creation of the Federation, putting up and helping to pay the expenses of Nyasa delegations in London. He came to be regarded by the Nyasas not only as their first university graduate and their best drafter of submissions to the Colonial Office, but as a national hero.

In 1953, when it was becoming apparent that the Gold Coast would soon become independent as Ghana, Banda moved there, to practise medicine in the Ashanti capital of Kumasi. This was the year the Federation came into being, and Banda, having unsuccessfully resisted its creation, opted out of politics. Through his stay in the Gold Coast, however, he acquired in the eyes of both Nyasas and white Rhodesians something of the mantle of Nkrumah.

By 1958 the blacks of Nyasaland were becoming seriously alarmed at political developments. The experience of the first five years of Federation had strengthened their initial objections. The promise of economic benefit was not fulfilled in a way that made any impact on them; the white Southern Rhodesians seemed bent on obtaining independence for the whole Federation and thus removing Colonial Office protection from the Nyasas. The Nyasaland Congress, led by a quarrelling mixture of elderly chiefs and young firebrands, faced a grim prospect: the British Government had promised to review the Federal constitution in 1960 and seemed committed then further to strengthen the hold of the white Federal electorate; it was therefore urgently necessary to persuade Britain to advance the constitutional position of the Africans in Nyasaland, to enable them to resist the Federal predators before the review; attempts by Congress to impress the Colonial Office with the urgency of this need had not borne fruit. The young Congress leaders decided that the only solution was to persuade Banda to return. With suitable publicity he could quickly be made the leader of a national crusade.

Some moderate whites also urged Banda to come back to Nyasaland. They hoped he could head off the clash between black and white: after decades in Britain he was loyal to the Crown and deeply conservative. He wanted not immediate independence for Nyasaland but an enlarged African share in government under continuing colonial rule. While the Nyasaland Congress aroused popular African expectations of the return of the saviour, reasonable whites and members of the Government hoped his arrival would have a calming influence.

Although in all three territories organisations existed called 'The African National Congress', each was quite independent; they had not got round to combining plans. Banda, however, just happened to return in July 1958 at the moment when all three were close to explosion and he provided a rallying-point for them all. The Southern Rhodesian and Federal Governments thought he was about to lead the congresses in a joint anti-Federal campaign. They saw him from the moment of his arrival as a menace to the Federation, to the white man and to civilised order.

In Nyasaland Banda found the situation tense. The Legislative Council there had been composed largely of officials plus a few white 'unofficials'. In 1956 for the first time Africans selected by the African provincial councils joined. The five Africans chosen were all Congress members, and two, Henry Chipembere and Kanyama Chiume, had immediately set about using the Legislative Council to demand Nyasaland's removal from the Federation. The Governor, Sir Robert Armitage, was having trouble even before Banda's return.

I had to preside over the new Legislative Council [he remembered]. We were a very undemocratic organisation, because there was a majority of officials. As the months went by Chiume and Chipembere became violently active in demanding that Nyasaland should be removed from the Federation. They even went so far as to have a motion introduced to advocate this. They knew that the review of the whole federal structure was going to be held in 1960 and it seemed to me inappropriate that a motion of this sort should be debated so far in advance of that examination. In my autocratic way as Governor as well as Speaker I refused to allow them to introduce their motion. But they got many other opportunities to air their view that the only way Nyasaland could progress was by getting a black government in control.

The colonial government's purpose in bringing Africans onto Legco was to educate them in the arts of governing. Chipembere and Chiume used their position instead to mount a fully-fledged opposition. Their speeches were largely designed as inspiration for the Congress. The official report of Legislative Council debates, Hansard, printed at the Government's expense, became a best-seller among educated Africans.

By the time Banda arrived Chipembere and Chiume had worked up nationwide excitement. He stepped onto the bridge of a fast-moving vessel which he could not at first control. Although he insisted on being president with complete authority over the Nyasaland Congress, he did not at first want to be troubled with the minutiae of administration and left much committee work to his colleagues, particularly Chipembere and Chiume. Not having spoken the local language, chi-Nyanja, for forty years, he delivered his speeches in English, with an interpreter who often spiced up his sentiments or removed modifying clauses. This did not diminish his impact and may even have increased it: he was the Nyasa messiah and spoke like a British ruler. His mob-oratory – calling for discipline and respect for whites

*A heroic return. Dr Banda raises his homburg, flanked by Kanyama Chiume (left) and Orton Chirwa, Nyasaland's only qualified African lawyer.*

but contemptuous of 'their *stupid* Federation' – gripped the Nyasa people and enhanced Congress's position as their national movement. For the past year Congress had been pressing for a new constitution for Nyasaland, on the grounds that it was patently unjust for 2.5 million Africans to have fewer representatives than seven thousand Europeans and ten thousand Indians. The British Government repeatedly promised constitutional proposals and then repeatedly failed to produce them. Banda roused the Nyasa people in a united demand that this blockage be removed.

The Congress, needing to build up its local organisation in villages throughout the country, faced a problem. The cleverest and most forceful young Africans usually had jobs in the towns. Chipembere, on being selected for the Legislative Council in 1956, had resigned from his government job as a district assistant, but most workers with responsible jobs could give little time to Congress. Local organisers in the villages had to be literate but they were rarely very clever or able. Frequently those who were were frustrated and bloody-minded in their attitude towards the Government. The official measures against which they found it easiest to raise popular feeling were regulations designed to prevent soil erosion and the spread of disease. Such regulations required farmers to hoe before the rains and to contour-ridge: hard work. By the time Banda arrived, local Congress leaders throughout the Federation were campaigning against agricultural regulations, and District Officers, appalled at rabble rousers' attempts to undo years of careful work, were sending in the police to enforce good husbandry.

The Government of Northern Rhodesia had been the most effective in the three territories at overcoming popular resistance to agricultural regulations. When the Northern Rhodesian Congress ran a campaign against cattle inoculation, the Government gave in, withdrew the inoculation teams, let the effects become apparent in the shape of thousands of dead cattle and let it be known that the family cattle of Harry Nkumbula, the Congress leader, were being inoculated. The Governor, Sir Arthur Benson, had been closely involved with Andrew Cohen in creating the Federation and believed in partnership. He persuaded Nkumbula to co-operate with the Government by standing in an election on a new (and immensely complicated) cross-voting franchise – and getting elected. Nkumbula, joint signatory with Banda of the 1949 paper attacking the proposed Federation, was now working with it. His moderation – over both agricultural regulation and the Northern Rhodesian franchise – was a principal reason for his losing popular support to a more extreme breakaway group from his own Congress, led by Kenneth Kaunda. Banda, though rational, conservative and well disposed towards the British Colonial Service, was not going to make Nkumbula's mistake.

Banda could not bring himself to attack agricultural regulations which he knew were sensible. He did, however, attack the role of the police and the chiefs' courts in enforcing them. Banda had no objection to eating with whites, including members of the Government – he and Sir Robert

Armitage, the Governor, got on well together – but the young Congress radicals were highly suspicious of social contact with Europeans, so Banda avoided it. Compared to some of his colleagues, Banda was no enthusiast for violence but, as he explained to the Government Secretary for African Affairs, John Ingram, the record of colonial policy in India and West Africa showed that pressure had to be applied to make the British carry out their declared aim of granting self-government.

Banda declined an invitation to lunch with the Governor but met him and senior officials and firmly told them his requirements. He had to demand complete political power but would of course settle for something less so long as it was sufficient to enable the African majority to speak for Nyasaland at the Federal review conference in 1960 and to secede from the Federation if necessary. This placed Sir Robert Armitage in a dilemma. He had been told when he was appointed Governor that his main task was to win support for the Federation. Furthermore, he later recalled:

> I was in extreme difficulty because Her Majesty's Government in London had no idea what constitutional advance would be suitable for Nyasaland. I got a letter from Alan Lennox-Boyd in which he said he was very sorry he hadn't been able to make any advance on these political matters, because the constitution of Northern Rhodesia was under discussion; that had to be settled first and he was having great trouble arguing with the Federal Prime Minister about it.

Banda's colleagues were strengthened in their view that the British Government had to be forced.

The growing tension comes out in Banda's own description of events at Mzimba in late August 1958. After he had addressed a meeting his car was pushed for more than a mile, mostly by singing women. They chose a route which went past the European club, the golf course and the police station, 'to show the Europeans that, at least on that Sunday, they [the Africans] were in control of Mzimba. I felt sorry for the veterinary surgeon and his wife who met my car coming from the other direction. The women ordered him to stop and the poor fellow meekly obeyed.' As they passed the police station, the men and women threatened to pull down the Union Jack; Banda forbade them. But he could not prevent the African women from making 'grossly insulting gestures' at a group of five Europeans at the golf course.

Dr Banda did not permit violence in his presence, but he relished the demonstration, to Europeans and Government, that he was a force to be reckoned with. He addressed meetings in every part of the country. Huge audiences came to hear him and gave vent to their excitement afterwards. On two of these occasions stones were thrown, causing damage to cars and some slight injuries to Europeans. Wherever he went – dressed always like an English city gentleman in dark suit, tie and homburg hat with a beige raincoat and brown leather gloves – the police relied on Banda's word to keep order. They had no means of controlling the vast crowds and the excitement his presence aroused. The security services were jumpy. They tried to find out what Congress was planning but the police reports of Banda's speeches, which represented him as determined to use force to bring about immediate African rule, were often based on the chi-Nyanja translation rather than on Banda's own words, and the informers, unable to write during the meetings, usually compiled their reports from memory afterwards. Banda later satisfied a judicial inquiry that the reports were exaggerated: what he had repeatedly said was that he had not brought self-government with him in his bag and that it would have to be striven for by negotiation and peaceful means. Between speaking tours he attended meetings with government officials, including the Governor.

In December 1958 Banda returned to Ghana – independent for almost two years – to attend Kwame Nkrumah's first Pan-African Congress. Two Northern Rhodesian leaders, Harry Nkumbula and Kenneth Kaunda, also went to Accra, and the delegates signed a declaration pledging to break up the Federation. The Federal Government became convinced that Banda and Kaunda reached an agreement in Ghana to 'hot up the tempo of violence'.

Sir Godfrey Huggins had been succeeded in 1956 as Federal Prime Minister by Sir Roy Welensky, who now felt that the Federation was faced by a rising tide of African opposition which had to be put down. Welensky was the odd character of the Rhodesian story. The thirteenth child of a Polish Jew and his Afrikaner wife, he described himself as '50 per cent Jewish, 50 per cent Polish and 100 per cent British'. His father had knocked around the world, making and losing money. By the time Roy was born the family had settled in Salisbury and lived in poverty. His mother died when he was eleven, he started work at fourteen, became a railwayman and, in his spare time, a heavyweight boxer. He was troublesome and combative, and the railways posted him to remote Broken Hill in Northern Rhodesia. There he built up the white railway workers' union. The railway had made Rhodesia. The copper from the mines at Ndola and Kitwe passed through Broken Hill, with Welensky often driving the engine. He moved on from union affairs to the Northern Rhodesian Legislative Council and was soon, like Todd, spotted by Huggins as a man of talent. Welensky was one of those who saw the rise of black nationalism as linked to an international Communist plot. 'We had much to lose,' he later wrote, 'the battle for Africa was already on.' Rhodesians regarded Welensky as a liberal. Britons did not. Lord Alport, a former Conservative minister and British High Commissioner to the Federation in 1960–63, recalled meeting him at Salisbury airport:

His ministers were assembled there; some were Africans, and of course the majority were Europeans; also representatives of his party both black and white. I noticed that as he walked along the ranks he shook hands with all the Europeans and none of the Africans.

Wclensky regarded the visit to Accra of Banda and Kaunda as part of a concerted plan.

Dr Banda, passing through Salisbury airport on his way back from Accra, greeted the crowd that came to meet him with his slogans '*Kwacha!*' (the dawn) and 'Freedom!' These were held by Europeans – no doubt rightly – to be anti-Federal cries. He addressed a meeting in Salisbury's African township of Highfields, urging Africans to go to prison in their millions 'singing Hallelujah' and added: 'They can send me to prison. They can kill me. I will never give up my fight for freedom.' Southern Rhodesian Africans, always nervous about the listening government agent, were not accustomed to such outspokenness. A few days later Banda told a meeting in Nyasaland, 'I put Salisbury on fire . . . I got Salisbury rocking, rocking, and got it awake out of its political sleep.' He was referring to his impact on the Africans, but on Sir Roy Welensky his impact was even more decisive. Welensky summoned Federal defence chiefs to his office, told them that serious trouble was coming in Nyasaland and that the Federal Government must be ready to play its part in maintaining internal security.

Internal security was not the Federal Government's job. When the Federation was being set up Huggins had wanted the police to come under Federal control. But the Africans in the two northern territories feared this

*Sir Roy Welensky and a new smelting plant he opened in his constituency, Broken Hill in Northern Rhodesia.*

above all else: they trusted the colonial Governors – but not Rhodesian whites – to run the police and the law fairly. So internal security in Northern Rhodesia and Nyasaland had been made the responsibility of the Governors, who could turn to each other for help, or to a neighbouring colony such as Tanganyika, or to the Colonial Office in London, or, at their discretion, to the Federal Government. Benson in Northern Rhodesia had previously complained of the Federal Government's attempts to take over territorial powers, and Dr Banda now warned the Chief Secretary of the Nyasaland Government that the one event that would arouse panic and mistrust among the Nyasaland blacks would be the arrival of Southern Rhodesian forces.

Sir Roy Welensky acted properly according to his lights. He feared the spread of African nationalism, which he equated with Communism and violent disorder, from Nyasaland to the rest of the Federation. So he arranged to have troops stand by and he had a senior staff officer of the Rhodesian Air Force visit Nyasaland to discuss with Europeans there, official and unofficial, the kind of reinforcements they might need if disorder broke out. Welensky thus planted the idea that Federal forces were available before the Governor of Nyasaland or his officials thought they needed help. Indeed Welensky formed the view that the Nyasaland Government was slow coming to its senses: 'I decided that it was time Armitage and I had a talk.' He offered to put an aircraft at Armitage's disposal. The Governor, however, would not be bullied. While Welensky set up an operations room to plan for the Rhodesian Air Force to move the army at short notice, Armitage declined to meet him and waited for the constitutional proposals from London which he hoped would go some way to calm the excessive boisterousness of Congress.

At the start of 1959, with only a year to go to the Federal review and still no news from London about constitutional advance for Nyasaland, Banda and his Congress colleagues chose to raise the temperature. Banda knew what he was doing: he wanted to provoke the Government to make some arrests – preferably including himself – so that the many Labour MPs and Scottish clergymen who knew him to be moderate and reasonable would have something to complain about. This way he would capture the attention of Parliament.

On 25 January 1959 an open-air Congress meeting was held outside the capital, Blantyre, to discuss the next steps. Banda by agreement stayed away. Some present favoured non-violent resistance on Gandhi's model. Some favoured violence against anti-Congress chiefs and Europeans and a few called for them to be murdered. Some wanted to plan what they should do after Banda and the other leaders were arrested. The meeting took no formal decision, but its conclusion was clear: Congress must defy and provoke.

Over the next few weeks Congress increased the number of meetings it held illegally, i.e. without first obtaining a permit. Initially the Government stood by, allowing the law to be defied, but it could not let such conduct go on. The police began to arrest local leaders who resisted orders to disperse their illegal meetings. Scuffles followed. On each occasion the police were overwhelmingly outnumbered and the crowd could easily have lynched them. But the Nyasaland Africans showed no animosity. When compelling a district commissioner to release prisoners, when breaking into a prison, when smashing windows and stoning cars, when taking over a provincial airport and preventing its use, the Africans ensured that injuries to whites remained minimal. The enemy was Federation, not the colonial government or the tiny white minority. Henry Chipembere and some of the younger Congress leaders tried to encourage violence against the British and they undoubtedly succeeded in frightening isolated Britons. Rumours of what had been decided at the meeting on 25 January – that a plot to murder prominent whites had been agreed – made people nervous, especially some young policemen and officials who were responsible for the safety of the whites in their areas. But no whites were killed.

By mid-February 1959 Dr Banda had still failed to get himself arrested. Sir Roy Welensky and some whites in Nyasaland were pressing the Governor to declare a State of Emergency, arrest 'troublemakers', bring in Federal (i.e. Southern Rhodesian) troops and thus restore law and order, but Armitage kept his nerve. He was at last promised that a minister would fly out from London with constitutional proposals. He hoped that Banda, when told, would put a stop to violence. Banda, however, equivocated. He did not wish to reduce the pressure on the Government, nor was he sure that he could; his young colleagues did not believe the proposals from London could bring them what they required. The Governor then changed his mind and summoned Southern Rhodesian troops to help keep order. This, Banda warned the Chief Secretary, would 'really cause trouble'. Now Banda took the step of refusing to condemn violence.

Thus Banda's ally in bringing the Nyasaland pot to the boil turned out to be Sir Roy Welensky. By pressing the Governor to accept Federal troops, Welensky gave Banda grounds for refusing to condemn violence. In an open letter to the Governor Banda wrote that the arrival of Rhodesian troops 'reveals clearly that the government of this country is only a puppet in the hands of the European settlers of Southern Rhodesia'. Nobody can say whether the ministerial visit would have led Banda, with his respect for Crown and constitution, try to stop violence or whether the terms so long gestating in the womb of the Colonial Office would have formed the basis for a compromise. But certainly the arrival of Southern Rhodesian troops, which Nyasas had always feared, escalated the conflict. The number and anger of African demonstrations increased. Congress members rolled logs across an airstrip, preventing rapid police reinforcement. In several towns and villages the police opened fire. Within a week five African protesters were killed. The Governor became convinced that the disorders were so widespread and difficult to contain that the ministerial visit must be cancelled. He declared a State of Emergency. Welensky had got his way. Emergencies were also declared, though with less reason, in Southern and

Northern Rhodesia. The Prime Minister of Southern Rhodesia, Sir Edgar Whitehead, went so far as to announce: 'It is a very ancient tradition of the British people that Governments should defer action against subversive movements until actual rioting or bloodshed has occurred. My Government does not subscribe to this tradition.'

In Nyasaland police and troops arrested 1,322 people. Dr Banda and the other Congress leaders were seized in the early hours of 3 March 1959. He was flown to Gwelo jail in Southern Rhodesia. Few resisted and the violence feared by the authorities did not happen. But the people were troubled. Why had leaders guilty of no crime been suddenly taken away by Southern Rhodesian soldiers? Crowds came to government offices and police stations to ask. Getting no satisfactory answers, they refused to go away. Police and army commanders, faced with frightened and angry crowds, felt obliged to disperse them. Some panicked, some opened fire, and within a week a further forty-eight Africans had been killed. As Dr Banda had intended, Westminster required an explanation.

The Colonial Secretary, Alan Lennox-Boyd, tried to provide one. Pressed by sceptical opposition questioners, who believed that Sir Roy Welensky had sent Rhodesian troops to take over this still British colony, Lennox-Boyd told the House of Commons: 'I have seen information that made it clear that plans had been made by Congress to carry out widespread violence and murder of Europeans, Asians and moderate African leaders; that in fact, a massacre was being planned.' Lennox-Boyd had seen summaries of informers' reports about the open-air Congress meeting of 25 January and seized on the most dramatic justification he could find for the declaration of an emergency. James Callaghan, the opposition spokesman on colonies, had some weeks earlier been in touch with Banda, and promptly commented on Lennox-Boyd's statement: 'The right hon. gentleman will believe anything.'

Sir Robert Armitage recalled:

> When I read that Lennox-Boyd had said in the House of Commons that a massacre was being planned and that was the main reason for the declaration of the State of Emergency I was staggered. In my broadcast earlier that morning I had made no reference to any massacre or murder plan or anything of that sort. I had been governed in my action all through by the escalating violence throughout the country. The Europeans had been warned to look after themselves and were quite capable of doing so. The people I was concerned with were Africans in government service who were being molested, their houses burnt, their places of work destroyed. They were the people who really concerned me when I decided to declare a State of Emergency.

In the events leading to the State of Emergency, a handful of Europeans had been slightly injured. A government response that had led to more than fifty Africans being killed (five in the week before the emergency, forty-eight after) seemed disproportionate. The Prime Minister, Harold Macmillan, decided to appoint a Commission of Inquiry. The Lord Chancellor, Lord Kilmuir, and the Deputy Prime Minister, R. A. Butler, chose the judge to head it: Sir Patrick Devlin. Macmillan, still the imperialist, was in the United States when the choice was made, and disapproved.

Colleagues explained that Devlin was a Conservative supporter, the cleverest judge in Britain, certain before long to rise to the House of Lords, that Selwyn Lloyd, the Foreign Secretary, and Butler had known him at Cambridge, that he had canvassed for the party at general elections: he was sound. Macmillan wanted a man with less incisive intelligence. Was not Devlin, he asked, 'Irish, a lapsed Catholic and deformed?'

Lord Kilmuir, the Lord Chancellor, in his capacity as Cabinet minister as well as head of the judiciary, had a talk with Devlin, who later recalled:

He said that it was an important enquiry, and that was why he was anxious that a judge do it. He said that it might involve finding to what extent Federation was a cause of the disturbances. He was perfectly frank about what the Government's policy was. He said, 'We believe in

*The Devlin commission. Left to right: E. T. (Bill) Williams, Fellow of Balliol College, Oxford, Sir Patrick Devlin, chairman, and Sir John Ure Primrose, a Scottish landowner. Not pictured is the fourth member, Sir Percy Wyn-Harris, former Governor of the Gambia.*

Federation, but of course it's open to you to find that the ordinary African does not. We hope you won't make that finding, but if you do, we shall just have to accept it.'

Within four months the report was written. Its main finding was that there had been no murder plot. Nevertheless Sir Patrick Devlin and his colleagues concluded that the Governor was justified in declaring a State of Emergency; in the mounting disorder he had to act or abdicate. Nyasaland, the enquiry found, was 'no doubt only temporarily, a police state . . . where it is unwise to express any but the most restrained criticism of government policy'. With regard to Dr Banda, the Government had been mistaken in stating that his private offers to compromise were insincere: 'We think many politicians who are truly prepared to compromise would still in public [press] their full demands'. In imposing the emergency Government officers had, according to the report, repeatedly broken the law for what were 'thought to be sound administrative reasons'; this law-breaking by Government had amazed and horrified Africans. To cap it all, 'even amongst the chiefs [who] are loyal to the Government and dislike Congress, we have not heard of a single one who is in favour of Federation . . . on this issue a deep and bitter division separates the Government from the people.'

No sooner had the Government received the Devlin report than it assembled all the skill it possessed to produce a rebuttal. At Chequers, the Prime Minister's country house, the Lord Chancellor and the Attorney-General, each accompanied by officials, were joined for a two-day drafting session by Sir Robert Armitage and a team from the Colonial Office. Their purpose was to publish a reply at the same time as the report. In form it was a despatch from the Governor to the Colonial Secretary; in substance it was a united effort by the Government to defend itself. Together they attempted to prove that murders had been planned, that Dr Banda had known and approved, and that his continued detention, along with the 1,321 others arrested, was essential. The unfortunate Governor, in order to protect the Colonial Secretary, had to pretend publicly that the alleged murder plot was a principal reason for his declaring a State of Emergency. The Attorney-General had to open a debate in the House of Commons by rejecting many of the findings on fact of a unanimous commission that included, as well as Devlin and others, a former African colonial governor.

Ministers and Governor pretended nothing was wrong. But the summer of 1959 was a turning-point. Not only the Devlin report on Nyasaland but also the Hola camp murders in Kenya compelled the Prime Minister to think again about colonial policy. Was it in his or his party's interest to be answerable to Parliament for the killing of black men in Africa largely for the benefit of white settlers? As it became increasingly clear that the whites of Rhodesia wanted not partnership but permanent supremacy and that the blacks wanted not partnership but majority rule, was Britain justified in forcing a middle way? Had African nationalism become so pervasive that delaying the transfer of power in the interest of the majority of Africans was no longer possible?

Macmillan did not announce a sudden change of policy, but in the months after the Devlin report was published the change was startling, carried through, like Macmillan's reversal of imperial policy in the Middle East after Suez, without at first admitting anything had changed. So, publicly, Macmillan stood by Alan Lennox-Boyd and the Federation. But following Devlin's finding that Banda and Congress were not guilty as charged – that the colonial government was at least equally guilty – Macmillan became convinced that Banda must be released and the political advance he and the majority in Nyasaland demanded must be granted; if they insisted on seceding from the Federation, they must be allowed to go. And, inevitably, what was conceded to Nyasaland had to be conceded to Northern Rhodesia too.

This meant axing the Federal Government of the pugnacious Sir Roy Welensky, who believed he had been promised that it was a permanent construction from which the northern territories would not be allowed to secede; it meant easing out Nyasaland and Northern Rhodesia in a way that avoided provoking the Federal Government into a unilateral declaration of independence. Welensky had the power to use the Federal and Southern Rhodesian armed forces. Had he done so to seize power in the northern territories, Britain could have overruled him only by force. The reversal of policy that dates from the Devlin report had, therefore, to be a delicate and slow operation. Many who took part had to be led to believe they were helping to shore up the Federation.

The principal decision happened by chance. Alan Lennox-Boyd had twice offered the Prime Minister his resignation: in response to both the Nyasaland Emergency and the Hola camp killings. Macmillan would have none of it. However, Lennox-Boyd had in addition informed both his own constituency association and the Prime Minister that he intended to retire from Parliament at the next election: his wife's family owned Guinness, the Dublin brewers of stout, and needed him to take over the managing directorship. So when the election came, a mere four months after the Devlin report, Macmillan had to find a new Colonial Secretary. Lennox-Boyd had tried as far as he could to delay African independence with the objective, as he explained, of giving the Africans extra time to learn the skills of government. Macmillan's choice as his successor, Iain Macleod, removed the brakes.

When Macmillan appointed Macleod Colonial Secretary, two British-ruled territories in Africa – Sudan and the Gold Coast – had reached independence and one, Nigeria, had a date in view. The remaining sixteen were thought to have some way to go. Macleod instituted policies which resulted in every remaining British territory in Africa, except Southern Rhodesia, becoming independent by 1968. He was the most brilliant of the younger generation of Conservatives. His oratory dominated both the House of Commons and the Party conference. No man in Britain had greater skill at presenting a difficult case to an unsympathetic audience – and winning them over.

Macmillan knew that he and Macleod were embarking on a policy which large sections of the party would find extremely difficult to accept. Lord Home remained Commonwealth Secretary:

> When I was in the Commonwealth Office [he remembered] and Macleod was in the Colonial Office, he was always for galloping along with independence as fast as he could. I took the view that every year gained gave the countries a better chance when they became independent to be viable. There was something to be said for both points of view. When one looks at some of the African countries, one realises that another five years of tuition wouldn't have done them any harm. But Macmillan was beginning for the first time to think that our destiny lay really in Europe, so I think he leaned rather towards the faster programme than the slower. If you want to put it in a nutshell, I think that Macmillan was a wind of change man and Macleod was a gale of change man.

In his memoirs Macmillan quotes the one-time Law Member of Lord Bentinck's Executive Council in India, Thomas Babington Macaulay, writing in 1851:

> Many politicians of our time are in the habit of laying it down as a self-evident proposition that no people ought to be free till they are fit to use their freedom. The maxim is worthy of the fool in the old story who resolved not to go into the water till he had learnt to swim. If men are to wait for liberty till they become wise and good in slavery they may indeed wait for ever.

Macmillan also quotes an unnamed colonial Governor:

> 'Are they ready', I asked, 'for this great change for which they are shouting so vigorously – freedom, freedom, freedom?'
>     'Oh no,' he replied, 'of course they are not ready for it.'
>     'When will they be ready?'
>     'Oh', he said, 'in perhaps fifteen or twenty years. They are learning fast, but it will take at least that time before their leaders are ready to take full responsibility.'
>     'What then would you advise?'
>     The Governor did not hesitate. 'I should give it to them at once – as soon as possible.'
>     When I expressed some surprise he developed an argument which seemed to me, as to him, unanswerable: 'If the fifteen or twenty years were to be applied in learning the job, in increasing their experience of local government or of central administration, why then I would be all for it. But that is not what will happen. All the most intelligent men capable of government will be in rebellion. I will have to put them in prison. There they will learn nothing about administration, only about hatred and

revenge. They will not be fruitful but wasted years; so I say give them independence now.'

The Devlin report, Macmillan's conversion and the replacement of Lennox-Boyd by Macleod all pointed to an immediate conclusion in central Africa. Dr Banda must be released. Sir Robert Armitage remembered how he received a summons just a month after the new Colonial Secretary had taken office:

At the end of December 1959, Macleod sent for me to meet him in Nairobi. He immediately told me that Banda had to be released soon and the other detainees later because my internal security reports indicated that there was no emergency in Nyasaland now which could enable him to defend the detentions before the UN Human Rights Commission. I was staggered by this approach. I had spent a long time building up the forces to overcome the destruction and the lack of authority caused by Banda's campaign. I argued vehemently. I pointed out that it would mean another intense security situation. I would have to call on Federal troops, at least to stand by to make certain there was no violence. Eventually I convinced him that Banda should not be released at once

Three weeks later I was absolutely astonished to receive a telegram from him to say that the Cabinet had agreed that Banda should be released as rapidly as possible and that there should be a rapid run-down of the rest of the detainees. This gave me and my advisers on security matters the greatest problem. How were we going to avoid a recurrence of the demonstrations and emergency that we had only recently come through? I was advised strongly that Banda's return at an early date would give rise to demonstrations which would lead to destruction and violence.

The Governor, backed by his police advisers, continued to hold out, and they had an opportunity to put their case to the man in charge. Macmillan decided to tour Africa, the first British Prime Minister to do so. He felt the need to see for himself, the better to handle the intense feeling African affairs now aroused in both the Conservative and Labour parties. His tour, in January 1960, included independent Ghana and about-to-be-independent Nigeria. Then, on his way to what was to be the climax in South Africa (see Introduction, p 13), he visited the Federation. Sir Robert Armitage recalled:

> I thought if the Prime Minister of the United Kingdom was coming to little Nyasaland, he might be prepared to listen to our representations. My Executive Council had long discussions with him on two separate occasions. I think we convinced him that the release of Banda should be somewhat postponed. We argued very strongly that Banda should be released to the United Kingdom and so kept out of contact with all his Congress party supporters in Nyasaland, to avoid the recurrence of demonstrations and violence.

Sir Roy Welensky spoke up vigorously in support of the Governor when Macmillan was in Salisbury and also appealed to Lord Home, who, as Commonwealth Secretary, was responsible for representing the views of the Federal Government in the British Cabinet. Home was convinced by Welensky's evidence from the police, intelligence reports, army chiefs, farmers, chambers of commerce: to release this man would be irresponsibly to expose innocent citizens, black as well as white, to a renewal of the stoning, roadblocks and mob-intimidation that had been escalating out of control in 1959. It was now 1960, the year when the Belgian Government abandoned the Congo, with its thousand-mile frontier with Northern Rhodesia. There the terror and anarchy Welensky and Home feared were to come true. Home became so convinced of the danger that Macmillan thought he would resign if Banda was released, but the Colonial Secretary and Prime Minister overruled both the men on the spot and the Commonwealth Secretary. If the release of Banda led, as predicted, to white women raped or killed and white property destroyed, Macmillan and Macleod would be swept from office. Macleod was so convinced of the need to change direction throughout Africa that Macmillan thought *he* would resign if Banda was not released.

The decision that kept both ministers in the Cabinet was that Banda, after thirteen months in prison, was to be set free in time to give evidence to an advisory commission on the future of the Federation that would be visiting Nyasaland in April 1960, and that Macleod would be present at his release to persuade him to prevent a renewal of violence. Sir Robert Armitage described the event he had fought so hard to avoid:

> I released Banda on 1 April 1960 by sending two of my officials in an aeroplane to Gwelo in Southern Rhodesia where his prison was, flying him back to Zomba airfield, putting him in a motor car, bringing him to Government House, having him taken to my private secretary's flat where he had a bath and a brush-up and breakfast and bringing him to see Macleod and me at 11 o'clock. I introduced Macleod to him. It was a very amiable meeting.

The discussion that followed between Macleod and Banda was decisive. Macleod promised rapid advance to majority rule. Banda in return promised to keep Nyasaland at peace. Each man trusted the other's ability and will to keep their bargain. Dr Banda was then invited to make a radio broadcast. As Sir Robert Armitage recalled:

> Banda said, 'I am back. His Excellency the Governor and the Secretary of State brought me back from Gwelo today and I have had a very friendly discussion with them here this morning. Tomorrow at their invitation I'll be back at Government House to begin preliminary discussions on our constitution and they have assured me that if everything is calm in the country we will have a round table conference. So I want to have peace.'

That meant the end of the Federation. Sir Robert Tredgold's original prediction came true: an African majority government in one territory could not share power with a white minority government in another. Dr Banda, perceiving this, insisted on Nyasaland's seceding. His action made it inevitable that Northern Rhodesia would secede too, leaving the Federation totally dismembered less than ten years after its creation.

Sir Roy Welensky, the former heavyweight boxing champion of Rhodesia, had missed his chance. When he became Prime Minister of the Federation in 1956 he could have increased African representation in the Federal Assembly, made provision for African promotion in the Federal Civil Service and army, sought out African audiences to persuade them that the Federation wanted their friendship and co-operation. His lack of the instinct for such a course was revealed by a remarkable discovery made by Harold Macmillan at the Federal review conference in London in December 1960. Welensky there met Banda and Kaunda for the first time. They were the leaders of majority opinion in two of the three countries in the Federation of which he had for four years been Prime Minister, but he had not previously found occasion to meet them. Todd and Benson had believed what they said about sharing power with qualified African voters and had acted on it. They had tried to absorb able Africans into the political élite. Welensky and the

Federal Cabinet said they were doing the same – to impress the British Parliament and international opinion – but were in fact as afraid of African advance as many of their white voters.

Whenever Welensky visited London between 1959 and 1963 he was invited to address the Conservative Party's Commonwealth Affairs committee, to whom he repeatedly explained with a wealth of detail how he had been cheated and deceived by their colleagues the Prime Minister and Colonial Secretary. Both Britain and the Federation rattled their sabres, Welensky at one point mobilising Federal troops, the British flying reinforcements to Nairobi to be on hand for action in the Federation. It never came to war, but British ministers dealing with central Africa often felt it had. Their every proposal was followed by a broadside from Salisbury, demanding the right to be consulted, insisting on changes, alleging bad faith, stirring up trouble in Parliament. Welensky put up only a brief fight to save Nyasaland, but he fought like a trapped tiger to hang on to Northern Rhodesia. Here Macleod had to make concessions, reducing the African proportion in the Lusaka assembly to the point at which Kenneth Kaunda threatened a renewal of violent resistance on the scale of Mau Mau. Macleod's Colonial Office colleagues were able to hold Kaunda back by convincing him that the Colonial Secretary was absolutely determined to bring Northern Rhodesia to independence. That determination was genuine and proves that Macleod *was* deceiving Welensky. The Conservative die-hards had long sensed it. In the House of Commons a backbench revolt broke out against Macleod's policies. In the House of Lords a remarkable episode occurred which permanently damaged his career.

Lord Salisbury was not merely head of the family that had produced two previous chief ministers – Burleigh in Tudor days and the Salisbury who had granted Rhodes his charter – he was also trusted and respected among Conservatives as hard working, subtle and totally dedicated to the Party. He had been Commonwealth Secretary when the Federation was being put together and had in 1957 resigned from the Cabinet over Macmillan's decision to release Archbishop Makarios from detention. In February 1961 he told the House of Lords that 'a miasma of mistrust' had arisen between the British and Federal Governments and that the blame lay with Iain Macleod, who, in spite of his remarkable intellect, bravery and resolution had adopted an entirely wrong approach to the white communities in Africa. By tradition the House of Lords is courteous and avoids attacks on members of the House of Commons, but Salisbury went on to a personal character analysis: Macleod was a master of bridge, a game in which a player's purpose was to outwit his opponents. This had been Macleod's attitude to the white people of Africa. He was unscrupulous. He had been 'too clever by half'.

Although Macmillan fully supported Macleod's policies, only seven months after this attack he removed him from the Colonial Office. By general agreement Macleod was the best speaker and one of the most able ministers in the party – until this time the front runner to be leader in his time. But twice in the next four years, when the leadership fell vacant, he was ruled out by the right wing of his party. The phrase that damned him because there was some truth in it was 'too clever by half'.

The downfall of the Federation took more of the time of the Prime Minister and the Cabinet and more space on newspaper front pages than any other single issue of the time. The ideas of Ruskin that had inspired Rhodes continued to move many Britons. They did not think of their cousins who settled overseas as escaping failure, seeking quick riches or oppressing natives, but as advancing a noble cause. The skill of Macmillan and the courage of Macleod overcame such feelings, but both men's careers were bruised. In the year of the break-up of the Federation Conservative back-benchers chanted, 'Macmillan must go,' and in October 1963, for this reason reason among others, he resigned.

Dr Banda, hero of the destruction of Federation, was soon leading Nyasaland towards independence as Malawi. Kenneth Kaunda, who had displaced Harry Nkumbula as leader of the nationalists in Northern Rhodesia, followed close behind him leading what was to be Zambia. The whites of Southern Rhodesia were surprised to find themselves left behind. Self-governing since 1923, regularly represented at conferences of Commonwealth Heads of Government, the Southern Rhodesian electorate believed they could have had independence in 1948, had they but asked. Now they were outraged to find that Britain was prepared to concede independence to black men with scarcely any experience of government, but not to them.

A new determination took hold of them. They wanted independence under their existing constitution with minority rule, the Land Apportionment Act and all the cushions to their way of life. Lord Home, first as Commonwealth Secretary and later as Prime Minister, explained to their leaders why Britain could not grant what they asked:

> There was a strong case for dominion status for Rhodesia [he recalled]. They had over the years made the grade in many ways. I think their relations with the Africans were pretty friendly, totally unlike South Africa. But we couldn't have persuaded the new Commonwealth countries to accept Rhodesia as a member. Nor could we have persuaded an old Commonwealth country like Canada. I used to have to tell the Rhodesian Prime Ministers, 'If you push this position you'll find yourself isolated: it won't be much fun; you'll be by yourselves, ostracised.'

Ghana and Nigeria as independent members of the Commonwealth made it plain – Kwame Nkrumah of Ghana was particularly explicit – that if Britain became the ally of the white Rhodesian minority resisting the right of Africans to rule themselves, the price would be high. The Commonwealth was evolving into a multi-racial grouping through which Britain attempted to retain a measure of imperial influence without any longer bearing the political and military costs. India's Prime Minister Jawaharlal Nehru insisted that Britain must grant independence only to a government approved by the majority of the population. Canada concurred and even Australia and New Zealand advised Britain not to give in to the Rhodesian demand. At the United Nations the pressure was ten times worse. Since the Suez invasion of 1956, the non-aligned group of nations had evolved into a powerful block. Led by Nehru, Nasser, Tito of Yugoslavia and Sukarno of Indonesia, their power to obstruct and embarrass Britain was substantial. If they produced evidence at the United Nations that Britain was conspiring with a white minority to grant independence to Southern Rhodesia under an *apartheid*-type constitution, not only the Russians and the Communist countries would vote Britain down, but the non-aligned countries too and even possibly, under Presidents Kennedy and Johnson, the United States. The mood of the world was now so strongly against the white Rhodesians that Britain's Conservative Government, while by no means unsympathetic to the cause, weighed the diplomatic costs in the balance and found them too high. British ministers told the Rhodesian white leaders that they could be granted independence only if they agreed to a new constitution which the African majority could be publicly shown to accept.

The Rhodesian electorate was by now thoroughly confused. They had supported the party of Huggins, Todd and Welensky, dutifully voting for what they considered liberal measures, in the belief that this was the way to secure both the Federation and full independence. By 1961 they had neither. Why, they asked, did Britain now want to impose black rule and chaos? Did Britain want to subject Rhodesia to Congo-type rape and murder? To Kenya-type tribal savagery? To the corruption and Marxism of a black dictatorship like Ghana? The whites of Southern Rhodesia were convinced that they could run what they considered their own country better than the British or the Africans. They had no more patience with Britain.


## From UDI to Zimbabwe, 1963–1980

A unilateral declaration of independence seemed at first glance a simple solution to the problems of Southern Rhodesia. Being landlocked, the settlers were safe from the Royal Navy. Equipped with their own air force and army, they felt able to deal with any but a major invasion, which Britain was ill-placed to mount. Above all Southern Rhodesians believed that the fellow-feelings of their British kith and kin would rule out any use of force.

Sir Roy Welensky and his United Federal Party were less certain. Though Britain's presence in Southern Rhodesia was limited to a diplomatic mission, they recognised that the territory's ties to Britain might make UDI awkward. Officers in the army and air force had sworn loyalty to the Queen; many of them might refuse to take orders from a rebel government. Judges too were appointed by the Queen to enforce laws passed by the British Parliament or its appointed instrument. They might refuse to enforce rebel laws. Trade and finance were largely arranged through London, and Welensky had been advised, when he asked for a report on the possible effects of 'a Boston tea-party', that Britain would be able to respond with 'an economic stranglehold'. So the élite who ran the country rejected UDI.

However the break-up of the Federation and the failure of the Southern Rhodesian élite to obtain independence by negotiation led the electorate to put a new group in power. Welensky and the lawyers and professionals who had served with him in government despised these 'cowboys', who called their party the Rhodesian Front and who elected as their leader and the Prime Minister of Southern Rhodesia one Ian Smith. Sir Roy Welensky recalled:

> When I was Federal Prime Minister Smith was my party whip and I think it's a clear indication of my opinion of him that I never promoted him. One of my ministers came to ask me whether I would give him a junior minister. I said, 'Yes, who do you want?' He said, 'Smith, Ian Douglas Smith,' and I said, 'You're mad. He can only talk about cattle, European education and daylight saving. He never does any work. No, I won't agree to that. But you can have anybody else.'

For Lord Home, who gave up his peerage in order to succeed Harold Macmillan as Britain's Prime Minister in 1963, Ian Smith was the fourth Southern Rhodesian Prime Minister with whom he had had to deal:

> Negotiating with him was a very different thing from anything I had done before. You had to repeat yourself a lot. He was a very difficult man to pin down and keep pinned down to a particular point, a very slow negotiator. When you made an arrangement with him or thought you'd got an arrangement, you would find on reassembling that he'd found some qualifications. And so it went on, a long, slogging, difficult process. He claimed that, during the negotiations for the 1961 constitution, British ministers had given a pledge that independence would follow. But that was simply not true and we denied it convincingly. We searched all the records and there wasn't the slightest suggestion anywhere that anybody had made such a promise. Mr Smith had no written evidence of it either. So he realised that he couldn't sustain that case. He had to agree in the end that he had made a mistake. It was a point that took some time. But when he said that he threatened UDI one had to believe that he meant it.

During the days of Federation Rhodesia's white voters had put up with the introduction of liberal measures because all seemed to be going well and they were happy to leave politics to the professionals. With the breakdown of Federation and the promise to grant independence to Malawi and Zambia, politics became a central concern of every white Rhodesian. Many, in particular the tens of thousands of post-war immigrants, felt that if they did not secure immediate independence their farms and factories and their ability to stay in a land where many of them had grown rich were at risk. The Kenyan settler community had been described as an officers' mess, the Rhodesian settlers, by contrast, as a sergeants' mess. Many of them knew that the granting of equal opportunities to Africans would quickly lose them their jobs and that they would not be able to sustain their high standard of living if they moved to Australia or New Zealand – or even South Africa. Most of them said they would never emigrate to Britain, a nation which – they felt – had lost the will to govern, was in rapid decline and had recently double-crossed them. Nevertheless, emigration had begun. The white population of Southern Rhodesia, more than 220,000 in 1962, fell below 210,000 by 1964: no cause for panic, but a worrying drop.

Ian Smith was from the small goldmining town of Selukwe, the first locally-born Prime Minister. He spoke for the small-time white farmers and artisans. Educated at Rhodes University, Grahamstown, in South Africa where like many Rhodesians he gave more time to sport than study, he returned to Selukwe to farm a large ranch with plenty of loyal black workers. Like an English country Tory MP, he was quiet, slow-spoken, little inclined to make his mind up until he had listened to his constituents. He shared their fears and knew that they and the party they had built up required him to secure independence at once – if possible by negotiating with Britain, otherwise by a unilateral declaration. For almost two years Smith tried negotiation, but Britain's Conservative Government held to its refusal to grant independence until Rhodesia was clearly launched on the road to majority rule.

Lord Home became convinced that he must stand firm or several African and Asian member-states would leave the Commonwealth, a blow that might have been almost as damaging for Britain as the Suez invasion. Smith maintained that the majority of Africans in Southern Rhodesia wanted independence under the existing constitution and proposed to hold a grand *indaba* (meeting) of chiefs to prove it. Since the chiefs were Government-appointed and -paid, such a test of African opinion could hardly be convincing. Smith had been pressing the *indaba* proposal on Home for some months and Home had been firmly resisting when their negotiations were interrupted by the British general election of 1964. Smith tried to take advantage of the interregnum by having a letter delivered to Britain's High Commissioner in Salisbury on polling day. It announced that the *indaba* would be held in a week's time and asked the British Government to 'kindly advise the names' of its observers. The message was quickly forwarded to London where officials contacted Home and his ministers at the polls before replying by telegram that Britain continued to require a more convincing test of African opinion.

Smith's trick merely brought the Conservative leadership and Britain's new Labour Government more firmly into alliance in warning him that UDI would be illegal, a revolt against the Crown and disastrous for Rhodesia.

Smith's own military commanders told him they would not oppose a British landing. If faced with conflicting instructions they would obey the Queen, from whom they had their commissions. Further, they warned, the Rhodesian air force could be quickly and easily put out of action by British bombers.

Harold Wilson, who became Britain's Labour Prime Minister in 1964, decided against the use of force if Smith went ahead. Wilson's party had won power with a parliamentary majority so small that he was bound soon to call a further election in the hope of securing a stable basis for governing. Some of the white Rhodesians had been wounded fighting for Britain in the Second World War. Smith himself had been in the Royal Air Force and a wound had rendered half his face immobile, making it difficult for him to smile. For Wilson to launch a war against these people would risk giving a popular campaign cause to his Conservative opponents. He therefore went to remarkable lengths to prevent Smith from going over the brink. In spite of misgivings in his Cabinet, Wilson flew to Salisbury in October 1965 and all but talked Smith into agreeing to set up an Anglo-Rhodesian royal commission to hammer out a joint solution. The British public saw him doing all he could to avoid UDI. He talked to all the principal figures in Rhodesia, including African nationalist leaders, who were brought out of detention to meet him, and Garfield Todd, whom Smith's government had restricted to his farm. In his efforts to win over the Rhodesians (and, more important to

*Joshua Nkomo at Gonakudzingwa, where he was restricted from 1964 till 1976, watching sanctions-busting trains go by on the line to Lourenço Marques. In the desert heat the steel hut became an oven.*

Wilson, floating voters in Britain) he announced that whatever happened Britain would not use force.

For Smith, who had for two years been dithering nervously on the brink of UDI, Wilson's assurance was the signal that he could safely take the plunge. He had held an election in which his party won all fifty A-roll (i.e. European) seats in the legislature – fifteen B-roll seats being the most striking gain Federation had brought the Southern Rhodesian Africans. He had swept Sir Roy Welensky and all members of his former 'liberal' élite out of the legislature. He had dismissed the GOC Rhodesian armed forces, Major-General John Anderson, who had indiscreetly told many people he was loyal to the Crown and hostile to UDI. He now tricked the Governor, Sir Humphrey Gibbs, into signing an undated declaration of a state of emergency.

On 11 November 1965, after receiving a final, desperate telephone call from Wilson trying still to talk him out of it, Smith led his Cabinet in signing their Proclamation of Independence, echoing phrases from America in 1776: 'Whereas in the course of human affairs history has shown that it may become necessary for a people to dissolve the political affiliations which have connected them with another people and to assume amongst other nations

*Ian Smith signs the Unilateral Declaration of Independence, watched by members of his cabinet. Seated by him is Clifford Dupont, soon to be appointed 'Officer Administering the Government', i.e. replacement Governor.*

The legally appointed Governor, Sir Humphrey Gibbs, at his desk in Government House.

the separate and equal status to which they are entitled . . .' The undated declaration of a state of emergency now proved its use, enabling Smith to impose immediate censorship and thus prevent publication in Rhodesia of the Governor's response, which was formally in the name of the Queen to dismiss Smith's Government. Sir Humphrey Gibbs, a quiet, gentlemanly Rhodesian farmer, once a school-friend at Eton of Lord Home, became briefly the centre of British hopes. On instructions from London he refused to leave Government House in case Smith's men should seize it in his absence. He thus challenged them to order him to be man-handled, which they decided not to do. The Chief Justice of Rhodesia, Sir Hugh Beadle, moved in to join him, so that together they could symbolise true law and order. When Smith's regime cut off the Governor's salary, car and telephone, Rhodesians loyal to the Crown, many of whom came to sign the Government House visitors' book, raised funds to help keep Sir Humphrey going. He maintained the imperial style, with formal black-tie dinners and the toast to the Queen now invested with unaccustomed meaning.

The Governor's opposition was formal. He did not lead any political movement of resistance to UDI. The Smith regime by-passed him by appointing an 'Officer Administering the Government' to sign the final authority on their acts. So UDI seemed to pass off smoothly in Rhodesia. Apart from the blank spaces editors chose to leave in their newspapers where the censors had ordered deletions, little appeared to change. The

British Government's diplomatic representative, the High Commissioner, departed, so the Governor and Chief Justice assumed the role of link between the illegal regime in Rhodesia and the Government in London. A settler community which had long been self-governing remained so. A significant change was, however, made in the constitution. Until UDI, amendment of certain clauses had required the assent of the Government in London or of all races in Rhodesia, including Africans, whose views were to be tested by referendum. The new regime provided for all clauses in the constitution to be amendable by a two-thirds majority in the legislature. Smith's party had a two-thirds majority and could therefore at will undo the liberal measures that had been introduced in the days of Federation. In this way UDI reopened the door to creeping *apartheid*.

Harold Wilson controlled Britain's Rhodesia policy himself. He was determined to put a stop to what he called the 'rebellion', even though he had announced publicly that his Government would not use force. He made it plain to the world – and, by and large, the world believed him – that Britain was committed to granting independence only to a regime that represented the majority of the population. African leaders were sceptical of Wilson's claim that he could succeed without going to war, but they could do little except protest.

Long historical experience had shown that economic sanctions do not succeed in bringing down governments or even in making them change their policies. In the Commonwealth Relations Office in Britain this was well understood. The officials in the Cabinet Office committee which had to prepare a response to UDI came up with sanctions because they could not think of anything else. They expected sanctions to be limited in their impact on Rhodesia because South Africa and Mozambique, Southern Rhodesia's two passageways to the sea, were unlikely to help enforce them. Mozambique, the shortest route to the sea for both Rhodesia's and Zambia's trade, was an impoverished territory whose largest source of revenue was the railway. Its colonial master, Portugal, almost as poor, could not afford to lose this income. The official view in London was that sanctions had to be imposed because Britain could not be seen to be doing nothing.

Wilson professed a more vigorous view. Having accepted the idea of sanctions with a sigh of relief, he had to believe they would work. Wilson even went so far as to tell his fellow Commonwealth Prime Ministers, meeting at Lagos, Nigeria, in January 1966, that sanctions would work in 'weeks rather than months'. This apparently sincere opinion from a clever and supposedly well-informed Englishman led African Commonwealth leaders temporarily to withhold the demand that Britain use force. It enabled Wilson to escape from Lagos with their complaints and anger deflected. To that extent economic sanctions worked.

African leaders accused the British Government of lack of determination in introducing sanctions in a piecemeal and half-hearted way. Their criticism was justified. Several priorities were more important to the Wilson

Government than defeating Smith. Wilson considered it essential to prove to his own (predominantly white) electorate that he was not guilty of excessive harshness towards the Rhodesian whites. He believed it was an issue that could lose him the next election. Balance-of-payments crises, notably in October 1965 and July 1966, were a far bigger danger to the Wilson Government than Rhodesia's UDI was. Wilson feared that the use of force could have led to an even worse currency crisis, like that caused by the Suez invasion of 1956, and that mismanaged sanctions could have had almost as damaging an effect. Avoiding a conflict with South Africa was a higher priority for the Wilson Government than defeating Smith because in 1965 Britain's exports to, and investment in, South Africa exceeded those for the whole of black Africa. Many countries at the United Nations demanded total economic sanctions against South Africa as the quick way to bring Rhodesia to its knees, but the British Board of Trade and Treasury argued that such a policy would be financially disastrous. Finally Zambia sent all its exports of copper and received virtually all its imports, particularly coal and oil, via Rhodesia. The first list of banned goods *from* Rhodesia, published immediately after UDI, deliberately omitted coal, on which the Zambian copper mines were dependent. When, after a month's delay and much protest, oil was added to the list of goods that must not be sold *to* Rhodesia, the unavoidable effect was also to cut off Zambia's supply. A vast Anglo-American relief operation was launched to buy lorries and improve the road from Zambia through Tanzania to the sea, and to fly oil in chartered aircraft which used up as much fuel on the journey as they delivered and which soon ploughed up Zambian airstrips. Total sanctions against Rhodesia might have destroyed not only Zambia's economy but also the country's fragile, new political structure. Harold Wilson and his colleagues had to persuade President Kenneth Kaunda to introduce measures which had an immediate and damaging effect on his country. It took time to plan ways to mitigate the damage and to persuade Kaunda that the measures proposed were capable of toppling the rebel regime. Smith commented: 'The British Government will forever stand condemned because of its policy of fighting the war of sanctions to the last Zambian.'

The story of the oil tanker, *Joanna V*, shows something of the difficulties into which sanctions led Britain. In January 1966 a South African company contracted a Greek called Nicos Vardinoyannis to deliver crude oil to customers to be specified later. In February Mr V (as he will henceforward be known) chartered a tanker to load 14,000 tons of crude in the Persian Gulf. The contract contained a clause, required by the Greek Government since oil had been added by Britain to the list of banned goods, forbidding shipment to Rhodesia. In March the tanker – now at sea – was sold for a sum in excess of its market value. The seller said he did not know the real identity of the buyers: 'For money like that, who asks questions?' In fact the buyer was a Panamanian company controlled by Mr V. The deal was done in New York by means of a letter of credit drawn in Johannesburg. Mr V next ordered the tanker to Dakar in West Africa where it was renamed *Joanna V* and was boarded by a new master, Mr V's younger brother George. He then conducted the ship round the southern tip of Africa towards the port of Beira in Mozambique, where an oil pipeline ran 189 miles inland to Rhodesia.

British aircraft-carriers and reconnaissance aircraft were by this time patrolling the sea near Beira. They spotted many suspected sanctions-busters, including the *Joanna V*. Their information led a British ship, HMS *Plymouth*, to intercept, only to be told that the *Joanna V* was not going to deliver oil to Beira but was merely calling there for bunkering. Britain asked Greece for authority to stop the tanker by force. This was refused, but the British Ambassador in Athens successfully pressed the Greek Government to act. It sent a telex to both Mr V, the owner, and his brother, the master, informing them that to unload oil for Rhodesia would be an infringement of a decree signed a few days earlier by King Constantine and would lead to court action and possibly heavy fines. The *Joanna V* dropped anchor near the oil-berth at Beira and Greece instructed its consul there to take legal action if he found oil was being unloaded for Rhodesia. Mr V, who lived in Athens, then asked for the vessel to be removed from the Greek register of shipping so that it could be registered in Panama.

British pressure was urgently applied to Panama, to Portugal, the governing power in Mozambique, and to the company that owned the pipeline. Portugal, while anxious to please its oldest ally, did not want anything to do with sanctions. Its Foreign Minister explained that under international law Portugal's duty was to 'ensure the free access of landlocked countries to the sea'. Further, if it ordered the pipeline company not to pump oil to Rhodesia it would be obliged to pay compensation. The pipeline company, registered in Lisbon, took its lead from the Portuguese Government.

Britain's diplomats had better luck in Panama. The day after the *Joanna V* was provisionally registered there – an event celebrated by the raising of the Panamanian flag on the vessel in Beira to the cheers of Portuguese by-standers and Rhodesian holiday-makers – Panama cancelled the registration. The British Government did better still at the United Nations, persuading the Security Council to instruct Britain itself to stop 'by force if necessary vessels reasonably believed to be carrying oil destined for Rhodesia'. This gave the Royal Navy's Beira patrol the legal right to board the ships of all countries, a greater power than the slave patrol off West Africa had had in the nineteenth century or the anti-immigrant Palestine patrol had had in the 1940s. The powers given to the Beira patrol and the style in which they were used gave a brief fillip to Britain's nautical pride: newspapers and television were full of it. Many, however, were unhappy that the source of these powers was the United Nations. Hitherto Harold Wilson had succeeded brilliantly in maintaining the support of the Conservative Party. Resort to the United Nations instantly weakened that support, on the grounds that Rhodesia was hard enough for Britain to handle alone without giving Russia, Egypt and others the standing to help formulate instructions. Once the UN had ordered Britain to stop oil on its way to Rhodesia via Mozambique, no logical bar existed to its instructing Britain to take other less convenient measures.

The immediate end of the *Joanna V* story was a British triumph. No oil flowed to Rhodesia through the Beira pipeline. The Navy's patrol was totally successful from 1966 until 1980. However, entrepreneurs simply found other routes. Road tankers and lorries laden with barrels drove nightly through the northern Transvaal into Rhodesia. Trainloads of petrol began regularly to make their way to Rhodesia from the BP refinery (half owned by the British Government) at Lourenço Marques in Mozambique. The 'BP' signs on the waggons and tankers were hastily painted over. This caused the British Government intense embarrassment, but they could do nothing about it: a company, even a wholly-owned subsidiary, has to obey the law of the country in which it operates.

In Rhodesia the price of petrol rose, but sanctions gave a boost to the local manufacture of electric stoves, refrigerators, records, record-players, clothes, fertilisers and other items. They were generally more expensive than the imported goods that were no longer available, but the Smith regime banned many imports, subsidised much of the new production, pushed up exports of minerals, especially nickel which was scarce on the world market, and by skilful management kept the economy apparently flourishing. Thanks to loans from South Africa and the quick eye of white Rhodesians for new opportunities in the market, the immediate effect of sanctions was a small domestic boom. According to world trade statistics, many Rhodesian exports fell to zero while the South African or Mozambiquan figures rose in precise compensation.

Tobacco was the Smith regime's biggest problem: most of it had been exported to Britain, but Britain could obtain plentiful supplies elsewhere. Smith created an agency to buy the crop and keep the farmers going, and to store the substantial proportion that it was not able by devious means to sell. In 1968 the authorities in Rhodesia paid many farmers for not growing tobacco. Smith himself took to smoking one cigarette a day after dinner 'to support home industries'. Sanctions also hit the British economy. New British cars, for example, vanished from Rhodesia, the lost business being taken up by French Peugeots, German Mercedes and Japanese Toyotas. Their purchasers plainly had no fear of fuel shortage.

In such circumstances ministers in London reluctantly concluded that they must try to come to terms. Wilson decided to put an end to a policy that was costing Britain dear but failing in its purpose. He persuaded Commonwealth heads of government to allow him three months to talk Smith into a settlement, and promised that if he failed no further offer of independence before majority rule would be made. On the basis he arranged to meet Smith in December 1966, a year after UDI, aboard a Royal Navy ship, HMS *Tiger*, off Gibraltar. The reason for the theatrical location was to keep away from journalists and television cameras and to avoid either admitting the rebel leader to Britain or submitting to his jurisdiction. The Governor's residence in Salisbury had provided an island of territory loyal to the Queen, in which British ministers and officials preparing for the *Tiger* talks were able to operate.

Although he did his best to sound tough and principled, what Wilson proposed was capitulation by Britain. It was dressed up in a thin covering of multi-racial and democratic 'guarantees', to give Wilson a chance to secure the support of the Commonwealth and the United Nations, but in all matters of substance Smith was offered complete autonomy: Britain would recognise Rhodesia's independence under the existing constitution, with a few amendments; most of the present ministers would remain in power, with a few additions including two Africans; and 'unimpeded progress towards majority rule' would be ensured by constitutional mechanisms a suburban solicitor would have had no difficulty side-stepping. When Barbara Castle in the British Cabinet complained that the terms amounted to a sell-out, the Prime Minister told her, according to Richard Crossman's diary: 'This is a British Government which has failed to reach its objectives painfully accepting the best agreed terms they could get for the voluntary winding-up of the rebellion by the rebels themselves, and since that is the case we can't quite expect the terms we would have imposed if we'd won.'

Once Smith had recommended this deal to his Cabinet colleagues, Wilson would urge it on Rhodesia's Africans with a fair chance, he believed, of securing the 'assent of the people of Rhodesia as a whole', thus enabling him to persuade the British Parliament and his fellow heads of government around the world to recognise the new state. Wilson thought he had got Britain off the hook.

Smith and his Cabinet were not, however, the cleverest of men. They stared uncomprehendingly at the substance they had been offered and quibbled about the packaging. During the interim period before independence was recognised, the Governor, Sir Humphrey Gibbs, would be formally in charge; was this a cunning scheme by Wilson to secure British control? The Cabinet who were to advise the Governor would have new members added; this meant some present members losing office, an unappealing prospect. Censorship would be removed and normal political activities allowed. A tribunal of Rhodesian judges (plus one Briton) would review the cases of Africans held without trial, releasing those it deemed unlikely to engage in intimidation. After independence, amendment of certain 'entrenched' clauses in the constitution would require the approval of the Privy Council in London (in theory a fearsome restraint, but in practice such 'external safeguards' have never prevented any state, once sovereign, from doing what it wanted). None of it would have deprived Smith and his supporters of their control of Rhodesia. But they saw danger where there was none – and turned the proposal down.

Wilson was in despair, obliged to continue with a costly policy of sanctions which was earning him nothing but complaints from the Afro-Asian and Commonwealth countries it had been intended to please. Why, they asked, were not sanctions enforced more effectively, why were they not extended to South Africa and Portugal, why were they not complemented by the use of force – if only to destroy the bridges over which Rhodesia's exports and imports continued to flow? The answer to these questions was that Britain was working harder to enforce sanctions than any other country and that the British Cabinet now realised the task it had undertaken was like blocking an infinitely large sieve hole by hole. And Britain did not want to risk starting a war which might last longer and divide British public opinion even more damagingly than the present policy was doing.

African nationalists, both in Rhodesia and in neighbouring countries, understood. Until Wilson's attempted sell-out on the *Tiger*, most of them had hoped that Britain would solve the Rhodesia problem for them. Increasingly after the *Tiger* talks, the Africans came to realise that Britain lacked either the power or the will. Though ill-prepared to do so, the nationalists had even before UDI begun to take the matter into their own hands by building up guerilla armies. Their early efforts were uniformly unsuccessful. Armed groups of Africans would cross the Zambezi from Zambia, and chiefs or local headmen in the pay of the Rhodesian authorities would spot them; whereupon Rhodesian army and airforce units would wipe the guerillas out. However, in August 1967 the Rhodesians were surprised to suffer significant casualties in a number of pitched battles. A year later President Kaunda of Zambia, originally a pacifist and follower of Gandhi, now anxious to avoid Rhodesian counter-attacks on his own country, commented:

> To expect Africans to remain docile under minority rule is not realistic . . . The people of the West have refused to help the freedom fighters . . . This leaves these young men and women with no choice but to go to the only area where they will be supplied, namely the East. So they go there to train in the use of weapons.

In March 1968 some 150 men, with Soviet, Czech and Chinese arms, were spotted 150 miles north-west of Salisbury. Soldiers were summoned from all parts of Rhodesia and took more than a month to overwhelm them, killing fifty-six and, according to the Smith regime's figures, losing five themselves (four white and one African). Another incursion in July 1968 involved a hundred guerillas who were quickly rounded up.

The principal effect of the first few years of guerilla activities was to force the Portuguese and South Africans into closer co-operation with the Rhodesians. The Governments of both neighbouring territories had tacitly helped Rhodesia defeat sanctions, to the profit of their own middlemen. Now their assistance – particularly that of South Africa – became more positive. When in August 1967 the African National Congress of South Africa announced at a press conference in Lusaka, the capital of Zambia, that it had formed a military alliance with Rhodesian nationalists to conquer both Salisbury and Pretoria, the South African Prime Minister, John Vorster, responded by publicly acknowledging that South African units were deployed in Rhodesia, helping to defeat the guerillas. He warned the Zambian Government that continued use of its territory as a guerilla base would lead to a retaliatory blow 'you will never forget'.

For Harold Wilson's Government the guerillas were an embarrassment. If they succeeded in blowing up power lines and bridges and stirring up African resistance to the illegal regime, then clearly they were assisting the British sanctions policy. By 1967, however, Harold Wilson's Government were no longer serious about making sanctions effective; the British continued to maintain them only because their withdrawal would attract international condemnation: they had become a charade to impress the African Commonwealth and the United Nations. While British warships continued to patrol off Beira, preventing oil from reaching the pipeline to Rhodesia, the British oil companies BP and Shell sent a delegation to tell Wilson's Cabinet colleague, Commonwealth Secretary George Thomson, that they were regularly delivering oil by other routes. They wanted – and received – assurance that they need not fear prosecution under the sanctions laws. Thomson sent the Prime Minister a minute of the conversation (which Wilson later said he had not read). The main British policy was not to make pressure on Smith's regime effective but to talk to him and persuade him to call off his rebellion on terms which would enable Britain to secure him international recognition. An effective guerilla movement from Zambia was the last thing Wilson wanted. His concern was to help the Governor keep open lines of communications with Ian Smith.

Therefore when Zambia protested to the British Government in August 1967 that South African forces had 'invaded Her Majesty's colony of Rhodesia', the British reply was to counter-complain that Zambia had allowed its territory to be used as a base for armed attacks on Rhodesia. The Zambian Ministry of Foreign Affairs commented that Britain appeared to be accusing Zambia of attempting to overthrow the Smith regime.

Harold Wilson's quest for talks and a settlement with Ian Smith received an ugly setback in March 1968. Smith was showing no inclination to talk. His detention camps and prisons contained most of the African nationalist leaders; his troops had the nationalists' attempts at invasion thoroughly under control; sanctions were being satisfactorily dealt with by his trade department and treasury. Effectively Rhodesia had secured its independence. The time had come for Smith to challenge the judges at last to acknowledge reality; to flush Sir Hugh Beadle out of his closet in the Governor's House. Smith's Justice Minister announced that three Africans, Victor Mlambo, James Dhlamini and Duly Shadreck, all sentenced to death for murder before UDI, would be hanged. The Officer Administering the Government, Clifford Dupont, signed the warrants.

Defence lawyers acting for the three men at once appealed on the grounds that Dupont was not competent to authorise a hanging. Only the Governor had that power. Executions not authorised by Sir Humphrey Gibbs would be tantamount to murder. The Rhodesian Court of Appeal decided that the Smith regime was effectively running the country and that to deny it the power to enforce the law would be ridiculous. The defence lawyers sought leave to take the case to Rhodesia's final court of appeal, the Judicial Committee of the Privy Council in London. The Minister of Justice, Desmond Lardner-Burke, informed the court that the Rhodesian Government would ignore an appeal outside Rhodesia. The Chief Justice, Sir Hugh Beadle, thereupon refused leave to appeal. The Justice Ministry announced that the hangings would proceed.

Britain could not acquiesce in such a development, which amounted to a court of judges appointed by the Queen legitimising the Smith regime. So, acting on the advice of her ministers in London, the Queen exercised her prerogative of mercy, reprieving the three men and commuting their sentences to life imprisonment. Sir Hugh Beadle announced in open court in Salisbury that the reprieve had no validity: 'Her Majesty is quite powerless in this matter'. He thus stripped away the last vestige of British authority in Rhodesia. Sir Humphrey Gibbs immediately ordered Beadle to quit Government House.

The Rhodesian Cabinet examined a further appeal from the three men to Clifford Dupont, but turned it down. On 6 March 1968 the men were hanged. Smith had now proved that, in internal affairs at least, his regime possessed all the attributes of sovereignty.

At the United Nations the hangings were described as 'assassinations' and the Smith regime as 'murderers' and 'international criminals'. Afro-Asian delegates demanded an intensification of sanctions and the Security Council passed the necessary binding resolution to require all nations to enforce them. On paper the United Nations had drawn the sanctions noose tighter round the neck of the Smith regime. In practice the regime had slipped the noose. British ministers had to say publicly that they supported the strengthening of sanctions, while in private they wished the international anger would die down, so they and Smith could resume talks.

And so, a mere five months after the hangings and the insult to the Queen that they represented, Harold Wilson was back on board ship in the Mediterranean. This time Ian Smith joined him on HMS *Fearless*. The terms Wilson offered resembled those offered on *Tiger*, except that then Britain had insisted on the test of Rhodesian opinion being conducted under an interim administration headed by the Governor. This condition, which had worried Smith and his colleagues, was now withdrawn; Britain was prepared to accept a test of opinion conducted under the aegis of the present Smith Cabinet, with two Africans added in unspecified roles.

The main problem looming over Harold Wilson was how to persuade the Labour Party, the Commonwealth and the UN to accept the settlement he proposed. In the House of Commons he was prepared to rely on Conserva-

*Harold Wilson and Ian Smith aboard HMS* Fearless.

tive votes to pass the necessary law, since it was clear that many Labour MPs would oppose him. However, as after *Tiger*, he was spared the effort. Smith's Cabinet and party saw no need to make even paper concessions to world opinion. They were winning, the world was tiring of sanctions, and what the Rhodesian Front now wanted was a constitution that openly provided for what they believed in: white rule for ever, Africans kept in their place and a public end to all links with Britain. The South African Government advised Smith that Rhodesia's desire for international recognition was awkward to meet so long as its relationship to the British Crown remained unclear. Once Rhodesia adopted a constitution that clarified its legal position, some country could surely be persuaded to recognise the new state; then South Africa would follow and other governments would flock in to put an end to the rebels' isolation: the best solution was to go all the way the United States had gone in 1776 and declare themselves a republic.

And so they did. In June 1969, the small, predominantly white electorate voted by referendum for a new republican constitution to take effect in March 1970. It used an apparently neat device to delay African political advance. Africans' wages in Rhodesia were very low and it was therefore uneconomic to collect income tax from them. Their main contribution to government revenue came through sales taxes and the part their work and low wages played in raising the taxable profits and incomes of whites; the new constitution tied representation to the proportion of total income tax paid by each race. It enabled Rhodesians to declare there was nothing racialist about the arrangement – 'When they pay the taxes they will get the votes' – while ensuring that for a hundred years or more the legislature would remain largely white. Even if the white legislators were so to change the tax laws as to make 99 per cent of income tax derive from Africans, the maximum African proportion in the House under this constitution would never rise above one half. The conservative American journal *National Review*, which at that time regularly took the side of the southern states of America against liberalising pressure from the Government and Supreme Court in Washington, described the new Rhodesian constitution as 'racist, despotic, immoral, unnecessary and imprudent'.

Wilson was now completely stumped. Commonwealth African states had forced him to agree to a formula that became known as NIBMAR – No Independence Before Majority African Rule. In his negotiations with Smith he had hoped that a combination of constitutional provisions for 'unimpeded progress to majority rule' after independence and a genuine test of African opinion, impartially conducted, would enable him to persuade his Commonwealth colleagues to abandon NIBMAR: they were sensible men and would settle for a modest advance, knowing that the complete victory they wanted was unattainable. The new Rhodesian constitution made it plain that Ian Smith's party would not accept such a compromise. For the British Government there remained no way forward.

In 1970 a Conservative Government was elected in Britain and decided to have one last try. Lord Home, who had resigned from the leadership of the party and was now Foreign Secretary, flew to Salisbury. His proposals were, inevitably, even less restrictive of the whites' discretion to run the country than Wilson's had been. Now the 'broad-based interim Government' that had become less broadly based between *Tiger* and *Fearless* was removed altogether; during the period of testing the views of the people, Smith's unchanged regime would remain in total charge. The safeguards against retrogressive amendment of the constitution were also weakened – by the removal of Wilson's 'external safeguard', the appeal to the Privy Council. 'Unimpeded progress to majority rule' was spelled out by a process that would clearly take many years and be vulnerable to decisions in the interim by the Rhodesian Parliament, determined to keep white voters securely in charge of their three-servant, two-car, one-swimming-pool society. Smith agreed to abandon the 'income-tax method' of regulating African advance, so Home could recommend the proposal to the British Parliament. He conceded precious little else to help Home win the support of the Commonwealth and the UN. Nevertheless, so desperate was the Conservative Party to put an end to its divisions and embarrassments over Rhodesia – constituency activists were inclined to back Smith while the liberal wing of the party wanted him crushed – that on 24 November 1971 'Proposals for a Settlement' were signed by Home and Smith.

Within minutes the shares of companies with large Rhodesian interests rose by millions of pounds on the London stock exchange. Within hours the limited stocks of champagne in Salisbury shops were sold out. Within weeks property values in Rhodesia had begun to rise. A deal had at last been done to end the rebellion. Smith was confident that the Royal Commission to test popular opinion on the subject – a feature common to the two Wilson proposals as well as to Home's – would produce a favourable result.

The Royal Commission had to do the work which a referendum could have done had the majority of Rhodesians been enfranchised and therefore listed on electoral rolls. The Labour Party and many Africans outside Rhodesia dismissed the exercise as a whitewash: since Home and Smith had signed, the commission was bound to say the people of Rhodesia approved. The impartiality of the assessment was ensured by appointing one of Britain's most senior judges, Lord Pearce, as chairman. He went methodically about his task. He sent seven teams of ex-colonial service and British local government officials around Rhodesia, with translators, blackboards and brightly coloured visual aids in cars flying the Union Jack to hold meetings, interview individuals and seek to discover attitudes.

Smith had said, immediately after signing his agreement with Home, 'We have the happiest Africans in the world.' The Pearce commission found this not to be so. Some political detainees were released for the period of opinion-testing and they quickly joined forces to set up a body, the African National Council, under the leadership of a tiny, little-known, black bishop, Abel Muzorewa. He became the respectable, law-abiding figurehead for a nation-wide campaign to rouse Africans against the proposals. The presence of the Pearce commission stimulated much of the political activity and bustle normally caused by a general election, which for the overwhelming majority of the Africans of Rhodesia was a new experience (the B-roll franchise being limited to a few thousand). Hooliganism and intimidation were unleashed, as well as political campaigning. For the first time ever the Africans of Southern Rhodesia had a voice in the future of their country; they could turn down the Smith–Home settlement. This was a substantial power for Britain to have secured for an otherwise disfranchised people. Its origin was curious. When seeking a negotiated independence in 1964, Smith had told Home that the Africans supported him and that he as much as Britain required that the independence terms must be 'acceptable to the people of the country as a whole'. The phrase became the central condition of all subsequent settlement proposals.

Lord Pearce's teams met 115,000 Africans, almost 6 per cent of the adult African population. The teams first explained the proposals and the benefits they offered and then asked for responses. In the towns the commissioners found their meetings with Africans noisy and hard to manage. Rejection of the terms was not a surprise. But Smith and his Cabinet were sure of the tribal areas, where the Government's district officers had spent the weeks since the settlement terms were signed explaining their benefits. Here the Pearce teams found their meetings orderly, their lectures on the meaning of the proposals heard in silence. Then surprisingly knowledgeable objections were constantly raised, usually in the form of polite questions; and the more negative and sceptical the questions, the more they aroused the approval of the meetings. The reason, in the words of the subsequent report, was that 'Mistrust of the intentions of the Government transcended all other considerations. Apprehension for the future stemmed from resentment at what they felt to be the humiliations of the past and the limitations of the policy on land, education and personal advancement.'

Even though they were told that the rejection of the proposals meant the continued operation of Smith's 1969 constitution, the Africans seized the opportunity which the presence of the Pearce commission gave them to tell the world – through the sudden influx of journalists and television crews – that they rejected any deal by which Britain recognised the authority over them of Smith and his white electorate. The Commission concluded that whites, coloureds and Asians favoured the settlement by fourteen to one, but added: 'We are equally satisfied, after considering all our evidence including that on intimidation, that the majority of Africans – thirty-six to one – rejected the proposals. In our opinion the people of Rhodesia as a whole do not regard the proposals as a basis for independence.' Like the Devlin commission, this one was headed by a British judge, included a retired Governor of an African colony among its members, and surprised the sceptics. Douglas-Home, on behalf of the British Government, reluctantly accepted the Pearce verdict and withdrew the proposals. He said that any settlement must now be worked out by the various parties in Rhodesia: in effect, the British Government washed their hands of the issue. They continued unenthusiastically to apply sanctions, but their role in Rhodesia was over. The repeated attempts to employ the limited leverage which historical accident had left to Britain had exhausted the interest of both Westminster and the British public.

Smith did his best to conceal his disappointment at the Pearce judgement. The expected boom and influx of white immigrants were denied him and the sanctions – by now an evident drag on the Rhodesian economy – continued. But he declared that the continuance of the 1969 constitution unamended was really best for Rhodesia.

Smith's white supremacist regime could now be made to retreat only by the Africans using force. Of this little effective sign was discernible. Indeed, not only were most of Rhodesia's African nationalist leaders locked up by Smith, they were also divided and ineffective. The leading African nationalist since the late 1940s was Joshua Nkomo, a huge, jovial man with enormous political skill. For more than twenty years he had ridden two horses that were all but impossible to keep together: he had inspired and responded to the nationalist demands of his supporters, while recognising that power lay with the whites, with whom it was therefore necessary to do deals. Thus Nkomo had been prepared to support the Federation in 1952, until he found that the young enthusiasts on whom he depended could not be persuaded that this was the best way to protect their people. His talks with Todd had led nowhere, because Todd lost *his* political base. And he had been prepared in 1961 to support a constitutional deal (including the fifteen B-roll seats) which was the last effort by the white liberal élitists to keep open the possibility of partnership, but again Nkomo had backed down. After such a history of manoeuvring, Nkomo inevitably lost the trust of many of the younger and more militant black nationalists. They had also objected to his spending a great deal of time abroad, building up international support according to him, living luxuriously according to them. He often happened to be abroad when the Government banned his movement and arrested his colleagues. He was a member, though this was not the reason for the split, of the minority Matabele tribe, and therefore not the first choice leader of the majority Shonas. But he was not easy to ditch. He had slowly established the trust of thousands of politically experienced Africans. He had acquired great skill at dealing with foreign governments and the United Nations. He was a witty, deft, relaxed speaker, not seeming over-clever, but easy-going and sympathetic.

In 1963 his movement had split, young radicals, whose leaders included Robert Mugabe, seeking to displace him. Nkomo hit back with the methods of a caucus professional. Each branch, each district, each typewriter was fought for. Before long the pro- and anti-Nkomo factions became engaged in a war in which they lost sight of their major enemy. Gang fights, petrol bombing, stoning and assaults spread around the country. White politicians crowed over this confirmation of their repeated assertion that the African nationalists were merely thugs. The friends and defenders of Rhodesian black nationalism could not deny that its two parties were seeking to win support by terror.

Smith banned the rival parties, ZAPU (Zimbabwe African People's Union) and ZANU (Zimbabwe African National Union). Both took their name from the extraordinary Zimbabwe ruins left by a former African civilisation (and, to confuse matters further, ZAPU was in the habit, each time it was banned, of relaunching itself under a new alias). Smith sent Nkomo and hundreds of his ZAPU supporters to a restriction camp in a desert area of eastern Rhodesia. Nkomo's ZANU enemies were dispersed by the regime in camps and prisons around the country. President Kaunda of Zambia described the rivalry of the Rhodesian nationalists as 'disgraceful'. He pressed those leading members of ZAPU and ZANU who were outside Rhodesia to sink their differences and unite against Smith. He was not successful.

After the rejection of the Home–Smith proposals, however, the effectiveness of the guerillas increased. Some leading members of the breakaway party, ZANU, had settled in exile in Tanzania. From there a rebel movement against the Portuguese government of Mozambique had, by the early 1970s, established control of areas adjacent to north-east Rhodesia. ZANU guerillas began to take advantage of this new base to open their own front, and it was through Mozambique that the most damaging guerilla activity against the Smith regime now developed. Their technique was learned from Communist China, where the leading ZANU guerillas were sent for training. A guerilla army must have friends in the area where it is to operate; the people must be taught why the guerillas are there and must be invited to help voluntarily; only when enough co-operate willingly will terror against the recalcitrant remainder pay off. Where the earlier ZAPU raids from Zambia had repeatedly been disclosed to the authorities by chiefs and headmen, in 1972–3 ZANU guerilla groups in the north-east evaded capture and built up sustained fear among white farming families.

Isolated white homes were riddled with gunfire at night. Cars on remote roads were ambushed. White farmers placed sandbags round the windows of their houses, moved their children's beds into internal passageways and kept loaded firearms with them at all times. The balance was beginning to shift. In north-eastern Rhodesia in 1972–3 for the first time African guerillas knew the score, the whites and their security forces did not.

The Smith regime sent thousands of soldiers to the north-east, threatened and punished the local Africans and herded them into 'new villages' to cut the guerillas off from food and information. The number of whites killed was small. The response of the security services was energetic and soon made life for the Africans in the area difficult, caught as they were between two armies, each demanding information and its denial to the other.

Some Rhodesian army officers had served in the British forces in Malaya and had learned the lesson of that campaign: to defeat a guerilla movement it is necessary to win the trust of the population whose support is the guerillas' lifeline. They argued for a Malaya-style 'hearts and minds campaign' – some liberal concessions that would convince the Africans that the Government was their friend. The proposal they pressed upon Smith was to begin talks with Bishop Muzorewa, whose leadership of the African National Council during the Pearce commission inquiries had given him the unique status of spokesman for all Rhodesia's Africans. If Smith and Muzorewa could agree on a joint white-African arrangement for running the country, the soldiers believed they could win back the support of tribesmen in the north-east and thus defeat the guerillas. As more Rhodesian forces were poured into the area, they began by reasonable treatment of Africans to gather the information they needed. The ZANU guerillas responded with greater ferocity: where the police beat up village schoolmasters and headmen thought to have concealed information about the guerillas, the ZANU men tortured and killed those thought to have given anything away. The man who had commanded Rhodesian forces during their successful defeat of the early incursions from Zambia, General Sam Putterill, said publicly that the war against terrorism could not be won by force alone: 'The ingredient that is missing is a positive dynamic programme designed to win the loyalty of all people, to create a national loyalty.'

Smith's party, the Rhodesian Front, would not have it. In its disappointment after the failure to secure the Home–Smith settlement, the party demanded not liberal concessions to Africans or talks with them but more use of force and the abolition of such liberal and multi-racial arrangements as survived from the days of Federation. Smith did as his party asked: laws were passed increasing the requirement on Africans to carry passes, limiting their freedom to enter towns, ending multi-racial access to public swimming-pools and post-office counters. Rhodesia was back on the road to *apartheid*.

Then Smith began to have doubts. Reluctantly he became converted to the need to talk to Muzorewa, though he offered little more than the terms Muzorewa had campaigned against in 1971. He tried to warn his party's hardliners that they were losing the support of the chiefs, their traditional, paid allies:

> These are fine old men, nature's gentlemen [he said]. They want to work with us, they are not interested in political power. They don't want to take over the Government. However they are embarrassed by petty *apartheid*, which they are unable to understand or explain away to other reasonable Africans. We must not deliberately create conditions that make local Africans our enemies.

Smith's half-hearted conversion came too late. On 25 April 1974 a *coup d'état* in Lisbon reversed Portugal's policy for Mozambique. Instead of determinedly holding the territory against African nationalists, the new Portuguese Government decided to withdraw and hand power to them. Where narrow regions of Mozambique had provided a friendly base for the ZANU guerillas, from April 1974 the whole country became available, exposing the whites of eastern Rhodesia to a long new frontier of vulnerability.

This, however, was not the only effect of Mozambique's independence. Equally important was its impact on the Government of South Africa. Hendrik Verwoerd, Prime Minister at the time of UDI, and John Vorster, his successor, had long been ambivalent towards the Smith regime. While they and the majority of South African voters were instinctively on the side of the whites, Smith's illegal actions and his failure to accept the proposals of Harold Wilson exposed South Africa to danger. The South African Government did not want black guerilla fighters on their borders and would greatly have preferred a moderate black regime in Rhodesia to one which continued to provoke black terrorism. Rhodesia's republican constitution had failed to win the regime the recognition of other states. South Africa had therefore not been called upon to keep its undertaking to be the second nation to recognise Rhodesia. The man who might have become South Africa's Ambassador in Salisbury remained the ADR – Accredited Diplomatic Representative. Both Verwoerd and Vorster had urged Smith to settle with Wilson. The Portuguese collapse now exposed South Africa to black nationalist governments in both Mozambique and Angola. Vorster was stimulated into making a major new effort to stop the violence on his northern frontier.

Vorster's response was not merely to seek to avoid conflict with Mozambique but to seek to put an end to all black–white conflict near South Africa. He launched a 'peace offensive' on black African states. An early recipient of his hospitality was Dr Hastings Banda, by now the eccentric dictator of Malawi, who was willing to accept South African money for his country and in return gave the South Africans some lessons in how to behave towards a black head of state. No *apartheid* laws could be applied to Banda when, sixty years after working in the mines and studying in South Africa, he returned to Pretoria and Johannesburg. But Banda was only a first step. Vorster's main target in his friendship campaign was the state from which the guerilla movements against Smith's regime had long been directed, Kenneth Kaunda's Zambia.

Kaunda is an unusual head of state. Though politically ruthless and calculating, he impressed all who met him as a genuinely good man, a sincere Christian, a believer in non-violence and a passionate opponent of racial discrimination. For him *apartheid* was evil, so terrible a crime that it had to be opposed by force. Many African leaders found it politically expedient to mouth such views. Kaunda convinced sceptics that he meant what he said. When, therefore, in 1968 he had first received friendly approaches from emissaries of Vorster, a former Nazi sympathiser and the most ruthless exponent of *apartheid*, Kaunda rejected their proposal of a meeting. But Vorster persisted and after the Lisbon coup in 1974 his efforts became more pressing. He spoke sympathetically of the new black regime in Mozambique – 'Whoever takes over will have a tough task. It will require exceptional leadership. I wish them well' – and wrote to Kaunda that he would like to see a three-to-five year transition period to majority rule in Rhodesia. This was exactly how Kaunda hoped UDI would end. A Vorster–Kaunda nutcracker began, therefore, to be applied – Vorster working to bring Smith to a negotiation, Kaunda working on the African nationalists.

Perhaps the oddest part of this process took place in Lusaka in November 1974. Vorster had persuaded Smith to allow Nkomo and his ZANU rivals out of detention or prison, where they had been kept for more than ten years, since before UDI. They were flown secretly to Lusaka to meet Kaunda and three other African heads of state, Julius Nyerere of Tanzania, Samora Machel of Mozambique and Seretse Khama of Botswana, who tried to persuade them of the terms on which they must agree to negotiate a settlement with Smith. It was on Kaunda's word alone that Smith released the detainees to go to Lusaka, and Kaunda duly sent them back. The presidential arm-twisting worked. The African nationalists agreed to take part in a constitutional conference with Smith on the Vorster–Kaunda terms of five years' power-sharing with the white regime before transition to majority rule. Smith, too, after his attempts to wriggle out of the arrange-

*John Vorster visits Ian Smith in Salisbury.*

ment had been firmly crushed by Vorster, agreed to deliver his first contribution to the deal: the release of persons detained without trial. In return guerilla hostilities were to cease. (This was reluctantly agreed by ZANU, whose operations from Mozambique were prospering.) Nkomo and a hundred other African nationalist leaders were set free, though three hundred more remained in detention. Christmas 1974 was celebrated with much joy in African areas of Rhodesia. Among those released who did not believe in the talks was the leading ZANU member Robert Mugabe. He had entered detention with two degrees, a BA and a BEd. While in detention, in addition to maintaining his position as one of ZANU's principal decision-makers, he acquired four more degrees, through London university external courses. He now left Rhodesia to take charge of ZANU's guerilla head-quarters in Mozambique.

The talks with Smith were a spectacularly-staged comic opera. In August 1975 the luxurious white railway carriage of the President of South Africa was parked in the middle of the bridge that spans the gorge a few hundred yards down river from the Victoria Falls, with as Wagnerian a view as any railway in the world. Here the mile-wide Zambesi tumbles a sudden three hundred feet, a thunderous mass of foam. To the south, in Rhodesia, were the Victoria Falls Hotel and the Elephant Hills Casino; to the north, in

Zambia, lay the Intercontinental Hotel – all of them invisible behind the dense vegetation watered by centuries of spray. Into the presidential carriage and the hotels came Vorster and Kaunda – to meet for the first time – and Smith and the African nationalists. Smith had come only because Vorster had bullied him and he did not want to seem intransigent. He had no intention of handing over to black rule in five years. If he agreed to such a proposal he knew he would be immediately thrown out by his party. Vorster and Kaunda, in the railway carriage, addressed the assembled antagonists with wise words about peace in the region, and then withdrew together, united by their ambitious match-making. Those left behind had nothing to say to each other. The Africans demanded majority rule at once, Smith would not think of it in his lifetime. Vorster and Kaunda tried to press their respective clients to a compromise, but none was possible. They might as well have been singing to the waterfall.

The principal failure was Kaunda's. He could not persuade the Rhodesian nationalists to agree on a joint position. Had he been able to offer Vorster a unified nationalist movement to which a secure and gradual transfer of power might be made, Vorster could have leaned heavily on Smith to come to terms with them. But Smith, Vorster and Kaunda all had in mind recent events surrounding the Portuguese departure from Angola. On the eve of independence war had broken out between rival wings of the nationalist movement and more than 100,000 Europeans had fled the country. Vorster could not ask Smith to expose his electorate to such a risk.

The divisions in the Rhodesian nationalist movement were based on rivalries of personality and ambition. Tribal conflict too was a factor, though not predominant in the early stages. The most important division, however, was over policy, and the main protagonists emerged as Robert Mugabe and Joshua Nkomo. Mugabe had been one of the young men discontented with Nkomo's leadership who broke away to form ZANU. When the Vorster–Kaunda initiative led to his release from detention, he quickly became the dominant ZANU organiser in Mozambique, taking charge of the recruitment of young men from inside Rhodesia, transporting and training them, above all emphasising political education. Mao Tse-Tung's ideas about the use of a guerilla army as the political educators of the people were brought to the Zimbabwe struggle by Mugabe. A bookish, scholarly, quiet-spoken man – whenever he is in London he scurries into bookshops to stock himself up for the literary famine of the coming months in Africa – he was once a schoolmaster and retains the air of one who knows. After the charismatic leadership of ZAPU by Nkomo, ZANU went to the other extreme, a collective leadership in which all issues were argued to a conclusion. In this environment Mugabe's immense power to read, digest and analyse gradually brought him to the top, though never unchallenged. What made him ZANU's leader was a single-minded clarity of vision. He became convinced by Mao's view that power comes from the barrel of a gun. He saw no hope of securing worthwhile gains from negotiating with Smith and was therefore the fiercest advocate of war to the end. He did not want ceasefires or talks till he could negotiate from strength. Opposed to him was Nkomo, always willing to seek a compromise, long reconciled to the improbability of defeating the whites in war, a flexible politican. His guerilla movement had not been as successful as Mugabe's, so he had the stronger motive for wanting talks.

The railway carriage episode was followed by direct negotiations between Smith and Nkomo. Smith now regarded Nkomo as the reasonable African with whom terms could be arranged. He wanted Nkomo in the Government as the smiling black face, father of the nationalist movement, who could secure international recognition – Britain's, South Africa's, even Zambia's – for a regime that would remain white-dominated. Nkomo turned him down. He had the backing of Kaunda only if he could negotiate his way to majority rule. Otherwise, reluctantly, the Zambian President recognised he must find a way to unite the Zimbabwean nationalists for war. Nkomo warned Smith that if he did not settle the guerillas would soon form a united front, backed by the 'front-line Presidents' of Zambia, Mozambique, Tanzania and Botswana, almost completely surrounding Rhodesia. Nkomo said: 'We hope the whites in Zimbabwe realise that unless they think fast they may have to run out in their pyjamas.' Smith said: 'I have listened for more than ten years to bragging about guerilla plans. The fact is that when guerillas entered Rhodesia by the hundred they were killed by the hundred. If in future they decide to come in by the thousand, they will be killed by the thousand.'

So far, apart from the north-eastern border area, Smith's own bragging had been justified. The towns where most of the whites lived were peaceful. Smith himself continued to walk unguarded through the streets of Salisbury. Passing blacks neither jostled nor molested him. Africans continued to volunteer to serve in the police and army where they bore the brunt of the war against the guerillas. Smith, therefore, failed to see the need to make significant concessions to Nkomo. The threatened alternative – international Communist backing for the Marxist Mugabe and his guerillas – was in Smith's eyes simply not capable of overthrowing him. Vorster warned him that the danger was growing, as did Nkomo, the British Foreign Secretary (who by 1976 was James Callaghan), and his own army officers. Smith, the man still in charge of the army, the police and the civil service in Rhodesia, sat in his beautiful garden, rocking in his chair, comfortable and secure. So yet another chance of a settlement slipped away. The nutcracker policy of Kaunda and the frontline Presidents pressing the nationalists from the north and east and Vorster pressing Smith from the south was tightening, but Smith counted on Vorster easing off his side of the squeeze.

For five years after the Home–Smith settlement of 1971 was rejected, Britain stood on the sidelines, recognising that its ability to influence events in Rhodesia was negligible. Sovereignty remained British, recognised as such by every government in the world. Britain continued to invest military and diplomatic effort in maintaining sanctions, the ships of the Beira patrol expensively preventing oil from being delivered to the pipeline and British embassy officials around the world maintaining a routine of visits to foreign ministries, the climax of which went something like the following:

British official: 'So you see, this evidence does appear to suggest that the [named] company within your jurisdiction has breached the sanctions regulations which, in pursuit of the UN resolution, your parliament has passed.'

Foreign Ministry official: 'We really are most grateful to the British authorities for drawing this to our attention. We will of course pass all these documents to the Ministry of Justice and should their inquiries appear to confirm the facts they will no doubt take the appropriate measures to instigate a prosecution.'

Nominally every country in the world, except South Africa and Portugal, backed Britain's efforts to secure compliance with the UN sanctions resolution. In practice every Government followed the British example and turned a blind eye to breaches. One Government even went so far as formally to revoke part of its sanctions law: in 1971 the United States President Richard Nixon signed a measure exempting Rhodesian chrome, ferrochrome and nickel. With the United States openly importing these products, Britain's ability to persuade other countries to enforce sanctions was further reduced. Nevertheless in all countries but Portugal and South Africa sanctions remained the law. To withdraw these sanctions would be to concede victory to Smith; neither Britain nor the UN could allow that. So British Governments, both Conservative and Labour, found their principal contribution to crushing the rebellion against the Queen to be the endless task of stopping the holes in the sieve, one by one.

Significant developments depended on the Vorster–Kaunda nutcracker. This first became really effective after a raid by Rhodesian troops some thirty miles into Mozambique in August 1976. In a camp at Pungwe from which they had been told a major incursion was about to be launched, they killed 1,200 ZANU supporters. Vorster had advised Smith against the raid. He rightly predicted that international opinion would see it as a massacre, condemn it as an illegal incursion into Mozambique's sovereign territory and attribute part of the blame to South Africa. His ability to maintain his peace offensive would be undermined if Smith and the Rhodesian army continued in this way.

Vorster's response to the raid was immediate. South African personnel serving in Rhodesia, including some fifty helicopter pilots and technicians whose role in the anti-guerilla operations was crucial, were ordered home. And South African Railways – which, after the recent closure of the Mozambique line by the independent regime of Samora Machel, provided the only route for much of Rhodesia's trade – suddenly found itself short of rolling stock. Rhodesian exports were delayed and some, like a consignment of citrus fruits, ruined. Imports, including arms, ammunition and oil, failed to arrive. The Pungwe raid led Vorster to put his foot on Smith's windpipe. Now, after eleven years in which all negotiations had been on terms dictated by Smith, the position was reversed.

Unlike those of Wilson, Vorster's sanctions worked. Smith's troops were soon short of fuel and ammunition. What was worse, the South African Prime Minister, three days after the Pungwe raid, had a statement released at the United Nations which concluded: 'A solution of the Rhodesian issue on the basis of majority rule with adequate protection for minority rights is acceptable to the South African Government.'

Smith could not believe it. Like his voters, he saw things in simple terms. If Communist-backed guerillas became a serious threat, if Cubans in Russian tanks began driving inland from the coast, South Africa and the West would come to Rhodesia's aid. Even Sir Roy Welensky seemed to agree: 'I can't see,' he said, 'that they would leave us to a sticky end.' This belief that they were ultimately safe because they were perceived by the American Government as the free world's final bastion against Communism was not totally without foundation. The US Government's lifting of sanctions on chrome and nickel had provided strong encouragement to Smith and his supporters. When Portugal's African empire collapsed in 1974 and Angola became independent, the consequent war between the wings of the nationalist movement produced further encouragement. The US Government gave covert support to the anti-Communist side in Angola and encouraged South Africa to send a well-equipped force of some two thousand men. Henry Kissinger, President Nixon's national security adviser, pursued this policy in spite of opposition in the US State Department. By late 1975 it appeared to be working: the South African army and its black Angolan allies were capturing town after town and approaching the capital, Luanda. The Communist-backed forces faced defeat.

At this point the entire scene changed. Large numbers of Cuban troops were flown in, eventually amounting to 15,000; the Soviet Union, Cuba's sponsor and ally, thus openly committed itself. The State Department warned Kissinger and the President of the damaging consequences throughout black Africa of becoming militarily allied with South Africa. The US Congress, fearing another Vietnam, would not allow Kissinger to match the Cuban force. America backed away. The result was, to the disgust of Vorster and Smith, that a regime friendly to Soviet Russia came to power in Angola.

Smith and his supporters, ever optimists, drew the lesson that the United States would not let the same thing happen in Rhodesia. This was correct. Smith hoped American determination to back his regime would be strengthened. It was not. Although Kissinger and Nixon had shown sympathy for white Rhodesia, once their allies lost Angola a new policy evolved and Kissinger himself came to southern Africa to carry it through.

Kissinger was learning the lesson that Vorster had learned: to preserve a stable South Africa it was no good provoking African nationalism. The sounder policy was a peace offensive, of which an essential part was the speedy ending of the struggle in Rhodesia before the guerilla movement there became so powerful that it threatened South Africa. More to the point for Kissinger, there must be no repeat of the Angolan situation, with the United States caught backing the wrong side and Cuban soldiers arriving to settle the issue. Henry Kissinger came to Africa to tell Ian Smith he must capitulate: an African majority regime must be installed and they must all learn to call the country Zimbabwe.

The meeting between Kissinger and Smith in the US embassy in Pretoria was in part no more than a repetition of what Home, Wilson and Vorster had been saying to Smith for some years: that he must accept majority rule. But Kissinger arrived equipped with Vorster's nutcracker. He brutally spelled out the weakness of Smith's position, with accurate details of the arms his military units were short of, the backlog of unsold exports, the consequent and desperate need for loans. Smith countered by explaining his plan to bring acceptable Africans into his Government, but Kissinger would have none of it. He handed Smith a five-point summary of the basis required by the United States and South Africa for a Rhodesian settlement. The first point read: 'Rhodesia agrees to majority rule within two years.' Smith said: 'You want me to sign my own suicide note.' An American official described Kissinger's technique as 'meat-axe diplomacy'. Kissinger forced Smith to say, for the first time, that he would assist in the speedy introduction of majority rule. The objective was to install a moderate black administration before it was too late. Until September 1976 Smith had agreed to the principle of majority rule, but had convinced himself and his electorate that in practice it could be held off for a long time, longer than they need worry about. Kissinger's meat-axe made him capitulate.

But only verbally. Smith still possessed reserves of ingenuity and obstinacy. Although his concession horrified his party and led to an immediate scurry of whites to leave Rhodesia – which was not altogether easy as property prices collapsed and the exchange control rules designed to combat sanctions impeded their attempts to take their money out – Smith was soon planning ways to ensure that the black Government when it came would be an acceptable one. Smith's principal objective was at all costs to exclude Robert Mugabe, the leader of ZANU, whom he saw as Rhodesia's Lenin: learned, ruthless and unshakable. While Nkomo, Muzorewa and others were prepared, in return for Smith's agreement to transfer power, to help devise ways to protect the white minority, Mugabe saw white minority rights as a racist concept. He said Smith and his ministers must be tried for war crimes (for which, like Mugabe, they were certainly responsible) and a new people's state created with neither private ownership of land nor private enterprise. Mugabe declared: 'If whites are prepared to obey the new black Government, they can stay. Otherwise they will have to leave and the gaps can quickly be filled from the socialist and other countries.' Rather than negotiate with Smith, Mugabe continued to press ahead towards victory in

*Robert Mugabe, right, greets supporters with the raised fist of the black power salute, Lusaka, February 1977.*

the guerilla war. Nkomo, who, along with Mugabe, had been bullied by the front-line presidents into an alliance called the Patriotic Front, showed his usual sensitivity to the way the tide was running and became less ready than before to talk privately with Smith.

Therefore the only candidate available to provide a Smith-dominated Government with an acceptable black face was the tiny bishop, Muzorewa. Smith's courtship of Muzorewa was slow and peripatetic. They met in Geneva, where the British held a conference in a forlorn effort to translate Kissinger's meat-axe diplomacy into a scheme all parties might accept. They met in the intervals between the trips of well-meaning emissaries to Rhodesia and the trips overseas of Muzorewa, of whom Smith said: 'He's out of the country so much he's almost a foreigner.' Between their meetings, Mugabe's ZANU guerillas from Mozambique increased their effectiveness and Nkomo's ZAPU began vigorously attracting young blacks from Matabeleland to be sent for military training in Zambia. Muzorewa's popularity in the country remained high largely because Africans were led to believe that if he joined the Government he could end the war.

Smith maintained his standing among the whites sufficiently to win a decisive general election victory, the policy with which he replaced his previous slogan 'No majority rule in my lifetime' being, in effect, 'Trust Smithy to make majority rule bearable'. He assured the voters that he could find a black leader who, to save himself from the guerilla onslaught, would prove co-operative. To enable Muzorewa to perform this role, Smith had to persuade Vorster to maintain the flow of war supplies. This proved as easy as Smith had anticipated. Vorster wanted to force Smith to settle; he did not want so to disable his army as to allow Mugabe's guerillas a triumph.

And so, in February 1978, Smith signed a deal with Muzorewa. It preserved twenty-eight seats for whites in an assembly of a hundred. Smith was delighted with this result, which gave Muzorewa and his colleagues the strongest motive for maintaining a powerful, white-led army. Otherwise, in Smith's words, they would be the first to get a bullet in the back. Smith conceded one-man one-vote for the remaining seventy-two seats, with an election to be held soon. This settlement gave far more to the blacks of Rhodesia than the offers of Wilson and Home. The British Foreign Secretary, David Owen, felt unable to reject what was undoubtedly a step in the right direction. The Conservative Party in the House of Commons was in favour of recognising the new regime, as was the majority in the US Senate.

*Bishop Abel Muzorewa (left) and Ian Smith look on as the constitution introducing one-man-one-vote in Rhodesia is formally approved.*

It looked as though Ian Smith had once again defied the world and got away with it.

For Joshua Nkomo this situation was agonising. He believed in a peaceful transfer of power with guarantees for Europeans and he desperately wanted to head the first black government of Zimbabwe. Furthermore, Smith now needed him because Muzorewa, although popular in the country, soon proved unable to persuade the guerillas to lay down their arms; his emissaries asking them to do so were killed. So Smith and Nkomo met secretly in Lusaka. Both President Kaunda and Smith thought Nkomo would be able to call off the guerillas and thus prove himself the man to lead the new Government. However, Nkomo failed to inform his Patriotic Front ally of this meeting with their common enemy and Mugabe, when he was told of it, was both suspicious and angry. He never again trusted Nkomo. He still believed that victory in war was the only way to secure real independence. Nkomo could not make peace without him.

In January 1979, when the details of Smith's new constitution were published, they showed that he had conceded less than had at first been supposed. While Parliament was to have a black majority, every other centre of power was to be left securely in white control. The army, the police, the civil service and the judiciary were each to be run by independent commissions, whose members were to be drawn from the senior ranks of the service with at least five years in their posts. Consequently Parliament could not for some years get its hands on any of the main levers of power. Further, Smith had secured Muzorewa's agreement to form, after the first election, a government of national unity with five whites in the Cabinet.

The Patriotic Front (with Nkomo now back in line), the front-line Presidents and the majority of African countries dismissed this as not true majority rule at all. Guerilla activities increased, no longer restricted to border areas. Whites travelling between towns in cars and lorries had to move in convoys with armed escorts. Nkomo's guerillas using heat-seeking rockets shot down two civil aircraft, killing over a hundred passengers – a terrible shock to whites hitherto sure both of their technical superiority and of Nkomo's complaisance. In a radio broadcast about this accomplishment, Nkomo giggled with triumph – instantly reversing the whites' perception of him. White men of all ages were compelled to serve in the security services, leading many businesses to collapse. In the tribal areas guerillas and security forces had killed between 20,000 and 50,000 Africans (estimates vary widely). Of the country's black population of seven million, one million had lost their homes; some lived as refugees in Mozambique and Zambia, some squatted in the towns, most lived in the Government's 'protected hamlets'. The guerillas had destroyed hundreds of schools and health centres. Diseases of both humans and animals that had for years been kept under control, including malaria and bilharzia, began to spread. Nevertheless, in the election in April 1979 Muzorewa won an impressive victory with sixty-seven per cent of the votes cast in a poll that was observed by the former

Colonial Secretary Alan Lennox-Boyd on behalf of the Conservative Party. He pronounced it reasonably fair (though other observers were less impressed). The guerillas had tried to prevent Africans from voting, but the Government claimed that of a black electorate of 2,826,000 sixty-four per cent voted. Even if this figure was an exaggeration, it appeared that a majority of black Rhodesians had endorsed not only Bishop Muzorewa but also Smith's new constitution (although in reality most were almost certainly voting for an end to the war). According to the criteria previously laid down by Britain, the Commonwealth and the UN – unimpeded progress to majority rule approved by the people of Rhodesia as a whole – Smith had at last passed the test. His Government, of which Muzorewa was the Prime Minister from April 1979, had an apparently strong case to be recognised as legitimate.

A few days after Bishop Muzorewa became Prime Minister, a general election in Britain gave power to the Conservatives under Mrs Margaret Thatcher. Their election manifesto had stated that, on the terms of Smith's new constitution, they would 'have the duty to return Rhodesia to a state of legality, move to lift sanctions and . . . ensure that the new independent state gains international recognition.' Mrs Thatcher made it clear she would not have Parliament pressed to renew the sanctions legislation when it came up for its annual review. She was fiercely anti-terrorist and keen to recognise Muzorewa's Government. The Foreign Office set about what officials there called 'the education of Maggie Thatcher'.

Slowly she was persuaded that if she recognised Muzorewa she would be alone. The Commonwealth, the United States (where President Jimmy Carter was much more pro-African than his predecessors), the vast majority at the United Nations were against her.

Our recognising the Muzorewa regime [her Foreign Secretary Lord Carrington later recalled] would have led to the most appalling problems starting with the isolation of Britain from the rest of the world, including the United States. It would have settled nothing and intensified the war leading to much more bloodshed. It would probably have brought the thing everyone had been most anxious to avoid, Soviet and Cuban involvement.

A particular problem lay ahead: in three months Mrs Thatcher was to accompany the Queen to a Commonwealth Heads of Government conference in Lusaka. It would not be nice for the Queen, or for Mrs Thatcher herself, if Britain were to be pilloried there for selling out to Smith's puppet; and some African countries might carry out their threat to demand Britain's expulsion from the Commonwealth. Even Malcolm Fraser, the Prime Minister of Australia, a conservative on most topics, let it be known he was strongly opposed to recognising Muzorewa. Mrs Thatcher decided to wait and think before acting.

The man mainly responsible for persuading her was Carrington, who had never thought his party's manifesto commitment made sense. In Zimbabwe-Rhodesia, as the new constitution required it to be called, and in Zambia and Mozambique the Governments were desperate for an end to the war. The numbers killed, the railways and roads cut, the economic disruption, the spreading disease were demoralising all three countries, which were desperately short of money and losing control of their own territories. Diplomats told Carrington that Presidents Kaunda and Machel were now so worried they would apply every possible pressure to make the Zimbabwe nationalists stop the war if a reasonably honourable settlement was available. This was welcome news to Mrs Thatcher: a chance for Britain to take the lead in the exercise of its legitimate authority. What was more, she could launch the British initiative herself at the Commonwealth heads of government meeting.

Many of the African and Asian Government leaders came to Lusaka in August 1979 prepared for a battle with Mrs Thatcher. Her initiative surprised and impressed them. The *Rhodesia Herald*, amazed at her *volte-face*, asked: 'Is Mrs Thatcher really a Labour Prime Minister in drag?' Carrington and his Foreign Office team skilfully caused their plan to be adopted by other Governments and thus put forward as a Commonwealth initiative. It stated that Britain alone was responsible for granting legal independence to Zimbabwe, that the successor Government must be chosen through elections supervised by Britain and that to this end Britain should call a constitutional conference to which all parties would be invited. In short the Rhodesia situation required an honest broker and Britain's residual legal authority, combined with its knowledge of all principal participants and its diplomatic skill, meant that Britain and Britain alone must perform the central role. All relevant Zimbabwe–Rhodesians were invited to Lancaster House in London, in the hope that this time the disaster could at last be brought to an end.

Carrington received much advice. The Kissinger meat-axe operation had bequeathed its lessons. Carrington's immediate predecessor as Foreign Secretary, Dr David Owen, had spent months touring Africa, sometimes with the US Secretary of State Cyrus Vance, working out the basis for a settlement. Their lesson was that the number of parties involved was so large and their positions were so unstable that negotiation was all but impossible: Nkomo's party or Mugabe's or Muzorewa's or Smith's could block a compromise. To prevent their doing so, Carrington could not negotiate or conciliate: he had to lead from the front. Britain, still with no soldier or policeman to enforce its will in Zimbabwe–Rhodesia, had to use the guerillas' success to put pressure on Smith and Muzorewa, and Machel's and Kaunda's desperate need for peace to put pressure on the Patriotic Front. The guerilla war had at last brought Britain the chance to exercise the etiolated residue of imperial authority in Rhodesia which since 1889 Governments in London had formally retained: the honest broker must behave like Palmerston.

It was by no means clear whether Carrington, the Foreign Secretary who had to conduct this exercise, was up to the job. An apparently languid aristocrat, he did not appear tough or persevering enough. He was the embodiment of the old Tory party which Mrs Thatcher had displaced. He was very rich but had not, as Mrs Thatcher preferred, earned his money and land: they were inherited. He had never been elected to the House of Commons or fought his way through the bustle of party conflict: he had arrived at the top by way of Eton, Sandhurst, the Grenadier Guards and the family peerage. Worst of all, he was a 'wet', a close supporter of the former Conservative Prime Minister Edward Heath. Mrs Thatcher and her school in the party stood for a competitive, tough society. He, in his patrician way, stood for sympathy and tolerance. Over Rhodesia her instincts were those of the party – well-disposed towards the 'game little bishop', deeply hostile to Nkomo and Mugabe, essentially on the side of the whites. At the Conservative Party conference in October 1979, demonstrators outside the hall held up 'Hang Carrington' placards and met with some sympathy from delegates. If the man who chaired the Rhodesia talks could not maintain the support of his own party and Prime Minister, the whole project was hopeless. Therefore, throughout what was to be a long process, Carrington reported every day to Mrs Thatcher. The Foreign Office professionals called these daily meetings Lord Carrington's 'other negotiations'. Her personal regard for him was sufficiently high for her to accept developments which, from officials or a less esteemed minister, she would have disdained.

The objective in which Mrs Thatcher and Lord Carrington were united was to get Britain shot of Rhodesia. For too many years Britain had been rudely criticised at international gatherings and obliged to use its limited stock of diplomatic cards to maintain ineffective sanctions, and the Conservative Party remained dangerously divided on the issue, requiring a constant waste of ministerial time to prevent revolts both at conference and in the House of Commons. A settlement followed by international recognition of the new regime would put an end to all that. However, where Wilson, Home, Kissinger, Owen and Vance had all failed, it was plain that success would not come easily.

The centrepiece of Carrington's scheme was an interim period. During it the Government of Southern Rhodesia would for the first time be in Britain's hands. This interval would be brief, just long enough for Britain to supervise elections and bring a new constitution into effect. A new Government would then take office and independence would be recognised by all. Carrington wanted the Patriotic Front to agree to his scheme, take part in the election and form part of the resulting Government. For him the ideal result would have been a Muzorewa–Nkomo Government with Mugabe acquiescing (if only because Zambia and Mozambique wanted peace and therefore refused ZANU sanctuary for its guerillas). This was known in the British team as the 'first-class solution'. An acceptable alternative, from the British point of view, was for the Patriotic Front to refuse the deal and walk out of the conference, but only after Britain had convinced Zambia and Mozambique of the genuineness of the offer. That way the Bishop would win the election and both wings of the Patriotic Front would be excluded from the country, impotently watching the world recognise a legitimate one-man one-vote regime. This was known in the British team as the 'second-class solution', which Carrington disliked as it might fail to end the war and it would be difficult to persuade Commonwealth and African Governments to support it. What Carrington and Mrs Thatcher both disliked about the first-class solution was that it opened the door to a terrorist like Nkomo – or, even worse, a Marxist terrorist like Mugabe – joining the Government. However the Prime Minister and Foreign Secretary agreed that they would accept either.

What Muzorewa and Smith wanted was recognition of their regime and the consequent lifting of sanctions. However, in raising the first item on his agenda, the future constitution, Carrington set out to split Muzorewa's delegation by isolating Smith. He said white control of the army, police and public services must be relaxed. Muzorewa, who saw his own power thereby increasing, soon agreed. Smith, however, dug his feet in: he would not agree to any diminution of white control beyond that conceded the previous year. During a meeting with the delegation, Carrington provoked a clash with Smith, so that he could remind them all of Smith's record of twisting other people's words and destroying agreements. Carrington loathed Smith, whom he regarded as like the worst extremists and racialists in his own party. Their exchanges became harsh and then venomous. Whether Carrington put on a show of fury or whether it was genuine, nobody could tell, not even Carrington himself, but he succeeded in conveying his contempt for Smith's inflexibility.

Muzorewa's other eleven advisers, including General Peter Walls the army commander, agreed to accept Carrington's terms. Smith was thus rendered insignificant. Conservative groups had enthusiastically greeted him in London. He was guest of honour at a party given by the Marquis of Salisbury. But, reduced to a minority of one in Muzorewa's delegation, he had no more to say, except a private complaint that Nkomo and Mugabe were 'far cleverer than my blacks'.

Walls told Smith that, although he thought the guerillas could not win, the regime's forces were at full stretch and Europeans were increasingly reluctant to be 'the last white to die for a black Government'. This could not go on. The Rhodesians needed a settlement. Smith did not disagree. He just could not bring himself to accept it.

The Patriotic Front attended the conference – the nineteenth-century splendour of London's Lancaster House at first making Mugabe uncomfortable – to prevent Britain recognising the Muzorewa regime. Lord Carrington later recalled that the threat to recognise the Muzorewa Government was the one card he had up his sleeve with Mugabe and Nkomo. If such recognition followed what Kaunda and Machel would hold to be an

unreasonable walk-out by the Patriotic Front, then the guerillas would soon find themselves without bases, as both Zambia and Mozambique were opposed to continued support for the war. Both countries had long been suffering more severely from the imposition of sanctions than had Rhodesia itself. Mugabe, therefore, attended the conference to prove to Kaunda and Machel that nothing could be gained from talks: they should refuse recognition to the Muzorewa regime, prevent Britain from recognising it and help the guerillas pursue the war.

Nkomo, as usual, was more ambiguous. He hoped to persuade Mugabe to take part in elections which he was sure the Patriotic Front would win. But Mugabe did not trust Lord Carrington a yard (as he later told him) and did not think the election scheme was 'on the level'. Although his military commander, Josiah Tongogara, like General Walls, thought the war could not be won for several years and therefore the Patriotic Front should seek a settlement, Mugabe still believed in the purifying effect of war, preparing the fighters and the people for fundamental change. Nevertheless he and Nkomo reluctantly agreed to some constitutional provisions to protect the whites (including twenty seats in a hundred-seat Parliament). From Mugabe this was an unexpected and major concession; it held open the possibility, if the black vote were divided, of the whites being kingmakers. Mugabe

*Lancaster House, London, September 1979. Left, Muzorewa, Smith and their delegation; facing, Lord Carrington and the British Foreign Office team; right, Nkomo, Mugabe and the Patriotic Front.*

*The joint leaders of the Patriotic Front, Joshua Nkomo and Robert Mugabe, together face the press in London.*

acquiesced because front-line presidents, particularly Nyerere of Tanzania, told him that such a provision had been included by the British in earlier independence constitutions, notably Kenya's, and to walk out in protest against it would justify the British recognising the Muzorewa regime.

Getting the constitution accepted by both sides took six weeks. Carrington then turned to the transition arrangements. The first difficulty was to persuade Bishop Muzorewa to stand down as Prime Minister, so that the Zimbabwe-Rhodesian army and police could come under the orders of the Governor. Muzorewa's objections, that he had only a few months earlier received the mandate of the people to govern the country and that his administration had shown itself capable of supervising an election, were irrefutable. His chance of winning the election would be greatly enhanced if he was the incumbent Prime Minister. Talking him out of his office was the hardest single task Carrington and his team faced. Over lunches and dinners at the homes of the British ministers involved, in the hotels where the Muzorewa delegation stayed, in the Foreign Office, in small meeting-rooms at Lancaster House, members of the British team put their case to Muzorewa and his colleagues: he was almost certain to win the election anyway; to persuade African states and the UN that it was not just a repeat of the previous election that they had rejected, it had to be under clear British control; to remove Mugabe totally from the scene, both as guerilla and as political heavyweight, he had to be persuaded to stand and be seen to be fairly defeated. Eventually the Bishop conceded.

The Patriotic Front were almost as difficult. They were not prepared to take part in elections supervised by a Rhodesian, white-led military machine that during the conference continued to bomb Zambia and Mozambique and kill their men. They demanded that their own armies must share with the Rhodesian army the task of supervising the election. Presidents Kaunda and Machel had their representatives in London apply strong pressure. The latest bombing raids had had disastrous consequences: roads and rail bridges were destroyed on all Zambian highways leading to Tanzania and Malawi; guerilla camps and arms dumps in Mozambique had been destroyed, along with some camps of the Mozambique army. The front-line presidents warned the Patriotic Front that they must compromise or they would be on their own. But Mugabe and Nkomo still could not agree to take part in an election that was supervised, as they saw it, by Smith's police. Since Carrington had won General Walls's agreement and Bishop Muzorewa's willingness to stand down only on this understanding, and since the only force in Rhodesia that had the remotest chance of supervising an election fairly was the present one, Carrington had little room for manoeuvre

The Patriotic Front plainly had a case, which they made to the Commonwealth Secretary-General and to several outside Governments, including that of the United States. Heavy pressure on Carrington eventually convinced him that to impress African and American opinion, and not least the black leaders who had helped President Carter win office, a non-Rhodesian military presence must be introduced to ensure impartiality. He persuaded the Cabinet to send a small British contingent to form part of a Commonwealth military monitoring force. Australia, New Zealand, Kenya and Fiji also agreed to send troops to assist in this task. The Patriotic Front wanted a UN force and the inclusion of soldiers from more African countries in a peacekeeping role. Carrington stood firm on the force's role being limited to monitoring – i.e. they were not there to shoot. Sir Terence Lewin, Britain's chief of defence staff, later defined their duty if hostilities broke out as 'to get the hell out of it'. No great concession was therefore granted when Carrington gradually agreed to increase the size of the force, until the Patriotic Front finally accepted it at 1,200 men. Commonwealth and UN observers were also to be present to report on the fair conduct of the election. As with the constitution, before he could persuade Nkomo and Mugabe to accept that these terms were the best he could offer, Carrington had to threaten to reach a separate settlement with the Muzorewa group and this time actually had measures introduced in the House of Commons to implement such a step. It was Carrington's readiness to accept this alternative – the second-class solution – that enabled him to browbeat the Patriotic Front into agreement.

The final topic was the ceasefire. On this even-handedness was imposs-

ible. Muzorewa's Government and Walls's army were in effective control of all the towns and much of the countryside. The Governor could function only with Walls's co-operation. On the other hand, the guerillas could not be expected to give up their arms and face the risk of massacre by Walls's troops. The ceasefire was therefore the subject most likely to make the Patriotic Front walk out. With the approval of the Prime Minister, Carrington asked Lord Soames, a fellow member of the Cabinet, former British ambassador to Paris and son-in-law of Winston Churchill, to accept the post of Governor, and in the midst of the ceasefire talks, when momentum was flagging and it did indeed seem likely that the Patriotic Front would walk out, Carrington decided to send Soames out to take up his task, once again applying pressure on Mugabe and Nkomo by threatening a British deal with Muzorewa. For a third time this tactic worked. Mugabe delayed. He flew with Nkomo to Dar es Salaam to meet the front-line presidents and persuade them that a walk-out was justified. But their need for peace overrode all his objections. Machel told Mugabe that if he walked out he could have a retirement villa in Mozambique but if he tried to base guerillas there they would be arrested and shot. Mugabe was compelled to agree to ceasefire terms concerning which he was extremely nervous.

Lord Soames took with him to Salisbury a deputy, Sir Anthony Duff, a military adviser, Major-General John Acland, a police adviser, Sir John Houghton, and an election commissioner, Sir John Boynton. Acland had charge of the Commonwealth Monitoring Force whose task was to disperse to remote parts of the country and 'assemble' the guerillas. Whites in Salisbury warned that the lightly-armed small units, entering unfamiliar territory full of armed, ill-disciplined black men, would be easy targets. Most of the units went to border areas that had been deserted as a result of the guerilla activities. The roads were overgrown, some were mined and some of the 'assembly points' proved to be old schools, hospitals or missions that had been bombed or blown up. Each unit's task was to raise the Union Jack and wait for guerillas far better armed and more numerous than themselves to arrive. Since Mugabe suspected that the British Government was in league with Smith and Muzorewa, his guerillas could not be counted on to be friendly to British soldiers.

As soon as a guerilla group was sighted approaching, the Monitoring Force officer in charge would walk out unarmed to meet them and offer them a cup of tea. Several of the young officers who performed this task were faced with guns pointed at them and thought they were about to be shot. None was though six were killed accidentally. Most of Nkomo's 6,000 ZAPU guerillas in the country soon gathered at the assembly points, where Nkomo instructed them by radio to stay so that the elections could be conducted freely. 'The war is over,' he told them. 'People must not be surrounded by armed men from any quarter.'

Mugabe's ZANU guerillas were a different matter. Tongogara, their commander, had told Walls, the Rhodesian army commander, that 15,000 were in the country and would come to the assembly points. To avoid gunfights the agreement stipulated that Walls must order his troops to return to their camps. But Tongogara died in a motoring accident immediately after the London conference and his undertaking was not kept by his men. Some 15,000 did indeed come to the assembly points, but many thousands more (estimates vary from 7,000 to 20,000) entered the country, hid their weapons and billeted themselves in twos and threes on villages, where their purpose was to prevent rival parties campaigning.

Walls told Soames that to put a stop to this infiltration the Rhodesian security forces must be redeployed. Army border patrols were resumed. Soames, only nominally in charge, could not have stopped Walls even had he wished to. But when Mugabe arrived in Salisbury in January, Soames summoned him to Government House, pitched into him and told him to get a grip on his forces. This was Soames's first meeting with Mugabe but the Governor felt he had no time for a courteous introduction. If the breach of the agreement by Mugabe's men led to battles with Walls's troops – many of whom were eager for another shot at the 'terrs', their abbreviation for terrorists – then the entire structure for a settlement that Carrington had painstakingly built could collapse in a couple of days. Soames asked Mugabe to order all his guerillas to report to the assembly points. Mugabe answered that he needed more time and that the trouble had been provoked by the security forces. Only when they were confined to their camps would he co-operate.

The meetings between Soames and Mugabe continued rough. At the next one Soames angrily laid out the evidence for his belief that Mugabe's guerillas had ambushed a bus in which sixteen Africans were killed. This was terrorism, Soames said, and it must stop. In any place where it continued, ZANU would be disqualified from the election. This time Mugabe agreed that instructions would be broadcast to his guerillas to report to the assembly points, but he did not broadcast them himself. As to banning the party, Mugabe warned, 'Nobody will play the fool with us. It does not matter how painful it may be, if forced to we will return to war. We will not be intimidated by anybody, including Soames.'

Complaints of intimidation continued to be levelled against ZANU. Nkomo had wanted the Patriotic Front to contest the election as a united party, but Mugabe turned him down. Over the years their two parties had become increasingly tribally based, Nkomo's ZAPU strongest among the minority Matabele, Mugabe's ZANU among the majority, the Shona. If they won as a united party, Mugabe would be saddled not only with Nkomo's moderate policies but also with his desire as the senior man to occupy the top post. By standing separately Mugabe's policy-making collective believed they could secure the bulk of the Shona votes. Nkomo complained: 'The word *intimidation* is mild. People are being terrorised. It is *fear*.' Nkomo privately urged Soames to ban ZANU.

Bishop Muzorewa made the same demand publicly. His majority in the last election had come from precisely the Shona areas where ZANU was now forcefully seeking support. Muzorewa said it had become impossible for his party to hold meetings or rallies in parts of Mashonaland. The teams sent out by Sir John Boynton, Soames's election commissioner and formerly chief executive of Cheshire County Council, confirmed Nkomo's and Muzorewa's complaints. They were British local government officers and former colonial civil servants and they reported that in eastern Rhodesia the scale of intimidation was substantial.

Soames's Foreign Office advisers regarded this information as a blessing in disguise. Banning Mugabe's party, even if only in the most troubled areas, was the best way, they thought, to secure an orderly succession. The Rhodesian administrators with whom they were having to work closely warned that if Mugabe won the election they would leave the country – and so would most qualified whites. ZANU's intimidation provided an excellent non-political reason for securing a satisfactory political result. General Walls, Ian Smith and the majority of white Rhodesians offered hearty endorsement. Providence had given Soames a convenient way to secure a Muzorewa-Nkomo-Smith coalition, just what he and Carrington and Mrs Thatcher desired.

The Governor hesitated. The Commonwealth election monitoring group, a predominantly Afro-Asian team of more than 100 observers from ten nations presided over by an Indian judge, aware of the pressure to ban ZANU, sent the Governor their report of what they had seen. All parties were using intimidation, but Nkomo's and Muzorewa's complaints that they could not hold meetings in some of the specified places were untrue: members of the group had attended such meetings. Perhaps, the Indian judge conjectured, the election commissioners were believing too much of what their colleagues, the white Rhodesian local government officers, were telling them. As for the complaints of Nkomo and Muzorewa, well they would, wouldn't they?

Soames called a large meeting of all his election advisers and the Commonwealth Military Monitoring Group's liaison officers ten days before the election. Its purpose was to determine whether ZANU's intimidation genuinely merited a ban. The threat of a ban had boosted the enthusiasm of the Rhodesian whites who were helping Soames run the country. It had also led Mugabe to try to reduce the level of intimidation, with some success. The question now was whether the Governor should act. On 10 February 1980 a massive bomb had exploded seconds after Mugabe's car had passed over it. Mugabe blamed the security forces for this near-assassination. To ban his party when others – perhaps even the Government – were engaging in comparable tactics might be hard to justify.

Soames knew that the security forces were doing many things he disapproved of but could not prevent. In London during the final negotiations the Patriotic Front had complained that South African troops were active in Rhodesia. Walls had assured Carrington they were not present in formed units – only a small number of individuals integrated into Rhodesian units. Carrington had said publicly: 'There will be no external involvement in Rhodesia under the British Governor. The position has been made clear to all the Governments concerned, including South Africa.' But when Soames arrived in Rhodesia he was embarrassed to find three companies of South African troops on the Rhodesian side of the border at Beit Bridge. Walls said they could not be asked to leave – they were essential for white morale and in case of emergency – and Soames reluctantly acquiesced. When reports of this South African intrusion appeared in the press, the British were accused of both hypocrisy and conspiracy. Only after subsequent diplomatic pressure from Britain were the units withdrawn.

Similarly Soames was vulnerable to criticism on account of the 16,000 military auxiliaries who were deployed in tribal areas. They were a militia recruited by Bishop Muzorewa in 1978 and regarded by most Africans as his personal force. They were deployed by Walls without Soames's consent and their conduct provoked many complaints of brutality which the Commonwealth Monitoring Group spent a lot of time investigating. Although Walls took strong action to restore discipline, the conduct of the auxiliaries made it awkward for Soames to ban ZANU alone. ZANU supporters had undoubtedly been guilty of political murders, but some of the ZANU 'intimidation' seemed attributable to the success of Mugabe's political education campaign in winning whole villages to refuse to admit his rivals. The longer Soames listened to the reports of the CMG and the election commissioners, the more he realised that, with intimidation coming from so many sources, the ban could not be imposed.

The Rhodesian whites working for him and his senior Foreign Office advisers were deeply disappointed by this decision. Soames, however, was beginning to think that to ban ZANU would be not only unjust but dangerous. It was plain that what most voters wanted above all was an end to the war. In April 1979 they had voted for Muzorewa to end it and he had failed. In February 1980, a mere ten months later, they were going to vote for Mugabe, because his was the party that if elected would end the war – and if not elected might have the power to continue it. The newspapers were predicting a three-way split of the votes between the parties of Mugabe, Muzorewa, and Nkomo and speculating on the likely coalition partners. On the day before the election, Soames called Mugabe in for a one-to-one chat, to tell him that the much-threatened ban was not to be imposed and to open

*After the election result – Lord Soames has just invited Robert Mugabe to form the Government.*

the way to a new relationship. Until that day Soames, who had been charming to all the other political leaders, had rudely bullied and hectored Mugabe. Now they talked for an hour and their laughter could be heard outside the office. Mugabe had believed that the only way to power was via the barrel of a gun. Unexpectedly in the Governor's room he learned that he could have it by the choice of the people. He was confident of winning. 'You stay on as Governor,' he said, 'and I'll be your Prime Minister.'

That day began the last of the love affairs that so often developed between the final British Governor and the first head of government at independence. Nehru's affair with the Mountbattens set the pattern; Nkrumah's with Arden-Clarke was the longest-lasting; this was the briefest. It began on the day before the election, 25 February 1980, and it was brought to an end by independence on 17 April. On independence night, to the embarrassment of whites and blacks alike, Mugabe said on television of Soames, 'I have ended up not only implicitly trusting but fondly loving him as well.' Most of those who had had power transferred to them by the British understood what he meant, though nobody else had dared publicly so to express it.

Nearly a million more Africans voted than in the previous election. Of the eighty African seats, Mugabe's ZANU captured fifty-seven, Nkomo's ZAPU twenty, all in Matabeleland, and Bishop Muzorewa only three. Mugabe, the Marxist revolutionary, had an overall majority and therefore became Prime Minister. Lord Carrington and Mrs Thatcher, Ian Smith and John Vorster were all horrified. General Walls, having failed to persuade Soames to ban Mugabe's party, sent a cable to Mrs Thatcher asking her to invalidate the election results on account of the intimidation of voters. Since the many official observers of the election all pronounced that the result was not significantly affected by intimidation, the request made no impression.

Walls and a group of army commanders had drawn up a contingency plan for a coup. They now invited Sir Anthony Duff, the deputy Governor, to join them in their operations room as, in full uniform, they outlined their scheme: surely Britain's interest, like theirs, lay in removing the black Marxist before it was too late? Mugabe, on Soames's advice, scotched the plan by inviting Walls to stay on as commander-in-chief, with the difficult task of integrating ZANU and ZAPU guerillas and the Rhodesian army into a single national force. In a mood of confusion and some hysteria he allowed himself to be talked out of his coup and into accepting this professional challenge which, if skilfully executed, might hold the country together.

Many of the whites were in a panic. They regarded Mugabe as the living devil, bent on robbing them of their property and taking away their privileges. Indeed it was precisely for these ends that he had wanted to continue the war. But the election and his new office revealed unexpected subtleties. Samora Machel had described to Mugabe how the commitment of his movement, FRELIMO, to Marxist egalitarianism in Mozambique had led to a prompt exodus of tens of thousands of whites from the country, with the result that public services and productive industry had gone into a

534 *End of Empire*

sharp decline. Machel had been unable to bring back the skills to create an economic recovery. Mugabe heeded the warnings. On the night of his election victory in a television broadcast on which he had received some advice from Soames, he called for reconciliation and promised that the law and individuals' rights, including property rights, would be respected. He invited some whites – as well as Joshua Nkomo and some other ZAPU members – to join his Cabinet. If he was still determined to destroy capitalism in Zimbabwe, as some of his ZANU colleagues were, he had plainly decided to do it slowly.

In Parliament Ian Smith sat on the opposition benches, sulky and laconic, but as safe to walk the streets as when he was Prime Minister – a living proof, considering that he had locked up most of them, of the new black ministers' tolerance.

\*     \*     \*

So, by a series of flukes, Rhodesia emerged as Zimbabwe. Rhodes's plan of an extra white-ruled province for South Africa was averted. Lords Carrington and Soames pulled off a remarkable coup. They brought this peculiar, rogue colony under just enough control to prevent the final departure of the British Empire from Africa going disastrously wrong. It nearly did. Had Wilson or Home pulled off their deals with Smith, Britain would have been blamed world-wide for adding five million blacks to the *apartheid* bastion in southern Africa. The two British Prime Ministers took steps that almost led to this result because they recognised Britain's impotence. Only the unimaginable stupidity of Ian Smith and his government saved Britain from the consequences of Wilson's and Home's realism.

Rescuing Southern Rhodesia's blacks from *apartheid* was one of the original objectives of the Federation of Rhodesia and Nyasaland in the days when Attlee and Gordon Walker and Cohen supported the scheme in 1950–51. To that extent the Federation, almost twenty years after it was closed down, succeeded in one of its principal purposes. Both in Southern Rhodesia and in Kenya the Colonial Office was determined to prevent white settlers from creating another South Africa. That the British Government eventually overruled their settlers in Africa – instead of actively supporting them as the French did in Algeria and the Portuguese in Angola and Mozambique – was not due to greater British wisdom. Until 1959 the British Conservative Government was determined to secure for the settlers in Kenya a continuing hold on power. Until 1971 British Governments, Conservative and Labour, wanted nothing more than to hand independence to whites in Southern Rhodesia, with Africans in the minority in all parts of public life. What swung British policy round was, first, the two massacres of 1959: the Nyasaland emergency and Hola. The British public and the United States would not allow the Empire to continue to massacre its subjects.

Equally important was the Commonwealth. The Indian Government had some standing to make its views known about Kenya – the Viceroy had been doing so since 1920 – and it intervened actively to encourage Indians to throw in their lot with the Kenyan nationalist movement. Over Rhodesia the involvement of the Commonwealth was, in the final stages, even more crucial. Repeatedly when Mrs Thatcher, Lord Carrington and Lord Soames had reached the end of their tether at what they considered the unreasonable demands of the African nationalists and their backers, the Commonwealth Secretary-General, Sridath Ramphal, intervened to explain to the British why the Africans felt as they did and how damaging could be the consequences of ignoring them. The Foreign Office, at such moments, saw the Commonwealth Secretariat as an interfering nuisance. But Commonwealth pressure was several times crucial in steering Britain away from minefields. A typical case was the land issue in Rhodesia. The British Government refused to pay the cost of buying white settlers' land. The Patriotic Front agreed that land-owners should be compensated, but were ready to walk out of the Lancaster House conference at the suggestion that the successor Government should pay. The Commonwealth Secretariat quickly called a weekend meeting, brought in the United States to argue for the principle and offer some money and thus induced the British to pay the bulk – as they had done in Kenya. Another case was the election. British officials were arguing passionately for the need to disqualify Mugabe's party, ZANU, in parts of the country. The Commonwealth Monitoring Group – whose presence in Rhodesia Carrington had strongly resisted – was a decisive force in persuading Soames that he must not do so. By such guidance from, among others, its former subjects was the British Empire saved from disaster.

Only after the election did the British realise how lucky it was for them that Mugabe had won. A government cobbled together of Muzorewa, Nkomo and Smith would have seemed like a British fix. Mugabe's many thousands of Chinese-trained guerillas would have resisted. The British flag-down would have been followed, as in Palestine, by a war. By handing over to Mugabe, the British succeeded not only in demonstrating that their belief in properly conducted elections was genuine, but, more important, they transferred power to a government capable of disciplining the largest guerilla movement and therefore holding the country together.

# Epilogue

## The Falklands

In 1982, when the important territories of the Empire had all become independent and the show was more or less over, the British demonstrated that the imperial will dies hard.

The Falklands, small islands in the south Atlantic so cold and windy that trees do not grow there, had once been of value to Britain as the nearest landfall for ships sailing round the stormy extremity of South America, Cape Horn. But since the opening of the Panama Canal in 1913 the islands were of no further strategic or commercial use. Argentina, their nearest neighbour, claimed them, and in the 1960s the British Government took part in talks with a view to eventual transfer of sovereignty.

However, the 1,800 inhabitants were Britons and did not want to be ruled from Buenos Aires. The British company which kept most of the Falklands sheep farmers going, deriving a small but steady profit from the sale of wool, made sure that their case was well presented to Members of Parliament. When a Foreign Office minister, Nicholas Ridley, explained to the House of Commons in 1980 that the Government was considering 'exchanging the title of sovereignty against a long lease of the islands back to Her Majesty's Government', MPs of all parties objected. Ridley had said: 'The essential is that we should be guided by the wishes of the islanders themselves', but that was unacceptable to MPs. 'Their wishes must be paramount' (Peter Shore, Labour). 'Leasing back undermines a perfectly valid title in international law' (Sir Bernard Braine, Conservative). 'There is no support in this House for the shameful schemes which have been festering in the Foreign Office for years for getting rid of these islands' (Russell Johnston, Liberal). 'There will never be a majority in this House to give these islands to the Argentine' (Tom McNally, Labour). 'It is almost always a great mistake to get rid of real estate for nothing' (Julian Amery, Conservative). The British Government, which had skilfully nursed the House of Commons into giving up colonies of substantial value, was now trapped into refusing to hand over so much as the paper title of one that was valueless.

In April 1982 Argentina's military junta, spurred by popular nationalist clamour, invaded the Falklands. Britain immediately responded with vigour. A huge naval task force set out on the 8,000-mile journey to recover the islands, protect the settlers from undemocratic rule and restore Britain's honour. Members of Parliament were all but unanimous in the view that they had no choice. The Government managed the operation better than its predecessors at Suez in 1956. It skilfully obtained the support of both the United States and the United Nations. The Argentine invasion was an act of piracy and Britain was upholding the rule of law.

Almost a thousand people were killed in recovering the right of 1,800 to live under British rule. The cost of the task force, and of the subsequent reinforcement of the Falklands to ensure that Argentina did not do the same again, led to cuts in British Government spending on domestic projects. The war proved by contrast the bravery of Clement Attlee when he resisted demands to keep India, and the even greater bravery of Iain Macleod when, placing Britain's interests above those of white settlers who had friends in the House of Commons, he refused to back demands for the British and their near relatives to retain sovereignty over Nyasaland, Northern Rhodesia and Kenya. The spirit that demanded Britain fight for the Falklands had been hovering, ready to arouse imperial pride, throughout the years the Empire was coming to an end. Generally it was held in check. British ministers and civil servants found it hard to understand the anger and hurt pride of the nationalisms that sprang up against British rule, but each war they launched – in Malaya, Kenya, Suez and Cyprus – and each war they narrowly avoided by getting out fast – in India, Palestine and Aden – reminded them of the terrible cost and risk of resisting by force. Equally the British observed the disastrous experiences of France in Indo-China and Algeria. The main reason most of the British Empire moved peacefully to independence was the strong feeling in Whitehall and Westminster that 'we don't want any more fighting for territories we are bound, before long, to lose'.

The gunboat spirit animated British policy dangerously often. Churchill's conduct in 1940–45 over India and in 1952–3 over Iran, Eden's in 1955–6 over Egypt, the assertions of junior ministers over Cyprus in 1955 and Aden in 1956, all caused unnecessary deaths. All ran counter to the general tendency of the British Empire to concede self-determination when it was firmly demanded and all came under Conservative Prime Ministers. It is easy, with hindsight, to be critical of them. But in reviewing the whole period what is more remarkable is the speed with which British governments adapted to change. In 1950 the most radical African political leader, Kwame Nkrumah, was not asking for independence, only self-government. Arthur Creech Jones, the Labour Colonial Secretary, then thought that the British Empire in Africa still had fifty years to run, before it would have completed its tasks of education and economic development. The speed-up that caused Britain to be rapidly moving out of all its substantial colonies ten years later resulted from a sudden shift in the political wind. The anti-colonial pressure that the United States had since Woodrow Wilson's time been trying to exert became effective thanks to British and French errors over Suez in 1956. The demands of African nationalism became irresistible because within twelve months Ghana was freely granted its independence. From then on, Britain was no longer prepared to go to war in order to stay in power or to protect white settlers. If a single characteristic animated the End of the British Empire more than its contemporaries and predecessors – and therefore made it more successful than them – it was the suppression, until 1982, of the Falklands spirit.

The reason was a sound business instinct. Settlers and small businessmen generally wanted to stay in the colonies where they enjoyed a style of life far higher than they could expect in Britain. The senior managers of large businesses, however, tended in the latter stages of Empire to be more pragmatic. They wanted profits and saw, from India, that British business did as well after independence as before. Consequently, while local managers in the colonies were often bitterly hostile to nationalist politicians, their head offices in London were usually neutral. Most of them would have preferred not to face the challenge of nationalism but, given no choice, they reacted in a way Lenin failed to predict: by bowing to the inevitable and making the best of it. Thus the profit motive, which had led to the creation of the Empire, led also to the final decision to let it go under, in most places, without a fight.

# Bibliography

The books listed are merely a selection from those I have found useful in work on *End of Empire*.

## Introduction and books relevant to several chapters

Carlton, David: *Anthony Eden*, Allen Lane, 1981, 528 pp. A perceptive critical biography.

Cross, Colin: *The Fall of the British Empire*, Hodder & Stoughton, 1968, 368 pp. An excellent, clear survey.

Eden, Anthony: *Full Circle*, Cassell, 1960, 619 pp. Well-argued chapters on Cyprus and Egypt, but what startling omissions!

Fieldhouse, D. K.: *The Colonial Empires*, Macmillan, 1982 (2nd edition), 476 pp. A useful, broad range.

Howard, Michael: *The Continental Commitment*, Penguin, 1974, 173 pp. Clear historical thinking on the conflict between defence of the empire and the need to fight in Europe.

Louis, Wm. Roger: *The British Empire in the Middle East, 1945–51*, Oxford, 1984, 803 pp. This American, a professor at the University of Texas at Austin, is by far the greatest scholar on the end of the British Empire.

Lyttelton, Oliver: *Memoirs of Lord Chandos*, Bodley Head, 1962, 446 pp. The Colonial Secretary 1951–4 is dull on Malaya and Rhodesia but reveals more than he means to on Kenya and Mau Mau.

Macmillan, Harold. Volumes III, IV and V of his memoirs are a rich source for diary extracts on colonial issues. Like Richard Crossman's diaries, what they mostly reveal is that the cleverest men in politics spend most of their time thinking about immediate challenges in the House of Commons.

Monroe, Elizabeth: *Britain's Moment in the Middle East*, Chatto & Windus, 1981, 254 pp. A wise and amazingly well-informed analysis.

Morris, James, (later known as Jan Morris): *Heaven's Command* (1837–97), *Pax Britannica* (1897) and *Farewell the Trumpets* (1897–1965), Penguin, 1979, 554 pp, 544 pp and 576 pp. For poetic insight, exquisite writing, eye-witness accounts of most of the interesting places, racy story telling, the sifting of a lifetime's purposeful reading, hilarious anecdotes and a feel for the imperial style, Morris is the tops.

Moyne, Lord, (Chairman): *West India: Royal Commission Report*, HMSO, 1945, 480 pp. The report the Government kept secret for five years says that nothing had been done to protect West Indians from the competition of alternative supplies of sugar.

Perham, Margery: *Colonial Sequence*, Methuen, 1970, 377 pp. The great teacher at Oxford of British colonial civil servants reveals in these essays on Africa between 1949 and 1969 that she managed, even in her later years, to understand the latest political developments – sometimes better than her ex-pupils who were dealing with them.

Seldon, Anthony: *Churchill's Indian Summer*, Hodder & Stoughton, 1981, 667 pp. An excellent review of the Conservative Government 1951–5.

## Chapter 1: India

Al Mujahid, Sharif: *Jinnah*, Quaid-i-Azam Academy, Karachi, 1981, 806 pp. A well-researched work-of-state.

Ali, Chaudhri Muhammad: *The Emergence of Pakistan*, Columbia, 1967. 418 pp. The most senior Muslim working for the government of India at partition describes events in which he played a central role.

Bolitho, Hector: *Jinnah*, Murray, 1954, 244 pp. Useful and rich in anecdotes, this book reveals how little is known or understood about Jinnah.

Chaudhuri, Nirad C.: *Clive of India*, Barrie & Jenkins, 1975, 446 pp. A brilliant writer returns to the original sources to argue that, by the standards of his time, Clive was not corrupt.

Collins, Larry and Lapierre, Dominique: *Freedom at Midnight*, Collins, 1975, 500 pp. Scholars affect to despise this book and it is certainly uncritical of Mountbatten, who gave tape-recorded interviews which form its main single source. But no other book makes India's independence so exciting, and much of the research, while journalistic rather than scholarly, is original and enterprising. The style, however, is prone to screech.

Dyer, R. E. H.: *Disturbances in the Punjab*, HMSO, 1920, 28 pp. Dyer's reply to Hunter (see below).

Feiling, Keith: *Warren Hastings*, Macmillan, 1954, 420 pp. The authoritative, modern defence.

Harris, Kenneth: *Attlee*, Weidenfeld & Nicolson, 1982, 630 pp. A new perspective on Attlee, Burma and Mountbatten.

Hodson, H. V.: *The Great Divide*, Hutchinson, 1969, 563 pp. The constitutional adviser to Viceroy Linlithgow provides the authoritative British version, drawing on full access to the Mountbatten papers.

Hunter, Lord (Chairman): *Report of the Committee appointed by the Government of India to investigate the disturbances in the Punjab, etc*, HMSO, 1920, 176 pp. The official report on the Amritsar massacre.

Ispahani, M. A. H.: *Qaid-e-Azam Jinnah as I knew him*, Forward Publications, Karachi, 1966, 244 pp. Recollections and letters assembled by an East Bengal political associate of Jinnah in his later years.

Khan, Mohammad Ayub: *Friends Not Masters*, Oxford, 1967, 275 pp. The senior Muslim in the Punjab Frontier Force in 1947, later became President of Pakistan.

Masani, R. P.: *Britain in India*, Oxford, 1960, 278 pp. A lively Congress-moderate perspective.

Mason, Philip: *A Matter of Honour, an account of the Indian army*, Cape, 1974, 580 pp. Former secretary of the Chiefs of Staff committee in India: enthusiastic but fair. (See also Woodruff, below.)

Middlemas, Keith and Barnes, John: *Baldwin*, Weidenfeld & Nicolson, 1969, 1149 pp. A splendid biography, showing that one Tory Prime Minister, at least, was not an imperialist so far as India was concerned.

Moore, R. J.: *Churchill, Cripps and India*, Oxford, 1979, 152 pp. Skilful use of Cabinet papers shows Cripps in a good light and makes sense of the 1942 mission.

Moore, R. J.: *Escape from Empire: the Attlee Government and the Indian Problem*, Oxford, 1983, 376 pp. Moore sorts out some puzzles in Hodson's masterly account (see above).

Pandey, B. N.: *Nehru*, Macmillan, 1976, 499 pp. A perceptive, well-informed biography.

Rosselli, John: *Lord William Bentinck*, Chatto & Windus, 1974, 384 pp. An intellectual biography of the great reforming Governor-General.

Seal, Anil: *The Emergence of Indian Nationalism*, Cambridge, 1968, 416 pp. A convincing and eloquent reinterpretation of the early years of the Indian National Congress.

Spear, Percival: *A History of India*, volume 2, Penguin, 1965, 284 pp. A useful general history.

Stephens, Ian: *Pakistan*, Pelican, 1964, 352 pp. Editor of the Calcutta *Statesman*, Stephens was passionately pro-Pakistan and a brilliant writer.

Taseer, Salmaan: *Bhutto*, Ithaca Press, 1979, 216 pp. High-quality journalism.

Tomlinson, B. R.: *The Indian National Congress and the Raj, 1929–1942*, Macmillan, 1976, 208 pp. Scholarly and valuable.

Tomlinson, B. R.: *The Political Economy of the Raj, 1914–1947*, Macmillan, 1979, 199 pp. A well-researched examination of the British mind in the last decades of the Raj.

Waley, S. D.: *Edwin Montagu: a memoir and an account of his visits to India*, Asia Publishing House, 1964, 343 pp. Particularly interesting on Montagu's reactions to the Amritsar massacre.

Wavell, Lord: *The Viceroy's Journal* (edited by Penderel Moon), Oxford, 1973, 528 pp. An honest man who reveals his own weaknesses, Wavell was treated outrageously by Churchill, who in effect destroyed him.

Woodruff, Philip (pseudonym of Philip Mason): *The Men who Ruled India*, volume 1 *The Founders*, 402 pp., volume 2 *The Guardians*, 386 pp., Cape, 1954. A personal, charming and brilliant history of the ICS, peppered with autobiography.


## Chapter 2: Palestine

Most of the books listed here are either pro-Zionist or pro-Palestinian. 'Facts' in some are often 'allegations' in others. Nobody has yet produced the masterly work that, through sympathy and understanding for all sides, is able to offer balanced judgements. Some come close, notably Simha Flapan and Y. Porath below.

Acheson, Dean: *Present at the Creation*, Hamish Hamilton, 1970, 798 pp. The Under-Secretary of State was close to Truman and is kind to him.

Bethell, Nicholas: *The Palestine Triangle*, Futura, 1980, 384 pp. Clear and lively journalism on the years 1935–48.

Bullock, Alan: *Ernest Bevin, Foreign Secretary*, Heinemann, 1983, 896 pp. In a great history of British foreign policy 1945–51, Bullock convincingly shows that Bevin was not driven by anti-semitism.

Cohen, Michael J.: *Palestine and the Great Powers 1945–48*, Princeton, 1982, 417 pp. Excellent up-to-date scholarship.

Flapan, Simha: *Zionism and the Palestinians*, Croom Helm, 1979, 361 pp. An Israeli of the modern school shows how leading Zionists were blind to the legitimate interests, even the existence, of the Palestinians.

Gilmour, David: *Dispossessed – the Palestinians 1917–1980*, Sidwick & Jackson, 1980, 242 pp. An eloquent statement of the Palestinian case.

Hadawi, Sami: *Bitter Harvest, Palestine 1914–1979*, Caravan Books, 1979, 326 pp. A Palestinian former tax administrator under the British tells a clear, well-documented story.

Hirst, David: *The Gun and the Olive Branch: the roots of violence in the Middle East*, Faber, 1977, repr. 1984, 475 pp. The *Guardian* correspondent in Beirut is an eloquent and informed pro-Palestinian.

Ingrams, Doreen (editor): *Palestine Papers, 1917–22*, Murray, 1972, 198 pp. A useful anthology of documents.

Kayyali, A. W.: *Palestine, a modern history*, Croom Helm, 1978, 243 pp. A scholarly history from a Palestinian viewpoint, ending in 1939.

Kimche, Jon: *The Second Arab Awakening*, Thames & Hudson, 1970, 288 pp. Kimche, a far-sighted journalist, was one of the first to open the eyes of his fellow Jews to the mind and needs of the Palestinians.

Laqueur, Walter (editor): *The Israel-Arab Reader: a documentary history of the Middle East conflict*, revised edition, Penguin, 1970, 591 pp.

Luttwak, Edward and Horowitz, Dan: *The Israeli Army*, Allen Lane, 1975, 461 pp. A gripping history of a remarkable institution.

Porath, Y.: *The Palestinian Arab National Movement*, vol 1 1918–1929, 406 pp., vol 2 1929–1939, 414 pp., Cass, 1977. The author is an Israeli, but the books have the fairness of true scholarship.

Samuel, Viscount: *Memoirs*, Cresset, 1945, 304 pp. Britain's first High Commissioner includes three bland chapters on Palestine.

Silver, Eric: *Begin*, Weidenfeld & Nicolson, 1984, 278 pp. Powerful insights into a strange, obsessive mind, shaped by the terrible experience of the holocaust.

Sykes, Christopher: *Crossroads to Israel*, Mentor, 1967, 413 pp. Son of the joint author of the Sykes-Picot agreement, he brings charm, wit and a long knowledge of Palestine to this history of the mandate.

Weizmann, Chaim: *Trial and Error*, Hamish Hamilton, 1949, 608 pp. The leading Zionist moderate tells his story elegantly but evasively.

Wilson, Evan M.: *Decision on Palestine*, Hoover Institution, 1979, 244 pp. The US State Department Palestine specialist in 1946–8 describes how strongly he and his colleagues pressed Truman to do the opposite of what he did.

Wilson, Harold: *The Chariot of Israel*, Weidenfeld/Michael Joseph, 1981, 406 pp. An odd book for an ex-Prime Minister of Britain: full of long extracts from official documents (very helpful) with a text of fervent Zionism.

## Chapter 3: Malaya

Clutterbuck, Richard: *The Long, Long War – The Emergency in Malaya 1948–60*, Cassell, 1966, 206 pp. The book of an intellectual soldier who served in Malaya.

Collis, Maurice: *Raffles*, Faber, 1966, 228 pp. Stylish hagiography.

Fitzgerald, C. P.: *A Concise History of East Asia*, Penguin, 1974, 372 pp. A profound scholar of China and south-east Asia provides a historical and regional context.

Means, Gordon P.: *Malaysian Politics*, University of London Press, 1970, 447 pp. A scholarly study of constitutional and political development.

Miller, Harry: *The Communist Menace in Malaya*, Harrap, 1954, 238 pp. and *Jungle War in Malaya: the campaign against Communism 1948–1960*, Barker, 1972, 220 pp. Two clear and lively accounts by a journalist and loyal Briton who was there throughout the emergency.

Miller, Harry: *Prince and Premier*, Harrap, 1959, 224 pp., a biography of Tunku Abdul Rahman, first Prime Minister of Malaya, written with the subject's assistance.

Purcell, Victor: *Malaya: Communist or Free?* Gollancz, 1954, 288 pp. A brilliant polemic against Templer and his policies by a former senior member of the Chinese Protectorate (the British administration for Chinese in Malaya till 1942).

Rahman, Tunku Abdul: *Looking Back*, Pustaka Antara, Kuala Lumpur, 1977, 380 pp. A political autobiography, based on a series of newspaper articles: not as good as Harry Miller's book.

Short, Anthony: *The Communist Insurrection in Malaya, 1948–1960*, Frederick Muller, 1975, 547 pp. The fullest and most authoritative work, likely to remain the standard authority. Based on full access to official sources in Malaya.

Stockwell, A. J.: *British Policy and Malay Politics during the Malayan Union Experiment, 1942–1948*, Malaysian Branch of the Royal Asiatic Society, Kuala Lumpur, 1979, 206 pp. An expanded Ph.D. thesis backed by extensive interviews in Malaya.

Thompson, Sir Robert: *Defeating Communist Insurgency*, Chatto & Windus, 1967, 171 pp. Sir Robert's Malayan experiences greatly impressed United States advisers and soldiers in Vietnam: if this was how the British did it, surely the same methods could work against the Viet Cong; but the circumstances were different.

## Chapter 4: Iran

Abrahamian, Ervand: *Iran Between Two Revolutions*, Princeton, 1982, 561 pp. A major work of political history.

Amirsadeghi, Hossein (editor): *Twentieth Century Iran*, Heinemann, 1977, 299 pp. Useful essays.

Avery, Peter: *Modern Iran*, Benn, 1967, 527 pp. A great Iranian scholar provides useful insights and analysis.

Cottam, Richard W.: *Nationalism in Iran*, Pittsburgh, 1979, 376 pp. An American scholar who served in the CIA during the 1953 coup in Iran provides the clearest and most balanced narrative.

Donoughue, Bernard and Jones, G. W.: *Herbert Morrison*, Weidenfeld, 1973, 696 pp. The Foreign Secretary when the Iranian crisis burst is shown frankly out of his depth.

Eisenhower, Dwight D.: *Mandate for Change*, Doubleday, 1963, 650 pp. The US President gives brief corroboration of the story told by Woodhouse and Roosevelt (see below).

Katouzian, Homa: *The Political Economy of Modern Iran*, Macmillan, 1981, 389 pp. Though dedicated to the memory of Dr Mussadeq, this is a fair, critical history.

Ledeen, Michael and Lewis, William: *Debacle: the American Failure in Iran*, Knopf, 1981, 256 pp. A vigorous statement of the tough American position.

Longhurst, Henry: *Adventure in Oil*, Sidgwick & Jackson, 1959, 286 pp. The story of the Anglo-Iranian Oil Company, later British Petroleum, chattily told.

Marlowe, John: *Iran*, Pall Mall, 1963, 144 pp. A clear introduction.

Roosevelt, Kermit: *Countercoup: the struggle for the control of Iran*, McGraw-Hill, 1979, 217 pp. The man who took over from Woodhouse (see below) and led the coup tells his story with the vividness of a thriller.

Woodhouse, C. M.: *Something Ventured*, Granada, 1982, 208 pp. Autobiography of the man who was in charge of the British effort to topple Mussadeq and restore power to the Shah: for a British public servant, amazingly open.

Wright, Sir Denis: *The English Amongst the Persians, 1787–1921*, Heinemann, 1977, 196 pp. A former British ambassador to Iran publishes for the first time extracts from the diaries of Sir Edmund Ironside, proving what for half a century Persians had claimed and the British denied, that this English general was behind Reza Shah's 1921 *coup d'état*.

## Chapter 5: Egypt

Earl of Cromer: *Modern Egypt*, Macmillan, 1908, 2 vols, 594 and 600 pp. A massive self-justification by Britain's great proconsul, written immediately on his return from Egypt. Does not mention the public hangings and floggings at Denshawai.

Killearn, Lord: *The Killearn Diaries*, Sidgwick & Jackson, 1972, 400 pp. Edited after his death, these are the daily diary entries of the ambassador who ordered King Farouk to change his Prime Minister or abdicate.

Lacouture, Jean and Simonne: *Egypt in Transition*, Methuen, 1958, 532 pp. This outstanding work of journalism and analysis includes particularly clear accounts of 'Black Saturday' in Cairo and of Nasser's speech nationalising the canal.

Lloyd, Selwyn: *Suez 1956*, Cape, 1978, 282 pp. The Foreign Secretary during the Suez crisis writes twenty-two years later with considerable candour, though inevitably seeking to conceal his own weakness in face of Eden.

McDermott, Geoffrey: *The Eden Legacy*, Frewin, 1969, 240 pp. One of the three Foreign Office men involved in planning the Suez invasion is more angry but less informative than the ministers who have written about it.

McLeave, Hugh: *The Last Pharaoh*, Michael Joseph, 1969, 319 pp. A lively biography of King Farouk.

Mansfield, Peter: *The British in Egypt*, Weidenfeld, 1971, 351 pp. A model for such a book: shows sympathetic understanding of both the Egyptians and the British.

Murphy, Robert: *Diplomat among Warriors*, Collins, 1964, 576 pp. Eisenhower's envoy to Eden at the start of the Suez crisis describes in particular his old friend Macmillan's bellicosity.

Neguib, Mohammed: *Egypt's Destiny*, Gollancz, 1955, 288 pp. The story of the general who displaced Farouk as head of state: an honourable soldier.

Nutting, Anthony: *No End of a Lesson*, Constable, 1967, 205 pp. The Minister of State at the Foreign Office who was close to Eden but resigned when his government used force against Egypt has produced far the best book on the Suez crisis: a masterpiece.

Thomas, Hugh: *The Suez Affair*, Weidenfeld, 1957, 259 pp. An interim history by a first-class historian.

Vatikiotis, P. J.: *A Modern History of Egypt*, Weidenfeld, 1969, 512 pp. Particularly useful on internal affairs.

Wavell, Lord: *Allenby*, Harrap, 1946, 383 pp. The life of Britain's High Commissioner in Egypt from 1919 to 1925 told by one who, while writing the book, was Commander-in-Chief, Middle East.


## Chapter 6: Aden

Gavin, R. J.: *Aden under British Rule*, Hurst, 1975, 472 pp. The standard work by the Professor of History, Ahmadu Bello University, Zaria, Nigeria.

Halliday, Fred: *Arabia without Sultans*, Penguin, 1974, 224 pp. Lit by the view that 'all capitalist business is blackmail' the book makes sense of the NLF, which most authors find baffling.

Hickinbotham, Tom: *Aden*, Constable, 1958, 242 pp. A former member of the Indian political service and Governor of Aden 1951–6 gives a fine feel for the place before the trouble started.

Holden, David: *Farewell to Arabia*, Faber, 1966, 268 pp. The work of an outstanding journalist.

Johnston, Charles: *The View from Steamer Point*, Collins, 1964, 224 pp. The Governor of Aden 1960–63 was a Foreign Office man transferred. His book provokes the question, would a Colonial Office man have pushed Aden so hard to adhere to the Federation?

Kelly, J. B.: *Arabia, the Gulf and the West*, Weidenfeld and Nicolson, 1980, 530 pp. Imperialist prejudice almost – but not quite – blunts the impact of profound scholarship.

Kirkman, W. P.: *Unscrambling an Empire*, Chatto & Windus, 1966. 214 pp. A former *Times* correspondent offers sharp and informed criticism of the merging of Aden into the South Arabian Federation.

Ledger, David: *Shifting Sands*, Peninsular, 1983, 232 pp. A former army intelligence officer in South Arabia and later a political officer at the High Commission, tells the story of the final years clearly and well.

Lunt, James: *The Barren Rocks of Aden*, Jenkins, 1966, 196 pp. The commander of the army of the South Arabian Federation reveals a sensitive eye for this strange territory.

Paget, Julian: *Last Post, Aden 1954–67*, Faber, 1969, 256 pp. A Lt-Colonel of the Coldstream Guards who served in Aden in 1965 gives a clear, soldier's-eye-view.

Trevaskis, Kennedy: *Shades of Amber*, Hutchinson, 1968, 256 pp. The High Commissioner 1963–5 makes the best possible case for the policy of backing the sultans.

Trevelyan, Humphrey: *The Middle East in Revolution*, Macmillan, 1970, 275 pp. Britain's last High Commissioner, brought in to prevent scuttle turning to disaster, writes with force and style.

## Chapter 7: Cyprus

Averoff-Tossizza, Evangelos: *Cyprus, A History of Lost Opportunities*, published in Greek, typescript of an English translation kindly loaned by the author. A long and detailed study by the Greek Foreign Minister 1956–63 of his involvement in Cypriot affairs during these years: clear and eloquent.

Crawshaw, Nancy: *The Cyprus Revolt*, Allen & Unwin, 1978, 447 pp. The fullest account in English, by a fair-minded journalist who covered much of the story.

Crouzet, François: *Le Conflit de Chypre*, Emile Bruylant, Brussels, 1973, 1187 pp. A historical masterpiece by a professor at the Sorbonne: every issue is argued with clarity, style and convincing worldly wisdom.

Durrell, Lawrence: *Bitter Lemons*, Faber, 1957, 256 pp. The novelist, who was press officer to Governors Armitage and Harding, makes one roar with laughter at the oddities and charm of Cypriot life, tangled amidst the violence.

Foot, Sir Hugh: *A Start in Freedom*, Hodder & Stoughton, 1964, 265 pp. Some well-told anecdotes by Britain's last Governor.

Grivas, George (edited by Charles Foley): *The Memoirs of General Grivas*, Longman, 1964, 226 pp. He was always right, far-sighted, brave and doing God's work: or so he says.

Kyle, Keith: *Cyprus*, Minority Rights Group, 1984, 23 pp. An excellent post-independence summary.

Stephens, Robert: *Cyprus, a Place of Arms*, Pall Mall, 1966, 232 pp. Good on the broader, eastern Mediterranean and strategic issues.

Storrs, Sir Ronald: *Orientations*, Nicholson & Watson, 1943, 532 pp. The Governor when Government House was burned down in 1931, in a chapter of some sixty pages, dazzles.

## Chapter 8: Gold Coast

Austin, Dennis: *Politics in Ghana 1946–1960*, Oxford, 1966, 459 pp. The standard work: subtle and well-written.

Bourret, F. M.: *Ghana, the Road to Independence, 1919–1957*, Oxford, 1960, 246 pp. Useful but lacking in feel for the place.

Fage, J. D.: *A History of West Africa*, Cambridge, 1969, 239 pp and *Ghana*, Wisconsin, 1959, 122 pp. Two clear, brief introductory texts.

Hargreaves, John D.: *The End of Colonial Rule in West Africa*, Macmillan, 1979, 141 pp. Thought-provoking essays.

James, C. L. R.: *Nkrumah and the Ghana Revolution*, Allison & Busby, 1977, 227 pp. A sympathetic view by one of Nkrumah's left-wing, West Indian political allies.

Kimble, David: *A Political History of Ghana, 1850–1928*, Oxford, 1963, 587 pp. A massive work of scholarship.

Lloyd, Christopher: *The Navy and the Slave Trade*, Longman, 1949, 314 pp. The remarkable story of the biggest task undertaken by the British navy in the nineteenth century.

Metcalfe, G. E.: *Maclean of the Gold Coast*, Oxford, 1962, 344 pp. A meticulous study of a worthy man, the first Governor of the British forts.

Nkrumah, Kwame: *Ghana*, Nelson, 1957, 310 pp. A better autobiography than might be expected from a politician in mid-career.

Pedler, Frederick: *Main Currents of West African History*, Macmillan, 1979, 301 pp. A readable broad survey.

Robinson, Ronald: 'Andrew Cohen' from *African Proconsuls* edited by L. H. Gann and P. Duignan, Hoover Institution, Stanford, 1978. Professor Robinson was Cohen's research assistant in the Colonial Office.

Rooney, David: *Sir Charles Arden-Clarke*, Collings, 1982, 222 pp. Makes good use of the papers of the last Governor.

Ward, W. E. F.: *A History of Ghana*, Allen & Unwin, 1966, 452 pp. Particularly good on African tribal matters.

Watson, Aiken (Chairman): *Report of the Commission of Enquiry into Disturbances in the Gold Coast*, HMSO, 1948, 83 pp. Deserves to be better known; an essential document for understanding the Labour Government's African policy.

## Chapter 9: Kenya

Bennett, George: *Kenya, a political history*, Oxford, 1963, 190 pp. A concise and clear account by an Oxford don of British rule from start to finish.

Clayton, Anthony: *Counter-Insurgency in Kenya*, Transafrica (Nairobi), 1976, 63 pp. A balanced review of a wide range of contentious writings.

Corfield, F. D.: *The Origins and Growth of Mau Mau*, HMSO, 1960, 321 pp. The official view: a diabolical evil for which Britain bore no blame.

Douglas-Home, Charles: *Evelyn Baring*, Collins, 1978, 433 pp. The author worked as a young assistant to Baring when he was Governor of Kenya and later became editor of *The Times*. He tries to be sympathetic to his subject, but honestly lays out many damaging revelations.

Evans, Peter: *Law and Disorder*, Secker & Warburg, 1956, 296 pp. A Dublin barrister who was in Kenya during the early years of the emergency calmly describes the decline in British standards of justice.

Goldsworthy, David: *Tom Mboya*, Heinemann, 1982, 308 pp. A subtle, well-written political biography.

Kariuki, Josiah Mwangi: *Mau Mau Detainee*, Oxford, 1963, 188 pp. The British authorities' extraordinary mixture of illegal violence and genuine effort at rehabilitation of detainees is convincingly and moderately described.

MacDonald, Malcolm: *Titans and Others*, Collins, 1972, 285 pp. The last Governor describes the final months of British rule and the striking growth in stature of Kenyatta.

Majdalany, Fred: *State of Emergency*, Longman, 1962, 239 pp. Written with the co-operation of the Colonial Office and Kenya Government, this is a popular and vivid attempt to spread the word that Mau Mau was the army of the devil.

Mboya, Tom: *Freedom and After*, Deutsch, 1963, 266 pp. Kenya's most brilliant politician writes part autobiography, part manifesto.

Murray-Brown, Jeremy: *Kenyatta*, Allen & Unwin, 1972, 381 pp. An excellent interim biography. Some years must still pass before a fully rounded judgement can be made, especially about his relations with Mau Mau.

Odinga, Oginga: *Not Yet Uhuru*, Heinemann, 1967, 323 pp. Lively testament of the Luo leader who called for Kenyatta's release from detention and later became his vice-president.

Rosberg, Jr, Carl G. and Nottingham, John: *The Myth of Mau Mau*, Praeger/Pall Mall, 1966, 427 pp. A convincing rebuttal of the view of most white settlers, of the British Government and of Nottingham himself when he was a DC during the emergency.

Slater, Montagu: *The Trial of Jomo Kenyatta*, Secker & Warburg, 1955, 255 pp. A useful summary, full of quotable extracts.

Wasserman, Gary: *Politics of Decolonisation*, Cambridge, 1976, 225 pp. A scholarly study of Kenya Europeans and the land issue, 1960–65.

## Chapter 10: Rhodesia

Blake, Robert: *A History of Rhodesia*, Eyre-Methuen, 1977, 430 pp. Clear, scholarly and full of insights: the work of a considerable historian.

Davidow, Jeffrey: *A Peace in Southern Africa*, Westview, 1984, 143 pp. The United States' diplomatic observer in Rhodesia in the last months of UDI has written a useful study of the 1979 London conference.

Devlin, Lord (Chairman): *Report of the Nyasaland Commission of Inquiry*, HMSO, 1959, 147 pp. If one marks state papers out of 100, this one gets 100: for distinguishing between matters of principle and of convenience with a sure touch; for leading to a prompt reversal of government policy; for being a joy to read.

Fisher, Nigel: *Iain Macleod*, Deutsch, 1973, 352 pp. The Minister of State at the Colonial Office under Macleod writes with affection.

Good, Robert C.: *UDI*, Faber, 1973, 368 pp. The US Ambassador to Zambia 1965–9 has written the best book on the early years of UDI

Keatley, Patrick: *The Politics of Partnership*, Penguin, 1963, 528 pp. The Federation described in a bustling, vivid, scholarly work by the then Commonwealth correspondent of the *Guardian*.

Lockhart, J. G. and Woodhouse, C. M.: *Rhodes*, Hodder & Stoughton, 1963, 511 pp. The first biography based on full access to Rhodes's papers.

Mason, Philip: *Year of Decision*, Oxford, 1960, 282 pp. Instant journalism of the highest quality by a former Indian Civil Servant.

Meredith, Martin: *The Past is Another Country*, Pan, 1979, 430 pp. The correspondent in Southern Africa of the *Observer* and later the *Sunday Times* tells the story of UDI splendidly, from start to finish.

Rotberg, Robert I.: *Black Heart*, California, 1977, 359 pp. Life of Sir Stewart Gore-Browne, a remarkable rich white settler in Northern Rhodesia who sided with the black man.

Sanger, Clyde: *Central African Emergency*, Heinemann, 1960, 343 pp. Fine insights and anecdotes by a Canadian journalist who spent much time in the Federation.

Shamuyarira, Nathan: *Crisis in Rhodesia*, Deutsch, 1965, 240 pp. The best book to convey the hope Federation represented and how it collapsed. The author, an African journalist, became a minister in Zimbabwe on independence.

Short, Philip: *Banda*, Routledge & Kegan Paul, 1974, 357 pp. An excellent biography. The only explanation for Banda's attempt to suppress it is that His Excellency the Life-President was becoming a megalomaniac.

Welensky, Sir Roy: *4,000 Days*, Collins, 1964, 383 pp. The Prime Minister of the Federation of Rhodesia and Nyasaland 1956–63 has written one of the most vituperative and bitter political memoirs of all time. His message is 'We wuz robbed'.

Wood, J. R. T.: *The Welensky Papers*, Graham Publishing, Durban, 1983, 1330 pp. A massive history of the Federation of Rhodesia and Nyasaland: a mine for scholars.

## Epilogue

Franks, Lord (Chairman): *Falklands Islands Review*, HMSO, 1983, 105 pp. The report of the committee that found nobody to blame for the start of the Falklands war.

Hastings, Max and Jenkins, Simon: *The Battle for the Falklands*, Michael Joseph, 1983, 372 pp. The best work of instant history I have read.

# Index

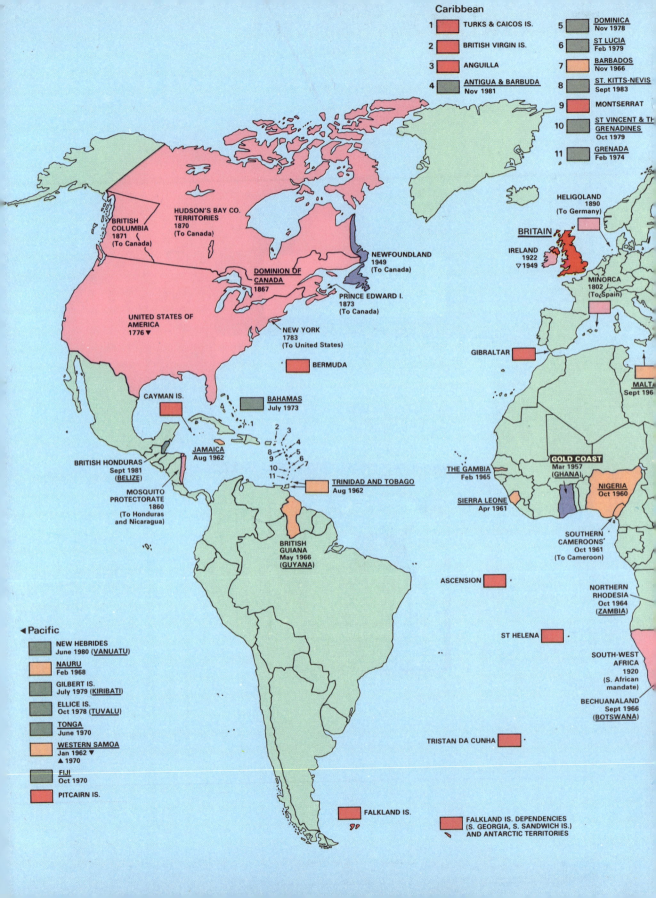